Contents

BPP LEARNING MEDIA

The BPP Learning Media Effective Study Package

Distance Learning from BPP Professional Education

You can access our exam-focussed interactive e-learning materials over the **Internet**, via BPP Learn Online, hosted by BPP Professional Education.

BPP Learn Online offers **comprehensive tutor support**, **revision guidance** and **exam tips**.

Visit www.bpp.com/acca/learnonline for further details.

Learning to Learn Accountancy

BPP's ground-breaking **Learning to Learn Accountancy** book is designed to be used both at the outset of your ACCA studies and throughout the process of learning accountancy. It challenges you to consider how you study and gives you helpful hints about how to approach the various types of paper which you will encounter. It can help you **focus your studies on the subject and exam**, enabling you to **acquire knowledge**, **practise and revise efficiently and effectively**.

How the BPP ACCA-approved Study Text can help you pass

How the BPP ACCA-approved Study Text can help you pass

Tackling studying

We know that studying for a number of exams can seem daunting, particularly when you have other commitments as well.

- We therefore provide guidance on **what you need to study efficiently and effectively** – to use the limited time you have in the best way possible

- We explain the **purposes** of the **different features** in the BPP Study Text, demonstrating how they help you and improve your chances of passing

Developing exam awareness

We never forget that you're aiming to pass your exams, and our Texts are completely focused on helping you do this.

- In the section **Studying P3** we introduce the key themes of the syllabus, describe the skills you need and summarise how to succeed

- The **Introduction** to each chapter of this Study Text sets the chapter in the context of the syllabus and exam

- We provide specific tips, **Exam focus points**, on what you can expect in the exam and what to do (and not to do!) when answering questions

And our Study Text is **comprehensive**. It covers the syllabus content. No more, no less.

Using the Syllabus and Study Guide

We set out the Syllabus and Study Guide in full.

- Reading the **introduction to the Syllabus** will show you what **capabilities** (skills) you'll have to demonstrate, and how this exam links with other papers.

- The topics listed in the **Syllabus** are the **key topics** in this exam. By quickly looking through the Syllabus, you can see the breadth of the paper. Reading the Syllabus will also highlight topics to look out for when you're reading newspapers or *student accountant* magazine.

- The **Study Guide** provides the **detail**, showing you precisely what you'll be studying. Don't worry if it seems a lot when you look through it; BPP's Study Text will carefully guide you through it all.

- Remember the Study Text shows, at the start of every chapter, which areas of the Syllabus and Study Guide are covered in the chapter.

Testing what you can do

Testing yourself helps you develop the skills you need to pass the exam and also confirms that you can recall what you have learnt.

- We include **Questions** within chapters, and the **Exam Question Bank** provides lots more practice.

- Our **Quick Quizzes** test whether you have enough knowledge of the contents of each chapter.

- Question practice is particularly important if English is not your first written language. ACCA offers an **International Certificate in Financial English** promoting language skills within the international business community.

Example chapter

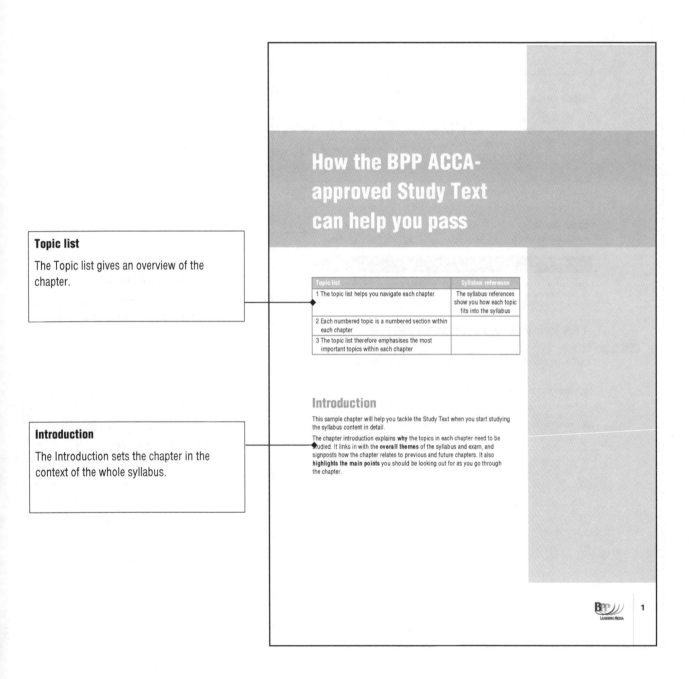

Topic list

The Topic list gives an overview of the chapter.

Introduction

The Introduction sets the chapter in the context of the whole syllabus.

How the BPP ACCA-approved Study Text can help you pass

Topic list	Syllabus reference
1 The topic list helps you navigate each chapter	The syllabus references show you how each topic fits into the syllabus
2 Each numbered topic is a numbered section within each chapter	
3 The topic list therefore emphasises the most important topics within each chapter	

Introduction

This sample chapter will help you tackle the Study Text when you start studying the syllabus content in detail.

The chapter introduction explains **why** the topics in each chapter need to be studied. It links in with the **overall themes** of the syllabus and exam, and signposts how the chapter relates to previous and future chapters. It also **highlights the main points** you should be looking out for as you go through the chapter.

1

Study guide

		Intellectual level
	We list the topics in ACCA's Study guide that are covered in each chapter	The intellectual level indicates the depth in which the topics will be covered

Exam guide

The Exam guide highlights ways in which the main topics covered in each chapter may be examined.

Knowledge brought forward from earlier studies

Knowledge brought forward boxes summarise information and techniques that you are **assumed to know** from your earlier studies. As the exam may test your knowledge of these areas, you should **revise** your previous study material if you are unsure about them.

1 Key topic which has a section devoted to it

FAST FORWARD   Fast forwards give you a **summary** of the content of each of the main chapter sections. They are listed together in the roundup at the end of each chapter to allow you to review each chapter quickly.

1.1 Important topic within section

The headings within chapters give you a good idea of the **importance** of the topics covered. The larger the header, the more important the topic is. The headers will help you navigate through the chapter and locate the areas that have been highlighted as important in the front pages or in the chapter introduction.

Study guide

The Study guide links with ACCA's own guidance.

Exam guide

The Exam guide describes the examinability of the chapter.

Knowledge brought forward

Knowledge brought forward shows you what you need to remember from previous exams.

Fast forward

Fast forwards allow you to preview and review each section easily.

Example

Examples show you how theory is put into practice.

Key term

Key terms are the core vocabulary.

Exam focus point

Exam focus points provide specific links to the exam.

Formula to learn

You must remember these formulae in the exam.

Question

Questions provide vital practice of what you've learnt.

Case Study

Case Studies link what you've learnt with the business environment.

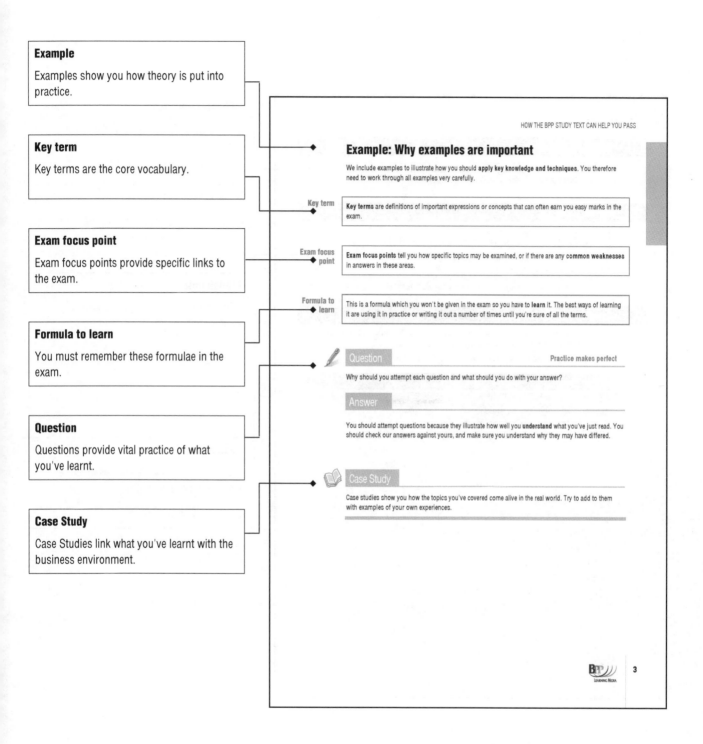

HOW THE BPP STUDY TEXT CAN HELP YOU PASS

Example: Why examples are important

We include examples to illustrate how you should **apply key knowledge and techniques**. You therefore need to work through all examples very carefully.

Key term

Key terms are definitions of important expressions or concepts that can often earn you easy marks in the exam.

Exam focus point

Exam focus points tell you how specific topics may be examined, or if there are any **common weaknesses** in answers in these areas.

Formula to learn

This is a formula which you won't be given in the exam so you have to **learn** it. The best ways of learning it are using it in practice or writing it out a number of times until you're sure of all the terms.

Question   Practice makes perfect

Why should you attempt each question and what should you do with your answer?

Answer

You should attempt questions because they illustrate how well you **understand** what you've just read. You should check our answers against yours, and make sure you understand why they may have differed.

Case Study

Case studies show you how the topics you've covered come alive in the real world. Try to add to them with examples of your own experiences.

Chapter Roundup

- Fast forwards give you a **summary** of the content of each of the main chapter sections. They are listed together in the roundup at the end of each chapter to allow you to review each chapter quickly.

Quick Quiz

1   What are the main purposes of the Quick Quiz?

2   What should you do if you get Quick Quiz questions wrong?

   A   Nothing as you now know where you went wrong
   B   Note the correct answer and go on to the next chapter
   C   Practise full questions on this topic when you revise
   D   Go back and look through the topic again to ensure you know it

Answers to Quick Quiz

1   The main purposes of the Quick Quiz are to check how much you've remembered of the topics covered and to practise questions in a variety of formats.

2   D   Go back and look through the topic again to ensure that you know it.

Now try the questions below from the Exam Question Bank

Number	Level	Marks	Time
Questions that give you practice of what you've learnt in each chapter	Examination	25	45 mins

Chapter Roundup

The Chapter Roundup lists all the Fast forwards.

Quick Quiz

The Quick Quiz speedily tests your knowledge.

Exam Question Bank

Each chapter cross-references to further question practice.

BPP
LEARNING MEDIA

BPP
LEARNING MEDIA

Learning styles

BPP's guide to studying, *Learning to Learn Accountancy*, provides guidance on identifying how you learn and the variety of intelligences that you have. We shall summarise some of the material in *Learning to Learn Accountancy*, as it will help you understand how to you are likely to approach the Study Text:

If you like	Then you might focus on	How the Study Text helps you
Word games, crosswords, poetry	Going through the detail in the Text	Chapter introductions, Fast forwards and Key terms help you determine the detail that's most significant
Number puzzles, Sudoku, Cluedo	Understanding the Text as a logical sequence of knowledge and ideas	Chapter introductions and headers help you follow the flow of material
Drawing, cartoons, films	Seeing how the ways material is presented show what it means and how important it is	The different features and the emphasis given by headers and emboldening help you see quickly what you have to know
Attending concerts, playing a musical instrument, dancing	Identifying patterns in the Text	The sequence of features within each chapter helps you understand what material is really crucial
Sport, craftwork, hands on experience	Learning practical skills such as preparing a set of accounts	Examples and question practice help you develop the practical skills you need

If you want to learn more about developing some or all of your intelligences, *Learning to Learn Accountancy* shows you plenty of ways in which you can do so.

Studying efficiently and effectively

What you need to study efficiently and effectively

Positive attitude

Yes there is a lot to learn. But look at the most recent ACCA pass list. See how many people have passed. They've made it; you can too. Focus on all the **benefits** that passing the exam will bring you.

Exam focus

Keep the exam firmly in your sights throughout your studies.

- Remember there's lots of **helpful guidance** about P3 in this first part of the Study Text.
- Look out for the **exam references** in the Study Text, particularly the types of question you'll be asked.

Organisation

Before you start studying you must organise yourself properly.

- We show you how to **timetable** your study so that you can ensure you have enough time to cover all of the syllabus – and revise it.
- Think carefully about the way you take **notes**. You needn't copy out too much, but if you can summarise key areas, that shows you understand them.
- Choose the notes **format** that's most helpful to you; lists, diagrams, mindmaps.
- Consider the **order** in which you tackle each chapter. If you prefer to get to grips with a theory before seeing how it's applied, you should read the explanations first. If you prefer to see how things work in practice, read the examples and questions first.

Active brain

There are various ways in which you can keep your brain active when studying and hence improve your **understanding** and **recall** of material.

- Keep asking yourself how the topic you're studying fits into the **whole picture** of this exam. If you're not sure, look back at the chapter introductions and Study Text front pages.
- Go carefully through every **example** and try every **question** in the Study Text and in the Exam Question Bank. You will be thinking deeply about the syllabus and increasing your understanding.

Review, review, review

Regularly reviewing the topics you've studied will help fix them in your memory. Your BPP Texts help you review in many ways.

- Important points are emphasised **in bold**.
- **Chapter Roundups** summarise the **Fast forward** key points in each chapter.
- **Quick Quizzes** test your grasp of the essentials.

BPP Passcards present summaries of topics in different visual formats to enhance your chances of remembering them.

Timetabling your studies

As your time is limited, it's vital that you calculate how much time you can allocate to each chapter. Following the approach below will help you do this.

Step 1   Calculate how much time you have

Work out the time you have available per week, given the following.

- The standard you have set yourself
- The time you need to set aside for work on the Practice & Revision Kit, Passcards, i-Learn and i-Pass
- The other exam(s) you are sitting
- Practical matters such as work, travel, exercise, sleep and social life

Hours

Note your time available in box A.   A [   ]

Step 2   Allocate your time

- Take the time you have available per week for this Study Text shown in box A, multiply it by the number of weeks available and insert the result in box B.   B [   ]
- Divide the figure in box B by the number of chapters in this Study Text and insert the result in box C.   C [   ]

Remember that this is only a rough guide. Some of the chapters in this Study Text are longer and more complicated than others, and you will find some subjects easier to understand than others.

Step 3   Implement your plan

Set about studying each chapter in the time shown in box C. You'll find that once you've established a timetable, you're much more likely to study systematically.

Short of time: Skim study technique

You may find you simply do not have the time available to follow all the key study steps for each chapter, however you adapt them for your particular learning style. If this is the case, follow the **Skim study** technique below.

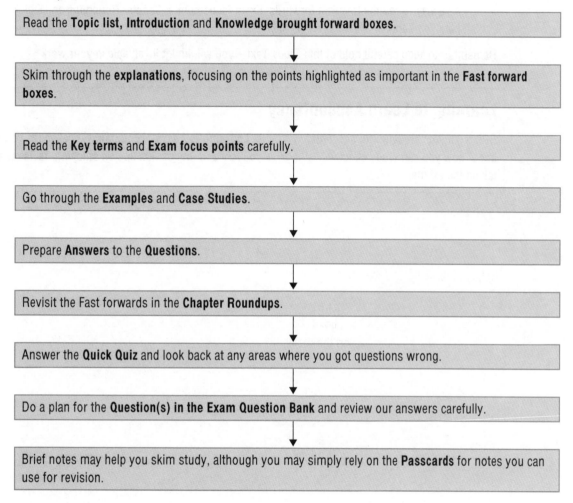

Read the **Topic list, Introduction** and **Knowledge brought forward boxes**.

Skim through the **explanations**, focusing on the points highlighted as important in the **Fast forward boxes**.

Read the **Key terms** and **Exam focus points** carefully.

Go through the **Examples** and **Case Studies**.

Prepare **Answers** to the **Questions**.

Revisit the Fast forwards in the **Chapter Roundups**.

Answer the **Quick Quiz** and look back at any areas where you got questions wrong.

Do a plan for the **Question(s) in the Exam Question Bank** and review our answers carefully.

Brief notes may help you skim study, although you may simply rely on the **Passcards** for notes you can use for revision.

Revision

When you are ready to start revising, you should still refer back to this Study Text.

- As a source of **reference** (you should find the index particularly helpful for this)
- As a way to **review** (the Fast forwards, Exam focus points, Chapter Roundups and Quick Quizzes help you here)

Remember to keep careful hold of this Study Text – you will find it invaluable in your work.

Learning to Learn Accountancy

BPP's guide to studying for accountancy exams, **Learning to Learn Accountancy**, challenges you to think about how you can study effectively and gives you lots and lots of vital tips on studying, revising and taking the exams.

Studying P3

Approaching P3

In this section we will attempt to summarise what the paper is designed to achieve and what you must do to pass it.

1 What the paper is about

Paper P3 is about business strategy. This is not a mainstream accountancy subject and you may be wondering why it forms part of your qualification. The answer to that question is that as a Chartered Certified Accountant you are likely to find yourself dealing with matters that are of strategic importance quite early in your career. You must therefore have a basic understanding of the way business strategy is conducted so that your input may be appropriate and properly considered.

Business strategy is a huge subject and your syllabus can only give you an introduction to it. The syllabus adopts the systems approach to understanding the way organisations work and therefore emphasises the importance of both the internal linkages between the various organisational components and the boundary-spanning links between the organisation and its environment. These two elements are reflected in the two main strategic issues dealt with by the syllabus: the external forces that influence the organisation's strategy and the internal forces and activities that sustain it.

Within this basic vision, the syllabus deals with three interconnected layers.

(a) The top layer is concerned with the overall strategic perspective, moving from the analysis of strategic position through strategic choices to strategic action.

(b) The middle layer expands on the basic idea of strategic implementation. The focus is on three linked aspects of business process management.

- Process improvement
- IS and e-business
- Quality methods

Each of these elements must be financially feasible and requires good project management: project management itself can be of strategic significance.

The middle layer is also a reminder that strategy may emerge from within the day-to-day activities of the organisation.

(c) The bottom layer of the model emphasises the importance of the human resource and, therefore, of effective human resource management

2 The skills you need

The study of business strategy is a work in progress. There is still vigorous debate, not only about how organisations should make their strategies but also about how they actually do make them.

Partly as a result of this, and partly as a result of the complexity of human behaviour there are few, if any, correct answers to business strategy problems. This means that the essence of your exam is not about things you can learn by heart, such as models and procedures; it is about **intelligent argument**: selecting and applying ideas and theories to realistic problems in order to reach sensible conclusions and suggestions.

All of the questions you will encounter in the exam will be of the scenario type. There will almost certainly be some marks for sensible numerical analysis, but there will not be many of them and they will be concentrated in question one. The rest of the marks will be entirely for written argument. The primary skills you must deploy therefore are those that relate to such answers.

(a) Careful reading and analysis of both scenarios and question requirements
(b) Marshalling of scenario facts and relevant theoretical models
(c) Synthesis and clear written expression of reasoned argument

Other papers in your syllabus have required these skills, but few to such an extent as this one. Many candidates find dealing with P3 questions extremely demanding and we can only recommend question practice as an essential part of your preparation.

3 How can you improve your chances of passing the paper?

- Your study must cover the entire syllabus. Question spotting is a very dangerous practice in any advanced exam and particularly so in this one since the clear intention of the Examiner is to set questions that require an integrated knowledge of the whole syllabus.

- Do not be put off by question one. Yes, it is very large and, yes, it is likely to cover a wide range of topics. However, experience shows that candidates who shy away from question one (perhaps leaving it until last) are unlikely to pass. Your BPP Practice and Revision Kit include plenty of practice examples.

- Do not waffle. It is difficult to produce a reasonable answer to a 25 mark question in much under two or three pages of manuscript but this does not mean that a high word count will bring high marks. Markers definitely prefer answers that are complete but brief. Think carefully about what you want to say and do not labour your points.

- Manage your time in the exam hall carefully. We have already referred to candidates who answer question one last – to do this without leaving yourself 90 minutes to answer it is foolish in the extreme.

4 Brought forward knowledge

Paper P3 assumes that you have a good knowledge of the syllabus for Paper F1 *Accountant in Business*. If you were exempt from this exam, you should spend some time considering its syllabus and study guide so as to identify any gaps in your knowledge. Both documents are available on the ACCA web site.

Syllabus

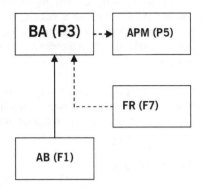

AIM

To apply relevant knowledge, skills, and exercise professional judgement in assessing strategic position, determining strategic choice, and implementing strategic action through beneficial business process and structural change; coordinating knowledge systems and information technology and by effectively managing quality processes, projects, and people within financial and other resource constraints.

MAIN CAPABILITIES

On successful completion of this paper, candidates should be able to:

A   Assess the strategic position of an organisation

B   Evaluate the strategic choices available to an organisation

C   Discuss how an organisation might go about its strategic implementation

D   Evaluate and redesign business processes and structures to implement and support the organisation's strategy taking account of customer and other major stakeholder requirements

E   Integrate appropriate information technology solutions to support the organisation's strategy

F   Apply appropriate quality initiatives to implement and support the organisation's strategy

G   Advise on the principles of project management to enable the implementation of aspects of the organisation's strategy with the twin objectives of managing risk and ensuring benefits realisation

H   Analyse and evaluate the effectiveness of a company's strategy and the financial consequences of implementing strategic decisions

I   The role of leadership and people management in formulating and implementing business strategy.

RELATIONAL DIAGRAM OF MAIN CAPABILITIES

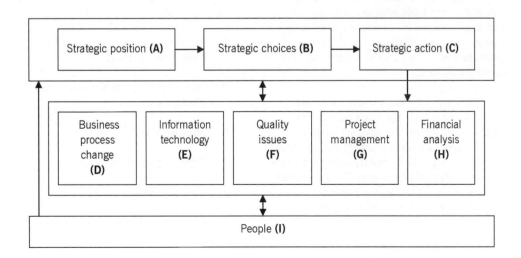

RATIONALE

The syllabus for Paper P3, *Business Analysis*, is primarily concerned with two issues. The first is the external forces (the behaviour of customers, the initiatives of competitors, the emergence of new laws and regulations) that shape the environment of an organisation. The second is the internal ambitions and concerns (desire for growth, the design of processes, the quality of products and services, the competences of employees, the financial resources) that exist within an organisation. This syllabus looks at both of these perspectives, from assessing strategic position and choice to identifying and formulating strategic action and its formulation. It identifies opportunities for beneficial change that involve people, finance and information technology. It examines how these opportunities may be implemented through the appropriate management of programmes and projects.

The syllabus begins with the assessment of strategic position and is concerned with the impact of the external environment, its internal capabilities and expectations and how the organisation positions itself. It examines how factors such as culture, leadership and stakeholder expectations shape organisational purpose. Strategic choice is concerned with decisions which have to be made about an organisation's future and the way in which it can respond to the influences and pressures identified in the assessment of its strategic position.

Strategic action concerns the implementation of strategic choices and the transformation of these choices into organisational action. Such action takes place in day-to-day processes and organisational relationships and these processes and relationships need to be managed in line with the intended strategy, involving the effective coordination of information technology, people, finance and other business resources.

Companies that undertake successful business process redesign claim significant organisational improvements. This simply reflects the fact that many existing processes are less efficient than they could be and that new technology makes it possible to design more efficient processes. For some writers, quality issues are at the heart of process improvement and the continual emergence of

models and concepts that focus on quality improvement merits its inclusion in this syllabus. Strategic planning and strategy implementation has to be subject to financial benchmarks. Financial analysis explicitly recognises this, reminding candidates of the importance of focusing on the key ratios and measures that may be used to assess the viability of a strategy and to monitor and measure its success.

Throughout, the syllabus recognises that successful strategic planning and implementation requires the effective recruitment, training, motivation and organisation of people.

DETAILED SYLLABUS

A   Strategic position

1. The need for, and purpose of, strategic and business analysis

2. Environmental issues affecting the strategic position of an organisation

3. Competitive forces affecting an organisation

4. Marketing and the value of goods and services

5. The internal resources, capabilities and competences of an organisation

6. The expectations of stakeholders and the influence of ethics and culture

B   Strategic choices

1. The influence of corporate strategy on an organisation

2. Alternative approaches to achieving competitive advantage

3. Alternative directions and methods of development

C   Strategic action

1. Organising and enabling success

2. Managing strategic change

3. Understanding strategy development

D   Business process change

1.   The role of process and process change initiatives

2.   Improving the processes of the organisation

3.   Software solutions

E   Information technology

1.   Principles of e-business

2.   E-business application: upstream supply chain management

3.   E-business application: downstream supply chain management

4.   E-business application: customer relationship management

F   Quality issues

1.   Quality control, quality assurance, and quality management systems

2.   Quality in the information systems development lifecycle

3.   Quality initiatives: Six-Sigma

G   Project management

1.   Identifying and initiating projects

2.   Managing and leading projects

3.   Monitoring, controlling and concluding projects

H   Financial Analysis

1.   The link between strategy and finance

2.   Finance decisions to formulate and support business strategy

3.   Financial implications of making strategic choices and of implementing strategic actions

I   People

1.   Strategy and people: leadership

2.   Strategy and people: performance management

3.   Strategy and people: reward management

4.   Strategy and people: job design

5.   Strategy and people: staff development

APPROACH TO EXAMINING THE SYLLABUS

The syllabus is assessed by a three-hour paper-based examination.

Section A
This section contains one multi-part question based on a case study scenario. The question is worth 50 marks. The question will be firmly based on capabilities defined in sections A, B and C of the syllabus, supported by capabilities defined in sections H and I of the syllabus. It will occasionally be supported by capabilities defined in sections D, E, F and G of the syllabus. The case study scenario will always include quantitative information, which might be financial data.

Section B
This section of the examination paper will contain three discrete questions, each worth 25 marks. The candidate must answer two questions in this section. **At least** two of the questions in this section will be based on capabilities defined in sections D, E, F, G and I of the syllabus. **At most**, one question in this section will be based on capabilities defined in sections A, B and C of the syllabus. Capabilities defined in section H of the syllabus may be used to support questions in this section.

Examination structure

Section A
One compulsory 50 mark question, possibly in several parts
Section B
Two out of three 25 mark questions
Total: 100 marks

Study Guide

A   STRATEGIC POSITION

1.   The need for, and purpose of, strategic and business analysis

a)   Recognise the fundamental nature and vocabulary of strategy and strategic decisions.[2]

b)   Discuss how strategy may be formulated at different levels (corporate, business level, operational) of an organisation.[2]

c)   Explore the Johnson, Scholes and Whittington model for defining elements of strategic management – the strategic position, strategic choices and strategy into action.[3]

d)   Analyse how strategic management is affected by different organisational contexts.[3]

e)   Compare three different strategy lenses (Johnson, Scholes and Whittington) for viewing and understanding strategy and strategic management.[3]

f)   Explore the scope of business analysis and its relationship to strategy and strategic management in the context of the relational diagram of this syllabus.[3]

2.   Environmental issues affecting the strategic position of an organisation

a)   Assess the macro-environment of an organisation using PESTEL.[3]

b)   Highlight the key drivers of change likely to affect the structure of a sector or market.[3]

c)   Explore, using Porter's Diamond, the influence of national competitiveness on the strategic position of an organisation.[2]

d)   Prepare scenarios reflecting different assumptions about the future environment of an organisation.[3]

3.   Competitive forces affecting an organisation

a)   Discuss the significance of industry, sector and convergence.[3]

b)   Evaluate the sources of competition in an industry or sector using Porter's five forces framework.[3]

c)   Assess the contribution of the lifecycle model and the cycle of competition to understanding competitive behaviour.[3]

d)   Analyse the influence of strategic groups and market segmentation.[3]

e)   Determine the opportunities and threats posed by the environment of an organisation.[2]

4.   Marketing and the value of goods and services

a)   Analyse customers and markets[2]

b)   Establish appropriate critical success factors for products and services[2]

c)   Explore the role of the value chain in creating and sustaining competitive advantage.[2]

d)   Advise on the role and influence of value networks.[3]

e)   Assess different approaches to benchmarking an organisation's performance.[3]

5.   The internal resources, capabilities and competences of an organisation

a)   Discriminate between strategic capability, threshold resources, threshold competences, unique resources and core competences.[3]

b)   Advise on the continuing need for cost efficiency.[3]

c)   Discuss the capabilities required to sustain competitive advantage.[2]

d)   Explain the impact of new product, process, and service developments and innovation in supporting business strategy.[2]

e) Discuss the contribution of organisational knowledge to the strategic capability of an organisation.[2]

f) Identify opportunities for managing the strategic capability of an organisation.[2]

g) Determine the strengths and weaknesses of an organisation and formulate an appropriate SWOT analysis.[2]

6. The expectations of stakeholders and the influence of ethics and culture

a) Advise on the implications of corporate governance on organisational purpose and strategy.[2]

b) Evaluate, through stakeholder mapping, the relative influence of stakeholders on organisational purpose and strategy.[3]

c) Assess ethical influences on organisational purpose and strategy.[3]

d) Explore the scope of corporate social responsibility.[3]

e) Assess the impact of culture on organisational purpose and strategy.[3]

f) Prepare and evaluate a cultural web of an organisation.[2]

g) Advise on how organisations can communicate their core values and mission.[3]

B   STRATEGIC CHOICES

1. The influence of corporate strategy on an organisation

a) Explore the relationship between a corporate parent and its business units.[2]

b) Assess the opportunities and potential problems of pursuing different corporate strategies of product/market diversification from a national, international and global perspective.[3]

c) Assess the opportunities and potential problems of pursuing a corporate strategy of

international diversity, international scale operations and globalisation.[3]

d) Discuss a range of ways that the corporate parent can create and destroy organisational value.[2]

e) Explain three corporate rationales for adding value – portfolio managers, synergy managers and parental developers.[3]

f) Explain and assess a range of portfolio models (the growth/share (BCG) matrix, the public sector portfolio matrix, market attractiveness/ SBU strength matrix, directional policy matrix, Ashridge Portfolio Display) that may assist corporate parents manage their business portfolios.[3]

2. Alternative approaches to achieving competitive advantage

a) Evaluate, through the strategy clock, generic strategy options available to an organisation.[3]

b) Advise on how price-based strategies, differentiation and lock-in can help an organisation sustain its competitive advantage.[3]

c) Explore how organisations can respond to hypercompetitive conditions.[2]

d) Assess opportunities for improving competitiveness through collaboration.[3]

3. Alternative directions and methods of development

a) Determine generic development directions (employing an adapted Ansoff matrix and a TOWS matrix) available to an organisation.[2]

b) Assess how internal development, mergers, acquisitions and strategic alliances can be used as different methods of pursuing a chosen strategic direction.[3]

c) Establish success criteria to assist in the choice of a strategic direction and method (strategic options).[2]

d) Assess the suitability of different strategic options to an organisation.[3]

e) Assess the feasibility of different strategic options to an organisation.[3]

f) Establish the acceptability of strategic options to an organisation through analysing risk and return on investment.[3]

C STRATEGIC ACTION

1. Organising and enabling success

a) Advise on how the organisation can be structured to deliver a selected strategy.[3]

b) Explore generic processes that take place within the structure, with particular emphasis on the planning process.[3]

c) Discuss how internal relationships can be organised to deliver a selected strategy.[2]

d) Discuss how external relationships (outsourcing, strategic alliances, networks and the virtual organisation) can be structured to deliver a selected strategy.[2]

e) Explore (through Mintzberg's organisational configurations) the design of structure, processes and relationships.[3]

2. Managing strategic change

a) Explore different types of strategic change and their implications.[2]

b) Determine the organisational context of change and use the cultural web to diagnose this organisational context.[3]

c) Establish potential blockages and levers of change.[2]

d) Advise on the style of leadership appropriate to manage strategic change.[2]

e) Specify organisational roles required to manage strategic change.[2]

f) Discuss levers that can be employed to manage strategic change.[2]

3. Understanding strategy development

a) Discriminate between the concepts of intended and emergent strategies.[3]

b) Explain how organisations attempt to put an intended strategy into place.[2]

c) Highlight how emergent strategies appear from within an organisation.[3]

d) Discuss how process redesign, quality initiatives and e-business can contribute to emergent strategies.[2]

e) Assess the implications of strategic drift and the demand for multiple processes of strategy development.[3]

D BUSINESS PROCESS CHANGE

1. The role of process and process change initiatives

a) Advise on how an organisation can reconsider the design of its processes to deliver a selected strategy.[3]

b) Appraise business process change initiatives previously adopted by organisations.[3]

c) Establish an appropriate scope and focus for business process change using Harmon's process-strategy matrix.[3].

d) Explore the commoditisation of business processes [3]

e) Advise on the implications of business process outsourcing [3]

f) Recommend a business process redesign methodology for an organisation.[2]

2. Improving the processes of the organisation

a) Evaluate the effectiveness of current organisational processes.[3]

b) Describe a range of process redesign patterns.[2]

c) Establish possible redesign options for improving the current processes of an organisation.[2]

d) Assess the feasibility of possible redesign options.[3]

e) Assess the relationship between process redesign and strategy.[3]

3. Software solutions

a) Establish information system requirements required by business users.[2]

b) Assess the advantages and disadvantages of using a generic software solution to fulfil those requirements.[2]

c) Establish a process for evaluating, selecting and implementing a generic software solution.[2]

d) Explore the relationship between generic software solutions and business process redesign.[2]

E   INFORMATION TECHNOLOGY

1.   Principles of e-business

a) Discuss the meaning and scope of e-business.[2]

b) Advise on the reasons for the adoption of e-business and recognise barriers to its adoption.[3]

c) Evaluate how e-business changes the relationships between organisations and their customers.[3]

d) Discuss and evaluate the main business and marketplace models for delivering e-business.[3]

e) Advise on the hardware and software infrastructure required to support e-business.[3]

f) Advise on how the organisation can utilise information technology to help it deliver a selected strategy.[3]

2.   E-business application: upstream supply chain management

a) Analyse the main elements of both the push and pull models of the supply chain.[2]

b) Discuss the relationship of the supply chain to the value chain and the value network.[2]

c) Assess the potential application of information technology to support and restructure the supply chain.[3]

d) Advise on how external relationships with suppliers and distributors can be structured to deliver a restructured supply chain.[3]

e) Discuss the methods, benefits and risks of e-procurement.[2]

f) Assess different options and models for implementing e-procurement.[2]

3.   E-business application: downstream supply chain management

a) Define the scope and media of e-marketing.[2]

b) Highlight how the media of e-marketing can be used when developing an effective e-marketing plan.[2]

c) Explore the characteristics of the media of e-marketing using the '6I's of Interactivity, Intelligence, Individualisation, Integration, Industry structure and Independence of location.[2]

d) Evaluate the effect of the media of e-marketing on the traditional marketing mix of product, promotion, price, place, people, processes and physical evidence.[3]

e) Assess the importance of, on-line branding in e-marketing and compare it with traditional branding.

4.   E-business application: customer relationship management

a) Define the meaning and scope of customer relationship management.[2]

b) Explore different methods of acquiring customers through exploiting electronic media.[2]

c) Evaluate different buyer behaviour amongst on-line customers.[3]

d) Recommend techniques for retaining customers using electronic media.[2]

e) Recommend how electronic media may be used to increase the activity and value of established, retained customers.[2]

f) Discuss the scope of a representative software package solution designed to support customer relationship management.[2]

F   QUALITY ISSUES

1.   Quality control, quality assurance and quality management systems

a) Discriminate between quality, quality assurance, quality control and a quality management system.[2]

b) Assess the relationship of quality to the strategy of an organisation.[3]

c) Appraise quality initiatives previously adopted by organisations.[2]

d) Advise on the structure and benefits of a quality management system and quality certification.[3]

2.   Quality in the information systems development lifecycle

a) Justify the need and assess the characteristics of quality in computer software and the implications of these characteristics for testing, liability and ownership.[3]

b) Discuss the stages of systems development through the medium of the V lifecycle model.[2]

c) Advise on how the V lifecycle model defines and partitions testing and contributes to improved computer software quality.[3]

d) Discuss how the process of computer software development process might be improved through the application of the Capability Maturity Model Integration (CMMI) process.[2]

3.   Quality Initiatives: Six Sigma

a) Define the scope, principles and objectives of Six Sigma.[2]

b) Discuss the team roles typically required by Six Sigma.[2]

c) Outline the Six Sigma problem-solving process (DMAIC).[2]

d) Discuss the significance and implications of measurement in the Six Sigma problem-solving process.[2]

e) Explain the application of Six Sigma within e-business, the value chain and process re-design.[2]

G   PROJECT MANAGEMENT

1.   Identifying and initiating projects

a) Determine the distinguishing features of projects and the constraints they operate in.[2]

b) Discuss the relationship between organisational strategy and project management.[2]

c) Identify and plan to manage risks [2]

d) Advise on the structures and information that have to be in place to successfully initiate a project.[3]

e) Assess the importance of developing a project plan and discuss the work required to produce this plan.[3]

f) Explain the relevance of projects to process re-design, e-business systems development and quality initiatives.[2]

2.   Managing and leading projects

a) Discuss the organisation and implications of project-based team structures.[2]

b) Establish the role and responsibilities of the project manager and the project sponsor.[2]

c) Identify and describe typical problems encountered by a project manager when leading a project.[2]

d) Advise on how these typical problems might be addressed and overcome.[3]

3. Monitoring, controlling and concluding projects

a) Monitor the status of a project and identify project risks, issues, slippage and changes and the likely achievement of business benefits.[2]

b) Formulate responses for dealing with project risks, issues, slippage and changes.[2]

c) Establish mechanisms for successfully concluding a project.[2]

d) Discuss the meaning and benefits of an end-project review, including benefits realisation.[2]

e) Evaluate how project management software may support the planning and monitoring of a project.[3]

H   FINANCIAL ANALYSIS

1. The link between strategy and finance

a) Explain the relationship between strategy and finance.[3]
   i)   Managing for value
   ii) Financial expectations of stakeholders
   iii) Funding strategies

2. Finance decisions to formulate and support business strategy

a) Determine the overall investment requirements of the business.[2]

b) Evaluate alternative sources of finance for these investments and their associated risks.[3]

c) Efficiently and effectively manage the current and non-current assets of the business from a finance and risk perspective.[2]

3. Financial implications of making strategic choices and of implementing strategic actions

a) Apply efficiency ratios to assess how efficiently an organisation uses its current resources.[2]

b) Apply appropriate gearing ratios to assess the risks associated with financing and investment in the organisation.[2]

c) Apply appropriate liquidity ratios to assess the organisation's short-term commitments to creditors and employees.[2]

d) Apply appropriate profitability ratios to assess the viability of chosen strategies.[2]

e) Apply appropriate investment ratios to assist investors and shareholders in evaluating organisational performance and strategy.[2]

I   PEOPLE

1. Strategy and people: leadership

a) Explain the role of visionary leadership and identify the key leadership traits effective in the successful formulation and implementation of strategy and change management.[3]

b) Apply and compare alternative classical and modern theories of leadership in the effective implementation of strategic objectives.[3]

2. Strategy and people: performance management

a) Explain how the effective recruitment, management and motivation of people is necessary for enabling strategic and operational success.[3]

b) Discuss the judgemental and developmental roles of assessment and appraisal.[3]

c)' Evaluate the concept of performance management and explore its relationship with strategic management.[3]

d) Advise on the relationship of performance management to performance measurement (performance rating) and determine the implications of performance measurement to quality initiatives and process re-design.[3]

3. Strategy and people: reward management

a) Explore the meaning and scope of reward management and reward practices.[2]

b) · Discuss and evaluate different methods of reward.[2]

c) Discuss and evaluate different techniques of reward and their relationship to job design, appraisal and deployment of staff.[2]

d) Explore the principles and difficulty of aligning reward practices with strategy.[2]

e) Advise on the relationship of reward management to quality initiatives, process re-design and the harnessing of e-business opportunities.[3]

4. Strategy and people: job design

a) Assess the contribution of four different approaches to job design (scientific management, job enrichment, Japanese management and re-engineering).[3]

b) Explain the human resource implications of knowledge work and post-industrial job design.[2]

c) Discuss the tensions and potential ethical issues related to job design.[2]

d) Advise on the relationship of job design to quality initiatives, process re-design, project management and the harnessing of e-business opportunities.[3]

5. Strategy and people: staff development

a) Discuss the emergence and scope of human resource development, succession planning and their relationship to the strategy of the organisation.[2]

b) Advise and suggest different methods of establishing human resource development.[3]

c) Advise on the contribution of competency frameworks to human resource development.[3]

d) Discuss the meaning and contribution of workplace learning, the learning organisation, organisation learning and knowledge management.[3]

READING LIST

ACCA's approved publishers:

BPP Professional Education
Contact number: +44(0)20 8740 2222
Website: www.bpp.com

Kaplan Publishing Foulks Lynch
Contact number: +44(0)118 989 0629
Website: www.kaplanfoulkslynch.com

Additional reading:

Accountancy Tuition Centre (ATC) International
Contact number: +44(0)141 880 6469
Website: www.atc-global.com

Primary Texts:

Johnson G, Scholes K and Whittington R, Exploring Corporate Strategy (seventh edition), Prentice Hall (2005)

Harmon P, Business Process Change, Morgan Kaufman Publishers (2003)

Chaffey D, E-Business and E-Commerce Management (second edition), Prentice Hall (2004)

Bratton J and Gold J, Human Resource Management, Palgrave Macmillan (2003)

Secondary texts:

Tricker R and Sherring-Lucas B, ISO 9001:2000, Butterworth Heinemann (2001)

Pande P and Holpp L, What is Six Sigma?, McGraw-Hill (2002)

Grundy T and Brown L, Strategic Project Management, Thomson Learning (2002)

Schwalbe K, Introduction to Project Management, Thomson Course Technology (2006)

The exam paper

The exam is a three-hour paper consisting of two sections. Fifteen minutes reading and planning time is allowed in addition to three hours writing time.

Section A will be a compulsory case study question with several requirements relating to the same scenario information. The question will usually assess and link a range of subject areas across the syllabus and will require students to demonstrate high-level capabilities to evaluate, relate and apply the information in the case study to the requirements.

Section B questions are more likely to assess a range of discrete subject areas from the main syllabus section headings; they may require evaluation and synthesis of information contained within short scenarios and application of this information to the question requirements.

The paper will have a global focus; no numerical questions will be set.

		Number of marks
Section A:	1 compulsory case study	50
Section B:	Choice of 2 from 3 questions (25 marks each)	50
		100

Analysis of pilot paper

Section A

1   Environmental analysis; financial and sector analysis; assessment of stated options

Section B

2   Principles of internal development, growth by acquisition and strategic alliances; and their application

3   Importance and characteristics of software quality; CMMI levels

4   Drawing a scenario-based value chain and explaining upstream and downstream supply chains

The pilot paper is reproduced in full below.

Pilot paper

Paper P3

Business Analysis

Time allowed

Reading and planning: 15 minutes
Writing: 3 hours

This paper is divided into two sections:

Section A – This ONE question is compulsory and MUST be attempted

Section B – TWO questions ONLY to be attempted

Do NOT open this paper until instructed by the supervisor.

During reading and planning time only the question paper may be annotated. You must NOT write in your answer booklet until instructed by the supervisor.

This question paper must not be removed from the examination hall.

Warning

The pilot paper cannot cover all of the syllabus nor can it include examples of every type of question that will be included in the actual exam. You may see questions in the exam that you think are more difficult than any you see in the pilot paper.

Section A – The ONE question in this section is compulsory and MUST be attempted.

The following information should be used when answering question 1.

The case study of this Business Analysis pilot paper is based on the one examined in Paper 3.5 – Strategic Business Planning and Development in June 2004. Slight amendments have been made to the scenario, questions and answers to reflect the Business Analysis syllabus and emphasis.

1   Introduction

Network Management Systems (NMS) is a privately owned hi-tech business set up in a location near London in 1993. NMS is the brainchild of a Canadian computer engineer, Ray Edwards. Ray is a classic hi-tech entrepreneur, constantly searching for ways to exploit technological opportunities and unafraid to take the risks associated with high technology start-ups. NMS's first product was a digital error detection box able to 'listen' to computer signals and detect faults. The original box, designed by Ray, was built on his kitchen table and manufactured in a garage. Ray is a flamboyant character and a committed entrepreneur. In his words an entrepreneur is "someone willing to work 18 hours a day for themselves … to avoid working eight hours a day for someone else!"

Structure of the business and key product areas

By 2006 NMS employed 75 full time employees in a new, purpose built factory and office unit. These employees were a mix of technically qualified engineers working in research and development (R&D), factory staff manufacturing and assembling the products and a small sales and service support team. In 2006, NMS had three distinct product/service areas.

One of the three products NMS produced was data communication components which it sold directly to original equipment manufacturers (OEMs) that used these components in their hardware. Both the OEMs and their customers were predominantly large international companies. NMS had established a good reputation for the quality and performance of its components, which were also competitively priced. However, NMS had less than 1% share of the UK market in this sector and faced competition from more than twenty suppliers, most of who also competed internationally. Furthermore, one of NMS's OEM customers accounted for 40% of its sales. The European market for data communications equipment had increased from $3.3 billion in 1999 to $8.0 billion in 2006. Forecasts for 2007 and beyond, predict growth from increased sales to currently installed networks rather than from the installation of new networks. The maturity of the technology means that product lifecycles are becoming shorter. Success comes from producing large volumes of relatively low priced reliable components. However, all new components have to be approved by the relevant government approval body in each country being supplied. Approval for new data communication equipment is both costly and time consuming.

NMS's second product area was network management systems – hence the name of the company. Fault detection systems were supplied directly to a small number of large end users such as banks, public utility providers and global manufacturers. NMS recognised the unique configuration of each customer and so it customised its product to meet specific needs and requirements. They have pioneered a "modular building block" design, which allows the customer to adapt standard system modules to fit their exact networking requirements. NMS products focused on solving network management problems and the success of its products was reflected in the award of the prestigious Government Award for Technology for "technological innovation in the prevention of computer data communication downtime". This was recognition of the excellence of the R&D engineers who developed the software and related hardware. It further enhanced NMS's reputation and enabled it to become a successful niche player in this low volume market with gross margins in excess of 40%. NMS only faces two or three competitors in a specialist market where there is no need to gain government approval for new products and systems.

Finally, the complexity of NMS products means that technical support is a third key business area. NMS has established a reputation for excellent technical support, reflecting Ray's continuing concern with customer care. However, it is increasingly difficult and costly to maintain this support because the company lacks a national network. All technical support is provided from its headquarters. This contrasts with the national and international distributed service structure operated by its large, international competitors.

Emerging problems

NMS's growth has made Ray increasingly concerned about the ability of NMS to identify market trends, scan its competitive environment and create marketing strategies and plans. NMS's market and sales planning only covers the year ahead. Larger competitors invest heavily in market research analysis and customer relationship marketing. Business-to-business marketing is becoming an increasingly complex and sophisticated activity in this sector.

Accurate sales forecasting is also a key input into production planning and scheduling. NMS manufactures 40% of the components used in its products. The rest of the components, including semiconductors and microprocessors, are bought in from global suppliers. Serious production problems result from periodic component shortages, creating significant delays in manufacturing, assembly, and customer deliveries. Furthermore, the growth of NMS has outstripped the largely manual control systems designed to support its production and sales operation.

Ray is acutely aware of his key role as founder and chairman of the firm. He is also finding the skills and attributes necessary for founding and growing the business are not appropriate in a mature business. He is heavily reliant on his extrovert personality and his ability to muddle through with informal, flexible systems. The limitation of this approach is now beginning to show. He is finding it increasingly difficult to cope with the day-to-day demands of running the business while at the same time planning its future. Functional departments in the shape of sales and marketing, technical (R&D), manufacturing and administration are in place but strategic planning, such as there is, is very much his responsibility.

Recruitment of high calibre staff is also a problem – NMS's small size and location means that it struggles to attract the key personnel necessary for future growth. Ray feels pressure on him to either develop the necessary skills himself, or to develop the right people with the right skills. In Ray's words, starting a business is like "building your own airplane and then teaching yourself how to fly".

One particular skill in short supply is the financial capability of dealing with growth. His negotiations with bankers and other financial intermediaries have become increasingly difficult and time consuming. The financial control information required to support growth and, more recently, to ensure survival is often inadequate. However, 2006 had started well, with NMS approached as a target for a possible acquisition by a major data communications company. The opportunity to realise some of the equity in the business had considerable appeal. Unfortunately, while protracted negotiations were taking place, a downturn in the global economy occured. Orders for NMS's products fell and the banks and venture capitalists supporting NMS through overdraft and long-term investment became much less sympathetic. The final insult occurred when Ray was approached by a venture capitalist with a management buyout proposal put together with NMS's financial director and sales manager. The value placed on the business was a derisory £50K. Ray was angry and hurt by the size of the offer and also at the disloyalty of his senior staff in seeking to buy the business. To make matters worse the uncertainty over the future of the business has led to a number of key members of staff deciding to leave the company. The financial director and sales manager are still both in post, but their future plans are uncertain. Financial data for NMS is presented in Table 1.

Ray's future at NMS

Ray is currently considering his future at NMS. He has identified three main exit options. The first is to personally lead the company out of its current problems, which he largely attributes to global economic slowdown, and to launch the business on the stock exchange as soon as its economic position improves. His second option is to sell the business for a figure which more accurately reflects its real value and to walk away and reflect on his future. His final option is to seek acquisition by one of his large customers (or competitors) and so become part of a much larger organisation. In such circumstances he would offer to stay on and develop NMS within the structures imposed by a parent organisation. By nature a fighter, the recent uncertainties over ownership and gloomy forecasts for the global economy have made him seriously reflect on his own priorities. His hands-on approach and involvement with all aspects of the business seems increasingly inappropriate for handling the problems of a hi-tech business such as NMS.

BPP
LEARNING MEDIA

Table 1: Financial data for Network Management Systems

	2004	2005	2006	2007 (forecast)
Sales	£'000	£'000	£'000	£'000
UK sales	4,500	6,300	6,930	6,235
Export sales	300	500	650	520
Total sales	4,800	6,800	7,580	6,755
Cost of sales	2,640	3,770	4,550	4,320
Gross margin	2,160	3,030	3,030	2,435
Expenses				
Administration	500	630	700	665
Distribution	715	940	945	885
Marketing	50	60	70	70
R&D	495	590	870	690
Overheads	200	280	320	325
Operating profit	200	530	125	-200
Sales Interest paid	25	120	150	165
Net profit	175	410	-25	-365
Financing				
Long-term liabilities	160	750	1,000	1,100
Share capital and reserves	375	605	600	575
Other information				
Employees	50	60	75	60
% of orders late	5	7	10	6
Order book	4,725	4,150	3,150	2,500

Required:

(a) Assess the macro-environment of NMS by undertaking a **PESTEL** analysis. (10 marks)

(b) Using appropriate models and financial and quantitative data from the scenario, provide an environmental and financial analysis of NMS, highlighting problem areas. (25 marks)

(c) Ray is considering three main exit options from the business as it currently exists. Assess each of the three identified exit options in terms of their ability to solve the problems highlighted in your analysis and in terms of Ray's future role in the business. (15 marks)

(50 marks)

Section B – TWO questions ONLY to be attempted

2   The Environment Management Society (EMS) was established in 1999 by environment practitioners who felt that environmental management and audit should have its own qualification. EMS has its own Board who report to a Council of eight members. Policy is made by the Board and ratified by Council. EMS is registered as a private limited entity.

EMS employs staff to administer its qualification and to provide services to its members. The qualification began as one certificate, developed by the original founding members of the Society. It has since been developed, by members and officers of the EMS, into a four certificate scheme leading to a Diploma. EMS employs a full-time chief examiner who is responsible for setting the certificate examinations which take place monthly in training centres throughout the country. No examinations are currently held in other countries.

If candidates pass all four papers they can undertake an oral Diploma examination. If they pass this oral they are eligible to become members. All examinations are open-book one hour examinations, preceded by 15 minutes reading time. At a recent meeting, EMS Council rejected the concept of computer-based assessment. They felt that competence in this area was best assessed by written examination answers.

Candidate numbers for the qualification have fallen dramatically in the last two years. The Board of EMS has concluded that this drop reflects the maturing marketplace in the country. Many people who were practitioners in environmental management and audit when the qualification was introduced have now gained their Diploma. The stream of new candidates and hence members is relatively small.

Consequently, the EMS Board has suggested that they should now look to attract international candidates and it has targeted countries where environmental management and audit is becoming more important. It is now formulating a strategy to launch the qualification in India, China and Russia.

However, any strategy has to recognise that both the EMS Board and the Council are very cautious and notably risk-averse. EMS is only confident about its technical capability within a restricted definition of environmental management and audit. Attempts to look at complementary qualification areas (such as soil and water conservation) have been swiftly rejected by Council as being non-core areas and therefore outside the scope of their expertise.

Required:

Internal development, acquisitions and strategic alliances are three development methods by which an organisation's strategic direction can be pursued.

(a)   **Explain the principles of internal development and discuss how appropriate this development method is to EMS.**   (8 marks)

(b)   **Explain the principles of acquisitions and discuss how appropriate this development method is to EMS.**   (8 marks)

(c)   **Explain the principles of strategic alliances and discuss how appropriate this development method is to EMS.**   (9 marks)

(25 marks)

3 CCT Computer Systems plc specialises in the development and implementation of software for the logistics industry. After experiencing a number of years of growth and profitability the company is continuing to report growth in turnover but, for the last five quarters, it has also reported small losses. An investigation into this has revealed that costs have risen greatly in systems development and support and consequently margins have been eroded in recently completed projects. It appears that this trend is going to continue. Many people within the company attribute this worsening financial performance to a perceived reduction in software quality. Here are three testimonies received during the investigation

Amelia Platt: Software Development Manager CCT Computer Systems plc
"You have to remember that the original logistics system was developed by Ilya Borisova (the founder of CCT) and three of his friends from university days. They did not build the software with expansion or maintenance in mind. Also, it is difficult to know what some of the programs actually do, so making changes is a nightmare. Programmers make changes to program code without really knowing what the knock-on effect will be."

Tony Osunda: General Manager QANDO logistics – a major customer
"We feel that the last project was most unsatisfactory. We specified our requirements very carefully but the delivered system did not work the way we wanted. We found it cumbersome to use and key areas of functionality were either wrong or missing altogether. After implementation, we asked for a number of changes so that the system would work as it should. We were originally asked to pay for these changes but we pointed out that they weren't really changes – they were things we had asked for all along. Eventually, CCT backed down and so we got the changes for free. The system works fine now, but it has been delivered late and we are still seeking compensation for this.

Carlos Theroux: One of the original programmers of the CCT logistics software solution: Now lead programmer CCT Computer Systems plc
"It is no fun here anymore. When we were smaller we could all dive in and solve the problems. When I joined we had three programmers, now we have one hundred and thirty. What do they all do? There is no work ethic. We all used to stay over until we got the problem solved. Now there is documentation, documentation and documentation. We have now adopted a formal project management method, more documentation! I am not sure this place suits me anymore."

Required:

(a) **A perceived reduction in software quality is blamed by many people for the decline in profitability at CCT. Discuss the importance and characteristics of software quality and explain how each of these characteristics might be measured.** (10 marks)

(b) **Explain the levels within the Capability Maturity Model Integration (CMMI) process and discuss their implications for CCT.** (15 marks)

(25 marks)

4   DRB Electronic Services operates in a high labour cost environment in Western Europe and imports electronic products from the Republic of Korea. It re-brands and re-packages them as DRB products and then sells them to business and domestic customers in the local geographical region. Its only current source of supply is ISAS electronics based in a factory on the outskirts of Seoul, the capital of the Republic of Korea. DRB regularly places orders for ISAS products through the ISAS web-site and pays for them by credit card. As soon as the payment is confirmed ISAS automatically e-mails DRB a confirmation of order, an order reference number and likely shipping date. When the order is actually despatched, ISAS send DRB a notice of despatch e-mail and a container reference number. ISAS currently organises all the shipping of the products. The products are sent in containers and then trans-shipped to EIF, the logistics company used by ISAS to distribute its products. EIF then delivers the products to the DRB factory. Once they arrive, they are quality inspected and products that pass the inspection are re-branded as DRB products (by adding appropriate logos) and packaged in specially fabricated DRB boxes. These products are then stored ready for sale. All customer sales are from stock. Products that fail the inspection are returned to ISAS.

Currently 60% of sales are made to domestic customers and 40% to business customers. Most domestic customers pick up their products from DRB and set them up themselves. In contrast, most business customers ask DRB to set up the electronic equipment at their offices, for which DRB makes a small charge. DRB currently advertises its products in local and regional newspapers. DRB also has a web site which provides product details. Potential customers can enquire about the specification and availability of products through an e-mail facility in the web site. DRB then e-mails an appropriate response directly to the person making the enquiry. Payment for products cannot currently be made through the web site.

Feedback from existing customers suggests that they particularly value the installation and support offered by the company. The company employs specialist technicians who (for a fee) will install equipment in both homes and offices. They will also come out and troubleshoot problems with equipment that is still under warranty. DRB also offer a helpline and a back to base facility for customers whose products are out of warranty. Feedback from current customers suggests that this support is highly valued. One commented that "it contrasts favourably with your large customers who offer support through impersonal off-shore call centres and a time-consuming returns policy". Customers can also pay for technicians to come on-site to sort out problems with out-of-warranty equipment.

DRB now plans to increase their product range and market share. It plans to grow from its current turnover of £5m per annum to £12m per annum in two years time. Dilip Masood, the owner of DRB, believes that DRB must change its business model if it is to achieve this growth. He believes that these changes will also have to tackle problems associated with

–   Missing, or potentially missing shipments. Shipments can only be tracked through contacting the shipment account holder, ISAS, and on occasions they have been reluctant or unable to help. The trans-shipment to EIF has also caused problems and this has usually been identified as the point where goods have been lost. ISAS does not appear to be able to reliably track the relationship between the container shipment and the Waybills used in the EIF system.

–   The likely delivery dates of orders, the progress of orders and the progress of shipments is poorly specified and monitored. Hence deliveries are relatively unpredictable and this can cause congestion problems in the delivery bay.

Dilip also recognises that growth will mean that the company has to sell more products outside its region and the technical installation and support so valued by local customers will be difficult to maintain. He is also adamant that DRB will continue to import only fully configured products. It is not interested in importing components and assembling them. DRB also does not wish to build or invest in assembly plants overseas or to commit to a long-term contract with one supplier.

Required:

(a)   **Draw the primary activities of DRB on a value chain. Comment on the significance of each of these activities and the value that they offer to customers.**   (9 marks)

(b)   **Explain how DRB might re-structure its upstream supply chain to achieve the growth required by DRB and to tackle the problems that Dilip Masood has identified.**   (10 marks)

(c)   **Explain how DRB might re-structure its downstream supply chain to achieve the growth required.**   (6 marks)

(25 marks)

Part A
Strategic position

Business
strategy

Topic list	Syllabus reference
1 What is strategy?	A1(a), (f) A6(g)
2 Levels of strategy in an organisation	A1(b)
3 Elements of strategic management	A1(c)
4 The importance of context	A1(d)
5 The strategy lenses	A1(e)

Introduction

This Study Text concerns the ACCA examination called **Business Analysis**.
Analysis, of various kinds, forms an important element of the wider activity of
strategic management. Despite its name, your syllabus deals with the full
scope of strategic management and we will provide you with complete
coverage in this Text. Section A of your syllabus is, in fact, largely concerned
with the analysis aspect of strategic management, but before we start to
discuss that in detail, we will give you an overview of how it fits in to the bigger
strategic picture. This is, broadly, the material specified in the first element of
syllabus Section A and will form the basis of this chapter.

The main reference for Sections A, B and C of your syllabus is the seventh
edition of *Exploring Corporate Strategy* by *Johnson, Scholes and Whittington*.
We shall make frequent reference to this book using the abbreviation **JS&W**.

Study guide

		Intellectual level
A1	**The need for, and purpose of, strategic and business analysis**	
(a)	Recognise the fundamental nature and vocabulary of strategy and strategic decisions	2
(b)	Discuss how strategy may be formulated at different levels (corporate, business level, operations) of an organisation	2
(c)	Explore the Johnson, Scholes and Whittington model for defining elements of strategic management – the strategic position, strategic choices and strategy into action	3
(d)	Analyse how strategic management is affected by different organisational contexts	3
(e)	Compare three different strategy lenses (Johnson, Scholes and Whittington) for viewing and understanding strategy and strategic management	3
(f)	Explore the scope of business analysis and its relationship to strategy and strategic management in the context of the relational diagram of this syllabus	3

Exam guide

This chapter covers fundamental concepts that are likely to be relevant to any exam question, though questions specifically aimed at this material are unlikely.

1 What is strategy?

FAST FORWARD

Strategy is the direction and scope of an organisation over the long term, which achieves advantage in a changing environment through its configuration of resources and competences with the aim of fulfilling stakeholder expectations. Strategic decisions are made under conditions of complexity and uncertainty; they have wide impact on the organisation and often lead to major change.

Strategy is difficult to define; it is a topic with several rather different aspects and the word is used to mean several rather different things. We are concerned with its meaning in relation to the higher management of organisations. This is a complex process (as will become clearer as you make your way through this Study Text), but examining some of its features will help us to develop an understanding of what is meant by strategy and strategic management.

Exam focus point

Business strategy is as much an art as it is a science. This is because it is concerned with the **behaviour of people,** both individually and in large numbers. It is a social science, in fact. This presents an **immediate problem for the typical student of accountancy**. People tend to choose accountancy as a career because they prefer working with hard facts to dealing with people, with all their messy, unpredictable feelings, motivations, and behaviours. If you recognise any part of yourself in this (rather tongue in cheek) description, it will be important for you to understand and accept some important facts about business strategy before you go any further.

(a) **Business strategy is not a finished artefact, it is a work in progress**. There is still vigorous debate, not only about how organisations *should* make their strategies but also about how they *actually do* make them.

(b) Partly as a result of this, and partly as a result of the complexity of human behaviour mentioned above, **there are few, if any, correct answers** to business strategy problems. This means that the essence of your exam is **not about things you can learn by heart**, such as models and procedures; it is about **intelligent argument**: selecting and applying ideas and theories to realistic problems in order to reach sensible conclusions and make reasonable suggestions.

(c) In this study text you will come across some ideas that are widely accepted and others that are not. It is important to understand that even these latter ideas may have something to offer. However, even the widely accepted ones are only useful if you apply them appropriately.

It is worth reviewing at this point the view of the relationship between strategy and accountancy taken by Ralph Bedrock, the Examiner for the old syllabus Paper 3.5. Writing on the new product development process in Student Accountant in January 2005, he said '... accountants, with their ability to subject proposals to robust analysis (have) an active and positive role to play in resource allocation.... An accountant's realism can balance the naturally optimistic marketeer.'

1.1 Defining strategy

JS&W explore the significance of strategy by considering the subject matter of **strategic decisions**. They discern **six general areas for decision-making** that will normally be regarded as strategic.

(a) The organisation's **long-term direction**: no specific timescale is envisaged, but you should think in terms in excess of one year and more probably of several years.

(b) The **scope of an organisation's activities**: this will include both the overall roles and purposes the organisation accepts for itself and the activities it undertakes in pursuit of them.

(c) For commercial organisations and for many not-for-profit organisations too, strategy will be about gaining some kind of **advantage in competition**.

(d) Strategic management in some organisations will take the form of **adapting their activities to fit the business environment**. In its simplest form, this will involve adapting products and services to gradually changing **customer requirements**.

(e) A contrasting approach will be to **exploit unique resources** and the organisation's **special competences** in particular. This approach sees the business environment as **something that can be changed** by the organisations' own actions.

(f) Strategic decisions are affected by the **values and expectations** of the organisation's **stakeholders**. Stakeholders are people who have a legitimate interest in what the organisation does.

These six considerations lead JS&W to suggest the definition of strategy given below.

Key term

> **Strategy** is the direction and scope of an organisation over the long term, which achieves advantage in a changing environment through its configuration of resources and competences with the aim of fulfilling stakeholder expectations.

1.2 Characteristics of strategic decisions

Having defined the matters that require decisions of a strategic nature, JS&W go on to describe some **important characteristics of the strategic decisions** themselves.

(a) Decisions about strategy are likely to be **complex** since there are likely to be a number of significant factors to take into consideration and a variety of possible outcomes to balance against one another.

(b) There is likely to be a high degree of **uncertainty** surrounding a strategic decision, both about the precise nature of current circumstances and about the likely consequences of any course of action.

(c) Strategic decisions have extensive impact on **operational decision-making**; that is, decisions at lower levels in the organisation.

(d) Strategic decisions affect the organisation as a whole and require processes that cross operational and functional boundaries within it. An **integrated approach** is therefore required.

(e) Strategic decisions are likely to lead to **change** within the organisation as resource capacity is adjusted to permit new courses of action. Changes with implications for **organisational culture** are particularly complex and difficult to manage.

1.3 Mission, goals and objectives

> **FAST FORWARD**
>
> Strategies are developed in order to achieve desired outcomes. These are inherent in the organisation's mission or defining purpose. Mission guides strategic decisions and provides values and a sense of direction.

The **Ashridge College model of mission** links business strategy to culture and ethics by including four separate elements in an expanded definition of mission.

(a) **Purpose**. Why does the organisation exist? Who does it exist for?

　(i) To create wealth for owners?
　(ii) To satisfy the needs of all stakeholders?
　(iii) To reach some higher goal such as the advancement of society?

(b) **Values** are the beliefs and moral principles that underlie the organisation's culture.

(c) **Strategy** provides the commercial logic for the company, and so addresses the following question: 'What is our business? What should it be?' Strategy in this sense is referred to by JS&W as 'business model' (see below).

(d) **Policies and standards of behaviour** provide guidance on how the organisation's business should be conducted. For example, a service industry that wishes to be the best in its market must aim for standards of service, in all its operations, which are at least as good as those found in its competitors.

1.3.1 The importance of mission for corporate strategy

Mission and values are taken seriously by many businesses, though some managers think the idea is no more than a **consultant-driven fad**. There are several reasons why a business should give serious consideration to establishing a clear concept of its corporate mission.

(a) **Values** are acknowledged as integral elements of consumers' buying decisions; this is shown by the attention paid to them in advertising, brand building and market research. Customers ask not only 'What do you sell?' but 'What do you stand for?'

(b) Studies into organisational behaviour show that **people are motivated by many things** other than money: employees are likely to be both more productive and more satisfied with their work when they feel that what they are doing has significance beyond the mere pursuit of a living.

(c) Some writers believe there is an empirical relationship between strong corporate values and profitability.

1.3.2 Mission statements

Mission statements are formal documents that state the organisation's mission. They are published within organisations in order to promote desired behaviour: support for strategy and purpose, adherence to core values and adoption of policies and standards of behaviour.

Some are suspicious of mission statements.

(a) They are often **public relations** exercises rather than an accurate portrayal of the firm's actual values.

(b) They can often be full of **generalisations** which are impossible to tie down to specific strategic implications.

(c) **They may be ignored** by the people responsible for formulating or implementing strategy.

1.3.3 Mission and planning

The mission statement can play an important role in the strategic planning process.

(a) **Inspires and informs planning**. Plans should further the organisation's goals and be consistent with its core values.

(b) **Screening**. Mission acts as a yardstick by which plans are judged.

(c) Mission also affects the **implementation** of a planned strategy in terms of the ways in which the firm carries out its business and the culture of the organisation.

1.3.4 Goals, objectives and targets

FAST FORWARD

> A structure of goals and objectives derive from mission and support it. All the parts of this structure should be mutually supportive.

An understanding of the organisation's mission is invaluable for setting and controlling the overall functioning and progress of the organisation. However, it is possible for an organisation to operate reasonably effectively even if most of the people within it have only an **intuitive or vague understanding of its purpose**. Most people's work is defined in terms of far more specific and immediate things to be achieved: if these things are related in some way to the wider purpose, the organisation will function. Loosely speaking, these 'things to be achieved' are the goals, objectives and targets of the various departments, offices, and individuals that make up the organisation. In more effective organisations **goal congruence** will be achieved: all these disparate goals, objectives and targets will be consistent with one another and will operate together to support progress with the mission.

Goals can be related in several ways: **hierarchically**, as in the pyramid structure outlined below; **functionally**, as when colleagues collaborate on a project; **logistically**, as when resources must be shared or used in sequence; and in **wider organisational senses**, as when senior executives make decisions about their operational priorities. A good example of the last category is the tension between long– and short-term priorities in such matters as the need contain costs while at the same time increasing productivity by investing in improved plant.

1.3.5 A hierarchy of objectives

A simple model of the relationship between the various goals, objectives and targets is a **pyramid** analogous to the traditional organisational hierarchy. At the top is the **overall mission**; this is supported by a small number of **wide ranging goals**, which may correspond to overall departmental or functional responsibilities. For a business, a primary, corporate objective will be the return offered to shareholders, however this is measured. There may be other primary objectives and there will certainly be supporting objectives for costs, innovation, markets, products and so on.

Each of the high level goals is supported in turn by more detailed, **subordinate goals**. These may correspond, perhaps, to the responsibilities of the senior managers in the function concerned. A more modern pattern is for the hierarchy (and indeed many other aspects of the organisation) to be based on major **value-creating processes** rather than on functional departments. We will return to this topic later in this Study Text. In any event, the pattern is continued downwards until we reach the **work targets** of individual members of the organisation.

We owe the concept of a hierarchy or cascade of objectives to the great management thinker and writer *Peter Drucker*, who outlined the system now known as **management by objectives** (MbO) in the middle of the twentieth century. MbO is still in use as a management tool, though no longer promoted as a universal solution. Its importance for this discussion of goals and objectives is that Drucker was the first to suggest that objectives should be SMART. This acronym originally stood for the qualities listed below.

Specific   **M**easurable   **A**chievable   **R**ealistic   **T**ime-related

Today, *realistic* is often replaced with *results-focused*, for two reasons.

(a)   The current pursuit of innovation as a route to competitive advantage makes it very important that managerial attention is directed towards **achieving results** rather than just **administering established processes**.

(b)   Realistic means much the same thing as achievable, anyway.

There are other variants: *achievable* may be replaced with *attainable*, which has an almost identical meaning, and *relevant* (meaning appropriate to the group or individual concerned) has been proposed as a third option for *R*.

Functions of objectives

(a)   **Planning**: objectives define what the plan is about.

(b)   **Responsibility**: objectives define the responsibilities of managers and departments.

(c)   **Integration**: objectives should support one another and be consistent; this integrates the efforts of different departments.

(d)   **Motivation**: the first step in motivation is knowing what is to be done. Objectives must be created for all areas of performance.

(e)   **Evaluation**: performance is assessed against objectives and control exercised.

1.4 The vocabulary of strategy

FAST FORWARD   Strategy has its own vocabulary, though usage varies. JS&W provide a very useful list.

The field of business strategy has its own vocabulary that you must become familiar with. Unfortunately, there is no generally accepted list of definitions and you may encounter a variety of usages. The key terms box below is based on the definitions used by *JS&W*.

Key terms

Mission is the organisation's overriding purpose; it reflects the values or expectations of stakeholders and answers the question 'what business are we in?'.

Vision or strategic intent is the future state desired by the organisation's strategists: they aim to guide the organisation's collective aspiration toward it.

A **goal** is a statement of a general aim or purpose that supports the mission. It *may* be qualitative in nature.

An **objective** is a more specific aim or purpose and will probably be quantified.

Strategic capability flows from resources and competences. **Unique resources and core competences** create **competitive advantage**. (We will define these terms more precisely later in this Study Text.)

A **business model** describes the structure of product, service and information flows between the parties involved.

Strategic control has two parts: monitoring the effectiveness of strategies and actions; and taking corrective action when required.

1.5 The business analysis syllabus

RELATIONAL DIAGRAM OF MAIN CAPABILITIES

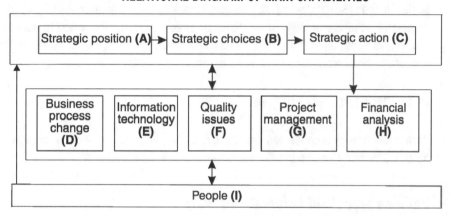

Section A1(f) of the Study Guide for your syllabus calls explicitly for understanding of the nature and scope of business strategy as envisioned by the syllabus and summarised in the relational diagram shown above.

This vision adopts the **systems approach** to understanding the way organisations work and therefore emphasises the importance of both the **internal linkages** between the various organisational components and the **boundary-spanning links** between the organisation and its environment. These two elements are reflected in the two main strategic issues dealt with by the syllabus: the external forces that influence the organisation's strategy and the internal forces and activities that sustain it.

The relational diagram shows the syllabus and, by extension, the nature of business strategy, as **three interconnected layers**.

The top layer is concerned with the **overall strategic perspective**, moving from the analysis of strategic position through strategic choices to strategic action.

The middle layer expands on the basic idea of strategic implementation. The focus is on **three linked aspects of business process management**.

- Process improvement
- IS and e-business
- Quality methods

Each of these elements must be **financially feasible** and requires good **project management**: project management itself can be of strategic significance, as is discussed later in this Study Text.

The middle layer is also a reminder that strategy may **emerge** from within the day-to-day activities of the organisation.

The bottom layer of the model emphasises the importance of the **human resource** to all the other aspects and, therefore, of effective human resource management

2 Levels of strategy in an organisation

FAST FORWARD

There are three main levels of strategy in an organisation.

- **Corporate**: the general direction of the whole organisation
- **Business**: how the organisation or its SBUs tackle particular markets
- **Operational/functional**: specific strategies for different departments of the business

Any level of the organisation can have objectives and devise strategies to achieve them. The strategic management process is multi-layered.

Hofer and Schendel refer to three levels of strategy: **corporate**, **business** and **functional** or **operational**. The distinction between corporate and business strategy arises because of the development of the **divisionalised** business organisation, which typically has a corporate centre and a number of **strategic business units** (SBUs) dealing with particular markets. *Chandler* described how four large US corporations found that the best way to divide strategic responsibility was to have the corporate HQ allocate resources and exercise overall financial control while the SBUs were each responsible for their own product-market strategies. Operational strategies are then developed for component parts of SBUs.

2.1 Corporate strategies

Key term

Corporate strategy is concerned with the overall purpose and scope of the organisation and how value will be added to the different parts (business units) of the organisation. *JS&W*

Defining aspects of corporate strategy

Characteristic	Comment
Scope of activities	Strategy and strategic management impact upon the whole organisation: all parts of the business operation should support and further the strategic plan.
Expectations of stakeholders	There may be a mission statement, but in any case, stakeholder expectations must be prioritised and managed.
Resources	Strategy involves choices about allocating or obtaining corporate resources now and in future.

2.2 Business-level strategy

Key term

Business strategy is about how to compete successfully in particular markets. *JS&W*

Business-level strategy is about the particular and distinct combination of products and markets dealt with by one business unit. A business unit might be a small, independent organisation or part of a larger one. In the first case, business and corporate strategy merge with one another; in the second, SBU level strategies must be co-ordinated with corporate strategy and with each other.

2.3 Operational strategies

Key term

Operational strategies are concerned with how the component parts of an organisation deliver effectively the corporate- and business-level strategies in terms of resources, processes and people *JS&W*

Much operational strategy is created by individual business functions and delivered by them.

Functional area	Comment
Marketing	Devising products and services, pricing, promoting and distributing them, in order to satisfy customer needs at a profit. Marketing and corporate strategies are interrelated.
Production	Factory location, manufacturing techniques, outsourcing and so on.
Finance	Ensuring that the firm has enough financial resources to fund its other strategies by identifying sources of finance and using them effectively.
Human resources management	Secure personnel of the right skills in the right quantity at the right time, and to ensure that they have the right skills and values to promote the firm's overall goals.
Information systems	A firm's information systems are becoming increasingly important, as an item of expenditure, as administrative support and as a tool for competitive strength. Not all information technology applications are strategic, and the strategic value of IT will vary from case to case.
R&D	New products and techniques.

Question

Levels of strategy

Ganymede Ltd is a company selling widgets. The finance director says: 'We plan to issue more shares to raise money for new plant capacity – we don't want loan finance – which will enable us to compete better in the vital and growing widget markets of Latin America. After all, we've promised the shareholders 5% profit growth this year, and trading is tough.'

Identify the **corporate**, **business** and **functional** strategies in the above statement.

Answer

The corporate objective is profit growth. The corporate strategy is the decision that this will be achieved by entering new markets, rather than producing new products. The business strategy suggests that those markets include Latin America. The operational or functional strategy involves the decision to invest in new plant (the production function) which is to be financed by shares rather than loans (the finance function).

3 Elements of strategic management

FAST FORWARD

JS&W suggest a three part structure for thinking about strategy.

- Strategic position
- Strategic choices
- Strategy into action

JS&W analyse strategic management into three main elements.

- **Strategic position**
- **Strategic choices**
- **Strategy into action**

If you refer back to the diagram of the syllabus relational model shown earlier in this chapter, you will see that these three elements form its top layer.

3.1 Strategic position

The strategic managers must attempt to understand the organisation's strategic position. There are **three main groups of influences** to consider: the environment; strategic capability and the expectations of stakeholders.

3.1.1 The environment

The environment of business includes wider political, economic, social, technological, environmentally conscious and legal forces as well as the more immediate pressures of business competition. It is both **complex** and subject to constant **change**, to an extent that probably precludes **complete understanding**. However, if the more salient aspects of the environment can be identified and described, they may be diagnosed into **opportunities** and **threats**.

3.1.2 Strategic capability

The organisation's **resources** and **competences** make up its strategic capability. This may be analysed into **strengths** and **weaknesses**; these influence, enable or constrain possible future strategic choices.

3.1.3 Stakeholders' expectations

Strategy is made in order to achieve the organisation's **purpose**. This may have a formal, even legal, definition and **corporate governance** may be a relevant issue. Consideration must also be given to the **expectations of stakeholder groups** that have a less formal relationship with the organisation. **Stakeholder power and interest** influence the direction in which strategy evolves, as do **ethical issues**.

3.2 Strategic choices

Strategic choices are made at both the **corporate** and **business unit** level. At the level of the business unit, these choices are about how to achieve **competitive advantage** and are based on an understanding of **customers and markets**. At the corporate level, strategy is primarily about **scope**: this is concerned with the overall product/business portfolio, the spread of markets and the relationship between business units and the corporate centre.

Strategic choices must also be made about the **direction** and **method** of development.

3.3 Strategy into action

Strategies must be made to work in practice. Major issues here include **structuring**, **enabling** and **change**.

(a)   **Structuring** includes processes, relationships, organisation structure and how these elements work together.

(b)   **Enabling** is the complex two-way process by which the organisation's resources are managed to both support and to create strategies.

(c)   **Change** is a very common feature of strategic development and the management of change is a most important feature of strategic implementation.

4 The importance of context

The **context of strategy** is the organisational setting in which it is developed. **Small businesses** tend to have limited resources and strong competition; **multinationals** are more concerned with problems of structure, resource allocation and logistics. **Public sector** and **not for profit** organisations are influenced by ideology, politics, and the influence of a range of stakeholders. Intangible aspects have become very important for companies dealing in physical products.

Exam focus point

Context is particularly important to you as a candidate for the P3 exam, since question settings will nearly always provide detailed contexts for the problems they feature. You must always consider the question context and make your answer clearly relevant to it.

Strategic management has many aspects and the relative importance of each of these aspects for individual organisations may vary considerably. For example, an organisation heavily influenced by national political activity, such as the UK National Health Service, is likely to find the management of conflicting stakeholder expectations of far greater significance than might a privately owned distributor of standard electrical components. Even within a single company, differences of industry and market are likely to require different business units to take different approaches to strategy.

4.1 Small businesses

Characteristic	Effect on strategic processes
Limited range of products in a limited market	Few problems of **scope**
Limited planning resources; ownership interest among managers	Strategy based on values and experience
Significant pressure from competitors	Exploitation of competences and resources, choice of competitive strategy and knowledge of market and competition all very important
Limited financial resources	Constant attention to building relationship with providers of funds, especially bankers

4.2 Multinationals

Characteristic	Effect on strategic processes
Diverse products, processes and markets	Problems of relationships, structure and control
Significant resources of all kinds	Allocation and co-ordination of resources
Multiple markets, operations and facilities	Great importance of logistics of manufacturing and supply

4.3 The public sector

The public sector has distinct strategic characteristics.

(a)   Influence of **ideology** on strategy

(b)   **External influence** and even control, especially by government

(c)   **Political constraints on funding and strategic choice** even for state-owned organisations with a commercial role

(d)   Requirement to provide a **universal service**

(e)   **Competition for resource inputs** within a political arena for non-commercial organisations

(f)   Need to demonstrate **best value** in outputs

(g)   Increasing need to demonstrate **improvement in social outcomes**

4.4 Not for profit organisations

Not for profit organisations also have their particular features.

(a)   Importance of underlying **values and purposes**

(b)   **Diverse sources of funds** that may have to be competed for

(c)   Potential for conflict between stakeholders and need for transparency of governance may require **centralised decision-making**.

4.5 Intangible products

There has been an element of strategic convergence between companies supplying **manufactures** on the one hand and those supplying **services** on the other. While the nature of the physical product is still strategically important for the manufacturer, it has become common for competitive advantage to depend as much on the customer's perception of the **intangibles** that are included in the complete market offering. Factors such as product information, after-sales service and brand values have become as strategically important to manufacturers as intangibles, such as staff competence and manner, have always been to providers of services.

5 The strategy lenses

FAST FORWARD

The study of business strategy is fairly new and opinion as to its nature and content is only just beginning to settle. The breadth of opinion about it can be analysed into three different approaches or 'lenses' for looking at individual strategies. These lenses are **strategy as design**, **strategy as experience** and **strategy as ideas**.

5.1 A brief history of the study of business strategy

The 1960s saw the use of the **case study** approach based on practical experience and common sense.

Also in the 1960s and extending into the 1970s, the highly rational **corporate planning approach** was popular. This incorporated operational research ideas and highly systematised analysis of the influences on the organisation's operations. At the same time, writers such as *Simon* and *Lindblom* were challenging rational decision models as unrealistic because of the impossibility of carrying out the full analysis of relevant factors that such models demanded. However, the planning model was popular and corporate planning departments were common in large organisations.

Subsequently, there was considerable **empirical research** aimed at establishing evidence for the likely outcomes of business decisions about products, markets and structures. At the same time, writers such as *Quinn* and *Mintzberg* argued that the sheer **complexity of the world severely limited the usefulness of the analytic approach**. These writers argued that strategic decisions were heavily influenced by experience, politics, culture and history and, as a result, tended to be sub-optimal.

In the 1980s, economic thinking led to the influential work of *Porter* on **competitive advantage** and the emergence of the **resource-based** view of the firm.

More recent ideas have focussed on the concept of the organisation as an organism, adapting to environmental forces through processes of **social interaction** that promote **innovation and change**.

5.2 The strategy lenses

Each of the approaches briefly outlined above has something to offer in understanding of what strategy is and what it is for. JS&W suggest that they can be summarised into **three lenses** through which strategy may be examined.

- Strategy as **design**
- Strategy as **experience**
- Strategy as **ideas**

5.2.1 Strategy as design

There is a widely held view of strategy as a **rational, top-down** process by which senior managers analyse and evaluate strategic constraints and forces in order to establish a clear and rational course of strategic action. This is a traditional view and one that appeals to managers: it is orthodox, logical and supportive of their own view of their role. It also appeals to stakeholders such as shareholders, banks, many employees and public servants.

However, this view makes a number of important assumptions that might be subject to debate. Some of these are given below.

(a) Managers are **rational decision-makers** and the strategic problems facing the organisation are susceptible to **rational analysis**.

(b) There are clear and explicit **objectives**.

(c) The organisation is a hierarchy in which strategy is an **exclusively management responsibility**.

(d) The organisation is also a **rational, almost engineered, system** that is capable of putting management's plans into effect.

The view of strategy as design is useful since it leads to the use of a number of tools and techniques that are both logical and practical. However, it does not describe the whole of strategic management.

5.2.2 Strategy as experience

This view sees strategy as an adaptation and extension of **what has worked in the past**. It is firmly based in the **experience** and **assumptions** of influential figures in the organisation and the ways of doing things approved by the organisation's cultural norms. We will discuss this idea of cultural norms later in this Study Text when we consider the **paradigm**.

Managers tend to **simplify** the complexity they face in order to be able to deal with it, selecting and using the elements of their knowledge and understanding that seem most relevant or important. This process is related to the habit of **exemplifying complex forces** in the form of their most important elements.

Thus, where there is an identifiable main competitor, this entity may come to represent competition in general. The problem here is that this may blind managers to emerging competitors that have the potential to dislocate the existing market structure.

Where there are choices or disputes about strategic options, these are resolved by negotiation and bargaining. The result is decisions that **satisfice rather than optimise** and strategies that develop in an incremental and adaptive way. Another feature of this view is that strategies are as likely to **emerge** from intermediate and lower levels of the organisational hierarchy as they are to be decided at its apex.

Mintzberg described an **emergent strategy** as one 'where patterns developed in the absence of intentions, or despite them'.

5.2.3 Strategy as ideas

This approach to strategy emphasises **innovation** and the need for **diversity of ideas** in the organisation: strategy can emerge from the way the people within the organisation handle and respond to the changing forces present both in the organisation and in the environment. Supporters of this view argue partly by analogy with evolutionary theory, suggesting that where there is diversity of approach, a change in environmental conditions is likely to be accommodated by one of the various methods, products or systems already in existence.

The role of senior managers is to create the **context and conditions** in which new ideas can emerge and the best ones survive and thrive. An important feature of this role is to avoid relying on either the design approach or the experience approach. The first tends to lead to over-emphasis on control, while the second tends to develop a kind of incremental momentum. In either case, innovation is unlikely and the result is **strategic drift**. Senior managers must take care to avoid pressure for conformity, particularly in the matter of cultural assumptions.

Not all of the factors that encourage innovation are under the control of managers, or even easily influenced by them.

(a)   **Boundaries** between the organisation and the environment should be **fluid** and **permeable**. Network organisations and those that co-operate widely with others are the model here. Staff should be encouraged to be in contact with and responsive to the changing environment. Attention should be paid to their **intuitions**.

(b)   **Informal interaction and co-operation** can be more innovative than carefully designed official systems.

(c)   Culturally, **questioning and challenge** are more valuable than **consensus**.

(d)   There should be deliberate support for personal projects and **experimentation**.

(e)   A degree of **ambiguity** in direction sanctions freedom of thought and effort.

Despite all this, there is a need for some degree of control. The aim is the achieve an 'adaptive tension' that will keep the organisation functioning without either resorting to machine-like procedure or descending into unproductive disarray. This can be achieved by the use of **simple rules**, which are general principles rather than detailed procedures. These rules should focus on important basic principles, such as the criteria to be used when ranking potential opportunities.

Chapter Roundup

- **Strategy** is the direction and scope of an organisation over the long term, which achieves advantage in a changing environment through its configuration of resources and competences with the aim of fulfilling stakeholder expectations. Strategic decisions are made under conditions of complexity and uncertainty; they have wide impact on the organisation and often lead to major change.

- Strategies are developed in order to achieve desired outcomes. These are inherent in the organisation's mission or defining purpose. Mission guides strategic decisions and provides values and a sense of direction.

- A structure of goals and objectives derive from mission and support it. All the parts of this structure should be mutually supportive.

- Strategy has its own vocabulary, though usage varies. JS&W provide a very useful list.

- There are many levels of strategy in an organisation.

  - **Corporate**: the general direction of the whole organisation
  - **Business**: how the organisation or its SBUs tackle particular markets
  - **Operational/functional**: specific strategies for different departments of the business

- JS&W suggest a three part structure for thinking about strategy.

  - Strategic position
  - Strategic choices
  - Strategy into action

- The **context of strategy** is the organisational setting in which it is developed. **Small businesses** tend to have limited resources and strong competition; **multinationals** are more concerned with problems of structure, resource allocation and logistics. **Public sector** and **not for profit** organisations are influenced by ideology, politics, and the influence of a range of stakeholders. Intangible aspects have become very important for companies dealing in physical products.

- The study of business strategy is fairly new and opinion as to its nature and content is only just beginning to settle. The breadth of opinion about it can be analysed into three different approaches or 'lenses' for looking at individual strategies. These lenses are **strategy as design**, **strategy as experience** and **strategy as ideas**.

Quick Quiz

1 What is strategy?

2 What are the four elements of the Ashridge model of mission?

3 What are the qualities of SMART objective?

4 What are the three elements of the JS&W model of strategy?

5 What are the three strategy lenses and what is the relationships between them?

Answers to Quick Quiz

1   The JS&W definition is worth committing to memory. Essential elements are **long-term direction** and **scope**; **advantage**; **changing environment**; **resources** and **competences**; and **stakeholder expectations**.

2   Purpose; values; strategy; and policies and standards of behaviour.

3   Specific, measurable, achievable, realistic (relevant, results-focused) time-related.

4   Strategic position, strategic choices, strategy into action.

5   The **design** lens shows strategy as a rational, top-down process under careful controls. This contrasts with the **experience** lens which presents strategy as an extension of what has worked in the past. The **ideas** lens suggests that strategy is formed by diversity of ideas, which leads to innovation. The ideas lens fills a gap left by the design and experience lenses and emphasises that much strategy is not dependant on managerial decisions.

Now try the questions below from the Exam Question Bank

Number	Level	Marks	Time
Q1	Preparation	n/a	15 mins

BPP LEARNING MEDIA

Environmental issues

Introduction

The changing environment is one of the essential elements of JS&W's definition of strategy and analysis of the environment is a fundamental part of the process of developing strategy. Traditionally, strategy in business has been seen as a process of adapting the firm to its environment: the importance of environmental analysis in this approach is obvious. Other views of strategy have emerged that place less emphasis on adaptation, but even when a firm sets out to dominate its environment it must have a full knowledge of the nature of that environment.

Study guide

		Intellectual level
A2	**Environmental issues affecting the strategic position of an organisation**	
(a)	Assess the macro-environment of an organisation using PESTEL	3
(b)	Highlight the key drivers of change likely to affect the structure of a sector or market	3
(c)	Explore, using Porter's Diamond, the influence of national competitiveness on the strategic position of an organisation	2
(d)	Prepare scenarios reflecting different assumptions about the future environment of an organisation	3
A3	**Competitive forces affecting an organisation**	
(a)	Discuss the significance of industry, sector and convergence	3
(b)	Evaluate the sources of competition in an industry or sector using Porter's five forces framework	3

Exam guide

This chapter, like the previous one, deals with wide topics that may be relevant to almost any exam question. However, it also covers some very specific models, such as **PESTEL** and the **five forces**, that you must study in detail. Environmental analysis is a well-established aspect of the theory of business strategy and examiners find it an easy topic to introduce into questions. It will be unusual to come across a question that deals exclusively with the environment, but it is common in this field for examiners to give a fair amount of environmental detail. Make sure you read question scenarios carefully and note the potential implications of the environmental background.

1 The organisation in its environment

All organisations are open systems: they exist within a complex environment and have a variety of interchanges with it, both receiving inputs and providing outputs. Organisations try to control the nature of their outputs, but very few of them can control more than a few of the inputs they receive. Understanding the nature of the environment and the changes taking place within it is therefore a vital part of business analysis.

1.1 Analysing the environment

FAST FORWARD

The environment may be divided for convenience into three concentric layers: the macro-environment; the industry or sector; and competitors and markets. The layers and the elements within them all interact with one another.

We will divide the environment into a variety of components in order to explain it. However, you should be aware that the environmental influences affecting an organisation do not come in neatly labelled packages; there are complex interactions between the elements we will discuss and you must always try to understand the broader picture when you are thinking about the environment.

Following JS&W, we will start our analysis of the environment by dividing it into three parts, each of which has its own particular tools or theories that provide a basis for thinking about it.

Environmental element	Basis of analysis
Macro-environment	PESTEL Key drivers of change Scenarios
Industry or sector	Five forces Cycles of competition
Competitors and markets	Strategic groups Market segments Critical success factors

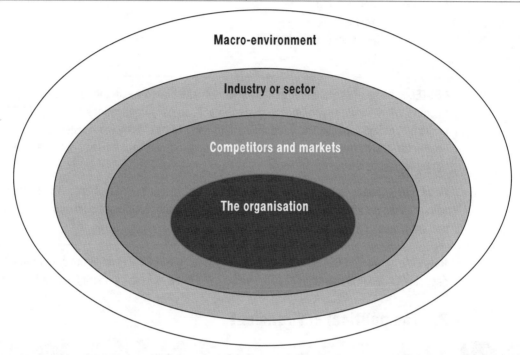

1.2 Environmental uncertainty

FAST FORWARD

Environmental uncertainty depends on the degree of **complexity** and the degree of **stability** present.

A large part of business strategy consists of making the organisation's interaction with its environment as efficient as possible. In the context of strategic management, therefore, the degree of **uncertainty** in the environment is of great importance. The greater the uncertainty, the greater the strategic challenge.

Uncertainty depends on **complexity** and **stability**: the more complex or dynamic the environment is, the more uncertain it is.

(a) An **uncomplicated**, **stable** environment can be dealt with as a matter of routine. The security and efficiency of a **mechanistic** or **bureaucratic** approach to management can be exploited. Since the future is likely to resemble the past, extrapolation from history is a satisfactory way of preparing for future events.

(b) Where the environment is **dynamic**, the management approach must emphasise response to rapid change. **Scenario planning**, **intuition** and a **learning approach** are all valid features of such a response.

(c) **Complexity** makes an environment difficult to understand. Diversity of operations and technological advance contribute to complexity. Complexity is difficult to analyse. It may be that it is best dealt with by a combination of **experience** and **extensive decentralisation**.

2 The macro-environment

The macro-environment may be analysed into six segments using the PESTEL framework.

Analysis of the macro-environment is commonly based on breaking it down into a handful of major aspects. Your syllabus requires you to be familiar with the PESTEL framework, which is based on six segments.

- **P**olitical
- **E**conomic
- **S**ocio-cultural
- **T**echnological
- **E**nvironmental protection
- **L**egal

Exam focus point

PESTEL is a useful checklist for general environmental factors – in the real world they are all **interlinked**, of course. Any single environmental development can have implications for all six PESTEL aspects. In particular, political, social and economic affairs tend to be closely intertwined. Do not, therefore, waste time in the exam trying to impose unnecessary divisions on your environmental analysis. The important thing is the substance, not the form.

Read a newspaper to keep yourself up with current relevant developments. The Section A case studies will be based on industries of global significance and recognisable as such, so you need to be familiar with current topics of importance.

Note. The acronym **PESTEL** is sometimes replaced by **SLEPT**, in which the environmental protection aspect is folded into the other five, or even by **STEEPLE**, where the extra E stand for **ethics**.

2.1 The political environment

Government is responsible for providing a stable framework for economic activity and, in particular, for maintaining and improving the physical, social and market infrastructure. Public policy on **competition** and **consumer protection** is particularly relevant to business strategy.

2.1.1 Government policy

Government policy affects the whole **economy**, and governments are responsible for enforcing and creating a **stable framework** in which business can be done. A report by the World Bank indicated that the quality of **government policy is important in providing** three things.

- Physical infrastructure (eg transport).
- Social infrastructure (education, a welfare safety net, law enforcement, equal opportunities).
- Market infrastructure (enforceable contracts, policing corruption).

However, it is **political change** which complicates the planning activities of many firms. Here is a checklist for case study use. It shows a sequence of considerations.

Consideration	Example
Possibility of political change	Effect on economic policies
Likely nature of impact	Change in taxes and interest rates
Consequences	Cash flow and availability of resources

Consideration	Example
Coping strategies	Cash flow planning
Influence on decision making	Lobbying and publicity

2.1.2 Public policy on competition

In a perfect monopoly, there is only one firm that is the sole producer of a good that has no closely competing substitutes, so that the firm controls the supply of the good to the market. The definition of a monopoly in practice is wider than this, because governments seeking to control the growth of monopoly firms will probably choose to regard any firm that acquires a major share of the market as a potential monopolist.

Monopoly generally exploits customers, but it may have both economic disadvantages and economic advantages.

(a) A **beneficial monopoly** achieves **economies of scale** in an industry where the **minimum efficient scale** is at a level of production that would mean having to achieve a large share of the total market supply. In these circumstances, monopoly may be tolerated but is likely to be regulated or even taken into government ownership. Many utilities, such as railways, telecomms and power generation fall into this category.

Key term

> **Economies of scale** arise when a business grows to the extent that it is able to increase its input of all four types of productive resource: land, labour, capital and enterprise. The effect is to cause the whole structure of short-run costs to fall.

(b) A monopoly would be detrimental to the public interest if **cost efficiencies** are not achieved. *Oliver Williamson* suggested that monopolies might be inefficient if 'market power provides the firm with the opportunity to pursue a variety of other-than-profit objectives'. For example, managers might instead try to maximise sales, or try to maximise their own prestige.

Consumer protection policies may be required.

(a) Control over markets can arise by firms eliminating the opposition, either by merging with or taking over rivals or preventing other firms from entering the market. When a single firm controls a big enough share of the market it can begin to behave as a monopolist even though its market share is below 100%.

(b) Several firms could behave as monopolists by agreeing with each other not to compete. This could be done in a variety of ways – for example by exchanging information, by setting common prices or by splitting up the market into geographical areas and operating only within allocated boundaries. Such a **collusive oligopoly** is called a cartel and is illegal in most jurisdictions.

 Case Study

In 2001 both *VW* and *Michelin* were made to pay heavy fines for monopolistic practices by the European Commission.

2.1.3 The Competition Commission in the UK

The activity of the Competition Commission in the UK is a good example of the way governments may approach the problem of monopoly. The Office of Fair Trading may ask the Competition Commission (CC) to investigate if any firm or group of firms controls 25% or more of the market, or the Secretary of State may do the same if any proposed takeover or merger would create a firm that controlled 25% or more of the market. The CC may also investigate proposed mergers where the assets involved exceed £70 million in value. The Commission will then investigate the proposed merger or takeover and recommend whether or not it should be allowed to proceed.

2.1.4 Anticipating changes in the law

- The governing party's election **manifesto** should be a guide to its political priorities, even if these are not implemented immediately.

- The government often publishes advance information about its plans for consultation purposes.

2.1.5 Political risk

The political risk in a decision is the risk that political factors will invalidate the strategy and perhaps severely damage the firm. Examples are wars, political chaos, corruption and nationalisation.

A **political risk checklist** was outlined by *Jeannet and Hennessey*. Companies should ask the following six questions.

1   How **stable** is the host country's political system?

2   How **strong** is the host government's commitment to specific rules of the game, such as ownership or contractual rights, given its ideology and power position?

3   How **long** is the government likely to remain in **power**?

4   If the present government is **succeeded**, how would the specific rules of the game change?

5   What would be the effects of any expected **changes** in the specific rules of the game?

6   In light of those effects, what **decisions and actions should be taken now**?

2.2 The economic environment

The **economic** environment affects firms at national and international level, both in the general level of economic activity and in particular variables, such as exchange rates, interest rates and inflation.

The economic environment is an important influence at **local and national level**.

Factor	Impact
Overall growth or fall in gross domestic product	Increased/decreased demand for goods (eg dishwashers) and services (holidays).
Local economic trends	Type of industry in the area. Office/factory rents. Labour rates. House prices.
Inflation	Low in most countries; distorts business decisions; wage inflation compensates for price inflation.
Interest rates	How much it costs to borrow money affects cash flow. Some businesses carry a high level of debt. How much customers can afford to spend is also affected as rises in interest rates affect people's mortgage payments.

Factor	Impact
Tax levels	Corporation tax affects how much firms can invest or return to shareholders. Income tax and VAT affect how much consumers have to spend, hence demand.
Government spending	Suppliers to the government (eg construction firms) are affected by spending.
The business cycle	Economic activity is always punctuated by periods of growth followed by decline, simply because of the nature of trade. The UK economy has been characterised by periods of boom and bust. Government policy can cause, exacerbate or mitigate such trends, but cannot abolish the business cycle. (Industries which prosper when others are declining are called counter-cyclical industries.)

The **forecast state of the economy** will influence the planning process for organisations which operate within it. In times of boom and increased demand and consumption, the overall planning problem will be to **identify** the demand. Conversely, in times of recession, the emphasis will be on cost-effectiveness, continuing profitability, survival and competition.

Impact of **international factors**

Factor	Impact
Exchange rates	Cost of imports, selling prices and value of exports; cost of hedging against fluctuations
Characteristics of overseas markets	Desirable overseas markets (demand) or sources of supply.
International capital markets	Generally, advanced economies accept that supply and demand set the value of their currencies, using interest rates only to control inflation.
Large multinational companies	MNCs have huge turnovers and significant political influence because of governments' desire to attract capital investment.
Government policy on trade/protection	Cost of barriers to trade, effect on supplier interests of free trade, erection of reciprocal barriers, possibility of dumping

 Case Study

World Trade Organisation data for 2004 indicate to total volume of world trade in goods and services combined of just under US $ 13,500 billion.

Fairly obviously, there is constant and large scale interaction between government and economy through the various aspects of **government economic policy**.

2.3 The sociocultural environment

FAST FORWARD

The **social and cultural** environment features long-term social trends and people's beliefs and attitudes

Key term

Demography is the study of human population and population trends.

Factors of importance to organisational planners

Factor	Comment
Growth	The rate of growth or decline in a national population and in regional populations.
Age	Changes in the age distribution of the population. In the UK, there will be an increasing proportion of the national population over retirement age. In developing countries there are very large numbers of young people.
Geography	The concentration of population into certain geographical areas.
Ethnicity	A population might contain groups with different ethnic origins from the majority. In the UK, about 5% come from ethnic minorities, although most of these live in London and the South East.
Household and family structure	A household is the basic social unit and its size might be determined by the number of children, whether elderly parents live at home and so on. In the UK, there has been an increase in single-person households and lone parent families.
Social structure	The population of a society can be broken down into a number of subgroups, with different attitudes and access to economic resources. Social class, however, is hard to measure (as people's subjective perceptions vary).
Employment	In part, this is related to changes in the workplace. Many people believe that there is a move to a casual flexible workforce; factories will have a group of **core employees**, supplemented by a group of insecure **peripheral employees**, on part time or temporary contracts, working as and when required. Some research indicates a 'two-tier' society split between **'work-rich'** (with two wage-earners) and **'work-poor'**. However, despite some claims, **most employees are in permanent, full-time employment.**
Wealth	Rising standards of living lead to increased demand for certain types of consumer good. This is why developing countries are attractive as markets.

Implications of demographic change

(a)   **Changes in patterns of demand**: an ageing population suggests increased demand for health care services: a young growing population has a growing demand for schools, housing and work.

(b)   **Location of demand**: people are moving to the suburbs and small towns.

(c)   **Recruitment policies**: there are relatively fewer young people so firms will have to recruit from less familiar sources of labour.

(d)   **Wealth and tax**. Patterns of poverty and hence need for welfare provisions may change. The tax base may alter.

2.3.1 Culture

Through contact with a particular culture, individuals learn a language, acquire values and learn habits of behaviour and thought.

(a)   **Beliefs and values**. Beliefs are what we feel to be the case on the basis of objective and subjective information (eg people can believe the world is round or flat). **Values** are beliefs which are relatively enduring, relatively general and fairly widely accepted as a guide to culturally appropriate behaviour.

(b)   **Customs:** modes of behaviour which represent culturally accepted ways of behaving in response to given situations.

(c) **Artefacts:** all the physical tools designed by human beings for their physical and psychological well-being: works of art, technology, products.

(d) **Rituals.** A ritual is a type of activity which takes on symbolic meaning, consisting of a fixed sequence of behaviour repeated over time.

The learning and sharing of culture is made possible by **language** (both written and spoken, verbal *and* non-verbal).

Underlying characteristics of culture

(a) **Purposeful.** Culture offers order, direction and guidance in all phases of human problem solving.

(b) **Learned.** Cultural values are transferred in institutions (the family, school and church) and through on-going social interaction and mass media exposure in adulthood.

(c) **Shared.** A belief or practice must be common to a significant proportion of a society or group before it can be defined as a cultural characteristic.

(d) **Cumulative.** Culture is handed down to each new generation. There is a strong traditional/historical element to many aspects of culture (eg classical music).

(e) **Dynamic.** Cultures adapt to changes in society: eg technological breakthrough, population shifts, exposure to other cultures.

Knowledge of the culture of a society is clearly of value to businesses in a number of ways.

(a) **Marketers** can adapt their products accordingly, and be fairly sure of a sizeable market. This is particularly important in export markets.

(b) **Human resource managers** may need to tackle cultural differences in recruitment. For example, some ethnic minorities have a different body language from the majority, which may be hard for some interviewers to interpret.

Culture in a society can be divided into **subcultures** reflecting social differences. Most people participate in several of them.

Subculture	Comment
Class	People from different social classes might have different values reflecting their position of society.
Ethnic background	Some ethnic groups can still be considered a distinct cultural group.
Religion	Religion and ethnicity are related.
Geography or region	Distinct regional differences might be brought about by the past effects of physical geography (socio-economic differences etc). Speech accents most noticeably differ.
Age	Age subcultures vary according to the period in which individuals were socialised to an extent, because of the great shifts in social values and customs in this century. ('Youth culture'; the 'generation gap').
Sex	Some products are targeted directly to women or to men.
Work	Different organisations have different corporate cultures, in that the shared values of one workplace may be different from another.

Cultural change might have to be planned for. There has been a revolution in attitudes to female employment, despite the well-publicised problems of discrimination that still remain.

Question   Club Fun

Club Fun is a UK company that sells packaged holidays. Founded in the 1960s, it offered a standard 'cheap and cheerful' package to resorts in Spain and, more recently, to some of the Greek islands. It was particularly successful at providing holidays for the 18-30 age group.

What do you think the implications are for Club Fun of the following developments?

- A fall in the number of school leavers
- The fact that young people are more likely now than in the 1960s to go into higher education
- Holiday programmes on TV which feature a much greater variety of locations
- Greater disposable income among the 18-30 age group

Answer

The firm's market is shrinking. There is an absolute fall in the number of school leavers. Moreover, it is possible that the increasing proportion of school leavers going to higher education will mean there will be fewer who can afford Club Fun's packages. That said, a higher disposable income in the population at large might compensate for this trend. People might be encouraged to try destinations other than Club Fun's traditional resorts if these other destinations are publicised on television.

2.3.2 Business ethics

The conduct of an organisation, its management and employees will be measured against **ethical standards** by the customers, suppliers and other members of the public with whom they deal.

We consider business ethics in detail elsewhere in this Study Text.

2.4 The technological environment

> **FAST FORWARD**
>
> Technological developments can affect all aspects of business, not just product and services.

The word 'technology' is used to mean three rather different things.

(a) **Apparatus** or equipment such as a TV camera

(b) **Technique**: for instance how to use the TV camera to best effect, perhaps in conjunction with other equipment such as lights.

(c) **Organisation**: for example the grouping of camera-operators into teams, to work on a particular project

Technology contributes to overall economic growth. The **production possibility curve** describes the total production in an economy. There are three ways in which technology can increase total output.

(a) Gains in **productivity** (more output per units of input)

(b) Reduced **costs** (eg transportation technology, preservatives)

(c) New types of **product**

Effects of technological change on organisations

(a) **The type of products or services that are made and sold**.

(b) **The way in which products are made** (eg robots, new raw materials).

(c) **The way in which services are provided.** For example, companies selling easily transportable goods, such as books and CDs can offer much greater consumer choice and are enjoying considerable success over the Internet.

(d) **The way in which markets are identified.** Database systems make it much easier to analyse the market place.

(e) **The way in which firms are managed.** IT encourages delayering of organisational hierarchies, homeworking, and better communication.

(f) **The means and extent of communications with external clients.** The financial sector is rapidly going electronic – call centres are now essential to stay in business, PC banking is on the way, and the Internet and interactive TV are starting to feature in business plans.

The impact of recent technological change also has potentially important social consequences, which in turn have an impact on business.

(a) **Homeworking.** Whereas people were once collected together to work in factories, home working will become more important.

(b) **Knowledge work.** Certain sorts of skill, related to interpretation of data and information processes, are likely to become more valued than manual or physical skills.

(c) **Services.** Technology increases manufacturing productivity, releasing human resources for service jobs. These jobs require **greater interpersonal skills** (eg in dealing with customers).

 Case Study

Ethanol in Brazil

The need to consider the general environment as an integrated whole and not as a group of separate influences is illustrated by the history of the ethanol fuel industry in Brazil.

Ethanol as an alternative or supplement to petroleum products for motor vehicle fuel came back into prominence in 2005 because of major demand-driven rises in the global price of oil. In January 2006, *The Financial Times* reported that Brazilian ethanol industry had been established in response to the oil crises of the 1970s. Subsidies for cane mills and price controls had helped to create a major industry. Here we see a problem that combines politics and economics being solved with a combination of politics, economics and technology.

During the 1980s, nearly all cars in Brazil were running on ethanol, so there was clearly a significant social effect in terms of acceptance. Unfortunately, in 1989, world sugar prices spiked and ethanol producers shifted their raw material (sugar cane) to the production of sugar. The price of ethanol was still controlled, so the inevitable result was a major shortage of fuels, which prejudiced consumers against it for a decade. Once again, politics, economics and social factors interact. A further prejudice was created against ethanol fuelled cars, focussing on their inferior performance. This has only recently been overcome by the introduction of higher technology 'flex fuel' cars that utilise a mix of ethanol and petrol to boost performance.

2.5 Environmental protection

FAST FORWARD

The **physical** environment is important for logistical reasons, as a source of resources, and because of increasing regulation.

The importance of physical environmental conditions

(a) **Resource inputs**. Managing physical resources successfully (eg oil companies, mining companies) is a good source of profits.

(b) **Logistics.** The physical environment presents logistical problems or opportunities to organisations. Proximity to road and rail links can be a reason for siting a warehouse in a particular area.

(c) **Government.** The physical environment is under government influence.

    (i) Local authority town planning departments can influence where a building and necessary infrastructure can be sited.

    (ii) Governments can set regulations about some of the organisation's environmental interactions.

(d) **Disasters.** In some countries, the physical environment can pose a major threat to organisations. The example of the earthquake in Kobe, Japan, springs to mind.

> **FAST FORWARD**
>
> The impact of business activity on the physical environment is now a major concern. Companies are under pressure to incorporate measures to protect the environment into their plans. This presents both challenges and opportunities, since some measures will impose costs, but others will allow significant savings. There is also a new range of markets for goods and services designed to protect or have minimum impact on the environment.

2.5.1 Environmental protection policy

Pressure on businesses for better environmental performance is coming from many quarters.

(a) **Green pressure groups** have increased their membership and influence dramatically.

(b) **Employees** are increasing pressure on the businesses in which they work for a number of reasons – partly for their own safety, partly in order to improve the public image of the company.

(c) **Legislation** is increasing almost by the day. Growing pressure from the green or green-influenced vote has led to mainstream political parties taking these issues into their programmes, and most countries now have laws to cover land use planning, smoke emission, water pollution and the destruction of animals and natural habitats.

(d) **Environmental risk screening** has become increasingly important. Companies in the future will become responsible for the environmental impact of their activities.

Such pressures as these have led to the establishment of 'environmental' awareness and policy as an important aspect of overall strategy. We thus have a slight **terminological problem** in that the 'environment' (in 'green' terms) has become an important part of the overall business 'environment'. Environmental protection is now a key aspect of **corporate social responsibility**.

2.5.2 Environmental audit

In the USA, **audits on environmental** issues have increased since the *Exxon Valdez* catastrophe in which millions of gallons of crude oil were released into Alaskan waters. The **Valdez principles** were drafted by the Coalition for Environmentally Responsible Economics to focus attention on environmental concerns and corporate responsibility.

- Eliminate pollutants and hazardous waste
- Conserve non-renewable resources
- Market environmentally safe products and services

- Prepare for accidents and restore damaged environments

- Provide protection for employees who report environmental hazards

- Companies should appoint an environmentalist to the board of directors, name an executive for environmental affairs and develop an environmental audit of global operations.

2.5.3 How green issues will impinge on business

Possible issues to consider are these.

- **Consumer demand** for products that appear to be environmentally friendly
- Demand for **less pollution** from industry
- Greater **regulation** by government and the EU (eg recycling targets)
- Demand that **businesses be charged** with the external cost of their activities
- Possible requirements to conduct **environmental audits**
- Opportunities to develop **products and technologies that** are environmentally friendly
- Taxes (eg landfill tax)

Martin Bennett and Peter James looked at the **ways in which a company's concern for the environment can impact on its performance**.

(a) **Short-term savings** through waste minimisation and energy efficiency schemes can be substantial.

(b) **Pressures on businesses** for environmental action are increasing.

(c) Companies with poor environmental performance may face **increased cost of capital** because investors and lenders demand a higher risk premium.

(d) There are a growing number of **energy and environmental taxes**, such as the UK's landfill tax.

(e) Accidents and long-term environmental effects can result in **large financial liabilities**.

(f) **Pressure group campaigns** can cause damage to reputation and/or additional costs.

(g) Environmental legislation may cause the **'sunsetting'** of products and opportunities for **'sunrise' replacements**.

(h) The cost of processing input which becomes **waste** is equivalent to 5-10% of some organisation's turnover.

(i) The phasing out of CFCs has led to markets for alternative products.

They go on to suggest six main ways in which business and environmental benefits can be achieved.

(a) **Integrating the environment into capital expenditure decisions** (by considering environmental opposition to projects which could affect cash flows, for example)

(b) **Understanding and managing environmental costs**. Environmental costs are often 'hidden' in overheads and environmental and energy costs are often not allocated to the relevant budgets.

(c) **Introducing waste minimisation schemes**

(d) **Understanding and managing life cycle costs.** For many products, the greatest environmental impact occurs upstream (such as mining raw materials) or downstream from production (such as energy to operate equipment). This has led to producers being made responsible for dealing with the disposal of products such as cars, and government and third party measures to influence raw material choices. Organisations therefore need to identify, control and make provision for environmental life cycle costs and work with suppliers and customers to identify environmental cost reduction opportunities.

(e)   **Measuring environmental performance.** Business is under increasing pressure to measure all aspects of environmental performance, both for statutory disclosure reasons and due to demands for more environmental data from customers.

(f)   **Involving management accountants in a strategic approach to environment-related management accounting and performance evaluation**. A 'green accounting team' incorporating the key functions should analyse the strategic picture and identify opportunities for practical initiatives. It should analyse the short-, medium- and long-term impact of possible changes in the following.

   (i)   Government policies, such as on transport
   (ii)   Legislation and regulation
   (iii)   Supply conditions, such as fewer landfill sites
   (iv)   Market conditions, such as changing customer views
   (v)   Social attitudes, such as to factory farming
   (vi)   Competitor strategies

Possible action includes the following.

   (i)   Designating an **'environmental champion'** within the strategic planning or accounting function to ensure that environmental considerations are fully considered.

   (ii)   Assessing whether **new data sources** are needed to collect more and better data

   (iii)   Making **comparisons** between sites/offices to highlight poor performance and generate peer pressure for action

   (iv)   Developing **checklists** for internal auditors

Such analysis and action should help organisations to better understand present and future environmental costs and benefits.

2.5.4 Renewable and non-renewable resources

Key term

> **Sustainability** involves developing strategies so that the company only uses resources at a rate that allows them to be replenished. At the same time, emissions of waste are confined to levels that do not exceed the capacity of the environment to absorb them.

Sustainability means that resources consumed are **replaced** in some way: for every tree cut down another is planted. Some resources, however, are inherently non-renewable. For example, oil will eventually run out, even though governments and oil firms have consistently underestimated reserves.

(a)   Metals can be recycled. Some car manufacturers are building cars with recyclable components.

(b)   An argument is that as the price of resources rise, market forces will operate to make more efficient use of them or to develop alternatives. When oil becomes too expensive, solar power will become economic.

John Elkington, chairman of the think-tank *SustainAbility Ltd*, has said that **sustainability** now embraces not only environmental and economic questions, but also social and ethical dimensions. He writes about the **triple bottom line**, which means 'business people must increasingly recognise that the challenge now is to help deliver simultaneously:

- Economic prosperity
- Environmental quality
- Social equity

Case Study

Elkington quotes the example of *Kvaerner*, the Norwegian construction company. An environmental report compiled by the company listed the following.

- A 1% reduction in absence due to sick leave is worth $30 million
- A 1% reduction in material and energy consumption is worth $60 million
- A 20% cut in insurance premiums would be worth $15 million

2.6 The legal environment

Laws come from common law, parliamentary legislation and government regulations derived from it, and obligations under EU membership and other treaties.

Legal factors affecting all companies

Factor	Example
General legal framework: contract, tort, agency	Basic ways of doing business; negligence proceedings; ownership; rights and responsibilities, property
Criminal law	Theft; insider dealing; bribery; deception; industrial espionage
Company law	Directors and their duties; reporting requirements; takeover proceedings; shareholders' rights; insolvency
Employment law	Trade Union recognition; Social Chapter provisions; possible minimum wage; unfair dismissal; redundancy; maternity; Equal Opportunities
Health and Safety	Fire precautions; safety procedures
Data protection	Use of information about employees and customers
Marketing and sales	Laws to protect consumers (eg refunds and replacement, 'cooling off' period after credit agreements); what is or isn't allowed in advertising
Environment	Pollution control; waste disposal
Tax law	Corporation tax payment; Collection of income tax (PAYE) and National Insurance contributions; VAT
Competition law	General illegality of cartels

Some legal and regulatory factors affect **particular industries**, if the public interest is served. For example, as already discussed, electricity, gas, telecommunications, water and rail transport may be subject to **regulators** who have influence over market access, competition and pricing policy (can restrict price increase).

This is for either of two reasons.

- The industries are, effectively, monopolies.
- Large sums of public money are involved (eg in subsidies to rail companies)

Gas deregulation in the UK

Government policy. Gas used to be a state monopoly in the UK. The industry was privatised as one company, British Gas. Slowly, the UK gas market was opened to competition: eventually, about 20 suppliers competed with British Gas.

Regulators. Ofgas regulates the gas industry. Ofgas has introduced a Code of Conduct requiring gas suppliers to train sales agents, allow for a cooling off period in new sales contracts and so on.

Contracts. When British Gas was privatised, it inherited 'take or pay contracts' requiring it to buy gas at a specific price from gas producers. Since that time, gas prices have fallen, and competitors have been able to benefit from this.

New markets. Government policy has also deregulated the electricity market, so that companies such as British Gas can now sell electricity.

3 Key drivers of environmental change

FAST FORWARD

Four aspects of globalisation are key drivers of change.

- Market globalisation grows as tastes converge and communications improve.
- Cost globalisation spreads as trade barriers fall and economies of scale and experience grow.
- Governments promote free trade and international standards.
- International competition promotes further trade and interaction.

JS&W, following *Yip*, identify four aspects of **globalisation** as **key drivers of change** in the macro-environment.

- Market globalisation
- Cost globalisation
- Government activity and policy
- Global competition

3.1 Market globalisation

Gradual **globalisation of markets** is taking place because of the interplay of a number of forces. It is impossible to isolate a simple chain of causation here.

(a) **Consumer tastes** are becoming more homogeneous in such matters as clothes and entertainment.

(b) As markets globalise, firms supplying them become **global customers** for their own inputs and seek **global suppliers**.

(c) **Improvements in global communications and logistics** reduce costs, make globalisation easier and allow the creation of global brands. The latter feeds back to the homogenisation of taste.

3.2 Cost globalisation

(a) **Economies of scale** are a major source of cost advantage: companies in some industries, such as some electronics manufacture, can continue to gain such economies even as they expand up to global size.

(b) **Experience effects** (discussed later in this Study Text) can continue to drive down costs in the same way.

(c) **Sourcing efficiencies** may be achieved by central procurement from global lowest-cost suppliers.

(d) Country-specific cost advantages, such as low labour costs or a favourable exchange rate, encourage purchasers to search globally for suppliers.

(e) **High costs of product development** can be spread over longer production runs if products are standardised and sold globally.

3.3 Government policy

The climate of government opinion has been increasingly sympathetic to **free trade**, though producer special interests and popular discontent continue to hamper it. **Technical standardisation** in both manufacturing and services has also encouraged increased trade, while some governments have been active in seeking foreign direct investment.

3.4 Global competition

Competitive forces seem to have had global effects

(a) Existing high levels of international trade encourage further interaction between competitors as a matter of routine.

(b) The existence of global competitors and global customers in an industry prompts purely national firms to start trading globally so as to be able to compete on an even footing.

4 The competitive advantage of nations

> **FAST FORWARD**
>
> Porter identifies four principal determinants of national competitive advantage.
>
> - **Factor conditions**
> - **Firm strategy structure and rivalry**
> - **Demand conditions**
> - **Related and supporting industries**

Exam focus point

Porter's diamond is a very important model. You should understand it in detail and be able to apply it in practice.

Michael Porter's The Competitive Advantage Of Nations, suggests that some nations' industries are more internationally competitive than others. For example, UK leadership in many heavy industries, such as ship-building, has been overtaken by Japan and Korea.

Porter does not believe that countries or nations as such are competitive, but rather that the conditions within a country may help firms to compete.

The original explanation for **national** success was the theory of **comparative advantage**. This held that **relative opportunity costs** determined the appropriateness of particular economic activities in relation to other countries.

Porter argues that comparative advantage is **too general a concept** to explain the success of individual companies and industries. He suggests that industries that require **high technology** and **highly skilled employees** are less affected than low technology industries by the relative costs of their inputs of raw materials and basic labour as determined by the national endowment of factors of production.

We must therefore look elsewhere for the determinants of national competitive advantage.

Porter identifies four principal factors, which are outlined in the diagram below. Porter refers to this as the **diamond**.

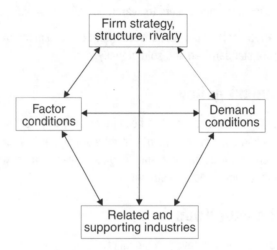

4.1 Analysing the diamond

4.1.1 Factor conditions

Factor conditions are a country's endowment of inputs to production.

- Human resources (skills, price, motivation, industrial relations)
- Physical resources (land, minerals, climate, location relative to other nations)
- Knowledge (scientific and technical know-how, educational institutions)
- Capital (amounts available for investment, how it is deployed)
- Infrastructure (transport, communications, housing)

Porter distinguishes between **basic** and **advanced** factors.

(a)   **Basic factors** are natural resources, climate, semiskilled and unskilled labour. They are inherent, or at best their creation involves little investment. They are **unsustainable** as a source of national competitive advantage, since they are widely available. For example, the wages of unskilled workers in industrial countries are undermined by even lower wages elsewhere.

(b)   **Advanced factors** are associated with a well-developed scientific and technological infrastructure and include modern digital communications infrastructure, highly educated people (eg computer scientists), university research laboratories and so on. They are necessary to achieve high order competitive advantages such as differentiated products and proprietary production technology.

An abundance of factors is not enough. It is the efficiency with which they are deployed that matters. The former USSR has an abundance of natural resources and a fairly well educated workforce, but was an economic catastrophe.

Porter also notes that **generalised factors**, such as transport infrastructure do not provide as decisive and sustainable bases for competitive advantage as **do specialised factors**. These are factors that are relevant to a limited range of industries, such as knowledge bases in particular fields and logistic systems developed for particular goods or raw materials. Such factors are integral to innovation and very difficult to move to other countries.

4.1.2 Demand conditions: the home market

The **home market determines how firms perceive, interpret and respond to buyer needs.** This information puts pressure on firms to innovate and provides a launch pad for global ambitions.

(a)   There are **no cultural impediments** to communication.

(b)   The **segmentation** of the home market shapes a firm's priorities: companies will be successful globally in segments which are similar to the home market.

(c)   **Sophisticated and demanding buyers** set standards.

(d)   **Anticipation of buyer needs:** if consumer needs are expressed in the home market earlier than in the world market, the firm benefits from experience.

(e)   The **rate of growth**. Slow growing home markets do not encourage the adoption of state of the art technology.

(f)   **Early saturation** of the home market will encourage a firm to export.

4.1.3 Related and supporting industries

Competitive success in one industry is linked to success in related industries. Domestic suppliers are preferable to foreign suppliers, as they offer continuing close co-operation and co-ordination. The process of innovation is also enhanced when suppliers are of high quality, since information is transmitted rapidly and problems are solved by joint effort.

4.1.4 Firm strategy, structure and rivalry

Management style and industrial structure. Nations are likely to display competitive advantage in industries that are culturally suited to their normal management practices and industrial structures. For example, German managers tend to have a strong bias towards engineering and are best at products demanding careful development and complex manufacturing processes. They are less successful in industries based on intangibles such as fashion and entertainment.

Strategy. Industries in different countries have different **time horizons**, funding needs and so forth.

(a)   **National capital markets** set different goals for performance. In Germany and Switzerland, banks are the main source of capital, not equity shareholders. Short-term fluctuations in share prices are not regarded as of great importance as funds are invested for the long term. In the USA, most shares are held by financial institutions whose own performance indicators emphasise short-term earnings growth.

(b)   National attitudes to **wealth** are important. The egalitarian Swedes are rarely successful in industries that have the potential to create individual fortunes but depend on new start-ups.

(c)   National culture affects industrial priorities through the relative prestige it allots to various industries and their leaders. Italy values fashion and furnishings, for instance, while in Israel the most prestigious industries are agriculture and those related to defence.

Domestic rivalry is important for several reasons.

•   There can be no special pleading about unfair foreign competition.
•   With little domestic rivalry, firms are happy to rely on the home market.

- Tough domestic rivals teach a firm about competitive success.
- Domestic rivalry forces firms to compete on grounds other than basic factors.
- Each rival can try a different strategic approach.

The promotion by government of one or two **'national champions'** who can reap major economies of scale in the domestic market is undermined by the vigorous domestic competition among high-performing global companies. Examples are the Swiss pharmaceutical industry and the US IT industry.

4.2 Influencing the diamond

A nation's competitive industries tend to be **clustered**. Porter believes **clustering** to be a key to national competitive advantage. A cluster is a linking of industries through relationships that are either vertical (buyer-supplier) or horizontal (common customers, technology, skills). For example, the UK financial services industry is clustered in London.

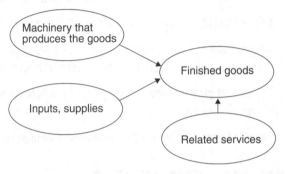

How does a country create a diamond of competitive advantage? Governments cannot compete: only firms can do that. Governments can influence the **context** in which an industry operates and can create opportunities and pressures for innovation.

(a)   Factors of production provide the seed corn. A large endowment of easily mined iron ore would suggest metal-working industries.

(b)   Related and supporting industries can also be a foundation, if the competences within them can be configured in a new way.

(c)   Government policy should support cluster development and promote high standards of education, research and commercially relevant technologies

(d)   Extraordinary demand in the *home market* based on national peculiarities and conditions can set the demand conditions determinant in the diamond.

It must be remembered that the creation of competitive advantage can take many years.

The **individual** firm will be more likely to succeed internationally if there is a **supporting cluster.** Firms should be prepared to invest in co-operative ventures in such fields as training, infrastructure and research. However, the cluster approach is not guaranteed to be successful.

 Case Study

Lack-lustre clusters

Time was when the only thing more fashionable than an Italian suit was the cluster that made it.

The small companies that both competed and co-operated with each other in industrial districts all over Italy – some making shoes, some clothing and others machine tools – were regarded as an example to the rest of the world. Their flexibility contrasted with slow-moving manufacturers that depended on mass production and suffered heavily in the recession of the early 1990s.

The pendulum always swings back and it has done so viciously in the case of Italy's clusters. The country faces an industrial crisis caused by the high euro and competition from low-wage countries. Companies making footwear, textiles and leather goods – specialisms of some northern regions – struggle to compete against China.

The problem goes deeper than labour costs and an expensive currency. The clusters are showing their age as a way to organise businesses in a mature economy. Some have become conservative and inward-looking, more focused on finding outlets for goods they have traditionally made locally than designing and marketing innovative products.

While the Lira could be devalued and competition with China was restrained by trade barriers, any structural weaknesses among the 500,000 companies in Italy employing fewer than 20 people remained hidden.

Italy is trying to adjust. Many industrial companies outsource some production to eastern European countries such as Romania and Slovakia and to China. Some industrial districts have taken similar steps. The Montebelluna cluster of companies producing sports shoes set up an industrial park in Romania. But clusters that do everything from weaving cloth to making clothes can find it harder to discard local jobs and craft skills in favour of production abroad than bigger manufacturers which have less at stake.

Small companies that mainly interact with others in their district may also lack the expertise to manage a global supply network, a comparative advantage of big companies.

Above all, clusters face the problem of being rooted in craft industries rather than value-added services such as design and marketing. In the days when consumers were less demanding, if was sufficient to buy in such services from agencies in Milan and Rome. But they must now compete with rivals that focus all their efforts on services instead of manufacturing.

(John Gapper, Financial Times, 26 May 2005)

If a firm wishes to compete in an industry in which there is no national competitive advantage, it can take a number of steps to succeed.

(a)   **Compete in the most challenging market,** to emulate domestic rivalry and to obtain information. If a firm can compete successfully in such a market, even if this only means carving out a small niche, it should do well elsewhere.

(b)   **Spread research and development** activities to countries where there is an established research base or industry cluster already.

(c)   Be prepared to **invest heavily in innovation**.

(d)   **Invest in human resources**, both in the firm and the industry as a whole. This might mean investing in training programmes.

(e)   **Look out for new technologies** which will change the rules of the industry. The UK with its large efficient research base should have some creative ideas.

(f)   **Collaborate with foreign companies.** American motor companies, successfully learned Japanese production techniques.

(g)   **Supply overseas companies**. Japanese car plants in the UK have encouraged greater quality in UK components suppliers. Inward investment provides important **learning opportunities** for domestic companies.

(h)   **Source components from overseas**. In the UK crystal glass industry, many firms buy crystal glass from the Czech Republic, and do the cutting and design work themselves. Conversely, firms can sell more abroad.

(i)   **Exert pressure on politicians** and opinion formers to create better conditions for the diamond to develop (eg in education).

5 The environment in the future

The past is not necessarily a good guide to the future. It may be so in simple static conditions, but more complex or dynamic environments require sophisticated techniques such as the use of leading indicators and scenarios.

5.1 Forecasts

Forecasting attempts to reduce the uncertainty managers face. In **simple and static conditions, the past is a relatively good guide** to the future, though, of course, this is not the case in dynamic or complex conditions.

(a)   **Time series analysis** uses past data to distinguish seasonal and other cyclical fluctuations from long term underlying trends. An example of the use of this approach is the UK's monthly inflation statistics which show a headline figure and the underlying trend.

(b)   **Regression analysis** is a quantitative technique to check any underlying correlations between two variables (eg sales of ice cream and the weather). The relationship between two variables may only hold between certain values. (You would expect ice cream consumption to rise as the temperature becomes hotter, but there is probably a maximum number of ice creams an individual can consume in a day, no matter how hot it is.)

5.2 Econometric models for medium-term forecasting

Econometrics is the study of economic variables and their interrelationships.

(a)   **Leading indicators** are indicators which change *before* market demand changes. For example, a sudden increase in the birth rate would be an indicator of future demand for children's clothes.

(b)   The ability to predict the span of time between a change in the indicator and a change in market demand is important. Change in an indicator is especially useful for demand forecasting when they reach their highest or lowest points (when an increase turns into a decline or vice versa).

5.3 Scenario building

Macro scenarios are used to consider possible future environmental conditions overall. **Industry scenarios** deal with an individual industry in more detail.

Because the environment is so complex, it is easy to become overwhelmed by the many factors. Firms therefore try to model the future and the technique is *scenario building*.

Key term

> A **scenario** is a detailed and consistent view of how the business environment of an organisation might develop in the future.   JS&W

Scenarios are built with reference to key influences and change drivers in the environment. They inevitable deal with conditions of high uncertainty, so they are not forecasts: they are, rather, internally consistent views of potential future conditions.

5.3.1 Macro scenarios

Macro scenarios use macro-economic or political factors, creating alternative views of the future environment (eg global economic growth, political changes, interest rates).

5.3.2 Building scenarios

Keeping the scenario process simple is the way to get most out of scenario building.

(a)   Normally a *team* is selected to develop scenarios, preferably of people from diverse backgrounds. The team should include 'dissidents' who challenge the consensus and some reference outsiders to offer different perspectives.

(b)   Most participants in the team draw on both general reading and specialist knowledge.

Steps in scenario planning (Mercer).

Step 1   **Decide on the drivers for change**

- Environmental analysis helps determine key factors.

- At least a ten year time horizon is needed, to avoid simply extrapolating from the present.

- Identify and select the important issues and degree of certainty required.

Step 2   **Bring drivers together into a viable framework**

- This relies almost on an intuitive ability to make patterns out of 'soft' data, so is the hardest part of the process.

- Items identified can be brought together as mini-scenarios.

- There might be many trends, but these can be grouped together.

- It is inappropriate to attempt to allocate probabilities

Step 3   Produce seven to nine mini-scenarios. The underlying logic of the connections between the items can be explored.

Step 4   Group mini-scenarios into two or three larger scenarios containing all topics.

- This generates most debate and in likely to highlight fundamental issues.

- More than three scenarios will confuse people.

- The scenarios should be complementary not opposite. They should be equally likely. There is no 'good' or 'bad' scenario.

- The scenarios should be tested to ensure they hang together. If not, go back to Step 1.

Step 5   **Write the scenarios**

- The scenarios should be written up in the form most suitable for managers taking decisions based on them.

- Most scenarios are qualitative rather than quantitative in nature.

Step 6   **Identify issues arising**

- Determine the most critical outcomes, or branching points which are critical to the long term survival of the organisation.

- Role play can be used to test what the scenarios mean to key actors in the future of the business.

5.3.3 Industry scenarios

Porter believes that the most appropriate use for scenario analysis is if it is restricted to an industry. An **industry scenario** is an internally consistent view of an **industry's** future structure. It is not a forecast, but a possibility. A set of scenarios would reflect the possible future implications of current uncertainties. Different competitive strategies may be appropriate to different scenarios.

Using scenarios to formulate competitive strategy

(a)   A strategy built in response to only one scenario is **risky**, whereas one supposed to cope with them all might be **expensive**.

(b)   Choosing scenarios as a basis for decisions about competitive strategy.

Approach	Comment
Assume the most probable	This choice puts too much faith in the scenario process and guesswork. A less probable scenario may be one whose **failure** to occur would have the **worst** consequences for the firm.
Hope for the best	A firm designs a strategy based on the scenario most attractive to the firm: this is wishful thinking.
Hedge	The firm chooses the strategy that produces **satisfactory** results under **all** scenarios. **Hedging, however, is not optimal**. The **low risk** is paid for by a **low reward**.
Flexibility	A firm taking this approach plays a 'wait and see' game. It is safer, but sacrifices first-mover advantages.
Influence	A firm will try and influence the future, for example by influencing demand for related products in order that its favoured scenario will be realised in events as they unfold.

6 Industry and sector

FAST FORWARD

> The immediate business environment of firms producing similar goods is called the **industry**. **Sector** may be used in a similar way in public and not-for-profit services.

The macro environment provides a general background of influences on the organisation. Closer in, we find the day-to-day environment of immediate business concerns: the industry or sector, competitors and markets. Taken together, these factors are sometimes called the **task environment**.

Key term

> An **industry** is a group of firms producing the same product or products that are close substitutes for one another.

The industry concept may be extended into the arena of **public** and **not for profit** services, though the term **sector** is normally used rather than **industry**. The terminology is a little vague in that, for example, 'the public sector' is also used to mean *all* public services of whatever kind.

For convenience, we will use the word 'industry' as shorthand to mean 'industry or sector', unless there are considerations that require us to be more specific.

Industries tend not to be stable: such features as location, products, customers and rate of growth all tend to be more or less variable. One important feature of this instability is the way in which the **boundaries** of an industry can change. Previously distinct industries can **converge**: their technologies, activities and products start to mingle or become complementary and their member firms start to compete or collaborate. This process can be supply-led or demand-led.

Supply-led convergence occurs where suppliers discover links with suppliers in other industries and move together to cooperate in building new markets. Such convergence is common in the public sector, where government departments are regularly merged and reorganised. Government can also promote supply-led convergence in the private sector, especially by deregulation, as has happened in the UK financial services industry. The development of e-commerce has provided manufacturers with a completely new route to consumers, eroding the boundaries of traditional retailing and distribution industries in the process.

Demand-led convergence occurs when customers treat the products of different industries as **substitutable**, as in the case of mobile and fixed line telephones, or **complementary**, as in the case of air travel and car hire.

7 Competitive forces

The **competitive environment** is structured by five forces: **threat of new entrants; substitute products**; the bargaining power of **customers**; the bargaining power of **suppliers; competitive rivalry**.

Exam focus point

The five forces is one of the three or four most important models in the field of strategy. You must study it carefully and be able to apply it. In particular, be aware that it can be very difficult in exam questions to decide which of the five categories properly describes a given strategic problem. Pay particular attention to the nature of the **substitutes**.

In discussing competition, *Porter* (*Competitive Strategy*) distinguishes between factors that characterise the nature of competition.

(a)   **In one industry compared with another** (eg in the chemicals industry compared with the clothing retail industry, some factors make one industry as a whole potentially more profitable than another (ie yielding a bigger return on investment).

(b)   Factors **within a particular industry** lead to the competitive strategies that individual firms might select.

Five **competitive forces** influence the state of competition in an industry, which collectively determine the **profit potential** of the industry as a whole. **Learn them.**

- The threat of **new entrants** to the industry
- The threat of **substitute** products or services
- The bargaining power of **customers**
- The bargaining power of **suppliers**
- The **rivalry** amongst current competitors in the industry

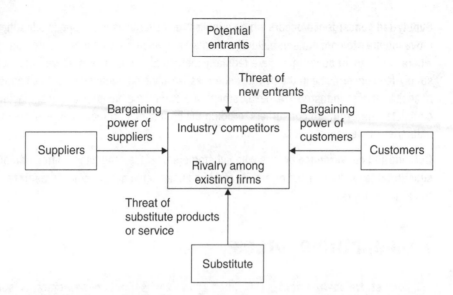

7.1 The threat of new entrants (and barriers to entry to keep them out)

A new entrant into an industry will bring extra capacity and more competition. The strength of this threat is likely to vary from industry to industry and depends on two things.

- The strength of the **barriers to entry**. Barriers to entry discourage new entrants.
- The likely **response of existing competitors** to the new entrant.

Barriers to entry

(a) **Scale economies**. High fixed costs often imply a high breakeven point, and a high breakeven point depends on a large volume of sales. If the market as a whole is not growing, the new entrant has to capture a large slice of the market from existing competitors. This is expensive (although Japanese companies have done this in some cases).

(b) **Product differentiation**. Existing firms in an industry may have built up a good brand image and strong customer loyalty over a long period of time. A few firms may promote a large number of brands to crowd out the competition.

(c) **Capital requirements**. When capital investment requirements are high, the barrier against new entrants will be strong, particularly when the investment would possibly be high-risk.

 Case Study

Large gas turbines

There are only three manufactures of engines for large air liners in the world: *General Electric*, *Pratt & Whitney* and *Rolls-Royce*. Such is the nature of the technology, the cost of entry for a new competitor would be tens of billions of dollars.

(d) **Switching costs**. Switching costs refer to the costs (time, money, convenience) that a customer would have to incur by switching from one supplier's products to another's. Although it might cost a **consumer** nothing to switch from one brand of frozen peas to another, the potential costs for the **retailer or distributor** might be high.

(e) **Access to distribution channels**. Distribution channels carry a manufacturer's products to the end-buyer. New distribution channels are difficult to establish, and existing distribution channels hard to gain access to.

(f) **Cost advantages of existing producers, independent of economies of scale** include:

    (i)   Patent rights

    (ii)   Experience and know-how (the learning curve)

    (iii) Government subsidies and regulations

    (iv) Favoured access to raw materials

Case Study

Japanese firms

A little while ago, it was assumed that, following the success of Japanese firms worldwide in motor vehicles (*Nissan, Honda, Toyota*) and consumer electronics (eg *Sony, JVC, Matsushita*), no Western companies were safe from Japanese competition. *Kao* (household goods), *Suntory* (drinks), *Nomura* (banking and securities) were seen as successors to firms such as *Procter and Gamble* and *Heineken*.

This has not happened: for example, Japanese pharmaceutical firms, such as *Green Cross*, have not achieved the world domination (anticipated in 1982). US and European firms are still dominant in this industry.

Perhaps cars and consumer electronics are the exception rather than the rule. The reason for this might be distribution. Normally, outsiders do not find it easy to break into established distribution patterns. However, distribution channels in cars and consumer electronics offered outsiders an easy way in.

(a) The car industry is vertically integrated, with a network of exclusive dealerships. Given time and money, the Japanese firms could simply build their own dealerships and run them as they liked, with the help of local partners. This barrier to entry was not inherently complex.

(b) Consumer electronics

    (i)   In the early years, the consumer electronics market was driven by technology, so innovative firms such as Sony and Matsushita could overcome distribution weaknesses with innovative products, as they had plenty to invest. This lowered entry barriers.

    (ii)   Falling prices changed the distribution of hifi goods from small specialist shops to large cut-price outlets. Newcomers to a market are the natural allies of such new outlets: existing suppliers prefer to shun 'discount' retailers to protect margins in their current distribution networks.

Japanese firms have not established dominant positions in:

(a) Healthcare, where national pharmaceuticals wholesalers are active as 'gatekeepers'

(b) Household products, where there are strong supermarket chains and global brands

(c) Cosmetics, where department stores and specialist shops offer a wide choice.

Entry barriers might be **lowered** by the impact of change.

- Changes in the environment
- Technological changes
- Novel distribution channels for products or services

7.2 The threat from substitute products

A **substitute product** is a good or service produced by **another industry** which satisfies the same customer needs.

> It is very easy to misunderstand the nature of substitute products: while they provide competition, they are **not** goods or services produced by competitors in the same industry.

 Case Study

The Channel Tunnel

Passengers have several ways of getting to London to Paris, and the pricing policies of the various industries transporting them there reflects this.

(a) 'Le Shuttle' carries cars in the Channel Tunnel. Its main competitors come from the *ferry* companies, offering a substitute service. Therefore, you will find that Le Shuttle sets its prices with reference to ferry company prices, and vice versa.

(b) Eurostar is the rail service from London to Paris/Brussels. Its main competitors are not the ferry companies but the *airlines*. Prices on the London-Paris air routes fell with the commencement of Eurostar services, and some airlines have curtailed the number of flights they offer.

7.3 The bargaining power of customers

Customers want better quality products and services at a lower price. Satisfying this want might force down the profitability of suppliers in the industry. Just how strong the position of customers will be depends on a number of factors.

- How much the customer buys

- How critical the product is to the customer's own business

- Switching costs (ie the cost of switching supplier)

- Whether the products are standard items (hence easily copied) or specialised

- The customer's own profitability: a customer who makes low profits will be forced to insist on low prices from suppliers

- Customer's ability to bypass the supplier (or take over the supplier)

- The skills of the customer purchasing staff, or the price-awareness of consumers

- When product quality is important to the customer, the customer is less likely to be price-sensitive, and so the industry might be more profitable as a consequence

 Case Study

The major UK supermarkets are regularly accused of abusing their buying power and the Competition Commission is asked to examine them at regular intervals. An investigation was carried out in 2000 and, further investigation was taking place while the first edition of this Study Text was being prepared.

7.4 The bargaining power of suppliers

Suppliers can exert pressure for higher prices. The ability of suppliers to get higher prices depends on several factors.

- Whether there are just **one or two dominant suppliers** to the industry, able to charge monopoly or oligopoly prices

- The threat of **new entrants** or substitute products to the **supplier's industry**

- Whether the suppliers have **other customers** outside the industry, and do not rely on the industry for the majority of their sales

- The **importance of the supplier's product** to the customer's business

- Whether the supplier has a **differentiated product** which buyers need to obtain

- Whether **switching costs** for customers would be high

7.5 The rivalry amongst current competitors in the industry

The **intensity of competitive rivalry** within an industry will affect the profitability of the industry as a whole. Competitive actions might take the form of price competition, advertising battles, sales promotion campaigns, introducing new products for the market, improving after sales service or providing guarantees or warranties. Competition can stimulate demand, expanding the market, or it can leave demand unchanged, in which case individual competitors will make less money, unless they are able to cut costs.

Factors determining the intensity of competition

(a) **Market growth**. Rivalry is intensified when firms are competing for a greater market share in a total market where growth is slow or stagnant.

(b) **Cost structure**. High fixed costs are a temptation to compete on price, as in the short run any contribution from sales is better than none at all. A perishable product produces the same effect.

(c) **Switching**. Suppliers will compete if buyers switch easily (eg Coke vs Pepsi).

(d) **Capacity**. A supplier might need to achieve a substantial increase in output capacity, in order to obtain reductions in unit costs.

(e) **Uncertainty**. When one firm is not sure what another is up to, there is a tendency to respond to the uncertainty by formulating a more competitive strategy.

(f) **Strategic importance**. If success is a prime strategic objective, firms will be likely to act very competitively to meet their targets.

(g) **Exit barriers** make it difficult for an existing supplier to leave the industry. These can take many forms.

   (i) Fixed assets with a low **break-up value** (eg there may be no other use for them, or they may be old)

   (ii) The cost of **redundancy payments** to employees

   (iii) If the firm is a division or subsidiary of a larger enterprise, the **effect of withdrawal on the other operations** within the group

   (iv) The **reluctance of managers** to admit defeat, their loyalty to employees and their fear for their own jobs

   (v) **Government pressures** on major employers not to shut down operations, especially when competition comes from foreign producers rather than other domestic producers

Question

The Tea Industry is characterised by oversupply, with a surplus of about 80,000 tonnes a year. Tea estates 'swallow capital, and the return is not as attractive as in industries such as technology or services'. Tea is auctioned in London and prices are the same in absolute terms as they were 15 years ago. Tea is produced in Africa and India, Sri Lanka and China. Because of the huge capital investment involved, the most recent investments have been quasi-governmental, such as those by the Commonwealth Development Corporation in ailing estates in East Africa. There is no simple demarcation between buyers and sellers. Tea-bag manufacturers own their own estates, as well as buying in tea from outside sources.

In 1997 tea prices were described in India at least as being 'exceptionally firm ... The shortage and high prices of coffee have also raised demand for tea which remains the cheapest of all beverages in spite of the recent rise in prices. Demand from Russia, Poland, Iran and Iraq are expected to rise.'

(a) Carry out a five forces analysis.

(b) Thinking ahead, suggest a possible strategy for a tea-grower with a number of estates which has traditionally sold its tea at auction.

Answer

(a) Here are some ideas. Barriers to entry are high. There are plenty of substitute products (coffee), competitive rivalry is high because of the difficulty of stockpiling products. Customer bargaining power is high, but supplier power is low: all it needs is capital, the right sort of land and labour.

(b) *Williamson and Magor* has begun to switch from selling tea at auction to consumer marketing. The firm is aiming to build up its own brand image in the UK and Germany, by offering – by mail order – unblended, specialist teas from its Indian estates. It advertised via Barclays Premier Card magazine; replies were used to set up a customer database. When the company's Earl Grey tea was recommended on BBC2's *Food and Drink,* these existing customers were targeted with a letter and a sample.

7.6 The impact of information technology on the competitive forces

FAST FORWARD

IT has characteristics that can affect all five competitive forces. These characteristics generally amount to communication improvements but IT can also be a substantial product in its own right.

Barriers to entry and IT

(a) **IT can raise entry barriers** by increasing economies of scale, raising the capital cost of entry (by requiring a similar investment in IT) or effectively colonising distribution channels by tying customers and suppliers into the supply chain or distribution chain.

(b) **IT can surmount entry barriers**. The use of IT can reduce the costs of selling and distribution and even substitute for traditional methods entirely. An example is the use of telephone banking, which sometimes obviates the need to establish a branch network.

Bargaining power of suppliers and IT

(a) **Increasing the number of** accessible **suppliers.** Supplier power in the past can derive from various factors such as geographical proximity and the fact that the organisation requires goods of a certain standard in a certain time. IT enhances supplier information available to customers.

(b) **Closer supplier relationships.** Suppliers' power can be *shared*. CAD can be used to design components in tandem with suppliers. Such relationships might be developed with a few key suppliers. The supplier and the organisation both benefit from performance improvement, but the relations are closer.

(c) **Switching costs.** Suppliers can be integrated with the firm's administrative operations, by a system of electronic data interchange.

Bargaining power of customers. IT can lock customers in.

(a) **IT can raise switching costs** by locking customers into networks.

(b) **Customer information systems** can enable a thorough analysis of marketing information so that products and services can be tailored to the needs of certain segments.

(c) Customers also have access to improved information; this can increase their bargaining power.

(d) Suppliers can gain access to larger number of customers, reducing their dependence on a few large buyers.

Substitutes. In many respects, **IT itself is the substitute product.** Here are some examples.

(a) Video-conferencing systems might substitute for air transport in providing a means by which managers from all over the world can get together in a meeting.

(b) IT is the basis for new leisure activities (eg computer games) which substitute for TV or other pursuits.

(c) E-mail substitutes for some postal deliveries.

IT and the state of competitive rivalry. In many industries, IT will enable newcomers to imitate existing products and services, though set up costs may limit this effect. The effect of the Internet may be to expand the size of the market.

(a) IT can be used in support of a firm's **competitive** strategy of cost leadership, differentiation or focus. These are discussed later in this text.

(b) IT can be used in a **collaborative** venture, perhaps to set up new communications networks. Some competitors in the financial services industry share the same ATM network.

7.7 Using the five forces model: a caution

The five forces model provides a comprehensive framework for analysing the competitive environment. However, it must be used with caution. Its very comprehensiveness can encourage a feeling of omniscience in those who use it: a sense that all factors have been duly considered and dealt with. Unfortunately, no one is actually omniscient. Any analysis must pursue as high a degree of **objectivity** as possible. If there is too much subjectivity, unfounded complacence will result.

The creation in the UK of direct motor insurance selling by *Direct Line Insurance* is a case in point. Existing motor insurers' view of the threat from new entrants was that the need to create a distribution network of local agents and brokers was an **effective barrier to entry**. Direct Line's centralised call-centre approach simply **bypassed the barrier**.

The effect of subjectivity appears at an early stage in any analysis using the five forces approach. It is necessary to define with great care just what **market** or **market segment** one is dealing with. For a large organisation, or one operating in a complex environment, this may be extremely difficult. **BPP's** UK provision of classroom training in accountancy is a good example. The market for training for potential ICAEW accountants is subject to considerable **customer** bargaining power, since there are a few large firms that predominate. ACCA and CIMA courses, on the other hand, are more subject to the rivalry of existing **competitors**, since, as well as other commercial training providers, universities and local technical colleges are also sources of competition.

The need for careful analysis is, perhaps, most demanding in the area of substitute products or services. It takes a particular alertness to discern potential substitutes in the early stages of their development.

7.8 Government

It is possible to view the influence of **government** as so great as to justify viewing it as a sixth force. The activities of government would normally be analysed using the PESTEL model but, as we have pointed out, the division of the general environment into these categories is arbitrary and it may be useful to reconsider government in the task environment context. There is also the consideration that competition itself is often the target of specific government policies, either to encourage it or, quite often, to restrict it.

Chapter Roundup

- The environment may be divided for convenience into three concentric layers: the macro-environment; the industry or sector; and competitors and markets. The layers and the elements within them all interact with one another.

- Environmental uncertainty depends on the degree of **complexity** and the degree of **stability** present.

- The macro-environment may be analysed into six segments using the PESTEL framework.

- Government is responsible for providing a stable framework for economic activity and, in particular, for maintaining and improving the physical, social and market infrastructure. Public policy on **competition** and **consumer protection** is particularly relevant to business strategy.

- The **economic** environment affects firms at national and international level, both in the general level of economic activity and in particular variables, such as exchange rates, interest rates and inflation.

- The **social and cultural** environment features long-term social trends and people's beliefs and attitudes

- Technological developments can affect all aspects of business, not just product and services.

- The **physical** environment is important for logistical reasons, as a source of resources, and because of increasing regulation.

- The impact of business activity on the physical environment is now a major concern. Companies are under pressure to incorporate measure to protect the environment into their plans. This presents both challenges and opportunities, since some measures will impose costs, but others will allow significant savings. There is also a new range of markets for goods and services designed to protect or have minimum impact on the environment.

- Four aspects of globalisation are key drivers of change.
  - Market globalisation grows as tastes converge and communications improve.
  - Cost globalisation spreads as trade barriers fall and economies of scale and experience grow.
  - Governments promote free trade and international standards.
  - International competition promotes further trade and interaction.

- Porter identifies four principal determinants of national competitive advantage.
  - **Factor conditions**
  - **Firm strategy structure and rivalry**
  - **Demand conditions**
  - **Related and supporting industries**

- The past is not necessarily a good guide to the future. It may be so in simple static conditions, but more complex or dynamic environments require sophisticated techniques such as the use of leading indicators and scenarios.

- The immediate business environment of firms producing similar goods is called the **industry**. **Sector** may be used in a similar way in public and not-for-profit services.

- The **competitive environment** is structured by five forces: **barriers to entry; substitute products**; the bargaining power of **customers**; the bargaining power of **suppliers; competitive rivalry**.

- IT has characteristics that can affect all five competitive forces. These characteristics generally amount to communication improvements but IT can also be a substantial product in its own right.

Quick Quiz

1   What are the three concentric layers that make up the environment?

2   What does PESTEL stand for?

3   Which four aspects of globalisation may be regarded as key drivers of change?

4   What are the four elements of Porter's diamond?

5   What is a leading indicator?

6   What are the five forces?

Answers to Quick Quiz

1   Macro-environment; industry or sector; and competitors and markets

2   Political, economic, socio-cultural, technological, environmental protection, legal

3   Market globalisation; cost globalisation; government activity and policy; global competition

4   Firm strategy, structure and rivalry; factor conditions; demand conditions; related and supporting industries

5   An economic quantity or effect that changes before market demand changes.

6   Threat of new entrants; substitute products; bargaining power of customers and suppliers; competitive rivalry

Now try the questions below from the Exam Question Bank

Number	Level	Marks	Time
Q2	Exam	8	15 mins

Competitors and customers

3

Topic list	Syllabus reference
1 Competition dynamics	A3(c), (d)
2 Marketing	A4(a)
3 Customers and segmentation	A4(a), A3(d)
4 Understanding the customer	A4(b)
5 Opportunities and threats	A3(e)

Introduction

Competitors and customers make up the inner layer of the environmental shell. A detailed knowledge of both is essential for the development of effective strategy. In particular, customer reaction is what determines an organisation's critical success factors.

In this chapter we start to deal with specific topics that may form the basis of questions.

Study guide

		Intellectual level
A3	**Environmental issues affecting the strategic position of an organisation**	
(c)	Assess the contribution of the lifecycle model and the cycle of competition to understanding competitive behaviour	3
(d)	Analyse the influence of strategic groups and market segmentation	3
(e)	Determine the opportunities and threats posed by the environment of an organisation	2
A4	**Marketing and the value of goods and services**	
(a)	Analyse customers and markets	2
(b)	Establish appropriate critical success factors for products and services	2

Exam guide

In this chapter we start to look at some very specific aspects of strategy. Much of the material, such as the discussion of the nature of marketing, is still background, but the more specific topics, such as market segmentation, critical success factors and customer analysis may have direct relevance to future examination questions.

1 Competition dynamics

> **FAST FORWARD**
>
> The dynamic nature of competition may be considered using a variety of concepts.
>
> - The **cycle of competition** describes the typical development of the relationship between an established firm and a new challenger.
>
> - **Hyper-competition** is an unstable state of constantly shifting short-term advantage.
>
> - The **industry life cycle** has four phases: inception, growth, maturity/shakeout and decline. Each phase has typical implications for customers, competitors, products and profits.
>
> - **Strategic group analysis** examines the strategic space occupied by groups of close competitors in order to identify potential competitive advantage

The five forces model is a very useful tool for analysing the nature of competition within an industry, but it is essentially static: it does not focus on the **dynamic nature** of the business environment. The nature of competition is that future developments are not controllable by a single firm; each competitor will exercise its own influence on what happens. The business environment is therefore subject to constant change. Strategic managers must attempt to forecast what form this change is likely to take since it is their responsibility to make plans that will be appropriate under future conditions. JS&W, quoting *D'aveni with Gunter* describe a typical **cycle of competition**.

1.1 Cycle of competition

1.1.1 The challenge

An **incumbent firm** already operating successfully in an industry improves existing **barriers to entry** and erects new ones. Any **challenger firm** wishing to enter the industry must attempt to overcome these barriers. This does not necessarily mean attacking the market leader head-on. This is a risky strategy in any case, because of the incumbent firms' resources in cash, promotion and innovation. Instead, the challenger may attack smaller regional firms or companies of similar size to itself that are vulnerable through lack of resources or poor management.

Military analogies have been used to describe the challenger's attacking options.

(a) The **head-on attack** matches the target's marketing mix in detail, product for product and so on. A limited frontal attack may concentrate on selected desirable customers.

(b) The **flank attack** is mounted upon a market segment, geographic region or area of technology that the target has neglected.

(c) The **encirclement attack** consists of as large number of simultaneous flank attacks as possible in order to overwhelm the target.

(d) The **bypass attack** is indirect and unaggressive. It focuses on unrelated products, new geographic areas and technical leap-frogging to advance in the market.

(e) **Guerilla attack** consists of a series of aggressive, short-term moves to demoralise, unbalance and destabilise the opponent. Tactics include drastic price cuts, poaching staff, political lobbying and short bursts of promotional activity.

 Case Study

Dolls

Between 2001 and 2004, *Mattel* lost 20% of its share of the worldwide fashion-doll segment to smaller rivals such as *MGA Entertainment*, creator of a hip new line of dolls called *Bratz*. MGA recognised what Mattel had failed to – that preteen girls were becoming more sophisticated and maturing more quickly. At younger ages, they were outgrowing *Barbie* and increasingly preferring dolls that looked like their teenage siblings and the pop stars they idolised. As the target market for Barbie narrowed from girls ages three to eleven to girls about three to five, the Bratz line cut rapidly into the seemingly unassailable Mattel franchise. Mattel finally moved to rescue Barbie's declining fortunes, launching a brand extension called *My Scene* that targeted older girls, and a line of hip dolls called *Flavas* to compete head-on with Bratz. But the damage was done. Barbie, queen of dolls for over 40 years, lost a fifth of her realm almost overnight – and Mattel didn't see it coming.

GS Day and PJH Schoemaker, Harvard Business Review, November 2005

1.1.2 The response

If the incumbent makes no response to the initial campaign, the challenger will widen its attack to other, related or vulnerable market segments, using similar methods to those outlined above. On the other hand, the incumbent may respond; this will often be by means that amount to reinforcing the barriers to entry, such as increasing promotional spending.

Military analogies have also been used to describe defensive strategies for market leaders.

(a) **Position defence** relies upon not changing anything. This does not work very well.

(b) **Mobile defence** uses market broadening and diversification.

(c) **Flanking defence** is needed to respond to attacks on **secondary markets** with growth potential.

(d) **Contraction defence** involves withdrawal from vulnerable markets and those with low potential. It may amount to surrender.

(e)   **Pre-emptive defence** gathers information on potential attacks and then uses competitive advantage to strike first. Product innovation and aggressive promotion are important features.

A challenger faced with such moves may decide to start a **price war**. The disadvantage of this is that it will erode its own margins as well as those of the incumbent, but it does have the potential to reshape the market and redistribute longer-term market share.

1.1.3 Fighting back

An incumbent faced with a vigorous and resourceful challenger may decide in turn to **attack the entrant's own base**, perhaps by cutting price in its strongest market. This may have the result of causing the challenger to move on towards entry into another attractive market as it seeks to expand.

1.1.4 Resource implications

Both attacking and defending require the deployment of cash and strategic skill. In particular, extending competition to new geographical and national markets can raise the risks and costs involved to an extent that inhibits rivalry.

1.1.5 Hypercompetition

It is possible for competition in an industry to cycle fairly slowly, with extended periods of stability. This allows the careful building of competitive advantages that are difficult to imitate. **Hypercompetition**, by contrast, is a condition of constant competitive change. It is created by frequent, boldly aggressive competitive moves. This state makes it impossible for a firm to create lasting competitive advantage; firms that accept this will deliberately disrupt any stability that develops in order to deny long-term advantage to their competitors. Under these conditions, continuing success depends on effective exploitation of a series of short-term moves.

1.2 The industry life cycle

FAST FORWARD   Industries may display a **lifecycle**: this will affect and interact with the five forces.

Later in this Study Text we will discuss the concept of the **product life cycle**: this is a well established strategic and marketing tool. It may be possible to discern an **industry life cycle**, which will have wider implication for the nature of competition and competitive advantage. This cycle reflects **changes in demand** and the **spread of technical knowledge** among producers. Innovation creates the new industry, and this is normally product innovation. Later, innovation shifts to **processes** in order to maintain margins. The overall progress of the industry lifecycle is illustrated below.

	Inception	Growth	Maturity/shakeout	Decline
Products	Basic, no standards established	Better, more sophisticated, differentiated	Superior, standardised	Varied quality but fairly undifferentiated
Competitors	None to few	Many entrants	Competition increases, weaker players leave	Few remain. Competition may be on price
Buyers	Early adopters, prosperous, curious must be induced	More customers attracted and aware	Mass market, brand switching common	Enthusiasts, traditionalists, sophisticates
Profits	Negative – high first mover advantage	Good, possibly starting to decline	Eroding under pressure of competition	Variable

The industry life cycle model is an important concept that may illuminate some aspects of strategic thought. Like other models, it has some value for analysis, for forecasting trends and for suggesting possible courses of action, but it would be a mistake to attempt to apply it to all industries at all times. Proper attention must always be paid to current circumstances and options.

1.3 Strategic group analysis

Five forces analysis deals with the competitive environment in broad **industry-wide** terms. It is possible to refine this by considering **strategic groups**. These are made up of organisations with similar strategic characteristics, following similar strategies or competing on similar bases. Such groups arise for a variety of reasons, such as barriers to entry or the attractiveness of particular market segments.

The **strategic space** pertaining to a strategic group is defined by two or three common strategic characteristics. Here are some examples of such characteristics.

- Product diversity
- Geographical coverage
- Extent of branding
- Pricing policy
- Product quality
- Distribution method
- Target market segment

A series of 2-axis maps may be drawn using selected pairs of these characteristics to define both the extent of the strategic space and any unfilled gaps that exist within it. (A similar technique is used for specific products and is illustrated later in this chapter: this is **product positioning**.)

The **identification of potential competitive advantage** is the reason for analysing strategic groups. It improves knowledge of competitors and shows gaps in the organisation's current segments of operations. It may also reveal opportunities for migration to more favourable segments. Strategic problems may also be revealed.

2 Marketing

FAST FORWARD

Marketing as a concept of the way business should be done must be distinguished from marketing as a business function. Operational marketing is the best developed form of the latter.

2.1 The nature of marketing

We have already remarked that the terminology used in the world of corporate strategy is sometimes rather imprecise. An important area of potential confusion arises in the relationship between 'strategic management' and 'marketing'. A number of ideas and models are shared between the two activities (to the extent that they are, in fact, separate activities), and many marketing authors write as though 'marketing' encompasses all of 'strategic management'. We reject this view: for our purposes, 'marketing' is an important area of business activity that makes a particular contribution to strategic management, but is ultimately subordinate to it.

What is marketing?

> **Marketing** is the management process responsible for identifying, anticipating and satisfying customer requirements profitably.
>
> *(Chartered Institute of Marketing)*

While useful in its way, the CIM definition is not the only one we might consider; in fact there are many. Here is what *Dibb, Simkin, Pride and Ferrel* have to say:

> Marketing consists of individual and organisational activities that facilitate and expedite satisfying exchange relationships in a dynamic environment through the creation, distribution, promotion and pricing of goods, services and ideas.

This is a more detailed definition and has the advantage of being very specific about the activities it includes under the umbrella term 'marketing'.

There is one important problem with both of these approaches to marketing and that is their tendency towards **over-inclusiveness**. We see this most clearly when we think about the activity we know as **production**. Taking the CIM definition first, if we ask 'Does the production function have anything to do with satisfying customer requirements profitably?' we must, if we are fair, answer 'Yes, it does.' If production is to the wrong standard, or at too great a cost, or late, customer satisfaction will be reduced. A very similar question could be asked about the phrase 'creation ... of goods...' in the definition of Dibb *et al*, and it would have to be answered in the same way. Now, it is clear that it would be going too far to suggest that production is a core marketing activity and should be controlled by the marketing director.

While it is not so obvious in the case of functions such as finance and human resource management, the same argument applies to them, if to a lesser extent. We are driven to the conclusion that neither definition we have looked at is much good at explaining the relationship between marketing as an activity and the other activities to be found in any given organisation.

The related term '**marketing concept**' is worth looking at if we wish to understand more deeply.

Philip Kotler, one of the best known of writers on marketing subjects says this:

> 'The marketing concept holds that the key to achieving organisational goals lies in determining the needs and wants of target markets and delivering the desired satisfactions more efficiently and effectively than the competition.

In Kotler's statement we see a clue to resolving the problem we have identified. It is necessary for us to strike a clear distinction between marketing as an **activity** and marketing as a **concept** of how an organisation should go about its business. The two definitions we examined earlier were related to the **concept**; we need to know about the **activity**.

2.2 Models of marketing

The material below is taken from the introduction to the syllabus for the CIM qualification. It therefore represents an authoritative view of just what marketing is.

> 'The type, or model, of marketing practised in any organisation depends on a number of factors, not least of which are the activities to be performed according to the nature of the business and the organisation's dominant orientation. Marketing activities in organisations can be grouped broadly into four roles.
>
> (a) **Sales support**: the emphasis in this role is essentially reactive: marketing supports the direct sales force. It may include activities such as telesales or telemarketing, responding to inquiries, co-ordinating diaries, customer database management, organising exhibitions or other sales promotions, and administering agents. These activities usually come under a sales and marketing director or manager.
>
> (b) **Marketing communications**: the emphasis in this role is more proactive: marketing promotes the organisation and its product or service at a tactical level. It typically includes activities such as providing brochures and catalogues to support the sales force.
>
> (c) **Operational marketing**: the emphasis in this role is for marketing to support the organisation with a co-ordinated range of marketing activities including marketing research; brand management; product development and management; corporate and marketing communications; and customer relationship management. Given this breadth of activities,

planning is also a function usually performed in this role but at an operational or functional level.

(d) **Strategic marketing**: the emphasis in this role is for marketing to contribute to the creation of competitive strategy. As such, it is practised in customer-focused and larger organisations. In a large or diversified organisation, it may also be responsible for the coordination of marketing departments or activities in separate business units.

Operational marketing activities.
- Research and analysis
- Contributing to strategy and marketing planning
- Managing brands
- Implementing marketing programmes
- Measuring effectiveness
- Managing marketing teams

The operational marketing role, where it exists, will be performed by a marketing function in a business.'

So, what is the relationship between marketing and strategic management? The two are closely linked since there can be no corporate plan which does not involve products/services and customers.

Corporate strategic plans aim to guide the overall development of an organisation. Marketing planning is subordinate to corporate planning but makes a significant contribution to it and is concerned with many of the same issues. The marketing department is probably the most important **source of information** for the development of corporate strategy. The corporate audit of product/market strengths and weaknesses, and much of its external environmental analysis is directly informed by the **marketing audit**.

Specific marketing strategies will be determined within the overall corporate strategy. To be effective, these plans will be interdependent with those for other functions of the organisation.

(a) The **strategic** component of marketing planning focuses on the direction which an organisation will take in relation to a specific market, or set of markets, in order to achieve a specified set of objectives.

(b) Marketing planning also requires an **operational** component that defines tasks and activities to be undertaken in order to achieve the desired strategy. The **marketing plan** is concerned uniquely with **products** and **markets**.

Marketing management aims to ensure the company is pursuing effective policies to promote its products, markets and distribution channels. This involves exercising strategic control of marketing, and the means to apply strategic control is known as the **marketing audit**. Not only is the marketing audit an important aspect of **marketing control**, it can be used to provide much information and analysis for the **corporate planning process**.

2.3 Marketing audit

Key term

> The CIM defines a **marketing audit** as 'a systematic assessment of the organisation's marketing objectives, strategies, organisation and performance'.

The CIM definition goes on to say that the first aspect of the marketing audit is an audit of the environment, something we have already discussed as part of the wider context of business strategy. However, the rest of the CIM's discussion is uncontentious, focussing, as it does, on purely marketing matters: strategy, organisation, systems, productivity and functions.

2.4 The marketing mix

> The marketing function aims to satisfy customer needs profitably through an appropriate **marketing mix.**
>
> The **marketing mix** comprises **product, price, place** and **promotion.** For **services**, this is extended to include **people**, **processes** and **physical evidence.**

Key term

> **Marketing mix:** 'the set of controllable variables and their levels that the firm uses to influence the target market'. These are **product**, **price**, **place** and **promotion** and are sometimes known as the four Ps.

The **marketing mix** is a very important concept: like so much else that bears the 'marketing' label, it is too important strategically to be left to the marketing department. Elements in the marketing mix **act partly as substitutes for each other** and they must be **integrated.** This is so the product can be positioned in the market to appeal to the customer. For example, a firm can raise the selling price of its products if it also raises product quality or advertising expenditure. Equally, a firm can perhaps reduce its sales promotion expenditure if it is successful in achieving a wider range and larger numbers of sales outlets for its product.

Exam focus point

> The **marketing mix** is a very useful basis for answering many questions that require you to advise on courses of action. While it is less likely that you will be required to discuss all of the variables, it is quite common to find that thinking about the relationship between two or three of them gives some useful insights. Make sure you are completely familiar with both the basic four Ps and the extra 3Ps of the service marketing mix.

2.5 Product

Key term

> A **product** (goods or services) is anything that satisfies a need or want. It is not a 'thing' with 'features' but a package of benefits.

From the firm's point of view the product element of the marketing mix is what is being sold, whether it be widgets, power stations, haircuts, holidays or financial advice. From the customer's point of view, a **product is a solution to a problem or a package of benefits.** Many products might satisfy the same customer need. On what basis might a customer choose?

(a)   **Customer value** is the customer's estimate of how far a product or service goes towards satisfying his or her need(s).

(b)   Every product has a price, and so the customer makes a **trade-off** between the **expenditure** and **the value offered**.

(c)   According to Kotler a customer must feel he or she gets a better deal from buying an item than by any of the alternatives.

The nature of the product

(a)   The **core product** is the most basic description of the product – a car is a means of personal transport. The **actual product** is the car itself, with all its physical features such as a powerful engine, comfortable seats and a sun roof. The **augmented product** is the car plus the benefits which come with it, such as delivery, servicing, warranties and credit facilities for buyers.

(b)   The **product range** consists of two dimensions.

(i)   **Width**. A car maker may have products in all parts, known as segments, of the market: luxury cars, family cars, small cheap cars, and so on.

(ii) **Depth**. It may then offer a wide variety of options within each segment – a choice of engines, colours, accessories and so on.

(c) **Benefits offered to the customer.** Customers differ in their attitudes towards new products and the benefits they offer.

Product issues in the marketing mix will include such factors as:

- Design (size, shape)
- Features
- Quality and reliability
- After-sales service (if necessary)
- Packaging

2.6 Place

Place deals with how the product is distributed, and how it reaches its customers. We discussed aspects of distribution from an operational perspective in Chapter 8.

(a) **Channel**. Where are products sold? In supermarkets, corner shops? Which sales outlets will be chosen?

(b) **Logistics.** The location of warehouses and efficiency of the distribution system is also important. A customer might have to wait a long time if the warehouse is far away. Arguably, the **speed of delivery** is an important issue in **place**.

A firm can distribute the product itself (direct distribution) or distribute it through intermediary organisations such as retailers. Key issues are:

(a) **Product push**: the firm directs its efforts to distributors to get them to stock the product.

(b) **Customer pull**: the firm persuades consumers to demand the product from retailers and distributors, effectively pulling the product through the chain.

2.7 Promotion

Many of the practical activities of the marketing department are related to **promotion**. Promotion is the element of the mix over which the marketing department generally has most control. A useful mnemonic is AIDA which summarises the aims of promotion.

- Arouse **Attention**
- Generate **Interest**
- Inspire **Desire**
- Initiate **Action** (ie buy the product)

Promotion in the marketing mix includes all marketing communications which let the public know of the product or service.

- Advertising (newspapers, billboards, TV, radio, direct mail, internet)
- Sales promotion (discounts, coupons, special displays in particular stores)
- Direct selling by sales personnel.
- Public relations

2.8 Price

The price element of the marketing mix is the only one which brings in revenue. Price is influenced by many factors.

(a) **Economic influences:** supply and demand; price and income elasticities

(b) **Competitors' prices.** Competitors include other firms selling the same type of product, as well as firm selling substitute products. Generally, firms like to avoid price wars.

(c)   **Quality connotations**. High price is often taken as being synonymous with quality, so pricing will reflect the a product's image. (Stella Artois lager was once marketed in the UK as being 'reassuringly expensive'.)

(d)   **Discounts**. These can make the product attractive to distributors.

(e)   **Payment terms** (eg offering a period of interest free credit)

(f)   **Trade-in allowances**

(g)   The stage in the **product life cycle**.

(i)   **Penetration pricing** is charging a low price to achieve early market share advantages

(ii)   **Skimming pricing** charging high prices early on to reap the maximum profits.

2.9 The extended marketing mix

This is also known as the service marketing mix because it is specifically relevant to the marketing of **services** rather than **physical products**. The intangible nature of services makes these extra three Ps particularly important.

2.9.1 People

The importance of employees in the marketing mix is particularly important in **service marketing**, because of the **inseparability** of the service from the service provider: the creation and consumption of the service generally happen at the same moment, at the interface between the server and the served. Front-line staff must be selected, trained and motivated with particular attention to customer care and public relations.

In the case of some services, the **physical presence** of people performing the service is a vital aspect of customer satisfaction. The staff involved are performing or producing a service, selling the service and also liaising with the customer to promote the service, gather information and respond to customer needs.

2.9.2 Processes

Efficient **processes** can become a marketing advantage in their own right. If an airline, for example, develops a sophisticated ticketing system, it can offer shorter waits at check-in or wider choice of flights through allied airlines. Efficient order processing not only increases customer satisfaction, but cuts down on the time it takes the organisation to complete a sale.

Issues to be considered include the following.

- Policies, particularly with regard to ethical dealings (a key issue for many consumers)
- Procedures, for efficiency and standardisation
- Automation and computerisation of processes
- Queuing and waiting times
- Information gathering, processing and communication times
- Capacity management, matching supply to demand in a timely and cost effective way
- Accessibility of facilities, premises, personnel and services

Such issues are particularly important in service marketing; because of the range of factors and people involved, it is difficult to standardise the service offered. Quality in particular specifications will vary with the circumstances and individuals.

Services are also innately **perishable**: their purchase may be put off, but they cannot be stored.

This creates a need for process planning for efficient work.

2.9.3 Physical evidence

Services are **intangible**: there is no physical substance to them. This means that even when money has been spent on them the customer has no **evidence of ownership**. These factors make it difficult for consumers to perceive, evaluate and compare the qualities of service provision, and may therefore dampen the incentive to consume.

Issues of intangibility and ownership can be tackled by making available a physical symbol or representation of the service product or of ownership, and the benefits it confers. For example, tickets and programs relating to entertainment; and certificates of attainment in training are symbolic of the service received and a history of past positive experiences.

Physical evidence of service may also be incorporated into the design and specification of the service environment by designing premises to reflect the quality and type of service aspired to. Such environmental factors include finishing, decor, colour scheme, noise levels, background music, fragrance and general ambience.

3 Customers and segmentation

3.1 Buyer behaviour

FAST FORWARD

> The decision to make a purchase can be very simple, very complex or somewhere between the two. Buyers do not always proceed rationally, though the motivation of industrial buyers may be more logical than that of consumers.

In marketing, a market is defined in terms of its **buyers** or **potential buyers**.

- **Consumer markets** (eg for soap powder, washing machines, TV sets, clothes)
- **Industrial markets** (eg for machine tools, construction equipment)
- **Government markets** (eg for armaments, and, in the UK, medical equipment)
- **Reseller markets**
- **Export markets**

3.1.1 Consumer goods

Consumer goods are in such a form that they can be used by the consumer without the need for any further commercial processing. Consumer goods are further classified according to the method by which they are purchased.

- **Convenience goods**
- **Shopping goods**
- **Speciality goods**

If an article has close substitutes, is purchased regularly in small amounts of low unit value, and the customer insists on buying it with the minimum of inconvenience, the article is called a **convenience good**. Convenience goods are everyday purchases such as toothpaste, bread, coffee, chocolate etc, and are likely to be produced by several manufacturers. Promoting a unique image for the product, for example by **branding**, is therefore important.

Shopping goods are goods for which customers are more discriminating. They usually have a higher unit value than convenience goods and are bought less frequently, usually from a specialist outlet with a wider range on offer. **Examples** of shopping goods are cars, furniture, hi-fi equipment, many clothes, household appliances such as washing machines and cookers.

When a manufacturer, either by product design or advertising, has become associated in the public mind with a particular product (eg *Rolls Royce* cars, *Wedgwood* pottery) the article produced is no longer a shopping good, but a **speciality good**, possessing a unique character which will make a customer go out of his way to ask for it by name and find a dealer who sells it.

3.1.2 Industrial or business-to-business markets

In industrial markets, the customer is another firm, such as for the sale of machine tools or consultancy advice. The industrial market, more than the consumer market, is influenced by the general state of the economy and the government's economic policy.

The demand for industrial goods and services is **derived** from the demand for the product or service to which they contribute. For example, the demand for aluminium is in part derived from the demand for cans, which might itself be derived from demand for the beer with which the cans will be filled.

Industrial buyers are more **rationally motivated** than consumers in deciding which goods to buy. Sales policy decisions by a supplier are therefore more important than sales promotion activities in an industrial market. Special attention should be given in selling to quality, price, credit, delivery dates, after-sales service, etc, and it is the importance of these rational motivations which make it difficult for an untried newcomer to break into an industrial goods market.

3.1.3 Organisational buying behaviour

The organisational buying behaviour process has some similarities with consumer buyer behaviour, but is supposedly more rational.

- How are needs recognised in a company?
- What is the type of buying situation?
- How is a supplier selected?
- How will performance be reviewed after purchase?

3.1.4 The decision-making unit

The **decision-making unit** (DMU) is a term used to describe the person or people who actually take the decision to buy a good or service. The marketing manager needs to know who in each organisation makes the effective buying decisions and how decisions are made: the DMU might act with formal authority, or as an informal group reaching a joint decision. Many large organisations employ specialist purchasing departments or 'buyers' – but the independence of the buyers will vary from situation to situation.

3.1.5 Factors in the motivation mix of business or government buyers

Business or government buyers are motivated as follows.

(a) **Quality**.

(b) **Price**. Where profit margins in the final market are under pressure, the buyer of industrial goods will probably make price the main purchasing motivation.

(c) **Budgetary control** may encourage the buying department to look further afield for potential suppliers to obtain a better price or quality of goods.

(d) **Fear of breakdown**. Where a customer has a highly organised and costly production system, he will clearly want to avoid a breakdown in the system, due to a faulty machine or running out of stocks of materials.

(e) **Credit**. The importance of credit could vary with the financial size of the buyer.

3.2 Market segmentation

Segments are groups of customers with similar needs that can be **targeted** with a distinctively **positioned** marketing **mix**. Both consumer and industrial markets can usefully be segmented and several bases exist for the process. The aim is to identify a coherent segment that is both **valid** and **attractive**.

Much marketing planning is based on the concepts of **segmentation and product positioning.** The purpose of segmentation is to identify target markets in which the firm can take a position. A market is not a mass, homogeneous group of customers, each wanting an identical product. Every market consists of potential buyers with different **needs** and different **buying behaviour**. These different customers may be **grouped into segments**. A different marketing approach will be taken by an organisation for each market segment.

Key term

> **Market segmentation** is 'the subdividing of a market into distinct and increasingly homogeneous subgroups of customers, where any subgroup can conceivably be selected as a target market to be met with a distinct marketing mix'.
>
> *Kotler*

There are two important elements in this definition of market segmentation.

(a) Although the total market consists of widely different groups of consumers, each group consists of people (or organisations) with **common needs and preferences**, who perhaps react to 'market stimuli' in much the same way.

(b) Each market segment can become a **target market for a firm**, and would require a unique marketing mix if the firm is to exploit it successfully.

Reasons for segmenting markets

Reason	Comment
Better satisfaction of customer needs	One solution will not satisfy all customers
Growth in profits	Some customers will pay more for certain benefits
Revenue growth	Segmentation means that more customers may be attracted by what is on offer, in preference to competing products
Customer retention	By targeting customers, a number of different products can be offered to them
Targeted communications	Segmentation enables clear communications as people in the target audience share common needs
Innovation	By identifying unmet needs, companies can innovate to satisfy them

Steps in segmentation, targeting and positioning identified by Kotler

Step 1 Identify **segmentation** variables and segment the market

Step 2 Develop segment profiles

⎱ Segmentation

Step 3 Evaluate the attractiveness of each segment

Step 4 Select the **target** segment(s)

⎱ Targeting

Step 5 Identify **positioning** concepts for each target segment

Step 6 Select, develop and communicate the chosen concept

⎱ Positioning

3.3 Identifying segments

An important initial marketing task is the **identification of segments** within the market. Segmentation applies more obviously to the consumer market, but it can also be applied to an **industrial market**.

(a) One basis will not be appropriate in every market, and sometimes two or more bases might be valid at the same time.

(b) One basis or segmentation variable might be superior to another in a hierarchy of variables. There are thus **primary and secondary segmentation variables.**

3.4 The bases for segmentation

Segmentation variables fall into a small number of categories.

3.4.1 Geographical segmentation

Geographical segmentation is very simple, but useful, especially in business-to-business marketing, which relies heavily on personal selling. It can be combined with socio-demographic segmentation (see below) .

3.4.2 Psychographic or lifestyle segmentation

Psychographic segmentation is not based on objective data so much as how people see themselves and their **subjective** feelings and attitudes towards a particular product or service, or towards life in general. It makes use of variables such as interests, activities, personality and opinions. This is very useful for many consumer goods, since they can be designed and promoted to appeal on the basis of such variables.

3.4.3 Behavioural segmentation

The behavioural approach segments buyers into groups based on their attitudes to and use of the product, and the **benefits** they expect to receive. It uses such variables as usage rate, impulse purchase, brand loyalty and sensitivity to marketing mix variables such as price, quality and promotion

Benefit segmentation of the toothpaste market						
Segment name	*Principal benefit sought*	*Demographic strengths*	*Special behavioural characteristics*	*Brands dis-proportionately favoured*	*Personality character-istics*	*Lifestyle characteristics*
The sensory segment	Flavour, product appearance	Children	Users of spearmint flavoured toothpaste	Colgate, Stripe	High self-involvement	Hedonistic
The Sociables	Brightness of teeth	Teens, young people	Smokers	Macleans, Ultra-Brite	High sociability	Active
The Worriers	Decay prevention	Large families	Heavy users	Crest	High hypochon-driasis	Conservative
The Independent Segment	Price	Men	Heavy users	Brands on sale	High autonomy	Value oriented

3.4.4 Socio-demographic segmentation

Socio-demographic segmentation is based on social, economic and demographic variables such as those below.

- Age
- Sex
- Income
- Occupation
- Education

- Religion
- Ethnicity/national origin
- Social class
- Family size

An example is the **ACORN** system which divides the UK into 17 groups covering a total of 54 different types of areas, that share common socio-economic characteristics. Unlike geographical segmentation, which is fairly crude, **geodemographics** enables similar groups of people to be targeted, even though they might exist in different areas of the country. These various classifications share certain characteristics, including:

- Car ownership
- Unemployment rates
- Purchase of financial service products
- Number of holidays
- Age profile

Age and sex present few problems but **social class** has always been one of the most dubious areas of marketing research investigation. 'Class' is a highly personal and subjective phenomenon, to the extent that some people are 'class conscious' or class aware and have a sense of belonging to a particular group.

From 2001 the UK Office for National Statistics used a new categorisation system, which reflects recent changes in the UK population.

New social class	Occupations	Example
1	Higher managerial and professional occupations	
1.1	Employers and managers in larger organisations	Bank managers, company directors
1.2	Higher professional	Doctors, lawyers
2	Lower managerial and professional occupations	Police officers
3	Intermediate occupations	Secretaries, clerical workers
4	Small employers and own-account workers	
5	Lower supervisory, craft and related occupations	Electricians
6	Semi-routine occupations	Drivers, hairdressers, bricklayers
7	Routine occupations	Car park attendants, cleaners

 Case Study

Capital One

Capital One's competitive advantage comes not from the brand strength of American Express, or the economies of scale that Citibank enjoys, or from its links with affinity groups such as those that benefit MBNA Bank. Its strength is in gathering and using data. 'It is the best data mining shop anywhere in the US', is the assessment of Eric Clemons, professor of marketing at Wharton Business School at the University of Pennsylvania.

Its special skill is spotting the patterns that identify 'micro-segments' in the market for consumer credit. Last year, the company offered thousands of variations of credit card. It also conducted 64,000 marketing tests on small groups of customers to gauge how new varieties would be received.

The ability to segment the credit card market more finely than its competitors, and customise products accordingly, is what sets Capital One apart. Many companies talk about mass customisation. The Virginia-based company really does it.

Financial Times, 14 May 2002

3.5 Segmentation of the industrial market

Industrial markets can be segmented with many of the bases used in consumer markets such as geography, usage rate and benefits sought. Additional, more traditional bases include customer type, product/technology, customer size and purchasing procedures.

(a) **Geographic location**. Some industries and related industries are clustered in particular areas. Firms selling services to the banking sector might be interested in the City of London.

(b) **Type of business** (eg service, manufacturing)

    (i) **Type of organisation.** Organisations in an industry as a whole may have certain needs in common. Employment agencies offering business services to publishers, say, must offer their clients personnel with experience in particular desk top publishing packages. Suitable temporary staff offered to legal firms can be more effective if used to legal jargon. Each different type of firm can be offered a tailored product or service.

    (ii) **Components manufacturers specialise in the industries of the firms to which they supply components.**

(c) **Use of the product.** In the UK, many new cars are sold to businesses, as benefit cars. Although this practice is changing with the viability of a 'cash alternative' to a company car, the varying levels of specification are developed with the business buyer in mind (eg junior salesperson gets an Escort, Regional Manager gets a Ford Mondeo).

(d) **Size of organisation**. Large organisations may have elaborate purchasing procedures, and may do many things in-house. Small organisations may be more likely to subcontract certain specialist services.

3.6 Segment validity

A market segment will only **be valid if it is worth designing and developing a unique** marketing mix for that specific segment. The following questions are commonly asked to decide whether or not the segment can be used for developing marketing plans.

Criteria	Comment
Can the segment be measured?	It might be possible to conceive of a market segment, but it is not necessarily easy to measure it. For example, for a segment based on people with a conservative outlook to life, can conservatism of outlook be measured by market research?
Is the segment big enough?	There has to be a large enough potential market to be profitable.
Can the segment be reached?	There has to be a way of getting to the potential customers via the organisation's promotion and distribution channels.

Criteria	Comment
Do segments respond differently?	If two or more segments are identified by marketing planners but each segment responds in the same way to a marketing mix, the segments are effectively one and the same and there is no point in distinguishing them from each other.
Can the segment be reached profitably?	Do the identified customer needs cost less to satisfy than the revenue they earn?
Is the segment suitably stable?	The stability of the segment is important, if the organisation is to commit huge production and marketing resources to serve it. The firm does not want the segment to 'disappear' next year. Of course, this may not matter in some industries.

3.7 Segment attractiveness

A segment might be valid and potentially profitable, but is it potentially **attractive?** For example a segment that has **high barriers to entry** might cost more to enter but will be less **vulnerable to competitors.** The most attractive segments will be those whose needs can be met by building on the company's strengths and where forecasts for demand, sales profitability and **growth** are favourable.

3.8 Target markets

FAST FORWARD

Companies select particularly attractive segments and approach them with a carefully designed marketing mix. This **concentrated** marketing approach is more affective than the **undifferentiated**, mass marketing method when customers are likely to exercise careful choice.

Because of limited resources, competition and large markets, organisations are not usually able to sell with equal efficiency and success to every market segment. It is necessary to select **target markets**. A target market is a particularly attractive segment that will be served with a distinct marketing mix. The marketing management of a company may choose one of the following policy options.

Key terms

Undifferentiated marketing: this policy is to produce a single product and hope to get as many customers as possible to buy it; that is, ignore segmentation entirely.

Concentrated marketing: the company attempts to produce the ideal product for a single segment of the market (eg Rolls Royce cars for the wealthy).

Differentiated marketing: the company attempts to introduce several product versions, each aimed at a different market segment. For example, manufacturers of soap powder make a number of different brands, marketed to different segments.

It is important to assess company strengths when evaluating attractiveness and targeting a market. This can help determine the appropriate strategy, because once the attractiveness of each identified segment has been assessed it can be considered along with relative strengths to determine the potential advantages the organisation would have. In this way preferred segments can be targeted.

The major **disadvantage of differentiated marketing** is the additional costs of marketing and production (more product design and development costs, the loss of economies of scale in production and storage, additional promotion costs and administrative costs etc). When the **costs of further differentiation of the market exceed the benefits** from further segmentation and **target marketing**, a firm is said to have **over-differentiated**.

The major **disadvantage of concentrated marketing** is the business risk of relying on a single segment of a single market. On the other hand, specialisation in a particular market segment can give a firm a profitable, although perhaps temporary, competitive edge over rival firms.

The choice between undifferentiated, differentiated or concentrated marketing as a marketing strategy will depend on the following factors.

(a)   The extent to which the product and/or the market may be considered **homogeneous**. **Mass marketing** may be 'sufficient' if the market is largely homogeneous (for example, for safety matches).

(b)   The **company's resources** must not be over extended by differentiated marketing. Small firms may succeed better by concentrating on one segment only.

(c)   The product must be sufficiently **advanced in its life cycle** to have attracted a substantial total market; otherwise segmentation and target marketing is unlikely to be profitable, because each segment would be too small in size.

3.9 Product positioning

FAST FORWARD

A product's **positioning** defines how it is intended to be perceived by customers and how it differs from current and potential competing products.

It is not always possible to identify a market segment where there is no direct competitor, and a marketing problem for the firm will be the creation of some form of **product differentiation** (real or imagined) in the marketing mix of the product. The aim is to make the customer perceive the product as different from its competitors.

A perceptual map of product positioning can be used to identify **gaps in the market**. This example might suggest that there could be potential in the market for a low-price high-quality bargain brand. A company that carries out such an analysis might decide to conduct further research to find out whether there is scope in the market for a new product which would be targeted at a market position where there are few or no rivals. (A firm successfully pursuing **cost leadership** might be in a good position to offer a **bargain brand**.)

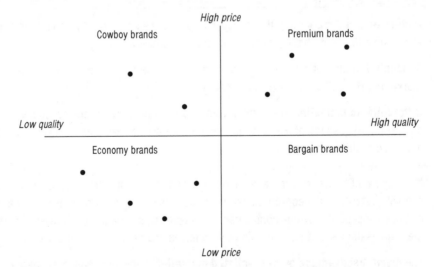

Similar matrices to explore possible product positions in terms of, for instance, attributes, applications, users, occasions for use and specific aspects of quality may be drawn to refine knowledge of product position.

4 Understanding the customer

4.1 The strategic customer

> The **strategic customer** is the entity that decides to make the purchase, not the end user.

Many goods and services are purchased not by their end users but by intermediaries such as retailers, sales agents and procurement department staff. Where this pattern applies, the supplier has to take account of the influence of the intermediary; indeed, **the intermediary is the strategic customer**, not the end user, and it is the intermediary's requirements that are of primary strategic importance. The requirements of the end user are important, but subordinate in many cases to those of the intermediary.

4.2 What customers value – critical success factors

> **Critical success factors** are product features that are **particularly valued by customers**.

Customers purchase products and services because they value the things the products and services provide them with. This may be a relatively simple satisfaction, as when motorists buy petrol, or it may include a wide range of **both tangible and intangible benefits**. Many products are, in fact, **complex packages of features** that their producers have worked hard to assemble. The intangibles among these features are often collectively referred to as **brand values**. Consider a wristwatch, for example. It would be a mistake to imagine that most wristwatches are bought because they tell the time. They are also articles of adornment that reflect the taste, self-image and status of the purchaser. The man who buys a *Breitling Aerospace* values the penumbra of adventure and glamour associated with aviation that the company's promotion works hard to create, for example, as well as the quality and style of the product. He probably also enjoys the purchase process also, if he buys from an expensively fitted, well-staffed shop in a premium location.

One of the reasons we gave for segmenting markets was that it allows the organisation to focus on a particular set of customer requirements or special needs. There is likely to be a wide range of opinion among customers as to the features of the organisation's market offerings that provide them with the greatest satisfaction, but, equally, it is also likely that **some features will be widely regarded as particularly important**. These features, the satisfactions they provide and the demands they make on the organisation's way of doing business constitute **critical success factors**: the organisation must get these things right if it is to be successful in what it does.

Thus, for a producer of luxury goods, manufacturing quality would undoubtedly be a critical success factor, but ensuring that an air of luxury pervaded its retail outlets would be just as important; to be sold in a discount chain such as *TK Maxx* would be to fail to provide one of the satisfactions sought by the target market segment.

Key term

> **Critical success factors** are those product features that are particularly valued by a group of customers and, therefore, where the organisation must excel to outperform competitors.   *JS&W*

There are important messages connected with this concept. First, value must be assessed **through the eyes of the customer**, not those of the designer or professional specialist. Second, **resources** should be deployed so as to achieve high performance in critical success factors.

4.3 Reviewing the customer portfolio

> The **customer base** is an asset to be invested in, as future benefits will come from existing customers, but not all customers are as important as others. It will help you in evaluating the customer portfolio if you consider the customer base as an asset worth investing in.

Case Study

(a) *Coca-Cola* paid $200m to *Pernod* of France, which, under contract, had effectively built a customer base for Coca-Cola, as well as building up a distribution network. Coca-Cola wanted to take charge of the marketing of Coke in France.

(b) Supermarket loyalty cards reward customers with bonus points, saving them money, or allowing them to redeem points for products according to how much they spend.

(c) Many banks lose money on student accounts, in the hope that they will earn it back later in the customer's life cycle.

As already mentioned, a **marketing audit** involves a review of an organisation's products and markets, the marketing environment, and its marketing system and operations. The profitability of each product and each market should be assessed, and the costs of different marketing activities established.

Information obtained about markets

(a) **Size of the customer base**. Does the organisation sell to a large number of small customers or a small number of big customers?

(b) **Size of individual orders**. The organisation might sell its products in many small orders, or it might have large individual orders. Delivery costs can be compared with order sizes.

(c) **Sales revenue and profitability.** The performance of individual products can be compared. An imbalance between sales and profits over various product ranges can be potentially dangerous.

(d) **Segments.** An analysis of sales and profitability into export markets and domestic markets.

(e) **Market share.** Estimated share of the market obtained by each product group.

(f) **Growth.** Sales growth and contribution growth over the previous four years or so, for each product group.

(g) Whether the **demand** for certain products is **growing, stable or likely to decline.**

(h) Whether **demand is price sensitive** or not.

(i) Whether there is a growing tendency for the market to become **fragmented**, with more specialist and 'custom-made' products.

Information about current marketing activities

- Comparative pricing
- Advertising effectiveness
- Effectiveness of distribution network
- Attitudes to the product, in comparison with competitors

4.4 Customer analysis

Key customer analysis calls for six main areas of investigation into customers. A firm might wish to identify which customers offer most profit. Small businesses are especially prone to overtrading.

Area	Detail
Key customer identity	• Name of each key customer • Location • Status in market • Products they make and sell • Size of firm (capital employed, turnover, number of employees)
Customer history	• First purchase date. • Who makes the buying decision in the customer's organisation? • What is the average order size, by product? • What is the regularity/ periodicity of the order, by product? • What is the trend in size of orders? • What is the motive in purchasing? • What does the customer know about the firm's and competitors' products? • On what basis does the customer reorder? • How is the useful life of the product judged? • Were there any lost or cancelled orders? For what reason?
Relationship of customer to product	• What does the customer use the product for? • Do the products form part of the customer's own service/product?
Relationship of customer to potential market	• What is the size of the customer in relation to the total end-market? • Is the customer likely to expand, or not? Diversify? Integrate?
Customer attitudes and behaviour	• What interpersonal factors exist which could affect sales by the firm and by competitors? • Does the customer also buy competitors' products? • To what extent may purchases be postponed?
The financial performance of the customer	How successful is the customer?

4.5 Customer profitability analysis (customer account profitability)

Customer profitability analysis is an analysis of the total sales revenue generated from a customer or customer group, less all the costs that are incurred in servicing that customer group.

Key term

Customer profitability analysis (CPA). 'Analysis of the revenue streams and service costs associated with specific customers or customer groups.' (CIMA *Official Terminology*)

'An immediate impact of introducing any level of strategic management accounting into virtually every organisation is to destroy totally any illusion that the same level of profit is derived from all customers'.
(Ward, *Strategic Management Accounting*)

Different customer costs can arise out of the following.

- Order size
- Sales mix
- Order processing
- Transport costs (eg if JIT requires frequent deliveries)
- Management time
- Cash flow problems (eg increased overdraft interest) caused by slow payers
- Order complexity (eg if the order has to be sent out in several stages)
- Stockholding costs can relate to specify customers
- The customer's negotiating strength

The total costs of servicing customers can vary depending on how customers are serviced.

(a) **Volume discounts**. A customer who places one large order is given a discount, presumably because it benefits the supplier to do so (eg savings on administrative overhead in processing the orders – as identified by an ABC system).

(b) **Different rates** charged by power companies to domestic as opposed to business users. This in part reflects the administrative overhead of dealing with individual customers. In practice, many domestic consumers benefit from cross-subsidy.

Remember

> Customer profitability is the 'total sales revenue generated from a customer or customer group, less all the costs that are incurred in servicing that customer or customer group.'

It is possible to analyse customer profitability over a single period but more useful to look at a longer time scale. Such a multi period approach fits in with the idea of **relationship marketing**, with its emphasis on customer retention for the longer term.

Customer profitability analysis focuses on profits generated by customers and suggests that **profit does not automatically increase with sales revenue**. CPA can benefit a company in the following ways.

- It enables a company to **focus resources** on the most profitable areas
- It identifies unexpected **differences in profitability** between customers
- It helps quantify the **financial impact** of proposed changes
- It helps highlight the **cost** of obtaining **new** customers and the **benefit** of retaining existing customers
- It helps to highlight whether **product** development or **market** development is to be preferred
- An appreciation of the costs of servicing clients assists in **negotiations** with customers

4.6 The customer lifecycle

We can refine our financial analysis by incorporating the concept of the **customer lifecycle**. This is less developed than the equivalent product and industry lifecycle models, but it can be useful to consider the following matters.

(a) **Promotional expense** relating to a single customer is likely to be heavily **front-loaded**: it is much cheaper to retain a customer than to attract one.

(b) It is likely that **sales** to a customer will start at a low level and increase to a higher level as the customer gains confidence, though this is not certain and will vary from industry to industry.

(c) A customer who purchases a basic or commodity product initially may move on to **more differentiated products** later.

(d)   In consumer markets, career progression is likely to provide the individual with steadily increasing amounts of disposable income, while the **family lifecycle** will indicate the ranging nature of likely purchases as time passes.

Any attempt to estimate lifecycle costs and revenues should also consider existing and potential **environmental impacts**, including, in particular, the likely actions of competitors and the potential for product and process innovation.

5 Opportunities and threats

The strategic influence of the environment may be summarised into lists of **opportunities** and **threats**.

It is important to remember the purpose of all the environmental analysis ideas that we have been talking about: they should provide input into the process of designing a **practical business strategy**.

One very useful way of thinking about the implications of environmental information is to consider it in terms of **opportunities and threats**.

5.1 Threats

For a commercial organisation, the most urgent threats are likely to emerge from within the immediate industry arena. The **five forces** model provides a good summary of the threats inherent here, supplemented by strategic group analysis. Recognising threats in the wider PESTEL environment is, perhaps, more difficult, since it covers such an enormous range of factors.

5.2 Opportunities

Opportunities may take the form of **strategic gaps**: these are potentially profitable aspects of the competitive environment that are not being exploited by rivals. JS&W give several examples of how these might arise.

(a)   Potential **substitutes** for existing products might be created. This is largely a technology-based opportunity, but an important route to the development of substitutes is the imaginative development of new uses for existing products and methods.

(b)   Other **strategic groups** may present opportunities, especially if there are changes in the macro-environment, such as deregulation or opening of new markets in developing countries.

(c)   It may be possible to target **different strategic customers**. In the case of consumer goods, the development of Internet selling means that they ultimate user is displacing the distributor as the strategic customer.

(d)   There may be potential to market **complementary products**. For example, capital goods manufacturers routinely offer credit services to assist the customer to buy.

(e)   New **market segments** may have potential, though there may be a need to adapt the product.

Chapter Roundup

- The dynamic nature of competition may be considered using a variety of concepts.

    - The **cycle of competition** describes the typical development of the relationship between an established firm and a new challenger.

    - **Hyper-competition** is an unstable state of constantly shifting short-term advantage

    - The **industry life cycle** has four phases: inception, growth, maturity/shakeout and decline. Each phase has typical implications for customers, competitors, products and profits

    - **Strategic group analysis** examines the strategic space occupied by groups of close competitors in order to identify potential competitive advantage

- Industries may display a **lifecycle**: this will affect and interact with the five forces.

- **Marketing** as a concept of the way business should be done must be distinguished from marketing as a business function. Operational marketing is the best developed form of the latter.

- The marketing function aims to satisfy customer needs profitably through an appropriate **marketing mix.**

  The **marketing mix** comprises **product**, **price**, **place** and **promotion**. For **services**, this is extended to include **people**, **processes** and **physical evidence**.

- The decision to make a purchase can be very simple, very complex or somewhere between the two. Buyers do not always proceed rationally, thought the motivation of industrial buyers may be more logical than that of consumers.

- **Segments** are groups of customers with similar needs that can be **targeted** with a distinctively **positioned** marketing **mix**. Both consumer and industrial markets can usefully be segmented and several bases exist for the process. The aim is to identify a coherent segment that is both **valid** and **attractive**.

- Companies select particularly attractive segments and approach them with a carefully designed marketing mix. This **concentrated** marketing approach is more affective than the **undifferentiated**, mass marketing method when customers are likely to exercise careful choice.

- A product's **positioning** defines how it is intended to be perceived by customers and how it differs from current and potential competing products.

- The **strategic customer** is the entity that decides to make the purchase, not the end user.

- **Critical success factors** are product features that are **particularly valued by customers**.

- The **customer base** is an asset to be invested in, as future benefits will come from existing customers, but not all customers are as important as others. It will help you in evaluating the customer portfolio if you consider the customer base as an asset worth investing in.

- **Customer profitability analysis** is an analysis of the total sales revenue generated from a customer or customer group, less all the costs that are incurred in servicing that customer group.

- The strategic influence of the environment may be summarised into lists of **opportunities** and **threats**.

Quick Quiz

1   What is hypercompetition?

2   What is a strategic group?

3   What are the seven elements of the marketing mix for services?

4   What is the main behavioural difference between consumers and industrial buyers?

5   What bases might be used to segment an industrial market?

6   What is meant by 'the strategic customer'?

7   What are critical success factors?

Answers to Quick Quiz

1   A condition of constant competitive change typified by frequent aggressive moves to establish temporary competitive advantage.

2   A group of businesses with similar strategic characteristics, following similar strategies or competing on similar bases.

3   Product, place, price, promotion, people, processes and physical evidence.

4   Generally, industrial buyers will approach purchase decisions in an entirely rational manner; this is frequently not the case with consumers, whose behaviour is influenced by emotional responses.

5   Geography, business type, product usage, organisation size.

6   The actual purchaser of output, not the eventual end user further down the supply chain.

7   Product features that are particularly valued by a group of customers and where the organisation must excel to outperform competitors.

Now try the question below from the Exam Question Bank

Number	Level	Marks	Time
Q3	Exam	20	36 mins

Strategic capability

4

Introduction

In this chapter we move deeper into highly examinable territory. It is a long chapter and contains a number of very important ideas and models. You should work through it with care. When you reach the last section, do not be tempted to dismiss the content as a simple mnemonic: both SWOT and TOWS have important things to say about potential strategic choices.

Study guide

		Intellectual level
A4	**Marketing and the value of goods and services**	
(c)	Explore the role of the value chain in creating and sustaining competitive advantage	2
(d)	Advise on the role and influence of value networks	3
(e)	Assess different approaches to benchmarking an organisation's performance	3
A5	**The internal resources, capabilities and competences of an organisation**	
(a)	Discriminate between strategic capability, threshold resources, threshold competences, unique resources and core competences	3
(b)	Advise on the continuing need for cost efficiency	3
(c)	Discuss the capabilities required to sustain competitive advantage	2
(d)	Explain the impact of new product, process and service developments and innovation ion supporting business strategy	2
(e)	Discuss the contribution of organisational knowledge to the strategic capability of an organisation	2
(f)	Identify opportunities for managing the strategic capability of an organisation	2
(g)	Determine the strengths and weaknesses of an organisation and formulate an appropriate SWOT analysis	2
B3	**Alternative directions and methods of development**	
(a)	Determine generic development directions (employing an adapted Ansoff matrix and a TOWS matrix) available to an organisation.	2

Exam guide

In this chapter we introduce some specific models that you must become very familiar with.
They are useful both for analysing data and structuring answers. The most important, by far, is the **value chain**: you must have this model at your fingertips.

1 The organisation's resources

FAST FORWARD

> A **position audit** is undertaken in order to give strategic managers a clear understanding of the organisation's **strategic capability**; that is, its resources, competences and the constraints that limit their use.

1.1 Strategic capability

Managers responsible for an organisation's strategy need a clear and detailed knowledge of its **strategic capability**.

Key term

> An organisation's ability to survive and prosper depends on its **strategic capability**; this is defined by the adequacy and suitability of its resources and competences.

The process of analysing and assessing the organisation's resources and competences is called **position audit**.

Key term

> **Position audit** is the part of the planning process that examines the current state of the business entity's strategic capability.

Much of the rest of this chapter is concerned with the tools and methods that can be used to carry out the task of position audit. However, we must first discuss **resource-based strategy** and look more closely at resources and competences.

1.2 Resources and limiting factors

FAST FORWARD

> **Resource audits** identify human, financial and material resources and how they are deployed.

A **resource audit** is a review of all aspects of the resources the organisation uses. The **Ms model** categorises the factors as follows.

Resource	Example
Machinery	Age. Condition. Utilisation rate. Value. Replacement. Technologically up-to-date? Cost.
Make-up	Culture and structure. Patents. Goodwill. Brands.
Management	Size. Skills. Loyalty. Career progression. Structure.
Management information	Ability to generate and disseminate ideas. Innovation. Information systems.
Markets	Products and customers.
Materials	Source. Suppliers and partnering. Waste. New materials. Cost. Availability. Future provision.
Men and women	Number. Skills. Efficiency. Industrial relations. Adaptability. Innovatory capacity. Wage costs. Proportion of total costs. Labour turnover.
Methods	How are activities carried out? Outsourcing, JIT.
Money	Credit and turnover periods. Cash surpluses/deficits. Short term and long term finance. Gearing levels.

Unique resources are particularly valuable and an important source of competitive advantage.

Key term

> A **unique resource** is one which is both better than its equivalent employed by competitors and difficult to imitate.

Resources are of no value unless they are organised into systems, and so a resource audit should go on to consider how well or how badly resources have been utilised, and whether the organisation's systems are effective and efficient.

1.3 Limiting factors

Every organisation operates under resource **constraints**.

Key term

> A limiting **factor** or **key factor** is 'a factor which at any time or over a period may limit the activity of an entity, often one where there is shortage or difficulty of supply.'

1.3.1 Examples

- A shortage of production capacity
- A limited number of key personnel, such as salespeople with technical knowledge
- A restricted distribution network
- Too few managers with knowledge about finance, or overseas markets
- Inadequate research design resources to develop new products or services
- A poor system of strategic intelligence
- Lack of money
- A lack of adequately trained staff

Case Study

North Sea oil exploration

In February 2006, *The Financial Times* reported that the North Sea oil exploration was being constrained by a shortage of the mobile drilling rigs used for exploration. The number of yards building rigs fell in the late 1990s as oil prices fell and there has been significant attrition of numbers from storm and operational damage. As a result, rigs built in the 1970s and laid-up are being brought back into service

Once the limiting factor has been identified, the planners should do two things.

- In the short term, make best use of the resources available.
- Try to reduce the limitation in the long term.

1.4 Resource-based strategy

FAST FORWARD

The resource-based approach to strategy starts from a consideration of capabilities and, in particular, of distinctive **competences** and **resources**.

Position-based strategy seeks to develop competitive advantage in a way that responds to the **nature of the competitive environment**: the firm **positions** its offering in response to the opportunities or threats it discerns.

A fundamentally different approach is **resource-based strategy**. This was developed in response to two problems with the positioning method.

(a)   Many environments are **too complex and dynamic** to permit continuing effective analysis and response.

(b)   Once an opportunity is discerned and an offering made, it is very easy for competitors to make similar offerings, thus rapidly eroding competitive advantage.

The resource-based view is that sustainable competitive advantage is only attained as a result of the **possession of distinctive resources**. These may be **physical resources**, such as the effective monopolisation of diamonds by *De Beers*, or, more typically in today's service economies, they may be **competences**.

1.5 Terminology

As is so often the case, the terminology used in the literature of resource-based strategy is not yet formalised. JS&W use their own very clear and specific set of terms when discussing resources and competences and your syllabus requires that you should understand and use these terms also.

Key terms

> **Strategic capability** is the adequacy and suitability of the resources and competences of an organisation for it to survive and prosper.
>
> **Tangible resources** are the physical assets of an organisation, such as plant, labour and finance.
>
> **Intangible resources** are non-physical assets such as information, reputation and knowledge.
>
> **Competences** are the activities and processes through which an organisation deploys its resources effectively.
>
> **Threshold capabilities** are essential for the organisation to be able to compete in a given market.
>
> **Threshold resources** and **threshold competences** are needed to meet customers' minimum requirements and therefore for the organisation to continue to exist.
>
> **Unique resources** and **core competences** underpin competitive advantage and are difficult for competitors to imitate or obtain.

This analysis requires some discussion.

(a) Note that way that JS&W use the word **capabilities** to denote a useful overall category that contains both resources and competences.

(b) Look carefully at the definitions of **tangible** and **intangible resources**. These are not the tangible and intangible *assets* you are familiar with as an accountant: the inclusion of labour and finance under tangible resources, for example, demonstrates this.

(c) A connected point is the definition of **competences;** make sure you appreciate the difference between a **competence** and an **intangible resource**. We might say that the relationship between the two is that a competence might well create, use or exploit an intangible resource (or a tangible one, for that matter). Thus, information is an **intangible resource**; the ability to make good use of it is a **competence**.

(d) We have said that **capabilities** consist of **resources** and **competences**. As you can see, this means that JS&W effectively give a choice of definition for **threshold resources** and **threshold competences**. Each has its own specific definition, but since each qualifies as a **threshold capability**, we could, presumably, also use that definition.

(e) JS&W do not provide a term to mean **unique resources** and **core competences** taken together as a class: we might speculate that **unique capabilities** or **core capabilities** could be used in this way, but it would probably be unwise to do this in the exam.

Exam focus point

> To some extent, the resource-based approach is diametrically apposed to the marketing concept since, instead of approaching strategy on the basis of giving customers what they want, it concentrates on exploiting what the business already has to offer.
>
> In fact, this distinction is largely theoretical, but it leads to some important ideas that you could use in the exam.
>
> (a) Where the marketing concept is adopted, it will still be necessary to deploy threshold capabilities in all critical areas and the possession of unique resources and core competences will enhance the market offering.
>
> (b) Conversely, where strategy is built on unique resources and core competences, marketing activities must be carried out with at least threshold competence if the customer is to be satisfied.
>
> (c) As a result, when a company clearly adheres to one approach or the other, the reasons for this may be more cultural then reasoned; the priority given to one idea or to the other may be embedded in the **paradigm** (see Chapter 5).

2 Cost efficiency

Cost efficiency is fundamental to strategic capability: the public sector demands value for money, while in the private sector, price competition makes cost efficiency fundamental to survival. Cost efficiency is achieved in four main ways.

- Exploitation of **scale economies**
- Control of the cost of **incoming supplies**
- **Careful design** of products and processes
- Exploitation of **experience effects**

2.1 The importance of cost efficiency

Cost efficiency is a fundamental aspect of strategic capability. It requires both the possession and efficient use of **appropriate resources** and the ability to **manage costs** so that they are under constant downward pressure. The requirement for cost efficiency applies equally in the public and private sectors.

(a) In the **public sector**, cost efficiency is demanded by the political imperative to provide improved and extended levels of service while containing or reducing the cost to the public finances.

(b) For a **commercial organisation**, cost efficiency permits the firm to offer extended benefits at the same price, the same benefits at a lower price, or a combination of the two.

In the private sector, a sufficient degree of cost efficiency might constitute a **core competence** in that it might enable a firm to achieve competitive advantage; we will return to this point when we discuss **generic strategies** later in this Study Text. Nevertheless, for many firms, cost efficiency is merely a **threshold competence**: it is required for mere survival and does not form the basis of advantage. There are two reasons for this.

(a) **Customers are sensitive to price**: when making their buying decision, they will seek a balance between the desirability of the product's features and the sacrifice involved in paying for it. This means that whatever the features of their particular product offerings, all suppliers must strive to provide proper **value for money**. Failure to do this is an invitation to the customer to go elsewhere.

(b) All firms operating in a given market will seek to drive down their costs in order to offer better value to the customer; the search for cost efficiency is a fundamental aspect of **competitive rivalry**.

2.2 Sources of cost efficiency

JS&W identify four main sources of cost efficiency.

2.2.1 Economies of scale

The effect of economies of scale is to reduce costs per unit as the scale of operations increases. They arise for a range of reasons, including the efficiencies generated by increased **specialisation** and the **spreading of fixed elements of cost** over a greater number of units of output. A full discussion of economies of scale is beyond the scope of your syllabus, but you should be aware that some industries possess more of the features that lead to their occurrence than do others. The high costs of plant in the motor vehicle and chemicals industries have made scale of output important, while other industries, such as tobacco and drinks have benefited from economies of scale in marketing and distribution. In other industries, such as textiles, economies of scale have been less important.

2.2.2 Supply costs

The prices paid for inputs from suppliers have an obvious effect on cost structures. Two important influences are transport costs and, therefore, proximity to sources of supply; and relationships with suppliers, including the ability to negotiate good prices. The second factor is greatly influenced by quantity purchased over time and is thus a further example of **scale economy**.

Supply costs are particularly important for firms that have little opportunity to add value. These include trading intermediaries and processors of commodities, such as some chemicals manufacturers. For many intermediaries, **market intelligence** is a key resource; knowledge of who needs to buy what, when and at which price, enables profitable trading. In obtaining this resource, personal contact and networking are being superseded by IT systems, whose effective use therefore becomes a threshold competence.

2.2.3 Design of products and processes

Well-designed and operated business processes can be a source of cost efficiency, minimising both direct and indirect costs. Examples include obvious matters such as labour productivity, materials yield and the careful control of working capital. JS&W also mention the **management of capacity-fill**. This problem is typical of service sectors such as transport or live entertainment, where there is no possibility of storing unfilled seats. This is, in fact, yet another kind of scale economy and is known in economic theory as the **utilisation of indivisibilities**.

Product design also affects the cost base and can have impact on costs beyond those of supplies and the production process. Aircraft, for example, are now commonly designed so as to minimise **lifetime costs**, with ease of servicing and repair built in.

2.2.4 Experience

You are probably familiar with the way the **learning curve** effect has been used for many years as a means of estimating the future manufacturing costs of existing products.

Case Study

Solar panels

Over the years, the solar industry has been able continuously to reduce the cost of silicon-based solar panels. For every doubling in cumulative production volume, the cost of modules has declined by about 20%.

The Economist Technology Quarterly, 10 March 2007

The principle can be extended to activities other than manufacturing, to the extent that the passage of time should allow any organisation to improve the cost efficiency of any of its activities and thus experience a continuing decline in real unit costs. This wider **experience curve** effect holds out the possibility of developing core competences through the acquisition of experience, though the probability that this will happen is low. There are other important considerations.

(a) There should be an advantage in being the **first mover** in a new market, in that it should give an opportunity to create an experience-based cost advantage lead over later-entering rivals.

(b) **Outsourcing** may allow an organisation to benefit from the experience of suppliers. Outsourcing is discussed in more detail later in this Study Text.

(c)   Since **competitive rivalry** prompts all the firms in an industry to seek cost advantage, as mentioned earlier, so it follows that they will all seek the experience advantages that come with growth. This will be particularly apparent during the growth phase of the industry lifecycle.

3 Strategic capability and sustainable competitive advantage

If strategy is to be based on strategic capabilities, those capabilities must have four qualities.

- **Value to buyers**
- **Rarity**
- **Robustness** (difficult for competitors to imitate)
- **Non-substitutability**

Under conditions of **hyper-competition**, organisations must possess **dynamic capabilities:** the ability to develop and adjust competences to cope with rapidly changing environmental pressures.

Even if we do not entirely accept the resource-based view of strategy, it is clear that unique resources and core competences are of great importance in creating and sustaining competitive advantage. JS&W suggest that if competitive advantage is to be based on strategic capabilities they must have four qualities.

- They must produce effects that are **valuable to buyers**.
- They must be **rare**.
- They must be **robust**.
- They must be **non-substitutable**.

The first of these points is almost self-evident, but it must not be overlooked. The remaining three relate to the definition of unique resources and core competences as being **difficult for competitors to imitate or obtain**.

We must now consider these aspects of strategic capability more closely.

3.1 The importance of customer needs

The first point to make is that strategic capability only exists to the extent that it contributes to the organisation's ability to **satisfy its customers' needs**. No matter how rare a resource or well developed a competence, it cannot create competitive advantage if customers do not value it or the things it enables the organisation to do.

3.2 Rarity

A single **unique resource** *may* have the potential to create competitive advantage by itself. Here are some examples.

(a)   A unique **tangible resource** in the form of ownership of extraction rights to an easily worked deposit of a scarce and valuable mineral

(b)   A unique **intangible resource** in the form of ownership of the copyright of a best-selling novel

(c)   A **core competence** in a dangerous and demanding process such as extinguishing oil well fires

3.3 Robustness

Robustness is the term JS&W use to mean that a resource is difficult for competitors to imitate. They point out that, generally, it is difficult to base competitive advantage simply on possession of tangible resources, since they can often be imitated or simply bought in. Robustness most frequently resides in the **competences** involved in linking activities and processes in ways that both satisfy the critical success factors defined by customer priorities and are difficult for competitors to imitate.

There are three main aspects of a **competence** that tend to make it **robust**.

(a) **Complexity** arises from the linkages between the activities the organisation undertakes and the way it organises them. It also appears when organisations develop **complex links with their customers**.

(b) The **culture and history** of the organisation provided tacit knowledge (see below) and capability in the form of an accepted, if ill-defined, way of doing things.

(c) **Causal ambiguity** occurs when the processes and linkages that produce the organisation's competences are difficult to discern and so competitors are **uncertain about how to imitate** them.

3.4 Non-substitutability

Substitutability of strategic capability has two forms and managers must be alert to the emergence of either, since both are a threat to even a competence that possesses the other three vital qualities.

(a) The substitute **product** you are familiar with from our earlier discussion of the **five forces**

(b) The substitute **competence**: an example is the deployment of expert systems as substitutes for expensive professional advisers.

3.5 Hypercompetition and dynamic capabilities

The nature of the strategic capabilities as we have discussed them so far is that they are **long-term phenomena**: tangible and intangible resources will be more valuable if they can be counted on to last a long time, while the development of core competences might well be expected to be a fairly protracted process.

Under conditions of **hypercompetition**, described earlier in this Study Text, strategic capability takes a different form. In order to deal with the rapid market changes seen under conditions of hypercompetition, firms must possess **dynamic capabilities**.

Key term

> **Dynamic capabilities** are an organisation's abilities to develop and change competences to meet the needs of rapidly changing environments.
>
> *JS&W*

Such capabilities demand the ability to change, to innovate and to learn. They can take many forms and may include such things as systems for new product development or the acquisition of market intelligence and the absorption of new skills and products acquired by merger or acquisition. Indeed, we might regard the ability to 'develop and change competences' as a competence in its own right – a higher-order competence, perhaps.

4 Knowledge

FAST FORWARD The aim of **knowledge management** is to capture, organise and make widely available all the knowledge the organisation possesses, whether **explicit** (in recorded form) or **tacit** (in people's heads).

Knowledge management is a relatively new concept in business theory. It is connected with the theory of the **learning organisation** and founded on the idea that knowledge is a major source of competitive advantage in business.

Studies have indicated that 20 to 30 percent of company resources are wasted because organisations are not aware of what knowledge they already possess. *Lew Platt,* Ex-Chief Executive of *Hewlett Packard,* has articulated this, saying 'If only HP knew what HP knows, we would be three times as profitable'.

Knowledge is thus seen as an important **resource** and may in itself constitute a **competence**: it can certainly **underpin** many competences.

Key term

> **Organisational knowledge** is the collective and shared experience accumulated through systems, routines and activities of sharing across the organisation.
> *JS&W*

4.1 Organisational learning

Organisational learning is particularly important in the increasing number of task environments that are both complex and dynamic. It becomes necessary for strategic managers to promote and foster a **culture that values intuition**, **argument from conflicting views and experimentation**. A willingness to back ideas that are not guaranteed to succeed is another aspect of this culture: there must be freedom to make mistakes.

The aim of **knowledge management** is to exploit existing knowledge and to create new knowledge so that it may be exploited in turn. This is not easy. All organisations possess a great deal of data, but it tends to be unorganised and inaccessible. It is often locked up inside the memories of people who do not realise the value of what they know. This is what *Nonaka* calls **tacit knowledge**. Even when it is made **explicit**, by being recorded in some way, it may be difficult and time consuming to get at, as is the case with most paper archives. This is where knowledge management technology (discussed below) can be useful. Another important consideration is that tacit knowledge is inherently more **robust** (in the sense explained in the previous Section) than explicit knowledge.

Nonaka and Takeuchi describe four ways in which knowledge moves within and between the tacit and explicit categories.

(a) **Socialisation** is the informal process by which individuals share and transmit their tacit knowledge.

(b) **Externalisation** converts tacit knowledge into explicit knowledge; this is a very difficult process to organise and control.

(c) **Internalisation** is the learning process by which individuals acquire explicit knowledge and turn it into their own tacit knowledge.

(d) **Combination** brings together separate elements of explicit knowledge into larger, more coherent systems; this is the arena for meetings, reports and computerised knowledge management systems.

4.2 Managing explicit knowledge

4.2.1 Data, information and knowledge

Data are simple facts that can be organised in a way that creates **information**. **Knowledge** is patterns of information that are strategically useful and context independent.

There is an important conceptual hierarchy underpinning knowledge management. This distinguishes between **data, information** and **knowledge**. The distinctions are not clear-cut and, to some extent, are differences of degree rather than kind. An understanding of the terms is best approached by considering the relationships between them.

We start with **data**. Data typically consists of individual facts, but in a business context may include more complex items such as opinions, reactions and beliefs. It is important to realise that a quantity of data, no matter how large, does not constitute **information**.

Information is data that is **organised** in some useful way. For instance, an individual credit sale will produce a single invoice identifying the goods, the price, the customer, the date of the sale and so on. These things are data: their usefulness does not extend beyond the purpose of the invoice, which is to collect the sum due. Even if we possess a copy of every invoice raised during a financial year, we still only have data. However, if we **process** that data we start to create information. For instance, a simple combination of analysis and arithmetic enables us to state total sales for the year, to break that down into sales for each product and to each customer, to identify major customers and so on. These are pieces of information: they are useful for the **management** of the business, rather than just inputs into its administrative systems.

Nevertheless, we still have not really produced any **knowledge**. Information may be said to consist of the **relationships between** items of data, as when we combine turnover with customer details to discover which accounts are currently important and which are not. We need to go beyond this in order to create knowledge.

The conceptual difference between data and information is fairly easy to grasp: it lies chiefly in the **processes** that produce the one from the other. The difference between information and knowledge is more complex and varies from setting to setting. This is not surprising, since knowledge itself is more complex than the information it derives from.

A good starting point for understanding the difference is an appreciation of the importance of pattern: knowledge tends to originate in the **discovery of trends or patterns in information**. To return to our invoicing example, suppose we found that certain combinations of goods purchased were typical of certain customers. We could then build up some interesting customer profiles that would enhance our market segmentation and this in turn might influence our overall strategy, since we could identify likely prospects for cross-selling effort.

Another important aspect of the differences between data, information and knowledge is the relevance of **context**. Our sales invoice is meaningless outside its context; if you, as a marketing person, found an invoice in the office corridor, it would be little more than waste paper to you, though no doubt, the accounts people would like it back. However, if you found a list of customers in order of annual turnover, that would be rather more interesting from a marketing point of view. The information is **useful outside of its original context** of the accounts office.

This idea also applies to the difference between information and knowledge. If you were a visitor to a company and found a copy of the turnover listing, it would really only be useful to you if you were trying to sell the same sort of thing to the same customers. Its value outside its context would be small. However, if you found a marketing report that suggested, based on evidence, that customers were becoming more interested in quality and less interested in price, that would be applicable to a wide range of businesses, and possibly of strategic importance.

Here is a table that summarises the progression from data to knowledge.

	Data	**Information**	**Knowledge**
Nature	Facts	Relationships between processed facts	Patterns discerned in information
Importance of context	Total	Some	Context independent
Importance to business	Mundane	Probably useful for management	May be strategically useful

There is one final important point to note here and that is that the **progression** from data to knowledge is not the same in all circumstances. The scale is moveable and depends on the general complexity of the setting. Something may be **information** within its own context. Something similar may be **knowledge** in a different context. The difference will often be associated with the scale of operations. Take the example of a customer going into insolvent liquidation with £200,000 outstanding on its account. For a small supplier with an annual turnover of, say, £10 million, a bad debt of this size would be of strategic importance and might constitute a threat to its continued existence. Advance notice of the possibility would be valuable **knowledge**. However, for a company operating on a global scale, the bad debt write-off would be annoying but still only one item in a list of bad debts – **data**, in other words.

4.2.2 Other ideas about knowledge

Individuals acquire knowledge in a variety of ways including those listed below.

- Education and training
- Experience of work
- Observation of others
- Informal exchanges such as coaching and brain storming

Davenport and Pansak echo our earlier description of the relationship between data, information and knowledge and suggest that people **create knowledge from information by four processes**.

- **Comparison** with earlier experience
- **Consequences**: the implication of information
- **Connections**: relationships between items
- **Conversation**: discussion with others

4.2.3 Knowledge management (KM) systems

FAST FORWARD

Knowledge must be managed in a way that makes it easily available. Systems include office automation, groupware, intranets, extranets, expert systems and data mining.

Recognition of the value of knowledge and understanding of the need to organise data and make it accessible have provoked the development of sophisticated IT systems. Such systems deal, by definition with **explicit knowledge**: that is, knowledge that is widely distributed. **Tacit knowledge** exists within individuals' brains and is not readily available, especially when its possession enhances power and status. Tacit knowledge only becomes available to the KM System when conscious decisions are taken to share it.

(a) **Office automation systems** are IT applications that improve productivity in an office. These include word processing and voice messaging systems.

(b) **Groupware**, such as **Lotus Notes** provides functions for collaborative work groups. In a sales context, for instance, it would provide a facility for recording and retrieving all the information relevant to individual customers, including notes of visits, notes of telephone calls and basic data like address, credit terms and contact name. These items could be updated by anyone who had contact with a customer and would then be available to all sales people.

Groupware also provides such facilities as messaging, appointment scheduling, to-do lists, and jotters.

(c) An **intranet** is an internal network used to share information using Internet technology and protocols. The **firewall** surrounding an intranet fends off unauthorised access from outside the organisation. Each employee has a browser, used to access a server computer that holds corporate information on a wide variety of topics, and in some cases also offers access to the Internet. Applications include company newspapers, induction material, procedure and policy manuals and internal databases.

  (a) Savings accrue from the **elimination of storage**, **printing** and **distribution of documents** that can be made available to employees online.

  (b) Documents online are often **more widely used** than those that are kept filed away, especially if the document is bulky (eg manuals) and needs to be searched. This means that there are improvements in productivity and efficiency.

  (c) It is much easier to **update information in electronic form**.

  When access to an intranet is extended to trusted external agencies, such as suppliers and customers, it becomes an **extranet**. Security is a major issue for extranets and may require firewalls, server management, encryption and the issue of digital certificates.

(d) An **expert system** is a computer program that captures **human expertise** in a limited domain of knowledge. Such software uses a knowledge base that consists of facts, concepts and the relationships between them and uses pattern-matching techniques to solve problems. For example, many financial institutions now use expert systems to process straightforward loan applications. The user enters certain key facts into the system such as the loan applicant's name and most recent addresses, their income and monthly outgoings, and details of other loans. The system will then:

  (i) Check the facts given against its **database** to see whether the applicant has a good previous credit record.

  (ii) Perform **calculations** to see whether the applicant can afford to repay the loan.

  (iii) Make a **judgement** as to what extent the loan applicant fits the lender's profile of a good risk (based on the lender's previous experience).

  (iv) **A decision is then suggested**, based on the results of this processing.

(e) IT systems can be used to store vast amounts of data in accessible form. A **data warehouse** receives data from operational systems, such as a sales order processing system, and stores them in its most fundamental form, without any summarisation of transactions. Analytical and query software is provided so that reports can be produced at any level of summarisation and incorporating any comparisons or relationships desired.

(f) The value of a data warehouse is enhanced when **datamining** software is used. True datamining software **discovers previously unknown relationships** and provides insights that cannot be obtained through ordinary summary reports. These hidden patterns and relationships constitute **knowledge**, as defined above, and can be used to guide decision making and to predict future behaviour. Datamining is thus a contribution to organisational learning.

Case Study

Wal-Mart

The American retailer Wal-Mart discovered an unexpected relationship between the sale of nappies and beer! Wal-Mart found that both tended to sell at the same time, just after working hours, and concluded that men with small children stopped off to buy nappies on their way home, and bought beer at the same time. Logically, therefore, if the two items were put in the same shopping aisle, sales of both should increase. Wal-Mart tried this and it worked.

Here is an amended version of our earlier table. This one includes the relevant IT systems.

	Data	**Information**	**Knowledge**
Nature	Facts	Relationships between processed facts	Patterns discerned in information
Importance of context	Total	Some	Context independent
Importance to business	Mundane	Probably useful for management	May be strategically useful
Relevant IT systems	Office automation Data warehouse	Groupware Expert systems Report writing software Intranet	Datamining Intranet Expert systems

We will conclude this section with an example of the modern approach to knowledge management. You will notice that the IT system eventually developed looks like something half way between groupware and a database. However, the strategic impact of the system and its ability to create new corporate knowledge mean that it is properly described as a knowledge management system.

Notice also that the knowledge originates with people who are fairly low down in the hierarchy and who would not normally be described as knowledge workers. This illustrates the very important principle that valuable knowledge can be found at all levels and is not the prerogative of an elite.

Case Study

Servicing *Xerox* copiers

Our story begins with researchers working on artificial intelligence who wanted to see if they could replace the paper documentation that Xerox technicians used on the road with an expert system.

The team found that it was indeed possible to build software that could do just that. But when they showed their first efforts to technicians, the response was underwhelming.

What kept technicians from finding fixes was not that the documentation was paper-based but that it didn't address all the potential problems. And not all problems were predictable. Machines in certain regions could react to extreme temperatures in different ways. A drink overturned in one part of a machine could wreak havoc in another seemingly unconnected part. Technicians could handle these mishaps quickly only if they had seen them before or if another technician had run into a similar problem and shared the results.

Once the conversations with technicians revealed this gap in information sharing, the researchers realised that AI was the wrong approach. What Xerox needed instead was knowledge management. It wasn't a smart computer program that was going to fix these things, it was sharing the best ways to make these repairs.

When the researchers realised they needed to look at the way technicians work, they spent time in the field, following the technicians from call to call. What they observed proved invaluable – knowledge sharing was already unofficially ingrained in the organisation. Most striking was not how technicians solved common problems, but what they did when they came up against a tricky, intermittent one. Often they called one another on radios provided by the company. And in informal gatherings they shared vexing problems and their fixes.

Meanwhile, another researcher was busy comparing the way French and U.S. technicians worked. He discovered that, while French technicians appeared to work from immaculate, uniform documentation put out by headquarters, their real solutions also came from a second set of documentation – notes they carried with them detailing what they'd learned. It was from that database that researchers started building the first laptop-based knowledge-sharing system.

The researchers took the first iteration to France and began a series of exhaustive sessions with the French experts in the Xerox headquarters outside Paris. In those sessions, something magical happened: The system took on the shape of the people working on it, evolving with each suggestion from the actual users.

But the worldwide customer service group didn't take the project seriously. Nobody believed that the knowledge of the technicians was really valuable. So, working stealthily, outside the realm of worldwide management, the research team gave laptops and the fledging program to 40 technician and matched them with a control group of technicians who relied solely on their own knowledge when fixing machines. After two months, the group with the laptops had 10 percent lower costs and 10 percent lower service time than those without – and the control group was jealous of those with the system.

By 1998, the system was officially deployed in the United States and began to make its way around the globe. Today it has more than 15,000 user tips, with more being added every day. The hope is that by 2002 it will be distributed worldwide to the company's 25,000 technicians. And already success stories abound. One technician in Montreal authored a tip about a 50-cent fuse-holder replacement that caused a chronic problem with a high-speed colour copier. A Brazilian technician had the same problem, and his customer wanted the $40,000 machine replaced. When he found the tip from Montreal, he fixed the machine in minutes. Current estimates have the system saving Xerox at least $7 million in time and replacement costs. It's tales like those that make senior management happy.

Adapted from Meg Mitchell, *www.darwinmag.com* February 2001.

5 Converting resources: the value chain

The **value chain** describes those activities of the organisation that add value to purchased inputs. Primary activities are involved in the production of goods and services. Support activities provide necessary assistance. **Linkages** are the relationships between activities.

The **value chain** model of corporate activities offers a bird's eye view of the firm and what it does. Competitive advantage arises out of the way in which firms organise and perform **activities** to add value.

5.1 Value activities

Key term

Value activities are the means by which a firm creates value in its products.

Activities incur costs, and, in combination with other activities, provide a product or service which earns revenue.

5.2 Example

Let us explain this point by using the example of a **restaurant**. A restaurant's activities can be divided into buying food, cooking it, and serving it (to customers). There is no reason, in theory, why the customers should not do all these things themselves, at home. The customer however, is not only prepared to **pay for someone else** to do all this but also **pays more than the cost of** the resources (food, wages and so on). The ultimate value a firm creates is measured by the amount customers are willing to pay for its products or services above the cost of carrying out value activities. A firm is profitable if the realised value to customers exceeds the collective cost of performing the activities.

(a)   Customers **purchase value**, which they measure by comparing a firm's products and services with similar offerings by competitors.

(b)   The business **creates value** by carrying out its activities either more efficiently than other businesses, or by combining them in such a way as to provide a unique product or service.

Question   **Value activities**

Outline different ways in which the restaurant can create value.

Answer

Here are some ideas. Each of these options is a way of organising the activities of buying, cooking and serving food in a way that customers will value.

(a)   It can become more efficient, by automating the production of food, as in a fast food chain.

(b)   The chef can develop commercial relationships with growers, so he or she can obtain the best quality fresh produce.

(c)   The chef can specialise in a particular type of cuisine (eg Nepalese, Korean).

(d)   The restaurant can be sumptuously decorated for those customers who value atmosphere and a sense of occasion, in addition to a restaurant's purely gastronomic pleasures.

(e)   The restaurant can serve a particular type of customer (eg celebrities).

5.3 The value chain

Porter (in *Competitive Advantage*) grouped the various activities of an organisation into a **value chain**. Here is a diagram.

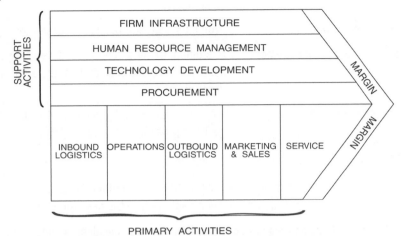

The **margin** is the excess the customer is prepared to **pay** over the **cost** to the firm of obtaining resource inputs and providing value activities. It represents the **value created** by the **value activities** themselves and by the **management of the linkages** between them.

<table>
<tr><td>**Exam focus point**</td><td>This diagram is worth **committing to memory** since the value chain model is an excellent basic description of how an organisation works. It is not just suitable for answering questions that require analysis of how an organisation works; it is also very useful as a kind of checklist for brainstorming a wide range of questions that require you to make suggestions for dealing with business problems. Work your way through the various activities asking yourself what could the organisation do about each one, if anything.</td></tr>
</table>

Primary activities are directly related to production, sales, marketing, delivery and service.

	Comment
Inbound logistics	Receiving, handling and storing inputs to the production system: warehousing, transport, stock control and so on
Operations	Converting resource inputs into a final product: resource inputs are not only materials. People are a resource, especially in service industries.
Outbound logistics	Storing the product and its distribution to customers: packaging, testing, delivery and so on; for service industries, this activity may be more concerned with bringing customers to the place where the service is available; an example would be front of house management in a theatre.
Marketing and sales	Informing customers about the product, persuading them to buy it, and enabling them to do so: advertising, promotion and so on
After sales service	Installing products, repairing them, upgrading them, providing spare parts and so forth

Support activities provide purchased inputs, human resources, technology and infrastructural functions to support the primary activities.

Activity	Comment
Procurement	All of the processes involved in acquiring the resource inputs to the primary activities (eg purchase of materials, subcomponents equipment)
Technology development	Product design, improving processes and resource utilisation
Human resource management	Recruiting, training, managing, developing and rewarding people; this activity takes place in all parts of the organisation, not just in the HRM department.
Firm infrastructure	Planning, finance, quality control, the structures and routines that make up the organisation's culture

Linkages connect the activities of the value chain.

(a) **Activities in the value chain affect one another**. For example, more costly product design or better quality production might reduce the need for after-sales service.

(b) **Linkages require co-ordination**. For example, Just In Time requires smooth functioning of operations, outbound logistics and service activities such as installation.

The value chain concept is an important tool in analysing the organisation's strategic capability, since it focuses on the overall means by which value is created rather than on structural functions or departments. There are two important, connected aspects to this analysis.

(a) It enables managers to establish the **activities** that are particularly important in **providing customers with the value they want**: this leads on to a consideration of where management attention and other resources are best applied, either to improve weakness or to further exploit strength. A further possible consequence would be decisions about outsourcing.

(b) This analysis can be extended to include an assessment of the **costs and benefits** associated with the various value activities.

5.4 The value chain, core competences and outsourcing

FAST FORWARD

Core competences are the basis for the creation of value; activities from which the organisation does not derive significant value may be outsourced.

The purpose of value chain analysis is to understand how the company creates value. It is unlikely that any business has more than a handful of activities in which it outperforms its competitors. There is clear link here with the idea of **core competences**: a core competence will enable the company to create value in a way that its competitors cannot imitate. These **value activities** are the basis of the company's unique offering.

There is a strong case for examining the possibilities of **outsourcing** non-core activities so that management can concentrate on what the company does best.

5.5 The value network

FAST FORWARD

The value network joins the organisation's value chain to those of its suppliers and customers.

Activities and linkages that add value do not stop at the organisation's **boundaries**. For example, when a restaurant serves a meal, the quality of the ingredients – although they are chosen by the cook – is determined by the grower. The grower has added value, and the grower's success in growing produce of good quality is as important to the customer's ultimate satisfaction as the skills of the chef. Similarly, the value received by a person buying a new car has been created by a **complex system** that includes several organisations' value chains. These would include the nominal manufacturer, their suppliers of parts and subsystems, *their* suppliers in turn, the retailer, the transport companies that delivered the car to the showroom and possibly others as well. A firm's value chain is connected to other value chains in what JS&W call a **value network**. (Porter used the term **value system**; value network is a better term since it emphasises the **interconnectedness of separate organisations**.)

> **The value network** is the set of inter-organisational links and relationships that are necessary to create a product or service. *JS&W*

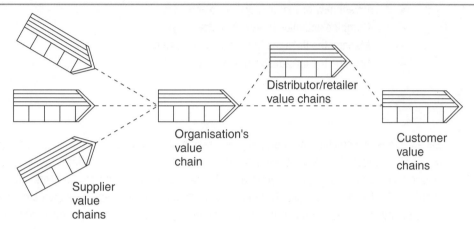

Value network

The value network is much the same thing as the supply chain, but with an emphasis on its value-creating capability.

Case Study

Supply chain improvements

Hagemeyer, a leading distributor of goods and services to businesses in Canada, Mexico and the USA, announced the adoption of new software intended to optimise their US supply chain. The new system will bring improvements in planning, purchasing and warehouse operations, including cross-docking and forecasting slow-moving lines.

Ferret.com.au, 21 March 2006

It may be possible to capture the benefit of some of the value generated both upstream and downstream in the value network. An obvious way to do this is by **vertical integration** through the acquisition of supplies and customers. This aspect of strategy is dealt with in more detail later in this Study Text.

It is possible for large and powerful companies to exercise less formal power over supplies and customers by using their **bargaining power** to achieve purchase and selling prices that are bias in their favour.

A more subtle advantage is gained by fostering good relationships that can promote **innovation** and the **creation of knowledge**.

Case Study

Toyota is well-known for close involvement with its suppliers. The company works with suppliers to improve their methods and the quality of their output; and to develop new, improved materials and components for input into its own operations. The relationship has benefits for all parties, but tends to be unequal, with Toyota dominating the operations of a large number of semi-captive suppliers.

Li & Fung aim for more equal relationships with the large number of clothing manufacturers they deal with. It guarantees to take at least 30% of a supplier's output in order to build a close relationship that can be built on to improve innovation and learning. But it also tries to limit its purchases to no more than 70% of a supplier's output in order to avoid creating a dependent organisation whose managers are influenced more by fear than by trust.

Using the value chain. A firm can secure competitive advantage in several ways.

- Invent new or better ways to do activities
- Combine activities in new or better ways
- Manage the linkages in its own value chain
- Manage the linkages in the value network

Question

Value chain

Sana Sounds is a small record company. Representatives from Sana Sounds scour music clubs for new bands to promote. Once a band has signed a contract (with Sana Sounds) it makes a recording. The recording process is subcontracted to one of a number of recording studio firms which Sana Sounds uses regularly. (At the moment Sana Sounds is not large enough to invest in its own equipment and studios.) Sana Sounds also subcontracts the production of records and CDs to a number of manufacturing companies. Sana Sounds then distributes the disks to selected stores, and engages in any promotional activities required.

What would you say were the activities in Sana Sounds' value chain?

Answer

Sana Sounds is involved in the record industry from start to finish. Although recording and CD manufacture are contracted out to external suppliers, this makes no difference to the fact that these activities are part of Sana Sounds' own value chain. Sana Sounds earns its money by managing the whole set of activities. If the company grows then perhaps it will acquire its own recording studios.

5.6 Section summary

- The value chain models how activities can be deployed to add value for the customer.
- Value chains are part of a value network.
- Firms can benefit by performing activities in a unique way and/or exploiting linkages.

6 Outputs: the product portfolio

Many firms make a number of different products or services. Each product or service has its own financial, marketing and risk characteristics. The combination of products or services influences the attractiveness and profitability of the firm.

6.1 The product life cycle

FAST FORWARD

The **product life cycle** concept holds that products have a life cycle, and that a product demonstrates different characteristics of profit and investment at each stage in its life cycle. The life cycle concept is a model, not a prediction. (Not all products pass through each stage of the life cycle.) It enables a firm to examine its portfolio of goods and services as a whole.

Case Study

Glaxo has for many years produced and profited from *Zantac* an anti-ulcer drug. Patents expire after a defined period: this means that other manufacturers will be able to produce and sell drugs identical to Zantac. Glaxo has been anticipating this development for a while and has invested in new drugs to provide income when returns from Zantac fall.

The profitability and sales of a product can be expected to change over time. The **product life cycle** is an attempt to recognise distinct stages in a product's sales history. Marketing managers distinguish between different aspects of the product.

(a) **Product class:** this is a broad category of product, such as cars, washing machines, newspapers' also referred to as the **generic product**.

(b) **Product form:** within a product class there are different forms that the product can take, for example five-door hatchback cars or two-seater sports cars; twin tub or front loading automatic washing machines; national daily newspapers or weekly local papers and so on.

(c) **Brand:** the particular type of the product form (for example Ford Escort, Vauxhall Astra; Financial Times, Daily Mail, Sun).

The product life cycle applies in differing degrees to each of the three cases. A product-class (eg cars) may have a long maturity stage, and a particular make or brand *might* have an erratic life cycle (eg Rolls Royce) or not. Product forms however tend to conform to the classic life cycle pattern.

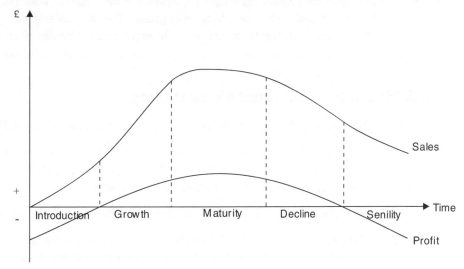

6.1.1 Introduction

- A new product takes time to find acceptance by would-be purchasers and there is a slow growth in sales. Unit costs are high because of low output and expensive sales promotion.

- There may be early teething troubles with production technology.

- The product for the time being is a loss-maker.

6.1.2 Growth

- If the new product gains market acceptance, sales will eventually rise more sharply and the product will start to make profits.

- Competitors are attracted. As sales and production rise, unit costs fall.

6.1.3 Maturity

The rate of sales growth slows down and the product reaches a period of maturity which is probably the longest period of a successful product's life. Most products on the market will be at the mature stage of their life. Profits are good.

6.1.4 Decline

Eventually, sales will begin to decline so that there is over-capacity of production in the industry. Severe competition occurs, profits fall and some producers leave the market. The remaining producers seek means of prolonging the product life by modifying it and searching for new market segments. Many producers are reluctant to leave the market, although some inevitably do because of falling profits.

6.1.5 The relevance of the product life cycle to strategic planning

In reviewing outputs, planners should assess products in three ways.

    (a)   The **stage of its life cycle** that any product has reached.

    (b)   The **product's remaining life**, ie how much longer the product will contribute to profits.

    (c)   How **urgent is the need to innovate**, to develop new and improved products?

 Case Study

Volkswagen product cycles

Under *Ferdinand Piech*, the desire to make rapid progress led to two important products, the *Golf* and the *Passat*, which moved through their model life cycles in parallel. They were redesigned together and reached obsolescence at the same time. This led to overload in show rooms when the new products were launched.

6.1.6 Difficulties of the product life cycle concept

    (a)   **Recognition**. How can managers recognise where a product stands in its life cycle?

    (b)   **Not always true**. The theoretical curve of a product life cycle does not always occur in practice. Some products have no maturity phase, and go straight from growth to decline. Some never decline if they are marketed competitively.

    (c)   **Changeable**. Strategic decisions can change or extend a product's life cycle.

    (d)   **Competition varies** in different industries. The financial markets are an example of markets where there is a tendency for competitors to copy the leader very quickly, so that competition has built up well *ahead* of demand.

6.2 Product portfolio models

Exam focus point

It has been common to analyse product portfolios using models such as the Boston Consulting Group (BCG) matrix. You will learn about such models in a later chapter. JS&W do not recommend their use in relation to portfolios of individual products, restricting them to the analysis of strategic business unit portfolios.

This means that where a question calls for some kind of product portfolio analysis, you should initially think in terms of the product life cycle. Nevertheless, there may be advantages in then considering the use of techniques such as the BCG matrix, perhaps making plain that you know of JS&W's opinion.

7 New products and innovation

7.1 Innovation

> **Innovation** can be a major source of competitive advantage but brings a burden of cost and uncertainty. To avoid waste, there should be a programme of assessment for major product development. The firm must decide whether to be a leader or a follower.

7.1.1 Innovation and competitive advantage

For many organisations, product innovation and being the **first mover** may be a major source of competitive advantage.

(a)   A reputation for innovation will attract **early adopters**, though it depends in part on promotional effort.

(b)   Customers may find they are locked in to innovative suppliers by unacceptable **costs of switching** to competitors.

(c)   The **learning** (or experience) **curve** effect may bring cost advantages.

(d)   The first mover may be able to **define the industry standard**.

(e)   A **price skimming** strategy can bring early profits that will be denied to later entrants.

(f)   Legal protection, such as patents, for intellectual property may bring important revenue advantages. This is particularly important in the pharmaceutical industry.

However, the first mover also has particular problems.

- Gaining regulatory approval where required
- Uncertain demand
- High levels of R&D costs
- Lower cost imitators
- Costs of introduction such as training sales staff and educating customers

Key term

> **PIMS** stands for Profit Impact of Marketing Strategy. The concept originated in a 1960s General Electric project to compare the profitability of GE SBUs. An extensive PIMS database of strategic actions and results is now administered by the American Strategic Planning Institute.

PIMS data indicate that there is a **negative correlation** between **profitability** and a high level of expenditure on **R&D**, perhaps because of the costs associated with these problems.

7.1.2 Technology and the value chain

Porter points out in *Competitive Advantage* that 'every value activity uses some technology to combine purchased inputs and human resources to produce some output.' He goes on to discuss the varied role of **information technology** and emphasises the often-overlooked importance of **administrative** or **office technology**. The significance of this for strategy lies in the area of **core competences.** Just as **R&D** is as much concerned with processes as with products, so improvement in the linkages of the value chain will enhance competitive advantage.

7.2 New product strategies

The development of new products might be considered an important aspect of a firm's competitive and marketing strategies.

(a)   New and innovative products can lower **entry barriers** to existing industries and markets, if new technology is involved.

(b)   The interests of the company are best met with a balanced product portfolio. Managers therefore must plan when to introduce new products, how best to extend the life of mature ones and when to abandon those in decline.

A strategic issue managers must consider is their approach to new product development.

(a)   **Leader strategy**. Do they intend to gain competitive advantage by operating at the leading edge of new developments? There are significant implications for the R&D activity and the likely length of product life cycles within the portfolio if this strategy is adopted. Also, **R&D costs** are likely to be heavy, with a significant reduction in potential profitability as a result.

(b)   **Follower strategy**. Alternatively they can be more pro-active, adopt a follower strategy, which involves lower costs and less emphasis on the R & D activity. It sacrifices early rewards of innovation, but avoids its risks. A follower might have to license certain technologies from a leader (as is the case with many consumer electronics companies). However, research indicates that this can be a **more profitable strategy** than being an innovator, especially when the follower is able to learn from the leader's mistakes.

A matrix of new product strategies and new market strategies can be set out as follows.

	Product		
	No technological change	*Improved technology*	*New technology*
Market unchanged	–	*Reformulation* A new balance between price/quality has to be formulated	*Replacement* The new technology replaces the old
Market strengthened (ie new demand from same customers)	*Remerchandising* The product is sold in a new way – eg by re-packaging	*Improved product* Sales growth to existing customers sought on the strength of product improvements	*Product line extension* The new product is added to the existing product line to increase total demand
New market	*New use* By finding a new use for the existing product, new customers are found	*Market extension* New customers sought on the strength of product improvements	*Diversification*

7.3 Types of 'new' products

Booz, Allen and Hamilton identified the following categories in a survey of 700 firms.

- New to the world   10%
- New product lines   20%
- Additions to product line   26%
- Repositionings   7%
- Improvements/revisions   26%
- Cost reductions   11%

7.4 Research and development

Research may be **pure, applied** or **development**. It may be intended to improve **products** or **processes**. New product development should be controlled by requiring strategic approval at key points of development.

R&D should support the organisation's strategy and be closely co-ordinated with marketing. There are distinct problems to managing R&D.

Here are some definitions culled from Statement of Standard Accounting Practice 13.

Key terms

> **Pure research** is original research to obtain new scientific or technical knowledge or understanding. There is no obvious commercial or practical end in view.
>
> **Applied research** is also original research work like (a) above, but it has a specific practical aim or application (eg research on improvements in the effectiveness of medicines etc).
>
> **Development** is the use of existing scientific and technical knowledge to produce new (or substantially improved) products or systems, prior to starting commercial production operations.

Many organisations employ **specialist staff** to conduct research and development (R&D). They may be organised in a separate functional department of their own. In an organisation run on a product division basis, R&D staff may be employed by each division.

7.5 Product and process research

There are two categories of R&D.

Key terms

> **Product research** is based on creating new products and developing existing ones, in other words the organisation's 'offer' to the market.
>
> **Process research** is based on improving the way in which those products or services are made or delivered, or the efficiency with which they are made or delivered.

Product research – new product development

The new product development process must be carefully controlled; new products are a major source of competitive advantage but can cost a great deal of money to bring to market. A screening process is necessary to ensure that resources are concentrated on projects with a high probability of success and not wasted on those that have poor prospects.

Cooper describes a typical modern product innovation screening process that he calls **Stage-Gate**™. This emphasises a cross-functional, prioritised, quality managed, project management approach consisting, typically, of five stages. Each stage begins with a **gate**; that is, a review meeting of managers who have the power either to kill the project or to allocate the resources necessary for it to progress to the next gate. Each gate incorporates the same three management elements.

(a) **Deliverables** are the results of the preceding stage's activity and are specified at its beginning.

(b) **Criteria** are applied by the decision makers to judge the progress of the project and decide whether or not to continue with it.

(c) **Outputs** are a **decision**, and such things as an **action plan**, a **budget** and a list of **deliverables** for the next gate.

A typical five stage process would look like this.

(a) The new idea is subjected to an initial screening to check such things as basic feasibility, strategic fit and marketability. Financial criteria are not usually applied at this stage. This is **Gate 1**.

(b) **Stage 1**. Preliminary investigation is likely to take less than a month and concentrates on preliminary assessment of market potential, technical implications and financial viability. Quick legal and risk assessments will also take place. This stage leads to **Gate 2**, which is similar to gate 1 in nature, but more rigorous. Gates 1 and 2 are probably operated by middle level managers since, in each case, the resources required to progress to the next stage are only moderate.

(c) **Stage 2**. It is now appropriate to **build a business case** for the project. The product is defined in detail and a full **marketing analysis** is carried out, featuring such processes as competitor analysis, user needs-and-wants studies, and value-in-use studies. There are also full **technical** and **manufacturing appraisals** and a detailed **financial analysis**. **Gate 3** assesses this business case and is probably operated by the company's senior management team, since approval at this stage will lead to heavy expenditure.

(d) **Stage 3**. The physical development of the product now proceeds, subject to a strict time schedule and budget of resources. Lengthy development phases may incorporate their own project management milestones to ensure control, but these are not formal gates in the Cooper sense. This stage leads to **Gate 4**, the **post development review**. The emphasis here is not on whether to proceed further but on ensuring that the project is on track and on reviewing the earlier work on feasibility using up to date information.

(e) **Stage 4**. This is the **testing and validation** stage and validates the entire commercial viability of the project. It may include **pilot production**, **field trials** and **test marketing**. **Gate 5** is **precommercialisation business analysis**. This gives top management the opportunity to check the work done in the testing and validation stage and apply final financial return and launch planning criteria.

(f) **Stage 5** is **full production** and **market launch**. Both must be carefully monitored and lead inexorably to the **post implementation review**, which considers the degree of success achieved by both the new product itself and the development process that led to its launch.

External to the **Stage-Gate**™ management process are **idea generation** and **strategy formulation**.

(a) **Idea generation**, to be effective requires a system to promote, and reward creativity and innovative ideas. You will find lots of ideas elsewhere in this Study Text about how this can be done. Cooper suggests a four point plan.

 (i) Nominate one manager to be the **focal point for ideas**.
 (ii) That manager establishes where ideas may **arise**.
 (iii) Those sources are **encouraged**.
 (iv) The ideas they produce are **captured**.

(b) **Strategy formulation**. A business should have a detailed new product strategy, specifying goals, priorities, funding and methods. This is a top management responsibility.

Cooper suggests that the basic process outlined above can be improved using features he calls the **six Fs**.

(a) **Flexibility** is incorporated by routing projects through an abbreviated process if they are small or low risk.

(b) **Fuzzy gates** have other conditions than open or closed: for example, a project may be given a **conditional approval** that depends on some future achievement, such as the receipt of a favourable legal report that is not yet available.

(c) **Fluidity** means that the stages are not sealed off from each other by the gates. For example, it may be permissible to order some long lead-time supplies needed for the next stage before the current one is complete. Assessment of **risk** is crucial here.

(d) **Focus** means considering portfolio management during the gate process, since resources saved by killing one project may then be redeployed to other, more promising ones.

(e) **Facilitation** of the whole process should be the full time responsibility of a manager who is charged with making the process (not the project) work.

(f) **Forever green**. The whole process can be used for other purposes than just new product development: it could, for instance be used on a proposal to extend premises.

Product research is not confined to dealing with new products. It has an important role in connection with **existing products**.

(a) **Value engineering** may be used to continue the development of existing products so that they use less costly components or processes without compromising the perceived value of the market offer.

(b) As products near the end of their **life cycle**, it may be possible to develop them for launch in a different market, or simply to extend their lives.

(c) Where products are being replaced by new versions it may be advantageous to ensure that the new products are **backwards compatible** with the installed base. This is an important consideration in software engineering, for example.

7.6 Process research

Process research involves attention to how the goods/services are produced. Process research has these aspects.

(a) **Processes** are crucial in service industries (eg fast food), where processes are part of the services sold.

(b) **Productivity**. Efficient processes save money and time.

(c) **Planning**. If you know how long certain stages in a project are likely to take, you can plan the most efficient sequence.

(d) **Quality management** for enhanced quality.

We will have a lot more to say about process development and quality later in this Study Text

An important aspect of process research is that advances are much more difficult to imitate then are product developments. Competitors can purchase and **reverse engineer** new products. With good physical security in place, they will find it much more difficult to imitate new processes.

The strategic role of R&D. R&D should support the organisation's chosen strategy. To take a simple example, if a strategy based on high quality and luxury has been adopted, it would be inappropriate to expend much effort on researching ways of minimising costs. If the company has a competence in R&D, this may form the basis for a strategy of product innovation. Conversely, where product lifecycles are short, as in consumer electronics, product development is fundamental to strategy.

7.7 Problems with R&D

(a) **Organisational**. Problems of authority relationships and integration arise with the management of R&D. The function will have to liase closely with marketing and with production, as well as with senior management responsible for corporate planning: its role is both strategic and technical.

(b) **Financial**. R&D is by nature not easily planned in advance, and financial performance targets are not easily set. Budgeting for long-term, complex development projects with uncertain returns can be a nightmare for management accountants.

(c) **Evaluation and control**. Pure research or even applied research may not have an obvious pay off in the short term. Evaluation could be based on successful application of new ideas, such as patents obtained and the commercial viability of new products.

(d) **Staff problems**. Research staff are usually highly qualified and profession-orientated, with consequences for the style of supervision and level of remuneration offered to them.

(e)   **Cultural problems**. Encouraging innovation means trial and error, flexibility, tolerance of mistakes in the interests of experimentation, high incentives etc. If this is merely a subculture in an essentially bureaucratic organisation, it will not only be difficult to sustain, but will become a source of immense 'political' conflict. The R&D department may have an 'academic' or university atmosphere, as opposed to a commercial one.

7.8 R&D and marketing

(a)   Customer needs, as identified by marketers, should be a vital input to new product developments.

(b)   The R&D department might identify possible changes to product specifications so that a variety of marketing mixes can be tried out and screened.

7.8.1 Intrapreneurship

FAST FORWARD

Intrapreneurship is entrepreneurship carried on at intermediate levels within the organisation.

The encouragement of intrapreneurship is an important way of promoting innovation. Such encouragement has many aspects.

(a)   Encouragement for individuals to achieve results in their own way without the need for constant supervision

(b)   A culture of risk-taking and tolerance of mistakes

(c)   A flexible approach to organisation that facilitates the formation of project teams

(d)   Willingness and ability to devote resources to trying out new ideas

(e)   Incentives and rewards policy that support intrapreneurial activity

 Case Study

Disney and Pixar

Organisational culture is an extremely important influence on innovation. A Financial Times report on *Disney's* purchase of *Pixar* in 2006 contrasted their distinct organisational styles.

'Disney has become a pathologically dysfunctional organisation. Like *IBM* of the 1970s or *AT&T* in the 1980s, Disney grew fat and bureaucratic in the 1990s, long after cementing its lucrative entertainment franchise. Some of Disney's problems are endemic to large corporations. When a company has 133,000 employees, it cannot be governed by human beings. Instead, it must rely on a culture to preserve its earlier entrepreneurialism, while focusing workers on the continuing mission.

Unfortunately, Disney's culture, like that of IBM and AT&T, encouraged inefficiency and stifled creativity. Over the past five years, Disney's shares have lost a third of their value and the company has become a corporate governance pariah. Many thought the low point was the fiasco surrounding Michael Ovitz, who left Disney with $140m after just 14 months. But more troubling was the release of the abysmal *Treasure Planet*, a film that cost about as much as Mr Ovitz and avoided universal ignominy only because so few people saw it.

To survive and prosper, large organisations must be divided into manageable pods, whose workers have independence and incentive. In contrast to Disney, Pixar was just such a free-standing, free-spirited group with a relaxed, open-plan office and no signs of managerial hierarchy. John Lasseter, Pixar's creative leader, wore Hawaiian shirts and rode a scooter inside. When Pixar won Oscars, employees displayed the statues proudly but dressed them in *Barbie* doll clothing. Whereas

Disney executives micromanaged films, including those with Pixar, Mr Lasseter let his crew run free and encouraged ideas.'

7.8.2 Market pull and technology push

Marketers would have us believe that the best way to competitive advantage is to find out what the market wants and give it to them. We might call this approach, when applied to innovation, **market pull**. Unfortunately, it tends merely to produce better versions of products that already exist. A more fruitful approach may be the 'product orientation', disdained by the marketing fraternity: the world is full of products that no-one asked for, including post-it notes and mobile phones that are also cameras. This approach we might call **technology push**.

Perhaps the most fruitful approach would be a combination of the two, where technologists try to solve customers' problems and marketers try to find applications for new and emerging technologies. Many new developments are, in fact, the result of **collaboration between suppliers and customers**.

 Case Study

Microsoft and Sony

A company's policy on innovation will be linked to its assessment of how the product lifecycle concept applies to its portfolio.

Microsoft has generally followed a policy of fairly limited incremental upgrades. Writing in the *Financial Times* on 19 May 2005, *John Gapper* pointed out that it had used this approach to gradually outflank *Apple's* OS, developing a credible alternative by steadily updating its *Windows* operating system. It followed a similar policy in upgrading its *Xbox* games console, releasing the *Xbox 360* only four years after the first Xbox.

Sony, on the other hand, has taken a longer view, working on a 10 year life cycle for video games consoles. This has led it to give its new *PlayStation 3* far greater imaging power than the Xbox 360 possesses. PlayStation 3's potential can only be realised by coupling it to a high-definition TV: the planned life of the product will give time for such TVs to become affordable and widely purchased.

8 Benchmarking

FAST FORWARD

Benchmarking enables a firm to meet industry standards by copying others, but it is perhaps less valuable as a source of innovation. It is a good way to challenge existing ways of doing things.

Key term

Benchmarking is the 'establishment, through data gathering, of targets and comparators, that permit relative levels of performance (and particularly areas of underperformance) to be identified. Adoption of identified best practices should improve performance. (CIMA *Official Terminology*)

CIMA's Official Terminology goes on to define several different types of benchmarking. Unfortunately, these definitions are not universally used, so we will use JS&W's categories.

Historical benchmarking is an internal comparison of current against past performance. This is unsatisfactory, since it can induce complacence; comparison with competitors is the real test of performance.

Industry/sector benchmarking compares like with like across the industry or similar providers in the public service. In the UK public sector, league tables are an obvious example of this approach. The limitation of this method is that the whole industry may be under-performing and in danger from substitute products provided by other industries.

Best-in-class benchmarking looks for best practice wherever it can be found. This involves making comparisons with similar features or processes in other industries. JS&W suggest that this approach can have a shock effect on complacent managers and lead to dramatic performance improvements

8.1 The benchmarking process

Benchmarking can be divided into stages.

Stage 1

The first stage is to **ensure senior management commitment** to the benchmarking process. This will only be genuinely available when the senior managers have a full appreciation of what is involved: senior people are quite capable of changing their minds when it becomes apparent that they did not anticipate the actual levels of cost or inconvenience, for example. The Board of E5E has actually proposed that a benchmarking exercise take place, but they will be as likely as any other senior management team to change their minds.

Stage 2

The areas to be benchmarked should be determined and objectives should be set. Note that here, the objectives will not be in the form of aspirations for improvement to specific processes and practices, but more in the nature of stating the extent and depth of the enquiry. In E5E, for example, under fundraising, it might be decided to look carefully specifically at the security of cash collections.

Stage 3

Key performance measures must be established. This will require an understanding of the systems involved, which, in turn, will require discussion with key stakeholders and observation of the way work is carried out. A simple example of how this stage would be carried out within E5E might be to examine the processes for assessing applications for research grants.

Stage 4

Select organisations to benchmark against. Internal benchmarking may be possible where, for example, there are local fund-raising branches or shops. Where internal departments have little in common, comparisons must be made against equivalent parts of other organisations. The aim will be to find an organisation that does similar things but which is not in competition with E5E. For example, another charity that undertakes educational work, but is not involved in medical research would provide a suitable benchmark for E5E's educational work. This is a kind of **functional benchmarking**, as defined by CIMA.

Stage 5

Measure own and others' performance. Negotiation should take place to establish just who does the measurement: ideally, a joint team should do it, but there may be issues of **confidentiality** or **convenience** that mean each organisation does its own measuring.

Stage 6

Compare performance. Raw data must be carefully analysed if appropriate conclusions are to be drawn. It will be appropriate to discuss initial findings with the **stakeholders** concerned: they are likely both to have useful comment to offer and to be anxious about the possibility of adverse reflection upon them. This may be particularly applicable to the volunteer staff within E5E, who may be sensitive about their amateur status.

Stage 7

Design and implement improvement programmes. It may be possible to import complete systems; alternatively, it may be appropriate to move towards a synthesis that combines various elements of best practice. Sometimes, improvements require extensive **reorganisation** and **restructuring**. In any event, there is likely to be a requirement for **training**. Improvements in administrative systems often call for investment in new equipment, particularly in IT systems.

Stage 8

Monitor improvements. The continuing effectiveness of improvements must be monitored. At the same time, it must be understood that **improvements are not once and for all** and that further adjustments may be beneficial.

8.2 Using benchmarking

Johnson and Scholes set out questions that should be asked when carrying out a benchmarking exercise as part of a wider strategic review.

- **Why** are these products or services provided at all?
- Why are they provided **in that particular way**?
- What are the examples of **best practice** elsewhere?
- How should activities be **reshaped** in the light of these comparisons?

They see three levels of benchmarking.

Level of benchmarking	Through	Examples of measures
Resources	Resource audit	Quantity of resources • revenue/employee • capital intensity Quality of resources • Qualifications of employees • Age of machinery • Uniqueness (eg patents)
Competences in separate activities	Analysing activities	Sales calls per salesperson Output per employee Materials wastage
Competences in linked activities	Analysing overall performances	Market share Profitability Productivity

Exam focus point

You could use the information above as the framework for an answer to a question about carrying out a benchmarking exercise. A May 2005 old syllabus Paper 3.5 question covered benchmarking in a medical charity, and its potential impact on staff. The question was fairly straightforward: 8 marks for the advantages and disadvantages, 13 for the stages of conducting a benchmarking exercise and 4 for implementing the benchmarking plan.

When selecting an appropriate **benchmark basis**, companies should ask themselves the following questions.

(a) Is it possible and easy to obtain reliable competitor information?

(b) Is there any wide discrepancy between different internal divisions?

(c)   Can similar processes be identified in non-competing environments and are these non competing companies willing to co-operate?

(d)   Is best practice operating in a similar environmental setting?

(e)   What is our timescale?

(f)   Do the chosen companies have similar objectives and strategies?

8.3 Reasons for undertaking benchmarking

Benchmarking has the following advantages.

(a)   **Position audit**. Benchmarking can assess a firm's existing position, and provide a basis for establishing standards of performance.

(b)   The comparisons are **carried out by the managers** who have to live with any changes implemented as a result of the exercise.

(c)   Benchmarking **focuses** on improvement in key areas and sets targets which are challenging but evidently achievable.

(d)   The sharing of information can be a **spur to innovation**.

(e)   The result should be **improved performance**, particularly in cost control and delivering value.

8.4 Drawbacks of benchmarking

Many companies have gained significant benefits from benchmarking but it is worth pointing out a number of possible dangers.

(a)   It can cloud perception of strategic purpose by attracting too much attention to the detail of what is measured, since it concentres on **doing things right** rather than **doing the right thing**: the difference between **efficiency** and **effectiveness**. A process can be efficient but its output may not be useful. A linked point is that the benchmark may be **yesterday's solution to tomorrow's problem**. For example, a cross-channel ferry company might benchmark its activities (eg speed of turnround at Dover and Calais, cleanliness on ship) against another ferry company, whereas the real competitor is the Channel Tunnel.

(b)   Benchmarking does not identify the **reasons** why performance is at a particular level, whether good or bad.

(c)   It is a **catching-up exercise** rather than the development of anything distinctive. After the benchmarking exercise, the competitor might improve performance in a different way.

(d)   It depends on **accurate** information about comparator companies.

(e)   It is not cost-free and can divert management attention.

(f)   It can become a hindrance and even a threat: sharing information with other companies can be a burden and a security risk.

 Case Study

A recent five year research programme by INSEAD business school identified the following five companies as likely to still be successful 10 or 20 years from now.

- *American International Group* (AIG), the US insurer
- *Heineken*, the Dutch brewer
- *Hewlett-Packard*, the US electronics manufacturer

- *JP Morgan*, the US bank
- *SGS Thomson*, the Franco-Italian semiconductor maker

The underlying premise of the study , as reported in the *Financial Times*, is that success or failure depends on a complex series of actions. Companies were compared on 12 capabilities – customer orientation, technical resources, market strategy and so forth. An overall score for effectiveness was calculated.

The study showed how the best companies go about their business, and allowed others to diagnose their shortcomings. To quote the project leader when talking about *IBM*: 'There was a time when it was the best at customer orientation. If we had had this tool 20 years ago, we could have seen it going wrong.'

9 Managing strategic capability

FAST FORWARD

> Managers must take great care not to disrupt strategic capability that arises from flexible, informal practices by trying to systematise and improve them. However, a policy of gradual extension and improvement of desirable activities may be useful and may be combined with culling of superfluous ones. Also, since much strategic capability is traceable to individual skill and ability, good HRM practice can help to create and improve it.

So far in this chapter we have concentrated on the analysis of strategic capability. We must now turn our attention to the problems of managing and improving it.

9.1 Limitation on the management of strategic capability

There is an important problem in the management of strategic capability, in that it can be very difficult to **understand** it properly. Quite often, core competences derive from **informal and flexible activities and processes** that are not subject to management from above: they simply exist. Sometimes, managers do not appreciate that these competences exist; where they do, they may or may not understand them or value them. Where managers recognise such competences, it is very important that they take great care with attempts to improve or even to formalise them. The former can be highly **disruptive**, while the latter can **eliminate the inherent flexibility** such competences tend to display.

9.2 Improving strategic capability

Despite the limitation discussed above, there may be opportunities to stretch existing capabilities and to add new ones.

(a) **Competences can be extended**. Competences that support existing business may be equally relevant to new activities.

(b) **Non-essential activities can cease**. It may be possible to make significant cost savings by abolishing, minimising or outsourcing current activities that do not support critical success factors.

(c) **Best practice can be extended**. Strategic capability identified in one part of the organisation might be introduced in other parts; though the difficulties associated with the management of change can make this very difficult.

(d) **Activities can be added and existing ones improved** in order to better support critical success factors.

(e) **Activities can be re-structured**. System overlaps and inconsistencies may require attention, particularly when there are marked differences between the requirements of the various market segments served.

(f)   **Weaknesses can be remedied**. Known weaknesses in resources or activities might have the potential to create competitive advantage if suitable market opportunities exist. Such weaknesses must then be remedied by suitable investment and management activity.

(g)   **External capability can be introduced** by acquisition and through alliances and joint ventures.

9.3 Developing competences through the human resource

Since much strategic capability resides in the organisation's staff in the form of their abilities and skills, human resource development can be particularly important in building that capability.

(a)   **Recruitment and selection** practice can be designed to emphasise the need for particular aptitudes, such as leadership or innovation.

(b)   **Training and development** can be targeted at specific requirements rather than generic skills.

(c)   **Individual strategic awareness** can be developed so that staff understand how their activities enhance strategic capability.

10 SWOT analysis

FAST FORWARD

The **SWOT analysis** combines the results of the environmental analysis and the internal appraisal into one framework for assessing the firm's current and future strategic fit, or lack of it, with the environment. It is an analysis of the organisation's strengths and weaknesses, and the opportunities and threats offered by the environment. Weirich's TOWS matrix emphasises the importance of threats and opportunities.

We examined the way in which **opportunities and threats** in the environment are detected and analysed in the previous chapter. In this chapter, we have discussed the analysis of the organisation's strategic capability; that is to say, its **strengths and weaknesses**. A complete awareness of the organisation's environment and its internal capacities is *necessary* for a rational consideration of future strategy, but it is not *sufficient*. The threads must be drawn together so that potential strategies may be developed and assessed. This is done in by combining the internal and external analyses into a **SWOT analysis** or **corporate appraisal**.

Key term

SWOT analysis summarises the key issues from the business environment and the strategic capability of an organisation that are most likely to impact on strategy development.   *JS&W*

10.1 The SWOT analysis

Effective SWOT analysis does not simply require a categorisation of information, it also requires some **evaluation of the relative importance** of the various factors under consideration.

(a)   These features are only of relevance if they are **perceived to exist by the consumers.** Listing corporate features that internal personnel regard as strengths/weaknesses is of little relevance if they are not perceived as such by the organisation's consumers.

(b)   In the same vein, threats and opportunities are conditions presented by the external environment and they should be independent of the firm.

The SWOT can now be used guiding strategy formulation.

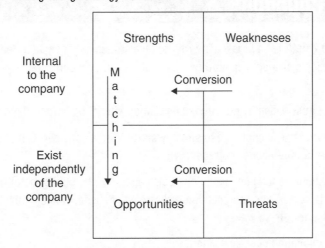

(a) **Match strengths with market opportunities**

Strengths that do not match any available opportunity are of limited use while opportunities which do not have any matching strengths are of little immediate value.

(b) **Conversion**

This requires the development of strategies that will convert weaknesses into strengths in order to take advantage of some particular opportunity, or converting threats into opportunities which can then be matched by existing strengths.

The SWOT technique can also be used for specific areas of strategy such as IT and marketing.

10.2 Weirich's TOWS matrix

Weirich, one of the earliest writers on corporate appraisal, originally spoke in terms of a **TOWS matrix** in order to emphasise the **importance of threats and opportunities**. This is therefore an inherently **positioning** approach to strategy. A further important element of Weirich's discussion was his categorisation of strategic options.

- SO strategies employ strengths to seize opportunities.
- ST strategies employ strengths to counter or avoid threats.
- WO strategies address weaknesses so as to be able to exploit opportunities.
- WT strategies are defensive, aiming to avoid threats and the impact of weaknesses.

One useful impact of this analysis is that **the four groups of strategies tend to relate well to different time horizons**. SO strategies may be expected to produce good short-term results, while WO strategies are likely to take much longer to show results. ST and WT strategies are more probably relevant to the medium term.

This consideration of time horizon may be linked to the **overall resource picture**: SO strategies can be profitable in the short term, generating the cash needed for investment in WT strategies, improving current areas of weakness so that further opportunities may be seized. ST and WT strategies are likely to be more or less resource-neutral, but care must be taken to achieve an overall balance.

Chapter Roundup

- A **position audit** is undertaken in order to give strategic managers a clear understanding of the organisation's **strategic capability**; that is, its resources, competences and the constraints that limit their use.

- **Resource audits** identify human, financial and material resources and how they are deployed.

- The resource-based approach to strategy starts from a consideration of capabilities and, in particular, of distinctive **competences** and **resources**.

- **Cost efficiency** is fundamental to strategic capability: the public sector demands value for money, while in the private sector, price competition makes cost efficiency fundamental to survival. Cost efficiency is achieved in four main ways.

  - Exploitation of scale economies
  - Control of the cost of income incoming supplies
  - Careful design of products and processes
  - Exploitation of experience effects

- If strategy is to be based on strategic capabilities, those capabilities must have four qualities.

  - **Value to buyers**
  - **Rarity**
  - **Robustness** (difficult for competitors to imitate)
  - **Non-substitutability**

  Under conditions of **hyper-competition**, organisations must possess **dynamic capabilities**: the ability to develop and adjust competences to cope with rapidly changing environmental pressures.

- The aim of **knowledge management** is to capture, organise and make widely available all the knowledge the organisation possesses, whether **explicit** (in recorded form) or **tacit** (in people's heads).

- **Data** are simple facts that can be organised in a way that creates **information**. **Knowledge** is patterns of information that are strategically useful and context independent.

- Knowledge must be managed in a way that makes it easily available. Systems include office automation, groupware, intranets, extranets, expert systems and data mining.

- The **value chain** describes those activities of the organisation that add value to purchased inputs. Primary activities are involved in the production of goods and services. Support activities provide necessary assistance. **Linkages** are the relationships between activities.

- Core competences are the basis for the creation of value; activities from which the organisation does not derive significant value may be outsourced.

- The value network joins the organisation's value chain to those of its suppliers and customers.

- The **product life cycle** concept holds that products have a life cycle, and that a product demonstrates different characteristics of profit and investment at each stage in its life cycle. The life cycle concept is a model, not a prediction. (Not all products pass through each stage of the life cycle.) It enables a firm to examine its portfolio of goods and services as a whole.

- **Innovation** can be a major source of competitive advantage but brings a burden of cost and uncertainty. To avoid waste, there should be a programme of assessment for major product development. The firm must decide whether to be a leader or a follower.

- Research may be **pure, applied** or **development**. It may be intended to improve **products** or **processes**. New product development should be controlled by requiring strategic approval at key points of development.

  R&D should support the organisation's strategy and be closely co-ordinated with marketing. There are distinct problems to managing R&D.

- **Intrapreneurship** is entrepreneurship carried on within the organisation at a level below the strategic apex.

- **Benchmarking** enables a firm to meet industry standards by copying others, but it is perhaps less valuable as a source of innovation. It is a good way to challenge existing ways of doing things.

- Mangers must take great care not to disrupt strategic capability that arises from flexible, informal practices by trying to systematise and improve them. However, a policy of gradual extension and improvement desirable activities may be useful and may be combined with culling of superfluous ones. Also, since much strategic capability is traceable to individual skill and ability, HRM can help to create and improve it.

- The **SWOT analysis** combines the results of the environmental analysis and the internal appraisal into one framework for assessing the firm's current and future strategic fit, or lack of it, with the environment. It is an analysis of the organisation's strengths and weaknesses, and the opportunities and threats offered by the environment. Weirich's TOWS matrix emphasises the importance of treats and opportunities.

Quick Quiz

1   What is a limiting factor?

2   What are core competence?

3   What four qualities enable a capability to form the basis of competitive advantage?

4   What is the difference between tacit and explicit knowledge?

5   What is a data warehouse?

6   What is the significance of the value chain?

7   Distinguish between product class and product form.

8   List the stages of the product life cycle.

9   What does PIMS data reveal about the relationship between high expenditure on R&D and profitability?

10 What are the three levels of benchmarking described by *Johnson and Scholes*?

11 What are the four types of strategy described by Weirich and based on the TOWS matrix?

Answers to Quick Quiz

1   Any factor that limits activity, usually because of a shortage.

2   Competences that underpin competitive advantage and that are difficult to imitate.

3   Value to buyers; rarity; robustness (difficulty of imitation); non-substitutability

4   Tacit knowledge exists only inside people's heads; explicit knowledge is recorded in some way.

5   A data warehouse receives data from operational systems and stores them in their most fundamental form, without any summarisation of transactions

6   The value chain illustrates how value is created by value activities and linkages.

7   Product class is a broad generic category, eg 'car'. Product form is a specific type within the class, eg 'executive saloon'.

8   Introduction, growth, maturity, decline.

9   There is a negative correlation between the two.

10 Resources; competences in separate activities; competences in limited activities.

11 SO   Strategies employ strengths to seize opportunities.
      ST   Strategies employ strengths to counter or avoid threats.
      WO   Strategies address weaknesses so as to be able to exploit opportunities.
      WT   Strategies are defensive, aiming to avoid threats and the impact of weaknesses.

Now try the questions below from the Exam Question Bank

Number	Level	Marks	Time
Q4	Exam	20	36 mins

Stakeholders, ethics and culture

Topic list	Syllabus reference
1 Ethics and the organisation	A6(c)
2 Social responsibility	A6(b), (d)
3 Corporate governance	A6(a)
4 The role of culture	A6(e), (f)

Introduction

Organisations are part of human society and, like individual people, are subject to rules that govern their conduct towards others. Some of these rules are **law** and enforced by legal sanction. Other rules fall into the realm of **ethics** or morality and are enforced only by the strength of society's approval or disapproval. The first section of this chapter is concerned with the strategic impact of ethical ideas on organisations.

The behaviour of organisations may also be considered in the light of notions of **corporate social responsibility**. This is a rather poorly defined concept. However, there does now seem to be widespread acceptance that commercial organisations should devote some of their resources to the promotion of wider social aims that are not necessarily mandated by either law or the rules of ethics.

The third section of this chapter is concerned with **corporate governance** and the mechanisms that may be installed to promote fair and honest behaviour at the strategic apex.

Finally, we conclude the chapter with a discussion of the influence of culture on the organisation and its people.

Study guide

		Intellectual level
A6	**The expectations of stakeholders and the influence of ethics and culture**	
(a)	Advise on the implications of corporate governance on organisational purpose and strategy	2
(b)	Evaluate, through stakeholder mapping, the relative influence of stakeholders on organisational purpose and strategy	3
(c)	Assess ethical influences on organisational purpose and strategy	3
(d)	Explore the scope of corporate social responsibility	3
(e)	Assess the impact of culture on organisational purpose and strategy	3
(f)	Prepare and evaluate a cultural web of an organisation	2
(g)	Advise on how organisations can communicate their core values and mission	3

Exam guide

The importance of the topics covered in this chapter is indicated by the emphasis laid on them by all professional bodies. There were regular questions on ethics and corporate governance in exams under the old syllabus and there is no reason to suppose that this will not continue into the future. Ethics is something that is relevant to all behaviour, so it could be included in a question on any topic.

Culture is also a very important and very examinable field.

1 Ethics and the organisation

> **Knowledge brought forward**
>
> The syllabus for *Paper F1 Accountant in Business* includes sections on ethics, governance and social responsibility. You should already be familiar with many of the basic ideas underpinning this chapter. Also, if you have already studied *Paper P1 Professional Accountant* you will have a detailed knowledge of these matters. Our coverage here is intended to provide a minimum of essential revision and new material relevant to the Business Analysis syllabus.

FAST FORWARD

Ethics is about right and wrong but it is not the same thing as law or the rules of religion. Cognitive approaches to ethics assume that objective moral truths can be established.

1.1 Ethics and business

Ethics is concerned with right and wrong and how conduct should be judged to be good or bad. It is about how we should live our lives and, in particular, how we should behave towards other people. Business life is a fruitful source of ethical dilemmas because its whole purpose is material gain, the making of profit. Success in business requires a constant, avid search for potential advantage over others and business people are under pressure to do whatever yields such advantage.

1.2 Non-cognitivism, ethical relativism and intuitionism

The approach called **non-cognitivism** suggests that all moral statements are essentially subjective and arise from the culture, belief or emotion of the speaker.

Non-cognitivism recognises the differences that exist between the rules of behaviour prevailing in different cultures. The view that right and wrong are culturally determined is called **ethical relativism** or **moral relativism**. This is clearly a matter of significance in the context of **international business**. Managers encountering cultural norms of behaviour that differ significantly from their own may be puzzled to know what rules to follow.

1.3 Cognitivism

Cognitivist approaches to ethics are built on the principle that objective, universally applicable moral truths exist and can be known. There are four important cognitivist theories to consider after we have looked at **law** and **religion** in relation to ethics.

(a) Religions are based on the concept of universally applicable principle but they cannot be regarded as reliable guides to ethical conduct since they differ so much between themselves, forming, in fact the basis of the moral relativist approach. This problem may be approached by asking how does God decide what is right and what is wrong? Presumably, it is not mere whim and **moral principles** are involved. The implication is that it is proper to seek to understand these reasons for ourselves and to use them as the basis of our moral code.

(b) Cognitivist ethics and law can be seen as parallel and connected systems of rules for regulating conduct. Both are concerned with right conduct and the principles that define it. However, ethics and law are not the same thing. Law must be free from ambiguity. However, unlike law, ethics can quite reasonably be an arena for debate, about both the principles involved and their application in specific rules. The law must be certain and therefore finds it difficult to deal with problems of conduct that are subject to opinion and debate. Another difference is that many legal rules are only very remotely connected with ethics, if at all, and some laws in some countries have been of debateable moral stature, to say the least.

1.4 Consequentialist ethics: utilitarianism

FAST FORWARD

Consequentialist ethics judges actions by their outcomes; deontology assumes the existence of absolute moral principles and ignores outcomes. Natural law is about rights and duties, while virtue ethics is based on moderation in behaviour and the idea of leading a harmonious life.

Ethical theory is not integrated: consequentialist, deontological and natural law based rules are capable of pointing to different conclusions. Partly as a result of this, **ethical dilemmas** can exist at all levels in the organisation.

The **consequentialist** approach to ethics is to make moral judgements about courses of action by reference to their outcomes or consequences. Right or wrong becomes a question of benefit or harm.

Utilitarianism is the best-known formulation of this approach and can be summed up in the '**greatest good**' principle. This says that when deciding on a course of action we should choose the one that is likely to result in the greatest good for the greatest number of people.

There is an immediate problem here, which is how we are to define what is good for people.

The utilitarian approach may also be questioned for its potential effect upon minorities. A situation in which a large majority achieved great happiness at the expense of creating misery among a small minority would satisfy the 'greatest good' principle. It could not, however, be regarded as ethically desirable.

However, utilitarianism can be a useful guide to conduct. It has been used to derive wide ranging rules and can be applied to help us make judgements about individual, unique problems.

1.5 Deontological ethics

Deontology is concerned with the application of universal ethical principles in order to arrive at rules of conduct, the word deontology being derived from the Greek for 'duty'. Whereas the consequentialist approach judges actions by their outcomes, deontology lays down *a priori* criteria by which they may be judged in advance. The definitive treatment of deontological ethics is found in the work of *Immanuel Kant*.

Kant suggested that if we make moral judgements about facts, the criteria by which we judge are separate from the facts themselves: the criteria come from within ourselves and are based on an intuitive awareness of the nature of good.

For Kant, moral conduct is defined by categorical imperatives. A **categorical imperative**, however, defines a course of action without reference to outcomes. We must act in certain ways because it is right to do so – right conduct is an end in itself.

Kant arrived at two formulations of the categorical imperative with which we should be familiar.

(a)   Never act in a way that you would condemn in others.

(b)   Do not treat people simply as means to an end. (Note that this does not preclude us from using people as means to an end as long as we, at the same time, recognise their right to be treated as autonomous beings. Clearly, organisations and even society itself could not function if we could not make use of other people's services.)

1.6 Natural law

Natural law approaches to ethics are based on the idea that a set of objective or 'natural' moral rules exists and we can come to know what they are. In terms of business ethics, the natural law approach deals mostly with rights and duties. Where there is a right, there is also a duty to respect that right. Unfortunately, the implications about duties can only be as clear as the rights themselves and there are wide areas in which disagreement about rights persists.

1.7 Duty and consequences

In their pure form, neither the duties of natural law nor Kant's categorical imperative will admit consideration of the consequences of our actions: we act in a certain way because we are obeying inflexible moral rules. Unfortunately, such an approach can have undesirable results. If people have absolute rights that we must respect whatever the circumstances, we may find that our actions in doing so harm the common good. An example is the accused person who commits an offence while on bail. The potential threat to public safety has to be balanced against the right of the individual to liberty. There is thus a great potential for conflict between courses of action based on the consequentialist approach and those based on deontology or natural law.

While individual cases are bound to provoke debate, it would be reasonable to suggest that an inflexible approach to rules of conduct is likely to produce ethical dilemmas. Deciding what to do when the arguments point in opposite directions is always going to be difficult. However, generally we do not have the option of doing nothing, and this is particularly true of business.

1.8 Virtue ethics

The virtue ethics approach consists of pursuing a harmonious or virtuous life and a rational judgement about what constitutes good. To some extent, this consists of avoiding extremes of any kind. For example, courage lies between cowardice at one end of the scale and foolhardiness at the other. The cultivation of appropriate virtues has been proposed as a route to ethical behaviour in business. For example, managers might cultivate a range of virtues such as honesty, courage, fairness and firmness.

1.9 Ethics and strategy

In this Study Text we have emphasised that what the organisation wishes to achieve – its **mission** – is fundamental to any focussed control of its activities. When we discussed the concept of mission we made passing reference to **policies and standards of behaviour**.

It is important to understand that if ethics is applicable to corporate behaviour at all, it must therefore be a fundamental aspect of **mission**, since everything the organisation does flows from that. Managers responsible for strategic decision making cannot avoid responsibility for their organisation's ethical standing. They should consciously apply ethical rules to all of their decisions in order to filter out potentially undesirable developments.

1.10 Ethical dilemmas

There are a number of areas in which the various approaches to ethics and conflicting views of a business's responsibilities can create **ethical dilemmas** for managers. These can impact at the highest level, affecting the development of policy, or lower down the hierarchy, especially if policy is unclear and guidance from more senior people is unavailable.

Dealing with **unpleasantly authoritarian governments** can be supported on the grounds that it contributes to economic growth and prosperity and all the benefits they bring to society in both countries concerned. This is a consequentialist argument. It can also be opposed on consequentialist grounds as contributing to the continuation of the regime, and on deontological grounds as fundamentally repugnant.

Honesty in advertising is an important problem. Many products are promoted exclusively on image. Deliberately creating the impression that purchasing a particular product will enhance the happiness, success and sex-appeal of the buyer can be attacked as dishonest. It can be defended on the grounds that the supplier is actually selling a fantasy or dream rather than a physical article.

Dealings with **employees** are coloured by the opposing views of corporate responsibility and individual rights. The idea of a job as property to be defended has now disappeared from UK labour relations, but there is no doubt that corporate decisions that lead to redundancies are still deplored. This is because of the obvious impact of sudden unemployment on aspirations and living standards, even when the employment market is buoyant. Nevertheless, it is only proper for businesses to consider the cost of employing labour as well as its productive capacity. Even employers who accept that their employees' skills are their most important source of competitive advantage can be reduced to cost cutting in order to survive in lean times.

Another ethical problem concerns **payments by companies to officials** who have power to help or hinder the payers' operations. In *The Ethics of Corporate Conduct, Clarence Walton* discusses to the fine distinctions which exist in this area.

(a) **Extortion**. Foreign officials have been known to threaten companies with the complete closure of their local operations unless suitable payments are made.

(b) **Bribery**. This is payments for services to which a company is not legally entitled. There are some fine distinctions to be drawn; for example, some managers regard political contributions as bribery.

(c) **Grease money**. Multinational companies are sometimes unable to obtain services to which they are legally entitled because of deliberate stalling by local officials. Cash payments to the right people may then be enough to oil the machinery of bureaucracy.

(d) **Gifts**. In some cultures (such as Japan) gifts are regarded as an essential part of civilised negotiation, even in circumstances where to Western eyes they might appear ethically dubious. Managers operating in such a culture may feel at liberty to adopt the local customs.

Business ethics are also relevant to competitive behaviour. This is because a market can only be free if competition is, in some basic respects, fair. There is a distinction between competing aggressively and competing unethically. The dispute between British Airways and Virgin centred around issues of business ethics.

1.11 The scope of corporate ethics

FAST FORWARD

Corporate ethics has three contexts.

- Interaction with national and international society
- Effects of routine operations
- Behaviour of individuals

If constructed with care, a corporate ethical code can be valuable.

Corporate ethics may be considered in three contexts.

- The organisation's interaction with **national** and **international society**
- The effects of the organisation's **routine operations**
- The behaviour of **individual members** of staff

Influencing society. The organisation operates within and interacts with the political, economic and social framework of wider society. It is both inevitable and proper that it will both influence and be influenced by that wider framework. Governments, individual politicians and pressure groups will all make demands on such matters as employment prospects and executive pay. Conversely, organisations themselves will find that they need to make their own representations on such matters as monetary policy and the burden of regulation. International variation in such matters and in the framework of **corporate governance** will affect organisations that operate in more than one country. It is appropriate that the organisation develops and promotes its own policy on such matters.

Corporate behaviour. The organisation should establish **corporate policies** for those issues over which it has direct control. Examples of matters that should be covered by policy include health, safety, labelling, equal opportunities, environmental effects, political activity, bribery and support for cultural activities.

Individual behaviour. Policies to guide the behaviour of individuals are likely to flow from the corporate stance on the matters discussed above. The organisation must decide on the extent to which it considers it appropriate to attempt to influence individual behaviour. Some aspects of such behaviour may be of strategic importance, especially when managers can be seen as representing or embodying the organisation's standards. Matters of financial rectitude and equal treatment of minorities are good examples here.

Corporate ethical codes. Organisations often publish corporate codes of ethical standards. Fundamentally, this is a good idea and can be a useful way of disseminating the specific policies we have discussed above. However, care must be taken over such a document.

(a) It should not be over-prescriptive or over-detailed, since this encourages a legalistic approach to interpretation and a desire to seek loopholes in order to justify previously chosen courses of action.

(b) It will only have influence if senior management adhere to it consistently in their own decisions and actions.

Ethical codes and policies on behaviour can, of course, be linked to and summarised in the **mission statement**.

Shell

'I am becoming sick and tired about lying.' Those are not the words shareholders want to hear from a senior executive. They are certainly not words anybody ever expected from an heir-apparent at *Royal Dutch/Shell*, one of the world's largest – and until recently, one of its most admired – oil companies.

And yet, as a new report is revealed this week, those words of exasperation did indeed come from a senior Shell executive. Walter van de Vijver, until recently the firm's head of exploration and production (E&P), wrote them in an angry e-mail to Sir Phillip Watts, then the firm's chairman, in November 2003 – fuming that he was tired of covering up for shortfalls in the firm's reserves that resulted from 'far too aggressive/ optimistic bookings'. Also, the overzealous booker was none other than Sir Phillip, who preceded him as head of E&P.

The overbooking finally caught up with both men when, in January, Shell was forced to reclassify a whopping fifth of its 'proved' resources. When preliminary investigations pointed the finger at the two men, both were forced out.

The Economist, 24 April 2004

2 Social responsibility

FAST FORWARD

There is a fundamental split of views about the organisation's relationship with its stakeholders and the nature of corporate responsibility.

- The **strong view** that a range of goals should be pursued
- The **weak view** that the business organisation is a purely **economic force**, subject to law

2.1 Stakeholders

FAST FORWARD

Stakeholders have an interest in what the organisation does.

Key term

Stakeholders: groups or individuals whose interests are directly affected by the activities of a firm or organisation

Here are some stakeholder groups.

Stakeholder group	Members
• Internal stakeholders	Employees, management
• Connected	Shareholders, customers, suppliers, lenders
• External	The government, local government, the public

Stakeholder groups can exert influence on strategy. The greater the power of a stakeholder group, the greater its influence will be. Each stakeholder group has different expectations about what it wants, and the expectations of the various groups will conflict. To some extent, the expectations of stakeholders will influence the organisation's mission. We will return to the subject of stakeholder expectations in Chapter 8 when we discuss the evaluation of strategic options.

2.1.1 Stakeholders' objectives

Here is a checklist of stakeholders' objectives. It is not comprehensive.

(a) **Employees and managers**

- Job security (over and above legal protection)
- Good conditions of work (above minimum safety standards)
- Job satisfaction
- Career development and relevant training

(b) **Customers**

- Products of a certain quality at a reasonable price
- Products that should last a certain number of years
- A product or service that meets customer needs.

(c) **Suppliers**: regular orders in return for reliable delivery and good service

(d) **Shareholders**: long-term wealth

(e) **Providers of loan capital (stock holders):** reliable payment of interest due and maintenance of the value of any security.

(f) **Society as a whole**

- Control pollution
- Financial assistance to charities, sports and community activities
- Co-operate with government in identifying and preventing health hazards

2.1.2 Competitors

Competitors can be stakeholders. You may find this easier to understand if you think of all the competitors in a given industry as stakeholders in that industry's overall status and the public's perception

 Case Study

Toyota and the Detroit auto makers

Toyota, the world's most profitable car manufacturer, has 15% of the US market, more than Chrysler and almost as much as Ford. Only General Motors, with 24% is significantly bigger.

> 'We understand that as Toyota's presence increases, expectations and demands will also rise,' president Katsuaki Watanabe told FORTUNE. Nuances will matter more then ever. When then-chairman Hiroshi Okuda in 2005 said Toyota might raise prices to take pressure off GM, the perceived condescension sparked outrage, followed by furious back-pedalling. **Okuda's remark betrayed Toyota's biggest fear: the financial collapse of one of the Detroit Three.** Jim Lentz tries his best to deflect such talk. 'We are all in this together,' he says of his US rivals. 'We wish them the best.'

(BPP emphasis)

Klex Taylor III, Fortune, 19 March 2007

2.1.3 Stakeholder risks

Stakeholder	Interests to defend	Response to risk
Internal Managers and employees (eg restructuring, relocation)	• Jobs/careers • Money • Promotion • Benefits • Satisfaction	• Pursuit of systems goals rather than shareholder interests • Industrial action • Negative power to impede implementation • Refusal to relocate • Resignation
Connected Shareholders (corporate strategy)	• Increase in shareholder wealth, measured by profitability, P/E ratios, market capitalisation, dividends and yield • Risk	• Sell shares (eg to predator) or replace management
Bankers (cash flows)	• Security of loan • Adherence to loan agreements	• Denial of credit • Higher interest charges • Receivership
Suppliers (purchase strategy)	• Profitable sales • Payment for goods • Long-term relationship	• Refusal of credit • Court action • Wind down relationships
Customers (product market strategy)	• Goods as promised • Future benefits	• Buy elsewhere • Sue
External Government	• Jobs, training, tax	• Tax increases • Regulation • Legal action
Interest/pressure groups	• Pollution • Rights • Other	• Publicity • Direct action • Sabotage • Pressure on government

How stakeholders relate to the management of the company depends very much on what **type of stakeholder** they are – internal, connected or external – and on the **level in the management hierarchy** at which they are able to apply pressure. Clearly a company's management will respond differently to the demands of, say, its shareholders and the community at large.

2.2 Balancing priorities

Cyert and March suggest that a business is actually run in the interests of an **organisational coalition** of stakeholders. Political processes managed by the strategic apex lead to a compromise on what the company's goals actually are. This usually results in a satisficing approach to balance the various priorities.

2.3 Stakeholder theory

We may discern two extreme approaches to stakeholder theory for profit-orientated business organisations.

Strong view	Weak view
Each stakeholder in the business has a legitimate claim on management attention. Management's job is to balance stakeholder demands.	Satisfying stakeholders such as customers *is* a good thing – but only because it enables the business to satisfy its primary purpose, the long term growth in owner wealth.

2.3.1 Problems with the strong stakeholder view

(a)   Managers who are accountable to everyone are, in fact, accountable to none.

(b)   If managers are required to balance different stakeholders' interests there is a danger that they will favour their own interests.

(c)   It confuses a stakeholder's interest in a firm with a person's citizenship of a state.

(d)   People have interests, but this does not give them rights.

2.4 Managing stakeholders

FAST FORWARD

An organisation's stakeholder relationships must be managed in accordance with their bargaining strength, influence, power and degree of interest. *Mendelow* summarises the possibilities in his stakeholder map. Stakeholders have three options: loyalty, exit and voice.

The way in which the relationship between company and stakeholders is conducted is a function of the parties' **relative bargaining strength** and the philosophy underlying **each party's objectives**. This can be shown by means of a spectrum.

2.4.1 Stakeholder mapping

Mendelow classifies stakeholders on a matrix whose axes are power held and likelihood of showing an interest in the organisation's activities. These factors will help define the type of relationship the organisation should seek with its stakeholders.

(a) **Key players** are found in segment D: strategy must be *acceptable* to them, at least. An example would be a major customer.

(b) Stakeholders in segment C must be treated with care. While often passive, they are capable of moving to segment D. They should, therefore be **kept satisfied.** Large institutional shareholders might fall into segment C.

(c) Stakeholders in segment B do not have great ability to influence strategy, but their views can be important in influencing more powerful stakeholders, perhaps by lobbying. They should therefore be **kept informed.** Community representatives and charities might fall into segment B.

(d) Minimal effort is expended on segment A.

Stakeholder mapping is used to assess the significance of stakeholder groups. This in turn has implications for the organisation.

(a) The framework of **corporate governance** should recognise stakeholders' levels of interest and power.

(b) It may be appropriate to seek to **reposition** certain stakeholders and discourage others from repositioning themselves, depending on their attitudes.

(c) Key **blockers** and **facilitators** of change must be identified.

Stakeholder mapping can also be used to establish **political priorities**. A map of the current position can be compared with a map of a desired future state. This will indicate critical shifts that must be pursued.

Exam focus point

Stakeholders and their influence are regular features of business strategy exam questions. An old syllabus question asked about stakeholder power and mentioned the Mendelow Matrix by name. It is always useful to at least mention specific theoretical models that are relevant to your answer if you can.

2.4.2 The internal and external coalitions

In *Power In and Around Organisations*, *Mintzberg* identifies groups that not only have an **interest** in an organisation but **power** over it.

The external coalition	The internal coalition
• Owners (who hold legal title)	• The chief executive and board at the strategic apex
• Associates (suppliers, customers, trading partners)	• Line managers
• Employee associations (unions, professional bodies)	• Operators
	• The technostructure
• Public (government, media)	• Support staff
	• Ideology (ie culture)

Each of these groups has three basic choices.

(a) **Loyalty**. They can do as they are told.

(b) **Exit**. For example by selling their shares, or getting a new job.

(c) **Voice**. They can stay and try to change the system. Those who choose **voice** are those who can, to varying degrees, influence the organisation. Influence implies a degree of power and willingness to exercise it.

Existing **structures and systems** can **channel stakeholder influence.**

(a)   They are the **location of power**, giving groups of people varying degrees of influence over strategic choices.

(b)   They are **conduits of information**, which shape strategic decisions.

(c)   They **limit choices** or give some options priority over others. These may be physical or ethical constraints over what is possible.

(d)   They **embody culture**.

(e)   They **determine the successful implementation** of strategy.

(f)   The **firm has different degrees of dependency** on various stakeholder groups. A company with a cash flow crisis will be more beholden to its bankers than one with regular cash surpluses.

Different stakeholders will have their own views as to strategy. As some stakeholders have **negative power**, in other words power to impede or disrupt the decision, their likely response might be considered. Note that this would be expected in the light of the **partisan mutual adjustment model** of decision making.

2.5 Corporate social responsibility

FAST FORWARD

> The extent to which an organisation recognises obligations to society in general is as much subject to debate as is its relationships with stakeholder groups.

Businesses, particularly large ones, are subject to increasing expectations that they will exercise **social responsibility**. This is an ill-defined concept, but appears to focus on the provision of **specific benefits to society in general**, such as charitable donations, the creation or preservation of employment, and spending on environmental improvement or maintenance. A great deal of the pressure is created by the activity of minority action groups and is aimed at businesses because they are perceived to possess extensive resources. The momentum of such arguments is now so great that the notion of social responsibility has become almost inextricably confused with the matter of ethics. It is important to remember the distinction. **Social responsibility** and **ethical behaviour** are **not the same thing**.

In this context, you should remember that a business managed with the sole objective of maximising shareholder wealth can be run in just as ethical a fashion as one in which far wider stakeholder responsibility is assumed. On the other hand, there is no doubt that many large businesses have behaved irresponsibly in the past and some continue to do so.

2.6 Against corporate social responsibility

Milton Friedman argued against corporate social responsibility along the following lines.

(a)   Businesses do not have responsibilities, only people have responsibilities. Managers in charge of corporations are responsible to the owners of the business, by whom they are employed.

(b)   These employers may have charity as their aim, but 'generally [their aim] will be to make as much money as possible while conforming to the basic rules of the society, both those embodied in law and those embodied in ethical custom.'

(c)   If the statement that a manager has social responsibilities is to have any meaning, 'it must mean that he is to act in some way that is not in the interest of his employers.'

(d)   If managers do this they are, generally speaking, spending the owners' money for purposes other than those they have authorised; sometimes it is the money of customers or suppliers that is spent and, on occasion, the money of employees. By doing this, the manager is, in effect, both raising taxes and deciding how they should be spent, which are functions of government, not of business. There are two objections to this.

(i)   Managers have not been democratically elected (or selected in any other way) to exercise government power.

(ii)   Managers are not experts in government policy and cannot foresee the detailed effect of such social responsibility spending.

Friedman argues that the social responsibility model is politically **collectivist** in nature and deplores the possibility that collectivism should be extended any further than absolutely necessary in a free society.

A second argument against the assumption of corporate social responsibility is that the **maximisation of wealth is the best way that society can benefit from a business's activities**.

(a)   Maximising wealth has the effect of increasing the tax revenues available to the state to disburse on socially desirable objectives.

(b)   Maximising shareholder value has a 'trickle down' effect on other disadvantaged members of society.

(c)   Many company shares are owned by pension funds, whose ultimate beneficiaries may not be the wealthy anyway.

2.7 The stakeholder approach to corporate social responsibility

The **stakeholder approach is based on the premise** that many groups have a stake in what the organisation does. This is particularly important in the business context, where shareholders own the business but employees, customers and government also have particularly strong claims to having their interests considered. This is fundamentally an argument derived from **natural law theory** and is based on the notion of individual and collective **rights**.

It is suggested that modern corporations are so powerful, socially, economically and politically, that **unrestrained use of their power will inevitably damage other people's rights**. For example, they may blight an entire community by closing a major facility, thus enforcing long term unemployment on a large proportion of the local workforce. Similarly, they may damage people's quality of life by polluting the environment. They may use their purchasing power or market share to impose unequal contracts on suppliers and customers alike. And they may exercise undesirable influence over government through their investment decisions. Under this approach, the exercise of corporate social responsibility constrains the corporation to act at all times as a good citizen.

Another argument points out that corporations exist within society and are **dependent upon it for the resources they use**. Some of these resources are obtained by direct contracts with suppliers but others are not, being provided by **government expenditure**. Examples are such things as transport infrastructure, technical research and education for the workforce. Clearly, corporations contribute to the taxes that pay for these things, but the relationship is rather tenuous and the tax burden can be minimised by careful management. The implication is that corporations should recognise and pay for the facilities that society provides by means of socially responsible policies and actions.

Henry Mintzberg (in *Power In and Around Organisations*) suggests that simply viewing organisations as vehicles for shareholder investment is inadequate.

(a)   In practice, he says, organisations are rarely controlled effectively by shareholders. Most shareholders are passive investors.

(b)   Large corporations can manipulate markets. Social responsibility, forced or voluntary, is a way of recognising this.

(c)   Moreover, as mentioned above, businesses do receive a lot of government support. The public pays for roads, infrastructure, education and health, all of which benefits businesses. Although businesses pay tax, the public ultimately pays, perhaps through higher prices.

(d)   Strategic decisions by businesses always have wider social consequences. In other words, says Mintzberg, the firm produces two kinds of outputs: **goods and services** and the **social consequences of its activities** (eg pollution).

2.8 Externalities

FAST FORWARD

There is particular concern over **externalities**, or the social and environmental costs of corporate activities.

If it is accepted that businesses do not bear the total social cost of their activities, then the exercise of social responsibility is a way of compensating for this. An example is given by the environment. Industrial pollution is injurious to health: if someone is made ill by industrial pollution, then arguably the polluter should pay the sick person, as damages or in compensation, in the same way as if the business's builders had accidentally bulldozed somebody's house.

In practice, of course, while it is relatively easy to identify statistical relationships between pollution levels and certain illnesses, mapping out the chain of cause and effect from an individual's wheezing cough to the dust particles emitted by Factory X, as opposed to Factory Y, is quite a different matter.

Of course, it could be argued that these external costs are met out of general taxation: but this has the effect of spreading the cost amongst other individuals and businesses. Moreover, the tax revenue may be spent on curing the disease, rather than stopping it at its source. Pollution control equipment may be the fairest way of dealing with this problem. Thus advocates of social responsibility in business would argue that business's responsibilities then do not rest with paying taxes.

Is there any justification for social responsibility outside remedying the effects of a business's direct activities. For example, should businesses give to charity or sponsor the arts? Several arguments have been advanced suggesting that they should.

(a)   If the **stakeholder concept** of a business is held, then the public is a stakeholder in the business. A business only succeeds because it is part of a wider society. Giving to charity is one way of encouraging a relationship.

(b)   Charitable donations and artistic sponsorship are a useful medium of **public relations** and can reflect well on the business. It can be regarded, then, as another form of promotion, which like advertising, serves to enhance consumer awareness of the business, while not encouraging the sale of a particular brand.

The arguments for and against social responsibility of business are complex ones. However, ultimately they can be traced to **different assumptions about society** and the relationships between the individuals and organisations within it.

Exam focus point

> The old syllabus Paper 3.5 June 2002 examination approached the idea of social responsibility from an unusual direction, asking for a discussion of the topic in relation to a hospital, rather than the usual commercial organisation. The problem here is that it becomes necessary to stand most of the arguments on their heads, since there is no doubt that considerations other than economic success are crucial to such an organisation. You must be prepared to **think** in the exam hall.

BPP
LEARNING MEDIA

2.9 The ethical stance

FAST FORWARD

An organisation's **ethical stance** is the extent to which it will exceed its minimum obligations to stakeholders. There are four typical stances.

- Short-term shareholder interest
- Long-term shareholder interest
- Multiple stakeholder obligations
- Shaper of society

Key term

An organisation's **ethical stance** is defined by *JS&W* as the extent to which it will exceed its minimum obligation to stakeholders and society at large.

JS&W illustrate the range of possible ethical stances by giving four illustrations.

- **Short-term shareholder interest**
- **Long-term shareholder interest**
- **Multiple stakeholder obligations**
- **Shaper of society**

2.10 Short-term shareholder interest

An organisation might limit its ethical stance to taking responsibility for **short-term shareholder interest** on the grounds that it is for **government** alone to impose wider constraints on corporate governance. This minimalist approach would accept a duty of obedience to the demands of the law, but would not undertake to comply with any less substantial rules of conduct. This stance can be justified on the grounds that going beyond it can **challenge government authority**; this is an important consideration for organisations operating in developing countries.

2.10.1 Long-term shareholder interest

There are two reasons why an organisation might take a wider view of ethical responsibilities when considering the **longer-term interest of shareholders**.

(a)   The organisation's **corporate image** may be enhanced by an assumption of wider responsibilities. The cost of undertaking such responsibilities may be justified as essentially promotional expenditure.

Case Study

The *Cooperative Bank* has estimated that it made £40m profit in 2003 as a result of its ethical policies.

Research showed that the Bank's ethical stance attracted business far in excess of that lost by turning away customers with poor human rights records or weak environmental performance.

(b)   The responsible exercise of corporate power may prevent a build-up of social and political **pressure for legal regulation**. Freedom of action may be preserved and the burden of regulation lightened by acceptance of ethical responsibilities.

2.10.2 Multiple stakeholder obligations

An organisation might accept the **legitimacy of the expectations of stakeholders other than shareholders** and build those expectations into its stated purposes. This would be because without appropriate relationships with groups such as suppliers, employers and customers, the organisation would not be able to function.

A distinction can be drawn between **rights** and **expectations**. The *Concise Oxford Dictionary* defines a right as 'a legal or moral entitlement'. One is on fairly safe interpretative ground with legal rights, since their basis is usually clearly established, though subject to development and adjustment. The concept of *moral* entitlement is much less well defined and subject to partisan argument, as discussed above in the context of **natural law**. There is, for instance, an understandable tendency for those who feel themselves aggrieved to declare that their *rights* have been infringed. Whether or not this is the case is often a matter of opinion. For example, in the UK, there is often talk of a 'right to work' when redundancies occur. No such right exists in UK law, nor is it widely accepted that there is a moral basis for such a right. However, there is a widespread acceptance that governments should make the prevention of large-scale unemployment a high priority.

Clearly, organisations have a duty to respect the **legal rights** of stakeholders other than shareholders. These are extensive in the UK, including wide-ranging **employment law** and **consumer protection law**, as well as the more basic legislation relating to such matters as contract and property. Where **moral entitlements** are concerned, organisations need to be practical: they should take care to establish just what *expectations* they are prepared to treat as *obligations*, bearing in mind their general ethical stance and degree of concern about bad publicity.

Acceptance of obligations to stakeholders implies that **measurement of the organisation's performance** must give due weight to these extra imperatives. For instance, as is widely known, *Anita Roddick* does not care to have the performance of *Body Shop* assessed in purely financial terms.

2.10.3 Shaper of society

It is difficult enough for a commercial organisation to accept wide responsibility to stakeholders. The role of **shaper of society** is even more demanding and largely the province of public sector organisations and charities, though some well-funded private organisations might act in this way. The legitimacy of this approach depends on the framework of corporate governance and accountability. Where organisations are clearly set up for such a role, either by government or by private sponsors, they may pursue it. However, they must also satisfy whatever requirements for financial viability are established for them.

3 Corporate governance

FAST FORWARD

> **Corporate governance** is the conduct of the organisation's senior officers. Abuses have led to a range of measures to improve corporate governance. Non-executive directors have a particular role to play.

Key term

> The conduct of an organisation's senior officers constitutes its **corporate governance**.

3.1 The governance framework

JS&W say that the most fundamental expectations of organisations concern who they should serve and how their direction and purposes should be determined. This is the province of corporate governance, which is also concerned with the supervision and accountability of executives.

Key term

> The **governance framework** describes whom the organisation is there to serve and how the purposes and priorities of the organisation should be decided.
>
> *JS&W*

3.1.1 The governance chain

FAST FORWARD

> Where the management of a business is separated from its ownership by the employment of professional managers, the managers may be considered to be the agents of the owners. **Agency theory** is concerned with adverse selection and moral hazard, the problems that arise as a result of the separation of ownership and control. In many organisations, corporate governance takes the form of a chain of responsibility and accountability.

Few large businesses are directly managed by their owners. In the case of larger companies, the shareholders may numerous and unlikely to wish to take part in the management of the company, viewing it simply as a vehicle for investment. Even where ownership is concentrated, large companies tend to be managed mostly by professional managers who have little ownership interest, if any.

In most large commercial organisations, the situation is even more complex in that governance is exercised through many links in a chain. Managers are accountable to more senior managers and so on up to the board of directors. The directors enjoy an element of autonomy, but in many cases they will effectively be accountable to the representatives of a few large institutional shareholders or perhaps those of a single venture capital company. The chain of accountability may then continue, with those representatives themselves accountable ultimately to the individual savers and investors that provide their funds.

This **separation of ownership from control** has been a feature of business for over a century and brings with it a recurring problem: the business should be managed so as to promote the economic interest of the shareholders as a body, but the power to manage lies in the hands of people who may use it to promote their own interests. How may such **conflicts of interest** be resolved and managers be made to favour the interest of the owners rather than their own?

This problem is not confined to the management of companies: it is the general problem of the **agency relationship** and occurs whenever one person (the **principal**) gives another (the **agent**) power to deal with his affairs. The relationship between principal and agent has been subjected to some quite abstruse economic and mathematical analysis; this area of study is called **agency theory**. It proceeds on the basis that principals and agents are rational utility maximisers.

Two important concepts are used to explain the things that can go wrong in the agency relationship: **adverse selection** and **moral hazard**.

Key term

> **Adverse selection** is the making of poor choices. It occurs perhaps most often because the chooser lacks the information necessary to make a good choice.

Adverse selection can be exacerbated in the agency relationship when the agent has an incentive to withhold information from the principal, thus creating **information asymmetry**. We see this in two important instances.

(a) **Appointment of the agent**: the principal attempts to appoint a competent and trustworthy agent, but potential agents thus have an incentive to conceal any evidence there may be that they are incompetent or untrustworthy.

(b) **Assessing the agent's performance**: the principal desires to reward the agent according to the standard of his performance, but the agent controls or is able to influence the information the principal uses to assess that performance.

Disclosure is thus a major them in corporate governance.

Key term

> **Moral hazard** arises whenever people are protected from the adverse consequences of their actions; they have no incentive to exercise correct judgement and are free to act in an irresponsible manner.

To protect a person from the adverse consequences of his behaviour is to encourage irresponsibility, hence the moral dimension of the concept.

Moral hazard is not confined to principal-agent relationships. It occurs in banking, for example, when government guarantee schemes allow bankers to make injudicious loans.

In the agency relationship, we are concerned with the use the agent makes of the authority with which he has been entrusted. Moral hazard will exist unless at least part of the agent's remuneration is contingent upon his making responsible use of his authority.

Agency theory is clearly relevant to the modern business organisation. The directors are the agents of the shareholders, employed to manage the business in the shareholders' interest. To do this they are given considerable power over the resources of the business. How can the shareholders be sure that they will not abuse this trust?

To a lesser extent, agency theory also applies within the organisation. The directors cannot do everything: as we have said, they must employ subordinate managers to put their plans into action. How can the directors be sure that those subordinates are not abusing their trust? They rely to an increasing extent on the initiative, skills, creativity and enthusiasm of quite junior members of the organisation, since this is what creates competitive advantage. They also depend on both motivating and empowering these employees. Therefore, the issue of trust comes to prominence.

Agency theory is thus very relevant to the fields of both performance measurement and executive compensation. **Moral hazard** can be reduced by making the rewards paid to the directors and managers contingent upon their satisfactory performance: the information asymmetry that leads to **adverse selection** can be reduced by making proper information about that performance available to the shareholders (in the case of the directors) and to the directors (in the case of the subordinate managers).

3.1.2 The board of directors

FAST FORWARD

There are four models of governance.

1   The Anglo-Saxon model is fast in action but may be short-termist and unresponsive to external criticism.

2   The Rhine model has more robust governance and takes a long view of investment.

3   The Japanese model values consensus, takes a very long view and makes decisions slowly. Accountability and governance may be poor.

4   The Latin model emphasises the role of the state: investment is likely to be for the very long-term but governance may suffer from political activity.

Most organisations will have some kind of governing body. In the private sector we are used to the concept of the board of directors; not for profit organisations are likely to have a board of trustees and, possibly, an executive committee of professional managers as well; while public sector organisations will usually have a similar body in overall charge.

The characteristics, role and functioning of boards of directors vary across the world: *Michel Albert* distinguishes three typical forms of corporate governance: the **Anglo-Saxon**, the **Rhine** and the **Japanese**. The first differs from the other two in that shares in such companies tend to be widely held in small quantities, which tends to permit significant autonomy to a small number of senior managers. In the other two models, top management is more **collective** in nature involving a larger team, and is responsible to a more stable body representing outside interests, such as founding family shareholders and trade unions in the Rhine model and large institutions in the Japanese models.

JS&W discuss a fourth model: this is the **Latin**, typical of France, Spain and Italy.

The Anglo-Saxon model

The Anglo-Saxon model is found in the UK, the USA and Australasia. There is a single level of board membership, which includes both executive and non-executive directors. The effectiveness of the non-executive directors in curbing the power of the executives varies. The wide spread of shareholding found in many large companies tends to limit the power of individual shareholders, though major institutional shareholders such as pension funds are becoming more assertive.

Corporate finance emphasises the dominant position of equity and relationships with banks tend to be contractually-based. This can lead to difficulties, since banks' own commercial considerations may lead them to withdraw funds. Shareholders thus assume most of the burden of financial risk and limit the extent of gearing as a result.

This kind of company tends to be very market-oriented, internationalised and able to raise and use large amounts of capital. However, it has been criticised for being unstable, for taking a short-term view of strategy and for poor standards of corporate governance.

The Rhine model

The Rhine model is found in such countries as Germany, The Netherlands and Switzerland; and, to some extent, in France. The two-tier board is common (and may be mandatory), with strong employee representation on the supervisory board and an emphasis on co-determination, or joint decision-making. There are robust procedures for corporate governance The supervisory board restrains the autonomy of the managerial professionals on the lower tier board.

Such companies have a long-term strategy with stable capital investment policies. However, they tend to be inflexible and slow to invest in new industries and international projects.

The Japanese model

Japanese business culture is respectful of consensus and rather patriarchal. Promotion to the board is decided by the Chairman after consultation, often with interested external parties such as bankers. Directors are expected to promote the interests of employees as a matter of course. Governance procedures tend to be secretive and can be corrupt, with weak accountability. A very long view is taken of industrial strategy and capital investment is stable, though there can be an element of financial speculation. Decision-making can be very slow.

Banks have extensive shareholdings as well as making loans and take a close interest in the management of the companies they finance. In times of difficulty they are more likely to promote change rather than simply withdrawing funds.

The Latin model

The Latin model features heavy state involvement in business and industrial strategy, with consistency between political, economic and administrative goals. Investment is very stable. However, government involvement can lead to over-emphasis on political priorities and over-intimate relations between directors, politicians and civil servants.

3.1.3 Governance and strategy

FAST FORWARD

The board must decide the extent of its involvement in the strategic process. If it decides on a stewardship role it must ensure that the organisation's activity is not directed to management's own ends rather than those of legitimate stakeholders. If it engages in the strategic process it must act independently of management and in a competent fashion.

Directors' involvement in the making of strategy may be limited to a stewardship role in which the board delegates the process to full-time executives, retaining only a final approval role. When this is done, the board must take steps to prevent the executives from pursuing their own interest rather than those of legitimate stakeholders.

There are a number of ways in which the board can engage in the strategic process: some of these are discussed elsewhere in this Study Text. Directors who take part in the making of strategy must be competent and have sufficient time to do so. They must ensure that they act independently in the interests of stakeholders and pay proper attention to personal and collective accountability and performance assessment.

3.2 The driving forces of governance development

Corporate governance issues came to prominence in the USA during the 1970s and in the UK and Europe from the late 1980s. There were several reasons why this happened.

(a) **Increasing internationalisation and globalisation** meant that investors, and institutional investors in particular, began to invest outside their home countries. This lead to calls for companies to operate in an acceptable fashion and to report corporate performance fairly.

(b) Issues concerning **financial reporting** were raised by many investors and were the focus of much debate and litigation. Shareholder confidence in many instances was eroded and, while focus solely on accounting and reporting issues is inadequate, the regulation of practices such as off-balance sheet financing has led to greater transparency and a reduction in risks faced by investors.

(c) An increasing number of **high profile corporate scandals** and collapses including *Polly Peck International*, *BCCI*, and *Maxwell Communications Corporation* prompted the development of governance codes in the early 1990s. However the scandals since then have raised questions about further measures that may be necessary.

3.3 Features of poor corporate governance

The scandals over the last 25 years have highlighted the need for guidance to tackle the various risks and problems that can arise in organisations' systems of governance.

3.3.1 Domination by a single individual

A feature of many corporate governance scandals has been boards dominated by a single senior executive with other board members merely acting as a rubber stamp. Sometimes the single individual may bypass the board to action his own interests. The report on the UK *Guinness* case suggested that the Chief Executive, *Ernest Saunders* paid himself a £3 million reward without consulting the other directors.

3.3.2 Lack of involvement of board

Boards that meet irregularly or fail to consider systematically the organisation's activities and risks are clearly weak. Sometimes the failure to carry out proper oversight is due to a **lack of information** being provided.

3.3.3 Lack of adequate control function

An obvious weakness is a **lack of internal audit.**

Another important control is **lack of adequate technical knowledge** in key roles, for example in the audit committee or in senior compliance positions. A rapid turnover of staff involved in accounting or control may suggest inadequate resourcing, and will make control more difficult because of lack of continuity.

3.3.4 Lack of supervision

Employees who are not properly supervised can create large losses for the organisation through their own incompetence, negligence or fraudulent activity. The behaviour of *Nick Leeson*, the employee who caused the collapse of *Barings* bank was not challenged because he appeared to be successful, whereas he was using unauthorised accounts to cover up his large trading losses. Leeson was able to do this because he was in charge of both dealing and settlement, a systems weakness or **lack of segregation of key roles** that featured in other financial frauds.

3.3.5 Lack of independent scrutiny

External auditors may not carry out the necessary questioning of senior management because of fears of losing the audit, and internal audit do not ask awkward questions because the chief financial officer determines their employment prospects. Often corporate collapses are followed by criticisms of external auditors, such as the *Barlow Clowes* affair, where poorly planned and focused audit work failed to identify illegal use of client monies.

3.3.6 Lack of contact with shareholders

Often board members may have grown up with the company but lose touch with the interests and views of shareholders. One possible symptom of this is the payment of remuneration packages that do not appear to be warranted by results.

3.3.7 Emphasis on short-term profitability

Emphasis on short-term results can lead to the **concealment of problems or errors,** or **manipulation of accounts** to **achieve desired results**.

3.3.8 Misleading accounts and information

Often misleading figures are symptomatic of other problems (or are designed to conceal other problems) but in many cases, poor quality accounting information is a major problem if markets are trying to make a fair assessment of the company's value. Giving out misleading information was a major issue in the UK's *Equitable Life* scandal where the company gave contradictory information to savers, independent advisers, media and regulators.

3.4 Risks of poor corporate governance

Clearly, the ultimate risk is of the organisation **making such large losses** that **bankruptcy** becomes inevitable. The organisation may also be closed down as a result of **serious regulatory breaches,** for example misapplying investors' monies.

4 The role of culture

Culture is important both in organisations and in the wider world. It is the knowledge, beliefs, customs and attitudes which people adhere to. In wider society it is affected by factors such as age, class, race and religion, while in organisations it is defined by assumptions, beliefs and artefacts. These, in turn, are influenced by history, management, structure and systems. The organisational iceberg concept show how culture relates to other aspects of the organisation. The **paradigm** is the common, basic assumptions and beliefs held by an organisation's decision-makers. Combined with the physical manifestations of culture, it makes up the **cultural web**.

4.1 Organisational culture

Key term

> The word, **culture** is used by sociologists and anthropologists to encompass 'the sum total of the beliefs, knowledge, attitudes of mind and customs to which people are exposed in their social conditioning.'

Through contact with a particular culture, individuals learn a language, acquire values and learn **habits of behaviour and thought**.

(a) **Beliefs and values**. Beliefs are what we feel to be the case on the basis of objective and subjective information (eg people can believe the world is round or flat). Values are beliefs which are relatively enduring, relatively general and fairly widely accepted as a guide to culturally appropriate behaviour.

(b) **Customs.** Customs are modes of behaviour which represent culturally accepted ways of behaving in response to given situations.

(c) **Artefacts.** Artefacts are all the physical tools designed by human beings for their physical and psychological well-being, including works of art, technology, products.

(d) **Rituals.** A ritual is a type of activity which takes on symbolic meaning; it consists of a fixed sequence of behaviour repeated over time.

The learning and sharing of culture is made possible by **language** (both written and spoken, verbal and non-verbal).

Knowledge of the culture of a society is clearly of value to businesses in a number of ways.

(a) **Marketers** can adapt their products accordingly, and be fairly sure of a sizeable market. This is particularly important in export markets.

(b) **Human resource managers** may need to tackle cultural differences in recruitment. For example, some ethnic minorities have a different body language from the majority, which may be hard for some interviewers to interpret.

Culture in a society can be divided into **subcultures** reflecting social differences. Most people participate in several of them.

Key term

> **Organisational culture** consists of the beliefs, attitudes, practices and customs to which people are exposed during their interaction with the organisation.

Culture is both internal to an organisation and external to it. The culture of an organisation is embedded in the culture of the wider society. Its importance to strategy is that it can predispose the organisation towards or away from a particular course of action.

All organisations will generate their own cultures, whether spontaneously or under the guidance of positive managerial strategy. *Schein* suggests that three aspects of culture can be distinguished in organisations.

(a) **Basic, underlying assumptions** which guide the behaviour of the individuals and groups in the organisation. These may include customer orientation, or belief in quality, trust in the organisation to provide rewards, freedom to make decisions, freedom to make mistakes and the value of innovation and initiative at all levels.

(b) **Overt beliefs** expressed by the organisation and its members, which can be used to condition the assumptions mentioned above. These beliefs and values may emerge as sayings, slogans and mottoes, such as IBM's motto, 'think'. They may emerge in a rich mythology of jokes and stories about past successes and heroic failures.

(c) **Visible artefacts** – the style of the offices or other premises, dress rules, visible structures or processes, the degree of informality between superiors and subordinates and so on.

Management can encourage this by selling a sense of the corporate mission, or by promoting the corporate image. It can reward the right attitudes and punish (or simply not employ) those who are not prepared to commit themselves to the culture.

An organisation's culture is influenced by many factors.

(a) **The organisation's founder**. A strong set of values and assumptions is set up by the organisation's founder, and even after he or she has retired, these values have their own momentum. Or, to put it another way, an organisation might find it hard to shake off its original culture. *Peters and Waterman* believed that 'excellent' companies began with strong leaders.

(b) **The organisation's history**. *Johnson and Scholes* state that the way an organisation works reflects the era when it was founded. Farming, for example, sometimes has a craft element to it. The effect of history can be determined by stories, rituals and symbolic behaviour. They legitimise behaviour and promote priorities. (In some organisations certain positions are regarded as intrinsically more 'heroic' than others.)

(c) **Leadership and management style**. An organisation with a strong culture recruits managers who naturally conform to it.

(d) **Structure and systems** affect culture as well as strategy.

4.2 The organisational iceberg

French and Bell described the **organisational iceberg** in which formal aspects are **overt** and informal aspects are **covert** or hidden, rather as the bulk of an iceberg is underwater.

Formal aspects

- Goals
- Terminology
- Structure
- Policies and procedures
- Products
- Financial resources

Informal aspects

- Beliefs and assumptions
- Perceptions, attitudes and feelings about the formal systems
- Values
- Informal interactions
- Group norms

A similar analysis was presented by *Hellriegel, Slocum and Woodman*.

4.3 The paradigm and the cultural web

4.3.1 The paradigm

The word **paradigm** was first used outside its original context by *Kuhn* and defined by him as 'an entire constellation of beliefs, values and techniques, and so on, shared by the members of a given community'. In a business context, it may be used to signify the **basic assumptions and beliefs** that an organisation's decision-makers **hold in common** and **take for granted**. Note that this is a slightly different concept from

culture. The paradigm represents **collective experience** and is used to make sense of a given situation; it is thus essentially conservative and inhibiting to innovation, while an innovative **culture** is entirely feasible.

4.3.2 The cultural web

Johnson and Scholes use the term **cultural web** to mean a combination of the assumptions that make up the **paradigm**, together with the **physical manifestations** of culture.

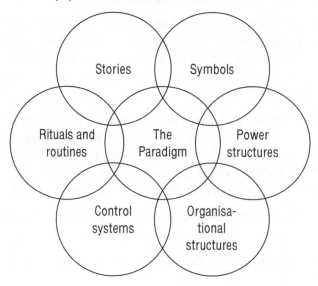

The cultural web

The cultural web model may be used to gain an understanding of an organisation's culture and thence the way its members **behave** and how its strategy develops. JS&W suggest that careful examination of each aspect of the web may lead to a brief summary of an organisation in cultural terms. Culture tends to be fairly simple, though manifested in complex ways: different but consistent elements may be discerned by investigating each constituent of the cultural web.

4.4 Culture and structure

> Harrison's four-fold classification of organisations, popularised by Handy, is a useful analysis of some common aspects of culture.
>
> - The **power** culture depends on the holder of centralised power.
> - The **role** culture is associated with bureaucracy and emphasises rules and procedures.
> - The **task** culture is focused on delivering the current goal.
> - The **existential** culture supports individual independence and aspiration.

Writing in 1972, *Roger Harrison* suggested that organisations could be classified into four types. His work was later popularised by *Charles Handy* in his book 'Gods of Management'. The four types are differentiated by their structures, processes and management methods. The differences are so significant as to create distinctive cultures, to each of which Handy gives the name of a Greek god.

Zeus is the god representing the **power culture**. Zeus is a dynamic entrepreneur who rules with snap decisions. Power and influence stem from a central source, perhaps the owner-directors or the founder of the business. The degree of formalisation is limited, and there are few rules and procedures, though this does not prevent the power-holders from exercising strict control. Such a firm is likely to be organised on a **functional** basis.

(a)   The organisation is capable of adapting quickly to meet change.

(b)   Personal influence decreases as the size of an organisation gets bigger. **The power culture is therefore best suited to smaller entrepreneurial organisations, where the leaders have direct communication with all employees**.

(c)   Subordinates succeed by successfully guessing how their superiors would want them to act.

Apollo is the god of the **role culture** or **bureaucracy**. Everything is orderly and legitimate. There is a presumption of **logic and rationality**.

(a)   These organisations have a formal hierarchical structure, and operate by well-established rules and procedures. Individuals are required to perform their job to the full, but not to overstep the boundaries of their authority. Individuals who work for such organisations tend to learn an expertise without experiencing risk; many do their job adequately, but are not over-ambitious.

(b)   **The bureaucratic style can be very efficient** in a stable environment, when the organisation is large and when the work is predictable.

Athena is the goddess of the **task culture.** Management is dedicated to achieving the current goal. Performance is judged by results.

(a)   The task culture is reflected in project teams and task forces. In such organisations, **there is no dominant or clear leader. The principal concern in a task culture is to get the job done**. Therefore the individuals who are important are the **experts** with the ability to accomplish a particular aspect of the task.

(b)   The task culture is well suited to complex, unstable environments.

(c)   Task cultures are expensive, as experts demand a market price.

(d)   Task cultures also depend on variety, and to tap creativity requires a tolerance of perhaps costly mistakes.

Dionysus is the god of the **existential culture**. In the three other cultures, the individual is subordinate to the organisation or task. **An existential culture is found in an organisation whose purpose is to serve the interests of the individuals within it**. These organisations are rare, although an example might be a partnership of a few individuals who do all the work of the organisation themselves (with perhaps a little secretarial or clerical assistance).

(a)   Barristers (in the UK) work through chambers. The clerk co-ordinates their work and hands out briefs, but does not control them.

(b)   Management in these organisations are often lower in status than the professionals and are labelled secretaries, administrators, bursars, registrars and chief clerk.

(c)   The organisation depends on the **talent of the individuals;** management is derived from the consent of the managed, rather than the delegated authority of the owners.

The descriptions above interrelate four different strands.

- The individual
- The type of the work the organisation does
- The culture of the organisation
- The environment

Organisational effectiveness perhaps depends on an appropriate fit of all of them.

Exam focus point

> Harrison's typology is really as much about structure and process as it is about culture. However, it is probably the best known of the various analyses of organisational culture and has been useful in many past questions, especially as a source of salient comment and suggestion worth one or two marks.

Case Study

Handy cites a pharmaceutical company which at one time had all its manufacturing subcontracted, until turnover and cost considerations justified a factory of its own. The company hired nine talented individuals to design and run the factory. Result:

(a)   The *design team* ran on a task culture, with a democratic/consultative leadership style, using project teams for certain problems. This was successful while the factory was being built.

(b)   After its opening, the factory, staffed by 400, was run on similar lines. There were numerous problems. Every problem was treated as a project, and the workforce resented being asked to help sort out 'management' problems. In the end, the factory was run in a slightly more autocratic way. Handy states that this is a classic case of an *Athenian* culture to create a factory being superseded by an *Apollonian* culture to run it. Different cultures suit different businesses.

Question

Which of Harrison's cultures would you say is prevalent in your office?

Question

Review the following statements. Ascribe each of them to one of the four approaches.

People are controlled and influenced by:

* the personal exercise of rewards, punishments or charisma;
* the impersonal exercise of economic and political power to enforce procedures and standards of performance;
* communication and discussion of task requirements leading to appropriate action, motivated by personal commitment, to achieve the goal;
* intrinsic interest and enjoyment in the activities to be done, and/or concern and caring for the needs of the other people involved.

Answer

* Power
* Role
* Task
* Existential

4.5 Culture, the environment and strategy

FAST FORWARD

Culture colours the organisation's view of its environment and hence influences its strategy. **Defenders** like low risk solutions and niche markets. **Prospectors** are more adventurous and concerned with results. **Analysers** try to balance risk and profits. **Reactors** do not have viable strategies. Deal and Kennedy analyse culture in terms of inherent risk in the industry and the speed with which feedback is available on strategic decisions. Denison assesses culture in terms of strategic orientation and environmental dynamism.

Culture is an important filter of information and an interpreter of it, as suggested in the diagrams below.

- Ignoring culture

- Including culture

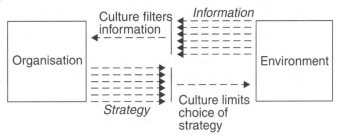

Culture filters and reconfigures environmental information. (A tragic example is the events in Waco, where members of the Branch Davidian cult interpreted environmental information about the FBI as presaging the end of the world.) At the same time culture filters out a number of strategic choices. For example, a firm might have a cultural predisposition against embarking on risky ventures. Another culture might have an ingrained 'Buy British' approach. Finally, **if culture is embodied in *behaviour*, existing behaviour may make a strategy incompatible with the culture and so impossible to implement**.

A model of culture which focuses specifically on a firm's approach to strategy was suggested by *Miles and Snow*, who outlined three strategic cultures, and a fourth 'non-strategic' culture.

(a) **Defenders like low risks, secure niche markets, and tried and trusted solutions**. These companies have cultures whose stories and rituals reflect historical continuity and consensus. Decision-taking is relatively formalised. There is emphasis on correct procedure. Personnel are drawn from within the industry.

(b) **Prospectors are organisations where the dominant beliefs are more to do with results** (doing the right things ie effectiveness). They seek to expand and increase market presence, and move into new areas.

(c) **Analysers try to balance risk and profits**. They use a core of stable products and markets as a source of earnings, like defenders, but move into areas that prospectors have already opened up. Analysers follow change, but do not initiate it.

(d) **Reactors**, unlike the three above, **do not have viable strategies**, other than living from hand to mouth.

The behaviour of defenders, analysers and prospectors arises largely because each type of firm is run by a different kind of **dominant coalition.** The defender tends to be run by accountants and engineers; the analyser by managers who are alive to both external developments and opportunities and the need for internal efficiency; prospectors tend to be run by entrepreneurs, designers and visionaries.

The behaviour of reactors arises because it does not have a coherent dominant coalition that has a clear view of what it wants to do.

Case Study

Miles and Snow's analysis was applied to the responses by the regional electricity companies (RECs) to takeover bids in the Autumn of 1995. (The RECs are responsible for supplying and distributing electricity.) As at October 1995, seven of the 12 RECs in England and Wales had received takeover bids. (*Financial Times,* 4 October 1995).

At privatisation they 'shared a common heritage and hence ... greater similarities than would be found in more well-established private sector market places'.

- The largest REC, Eastern Group, 'embraced' the possibility of an alliance with Hanson. Eastern exhibits the characteristics of a 'prospector'. Its chief executive is 'non-REC' 'with a North American corporate pedigree and a greater interest in activities outside the traditional REC field'.

- Norweb and Midlands were 'cautious prospectors' which allow significant degrees of decentralisation, and a 'willingness to bring in executives with experience external to the industry'. They countenance 'strategic alliances'.

- Many of the RECs 'have demonstrated classical defender strategies'. They have specific features.

  - Hierarchical company structures

  - Board membership drawn from within the industry

  - Incremental growth, rather than more rapid growth by entering new business areas; little enthusiasm for diversification

Denison's model uses a grid to assess the relationship of culture with the environment. There are two dimensions.

(a)   How orientated is the firm to the environment rather than to its internal workings? (An internal orientation is not always a bad thing, eg maintaining the safety of a nuclear installation.)

(b)   To what extent does the environment offer stability or change?

		Organisation's strategic orientation	
		Internal	*External*
Environmental responses	*Stability*	Consistency	Mission
Required	*Change/flexibility*	Involvement	Adaptability

There are thus four possible cultures.

(a)   **Consistency culture**. This exists in a stable environment, and its structure is well integrated. Management are preoccupied with efficiency. Such cultures are characterised by formal ways of behaviour. Predictability and reliability are valued. This has some features in common with the Apollonian culture.

(b)   **Mission culture**. The environment is relatively stable, and the organisation is orientated towards it (eg 'customers'). A mission culture, whereby members' work activities are given meaning and value, is appropriate. For example, hospitals are preoccupied with the sick: inevitably their values are 'customer' orientated. A church is concerned with saving souls.

(c)   **Involvement culture**. This is similar to clan control identified in an earlier chapter. The basic premise behind it is that the satisfaction of employees' needs is necessary for them to provide optimum performance. An example might be an orchestra, whose performance depends on each individual. Involvement and participation, as discussed in an earlier chapter, are supposed to create a greater sense of commitment and hence performance. For example, if you train people well enough, it is assumed that they will perform well. An involvement culture might take a 'human relations' approach to management.

(d)   **Adaptability culture**. The company's strategic focus is on the external environment, which is in a state of change. Corporate values encourage inquisitiveness and interest in the external environment. Fashion companies are an example: ideas come from a variety of sources. Customer needs are fickle and change rapidly.

Question

(a)   What do you think is the most significant contrast between Denison's model and Harrison's model?
(b)   Which is better?

Answer

(a)   Harrison's model places much more emphasis on organisation structure and systems, which both determine and are determined by culture. This model describes actual cultures. Denison's model describes *ideal* cultures, and is more concerned with the environment and a firm's external orientation than its structure. Denison suggests that if the environment is stable *and* the business is most effective with an internal orientation, *then* a consistency culture will be *best* etc.

(b)   It depends on what you wish to use each model for.

4.5.1 Culture and risk

Deal and Kennedy (*Corporate Cultures*) consider cultures to be a function of the willingness of employees to take **risks**, and how quickly they get **feedback** on whether they got it right or wrong.

High risk

BET YOUR COMPANY CULTURE ('Slow and steady wins the race') Long decision-cycles: stamina and nerve required eg oil companies, aircraft companies, architects	HARD 'MACHO' CULTURE ('Find a mountain and climb it') eg entertainment, management consultancy, advertising
PROCESS CULTURE ('It's not what you do, it's the way that you do it') Values centred on attention to excellence of technical detail, risk management, procedures, status symbols eg banks, financial services, government	WORK HARD/PLAY HARD CULTURE ('Find a need and fill it') All action - and fun: team spirit eg sales and retail, computer companies, life assurance companies

Slow feedback (left)   *Fast feedback* (right)

Low risk

4.5.2 Excellence, culture and motivation

Peters and Waterman, in their book *In Search of Excellence,* found that the 'dominance and coherence of culture' was an essential feature of the 'excellent' companies they observed. A 'handful of guiding values' was more powerful than manuals, rule books, norms and controls formally imposed (and resisted). They commented: 'If companies do not have strong notions of themselves, as reflected in their values, stories, myths and legends, people's only security comes from where they live on the organisation chart.'

Peters and Waterman also discuss the central importance of *positive reinforcement* in any method of motivation as critical. 'Researchers studying motivation find that the prime factor is simply the self-perception among motivated subjects that they are in fact doing well ... Mere association with past personal success apparently leads to more persistence, higher motivation, or something that makes us do better.'

Peters and Waterman argue that employees can be 'switched on' to extraordinary loyalty and effort in the following cases.

(a) **The cause is perceived to be in some sense great**. Commitment comes from believing that a task is inherently worthwhile. Devotion to the *customer,* and the customer's needs and wants, is an important motivator in this way.

(b) **They are treated as winners**. 'Label a man a loser and he'll start acting like one.' Repressive control systems and negative reinforcement break down the employee's self-image.

(c) **They can satisfy their dual needs, both to** be a conforming, secure part of a successful team to be stars in their own right.

This means applying control (through firm central direction, and shared values and beliefs) but also allowing maximum individual autonomy (at least, the illusion of control) and even competition between individual or groups within the organisation. Peters and Waterman call this *loose-tight* **management**. Culture, peer pressure, a focus on action, customer-orientation and so on are 'non-aversive' ways of exercising control over employees. In other words, the control system used is **cultural control**.

4.5.3 Cultural characteristics of dynamic companies

FAST FORWARD

Pümpin emphasises that companies cannot be good at everything. Hence their cultures must support their chosen **strategic excellence positions**.

Pümpin defines a dynamic company as one that 'considerably increases the benefits for its stakeholders within a relatively short time.' He notes that the culture of such firms emphasises four main aspects of business.

- **Expansion**. Rapid growth is eagerly sought.
- **Speed**. Time is seen as a vital resource.
- **Productivity**. Management is lean.
- **Risk-taking**. The possibility of failure is accepted.

Since it is not possible to emphasise everything, dynamic companies often display weaknesses in other important areas of culture.

- Customer service
- Innovation
- Technology
- Attitude to the workforce, including trust and respect
- Company spirit, including loyalty and identification

4.5.4 Strategic excellence positions and culture

Pümpin calls a specific superior capability a **strategic excellence position** (SEP). This is similar to what is generally known as a **competence**. SEPs fall into three categories.

- **Product-related**, such as technical superiority
- **Market-related**, such as an excellent image
- **Functional**, such as a cost-cutting production method

Once again, Pümpin asserts that it is not possible to be excellent at everything and that companies must decide where they will aim to excel.

There is a close relationship between a company's culture and its SEPs in that a SEP can only be developed if the company has an appropriate system of values. The aim of developing a SEP is to achieve above average capability in a specific field. This can only be done if the corporate culture emphasises the importance of that field.

 Case Study

In the 1960s, John De Lorean, then working for General Motors, emphasised the importance of developing smaller cars. This was an accurate strategic analysis but the strategy was never properly implemented because of GM's then prevailing corporate culture, which emphasised full-sized cars.

Chapter Roundup

- Ethics is about right and wrong but it not the same thing as law or the rules of religion. Cognitive approaches to ethics assume that objective moral truths can be established.

- Consequentialist ethics actions by their outcomes; deontology assumes the existence of absolute moral principles and ignores outcomes. Natural law is about rights and duties, while virtue ethics is based on the moderation in behaviour and the idea of leading a harmonious life.

  Ethical theory is not integrated: consequentialist, deontological and natural law based rules are capable of pointing to different conclusions. Partly as a result of this, **ethical dilemmas** can exist at all levels in the organisation.

- Corporate ethics has three contexts.

  - Interaction with national and international society
  - Effects of routine operations
  - Behaviour of individuals

  If constructed with care, a corporate ethical code can be valuable.

- There is a fundamental split of views about the organisation's relationship with its stake holders and the nature of corporate responsibility.

  - The **strong view** that a range of goals should be pursued
  - The **weak view** that the business organisation is a purely **economic force**, subject to law

- Stakeholders have an interest in what the organisation does.

- An organisation's stakeholder relationships must not be managed in accordance with their bargaining strength, influence, power and degree of interest. *Mendelow* summarises the possibilities in his stakeholder map. Stakeholders have three options: loyalty, exit and voice.

- The extent to which an organisation recognises obligations to society in general is as much subject to debate as is its relationships with stakeholder groups.

- There is particular concern over **externalities**, or the social and environmental costs of corporate activities.

- An organisation's **ethical stance** is the extent to which it will exceed its minimum obligations to stakeholders. There are four typical stances.

  - Short-term shareholder interest
  - Long-term shareholder interest
  - Multiple stakeholder obligations
  - Shaper of society

- **Corporate governance** is the conduct of the organisation's senior officers. Abuses have led to a range of measures to improve corporate governance. Non-executive directors have a particular role to play.

- Where the management of a business is separated from its ownership by the employment of professional managers, the managers may be considered to be the agents of the owners. **Agency theory** is concerned with adverse selection and moral hazard, the problems that arise as a result of the separation of ownership and control. In many organisations, corporate governance takes the form of a chain of responsibility and accountability.

- There are four models of governance.

  1 The Anglo-Saxon model is fast in action but may be short-termist and unresponsive to external criticism.

  2 The Rhine model has more robust governance and takes a long view of investment.

  3 The Japanese model values consensus, takes a very long view and makes decisions slowly. Accountability and governance may be poor.

  4 The Latin model emphasises the role of the state: investment is likely to be for the very long-term but governance may suffer from political activity.

- The board must decide the extent of its involvement in the strategic process. If it decides on a stewardship role it must ensure that the organisation's activity is not directed to management's own ends rather than those of legitimate stakeholders. If it engages in the strategic process it must act independently of management and in a competent fashion.

- Culture is important both in organisations and in the wider world. It is the knowledge, beliefs, customs and attitudes which people adhere to. In wider society it is affected by factors such as age, class, race and religion, while in organisations it is defined by assumptions, beliefs and artefacts. These, in turn, are influenced by history, management, structure and systems. The organisational iceberg concept shows how culture relates to other aspects of the organisation. The paradigm is the common, basic assumptions and beliefs held by an organisation's decision-makers. Combined with the physical manifestations of culture, it makes up the **cultural web**.

- Harrison's four-fold classification of organisations, popularised by Handy, is a useful analysis of some common aspects of culture.

  - The **power** culture depends on the holder of centralised power.
  - The **role** culture is associated with bureaucracy and emphasises rules and procedures.
  - The **task** culture is focused on delivering the current goal.
  - The **existential** culture supports individual independence and aspiration.

- Culture colours the organisation's view of its environment and hence influences its strategy. **Defenders** like low risk solutions and niche markets. **Prospectors** are more adventurous and concerned with results. **Analysers** try to balance risk and profits. **Reactors** do not have viable strategies. Deal and Kennedy analyse culture in terms of inherent risk in the industry and the speed with which feedback is available on strategic decisions. Denison assesses culture in terms of strategic orientation and environmental dynamism. Combined with the physical manifestations of culture, it makes up the **cultural web**.

- Pümpin emphasises that companies cannot be good at everything. Hence their cultures must support their chosen **strategic excellence positions**.

Quick Quiz

1 What is an organisation's ethical stance?

2 Why might an organisation act to secure long-term shareholder interests?

3 What is a right?

4 When should ethical considerations be included in performance measures?

5 What is corporate governance?

6 What is an externality?

7 What are the main influences on organisational culture, according to Schein?

8 What is the paradigm, in JS&W's terms?

9 Describe Harrison's analysis of organisations.

10 How did Miles and Snow analyse strategic culture?

Answers to Quick Quiz

1 The extent to which it will exceed its minimum obligation to shareholders

2 To improve corporate image and forestall legal regulation

3 A legal or moral entitlement

4 When moral expectations are accepted as obligations

5 The conduct of the organisation's senior officers

6 A social or environmental cost of the organisation's activities not borne by the organisation

7 Many factors, including the founder, history, management style, structure, systems

8 The common, basic assumptions and beliefs held by an organisation's decision-makers

9 Harrison analysed organisations into four types based on their structure and culture.

   - Organisations structured around a dynamic leader displaying a **power culture**

   - The **role culture** is typical of bureaucracy

   - Organisations that are run by project teams or have a matrix structure tend to display the **task culture**.

   - The **existential culture** pervades the loose organisation which exists to serve the interests of its principal members.

10 Defenders like low risks and secure markets. Prospectors constantly seek improved results. Analysers try to balance risk and profit. Reactors live from hand to mouth.

Now try the questions below from the Exam Question Bank

Number	Level	Marks	Time
Q5	Examination	20	36 mins

Part B
Strategic choices

Strategic options

Topic list	Syllabus reference
1 Corporate strategy	B1(a)
2 Diversity of products and markets	B1(b), (c)
3 International diversification	B1(b), (c)
4 The corporate parent and value creation	B1(d), (e)
5 The corporate portfolio	B1(f)
6 Business unit strategy: generic strategies	B2(a)
7 Sustaining competitive advantage	B2(b), (c), (d)
8 Using the value chain in competitive strategy	B2
9 Product-market strategy: direction of growth	B3(a)
10 Method of growth	B3(b)
11 Strategy and market position	B2
12 Success criteria	B3(c), (d), (e), (f)

Introduction

In this chapter we will examine the various strategic options that present themselves to the organisation. The process of making choices from among these options should, of course, be illuminated by the analyses of environmental and internal factors that we have already discussed.

There are two main areas to cover in our examination of strategic options; these are, first, the role of the corporate headquarters of an organisation that is made up of a number of business units; and, second, the strategies available to the business units themselves in their own separate industries and sectors. The second area is equally applicable to smaller organisations that are, effectively, independent businesses operating on their own account and not subject to any form of hierarchical supervision.

Study guide

		Intellectual level
B1	**The influence of corporate strategy on an organisation**	
(a)	Explore the relationship between a corporate parent and its business units	2
(b)	Assess the opportunities and potential problems of pursuing different corporate strategies of product/market diversification from a national, international and global perspective	3
(c)	Assess the opportunities and potential problems of pursuing a corporate strategy of international diversity, international scale operations and globalisation	3
(d)	Discuss a range of ways that the corporate parent can create and destroy organisational value	2
(e)	Explain three corporate rationales for adding value – portfolio managers, synergy managers and parental developers	3
(f)	Explain and assess a range of portfolio models (the growth/share (BCG) matrix, the public sector portfolio matrix, market attractiveness/SBU strength matrix, directional policy matrix, Ashridge Portfolio Display) that may assist corporate parents manager their business portfolios	3
B2	**Alternative approaches to achieving competitive advantage**	
(a)	Evaluate, through the strategy clock, generic strategy options available to an organisation	3
(b)	Advise on how price-based strategies, differentiation and lock-in can help an organisation sustain its competitive advantage	3
(c)	Explore how organisations can respond to hypercompetitive conditions	2
(d)	Assess opportunities for improving competitiveness through collaboration	3
B3	**Alternative directions and methods of development**	
(a)	Determine generic development directions (employing an adapted Ansoff matrix and a TOWS matrix) available to an organisation	2
(b)	Assess how internal development, mergers, acquisitions and strategic alliances can be used as different methods of pursuing ac hosen strategic direction	3
(c)	Establish success criteria to assist in the choice of a strategic direction and method (strategic options)	2
(d)	Assess the suitability of different strategic options to an organisation	3
(e)	Assess the feasibility of different strategic options to an organisation	3
(f)	Establish the acceptability of strategic options to an organisation through analysing risk and return on investment	3

Exam guide

This is another chapter that is packed with highly examinable material. In particular, it is very common in business strategy exams to be confronted with a complex scenario and be required to suggest sensible courses of action, with reasonable justification. It is very important, therefore to understand the general circumstances in which a particular strategic option is appropriate. It is not sufficient to be able to describe the options without understanding when they are to be recommended. The chapter concludes with a discussion of success criteria: these are the criteria against which possible courses of action are judged and they draw together the threads of choice we emphasise above. Pay diligent attention to the nature of these criteria: they are not as simple as they might seem to be.

1 Corporate strategy

Many large businesses consist of a corporate parent and a number of SBUs. The defining characteristic of the corporate parent is that it has no direct contact with the buyers or competitors, its role being to manage the overall scope of the organisation in terms of diversity of products, markets and international operations.

Many organisations consist, essentially, of a number of strategic business units (SBUs) and a **corporate parent**. Each SBU has its own products, with which it serves its own market sector, and its managers are, to a greater or lesser extent, responsible for its overall success (or failure). In very large organisations, SBUs may be grouped into **divisions**, with divisional managers providing an intermediate level of management between the SBU and the corporate parent.

The defining feature of the **corporate parent** is that it has no direct contact with buyers and competitors. Its role is generally to manage the **scope of the organisation**. There are two main, linked subjects for decisions about scope.

- Diversity of products and markets
- International and geographic diversity

The processes involved in making and implementing these decisions are complex and the role of the corporate parent is of very great importance to the success or failure of the organisation. In our consideration of the corporate centre we will also, therefore, examine the ways in which it can **create or destroy value**.

Your syllabus is very clear in its separate treatment of the corporate parent and its SBUs, and this is also apparent in *Exploring Corporate Strategy*, upon which much of the syllabus is explicitly based. This distinction was less clear in the old syllabus and represents a new and inviting area for the Examiner to set questions on. You must therefore understand the differences between these two aspects of strategy and be able to recognise which is required by question scenarios. The picture will, of course, be complicated by the Examiner, possibly by presenting questions about companies that consist of a single business unit. In this case, the strategic managers will have to develop both corporate and business-level strategies.

2 Diversity of products and markets

Diversity of products and markets may be advantageous for three reasons.

- **Economies of scope** may arise in several forms of **synergy**.
- **Corporate management skills** may be extendible.
- **Cross-subsidy** may enhance **market power**.

Related diversification, whether horizontal or vertical, usually works better than conglomerate, or unrelated, diversification.

The corporate parent controls the extent of product and market **diversification** undertaken by the organisation as a whole. *JS&W* suggest three reasons why diversification may be advantageous.

(a) **Economies of scope** (as opposed to economies of scale) may result from the **greater use of under-utilised resources**. These benefits are often referred to as **synergy** and can take several forms.

    (i) **Marketing synergy** is achieved by extending the use of marketing facilities such as distribution channels; sales staff and administration; and warehousing. For example the UK Automobile Association offers loans to customers as well as breakdown services.

    (ii) **Operating synergy** arises from the better use of operational facilities and personnel, bulk purchasing, and a greater spread of fixed costs whereby the firm's competence can be transferred to making new products. For example, although there is very little in common between sausages and ice cream, both depend on a competence of refrigeration.

    (iii) **Investment synergy** comes from the wider use of a common investment in fixed assets, working capital or research, such as the joint use of plant, common raw material stocks and transfer of research and development from one product to another

    (iv) **Management synergy** is the advantage to be gained where management skills concerning current operations are easily transferred to new operations because of the similarity of problems in the two industries.

(b) **Corporate management skills** may be extendible across a range of unrelated businesses. In a way this is also a kind of synergy, in which the corporate parent represents the resource that can be more intensively utilised. This kind of approach is commonly seen in consumer goods groups that deploy brand management skills across a diverse range of products and markets. *Virgin* is a good example.

(c) Diversification can increase **market power** *via* cross-subsidisation. A high margin business can subsidise a low margin one, enabling it to create a price advantage over its rivals and building market share. Eventually, it may achieve a dominant position that enables it to increase its prices and recoup earlier group losses.

JS&W also discuss **three questionable reasons** that may be advanced to justify a policy of diversification.

(a) **Response to environmental change** can be justified as a reason to diversify if it is undertaken in order to protect existing shareholder value by, for example, responding to the emergence of new and threatening technology developments. However, the environmental change reasoning is sometimes used as a cover for what is actually a move to protect the interests of top management; typically, this will lead to ill-considered acquisitions that destroy value.

(b) **Risk spreading** can be valid reason for an owner-managed business to diversify, but modern financial theory suggests that shareholders in large corporations can manage their risk exposure better themselves by diversifying their own portfolios.

(c) The **expectations of powerful stakeholders** can lead to inappropriate strategies generally. JS&W give the example of *Enron*, whose strategic managers were under pressure from the stock market to deliver continuing growth in revenues and responded with ill-considered diversification

2.1 Related diversification

Key term

> **Related diversification** is development beyond current products and markets but within the capabilities or value network of the organisation. *JS&W*

The **argument from synergy** is often used to justify related diversification. However, achieving synergy can be difficult and requires considerable strategic skill, both to recognise synergistic potential and to achieve it in practice. Simply undertaking more and more value activities is not necessarily a route to improved performance: each activity undertaken must be **managed in a skilful and appropriate manner**. A number of very large corporations have actually de-merged with success. Also, the **management of external relationships** with suppliers, customers and collaborators is emerging as an effective alternative to expansion.

Horizontal integration makes use of current capabilities by development into activities that are competitive with or directly **complementary** to a company's present activities. An example would be a TV company that moved into film production.

Vertical integration occurs when a company expands backwards or forwards within its existing value network and thus becomes its own supplier or distributor. For example, **backward integration** would occur if a milk processing business acquired its own dairy farms rather than buying raw milk from independent farmers. If a cloth manufacturer began to produce shirts instead of selling all of its cloth to other shirt manufacturers, that would be **forward integration**.

Vertical integration has its greatest potential for success when **the final customer's needs are not being properly satisfied**. If there is potential for improving the satisfaction of the end user by improving the links in the value network, then an integration strategy may succeed. Examples would be where there is a premium on speed, as in the marketing of fresh foodstuffs, or when complex technical features require great attention to quality procedures.

2.1.1 Advantages of vertical integration

- A **secure supply of components** or **materials,** hence lower supplier bargaining power
- **Stronger relationships** with the final consumer of the product
- A share of the **profits** at all stages of the value network
- More effective pursuit of a **differentiation strategy**
- Creation of **barriers to entry**

We will return to the management of the supply chain later in this Study Text.

 Case Study

Kumio Nakamura, president of *Matsushita* has said that, 'the vertical integration of Japanese manufacturers is a huge advantage because it enables us to move from development to production in a short time.'

2.1.2 Disadvantages of vertical integration

(a) **Overconcentration.** A company places 'more eggs in the same end-market basket' (Ansoff). Such a policy is fairly inflexible, more sensitive to instabilities and increases the firm's dependence on a particular aspect of economic demand.

(b) The firm **fails to benefit from any economies of scale or technical advances** in the industry into which it has diversified. This is why, in the publishing industry, most printing is subcontracted to specialist printing firms, who can work machinery to capacity by doing work for many firms.

Case Study

(a) **Horizontal integration**. Since water and electricity distribution were privatised in the UK, there have been a number of changes. Regional water companies have purchased **regional electricity distribution** firms. For example, *Norweb* has been bought by *North West Water*. Although the businesses are very different, they have a very similar customer base, and cost savings can be achieved by shared billing, accounts management and soon.

(b) **Vertical integration**. Before privatisation, the UK electricity industry was a state-owned monopoly, vertically integrated from power generation to distribution. Privatisation effectively split up these two businesses, to introduce competition in power generation, so that the regional distribution companies could buy from a number of suppliers. However, the power distribution companies sought to buy a regional distribution company, giving them a captive market: National Power was set to buy Southern Electric, but the bid was blocked by the government on the grounds that it would inhibit competition.

2.2 Unrelated diversification

Key term

> **Unrelated diversification** is the development of products or services beyond the current capabilities or value network.
>
> *JS&W*

Unrelated diversification produces the type of company known as a **conglomerate**. Conglomerate diversification has been a key strategy for companies in Asia, particularly South Korea, where the *chaebol*, as they are known, have provided better markets for capital and managerial skills than were available in the economy generally. Conglomerate diversification can also succeed when managed by particularly talented strategic leaders deploy an effective **dominant logic;** dominant logic is the term used by *Prahalad and Bettis* to signify a cognitive orientation or world-view based on sound judgement and experience.

Potential advantages of conglomerate diversification

Bear in mind our discussion of questionable reasons for diversification when considering these points.

(a) **Risk-spreading.** Entering new products into new markets can compensate for the failure of current products and markets.

(b) **Improved profit opportunities**. An improvement of the **overall profitability and flexibility** of the firm may arise through acquisition in industries with better prospects than those of the acquiring firms.

(c) **Escape** from a declining market

(d) **Use a company's image and reputation** in one market to develop into another where corporate image and reputation could be vital ingredients for success

Potential disadvantages of conglomerate diversification

(a) The **dilution of shareholders' earnings** if diversification is into growth industries with high P/E ratios.

(b) **Lack of a common identity and purpose** in a conglomerate organisation. A conglomerate will only be successful if it has a high quality of management and financial ability at central headquarters, where the diverse operations are brought together.

(c) **Failure in one of the businesses will drag down the rest**, as it will eat up resources.

(d)   **Lack of management experience**. Japanese steel companies have diversified into areas completely unrelated to steel such as personal computers, with limited success.

The previous Examiner's suggested solution to a question in the old Paper 3.5 syllabus December 2004 exam includes this interesting passage:

Michael Porter is one of the fiercest critics of groups ... who diversify through acquisition into many different businesses and industries and who, as a consequence, add little, if any value, to the companies in the group acting independently. He suggests such groups ask themselves what value does an individual company get through being part of the group and, in particular, what value does the corporate HQ add to their activities. Executives in such groups often claim that their diversification strategies lessen risk for their shareholders by creating a portfolio of companies. Porter dismisses this, arguing that any risk spreading should be left to the shareholder – having companies in a group, with little synergy with one another, or even worse, negative synergy, actually destroys shareholder value. Acquisition of a company may achieve significant one-off re-organisation benefits, through cost savings, but these benefits are not sustained over a period of time. Importantly, he argues that cost reduction is not a strategy in itself but must be part of a strategy designed to achieve competitive advantage – in his terms by either cost leadership or differentiation. Real value through acquisition will only be achieved if the enlarged group is then able to share resources or transfer learning from one part of the organisation to another.

2.3 Diversity and strategic success

JS&W's summary of the results of research into the impact of diversification on strategic performance tells us that organisations undertaking a **limited degree of related diversification are likely to perform better** than those that remain undiversified. However, as the degree of diversification **increases**, the rate of performance improvement is likely to **reduce** and may then become negative as the organisation becomes extensively diversified into unrelated fields.

3 International diversification

Despite wide-ranging measures to liberalise trade and the resulting major growth in world trade, there has been little globalisation of services. Language differences and restrictions on population movement hamper the growth of international markets for labour, even when it is highly skilled.

3.1 Globalisation

Since 1945, the volume of world trade has increased. There have been several factors at work.

(a)   **Import substitution.** A country aims to produce manufactured goods which it previously imported, by protecting local producers. This has had limited success.

(b)   **Export-led growth.** The success of this particular strategy has depended on the existence of open markets elsewhere. Japan, South Korea and the other Asian 'tiger' economies (eg Taiwan) have chosen this route.

(c)   **Market convergence**. Transnational market segments have developed whose characteristics are more homogeneous than the different segments within a given geographic market. **Youth culture** is an important influence here.

This has meant a proliferation of suppliers exporting to, or trading in, a wider variety of places. In many domestic markets it is now likely that the same international companies will be competing with one another. However, the existence of global markets should not be taken for granted in terms of **all** products and services, or indeed in **all** territories.

(a)   Some **services** are still subject to managed trade (for example, some countries prohibit firms from other countries from selling insurance). Trade in services has been liberalised under the auspices of the World Trade Organisation.

(b)   **Immigration.** There is unlikely ever to be a global market for labour, given the disparity in skills between different countries and restrictions on immigration.

(c)   The market for some goods is much more globalised than for others.

   (i)   Upmarket luxury goods may not be required or afforded by people in developing nations.

   (ii)   Some goods can be sold almost anywhere, but to limited degrees. Television sets are consumer durables in some countries, but still luxury or relatively expensive items in other ones.

   (iii)   Other goods are needed almost everywhere. In oil a truly global industry exists in both production (eg North Sea, Venezuela, Russia, Azerbaijan, Gulf states) and consumption (any country using cars and buses, not to mention those with chemical industries based on oil).

3.2 Management orientation

FAST FORWARD

Perlmutter identifies four orientations in the management of international business.

- **Ethnocentrism** is a home country orientation
- **Polycentrism** adapts totally to local environments
- **Geocentrism** adapts only to add value. It 'thinks globally, acts locally'.
- **Regiocentrism** recognises regional differences

3.2.1 Ethnocentrism

Key term

Ethnocentrism is a **home country orientation**. The company focuses on its domestic market and sees exports as secondary to domestic marketing.

This approach simply ignores any inter-country differences which exist. Ethnocentric companies will tend to market the same products with the same marketing programmes in overseas countries as at home. Marketing management is centralised in the home country and the marketing mix is standardised. There is no local market research or adaptation of promotion. As a result, market opportunities may not be fully exploited and foreign customers may be alienated by the approach.

 Case Study

Pepsi experienced customer alienation when it attempted to mechanically import its global 'younger challenger to *Coke's* image into Russia. It lost ground to an obscure Swiss rival, *Herschi*, which used Russian sports stars and celebrities in its campaign.

3.2.2 Polycentrism

Key term

With **polycentrism**, objectives are formulated on the assumption that it is necessary to adapt almost totally the product and the marketing programme to each local environment. Thus the various country subsidiaries of a multinational corporation are free to formulate their own objectives and plans.

The polycentric company believes that each country is unique. It therefore establishes largely independent local subsidiaries and decentralises its marketing management. This can produce major increases in turnover but the loss of economies of scale can seriously damage profitability. Such companies tend to think of themselves as **multinationals**. (Later in this chapter we introduce a slightly different polycentric company: the **transnational**.)

3.2.3 Geocentrism and regiocentrism

Key term

> **Geocentrism** and **regiocentrism** are syntheses of the two previous orientations. They are based on the assumption that there are both similarities and differences between countries that can be incorporated into regional or world objectives and strategies.

Geocentrism and **regiocentrism** differ only in geographical terms: the first deals with the world as a unity while the second considers that there are differences between regions. Bearing this in mind, we will speak in terms of geocentrism only, for simplicity.

Geocentrism treats the issues of standardisation and adaptation on their merits so as to formulate objectives and strategies that exploit markets fully while minimising company costs. The aim is to create a global strategy that is fully responsive to local market differences. This has been summed up as: 'think globally, act locally'.

Geocentric companies use an integrated approach to marketing management. Each country's conditions are given due consideration, but no one country dominates. A great deal of experience and commitment are required to make this approach work. A strong, globally recognised brand is a major aspect of the marketing approach. Geocentrically oriented companies both promote and benefit from **market convergence**.

3.3 Developing the global business

FAST FORWARD

Ohmae describes five stages in the evolution of a global business.

- **Exporting** is an extension of home sales, using foreign intermediaries. It is low risk and **ethnocentric**.

- **Overseas branches** arise when turnover is large enough. It requires greater investment and is still **ethnocentric**.

- **Overseas production** exploits cheap labour and reduces exporting costs. The orientation is still **ethnocentric** and the business is still largely run from its HQ.

- **Insiderisation** is a shift to **polycentrism**, with full functional organisations being set up overseas. This reduces exchange rate and political risk but economies of scale may be lost and there may be problems of co-ordination. The company is a **multinational**.

- **The global company** takes a world view while recognising total differences: it has a **geocentric** orientation. It integrates learning, skills and competences to achieve global efficiencies while retaining local responsiveness.

Ohmae offers five reasons for globalisation.

- **Customer:** market convergence
- **Company:** economies of scale
- **Competition:** keeping up
- **Currency:** exchange rate risk
- **Country:** absolute and comparative advantage; local orientation

Following *Ohmae*, we may describe five stages in the evolution of global business operations. These may be related to Perlmutter's classification of orientations.

(a)   **Exporting**. The product is saleable in overseas markets and they are exploited by means of foreign intermediaries such as agents and distributors. Foreign sales are a profitable extension of domestic operations. Little or no adjustment is made to the product in order to reap economies of scale. This is a low risk strategy, since there is little financial commitment, but the company is very much dependent on the effort and motivation of its foreign intermediaries. The management orientation in **ethnocentric**.

(b)   **Overseas branches**. Existing and potential export sales are high enough to justify largely replacing the foreign intermediaries with the company's own foreign sales and service branches. Financial commitment increases with increasing business, as does exchange rate and political risk. If the company is aiming to achieve globalisation, it is at this stage that it begins to acquire the local knowledge and experience that it will need. However, the management orientation is still **ethnocentric**.

(c)   **Overseas production**. Export sales are now so high that shipping and other exporting-related costs represent an opportunity for savings by establishing overseas production. At the same time, overseas production can exploit cheap labour and other resources. The company's management orientation is still largely **ethnocentric**. Some functions, such as R&D and marketing are centralised and there is centralised control of manufacturing operations with regular reports to headquarters. World-wide synergies and economies of scale are sought and decisions on adapting to local conditions are made at headquarters. Products are still largely standardised.

(d)   **Insiderisation**. The company clones itself in its overseas markets, completing the corporate functionality in each location rather than restricting itself to marketing. The aim is to develop a full marketing capability and offer products suited to local requirements. The management is shifting to a **polycentric** orientation and thinks of itself as a **multinational**. This approach reduces exchange rate and political risk but requires financial commitment. Economies of scale will be lost and there may be inefficiencies of co-ordination.

(e)   **The global company**. The global company differs from the multinational in that it has a **geocentric** management orientation. It takes a world view while recognising local differences and similarities. It minimises its local adaptation of product and the rest of the marketing mix to those things that actually add customer value and it makes use of the best of its global facilities and people to promote overall excellence. It is likely to centralise functions such as R&D, finance and HR, though not necessarily all in the same place. At the same time its operations will be controlled locally. The primary skill of the global company is to integrate learning, skills, competences and technologies in order to achieve global efficiencies combined with local responsiveness. It manages the value chain so that each part is centred in an optimal location. It is subject to a number of problems.

- Differing cultural values may undermine the global corporate identity.
- Senior executives with the right mix of attitudes and skills are likely to be scarce.
- It is subject to a wide range of environmental risks, particularly political ones.

Ohmae suggests there are five reasons why companies are moving towards the global stage. He calls these the **five Cs**.

(a)   **Customer**. Market convergence is driven by widespread customer demand for products with similar characteristics.

(b)   **Company**. The search for economies of scale drives expansion towards the global scale.

(c) **Competition**. The very existence of global competitors motivates companies to expand for reasons of prestige and competitiveness. They may also be amenable to cost-reducing strategic alliances.

(d) **Currency**. Exchange rate risk can be managed most easily when a company has major cash flows in the countries in which it operates.

(e) **Country**. Multiple locations enable a company to exploit both absolute and comparative advantage. They also enable it to promote itself as locally oriented in each country, thus enhancing its image with the local government and markets.

There are other factors encouraging the globalisation of world trade.

(a) **Financial factors** such as Third world debt; often lenders require the initiation of economic reforms as a condition of the loan. This can lead to a reduction in local protectionism and a consequent increase in trade

(b) **Country/continent** connections, such as that between the UK and the Commonwealth which foster trade and tourism.

(c) **Legal and regulatory factors** such as industrial standards and protection of intellectual property, which encourage the development and spread of standardised technology and design.

(d) **Markets** trading in international commodities; commodities are not physically exchanged, only the rights to ownership. A buyer can, thanks to efficient systems of trading and modern communications, buy a commodity in its country of origin for delivery to a specific destination at some future time.

(e) **The Internet**; major companies are developing on line systems of internal co-ordination and procurement.

(f) **Government policy** in many countries seeks to control the balance of payments by discouraging imports. Government policy towards importers will also reflect their quite proper desire to expand their economies and hence employment and the local standard of living. Local manufacture may thus be the only way to access some markets.

3.4 Designs for global businesses

FAST FORWARD

Bartlett and Ghoshal discern four types of organisations, depending on the strength or weakness of pressure to globalise and need for local adaptation.

- Global environment; geocentric; global product divisions
- International environment; ethnocentric; international division
- Transnational environment; polycentric; integrated systems and structures
- Multinational environment; polycentric; national or regional divisions

Bartlett and Ghoshal find that the pressures driving globalisation exist independently of the need for local responsiveness; and that both vary from industry to industry. The relationship between these pressures influences both the management orientation and the structure of the company that operates internationally.

(a) The **global company**, if active in more than one industry, is likely to be organised in product divisions with global scope.

(b) Companies operating in industries that require **little local differentiation** and at the same time are not subject to pressure for globalisation will tend to be structured with an international or export division.

(c)   The **multinational environment** drives a polycentric orientation, with largely autonomous local operating companies.

(d)   The **transnational environment** is particularly difficult to respond to. Global scale is desirable but local conditions require differentiated approaches. The structural response may be the **global heterarchy**. Each regional or national unit achieves global scale and influence within the overall organisation by exploiting its specialised competences on behalf of the whole company. Some headquarters functions, such as R&D may be diffused across the organisation. The role of the global strategic apex is to promote a corporate culture and shared values that will promote co-operation and co-ordination. JS&W call this type of company a **transnational**: we will discuss it in more detail later in this Study Text.

	Low requirement for local adaptation and responsiveness	**High requirement for local adaptation and responsiveness**
High pressure to globalise	**Global environment** Geocentric orientation Global product divisions (Chemicals, construction)	**Transnational environment** Polycentric orientation Integrated systems and structures (Pharmaceuticals, motor vehicles)
Low pressure to globalise	**International environment** Ethnocentric orientation International division (Paper, textiles)	**Multinational environment** Polycentric orientation National or regional divisions (Fast food, tobacco)

3.5 Market selection

In making a decision as to which market(s) to enter the firm must start by establishing its objectives. Here are some examples.

(a)   What proportion of total sales will be overseas?

(b)   What are the longer term objectives?

(c)   Will it enter one, a few, or many markets? In most cases it is better to start by selling in countries with which there is some familiarity and then expand into other countries gradually as experience is gained. Reasons to enter fewer countries at first include the following.

- Market entry and market control costs are high
- Product and market communications modification costs are high
- There is a large market and potential growth in the initial countries chosen
- Dominant competitors can establish high barriers to entry

(d)   What types of country should it enter (in terms of environmental factors, economic development, language used, cultural similarities and so on)? Three major criteria should be as follows.

- Market attractiveness
- Competitive advantage
- Risk

The matrix below can be used to bring together these three major criteria and assist managers in their decisions.

Evaluating which markets to enter

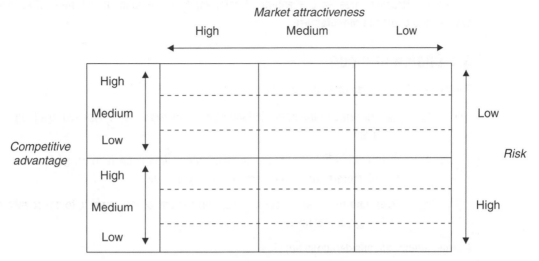

Source: Kotler

(a) **Market attractiveness**. This concerns such indicators as GNP/head and forecast demand, and market accessibility.

(b) **Competitive advantage**. This is principally dependent on prior experience in similar markets, language and cultural understanding.

(c) **Risk**. This involves an analysis of political stability, the possibility of government intervention and similar external influences.

The best markets to enter are those located at the top left of the diagram. The worst are those in the bottom right corner. Obtaining the information needed to reach this decision requires detailed and often costly international marketing research and analysis. Making these decisions is not easy, and a fairly elaborate screening process will be instituted.

In international business there are several categories of risk.

(a) **Political risk** relates to factors as diverse as wars, nationalisation, arguments between governments etc.

(b) **Business risk.** This arises from the possibility that the business idea itself might be flawed. As with political risk, it is not unique to international marketing, but firms might be exposed to more sources of risk arising from failures to understand the market.

(c) **Currency risk.** This arises out of the volatility of foreign exchange rates. Given that there is a possibility for speculation and that capital flows are free, such risks are increasing.

(d) **Profit repatriation risk.** Government actions may make it hard to repatriate profits.

3.6 Modes of entry to foreign markets

FAST FORWARD

Modes of entry to foreign markets vary widely and include:

- Direct and indirect exporting
- Wholly owned overseas production
- Contract manufacture
- Joint ventures

The most suitable mode of entry depends on

- Marketing objectives
- Mode availability
- HR requirements
- Risks
- Firm size
- Mode quality
- Market research feedback
- Control needs

If an organisation has decided to enter an overseas market, the way it does so is of crucial strategic importance. Broadly, three ways of entering foreign markets can be identified: **indirect exports**, **direct exports** and **overseas manufacture**.

3.7 Choice of mode

The most suitable mode of entry varies:

(a)   **Among firms in the same industry** (eg a new exporter as opposed to a long-established exporter)

(b)   **According to the market** (eg some countries limit imports to protect domestic manufacturers whereas others promote free trade)

(c)   **Over time** (eg as some countries become more, or less, hostile to direct inward investment by foreign companies).

A large number of considerations apply.

Consideration	Comment
The firm's marketing objectives	These relate to volume, time scale and coverage of market segments. Thus setting up an overseas production facility would be inappropriate if sales are expected to be low in volume.
The firm's size	A small firm is less likely than a large one to possess sufficient resources to set up and run a production facility overseas.
Mode availability	Some countries only allow a restricted level of imports, but will welcome a firm if it builds manufacturing facilities which provide jobs and limit the outflow of foreign exchange.
Mode quality	All modes may be possible in theory, but some are of questionable quality or practicality. The lack of suitably qualified distributors or agents would preclude the export, direct or indirect, of high technology goods needing installation, maintenance and servicing by personnel with specialist technical skills.
Human resources requirements	When a firm is unable to recruit suitable staff either at home or overseas, indirect exporting or the use of agents based overseas may be the only realistic option.
Market feedback information	In some cases a firm can receive feedback information about the market and its marketing effort from its sales staff or distribution channels. In these circumstances direct export or joint ventures may be preferred to indirect export.
Learning curve requirements	Firms which intend a heavy future involvement in an overseas market might need to gain the experience that close involvement in an overseas market can bring. This argues against the use of indirect exporting as the mode of entry.
Risks	Firms might prefer the indirect export mode as assets are safer from expropriation.
Control needs	Production overseas by a wholly owned subsidiary gives a firm absolute control while indirect exporting offers only limited control over the marketing mix to the exporter.

3.8 Exporting

Goods are made at home but sold abroad. It is the easiest, cheapest and most commonly used route into a new foreign market.

3.8.1 Advantages of exporting

(a) Exporters can **concentrate production** in a single location, giving **economies of scale** and **consistency of product quality**.

(b) Firms lacking experience can try international marketing on a **small scale**.

(c) Firms can **test** their international marketing plans and strategies before risking investment in overseas operations.

(d) Exporting **minimises operating costs**, administrative overheads and personnel requirements.

3.8.2 Indirect exports

Indirect exporting is where a firm's goods are sold abroad by other organisations who can offer greater market knowledge.

(a) **Export houses** are firms which facilitate exporting on behalf of the producer. Usually the producer has little control over the market and the marketing effort.

(b) **Specialist export management firms** perform the same functions as an in-house export department but are normally remunerated by way of commission.

(c) **UK buying offices of foreign stores and governments**.

(d) **Complementary exporting** ('piggy back exporting') occurs when one producing organisation (the carrier) uses its own established international marketing channels to market (either as distributor, or agent or merchant) the products of another producer (the rider) as well as its own.

3.8.3 Direct exports

Direct exporting occurs where the producing organisation itself performs the export tasks rather than using an intermediary. Sales are made directly to customers overseas who may be the wholesalers, retailers or final users.

(a) **Sales to final user**. Typical customers include industrial users, governments or mail order customers.

(b) Strictly speaking an **overseas export agent** or distributor is an overseas firm hired to effect a sales contract between the principal (ie the exporter) and a customer. Agents do not take title to goods; they earn a commission (or profit).

(c) **Company branch offices abroad**. A firm can establish its own office in a foreign market for the purpose of marketing and distribution as this gives greater control.

A firm can manufacture its products overseas, either by itself or by using an overseas manufacturer.

3.9 Overseas production

Benefits of overseas manufacture

- A **better understanding of customers** in the overseas market.
- **Economies of scale** in large markets.
- **Production costs are lower** in some countries than at home.
- **Lower storage and transportation costs**.
- **Overcomes the effects of tariff and non-tariff barriers**.
- Manufacture in the overseas market **may help win orders from the public sector**.

3.9.1 Contract manufacture

Licensing is a quite common arrangement as it avoids the cost and hassle of setting up overseas.

In the case of **contract manufacture** a firm (the contractor) makes a contract with another firm (the contractee) abroad whereby the contractee manufactures or assembles a product on behalf of the contractor. Contract manufacture is suited to **countries** where the **small size of the market** discourages investment in plant and to **firms** whose main **strengths are in marketing** rather than production.

Advantages of contract manufacture

- No need to invest in plant overseas
- Lower risks associated with currency fluctuations
- Lower risk of asset expropriation is minimised
- Control of marketing is retained by the contractor
- Lower transport costs and, sometimes, lower production costs

Disadvantages of contract manufacture

- Suitable overseas producers cannot always be easily identified
- The need to train the contractee producer's personnel
- The contractee producer may eventually become a competitor
- Quality control problems in manufacturing may arise

3.9.2 Joint ventures

Some governments discourage or even prohibit foreign firms setting up independent operations. so joint ventures are the only option. That said, a joint venture with an indigenous firm provides local knowledge, quickly.

3.9.3 Wholly owned overseas production

Production capacity can be built from scratch, or, alternatively, an existing firm can be acquired.

(a) **Acquisition** has all the benefits and drawbacks of acquiring a domestic company.

(b) **Creating new capacity** can be beneficial if there are no likely candidates for takeover, or if acquisition is prohibited by the government.

Advantages

(a) The firm does **not have to share its profits** with partners of any kind.

(b) The firm does **not have to share or delegate decision-making**.

(c) There are **none of the communication problems** that arise in joint ventures.

(d) The firm is able to operate completely **integrated** international systems.

(e) The firm gains a more **varied experience** from overseas production.

Disadvantages

(a) The **investment** needed prevents some firms from setting up operations overseas.

(b) Suitable **managers** may be **difficult to recruit** at home or abroad.

(c) Some overseas **governments discourage**, and sometimes prohibit, **100% ownership** of an enterprise by a foreign company.

(d) This mode of entry **forgoes the benefits of an overseas partner's market knowledge**, distribution system and other local expertise.

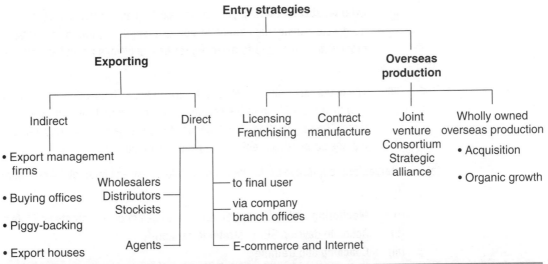

	Exporting	**Overseas production**
Advantages	Concentrates production; small start possible; minimises overheads	Lower distribution costs; overcomes trade barriers; possibly lower production costs
Key issues	Exchange rates, protectionism	Political risk; partnership; managing overseas facilities; more risky
Involvement	Usually less involved, but an exporter might depend on the **overseas** market	Usually more involved, but overseas subsidiaries might act independently: varying levels of control and risk

4 The corporate parent and value creation

FAST FORWARD

There are three value-creating roles for the corporate parent.

- **Envisioning corporate intent**, communicating the vision to stakeholders and SBU managers, and acting in accordance with it.

- **Intervention** to improve performance.

- Provision of **services**, **resources** and **expertise**.

Portfolio managers create value by applying financial discipline. They keep their own costs low.

Synergy managers peruse economies of scope through the shared use of competences and resources.

Parental developers add value by deploying their own competences to improve their SBUs' performance.

Earlier in this chapter we mentioned Porter's views on conglomerate diversification and its potential to destroy value.

We have said that the defining feature of the corporate parent is that it has no direct contact with buyers and competitors. How then, does it create value?

4.1 Value creation

JS&W propose **three main value-creating roles** for the corporate parent.

(a) **Envisioning** is the process of creating a clear vision of **corporate intent**. This is important for three reasons.

    (i) The **corporate parent** itself needs a clear view of its own role if it is to avoid wasteful activity.

(ii) **External stakeholders** in general and existing and potential **investors** in particular need a clear understanding of corporate intent if they are to understand what the organisation does and to make appropriate decisions about their relationships with it.

(iii) The **managers** responsible for the performance of individual SBUs need to know how their work fits in to the corporate scheme so that they know what is expected of them. Their motivation also depends to some extent on having a reasonable belief that the corporate parent knows what it is doing.

(b) **Intervention** to improve performance or develop business strategy takes a number of forms.

(i) **Monitoring and control** of performance against plans, targets and intentions
(ii) Action to develop SBUs' **strategic capability**
(iii) **Coaching** and **training**
(iv) Promoting **collaboration** between SBUs and the creation of **synergies**

(c) The corporate parent may provide **services**, **resources** and **expertise** to its SBUs.

(i) Financial assistance
(ii) Resource sharing
(iii) Managerial assistance
(iv) Central services, such as HRM, purchasing and treasury
(v) Knowledge creation and management
(vi) Access to external networks

It might be argued that external market forces and mechanisms such as takeover-enforced management change are capable of dealing with these issues without incurring the overhead cost associated with the existence of a corporate parent. JS&W suggest that the corporate parent is likely to produce better results since it has both access to inside information and the co-operation of the SBU managers.

4.2 Value destruction

The existence of a the corporate parent imposes **costs** related to its size, therefore **it must create value at least equal to these costs** if it is to be worth having. This may be challenging. In addition, the activities of the corporate parent may be economically disadvantageous.

(a) The corporate hierarchy provides an arena for **managers' political ambition**. There is power to be achieved, but at a distance from the commercial realities of life in the SBUs. This is attractive to many.

(b) The **size and complexity** of a very large corporation can hinder or obscure the development of a clear and useful **corporate vision**.

(c) Corporate processes and hierarchy can **slow decision-making**, **stunt enterprise** and **absorb the energies** of SBU managers. This has the effect of blunting market responsiveness and harming overall efficiency.

4.3 Strategic rationale

JS&W identify three approaches to value creation that the corporate parent might adopt. They call these approaches **strategic rationales**.

4.3.1 Portfolio managers

The **portfolio manager** provides a service to investors by applying financial disciplines. It seeks out **undervalued companies** as purchase targets, acquires them, and improves their value and performance. Improvement may be achieved by asset stripping (the sale of attractive but inessential fixed assets), by disposing of under-performing elements or by installing new management. Portfolio managers **keep their own costs low** and provide **few central services**. Their SBUs are largely autonomous and their managers are judged by financial results. Typically, this type of corporate parent presides over a **widely diversified conglomerate**; our earlier remarks about diversification and strategic success apply here.

4.3.2 Synergy managers

The **synergy manager**, reasonably enough, pursues economies of scope; that is, the benefits of synergy. We have already discussed potential sources of synergy: here we may simply remark that the synergy manager aims to achieve high efficiency in the **shared use of resources and competences**. To do this, it must overcome some difficulties

(a) The **costs** involved in sharing
(b) The impact of **self-interest** among SBU managers
(c) **Incompatibility of systems and culture** among SBUs
(d) Variation in **local conditions**

Synergy managers must be **determined** if they are to achieve their goals. The central staff must integrate and control the efforts of the SBUs, which means they must be familiar with all of their operations and may reduce managerial motivation within the SBUs. The corporate parent must also be realistic about its ability to leverage the resources and competences it believes to offer synergistic benefits: it is easy to become subject to the **illusion of synergy**.

4.3.3 Parental developers

The **parental developer** adds value to its SBUs by deploying its own specific competences to aid them in their operations and development. To do this requires certain qualities in the corporate parent.

(a) It must have **actual, demonstrable competences** to deploy, otherwise its efforts will be mere interference and a distraction to the SBUs.

(b) Since it is unlikely that it can be equally good at everything, it must be prepared to divest itself of capabilities that can be **provided externally at lower cost**.

(c) It must have sufficient understanding of its SBUs to discern genuine **opportunities for intervention**.

The parental developer may encounter a problem in the form of a high-performing SBU that offers no opportunities for the deployment of its competences. Logically, it would dispose of this business, since its relationship with it can only be one of adding cost, but the likelihood of any corporate parent actually doing this seems low. Alternatively, it could attempt to change its role in respect of such a SBU and become a portfolio manager or synergy manager. The danger of doing this is the potential for loss of focus and confusion as to just what it should be doing.

Case Study

Corporate headquarters

'The corporate head office should be fit for purpose, and justify itself in terms of added value,' says Michael Goold, founding director of the Ashridge strategic management centre in London. A dictatorial and over-mighty headquarters is unlikely to provide the support that the rest of the organisation needs.

In the late 1980s and early 1990s there was a joke about the so-called 'inverse atrium rule' of head offices: the grander the corporate setting, the more trouble that organisation was likely to be in. Empire builders have long aimed to intimidate both competitors and colleagues with imposing HQs. It is an ancient human instinct , embodied, as every schoolchild knows (or at least used to know), by Shelley's Ozymandias, 'king of kings', whose resonant challenge to all-comers was: 'Look on my works, ye mighty, and despair!'

In a recent article in the *Strategic Management Journal*, Mr Goold, with Harvard's David Collis and Ashridge's David Young, describes four main roles that an effective head office has to perform.

First, there is unavoidable governance and compliance activity. While more people are needed for this than in the past, owing to today's more onerous regulatory environment, Mr Goold warns against over-engineering. 'There is a danger that you end up double-checking everything, that there is too much monitoring going on, slowing down the work,' he says. 'This aspect of head office should be as lean and mean as possible.'

A second function of HQ is the 'value-added parenting' of other corporate activity, offering supports to the executives from the centre. The acid test here is that the cost of this parenting should be less than the value it is generating in the rest of the business.

A third element of head office's work are shared services – HR, call centres, facilities management – many of which have been outsourced in recent years, or handed back to business units. And the fourth role is that of the 'core resource unit'– an example would be the research and development team in a pharmaceutical business.

While cutting out waste and duplication is obviously a good idea, it does not follow that headquarters should always be shrinking. As Mr Goold *et al* argue: 'Simply reducing the size of the headquarters is no guarantee of improved performance. Indeed, companies with larger headquarters typically outperform those with smaller headquarters.' On the other hand, globalisation may require leadership to be 'distributed' around the world. 'Core resource units' do not have to sit in the same building as compliance teams.

Stephan Stern, Financial Times, 10 April 2007

5 The corporate portfolio

FAST FORWARD

A parent may deploy four policies towards its SBUs

- Build
- Hold
- Harvest
- Divest

The SBU portfolio must be managed against three criteria

- Balance
- Attractiveness
- Strategic fit

Matrix-based models are used to manage **portfolios:** the Ashridge model is the only one to address strategic fit and assumes the **parental developer** approach is used.

A corporate parent of any type will have to make decisions about acquiring, nurturing and disposing of subsidiaries.

Four **major strategies** can be pursued with respect to products, market segments and, indeed, SBUs.

(a) **Build**. A build strategy forgoes short term earnings and profits in order to increase market share.

(b) **Hold**. A hold strategy seeks to maintain the current position.

(c) **Harvest**. A harvesting strategy seeks short-term earning and profits at the expense of long-term development.

(d) **Divest**. Divestment reduces negative cash flow and releases resources for use elsewhere.

A number of strategic tools have been developed to assist the decision process. These tools help the corporate parent to manage its portfolio of SBUs against of three criteria.

(a) **Balance** in relation to markets and corporate needs
(b) **Attractiveness** in terms of profitability and growth
(c) **Strategic fit**, in terms of potential synergy and parenting capability

The balance and attractiveness criteria are addressed by a range of matrix-based tools; strategic fit is the subject of a single model, the Ashridge portfolio display.

5.1 The Boston classification

FAST FORWARD

> The **Boston classification** classifies business units in terms of their capacity for growth within the market and the market's capacity for growth as a whole.

The **Boston Consulting Group** (BCG) developed a matrix based on empirical research that assesses businesses in terms of potential cash generation and cash expenditure requirements. SBUs are categorised in terms of **market growth rate** and **relative market share**.

Key term

> **Market share:** 'One entity's sale of a product or service in a specified market expressed as a percentage of total sales by all entities offering that product or service.'

(a) Assessing rate of **market growth** as high or low depends on the conditions in the market. No single percentage rate can be set, since new markets may grow explosively while mature ones grow hardly at all. High market growth rate can indicate good opportunities for profitable operations. However, intense competition in a high growth market can erode profit, while a slowly growing market with high barriers to entry can be very profitable.

(b) **Relative market share** is assessed as a ratio: it is market share compared with the market share of the **largest competitor**. Thus a relative market share greater than unity indicates that the SBU is the market leader. BGG settled on market share as a way of **estimating costs** and thus **profit potential**, because both costs and market share are connected with **production experience**: as experience in satisfying a particular market demand for value increases, market share can be expected to increase also, and costs to fall. The connection between lower costs and higher market share was independently confirmed by PIMS studies.

		Market share	
		High	Low
Market growth	High	Stars	Question marks
	Low	Cash cows	Dogs

The portfolio should be balanced, with cash cows providing finance for stars and question marks; and a minimum of dogs.

(a) In the short term, **stars** require capital expenditure in excess of the cash they generate, in order to maintain their position in their competitive growth market, but promise high returns in the future. Strategy: **build**.

(b) In due course, stars will become **cash cows**. Cash cows need very little capital expenditure, since mature markets are likely to be quite stable, and they generate high levels of cash income. Cash cows can be used to finance the stars. Strategy: **hold** or **harvest** if weak.

(c) **Question marks** must be assessed as to whether they justify considerable capital expenditure in the hope of increasing their market share, or should they be allowed to die quietly as they are squeezed out of the expanding market by rival products? Strategy: **build** or **harvest**.

(d) **Dogs** may be ex-cash cows that have now fallen on hard times. Although they will show only a modest net cash outflow, or even a modest net cash inflow, they are cash traps which tie up funds and provide a poor return on investment. However, they may have a useful role, either to complete a product range or to keep competitors out. There are also many smaller niche businesses in markets that are difficult to consolidate that would count as dogs but which are quite successful. Strategy: **divest** or **hold**.

The BCG matrix must be used with care.

(a) It may be difficult to define 'high' and 'low' on both axes of the matrix.

(b) The matrix has been used to assess **products** rather than **SBUs**, but JS&W say this should not be done; nor should it be applied to broad markets that include many market segments. They do, however, recommend it for assessing a **portfolio of international operations**, though with three caveats.

  (i) The permitted forms of activity and ownership vary from country to country.
  (ii) Political risk is not considered.
  (iii) Shared resources are not considered

(c) The matrix is built around cash flows but **innovative capacity** may be the critical resource.

 Case Study

Google

Until recently, the weight of investor opinion held that Google's only significant business – delivery of context-specific online advertising – was a star and was positioned to remain one for many years to come.

The internet has so far attracted only about $US10bn of the $US250bn spent worldwide on advertising each year, and Google has proved its ability to translate its dominant position in the online ad market into a river of cash.

Google's revenues grew about 85 per cent to $US6bn in 2005 and are forecast to grow a further 50 per cent in 2006, according to Wall Street forecasts. The firm is expected to generate about US$2bn in cash from operations in 2006.

Nothing that was said on Tuesday by Google CFO George Reyes signalled any material change to that outlook. As can be seen in the consensus forecast for 2006 revenues, the market has already factored in the slower future growth rates that Reyes mentioned.

But if there is a message to take away from the Reyes comments, which were distorted in initial reports and further obscured by a 'clarifying' press release later on Tuesday, it is that context-specific online ad placement may not quite be the business that Google's more fervent admires believe it to be.

In fact, it may be already well on the way to becoming a cash cow (for Google at least, given its already dominant share) rather than a star.

This was certainly the implications of Reyes' comments that future revenue growth for Google's core business was likely to be organic, that is, to come from higher traffic, higher online advertising spending or increased market share.

Stephen Ellis, The Australian, 4 March 2006

Exam focus point

You should now think back to our discussion of the product life cycle in this Study Text. We noted there that JS&W do not recommend the use of the BCG matrix for product portfolio purposes and recommended that you should initially think in terms of the product life cycle when answering questions that call for the analysis of product portfolios.

However, we also said that the BCG matrix has traditionally been used for this purpose and that you might consider using it in such a question. A note about JS&W's view might be worth an extra mark.

5.2 The public sector portfolio matrix

FAST FORWARD

The public sector portfolio matrix classifies activities in terms of their popularity and the resources available for them.

Montanari and Bracker proposed a matrix for the analysis of services provided by public sector bodies. This might be applied at the level of local or national government, or an executive agency with a portfolio of services. The axes are an assessment of service efficiency and public attractiveness: naturally, political support for a service or organisation depends to a great extent on the extent to which the public need and appreciate it.

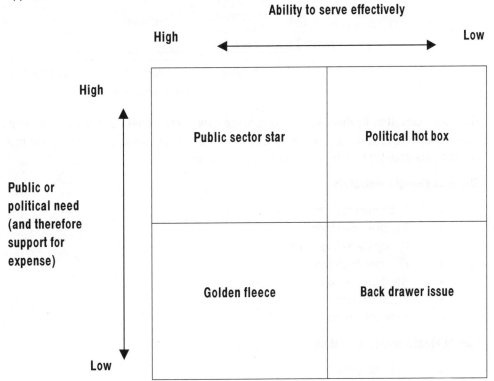

(a) A **public sector star** is something that the system is doing well and should not change. They are essential to the viability of the system.

(b) **Political hot boxes** are services that the public want, or which are mandated, but for which there are not adequate resources or competences.

(c) **Golden fleeces** are services that are done well but for which there is low demand. They may therefore be perceived to be undesirable uses for limited resources. They are potential targets for cost cutting.

(d) **Back drawer issues** are unappreciated and have low priority for funding. They are obvious candidates for cuts, but if managers perceive them as essential, they should attempt to increase support for them and move them into the **political hot box** category.

5.3 The General Electric Business Screen

FAST FORWARD

> The GE and Shell matrices are based on the enterprise's competitive capacity and the market's attractiveness.

The approach of the GE Business Screen (GEBS) is similar to that of the BCG matrix. The GEBS includes a broader range of company and market factors. A typical example of the GE matrix is provided below.

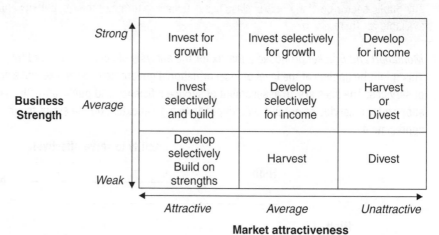

This matrix **classifies businesses** according to **industry attractiveness** and **company strengths**. The approach aims to consider a variety of factors that contribute to both these variables. The lists below are not complete: they are merely examples of relevant factors.

Business strength indicators

- Good market share
- Effective sales force
- Strong marketing activity
- Effective innovation
- Good distribution
- Brand strength
- Financial strength

Market attractiveness indicators

- The five forces
- Overall size
- Growth rate
- Cyclicality
- Overall profitability

- Inflation rate
- General environmental issues

The broader approach of the GE matrix emphasises the attempt to match competences within the company to conditions within the market place. Difficulties associated with measurement and classification mean that again the results of such an exercise must be interpreted with care.

JS&W suggest that this analysis could be used to assess competitive position in the same product market across national market boundaries. To do this it would be necessary to include such considerations as barriers to trade, political risk, economic stability and business regulation when considering market attractiveness. The horizontal axis would become **country attractiveness** and the vertical axis would show a combination of competitive strength and the compatibility of the company with the country. The high-high segment would represent primary investment opportunities, the two high/medium segments would be secondary opportunities and the two high/low segments together with the medium/medium segment would represent tertiary opportunities.

5.4 The Shell directional policy matrix

There have been several other matrices designed as guides to strategy. The **Shell directional policy matrix** is similar to the GEBS in that its classifications depend upon **managerial judgement** rather than simple **numerical scores**, as in the BCG matrix. Its axes are **competitive capability** and **prospects for sector profitability**. Clearly, these measures are very similar to those used in the GEBS.

Prospects for sector profitability

		Unattractive	Average	Attractive
	Weak	Disinvest	Phased withdrawal	Double or quit
Enterprise's competitive capabilities	Average	Phased withdrawal	Custodial Growth	Try harder
	Strong	Cash generation	Growth Leader	Leader

The Shell directional policy matrix

5.5 The Ashridge portfolio display

FAST FORWARD

The Ashridge model assesses the benefit SBUs can derive from a corporate parent playing the parental developer role. Heartland businesses both have CSFs that fit the parent's resources and competences *and* provide opportunities for good use of them. Alien businesses have neither quality. Ballast businesses are well-understood by the parent but need little assistance. Value trap businesses need help but of kinds the parent cannot provide.

As mentioned earlier, the Ashridge portfolio display is concerned with **strategic fit**, that is, the role of the corporate parent and the suitability of the range of SBUs it manages. The concept is based on the **parental developer** approach to the role of the corporate parent discussed earlier in this chapter. The principles embodied in the model can be approached from two directions.

    (a)   Corporate parents should build portfolios of businesses that they can develop effectively.

    (b)   Corporate parents should seek to build parenting skills that are relevant to their portfolios.

The coherence of the corporation overall may be assessed by reference to two variables.

    (a)   '**Feel**': The degree of fit between the parent's skills, resources and other characteristics and the SBUs' CSFs

    (b)   '**Benefit**': the degree of fit between the opportunities the SBUs present for parenting and the parent's skills resources and other characteristics

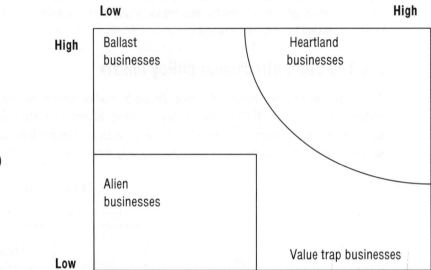

Benefit (fit between SBU **opportunities** and parental skills etc)

    (a)   **Heartland businesses** can benefit from the attention of the parent without risk of harm from unsuitable developments.

    (b)   **Ballast businesses** are well-understood by the parent, but need little assistance. They would do just as well if they were independent businesses. They should bear as little central cost as possible.

    (c)   **Value trap businesses** provide good opportunities for parenting, but these opportunities do not relate to the SBU's CSFs. They should only be retained if they can be moved into the heartland; this will require the parent to acquire new skills and resources.

    (d)   **Alien businesses** have no place in the portfolio. They need the attention of a skilled parent, but the actual parent does not have the skills and resources required to help them.

This analysis reverses the usual approach to portfolio management: it does not ask what the value of the SBUs is to the centre, but what value the centre can add to the SBUs. This raises two questions.

    (a)   Is the **cost burden** of the parent **commensurate with the value it adds**? For example, if the corporate parent's role is limited to, say, relations with the financial markets, it should be small and economically run.

    (d)   If a corporate parent has a justifiably interventionist role, **how many SBUs can it parent effectively**?

The trend in business recent years has been decentralisation of decision-making and a move towards **facilitiation** by the parent rather than active intervention. A similar trend towards privatisation and deregulation has been apparent in the public sector.

6 Business unit strategy: generic strategies

Business unit strategy involves a choice between being the lowest cost producer (**cost leadership**) making the product different from competitors' products in some way (**differentiation**) or specialising on a segment of the market (**focus**, by addressing that segment by a strategy of cost leadership or differentiation). **Porter** believes that a firm *must* choose one of these or be **stuck-in-the-middle**.

Competitive advantage is anything which gives one organisation an edge over its rivals. *Porter* argues that a firm should adopt a competitive strategy intended to achieve competitive advantage for the firm.

Competitive strategy means 'taking offensive or defensive actions to create a dependable position in an industry, to cope successfully with ... competitive forces and thereby yield a superior return on investment for the firm. Firms have discovered many different approaches to this end, and the best strategy for a given firm is ultimately a unique construction reflecting its particular circumstances'. (Porter)

6.1 The choice of competitive strategy

Porter believes there are three **generic strategies** for competitive advantage.

Cost leadership means being the lowest cost producer in the industry as a whole.

Differentiation is the exploitation of a product or service which the *industry as a whole* believes to be unique.

Focus involves a restriction of activities to only part of the market (a segment).

- Providing goods and/or services at lower cost (**cost-focus**)
- Providing a differentiated product or service (**differentiation-focus**)

Cost leadership and differentiation are industry-wide strategies. Focus involves segmentation but also the pursuit, **within the chosen segment only**, of a strategy of cost leadership or differentiation.

Porter's generic strategy model is one of a handful of truly vital theories that you **absolutely must master** for your exam. Study this section with great care and understand the implications of each strategy for the companies that might adopt them. Understanding this area of theory will not only equip you to make sensible suggestions in your answers to many questions, it will also enable you to appreciate important background detail in a wide range of question scenarios.

6.1.1 Cost leadership

A cost leadership strategy seeks to achieve the position of lowest-cost producer in the **industry as a whole**. By producing at the lowest cost, the manufacturer can compete on price with every other producer in the industry, and earn the higher unit profits, if the manufacturer so chooses.

How to achieve overall cost leadership

(a)   Set up production facilities to obtain **economies of scale**.

(b)   Use the **latest technology** to reduce costs and/or enhance productivity (or use cheap labour if available).

(c)   In high technology industries, and in industries depending on labour skills for product design and production methods, exploit the **learning curve effect**. By producing more items than any other competitor, a firm can benefit more from the learning curve, and achieve lower average costs.

(d)   Concentrate on improving productivity.

(e)   **Minimise overhead costs.**

(f)   **Get favourable access to sources of supply**.

Classic examples of companies pursuing cost leadership are *Black and Decker* and *South West Airlines*. Large out-of-town stores specialising in one particular category of product are able to secure cost leadership by economies of scale over other retailers. Such shops have been called **category killers**; an example is *PC World*.

 Case Study

Watermark is a supplier of catering and other services to airlines. It had a good six months in the first half of 2005, with turnover increasing from £30.5m to $35.2m and profits rising from £1.6m to £2.4m. John Caulentt, the CEO, declared that the company's business was, in essence, finding savings in the airlines' supply chain: 'we can sell the savings to our clients and keep some of it for ourselves',

6.1.2 Differentiation

A differentiation strategy assumes that competitive advantage can be gained through **particular characteristics** of a firm's products. Products may be divided into three categories.

(a)   **Breakthrough products** offer a radical performance advantage over competition, perhaps at a drastically lower price (eg float glass, developed by *Pilkington*).

(b)   **Improved products** are not radically different from their competition but are obviously superior in terms of better performance at a competitive price (eg microchips).

(c)   **Competitive products** derive their appeal from a particular compromise of cost and performance. For example, cars are not all sold at rock-bottom prices, nor do they all provide immaculate comfort and performance. They compete with each other by trying to offer a more attractive compromise than rival models.

How to differentiate

(a)   **Build up a brand image** (eg Pepsi's blue cans are supposed to offer different 'psychic benefits' to Coke's red ones).

(b)   **Give the product special features** to make it stand out (eg Russell Hobbs' Millennium kettle incorporated a new kind of element, which boils water faster).

(c)   **Exploit other activities of the value chain** (see Section 4 below).

Generic strategies and the five forces

Competitive force	Advantages		Disadvantages	
	Cost leadership	Differentiation	Cost leadership	Differentiation
New entrants	Economies of scale raise entry barriers	Brand loyalty and perceived uniqueness are entry barriers		
Substitutes	Firm is not so vulnerable as its less cost-effective competitors to the threat of substitutes	Customer loyalty is a weapon against substitutes		
Customers	Customers cannot drive down prices further than the next most efficient competitor	Customers have no comparable alternative Brand loyalty should lower price sensitivity		Customers may no longer need the differentiating factor Sooner or later customers become price sensitive
Suppliers	Flexibility to deal with cost increases	Higher margins can offset vulnerability to supplier price rises	Increase in input costs can reduce price advantages	
Industry rivalry	Firm remains profitable when rivals go under through excessive price competition	Unique features reduce direct competition	Technological change will require capital investment, or make production cheaper for competitors Competitors learn via imitation Cost concerns ignore product design or marketing issues	Imitation narrows differentiation

6.1.3 Focus (or niche) strategy

In a focus strategy, a firm concentrates its attention on one or more particular segments or niches of the market, and does not try to serve the entire market with a single product.

 Case Study

A good example of a niche strategy is that adopted by the makers of *Sibelius 7*, a computer system for composers of music. Contrary to most other developments in software, *Sibelius 7* requires dedicated hardware to work effectively: it cannot be run on a PC or Mac with a soundcard. Users of the software have to buy hardware too.

(a) A **cost focus strategy:** aim to be a cost leader for a particular segment. This type of strategy is often found in the printing, clothes manufacture and car repair industries.

(b) A **differentiation focus strategy:** pursue differentiation for a chosen segment. Luxury goods suppliers are the prime exponents of such a strategy.

Ben and Jerry's ice cream is a good example of a product offering based on differentiation focus.

Case Study

In 2005, *The Financial Times* reported on Tyrrells' Potato Chips, a niche manufacturer of crisps that uses potatoes produced on its own farm. William Chase, owner of the company, set it up in part to escape from dependence on the major supermarkets and in part to add extra value to his basic product, potatoes. Major feature of his strategy is to sell mainly though small retailers at the upper end of the grocery and catering markets. The Financial Times summarises the Tyrrells' strategy under six headings.

- **Branding**. Tyrrells' marketing taps into the public's enthusiasm for 'authenticity' and 'provenance'. Its crisp packets tell the story of Tyrrells'. Pictures of employees growing potatoes on the Herefordshire farm and then cooking them illustrate the journey from 'seed to chip'.

- **Quality**. Tyrrells' chips are made from traditional varieties of potato and 'hand-fried' in small batches.

- **Distribution**. Tyrrells' sells directly to 80 per cent of its retail stockists. Students from a local agricultural college are employed to trawl through directories and identify fine-food shops to target with samples. After winning their business, Tyrrells' develops the relationship though personal contact.

- **Diffusion strategy**. Selling to the most exclusive shops cerates a showcase for Tyrrells' to target consumers who are not sensitive to price, allowing it to grow profitably.

- **New product development**. Tyrrells' is constantly bringing out new flavours and products. Experimental recipes are produced in sample runs and given free to shops to test with customers. Recent introductions include apple chips, honey glazed parsnips and Ludlow sausage with wholegrain mustard.

- **Exporting**. This has created a further sales channel through fine-food stores. Yet it has also forced greater dependency on distributors, introducing an unwelcome layer between itself and its customers.

Porter suggests that a focus strategy can achieve competitive advantage when '**broad-scope**' businesses fall into one of two errors.

(a) **Underperformance** occurs when a product does not fully meet the needs of a segment and offers the opportunity for a **differentiation focus** player.

(b) **Overperformance** gives a segment more than it really wants and provides an opportunity for a **cost focus** player.

Advantages

(a) A niche is more secure and a firm can insulate itself from competition.

(b) The firm does not spread itself too thinly.

(c) Both cost leadership and differentiation require **superior performance** – life is easier in a niche, where there may be little or no competition.

Drawbacks of a focus strategy

(a) The firm sacrifices economies of scale which would be gained by serving a wider market.

(b) Competitors can move into the segment, with increased resources (eg the Japanese moved into the US luxury car market, to compete with Mercedes and BMW).

(c) The segment's needs may eventually become less distinct from the main market.

6.2 Which strategy?

Although there is a risk with any of the generic strategies, Porter argues that a firm *must* pursue one of them. A **stuck-in-the-middle** strategy is almost certain to make only low profits. 'This firm lacks the market share, capital investment and resolve to play the low-cost game, the industry-wide differentiation necessary to obviate the need for a low-cost position, or the focus to create differentiation or a low-cost position in a more limited sphere.'

It is also important that both cost leadership and differentiation require superior performance. Therefore, most businesses should pursue some form of focus strategy as it is easier to dominate a niche than a complete market.

Question	Hermes Telecommunications plc

The managing director of Hermes Telecommunications plc is interested in corporate strategy. Hermes has invested a great deal of money in establishing a network which competes with that of Telecom UK, a recently privatised utility. Initially Hermes concentrated its efforts on business customers in the South East of England, especially the City of London, where it offered a lower cost service to that supplied by Telecom UK. Recently, Hermes has approached the residential market (ie domestic telephone users) offering a lower cost service on long-distance calls. Technological developments have resulted in the possibility of a cheap mobile telecommunication network, using microwave radio links. The franchise for this service has been awarded to Gerbil phone, which is installing transmitters in town centres and at rail stations.

What issues of competitive strategy have been raised in the above scenario, particularly in relation to Hermes Telecommunications plc?

Answer

(a) Arguably, Hermes initially pursued a cost-focus strategy, by targeting the business segment.

(b) It seems to be moving into a cost leadership strategy over the whole market although its competitive offer, in terms of lower costs for local calls, is incomplete.

(c) The barriers to entry to the market have been lowered by the new technology. Gerbil phone might pick up a significant amount of business.

6.3 Conceptual difficulties with generic strategy

In practice, it is rarely simple to draw hard and fast distinctions between the generic strategies as there are conceptual problems underlying them.

(a) **Cost leadership**

(i) **Internal focus.** Cost refers to internal measures, rather than the market demand. It can be used to gain market share: but it is the **market share which is important,** not cost leadership as such.

(ii)   **Only one firm.** If cost leadership applies cross the whole industry, only one firm will pursue this strategy successfully. However, the position is not clear-cut.

- More than one firm might **aspire** to cost leadership, especially in dynamic markets where new technologies are frequently introduced.

- The boundary between cost leadership and cost focus might be blurred.

- Firms competing market-wide might have different competences or advantages that confer cost leadership in different segments.

(iii)   **Higher margins can be used for differentiation.** Having low costs does *not* mean you have to charge lower prices or compete on price. A cost leader can choose to 'invest higher margins in R&D or marketing'. Being a cost leader arguably gives producers more freedom to choose *other* competitive strategies.

(b)   **Differentiation**. Porter assumes that a differentiated product will always be sold at a **higher price**.

(i)   However, a **differentiated product** may be sold at the same price as competing products in order to **increase market share.**

(ii)   **Choice of competitor.** Differentiation from whom? Who are the competitors? Do they serve other market segments? Do they compete on the same basis?

(iii)   **Source of differentiation**. This can include **all** aspects of the firm's offer, not only the product. Restaurants aim to create an atmosphere or 'ambience', as well as serving food of good quality.

Focus probably has fewer conceptual difficulties, as it ties in very neatly with ideas of market segmentation. In practice most companies pursue this strategy to some extent, by designing products/services to meet the needs of particular target markets.

'Stuck-in-the-middle' is therefore what many companies actually pursue quite successfully. Any number of strategies can be pursued, with different approaches to **price** and the **perceived added value** (ie the differentiation factor) in the eyes of the customer.

6.4 The strategy clock

FAST FORWARD

> The strategy clock develops Porter's theory, analysing strategies in terms of **price** and **perceived value added**.

Porter's basic concept of generic strategies has been the subject of further discussion. JS&W, quoting *Bowman,* describe the strategic options using the **strategy clock.**

The eight strategies shown on the clock represent different approaches to creating value for the customer and each customer will buy from the provider whose offering most closely matches his own view of the proper relationship between price and perceived benefits.

Each position on the clock has its own **critical success factor**, since each strategy is defined in market terms. Positions 1 and 2 will attract customers who are price conscious above all, with position 2 giving a little more emphasis to serviceability. These are typical approaches in commodity markets. By contrast, strategies 4 and 5 are relevant to consumers who require a customised product.

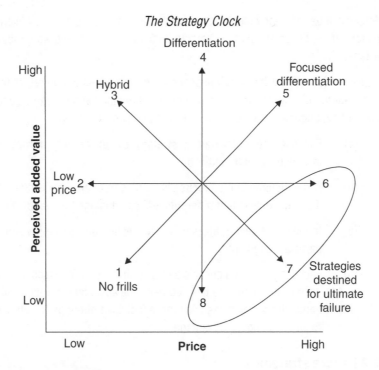

The Strategy Clock

6.4.1 Price-based strategies

Strategies 1 and 2 are price-based strategies.

(a)   A **no frills** strategy is appropriate under several conditions. It can be used for commodity-like products and the most price-conscious customers. It is also suitable where customers' switching costs are low and where there is little opportunity for competition on product features. This strategy may be used for market entry, to gain experience and build volume. This was done by Japanese car manufacturers in the 1960s.

(b)   A **low price** strategy offers better value than competitors. This can lead to price war and thence to reduced margins and lack of reinvestment for all players and Porter's generic strategy of **cost leadership** is appropriate to a firm adopting this strategy.

6.4.2 Differentiation strategies

Strategies 3, 4 and 5 are all differentiation strategies. Each one represents a different trade-off between market share (with its cost advantages) and margin (with its direct impact on profit). Differentiation can be created in three ways.

- Product features
- Marketing, including powerful brand promotion
- Core competences

The **hybrid** strategy seeks both differentiation and a lower price than competitors. The cost base must be low enough to permit reduced prices and reinvestment to maintain differentiation. This strategy may be more advantageous than differentiation alone under certain circumstances.

- If it leads to growth in market share
- If differentiation rests on core competences and costs can be reduced elsewhere
- If a low price approach is suited to a particular market segment
- Where it is used as a market entry strategy

The basic **differentiation** strategy comes in two variants, depending on whether a price premium is charged or a competitive price is accepted in order to build market share. The pursuit of a differentiation strategy requires detailed and accurate **market intelligence**. The **strategic customers** and their preferences must be clearly identified, as must the competitors and their likely responses. The chosen basis for differentiation should be inherently difficult to imitate, and will probably need to be developed over time.

A strategy of **focussed differentiation** seeks a high price premium in return for a high degree of differentiation. This implies concentration on a well-defined and probably quite restricted market segment. **Centres of excellence** in the public sector pursue a similar strategy.

(a)   Focus is a common start-up strategy: expansion may prompt or require a gradual move to a less focussed differentiation.

(b)   It is difficult to pursue focus with only part of an organisation: the less focussed part, even if it is to some extent differentiated, can damage the brand values of the focussed part.

(c)   In the public sector, stakeholders expecting universal provision will object to focus on particular segments.

(d)   Focus is aimed at a specific segment: if the non-focussed product is improved enough to become acceptable to this segment, the advantage of focus will be eroded. Alternatively, competitors may make even more focussed offerings to sub-segments, again eroding the focusser's original advantage

6.4.3 Failure strategies

Combinations 6, 7 and 8 are likely to result in failure.

6.5 The TOWS matrix

We have already discussed the TOWS matrix and Weihrich's classification of strategies based upon it. Consideration of the characteristics of each of these general classes of strategy might be a useful adjunct to use of the strategy clock, particularly when considering cash flow and the availability of resources.

7 Sustaining competitive advantage

FAST FORWARD

Different policies are required to sustain differentiation or price-based strategies. Lock-in is achieved when a product becomes the industry standard.

When we discussed competition in Chapter 3, we said that the business environment might be sufficiently stable to permit a build-up of **sustainable competitive advantage**. Alternatively, there might be **hypercompetition** and a need for rapid innovation and response to competitive moves. In Chapter 4, we went on to consider the **strategic capabilities** needed under these varying conditions. We will now consider the ways in which businesses can **form strategies** to respond to these two different conditions.

7.1 Sustaining price-based strategies

(a)   **Low margins** can be sustained either by increased volumes or by cross-subsidisation from another business unit.

(b)   A **cost leader** can operate at a price advantage, but to be sustainable, cost leaders must constantly and aggressively drive down all of their costs.

(c)   A cost leader or a company with extensive financial resources can win a **price war**.

(d)   A **no-frills strategy** can succeed in the long term if it is aimed at a segment that particularly appreciates low price.

7.2 Sustaining differentiation

Sustaining differentiation is difficult. To begin with, it is more than just being *different*: the difference must be **valued by customers**. Secondly, a difference that a competitor can easily imitate gives no sustainable advantage.

(a) **Attempts at imitation can be obstructed** by, for example, securing preferred access to customers or suppliers through bidding or licensing procedures.

(b) Some resources are **inherently immobile**. This can be the result of **intangibility**, as in the case of brands; high customer switching costs, as with proprietary technology; or **co-specialisation**, which occurs when organisations' value chains are intimately linked.

(c) **Cost advantage** can be used to sustain differentiation rather than price advantage by investing in innovation, brand management or quality improvement.

7.3 Lock-in

Lock-in is achieved in a market when a company's product becomes the **industry standard**. Direct competitors are reduced to minor niches and **compatibility** with the industry standard becomes a prerequisite for complementary products. *Microsoft* has achieved this position in the market for PC operating systems and is only challenged by *Linux* because the latter product is free to use. *Sony* regularly attempts to establish industry standards in order to achieve market dominance, with varying degrees of success. The original *Walkman* became the industry standard, but the *Betamax* video recording standard lost to *VHS*. The concept of lock-in is equally applicable to companies following strategies of cost leadership or differentiation.

Factors affecting lock-in

(a) **Perception of dominance**: potential competitors and suppliers of complementary products will only conform to an attempt to set standards if they perceive the standard-setter as dominant in the market, usually in terms of market share.

(b) **First mover advantage**: a standard is more likely to be set early in the lifecycle of a new product than when it is mature.

(c) **Self-reinforcement**: once dominance is achieved, conforming with the standard becomes necessary for survival.

(d) **Fierce defence**: a firm that achieves lock-in will defend its position vigorously. *Visa* threatened to impose coercive settlement fees on its top 100 card issuers if they attempted to move their operations to *MasterCard*.

Lock-in is also known as the **delta model**, which is the term used by *Hax and Wilde*, who described it in their book of the same name.

7.4 Strategy and hypercompetition

FAST FORWARD

> **Hypercompetition** makes it impossible to create lasting advantage with a steady policy: a series of short term moves is required. These include repositioning on the strategy clock, counter attack, imitation and attacks on barriers to entry.

We discussed **hypercompetition** in Chapter 3. There we said that it was a condition of constant competitive change created by frequent, boldly aggressive competitive moves. This makes it **impossible to create lasting competitive advantage**. Under these conditions, continuing success depends on the dynamic capabilities discussed in Chapter 4 and on the effective exploitation of a series of short-term moves. Here are some examples.

7.4.1 Repositioning on the strategy clock

Repositioning may be possible. For example, a firm using a no frills strategy may move towards higher quality combined with a low price; that is from position 1 on the clock to position 2. Similarly, a differentiator may attempt to create a new market segment or niche and move towards a more focussed kind of differentiation

7.4.2 Counterattacking against market-based moves

Market-based strategies that work under less competitive conditions are often successfully counterattacked.

(a)   **First mover advantage can be undermined** by leapfrogging into the lead with an improved product or making a flank attack on a new segment.

(b)   **Product/market moves can be imitated**, thus preventing the competitor from achieving advantage.

7.4.3 Attacking barriers to entry

(a)   **Rapid technological advance** shortens lifecycles and can allow competitors to outflank an initially **robust** strategic capability.

(b)   Attempts to dominate particular market segments or geographic markets may be overcome in several ways.

   (i)   **Economies of scale** in a market can be countered by utilising the effects of similar economies achieved from a dominant position in another one. An example would be entering a foreign market with an undifferentiated product already established in the home market. **Cross subsidy** can also be used, perhaps to enable initial price competition.

   (ii)   Dominance of the market's current pattern of **distribution** can be overcome by developing a different approach, such as selling by mail order rather than through retail outlets.

(c)   Small competitors can **avoid direct confrontation** with resource-heavy dominant players by concentrating on niches, building trading alliances and by merging with other small companies.

7.4.4 Principles of hypercompetitive strategy

(a)   **Pre-empt imitation and remain unpredictable** by competing in new ways. This may involve destroying current advantages in order to develop new ones.

(b)   To attack **competitors' weaknesses** is to provoke them to overcome them.

(c)   A **series of small moves** disguises the strategy and provides a succession of temporary advantages.

(d)   **Misleading signals** of strategic intent can be used to confuse.

7.5 Collaboration as a strategy

FAST FORWARD

> **Collaboration** may be a valid strategic option, reducing costs and building or overcoming barriers to entry.

Organisations do not only compete. **Collaboration** between buyers and sellers and between potential competitors can reduce costs below those of operating independently.

(a) Buyers and sellers may collaborate to ensure high quality, share the cost of research or reduce stock levels, for example. Where high quality is of great important, becoming an **accredited supplier** can be difficult, but will **enhance selling power**.

(b) Collaboration between members of a fragmented market **increases buying power**, as when small retailers co-operate to buy in large quantities.

(c) Collaboration between suppliers in an industry over such matters as marketing and research and development can help to **build barriers** to entry and against substitutes.

(d) On the other hand, collaboration may be the best way to obtain entry to some foreign markets; **aspiring entrants** can obtain local knowledge and access to the local infrastructure. Indeed, some governments require entrants to take a local partner.

(e) Suppliers may collaborate with consumers for a variety of reasons: examples include self-assembly of furniture and self-assessment of tax liability. Such **co-production** can help to hold down **costs** and increase a sense of **ownership**.

(f) **Knowledge sharing** may be required in the public sector, as a form of best practice. Also, collaboration may be required to improve standards, secure best value from spending or solve problems that cut across agency boundaries.

8 Using the value chain in competitive strategy

FAST FORWARD

The value chain can be used to design a competitive strategy, by deploying the various activities strategically.

The value chain model can be used to analyse a business's operations in order to establish where it achieves **competitive advantage through the creation of value**. It can also show where there is potential for **improved value addition** (especially in relationship to competitors) and where activities are being performed that do not add value; the aim here should be to eliminate such activities, or at least to reconfigure them so that they do contribute some value. However, using the value chain in this way, as with using any strategic management tool, requires careful thought and sound judgement. This may well involve the use of other strategic concepts, such as differentiation, competences and critical success factors, focussing the strategist's attention on areas where they might be applied.

8.1 Other uses of the value chain

As well as using the value chain to establish where it creates value for the customer, an organisation can also use the model in other strategically valuable ways.

- Identification of critical success factors
- Identification of activities suitable for out sourcing
- Identification of areas where value activities are not mutually supporting
- Identification of opportunities to use information strategically

9 Product-market strategy: direction of growth

FAST FORWARD

Product-market strategies involve determining which products should be sold in which markets, by market penetration, market development, product development and diversification. Diversification is assumed to be risky, especially diversification that is entirely unrelated to current products and markets. Alliances of various kinds are a possible approach to diversification. Withdrawal may be a valid option.

Key term

> **Product-market mix** is a short hand term for the **products and services** a firm sells (or a service which a public sector organisation provides) and the **markets** it sells them to.

9.1 The importance of market share

Like some of the portfolio matrix tools we looked at in the last chapter, the PIMS framework regards **competitive strength** and **market attractiveness** as important determinants of profitability. However, perhaps the single most significant factor to emerge from the PIMS data is the link between profitability and **relative market share**. You will recall that relative market share was one of the axes of the **BCG matrix**.

There is a definite, observable correlation between market share and return on investment. This is probably the result of lower costs resulting from **economies of scale**. Economies of scale due to increasing market share are particularly evident in **purchasing** and the **utilisation of fixed assets.**

 Case Study

Vodafone

Mark Ritson, a marketing academic with a particular expertise in branding, discussed Vodafone in his weekly column in *Marketing* in March 2006. The company had been forced to write down its book value by £28bn and Professor Ritson analysed the pressures that had led to this evidence of strategic failure. After mentioning competitive pressure, failure to develop internet telephony and a fixation on 3G, he turned to the scale of Vodafone's operations.

'Perhaps most problematic of all is Vodafone's size. There are advantages in having 180m customers in 27 countries, but there is also a crucial trade-off between scale economies and brand focus. Many analysts now believe Vodafone is simply too big and too cumbersome to succeed.

'For all the talk of global brands, there are two key caveats to remember. First, most customers usually prefer national or local brands to bland global offerings. Second, most marketing managers can't build a national brand successfully, let along a global one.'

9.2 Product-market mix

Ansoff drew up a **growth vector matrix**, describing how a combination of a firm's activities in current and new markets, with existing and new products can lead to **growth**. Ansoff's original model was a 4 cell matrix based on product and market, shown as the heart of the diagram below. *Lynch* (*Corporate Strategy*) has produced an enhanced model that he calls the **market options matrix.** This adds the external options shown in the diagram. Withdrawal, demerger and privatisation are discussed at the end of this section.

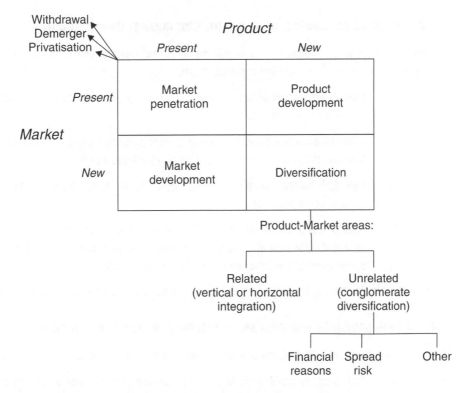

Note the obvious family resemblance between the basic Ansoff Matrix and the new product strategy matrix presented earlier in this Study Text.

9.2.1 Current products and current markets: market penetration

Market penetration. The firm seeks to do four things.

(a) **Maintain or to increase its share** of current markets with current products, eg through competitive pricing, advertising, sales promotion

(b) Secure dominance of growth markets

(c) Restructure a mature market by driving out competitors

(d) Increase usage by existing customers (eg airmiles, loyalty cards)

This is a relatively **low risk** strategy since it requires no capital investment. As such it is attractive to the unadventurous type of company.

9.2.2 Consolidation

To consolidate is to seek to maintain current market share. This may be an appropriate strategy when the firm is already the market leader; if availability of funds is limited; or when an owner-manager is approaching retirement or wishes to avoid the loss of personal control that is a likely consequence of growth. Also, if it seems that profitability does **not** correlate with market share, consolidation may be a sensible option.

(a) Consolidation does not mean neglect. It is unlikely that competitors will halt their efforts, so the firm must continue to enhance its market offer in order to maintain its relative position.

(b) PIMS data indicates that **high product quality** is important if a consolidation strategy is to succeed. It can compensate to some extent for both a low market share and a low level of marketing expenditure.

9.2.3 Present products and new markets: market development

Market development is the process by which the firm seeks new markets for its current products. There are many possible approaches. Here are some examples.

(a) **New geographical areas** and export markets (eg a radio station building a new transmitter to reach a new audience).

(b) **Different package sizes** for food and other domestic items so that both those who buy in bulk and those who buy in small quantities are catered for.

(c) **New distribution channels** to attract new customers (eg organic food sold in supermarkets not just specialist shops

(d) **Differential pricing policies** to attract different types of customer and create **new market segments**. For example, travel companies have developed a market for cheap long-stay winter breaks in warmer countries for retired couples.

This approach to strategy is also low in risk since it also requires little capital investment.

9.2.4 New products and present markets: product development

Product development is the launch of new products to existing markets. This has several advantages.

(a) The company can exploit its existing marketing arrangements such as promotional methods and distribution channels at low cost.

(b) The company should already have good knowledge of its customers and their wants and habits.

(c) Competitors will be forced to respond.

(d) The cost of entry to the market will go up.

This strategy is **riskier** than both market penetration and market development since it is likely to require **major investment** in the new product development process and, for physical products, in suitable production facilities.

 Case Study

One of the hottest consumer items in early 2006 was the 'High Definition Ready' television set, despite the fact that HD broadcasts are only available by subscription to Sky, the satellite TV company or Telewest, a regional cable company. Some experts felt it was unlikely that HDTV would ever be available by terrestrial broadcast since the signal takes up four times as much bandwidth as current channels. However the BBC started terrestrial HDTV trials in mid-2006.

9.2.5 New products: new markets (diversification)

Diversification occurs when a company decides to make **new products for new markets**. It should have a clear idea about what it expects to gain from diversification.

(a) **Growth.** New products and new markets should be selected which offer prospects for growth which the existing product-market mix does not.

(b) **Investing surplus** funds not required for other expansion needs, bearing in mind that the funds could be returned to shareholders. Diversification is a high risk strategy, having many of the characteristics of a new business start-up. It is likely to require the deployment of **new competences**.

 Case Study

Johnson Wax

When you think 'platform,' you probably think 'software' – with *Microsoft Windows* dominating the pack. But *any* product, not just software, can become a platform. What's required is imagination. Consider how *SC Johnson & Son*, the multibillion-dollar consumer products company, managed to 'platform' its way from floors to shaving cream to candles – and much, much more.

Samuel Curtis Johnson started the company in 1886 when he purchased the parquet flooring division of the *Racine Hardware Company*. After laying floors, Johnson would finish the wood with a special wax of his own creation, which became very popular with customers. Their repeated requests to buy extra wax led Johnson to develop *Johnson's Prepared Wax* and move into consumer products.

Another product – a paste blended with wax that created a spectacular sheen – also looked very promising, but there seemed to be no convenient way for customers to use it. Then the company discovered aerosol can technology (first patented by Erik Rotheim of Norway in 1927), put the wax and paste mix into pressurized cans, and launched *Pledge* – the first sprayable furniture polish for home use.

The company soon realised it could fill aerosol cans with anything sprayable: Scented liquid became *Glade*, an air freshener now available in more than a dozen fragrances; DEET was combined with other to create an insect repellent *Off!*, which is still the category leader. Later, company scientists working on shaving technologies discovered that gel was a better lubricant for skin than traditional shaving cream. But how to dispense gel from an aerosol can? They solved this dilemma by introducing an expandable bladder in the bottom of the can; when the company launched *Edge*, it found a whole new market.

Meanwhile, *Off!* led to plug-in insect repellents and, through another route, to DEET-infused candles. Lanterns based on the candle technology now use Off! cartridges as well. In short, SC Johnson advanced from indoor parquet floors to outdoor insect-repelling lanterns by thinking of aerosol technology as a platform rather than simply as a way to put wax on wood.

J Svikla and A Paoni, Harvard Business Review, October 2005

We discuss divisionalisation and the role of the corporate headquarters further in Chapter 9.

9.3 Diversification and synergy

Synergy combined results produce a better rate of return than would be achieved by the same resources used independently. Synergy is used to justify diversification.

9.3.1 Obtaining synergy

Synergy is probably difficult to achieve in practice when one company takes over another. All too often, the expectations of synergy that help to justify a business combination fail to materialise. Synergy is probably more discussed in takeover bids than actually implemented.

🖊 Question   Diversification

A large organisation in road transport operates nationwide in general haulage. This field has become very competitive and with the recent down-turn in trade, has become only marginally profitable. It has been suggested that the strategic structure of the company should be widened to include other aspects of physical distribution so that the maximum synergy would be obtained from that type of diversification.

Suggest two activities which might fit into the suggested new strategic structure, explaining each one briefly. Explain how each of these activities could be incorporated into the existing structure. State the advantages and disadvantages of such diversification.

Answer

The first step in a suggested solution is to think of how a company operating nationwide in general road haulage might diversify, with some synergistic benefits. Perhaps you thought of the following.

(a)   To move from **nationwide to international haulage**, the company might be able to use its existing contacts *with* customers to develop an international trade. Existing administration and depot facilities in the UK could be used. Drivers should be available who are willing to work abroad, and the scope for making reasonable profits should exist. However, international road haulage might involve the company in the purchase of new vehicles (eg road haulage in Europe often involves the carriage of containerised products on large purpose-built vehicles). Since international haulage takes longer, vehicles will be tied up in jobs for several days, and a substantial investment might be required to develop the business. In addition, in the event of breakdowns, a network of overseas garage service arrangements will have to be created. It might take some time before business builds up sufficiently to become profitable.

(b)   Moving from general haulage to **speciality types of haulage**, perhaps haulage of large items of plant and machinery, or computer equipment. The same broad considerations apply to speciality types of haulage. Existing depot facilities could be used and existing customer contacts might be developed. However, expertise in specialist work will have to be 'brought in' as well as developed within the company and special vehicles might need to be bought. Business might take some time to build up and if the initial investment is high, there could be substantial early losses.

9.4 Other strategies

Withdrawal may be an appropriate strategy under certain circumstances.

(a)   Products may simply disappear when they reach the end of their life cycles.

(b)   Underperforming products may be weeded out.

(c)   Sale of subsidiary businesses for reasons of corporate strategy, such as finance, change of objectives, lack of strategic fit.

(d)   Sale of assets to raise funds and release other resources.

Exit barriers make this difficult.

(a)   Cost barriers include redundancy costs and the difficulty of selling assets.

(b)   Managers might fail to grasp the idea of decision-relevant costs ('we've spent all this money, so we must go on').

(c)   Political barriers include government attitudes. Defence is an example.

(d)   Marketing considerations may delay withdrawal. A product might be a loss-leader for others, or might contribute to the company's reputation for its breadth of coverage.

(e)   Psychology. Managers hate to admit failure, and there might be a desire to avoid embarrassment.

(f)   People might wrongly assume that carrying on is a low risk strategy.

Divestment and **demerger** have become more common as companies seek to reverse the diversification strategies they once pursued. There are several reasons for this.

(a)   To **rationalise** a business as a result of a strategic appraisal, perhaps as a result of portfolio analysis. Another reason might be to concentrate on core competences and synergies.

(b)   To sell off **subsidiary companies** at a profit, perhaps as an exit route after managing a turn-round.

(c)   To allow market valuation to reflect growth and income prospects. Where a low growth, steady income operation exists alongside a potentially high growth new venture, the joint P/E is likely to be too high for the cash cow and too low for the star. The danger is that a predator will take over the whole operation and split the business in two, allowing each part to settle at its own level.

(d)   Satisfy investors: diversified conglomerates are unfashionable. Modern investment thinking is that investors prefer to provide their own portfolio diversification.

(e)   To **raise funds** to invest elsewhere or to reduce debt.

Case Study

Philips, the Dutch manufacturer of consumer electronics, divested some non-core businesses in order to concentrate on core businesses as a strategy for improving profitability. It sold its production of white goods (large kitchen appliances) to an American firm, *Whirlpool*. There was overcapacity in the market. Philips was suffering from declining profitability and did not have the resources to invest in all its product ranges.

Demerger can realise underlying asset values in terms of share valuation. ICI's demerger of its attractive pharmaceuticals business led to the shares in the two demerged companies trading at a higher combined valuation than those of the original single form.

Privatisation has been pursued by governments all over the world to raise funds and transform culture and performance.

10 Method of growth

FAST FORWARD

The **method of growth** can vary.

-    Companies can grow organically, building up their own products and developing their own market.

-    They may choose to acquire these ready-made by buying other companies. Acquisitions are risky because of the incompatibility of different companies.

-    Many firms grown by other means, such as joint ventures, franchising and alliances.

10.1 Organic growth

Organic growth (sometimes referred to as **internal development**) is the primary method of growth for many organisations, for a number of reasons. Organic growth is achieved through the development of internal resources.

10.1.1 Reasons for pursuing organic growth

(a)   **Learning.** The process of developing a new product gives the firm the best understanding of the market and the product.

(b)   **Innovation.** It might be the only sensible way to pursue genuine technological innovations, and exploit them. (Compact disk technology was developed by Philips and Sony, who earn royalties from other manufacturers licensed to use it.)

(c)   There is **no suitable target for acquisition.**

(d)   Organic growth can be **planned more meticulously** and offers little disruption.

(e)   It is often **more convenient** for managers, as organic growth can be financed easily from the company's current cash flows, without having to raise extra money.

(f)   The **same style of management and corporate culture** can be maintained.

(g)   **Hidden or unforeseen losses are less likely** with organic growth than with acquisitions.

(h)   **Economies of scale** can be achieved from more **efficient use of central head office** functions such as finance, purchasing, personnel and management services.

10.1.2 Problems with organic growth

(a)   **Time** – sometimes it takes a long time to descend a **learning curve**.

(b)   **Barriers to entry** (eg distribution networks) are harder to overcome: for example a brand image may be built up from scratch.

(c)   The firm will have to **acquire the resources independently.**

(d)   Organic growth may be **too slow for the dynamics of the market.**

Organic growth is probably ideal for market penetration, and suitable for product or market development, but it might be a problem with extensive diversification projects.

10.2 Acquisitions and mergers

10.2.1 The purpose of acquisitions

(a)   **Marketing advantages**

- Buy in a new product range
- Buy a market presence (especially true if acquiring a company overseas)
- Unify sales departments or to rationalise distribution and advertising
- Eliminate competition or to protect an existing market

(b)   **Production advantages**

- Gain a higher utilisation of production facilities
- Buy in technology and skills
- Obtain greater production capacity
- Safeguard future supplies of raw materials
- Improve purchasing by buying in bulk

(c) **Finance and management**

- Buy a high quality management team, which exists in the acquired company
- Obtain cash resources where the acquired company is very liquid
- Gain undervalued assets or surplus assets that can be sold off
- Obtain tax advantages (eg purchase of a tax loss company)

(d) **Risk-spreading**

(e) **Independence**. A company threatened by a take-over might take over another company, just to make itself bigger and so a more expensive target for the predator company.

(f) **Overcome barriers to entry**

Many acquisitions **do** have a logic, and the **acquired company can be improved** with the extra resources and better management. Furthermore, much of the criticisms of **takeovers** has been directed more against the notion of **conglomerate diversification** as a strategy rather than takeover as a **method of growth**.

 Case Study

Proctor and Gamble

In early 2005, *Proctor & Gamble* bought *Gillette* for just over $US 50 billion. Stock market analysts and industry gurus whooped with delight. Warren Buffett, whose investment company *Berkshire Hathaway* owns nearly 10% of Gillette promised to invest more in the new form.

In 2001 P&G bought *Clairol* for $US 55 billion and in 2004, bought *Wella* for $US 6.9 billion. At the same time, P&G has disposed of some under performing-brands, such as *Oxydol* and *Sunny Delight.*

Advocates of size think that a big company can leverage scale to cut costs, then use these savings to invest more in advertising and innovation and so gain even more scale. But there are also diseconomies of scale. Giant firms can find it more difficult to move quickly and their costs can balloon. In particular, mergers take discouragingly long to complete. P&G is still far from finished in integrating Wella, for example.

Adapted from *The Economist, 5 February 2005*

10.2.2 Problems with acquisitions and mergers

(a) **Cost**. They might be too expensive, especially if resisted by the directors of the target company. Proposed acquisitions might be referred to the government under the terms of anti-monopoly legislation.

(b) **Customers** of the target company might resent a sudden takeover and consider going to other suppliers for their goods.

(c) **Incompatibility**. In general, the problems of assimilating new products, customers, suppliers, markets, employees and different systems of operating might create 'indigestion' and management overload in the acquiring company. A proposed merger between two UK financial institutions was called off because of incompatible information systems.

(d) **Asymmetric information**. *John Kay* suggests that the acquisitions market for companies is rarely efficient.

    (i) The existing management 'always knows more about what is for sale than the potential purchaser. ... Successful bidders are often only the people who were willing to pay too much – that is the reason why their bid succeeds'.

(ii)   'At the same time, good buys may be ignored, because there is no potential purchaser confident that he really is making a good buy.'

(e)   **Driven by the personal goals** of the acquiring company's managers, as a form of sport, perhaps.

(f)   **Corporate financiers and banks** have a stake in the acquisitions process as they can charge fees for advice.

(g)   **Poor success record of acquisitions.** Takeovers benefit the shareholders of the acquired company often more than the acquirer. According to the Economist Intelligence Unit, there is a consensus that fewer than half all acquisitions are successful.

(h)   **Firms rarely take into account non-financial factors**. A survey by London Business School examining 40 acquisitions (in the UK and USA) revealed some major flaws.

(i)   All acquirers conducted financial audits, but only 37% conducted anything approaching a management audit: despite detailed audits of equipment, property, finances etc, few bothered with people.

(ii)   Some major problems of implementation relate to **human resources and personnel issues** such as morale, performance assessment and culture. Especially in service industries and 'knowledge-based' or creative businesses, many of the firm's assets are effectively the staff. If key managers or personnel leave, the business will suffer.

 Case Study

Acquisitions research

Acquisitions are a financial disaster for shareholders, new research suggests.

A study of the performance of large takeovers completed between 1977 and 1994 has found that in the five years after a deal, the total return on investment underperformed by an average of 26 per cent, compared with shares in companies of similar size.

The research, by Alan Gregory and John Matako, of the University of Exeter's new Centre for Finance and Investment, showed that the effect of acquisitions on share price and dividends varied according to whether the bids were hostile or non-hostile and whether they were equity–financed or cash backed.

The underperformance on share-based deals is 36 per cent over five years, relative to unacquisitive companies.

Agreed bids also generated negative returns, with shareholders doing 27 per cent less well. Agreed share-based deals led to underperformance of 37 per cent.

Cash financing or bidder hostility were not enough on their own to make a profit likely, the report found However, bids that are cash-backed and hostile have a better chance of creating, rather than destroying, shareholder value.

On a low sample, the academics found that a successful hostile cash bids generated an average 50 per cent increase in the profitability of shares in the five years after the bid. Share-based bids perform poorly because shares in the acquiring companies are overvalued in the first place, Dr Gregory suggested.

He added that the process of gaining co-operation from the target board might also increase the cost, as executives might have to be persuaded to agree only if the acquirer offers over-generous terms. Unnecessary cost may be incurred if executives in an acquired company retain their jobs after completion of deals, he said.

The Times, 18 October 2004

10.3 Joint ventures and franchising

Short of mergers and takeovers, there are other ways by which companies can co-operate.

(a)   **Consortia:** organisations co-operate on specific business areas such as purchasing or research.

(b)   **Joint ventures:** Two firms (or more) join forces for manufacturing, financial and marketing purposes and each has a share in both the equity and the management of the business.

   (i)   **Share costs**. As the capital outlay is shared, joint ventures are especially attractive to smaller or risk-averse firms, or where very expensive new technologies are being researched and developed (such is the civil aerospace industry).

   (ii)   **Cut risk**. A joint venture can reduce the risk of government intervention if a local firm is involved (eg *Club Mediterranée* pays much attention to this factor).

   (iii) Participating enterprises **benefit from all sources of profit**.

   (iv)   **Close control** over marketing and other operations.

   (v)   Overseas joint ventures provide **local knowledge, quickly**.

   (vi)   **Synergies**. One firm's production expertise can be supplemented by the other's marketing and distribution facility.

(c)   A **licensing agreement** is a commercial contract whereby the licenser gives something of value to the licensee in exchange for certain performances and payments.

   (i)   The licenser may provide rights to produce a patented product or to use a patented process or trademark as well as advice and assistance on marketing and technical issues.

   (ii)   The licenser receives a **royalty**.

(d)   **Subcontracting** is also a type of alliance. Co-operative arrangements also feature in supply chain management, JIT and quality programmes.

10.3.1 Disadvantages of joint ventures

   (a)   **Conflicts of interest** between the different parties.

   (b)   **Disagreements** may arise over profit shares, amounts invested, the management of the joint venture, and the marketing strategy.

   (c)   One partner may wish to **withdraw** from the arrangement.

   (d)   There may be a temptation to neglect **core competences**. Acquisition of competences from partners may be possible, but alliances are unlikely to create new ones.

 Case Study

SGS-Thompson's semiconductor manufacturing facility in Shenzhen, China (cost US$110m) was a joint venture. There were many problems, including the unsuitable site, selected by the Chinese partner. By 1996, according to *The Economist*, morale was at rock bottom and the partners did not trust each other. 'Vendors were ripping us off, the government was robbing us blind, key employees were on the take.' The situation has now improved.

10.3.2 Franchising

Franchising is a method of expanding the business on less capital than would otherwise be possible. For suitable businesses, it is an **alternative business strategy to raising extra capital** for growth. Franchisers include *Budget Rent-a-car, Dyno-rod, Express Dairy, Holiday Inn, Kall-Kwik Printing, KFC, Prontaprint, Sketchley Cleaners, Body Shop* and even *McDonald's*. The franchiser and franchisee each provide different inputs to the business.

(a)   The **franchiser**

- Name, and any goodwill associated with it
- Systems and business methods
- Support services, such as advertising, training and help with site decoration

(b)   The **franchisee**

- Capital, personal involvement and local market knowledge
- Payment to the franchiser for rights and for support services
- Responsibility for the day-to-day running, and the ultimate profitability of the franchise.

10.3.3 Disadvantages of franchising

(a)   The **search for competent candidates** is both costly and time consuming where the franchiser requires many outlets (eg McDonald's in the UK).

(b)   **Control** over franchisees (McDonald's franchisees in New York recently refused to co-operate in a marketing campaign).

10.4 Alliances

Exam focus point

> A Section B question in the Pilot Paper offered 25 marks for an explaining the principles of internal development, acquisitions and strategic alliances, and how they might be applied to the scenario.

Some firms enter long-term **strategic alliances** with others for a variety of reasons.

(a)   They share development costs of a particular technology.

(b)   The regulatory environment prohibits take-overs (eg most major airlines are in strategic alliances because in most countries – including the US – there are limits to the level of control an 'outsider' can have over an airline).

(c)   Complementary markets or technology.

(d)   **Learning.** Alliances can also be a 'learning' exercise in which each partner tries to learn as much as possible from the other.

(e)   **Technology**. New technology offers many uncertainties and many opportunities. Such alliances provide funds for expensive research projects, spreading risk.

(f)   **The alliance itself can generate innovations**.

(g)   The alliance can involve **'testing' the firm's core competence** in different conditions, which can suggest ways to improve it.

(h)   Regulation may prevent take over.

Strategic alliances only go so far, as there may be disputes over control of strategic assets.

10.4.1 Choosing alliance partners

Hooley et al suggest the following factors should be considered in choosing alliance partners.

Drivers	What benefits are offered by collaboration?
Partners	Which partners should be chosen?
Facilitators	Does the external environment favour a partnership?
Components	Activities and processes in the network
Effectiveness	Does the previous history of alliances generate good results? Is the alliance just a temporary blip? For example, in the airline industry, there are many strategic alliances, but these arise in part because there are legal barriers to cross-border ownership.
Market-orientation	Alliance partners are harder to control and may not have the same commitment to the end-user.

 Case Study

In January 2006 *Siemens* and *General Electric* announced that they would co-operate in the launch of a new GE-developed security device for shipping containers. The two companies are the largest conglomerates in Europe and the USA respectively.

The product, called *Commerce Guard*, will have first mover advantage, but GE believes Siemens' strength in Europe makes co-operation necessary if the product is to achieve a high level of penetration globally.

Alliances have some limitations

(a) **Core competence.** Each organisation should be able to focus on its core competence. Alliances do not enable it to create new competences.

(b) **Strategic priorities.** If a key aspect of strategic delivery is handed over to a partner, the firm loses flexibility. A core competence may not be enough to provide a comprehensive customer benefit.

10.4.2 IS based alliances

The cost of major IS based methods of working, combined with their inherent communications capability have made alliances based on IS a natural development. There are four common types.

(a) **Single industry partnerships**: for example, UK insurance brokers can use a common system called IVANS to research the products offered by all of the major insurance companies.

(b) **Multi-industry joint marketing partnerships**: some industries are so closely linked with others that it makes sense to establish IS linking their offerings. A well-known example is holiday bookings, where a flight reservation over the Internet is likely to lead to a seamless offer of hotel reservations and car hire.

(c) **Supply chain partnerships:** greater and closer co-operation along the supply chain has led to the need for better and faster information flows. Electronic data interchange between customers and suppliers is one aspect of this improvement, perhaps seen most clearly in the car industry, where the big-name manufacturers effectively control the flow of inputs from their suppliers.

(d)   **IT supplier** partnerships: a slightly different kind of partnership is not uncommon in the IT industry itself, where physical products have their own major software content. The development of these products requires close co-operation between the hardware and software companies concerned.

11 Strategy and market position

FAST FORWARD

Strategies may be based upon market position, as leader, challenger, follower or nicher.

So far in this chapter we have considered the broader aspects of strategy as they affect the overall stance of the organisation. In this section we will examine some of the options that apply most appropriately to the strategic management of individual products or brands. An appreciation of scale is important when considering strategy. The strategies we discuss below may be regarded as detailed strategy for a major global organisation. On the other hand, they may constitute the essence of corporate strategy for a smaller company.

Most of the material in this section is based on *Strategic Marketing Management* by *Wilson, Gilligan and Pearson*.

11.1 Strategies for market leaders

PIMS research has revealed the advantages of being the market leader. A company in this position may try to do three things.

(a)   **Expand the total market** by seeking increased usage levels; and new uses and users. These aims correspond to market penetration and market development.

(b)   **Protect the current market share**. The most common way of doing this is by means of continuous product innovation.

(c)   **Expand market share**. This may be pursued by enhancing the attractiveness of the product offering in almost any way, including increased promotion, aggressive pricing and improved distribution.

Military analogies have been used to describe defensive strategies for market leaders. These were described earlier in this Study Text.

11.2 Strategies for market challengers

The market challenger seeks to **build market share** in the hope of eventually overtaking the existing leader. However, this does not necessarily mean attacking the market leader head-on. This is a risky strategy in any case, because of the leader's resources in cash, promotion and innovation. Instead, the challenger may attack smaller regional firms or companies of similar size to itself that are vulnerable through lack of resources or poor management.

Military analogies have also been used to describe the challenger's attacking options. These were described earlier in this Study Text.

11.3 Strategies for market followers

The market follower accepts the status quo and thus avoids the cost and risk associated with innovation in product, price or distribution strategy. Such a **me-too** strategy is based on the leader's approach. This can be both profitable and stable. However, to be consistently successful, such a strategy must not simply imitate. The follower should compete in the most appropriate segments, maintain its customer base and ensure that its turnover grows in line with the general expansion of the market. It should be aware that it may constitute an attractive target for market challengers. The follower must therefore control its costs and exploit appropriate opportunities.

11.4 Strategies for market nichers

Avoiding competition by **niching** is a profitable strategy for small firms generally and for larger organisations where competition is intense. The key to niching is **specialisation**, but there are other considerations.

(a) The chosen market must have some growth potential while being uninteresting to major competitors.

(b) The firm must be able to serve its customers sufficiently well to build up sufficient goodwill to fend off any attacks.

(c) It must be possible to build up sufficient size to be profitable and purchase efficiently.

Serving a single niche can be risky: a sudden change in the market can lead to rapid decline. **Multiple niching** can overcome this problem.

12 Success criteria

FAST FORWARD

Strategies are evaluated according to their **suitability** to the firm's strategic situation, their **feasibility** in terms of resources and competences and their **acceptability** to key stakeholders groups (eg shareholders).

Organisations must select strategies to pursue in a rational way. JS&W suggest three **success criteria** to guide strategy choice.

- Suitability
- Feasibility
- Acceptability

12.1 Suitability

Suitability relates to the **strategic logic** of the strategy. The strategy should fit the organisation's current strategic position and should satisfy a range of requirements.

- **Exploit** strengths: that is, **unique** resources and **core competences**
- **Rectify** company **weaknesses**
- **Neutralise** or deflect environmental **threats**
- Help the firm to **seize opportunities**
- **Satisfy the goals** of organisation
- **Fill the gap** identified by gap analysis
- Generate/maintain **competitive advantage**
- Involve an acceptable level of **risk**
- Suit the **politics** and corporate **culture**

A number of techniques can be used to assess suitability. These are discussed below.

12.1.1 Life cycle analysis

FAST FORWARD

The A D Little lifecycle/portfolio matrix assesses suitability in terms of **industry maturity** and **competitive position**.

The **product life cycle** concept may be used to assess potential strategies.

The **industry life cycle** may be combined with an appraisal of the company's strength in its markets using a **life cycle/portfolio matrix**. This was originally designed by consultants **Arthur D Little**.

STAGES OF INDUSTRY MATURITY

	Embryonic	Growth	Mature	Ageing
Dominant	Fast grow Start up	Fast grow Attain cost leadership Renew Defend position	Defend position Attain cost leadership Renew Fast grow	Defend position Focus Renew Grow with industry
Strong	Start up Differentiate Fast grow	Fast grow Catch up Attain cost leadership Differentiate	Attain cost leadership Renew, focus Differentiate Grow with industry	Find niche Hold niche Hang in Grow with industry Harvest
Favourable	Start up Differentiate Focus Fast grow	Differentiate, focus Catch up Grow with industry	Harvest, hang in Find niche, hold niche Renew, turnaround Differentiate, focus Grow with industry	Retrench Turnaround
Tenable	Start up Grow with industry Focus	Harvest, catch up Hold niche, hang in Find niche Turnaround Focus Grow with industry	Harvest Turnaround Find niche Retrench	Divest Retrench
Weak	Find niche Catch up Grow with industry	Turnaround Retrench	Withdraw Divest	Withdraw

(left axis label) COMPETITIVE POSITION

The position of the company on the **industry maturity** axis of this matrix depends on the assessment of eight factors including market growth rate, growth potential and number of competitors. Each stage has its own strategic implications. For instance, an ageing market will be subject to falling demand, so heavy marketing expenditure is unlikely to be justified.

Competitive position

(a)   A **dominant** position allows the company to exert influence over the behaviour of competitors. It is rare in the private sector.

(b)   A **strong** position gives considerable freedom of choice over strategy.

(c)   A **favourable** position arises in a fragmented market, often when the company has strengths to exploit.

(d)   A **tenable** position is vulnerable to competition and profitability may depend on specialisation.

(e)   A **weak** position arises from inability to compete effectively. Firms of any size can find themselves in this condition.

12.1.2 Business profile analysis

In **business profile analysis** the expected effects of a strategy on the corporation are forecast. A business profile is then created by scoring the forecast state against the favourable parameters established by the empirical findings of PIMS research. There are eleven of these parameters; they relate to market position, financial strength, quality and operational efficiency. The forecast profile may be compared with the current profile in order to assess the proposed strategy for suitability.

12.1.3 Strategy screening

It is not enough merely to assess strategies for suitability. Eventually choices must be made. Such choices may be assisted by **strategy screening** methods, which include **ranking, decision trees** and **scenario planning**. Ranking and decision trees are dealt with later in this Study Text. Scenarios have already been described. Potential strategies may be screened by assessing their suitability against each potential scenario. This leads not so much to a choice as to the establishment of a series of **contingency plans**.

12.1.4 Consistency

Strategies must be internally consistent: generic strategy, market options choice and method of development must all work together satisfactorily. For example a strategy of cost leadership would not be supported by a decision to acquire a chain of luxury distributors.

12.1.5 The TOWS matrix

The TOWS matrix was discussed earlier in this Study Text. We noted that *Weirich* categorised strategies into four groups that linked strengths, weaknesses, opportunities and threats in a logical fashion. There is an **inherent suitability** about strategies that fall into these groups, since they are founded on the fundamentals of the organisation's strategic position.

JS&W (and your new syllabus) discern a logical link between the Ansoff Matrix and the TOWS matrix, since detailed strategic options based on the former may be validated and even generated by considering the latter. Thus, for example, a specific market development opportunity might exploit an under-used strength: this is an SO strategy.

12.2 Feasibility

Feasibility asks whether the strategy can be implemented and, in particular, if the organisation has adequate **strategic capability**.

- Enough **money**
- The **ability** to deliver the goods/services specified in the strategy
- The ability to deal with the likely **responses that competitors** will make
- Access to **technology, materials and resources**
- Enough **time** to implement the strategy

Strategies which do not make use of the existing competences and which therefore call for new competences to be acquired, might not be feasible, since gaining competences takes time and can be costly.

Two important financial approaches to assessing the feasibility of particular strategies are **funds flow** analysis and **breakeven** analysis. The principles of both should be familiar to you from your earlier studies in financial and management accounting.

Resource deployment analysis makes a wider assessment of feasibility in terms of **resources** and **competences.** The resources and competences required for each potential strategy are assessed and compared with those of the firm. A two stage approach may be followed.

(a) Does the firm have the necessary resources and competences to achieve the **threshold** requirements for each strategy?

(b) Does the firm have the core competences and **unique resources** to maintain **competitive advantage**?

When assessing feasibility in this way, it is important to remember that it may be possible to acquire new competences and resources or to stretch existing ones. Such innovation is likely to be difficult to imitate.

12.3 Acceptability

The acceptability of a strategy depends on expected performance outcomes and the extent to which these are acceptable to stakeholders.

(a) **Financial considerations**. Strategies will be evaluated by considering how far they contribute to meeting the dominant objective of increasing shareholder wealth.

- Return on investment
- Profits
- Growth
- EPS
- Cash flow
- Price/Earnings
- Market capitalisation
- Cost-benefit analysis

Profitability analysis techniques include **forecast ROCE**, **payback period** and **NPV**, all of which you should be familiar with. These methods should not be overemphasised.

(i) They are developed for assessing **projects** where cash flows are predictable. This is unlikely to be easy with wider **strategies**.

(ii) There may be **intangible** costs and benefits associated with a strategy, such as an enhanced product range or image or a loss of market share. **Cost-benefit analysis** is probably more appropriate for dealing with such development. See below.

Shareholder value analysis has the potential to provide a more realistic assessment of overall strategy than traditional financial measures such as NPV and forecast FOCE. This is because its emphasis on value management and understanding the organisation's system of value drivers requires managers to take an integrated view of current and potential future strategies and their overall effects.

(b) **Customers** may object to a strategy if it means reducing service, but on the other hand they may have no choice.

(c) **Banks** are interested in the implications for cash resources, debt levels and so on.

(d) **Government**. A strategy involving a takeover may be prohibited under competition legislation.

(e) **The public**. The environmental impact may cause key stakeholders to protest. For example, out of town superstores are now frowned upon by national and local government in the UK.

(f) **Risk**. Different shareholders have different attitudes to risk. A strategy which changed the risk/return profile, for whatever reason, may not be acceptable. Financial ratio projections and sensitivity analysis may be useful in the assessment of risk.

Exam focus point	Risk and return are particular important to investors. The old Paper 3.5 syllabus Section A case study in June 2004 included a requirement to evaluate three possible exit strategies for an owner-manager. The Examiner's suggested solution emphasised the balance of risk and return in each option.

Cost-benefit analysis may be an appropriate approach to acceptability where intangible effects are important, which is particularly the case in the public sector. This type of analysis attempts to put a monetary value on intangibles such as safety and amenity so that the impact of a strategy on all parties may be assessed.

12.4 Strategy selection

12.4.1 Planning and enforced choice

The techniques dealt with in this chapter are appropriate to the use of the rational model and may be useful when less formal approaches are taken. They also have a role when strategic developments are **imposed from outside** the organisation. This may come about, for instance, as a result of a major change in the environment, as when the oil shocks of the 1970s stimulated off-shore production, or because of the influence of a dominant stakeholder. A good example of the second possibility was the effect of *Marks and Spencer's* decision to cease buying from *William Baird*, a UK clothing manufacturer. This led to plant closures, reorganisation and a management buyout offer.

Formal evaluation of imposed strategy

(a) The first role of formal evaluation is to assess the degree of **risk** inherent in the imposed strategy. This may indicate that a medium-term programme to reduce risk is required; this could be incorporated into the overall plan.

(b) Secondly, techniques such as **scenario planning** can be used to establish contingency plans in case the imposed strategy leads to unacceptably low performance.

12.5 Real options

The analysis and use of **financial options** as business tools is not examinable in paper P3. However, the option concept is very useful in the context of selecting strategies. The selection of a particular course of strategic action may offer **options for future strategy**. The availability of such an option should be considered when evaluating strategies.

A possible course of action may open up further possibilities: one important case is the possibility of making further, follow-on investments. This is equivalent to a call option in financial strategy. For example, if a manufacturing business decides to open a retail outlet, it acquires the option to stock complementary products from other manufacturers. If the NPV of the basic outlet strategy is assessed as negative, this negative sum represents the price of the option to expand the range at a future date.

Using this type of conceptual approach allows more subtle evaluation of possible strategies to be undertaken and permits more sophisticated choices to be made between alternatives. In particular, the option to abandon a chosen strategy at low cost will make that strategy more attractive than one with a high cost of abandonment. This choice might rise where there are two possible approaches to manufacturing a new product.

(a) Purchase of high efficiency, highly specialised machinery
(b) Purchase of lower efficiency, general purpose machinery

Option (a) may offer lower costs if the venture succeeds, but the ability to use option (b)'s machinery for another purpose reduces its cost of abandonment should the venture fail.

Chapter Roundup

- Many large businesses consist of a corporate parent and a number of SBUs. The defining characteristic of the corporate parent is that it has no direct contact with the buyers or competitors, its role being to manage the overall scope of the organisation in terms of diversity of products, markets and international operations.

- Diversity of products and markets may be advantageous for three reasons.

    - **Economics of scope** may arise in several forms of **synergy**.
    - **Corporate management skills** may be extendible.
    - **Cross-subsidy** may enhance **market power**.

    Related diversification, whether horizontal or vertical usually works better than conglomerate, or unrelated, diversification.

- Despite wide-ranging measures to liberalise trade and the resulting major growth in world trade, there has been little globalisation of services. Language differences and also, restrictions on population movement hamper the growth of international markets for labour, even when it is highly skilled.

- Perlmutter identifies four orientations in the management of international business.

    - **Ethnocentrism** is a home country orientation
    - **Polycentrism** adapts totally to local environments
    - **Geocentrism** adapts only to add value. It 'thinks globally, acts locally'.
    - **Regiocentrism** recognises regional differences

- Ohmae describes five stages in the evolution of a global business.

    - **Exporting** is an extension of home sales, using foreign intermediaries. It is low risk and **ethnocentric**.

    - **Overseas branches** arise when turnover is large enough. It requires greater investment and is still **ethnocentric**.

    - **Overseas production** exploits cheap labour and reduces exporting costs. The orientation is still **ethnocentric** and the business is still largely run from its HQ.

    - **Insiderisation** is a shift to **polycentrism**, with full functional organisations being set up overseas. This reduces exchange rate and political risk but economies of scale may be lost and there may be problems of co-ordination. The company is a **multinational**.

    - **The global company** takes a world view while recognising total differences: it has a **geocentric** orientation. It integrates learning, skills and competences to achieve global efficiencies while retaining local responsiveness.

    Ohmae offers five reasons for globalisation.

    - **Customer:** market convergence
    - **Company:** economies of scale
    - **Competition:** keeping up
    - **Currency:** exchange rate risk
    - **Country:** absolute and comparative advantage; local orientation

- Bartlett and Ghoshal discern four types of organisations, depending on the strength or weakness of pressure to globalise and need for local adaptation.

    - Global environment; geocentric; global product divisions
    - International environment; ethnocentric; international division

- – Transnational environment; polycentric; integrated systems and structures
- – Multinational environment; polycentric; national or regional divisions

- Modes of entry to foreign markets vary widely and include

  - – Direct and indirect exporting
  - – Wholly owned overseas production
  - – Contract manufacture
  - – Joint ventures

  The most suitable mode of entry depends on

  - – Marketing objectives
  - – Mode availability
  - – HR requirements
  - – Risks
  - – Firm size
  - – Mode quality
  - – Market research feedback
  - – Control needs

- There are three value-creating roles for the corporate parent.

  - – **Envisioning corporate intent**, communicating the vision to stakeholders and SBU managers, and acting in accordance with it.

  - – **Intervention** to improve performance.

  - – Provision of **services, resources** and **expertise**.

  Portfolio managers create value by applying financial discipline. They keep their own costs low.
  Synergy managers peruse economics of scope through the shared use of competences and resources.
  Parental developers add value by deploying their own competences to improve their SBUs' performance.

- A parent may deploy four policies towards its SBUs

  - Build
  - Hold
  - Harvest
  - Divest

  The SBU portfolio must be managed against three criteria

  - Balance
  - Attractiveness
  - Strategic fit

  Matrix-based models are used to manage **portfolios**: the Ashridge model is the only one to address strategic fit and assumes the **parental developer** approach is used.

- The **Boston classification** classifies business units in terms of their capacity for growth within the market and the market's capacity for growth as a whole.

- The public sector portfolio matrix classifies activities in terms of their popularity and the resources available for them.

- The GE and Shell matrices are based on the enterprise's competitive capacity and the market's attractiveness.

- The Ashridge model assesses the benefit SBUs can derive from the corporate parent playing the parental developer role. Heartland businesses both have CSFs that fit the present's resources and competences *and* provide opportunities for good use of them. Alien businesses have neither quality. Ballast businesses are well-understood by the parent but need little assistance. Value trap businesses need help but of kinds the parent cannot provide.

- **Business unit strategy** involves a choice between being the lowest cost producer (**cost leadership**) making the product different from competitors' products in some way (**differentiation**) or specialising on a segment of the market (**focus**, by addressing that segment by a strategy of cost leadership or differentiation). **Porter** believes that a firm *must* choose one of these or be **stuck-in-the-middle**.

- The strategy clock develops Porter's theory, analysing strategies in terms of **price** and **perceived value added**.

- Different policies are required to sustain differentiation or price-based strategies. Lock-in is achieved when a product becomes the industry standard.

- **Hypercompetition** makes it impossible to create lasting advantage with a steady policy: a series of short term moves is required. These include repositioning on the strategy clock, counter attack, imitation and attacks on barriers to entry.

- **Collaborations** may be a valid strategic option, reducing costs and building or overcoming barriers to entry.

- The value chain can be used to design a competitive strategy, by deploying the various activities strategically.

- **Product-market** strategies involve determining which products should be sold in which markets, by market penetration, market development, product development and diversification. Diversification is assumed to be risky, especially diversification that is entirely unrelated to current products and markets. Alliances of various kinds are a possible approach to diversification. Withdrawal may be a valid option.

- The **method of growth** can vary.

  - Companies can grow organically, building up their own products and developing their own market.

  - They may choose to acquire these ready-made by buying other companies. Acquisitions are risky because of the incompatibility of different companies.

  - Many firms grown by other means, such as joint ventures, franchising and alliances.

- Strategies may be based upon market position, as leader, challenger, follower or nicher.

- Strategies are evaluated according to their **suitability** to the firm's strategic situation, their **feasibility** in terms of resources and competences and their **acceptability** to key stakeholders groups (eg shareholders).

- The A D Little lifecycle/portfolio matrix assesses suitability in terms of **industry maturity** and **competitive position**.

Quick Quiz

1   What is related diversification?

2   What is geocentrism?

3   What are JS&W's three strategic rationales for corporate parents?

4   What are the axes of the BCG matrix?

5   What are the axes of the Ashridge portfolio display?

6   What are Porter's three generic strategies?

7   What are the axes against which the strategy clock is constructed?

8   What is lock-in?

9   What is the me-too strategy?

10 What criteria are used to assess strategies?

Answers to Quick Quiz

1   Development beyond current products and markets but within the capabilities or value network of the organisation.

2   A synthesis of ethnocentrism and polycentrism that treats issues of standardisation and adaptation on their merits.

3   Portfolio manager, synergy manager, parental developer.

4   Market growth rate and relative market share.

5   Fit between SBU opportunities and parental skills and resources (benefit) and fit between CSFs and parental skills and resources (feel).

6   Cost leadership, differentiation, focus.

7   Price and perceived value added.

8   The product becomes the industry standard.

9   The market follower accepts the status quo and avoids the cost and risk associated with innovation.

10 Suitability in terms of strategic logic; feasibility in terms of resources required; and acceptability to shareholders.

Now try the questions below from the Exam Question Bank

Number	Level	Marks	Time
Q6	Preparation	n/a	36 mins

Part C
Organising and enabling success

Organising for success

Topic list	Syllabus reference
1 Challenges and concepts	C1
2 Types of structure	C1 (a)
3 Processes	C1 (b)
4 Relationships	C1 (c), (d)
5 Stereotypical configurations	C1 (e)
6 Configuration and strategy	C1

Introduction

The static pyramidal hierarchy has formed the basis of ideas about organisation structure for many years. This structural form has the advantage of being easily understood and of providing clear lines of responsibility and communication. However, the challenges of the modern business environment have led not only to new structural designs, but also to a complete re-evaluation of basic assumptions about organisation structure.

Study guide

		Intellectual level
C1	**Organising and enabling success**	
(a)	Advise on how the organisation can be structured to deliver a selected strategy	3
(b)	Explore generic processes that take place within the structure, with particular emphasis on the planning process	3
(c)	Discuss how internal relationships can be organised to deliver a selected strategy	2
(d)	Discuss how external relationships (outsourcing, strategic alliances, networks and the virtual organisation) can be structured to deliver a selected strategy	2
(e)	Explore (through Mintzberg's organisational configurations) the design of structure, processes and relationships	3

Exam guide

Questions on structure were fairly uncommon under the old syllabus. However, JS&W's fresh approach, emphasising processes and relationships casts a new light on this rather specialised topic and brings it into the mainstream of strategic thinking. You cannot afford to neglect this chapter. We can expect questions that demand input on structure ranging from passing comment all the way up to detailed proposals for change and development.

1 Challenges and concepts

FAST FORWARD

> Globalisation, other aspects of rapid environmental change and, above all, the need to **exploit knowledge** make the **structures**, **processes** and **relationships** that make up configurations vital for strategic success.

JS&W identify three major groups of challenges for twenty first century organisation structures.

(a) The rapid pace of **environmental change** and increased levels of **environmental uncertainty** demand flexibility of organisational design.

(b) The creation and exploitation of **knowledge** requires effective systems to link the people who have knowledge with the applications that need it.

(c) **Globalisation** creates new types and a new scale of technological complexity in communication and information systems; at the same time, diversity of culture, practices and approaches to personal relationships bring their own new problems of organisational form.

Of these three sets of issues, the need to capture, organise and exploit knowledge is probably the most pressing for most organisations. An important element of response to this need is therefore an emphasis on the importance of facilitating effective **processes** and **relationships** when designing **structures**. JS&W use the term **configuration** to encompass these three elements.

1.1 Organisational configuration

An organisation's **configuration** consists of the structures, processes, and relationships through which it operates.

JS&W

(a) **Structure** has its conventional meaning of organisation structure.

(b) **Processes** drive and support people: they define how strategies are made and controlled; and how the organisation's people interact and implement strategy.

(c) **Relationships** are the connections between people within the organisation and between those inside it and those on the outside.

Effective processes and relationships can have varying degrees of formality and informality and it is important that formal relationships and processes are aligned with the relevant informal ones.

It is very important to be aware that structures, processes and relationships are **highly interdependent**: they have to work together intimately and consistently if the organisation is to be successful.

2 Types of structure

An organisation's formal structure reveals much about it.

(a) It shows who is **responsible** for what

(b) It shows who **communicates** with whom, both in procedural practice and, to great extent, in less formal ways.

(c) The upper levels of the structure reveal the **skills the organisation values** and, by extension, the **role of knowledge and skill** within it.

JS&W review seven basic structural types.

- Functional
- Multidivisional
- Holding company
- Matrix
- Transnational
- Team
- Project

2.1 The functional structure

In a functional structure, people are organised according to the type of work that they do.

In a functional organisation structure, departments are defined by their **functions,** that is, the work that they do. It is a traditional, common sense approach and many organisations are structured like this. Primary functions in a manufacturing company might be production, sales, finance, and general administration. Sub departments of marketing might be selling, advertising, distribution and warehousing.

Functional departmentation

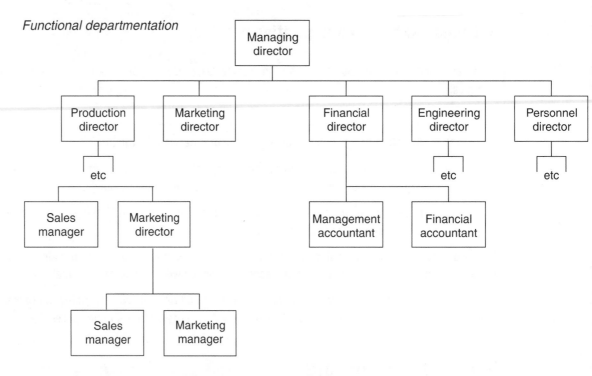

2.1.1 Advantages of functional departmentation

- It is based on work specialism and is therefore logical.
- The firm can benefit from economies of scale.
- It offers a career structure.

2.1.2 Disadvantages

- It does not reflect the actual business processes by which **value is created**.
- It is hard to identify where profits and losses are made on individual products.
- People do not have an understanding of how the *whole* business works.
- There are problems of co-ordinating the work of different specialisms.

2.2 The multi-divisional and holding company structures

FAST FORWARD

The multi-divisional structure divides the organisation into semi-autonomous divisions that may be differentiated by territory, product, or market. The holding company structure is an extreme form in which the divisions are separate legal entities.

(a) Divisionalisation is the division of a business into **autonomous regions** or product businesses, each with its own revenues, expenditures and profits.

(b) Communication between divisions and head office is restricted, formal and related to performance standards. Influence is maintained by headquarters' power to hire and fire the managers who are supposed to run each division.

(c) Divisionalisation is a function of organisation size, in numbers and in product-market activities.

Mintzberg believes there are inherent problems in divisionalisation.

(a) A division is partly **insulated** by the holding company from shareholders and capital markets, which ultimately reward performance.

(b)   The economic advantages it offers over independent organisations 'reflect fundamental inefficiencies in capital markets'. (In other words, different product-market divisions might function better as independent companies.)

(c)   The divisions are **more bureaucratic** than they would be as independent corporations, owing to the performance measures imposed by the strategic apex.

(d)   Headquarters management have a tendency to **usurp divisional profits** by management charges, cross-subsidies, head office bureaucracies and unfair transfer pricing systems.

(e)   In some businesses, it is impossible to identify completely independent products or markets for which divisions would be appropriate.

(f)   Divisionalisation is only possible at a fairly senior management level, because there is a limit to how much independence in the division of work can be arranged.

(g)   It is a halfway house, relying on personal control over performance by senior managers and enforcing cross-subsidisation.

(h)   Many of the problems of divisionalisation are those of **conglomerate diversification**. Each business might be better run independently than with the others. The different businesses might offer different returns for different risks which shareholders might prefer to judge independently.

The multi-divisional structure might be implemented in one of **two forms**.

(a)   **Simple divisionalisation**

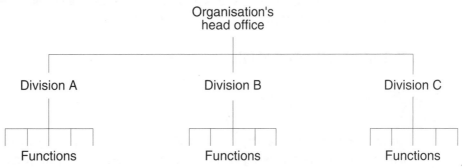

This enables concentration on particular product-market areas, overcoming problems of functional specialisation at a large scale. Problems arise with the power of the head office, and control of the resources. Responsibility is devolved, and some central functions might be duplicated.

(b)   The **holding company** (group) structure is a radical form of divisionalisation. **Subsidiaries are separate legal entities**. The holding company can be a firm with a permanent investment or one that buys and sells businesses or interests in businesses: the subsidiaries may have other shareholders.

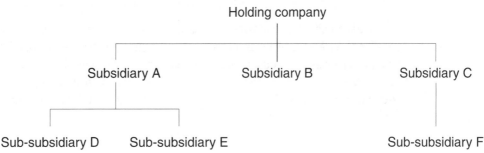

Divisionalisation has some advantages, despite the problems identified above.

- (a) It focuses the attention of subordinate management on business performance and results.

- (b) **Management by objectives** is the natural control default.

- (c) It gives more authority to junior managers, and therefore provides them with work that grooms them for more senior positions in the future.

- (d) It provides an organisation structure which reduces the number of levels of management. The top executives in each division should be able to report direct to the chief executive of the holding company.

2.3 The matrix structure

Matrix structures attempt to ensure co-ordination across functional lines by the embodiment of dual authority in the organisation structure

Matrix structure provides for the formalisation of management control between different functions, whilst at the same time maintaining functional departmentation. It can be a mixture of a functional, product and territorial organisation.

A golden rule of classical management theory is **unity of command**: an individual should have one boss. (Thus, staff management can only act in an advisory capacity, leaving authority in the province of line management alone.) Matrix and project organisation may possibly be thought of as a reaction against the classical form of bureaucracy by establishing a structure of **dual command** either temporary (in the form of projects) or permanent (in the case of matrix structure).

2.4 Matrix organisation

Case Study

Matrix management first developed in the 1950s in the USA in the aerospace industry. *Lockheed*, the aircraft manufacturers, were organised in a functional hierarchy. Customers were unable to find a manager in Lockheed to whom they could take their problems and queries about their particular orders, and Lockheed found it necessary to employ 'project expediters' as customer liaison officials. From this developed 'project co-ordinators', responsible for co-ordinating line managers into solving a customer's problems. Up to this point, these new officials had no functional responsibilities.

Owing to increasingly heavy customer demands, Lockheed eventually created 'programme managers', with authority for project budgets and programme design and scheduling. These managers therefore had functional authority and responsibilities, thus a matrix management organisation was created.

The matrix organisation imposes the multi-disciplinary approach on a permanent basis. For example, it is possible to have a product management structure superimposed on top of a functional departmental structure in a matrix; product or brand managers may be responsible for the sales budget, production budget, pricing, marketing, distribution, quality and costs of their product or product line, but may have to co-ordinate with the R&D, production, finance, distribution, and sales departments in order to bring the product on to the market and achieve sales targets.

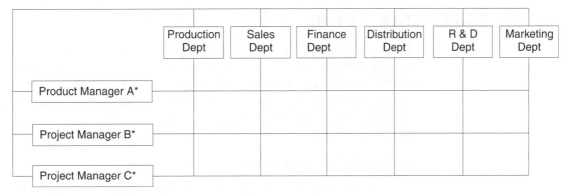

	Production Dept	Sales Dept	Finance Dept	Distribution Dept	R & D Dept	Marketing Dept
Product Manager A*						
Project Manager B*						
Project Manager C*						

* The product managers may each have their own marketing team; in which case the marketing department itself would be small or non-existent.

The authority of product managers may vary from organisation to organisation.

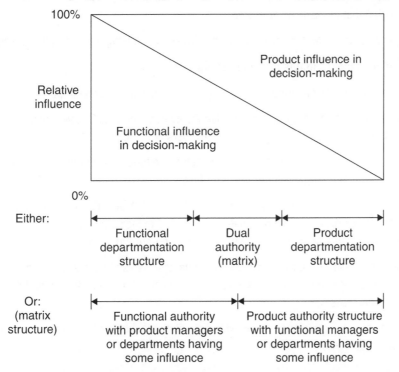

Once again, the division of authority between product managers and functional managers must be carefully defined.

Matrix management thus **challenges classical ideas** about organisation by rejecting the idea of one person, one boss.

A subordinate cannot easily take orders from two or more bosses, and so an arrangement has to be established, perhaps on the following lines.

(a)   A subordinate takes orders from one boss (the functional manager) and the second boss (the project manager) has to ask the first boss to give certain instructions to the subordinate.

(b)   A subordinate takes orders from one boss about some specified matters and orders from the other boss about different specified matters. The authority of each boss would have to be carefully defined. Even so, good co-operation between the bosses would still be necessary.

2.4.1 Advantages of a matrix structure

(a)   It offers greater **flexibility**. This applies both to **people,** as employees adapt more quickly to a new challenge or new task, and develop an attitude which is geared to accepting change; and to **task and structure**, as the matrix may be short-term (as with project teams) or readily amended (eg a new product manager can be introduced by superimposing his tasks on those of the existing functional managers). Flexibility should facilitate efficient operations in the face of change.

(b)   It should improve **communication** within the organisation.

(c)   Dual authority gives the organisation **multiple orientation** so that functional specialists do not get wrapped up in their own concerns.

(d)   It provides a **structure for allocating responsibility to managers for end-results**. A product manager is responsible for product profitability, and a project leader is responsible for ensuring that the task is completed.

(e)   It provides for **inter-disciplinary co-operation** and a mixing of skills and expertise.

A matrix organisation is most suitable in the following situations.

(a)   There is a fairly large number of different functions, each of great importance.

(b)   There could be communications problems between functional management in different functions (eg marketing, production, R&D, personnel, finance).

(c)   Work is supposed to flow smoothly between these functions, but the communications problems might stop or hinder the work flow.

(d)   There is a need to carry out uncertain, interdependent tasks. Work can be structured so as to be **task centred**, with task managers appointed to look after each task, and provide the communications (and co-operation) between different functions.

(e)   There is a need to achieve common functional tasks so as to achieve savings in the use of resources – ie product divisions would be too wasteful, because they would duplicate costly functional tasks.

(f)   There are many geographic areas with distinct needs, but the firm wishes to exploit economies of scale.

2.4.2 Disadvantages of matrix organisation

(a)   Dual authority threatens a **conflict** between managers. Where matrix structure exists it is important that the authority of superiors should not overlap and areas of authority must be clearly defined. A subordinate must know to which superior he is responsible for each aspect of his duties.

(b)   One individual with two or more bosses is more likely to suffer **role stress** at work.

(c)   It is sometimes more **costly** – eg product managers are additional jobs which would not be required in a simple structure of functional departmentation.

(d)   It may be **difficult for the management to accept** a matrix structure. It is possible that a manager may feel threatened that another manager will usurp his authority.

(e)   It required consensus and agreement which may slow down decision-making.

2.5 The transnational structure

FAST FORWARD

The transitional structure attempts to reconcile global scope and scale with local responsiveness.

Earlier in this Study Text, we discussed designs for global business. We now return to that topic.

In international strategy it has been difficult to combine **responsiveness to local conditions** with the degree of co-ordination necessary to achieve major **economies of scale**. The essence of the extreme case of the problem is an enforced choice between a low-cost product originally specified for a single market (typically the USA), which is potentially uninteresting or even actively shunned in other markets, and a range of low volume, and therefore high-cost, products, each specified for and produced in a single national market. These two cases are known as the **global** and the **multidomestic** approaches to organisation and they have their own characteristic organisational structures. The global approach leads to **global divisions**, each responsible for the worldwide production and marketing of a related group of standardised products. The multidomestic approach leads to the setting up or acquisition of local subsidiaries, each with a great deal of autonomy in design, production and marketing.

The **transnational structure** attempts to combine the best features of these contrasting approaches in order to create **competences of global relevance**, **responsiveness to local conditions** and **innovation and learning** on an organisation-wide scale. *Bartlett and Ghoshal* describe it as a **matrix** with two important general features.

(a)   It responds specifically to the challenges of globalisation.

(b)   It tends to have a high proportion of fixed responsibilities in the horizontal lines of management.

The transnational has three specific operational characteristics.

(a)   National units are **independent operating entities**, but also provide capabilities, such as R&D, that are utilised by the rest of the organisation.

(b)   Such shared capabilities allow national units to achieve global, or at least regional, **economies of scale**.

(c)   The global corporate parent adds value by establishing the **basic role of each national unit** and then supporting the **systems, relationships and culture** that enable them to work together as an effective network.

If it is to work, the transnational structure must have very clearly defined managerial roles, relationships and boundaries.

(a)   **Managers of global products or businesses** have responsibilities for strategies, innovation, resources and transactions that transcend both national and functional boundaries.

(b)   **Country managers** must feed back local requirements and build unique local competences.

(c)   **Functional managers** nurture innovation and spread best practice.

(d)   **Managers at the corporate parent** lead, facilitate and integrate all other managerial activity. They must also be talent spotters within the organisation.

2.5.1 Disadvantages of the transnational structure

The transnational structure makes great demands on its managers both in their immediate responsibilities and in the complexity of their relationships within the organisation. The complexity of the organisation can lead to the difficulties of control and the complications introduced by internal political activity.

2.6 The team-based structure

Both team and project based structures extend the matrix approach by using cross-functional teams. The difference is that projects naturally come to an end and so project teams disperse.

A team-based structure extends the matrix structures' use of both vertical functional links and horizontal, activity-based ones by utilising **cross-functional teams**. Business processes are often used as the basis of organisation, with each team being responsible for the processes relating to an aspect of the business. Thus, a purchasing team might contain procurement specialists, design and production engineers and marketing specialists in order to ensure that outsourced sub-assemblies were properly specified and contributed to brand values as well as being promptly delivered at the right price.

2.7 The project-based structure

The project-based structure is similar to the team-based structure except in that projects, by definition, have a **finite life** and so, therefore, do the project teams dealing with them. This approach is very flexible and is easy to use as an adjunct to more traditional organisational forms. Management of projects is a well-established discipline with its own techniques. It requires clear project definition if control is to be effective and comprehensive project review if longer-term learning is to take place. We deal with project management in more detail later in this Study Text.

2.8 Choosing a structure

An organisation structure must provide means of exercising appropriate **control**; it must also respond to the three challenges identified earlier: **rapid change**, **knowledge management** and **globalisation**.

JS&W summarise the seven basic types in a table. They emphasis that no single model of organisation is suitable for all purposes: managers must make choices as to which challenges they regard as most pressing.

	Control	Change	Knowledge	Globalisation
Functional	* * *	*	* *	*
Multidivisional	* *	* *	*	* *
Holding	*	* * *	*	* *
Matrix	*	* * *	* * *	* * *
Transnational	* *	* * *	* * *	* * *
Team	*	* *	* * *	*
Project	* *	* * *	* *	* *

Goold and Campbell propose nine tests that may be used to assess proposed structures. The first four relate to the organisation's **objectives** and the **restraints** under which it operates.

(a) **Market advantage**: where processes must be closely co-ordinated in order to achieve market advantage, they should be in the same structural element.

(b) **Parenting advantage**: the structure should support the parenting role played by the corporate centre. For example, a 'portfolio manager' would need only a small, low cost corporate centre. See Chapter 6 for a full discussion of parenting roles.

(c) **People test**: the structure must be suited to the skills and experience of the people that have to function within it. For example, skilled professionals used to a team-working approach might be frustrated by a move to a functional hierarchy.

(d) **Feasibility test**: this test sweeps up all other constraints, such as those imposed by law, stakeholder opinion and resource availability.

The tests forming the second group are matters of **design principle**.

(a) **Specialised cultures**: specialists should be able to collaborate closely.

(b) **Difficult links**: it is highly likely that some inter-departmental links will be subject to friction and strain. A good example would be the link between sales and production when there are frequent problems over quality and delivery. A sound structure will embody measures to strengthen communication and co-operation in such cases.

(c) **Redundant hierarchy**: the structure should be as flat as is reasonably attainable.

(d) **Accountability**: effective control requires clear lines of accountability.

(e) **Flexibility**: the structure must allow for requirements to change in the future, so that unexpected opportunities can be seized, for example.

3 Processes

Control processes determine how organisations function. They may be analysed according to whether they deal with inputs or outputs and whether they involve direct management action or more indirect effects. Balanced scorecards are direct output-based processes.

Processes are an important part of how organisations work. JS&W analyse them into four categories according to whether they deal with inputs or outputs and whether they operate by direct contact or through more indirect means. You should note that all of the processes discussed here are **control** processes.

3.1 Types of control process

	Input	Output
Direct	Supervision	Performance targets
	Planning processes	Balanced scorecard
Indirect	Cultural processes	Internal markets
	Self-control	

3.2 Input controls

3.2.1 Supervision

Direct supervision can be used for strategic control in addition to its traditional lower-level role. It is often used for overall control in small organisations and in larger ones displaying little complexity. This technique requires that the managers thoroughly understand all aspects of the business. Direct personal control is also used in a crisis when firm and rapid action is vital.

3.2.2 Planning processes

'Planning processes' is the phrase JS&W use to mean **budgetary control**. They also regard schemes for the standardisation of work processes, such as ISO 9000 certification, and IT-based enterprise resource planning systems as falling into this category. Simple and stable environments are best for this kind of approach. If different business units are faced by markedly different strategic imperatives, standardised planning systems are less applicable.

3.2.3 Self-control

Control can be exercised indirectly by promoting a high degree of **employee motivation**. When combined with autonomy, this can lead to both the exploitation of knowledge and effective co-ordination of activities by individuals interacting with one another. The role of management is then not to supervise but to provide appropriate channels for interaction and for knowledge creation and information use.

Leadership is of fundamental importance to this technique, and depends particularly on providing role models, supporting autonomous processes and providing resources.

3.2.4 Cultural processes

Cultural control processes are **indirect** and **internalised by employees** as they absorb the prevailing culture and its norms of behaviour and performance. Culturally conditioned behaviour can provide effective response to environments that are both dynamic and complex; it can be just as effective in a bureaucracy as in an informal, innovative, project-based organisation, for example. Training and development systems are an important aspect of the cultural control system.

Cultural processes also form important **links between organisations**, especially those that are highly dependent on the talent and knowledge of the people working in them; such people need an element of discussion, debate and cross-fertilisation in order for them to work effectively.

There is also a negative aspect to cultural processes, in that they can create **rigidities** of thought and behaviour, fossilising what was successful once, but may come to form an obstacle to progress.

3.3 Output controls

3.3.1 Performance targets

Performance can be judged against pre-set targets or **key performance indicators** (KPIs). This system is objective and permits the establishment of a hierarchy of supporting objectives that cascades down through the managerial structure. Managers are then free to organise their work and staff in as they think best, so long as they achieve the targets set for them.

The extensive autonomy of method permitted by this system makes it useful in **large organisations** where the centre cannot possibly control everything in detail. It is also useful in **regulated markets**, such as privatised utilities. These tend to retain strong monopolistic tendencies that are kept in check by external regulators' setting of targets for key indicators such as service levels.

In the **public sector**, control of inputs has been traditional, but there has been a move towards targets for outputs in order to improve services.

A problem with performance targets is that it can be difficult to identify appropriate KPIs. High-level financial KPIs, such as ROI, are well-established and present no difficulty. However, even where data is easily expressed in quantitative form, non-financial targets that are actually useful can be difficult to define. The problem is even greater with aspects of performance that are **largely qualitative**, such as customer satisfaction. As a result, attention tends to be directed towards the easily measured financial aspects of performance.

3.3.2 The balanced scorecard

The **balanced scorecard** approach emphasises the need for a broad range of KPIs and builds a rational structure that reflects longer term prospects as well as immediate performance.

The balanced scorecard focuses on **four different perspectives**.

Perspective	Question	Explanation
Customer	What do existing and new customers value from us?	Gives rise to targets that matter to customers: cost, quality, delivery, inspection, handling and so on.
Internal business	What processes must we excel at to achieve our financial and customer objectives?	Aims to improve internal processes and decision making.
Innovation and learning	Can we continue to improve and create future value?	Considers the business's capacity to maintain its competitive position through the acquisition of new skills and the development of new products.
Financial	How do we create value for our shareholders?	Covers traditional measures such as growth, profitability and shareholder value but set through talking to the shareholder or shareholders direct.

Performance targets are set once the key areas for improvement have been identified, and the balanced scorecard is the **main monthly report**.

The scorecard is **balanced** in the sense that managers are required to think in terms of all four perspectives, to **prevent improvements being made in one area at the expense of another**.

Kaplan and Norton, who first described the balanced scorecard, recognise that the four perspectives they suggest may not be perfect for all organisations: it may be necessary, for example, to add further perspectives related to the environment or to employment.

3.3.3 Problems

As with all techniques, problems can arise during application.

Problem	Explanation
Conflicting measures	Some measures in the scorecard such as research funding and cost reduction may naturally conflict. It is often difficult to determine the balance which will achieve the best results.
Selecting measures	Not only do appropriate measures have to be devised but the number of measures used must be agreed. Care must be taken that the impact of the results is not lost in a sea of information. The innovation and learning perspective is, perhaps, the most difficult to measure directly, since much development of human capital will not feed directly into such crude measures as rate of new product launches or even training hours undertaken. It will, rather, improve economy and effectiveness and support the achievement of customer perspective measures.
Expertise	Measurement is only useful if it initiates appropriate action. Non-financial managers may have difficulty with the usual profit measures. With more measures to consider this problem will be compounded.
Interpretation	Even a financially-trained manager may have difficulty in putting the figures into an overall perspective.

The scorecard should be used **flexibly**. The process of deciding **what to measure** forces a business to clarify its strategy. For example, a manufacturing company may find that 50% – 60% of costs are represented by bought-in components, so measurements relating to suppliers could usefully be added to the scorecard. These could include payment terms, lead times, or quality considerations.

3.3.4 Linkages

Disappointing results might result from a **failure to view all the measures as a whole**. For example, increasing productivity means that fewer employees are needed for a given level of output. Excess capacity can be created by quality improvements. However these improvements have to be exploited (eg by increasing sales). The **financial element** of the balanced scorecard 'reminds executives that improved quality, response time, productivity or new products, benefit the company only when they are translated into improved financial results', or if they enable the firm to obtain a sustainable competitive advantage.

The vertical vector

Kaplan and Norton's original perspectives may be viewed as hierarchical in nature, with a **vertical vector** running through the measures adopted.

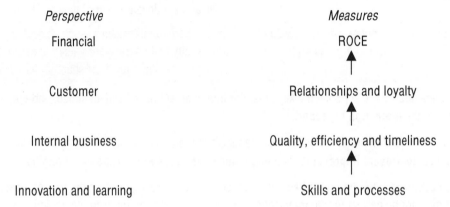

3.3.5 Market processes

Organisations are used to market relationships with entities, such as suppliers, outside the boundaries of their own systems. Attempts have been made to bring the responsiveness, self-regulating discipline and efficiency of the market **inside those boundaries**. Examples include autonomous **central service** units such as IT consultancy and the use of **transfer pricing** between divisions. Market solutions are particularly useful in complex or dynamic environments. They have also been used to promote innovation and responsiveness to local needs in the UK National Health Service as a replacement for centralised control.

3.3.6 Problems with market control processes

- Excessive management time spent bargaining
- Tendency for the creation of new bureaucracy to monitor effects
- Dysfunctional competition and legalistic contracting
- Destruction of cultures of collaboration

4 Relationships

Organisational relationships may be analysed into two categories: internal and external. Internal relationships concerning responsibility and authority for decision-making are particularly important.

4.1 Internal relationships

There are two important issues in internal relationships.

- The degree of centralisation
- The way the centre relates to the business units

4.1.1 Centralisation

FAST FORWARD

Centralisation offers control and standardisation; **decentralisation** utilises talent and local knowledge

Key terms

Centralisation means a greater degree of central control.

Decentralisation means a greater degree of delegated authority to regions or sub-units.

4.1.2 Advantages of centralisation

Advantage	Comment
Control	Senior management can exercise greater control over the activities of the organisation and co-ordinate their subordinates or sub-units more easily.
Standardisation	Procedures can be standardised throughout the organisation.
Corporate view	Senior managers can make decisions from the point of view of the organisation as a whole, whereas subordinates would tend to make decisions from the point of view of their own department or section.
Balance of power	Centralised control enables an organisation to maintain a balance between different functions or departments.
Experience counts	Senior managers ought to be more experienced and skilful in making decisions.
Lower overheads	When authority is delegated, there is often a duplication of management effort (and a corresponding increase in staff numbers) at lower levels of hierarchy.
Leadership	In times of crisis, the organisation may need strong leadership by a central group of senior managers.

4.1.3 Advantages of decentralisation

Advantage	Comment
Workload	It reduces the stress and burdens of senior management.
Job	It provides subordinates with greater job satisfaction by giving them more say in making decisions which affect their work.
Local knowledge	Subordinates may have a better knowledge than senior management of 'local' conditions affecting their area of work.
Flexibility and speed	Delegation should allow greater flexibility and a quicker response to changing conditions. If problems do not have to be referred up a scalar chain of command to senior managers for a decision, decision-making will be quicker.
Training	Management at middle and junior levels are groomed for eventual senior management positions.
Control	By establishing appropriate sub-units or profit centres to which authority is delegated, the system of control within the organisation might be improved.

4.2 Contingency approach

Centralisation suits some functions more than others.

- The **research and development function** might be centralised into a single unit, as a resource for each division.

- Sales departments might be decentralised on a territorial basis.

4.2.1 Strategic management relationships

> Goold and Campbell identified three major approaches to running divisionalised conglomerates: **strategic planning**, **strategic control** and **financial control**.

A vital feature of the relationship between the corporate centre and its business units is how responsibility for strategic decisions is divided between them.

There are **three generally accepted possible roles for the centre**.

- Determination of overall strategy and the allocation of resources
- Controlling divisional performance
- Provision of central services

All three of these roles have been subject to debate.

Centralised determination of strategy has been challenged as inappropriate in a diversified conglomerate. Similarly, **resource allocation**, it has been suggested, is the proper role of **capital markets**; and the rigour of the vetting carried out by central staffs has been questioned.

Controlling divisional performance is subject to all the arguments for and against decentralisation already discussed. The ability of the centre to prevent **strategic drift** has been questioned, though the radical market alternative can only work in drastic ways, such as takeover.

Centralised provision of certain **services**, such as legal and HR departments, is promoted as enhancing efficiency through the attainment of economies of scope. However, it is also suggested that many of these services can be contracted for locally at no greater cost and with the advantage of precluding any tendency to empire-building at the centre.

4.2.2 Research

Goold and Campbell researched the role of the centre in 16 British-based conglomerates. They concentrated on the first two roles summarised above, which they referred to as **planning influence** and **control influence**. The variation in these roles allowed the identification of eight distinct **strategic management styles**.

Planning influence was exercised in a variety of ways, but a fairly smooth spectrum of styles was observable, ranging from minimal, where the centre is little more than a holding company, to highly centralised, where the managers in the business units have responsibility only for operational decisions.

Control influence was exercised by the agreement of **objectives**, the monitoring of **results** and the deployment of **pressures and incentives**. This gave rise to three distinct categories of control influence: **flexible strategic**, **tight strategic** and **tight financial**.

Of the eight strategic management styles they defined, Goold and Campbell found that three of them were particularly common; each was associated with one of the three **control influence** categories mentioned above and with a different degree of **planning influence**.

Exam focus point

> You should note that this analysis of strategic management styles is completely separate from JS&W's description of the three corporate rationales, discussed earlier in this Study Text.

4.3 Strategic management styles

4.3.1 Strategic planning

The strategic planning style is associated with the flexible strategic type of control influence and a fairly high degree of central planning influence. The **centre establishes extensive planning processes** through which it works with business unit managers to make substantial contributions to strategic thinking, often with a unifying overall corporate strategy. Performance targets are set in broad terms, with an **emphasis on longer-term strategic objectives**. Such organisations build linked international businesses in core areas. Business units tend to follow bold strategies and often achieve above industry average **growth** and **profitability**.

4.3.2 Strategic control

The strategic control style involves a **fairly low degree of planning influence** but uses **tight strategic control**. The centre prefers to leave the planning initiative to the business unit managers, though it will review their plans for acceptability. **Firm targets are set** for a range of performance indicators and performance is judged against them. The centre concentrates on rationalising the portfolio. Such companies achieve **good profits** but are **less successful at achieving growth**.

4.3.3 Financial control

The centre exercises influence almost entirely through the budget process. It takes little interest in business unit strategy and controls through profit targets. Careers are at stake if budgets are missed. Strategies are **cautious** and rarely global. Business unit managers tend to sacrifice market share to achieve high profits. As a result, these companies produce **excellent profits**, but **growth comes mainly from acquisitions**.

Question   Head office

XYZ has over 500 profit centres (ranging from baggage handling equipment to stockings) and revenues of £7bn. Head office staff amount to 47. Each profit centre must provide the following.

(a)   The *annual profit plan*. This is agreed in detail every year, after close negotiation. It is regarded as a commitment to a preordained level of performance.

(b)   A *monthly management report*, which is extremely detailed (17 pages). Working capital is outlined in detail. Provisions (the easiest way to manipulate accounts) are highlighted.

Is XYZ a strategic planner, a strategic controller or a financial controller?

Answer

Financial controller.

4.4 External relationships

FAST FORWARD

> Extended relationships are increasingly co-operative rather than adversarial. Various forms of partnership, alliance, consortium may lead to the development of a network organisation.

Traditionally, external commercial relationships have been to a greater or lesser extent **adversarial**, in that each organisation has attempted to obtain for itself as much as possible of the value created overall in the value network. While this is still characteristic of most external relationships, many new ones have been created that focus more on **co-operation** than rivalry.

4.4.1 Alliances

The very great cost advantages available from economies of scale are a major driver of expansion. Indeed, the minimum efficient scale for capital intensive industries such as motor vehicle manufacture is so high that operations on at least a continental scale are necessary to achieve it. Such a degree of expansion requires huge amounts of capital; various forms of **complex organisation** result from the pressure to pool resources. These include **partnerships**, **alliances**, **consortia** and the unintegrated structures resulting from **takeovers** and **mergers**. An example of the latter is given by the merger between *Daimler* and *Chrysler*, which was a takeover by Daimler in all but name, and which preserved much of the structure of the two companies involved, to the extent of having two chief executives.

 Case Study

In February 2007 the *Financial Times* reported that *Daimler Chrysler* had 'opened the door to the total or partial sale of its Detroit-based *Chrysler* unit, acknowledging the short comings of one of the most ambitious transatlantic business mergers'.

The various forms of partnership structure were discussed in Chapter 6 in the context of strategic options. Structures such as franchises and joint ventures inevitably depend on the **management of relationships**, though the legal form can vary from loose co-operation on more or less market terms to joint ownership.

The legal form of these complex organisations is of less importance than the degree of co-operation actually achieved, and will anyway vary between the jurisdictions involved. Co-operation may be possible in any of the activities in the value chain. If co-operation is to convey mutual benefit, it must place both parties in a stronger position to achieve one or more of their strategic objectives, without at the same time undermining their ability to achieve others. A good example is **airline code sharing**.

Code sharing is a commercial agreement that allows an airline to put its two-letter identification code on the flights of another airline as they appear in computerised reservations systems. The airlines can then sell tickets for journeys that involve two or more flights without operating all the flights themselves. For example, *US Airways* and the German airline *Deutsche BA* operate code share flights from the USA to destinations in Germany. Customers fly on a US Airways aircraft between the US and Munich, and on Deutsche BA aircraft from Munich to Berlin, Cologne/Bonn, Dusseldorf and Hamburg, still using the US Airways ticket designator. Airlines that share codes typically co-ordinate schedules to minimise connection times and provide additional customer services, such as one-stop check-in and baggage checked through to the final destination.

The main problem of such structural relationships is the integration of knowledge to create a successful product. This becomes more difficult as the number of partners increases.

4.4.2 Network organisations

The idea of a **network structure** is applied both within and between organisations. Within the organisation, the term is used to mean something that resembles both the **organic** organisation discussed later in this chapter and the structure of informal relationships that exists in most organisations alongside the formal structure. Such a loose, fluid approach is often used to achieve innovative response to changing circumstances.

The network approach is also visible in the growing field of **outsourcing** as a strategic method. Complex relationships can be developed between firms, who may both buy from and sell to each other, as well as the simpler, more traditional practice of buying in services such as cleaning. Writers such as *Ghoshal and Bartlett* point to the likelihood of such networks becoming the corporations of the future, replacing formal organisation structures with innovations such as **virtual teams**. Virtual teams are interconnected groups of people who may not be in the same office (or even the same organisation) but who:

- Share information and tasks
- Make joint decisions
- Fulfil the collaborative function of a team

Organisations are now able to structure their activities very differently:

(a) **Staffing.** Certain areas of organisational activity can be undertaken by freelance or contract workers. *Charles Handy's* shamrock organisation (see below) is gaining ground as a workable model for a leaner and more flexible workforce, within a controlled framework. The question is: how can this control be achieved?

(b) **Leasing of facilities** such as machinery, IT and accommodation (not just capital assets) is becoming more common

(c) **Production** itself might be outsourced, even to offshore countries where labour is cheaper. (This, and the preceding point, of course beg the question: which assets and activities do companies retain, and which ones do they 'buy-in'?)

Interdependence of organisations is emphasised by the sharing of functions and services. Databases and communication create genuine interactive sharing of, and access to, common data.

JS&W give four examples of network organisation structures.

(a) **Teleworking**, which combines independent work with connection to corporate resources.

(b) **Federations of experts** who combine voluntarily. This is common in the entertainment industry.

(c) **One stop shops** for professional services in which a package of services is made available by a co-ordinating entity. The point of access to such a conglomerate might be a website.

(d) **Service networks** such as the various chains of franchised hotel that co-operate to provide centralised booking facilities.

Network structures are also discerned between competitors, where **co-operation on non-core competence matters** can lead to several benefits.

- Cost reduction
- Increased market penetration
- Experience curve effects

Typical areas for co-operation between **competitors** include R&D and distribution chains. The spread of the *Toyota* system of manufacturing, with its emphasis on JIT, quality and the elimination of waste has led to a high degree of integration between the operations of industrial **customers** and their **suppliers**.

4.5 The shamrock organisation

FAST FORWARD

The shamrock organisation, or flexible firm, has a core of permanent managers and specialist staff supplied by a contingent workforce of contractors and part-time and temporary workers. This form is popular during recessions.

Largely driven by pressure to reduce personnel costs and to adapt to new market imperatives, there has been an increase in the use of part-time and temporary contracts of employment. These allow rapid down-sizing in times of recession or slow growth and can save on the costs of benefits such as pensions, holiday pay and health insurance. The growth in the proportion of the workforce employed on such less-favourable contracts has attracted political attention but continues. It has produced the phenomenon of the **flexible firm** or, as *Handy* calls it, the **shamrock organisation**.

Handy defines the **shamrock organisation** as a 'core of essential executives and workers supported by outside contractors and part-time help'. This structure permits the buying-in of services as needed, with consequent reductions in overhead costs. It is also known as the **flexible firm**.

The first leaf of the shamrock is the **professional core**. It consists of professionals, technicians and managers whose skills define the organisation's core competence. This core group defines what the company does and what business it is in. They are essential to the continuity and growth of the organisation. Their pay is tied to organisational performance and their relations will be more like those among the partners in a professional firm than those among superiors and subordinates in today's large corporation.

The next leaf is made up of **self-employed professionals or technicians** or smaller specialised organisations who are hired on contract, on a project-by-project basis. They are paid in fees for results rather than in salary for time. They frequently **telecommute**. No benefits are paid by the core organisation, and the worker carries the risk of insecurity.

The third leaf comprises the **contingent work force**, whose employment derives from the external demand for the organisation's products. There is no career track for these people and they perform routine jobs. They are usually temporary and part-time workers who will experience short periods of employment and long periods of unemployment. They are paid by the hour or day or week for the time they work.

A fourth leaf of the shamrock may exist, consisting of **consumers** who do the work of the organisation. Examples are shoppers who bag their own groceries and purchasers of assemble-it-yourself furniture.

This type of organisation provides three kinds of flexibility.

(a) **Personnel costs** can respond to market conditions of supply and demand for different types of labour and to the employer's financial position.

(b) Overall **personnel numbers** can be changed as required.

(c) The **skills** available can be modified fairly rapidly and multi-skilling can be encouraged.

There are other implications for employment patterns.

(a) All staff will have to be prepared to widen their availability, possibly moving from site to site as required.

(b) Staff must accept varying patterns of working hours, perhaps working on **annual hours** contracts which require extended shifts in busy times balanced with shorter ones in slack times.

(c) Contracts of employment will be far less prescriptive of duties and responsibilities.

4.6 The virtual organisation

A virtual organisation is a geographically distributed network with little formal structure, probably held together by IT applications, partnerships and collaboration.

The idea of a **virtual organisation** or **cybernetic corporation** has attracted considerable attention as the usefulness of IT for communication and control has been exploited. The essence of the virtual organisation is the electronic linking of spatially dispersed components.

While there is some disagreement among academics as to a precise definition of the virtual organisation, a consensus exists with regard to **geographical dispersion** and the centrality of **information technology** to the production process. Many also agree that the virtual organisation has a temporary character. Other characteristics are a **flexible structure** and a **collaborative culture**.

However, an organisation is not a virtual organisation merely because it uses IT extensively and has multiple locations. Many academics would exclude organisations that use communications extensively, but not in a way **critical to completing the production process**.

Key term

> A **virtual organisation** is a temporary or permanent collection of geographically dispersed individuals, groups, organisational units (which may or may not belong to the same organisation), or entire organisations that depend on electronic linking in order to complete the production process.

JS&W use the term rather less rigorously, to mean any network organisation that is 'held together not through formal structure and physical proximity of people, but by partnership, collaboration and networking'.

5 Stereotypical configurations

In Section 1 we pointed out that it is very important to be aware that structures, processes and relationships are **highly interdependent**: they have to work together intimately and consistently if the organisation is to be successful. This means, among other things, that the basic assumptions and characteristics of the three components must be more or less compatible, since they have to integrate so closely. Thus, it might be difficult to combine a strict **financial control** style of leadership at the corporate parent with a **transnational** structural approach, or to use **cultural control** throughout the **shamrock organisation**, simply because of the use of temporary workers.

As a result of this need for compatibility, the number of successful overall configurations is small. *Mintzberg* identifies only **six ideal types**. Of these, five fit neatly into a taxonomy based on their five main structural components; the sixth, less so.

FAST FORWARD

> *Henry Mintzberg's* theory of organisational configuration is a way of expressing the main features by which both formal structure and power relationships are expressed in organisations. He suggests that there are five ideal types of organisation, each of which configures five standard components in a significantly different way. Each component of the organisation has its own **dynamic**, which **leads to a distinct type of organisation**. The sixth type is the missionary organisation.

The five components

(a) The **strategic apex** wishes to retain control over decision-making. It achieves this when the co-ordinating mechanism is **direct supervision**. The force this most relates to is the **force for direction** (in other words for the need for people to be told what to do).

(b) The **technostructure's** reason for existence is the design of **procedures** and **standards**. For example, the preparation of accounts is highly regulated. This acts as a **force for efficiency**.

(c) The members of the **operating core** seek to minimise the control of administrators over what they do. They prefer to work autonomously, achieving what other co-ordination is necessary by **mutual adjustment**. As professionals, they rely on outside training (such as medical training) to standardise skills. This corresponds to the **force for proficiency.**

(d) The managers of the **middle line** seek to increase their **autonomy** from the strategic apex, and to increase their control over the operating core, so that they can concentrate on their own segment of the market or with their own products. This corresponds to the **force for concentration** (on individual product areas).

(e) **Support staff** only gain influence when their expertise is vital. **Mutual adjustment** is the co-ordinating mechanism. This corresponds to the **force for learning**.

The **forces for co-operation and competition** largely describe how these elements relate to each other.

5.1 The simple structure (or entrepreneurial) structure

The **strategic apex** wishes to retain control over decision-making, and so exercises what Mintzberg describes as a **pull to centralise**. Mintzberg believes that this leads to a **simple structure**.

(a)   **The simple structure is characteristic of small, young organisations**.

(b)   In small firms, a single entrepreneur or management team will dominate (as in the power culture). If it grows, the organisation might need more managerial skills than the apex can provide. Strategies might be made on the basis of the manager's hunches.

(c)   Centralisation is advantageous as it reflects management's full knowledge of the operating core and its processes. However, senior managers might intervene too much.

(d)   It is risky as it depends on the expertise of one person. Such an organisation might be prone to **succession crises**. Who takes over if the boss dies? This problem is often encountered in family businesses.

(e)   This structure can handle an environment that is relatively simple but fast moving, where standardisation cannot be used to co-ordinate activities.

(f)   **Co-ordination is achieved by direct supervision**, with few formal devices. It is thus flexible.

(g)   This structure has its own particular characteristics : wide span of control; no middle line and hence minimal hierarchy; and no technostructure, implying little formalisation or standardisation of behaviour.

5.2 The machine bureaucracy

The **technostructure** exerts a pull for standardisation of work processes. It creates a **machine bureaucracy**.

(a)   This is the classic bureaucracy, working on a sophisticated and well-tuned set of **rules and procedures**. Machine bureaucracies are associated with routine technical systems and repetitive tasks. The bureaucracy can function if people leave, as jobs are designed precisely.

(b)   **The technostructure is the key part**. Power rests with analysts who standardise other people's work. The key management philosophy is **scientific management**.

(c)   The work of the operating core is highly standardised. Direct supervision by the strategic apex is limited as **standardisation of work processes ensures co-ordination**.

(d)   There is a strong emphasis on the **division of labour**, and in particular **on control**. Uncertainty has to be eliminated. The elaborate middle line monitors and directs the operating core. Outsourcing would be embraced reluctantly so the firm employs its own legal and PR specialists. (For example, many big firms have a central legal department.)

(e)   Formal communication is most important. Authority is hierarchical.

(f)   Conflict is rife between different departments, between line and staff, and between operating core and management.

(g)   The environment must be simple and stable.

(h)   The machine bureaucracy is the most efficient structure for integrating sets of simple and repetitive tasks.

(i)   Machine bureaucracies cannot adapt rapidly they are designed for specialised purposes. They are driven by performance, not problem solving.

5.3 The professional bureaucracy

The **operating core** has a pull for standardisation, not of work processes but of **individual skills**. A machine bureaucracy would lay down exactly how financial transactions should be posted, whether people understood them or not. A **professional bureaucracy** would employ accountants who should know what is involved. The operating core seeks to minimise the influence of administrators (mainly the middle line and technostructure) over work. Examples are hospitals and accountancy firms.

(a) It hires trained specialists who are all imbued with the skills and values of the profession. A school is an example. Teachers' work in the classroom is not directly supervised but all teachers are trained.

(b) **Co-ordination is achieved by standardisation of skills**, which originate outside its structure. (Teacher training occurs at independent colleges.)

(c) **Power is often based on expertise**, not formal position in the organisation hierarchy.

(d) Work processes are **too complex** to be standardised by a technostructure.

(e) The **operating core** is the key part. There is an elaborate support staff to service it. A technostructure might exist for budgeting, but not for designing work processes.

(f) Work is decentralised. **Professionals control their own work**, and seek collective control over the administrative decisions which affect them.

(g) There might be **two** organisation hierarchies: one, relatively informal, for the operating core doing the work; another, more formal for the support staff. An example is a barristers' chambers. Barristers are co-ordinated by their head clerk, but they retain collective authority over the clerk. The clerk, on the other hand, will exercise direct control over secretarial services.

(h) Professional administrators also manage much of the organisation's boundary.

(i) It can be democratic.

(j) The professional bureaucracy cannot always cope with any variations of standards, as control is exercised through training.

Question
Bureaucracy

How would a machine bureaucracy and a professional bureaucracy ensure that accounting transactions are correctly posted?

Answer

The machine bureaucracy would devise very precise procedures and rule-books telling untrained clerks exactly what to do in any situation.

The professional bureaucracy would employ trained and perhaps qualified accounts staff, whose professional training would give them the expertise to make the right decision.

5.4 The divisional (or diversified) form

The middle line seeks as much autonomy for itself as possible. It exerts a **pull to balkanise** (ie to split into small self-managed units). The result is the **divisional form**, by which autonomy is given to managers lower down the line. The prime co-ordinating mechanism is **standardisation of outputs**: these are usually performance measures such as profit, which are set by the strategic apex.

(a)   Divisionalisation is the division of a business into **autonomous regions** or product businesses, each with its own revenues, expenditures and profits.

(b)   Because each division is monitored by its objective performance towards a single integrated set of goals determined by the strategic apex, **each division is configured as a machine bureaucracy**.

(c)   Communication between divisions and head office is restricted, formal and related to performance standards. Influence is maintained by headquarters' power to hire and fire the managers who are supposed to run each division.

(d)   Divisionalisation is a function of organisation size, in numbers and in product-market activities.

5.5 The adhocracy

The **support staff** exert a pull of their own, towards **collaboration**. The **adhocracy** does not rely on standardisation to co-ordinate its activities, yet it is much more complex than the simple structure which also does not use standardisation.

(a)   The adhocracy is **complex and disorderly**. There is little formalisation of behaviour. Specialists are deployed in market-based project teams which group together and disperse as and when a project arises and ends. Co-ordination is informal, by mutual adjustment.

(b)   The adhocracy relies on the expertise of its members, **but not through standardised skills**. Instead, the *mix* of skills is important. For example, a film is made by a director, actors, camera people, set designers and so on.

(c)   A matrix structure might exist, but there are a large number of management roles such as project managers. Managers do not plan or supervise, but co-ordinate.

(d)   Decision-making power depends on the type of decision and the situation in which it is made, rather than level in hierarchy. 'No-one ... monopolises the power to innovate'.

(e)   Strategy is hard to determine in the adhocracy. It depends partly on the projects that come along (like a film studio). The strategic apex does not *formulate* strategies, but is engaged in battles over strategic *choices* (eg which films shall we make?) and liaisons with the outside parties.

(f)   The adhocracy is positioned in a dynamic and complex environment.

(g)   The adhocracy is driven to bureaucratise itself as it ages. The organisation will eventually **specialise in what it does best**, driving it to more stable environmental conditions and predictable work processes, leading perhaps to a professional bureaucracy.

The adhocracy is concerned with **innovation**.

(a)   The **operating adhocracy** seeks to **innovate** to serve its clients, whereas the professional bureaucracy seeks perfection. (Mintzberg uses an analogy of a theatre company. An adhocratic theatre company produces new plays. A professional bureaucratic one would seek to produce ever more perfect renditions of Shakespeare.) The operating core is retained.

(b)   The **administrative adhocracy** innovates to serve its **own convenience**. Note that the operating core is split off, frequently subcontracted or automated, or even forms a separate organisation. The support staff are important, a central pool of expert talent from which project teams are drawn.

Adhocracies sometimes exist because the complexity of their technical systems require a trained support staff to operate them.

(a) The adhocracy is an ambiguous environment for work. This elicits complex human responses, as many people dislike ambiguity.

(b) The adhocracy is not suitable for **standardised** work; it is better at dealing with unique projects.

(c) It has a high cost of communication, and workloads are unbalanced.

5.6 Concluding thoughts

The usefulness of Mintzberg's theory of structural configuration is that it covers many issues, over and above formal organisation structure.

- The type of work the organisation does (customised or standardised)
- The complexity it has to deal with (simple or complex)
- The environment (stable or dynamic)

We can summarise some of these in the table below.

	Co-ordination mechanism	Key part	Environment	Possible characteristics
Simple	Direct supervision	Strategic apex	Simple/dynamic (even hostile)	Small, young, centralised, personality-driven. Crisis of leadership
Machine bureaucracy	Standardised work processes	Techno-structure	Simple/stable	Old, large, rule-bound, specialised
Professional bureaucracy	Standardised skills	Operating core	Complex/stable	Decentralised, emphasis on training
Divisional form	Standardised outputs	Middle line	Varies; each division is shielded to a degree	Old, large, divisions are quasi-autonomous, decentralised, bureaucratic
Adhocracy	Mutual adjustment	Support staff	Complex/dynamic	High automated, 'organic'

5.6.1 The missionary organisation

Mintzberg mentions one other co-ordinating factor: **mission**. A **missionary organisation** is one welded together by ideology or culture. There is job rotation, standardisation of values (*norms*) and little external control (eg like a religious sect). This relates to ideology, the **force for co-operation**. This kind of configuration features simple systems and network relationships in team structures. It works well in a simple and static environment

| Question | Organisation configurations |

Which organisation configurations are suggested in the following cases?

(a) Creation Ltd provides public relations services to clients. It is run by five partners, with a staff of copy editors, designers, party-throwers and people with contacts in the press. Clients contact one of the partners who assembles a team to solve the client's problem, though the partner does not direct the solution.

(b) The St Imelda Hospital is involved in providing physiotherapy to accident victims. It recruits trained physiotherapists, each of whom is allocated a patient. The hospital does not determine exactly what sort of treatments should be used.

Answer

(a)   Adhocracy
(b)   Professional bureaucracy

6 Configuration and strategy

FAST FORWARD

> *Chandler* concluded that structure is determined by strategy. JS&W suggest that practical combinations of structures, processes and relationships are few and those that succeed tend to be robust and difficult to change because their dynamic interactions tend to produce **reinforcing cycles of behaviour**. Strategy and structure thus tend to support and preserve one another.

There has been debate as to which of strategy and structure is the **independent variable** and which the **dependent**. *Chandler* concluded that structure was determined by strategy, but it has been suggested that once a large organisation has settled into a particular structural form, the hierarchical, communication and cultural practices associated with that form will predispose it towards a particular strategic stance. JS&W expand on this suggestion with their description of **reinforcing cycles** and **configuration dilemmas**.

6.1 Reinforcing cycles

The very fact that there are only six ideal types of organisational configuration indicates that the three strands, structure, processes and relationships, are constrained in the ways in which they can combine effectively in practice. They do not offer a menu of independent choices; only certain combinations work. JS&W say 'configurations found in practice tend to be very **cohesive**, **robust** and **difficult to change**' (original emphasis).

This tendency is explained by the **dynamic interaction** between the various elements of configuration, environment and strategy. This interaction leads to **reinforcing cycles** of behaviour that tend to preserve the *status quo*. Thus, for example, a **machine bureaucracy** will seek out stable environmental conditions in which to compete with a standardised, cost effective product; this will make good use of its standardised processes and tight management and reinforce its defensive culture – which will predispose it to seek out stable environmental conditions.

This interdependence can strengthen the organisation, but the danger is that it can lead to strategic drift if one of the elements involved is changed. The circle of reinforcement is broken and the organisation may decline until a new reinforcing cycle is developed.

This tendency for things to get worse before they get better is illustrated by the **change and performance J curve**. Change tends to lead to a fall in performance that continues until a set of reinforcing factors is assembled; only then can performance improve past its original level.

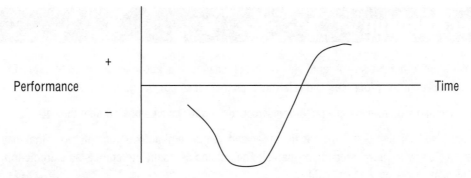

The change and performance J curve

There is an important lesson here for the **management of change**, which is that attention must be paid simultaneously to all three of structure, process and relationships if the change is to be carried through successfully.

6.2 Configuration dilemmas

Even within the six stereotypical configurations there will be **problems of optimisation**, since many of the features that might be adopted have both advantages and disadvantages. Some of these problems can be resolved into simple choices, but most require a balance to be struck between opposed extreme positions.

A **hierarchical structure** may be necessary for direction and control, but is less good than a **network approach** for fostering learning and innovation. Similarly, **vertical lines of acc**ountability may push subordinates to greater efforts, but this may at the expense of **horizontal relationships**.

Empowerment can promote the use of initiative, but is difficult to combine with overall control and may lead to chaotic activity. Similar considerations apply to centralisation, as discussed earlier in this chapter.

Dilemmas such as these may be managed in three ways.

(a) The organisation may be **divided** and different approaches used in each part. For example, the accounting and HRM departments may function best if organised in a standardised, bureaucratic way, while the adhocracy may provide a more effective model for such activities as marketing and R&D. This has been called the **dual core** approach.

(b) A **combination** of features may be possible, if difficult to achieve. JS&W give the examples of ABB and Unilever, which are said to be 'networked multidivisionals'.

(c) Frequent **reorganisation** may be used to prevent any particular approach from becoming dominant in the longer term.

Chapter Roundup

- Globalisation, other aspects of rapid environmental change and, above all, the need to **exploit knowledge** make the **structures**, **processes** and **relationships** that make up configurations vital for strategic success.

- In a functional structure, people are organised according to the type of work that they do.

- The multi-divisional structure divides the organisation into semi-autonomous divisions that may be differentiated by territory, product, or market. The holding company structure is an extreme form in which the divisions are separate legal entities.

- **Matrix structures** attempt to ensure co-ordination across functional lines by the embodiment of dual authority in the organisation structure

- The transitional structure attempts to reconcile global scope and scale with local responsiveness.

- Both team and project based structures extend the matrix approach by moving cross-functional teams. The difference is that projects naturally come to an end and project teams disperse.

- Control processes determine how organisations function. They may be analysed according to whether they deal with inputs or outputs and whether they involve direct management action or more indirect effects. Balanced scorecards are direct output-based processes.

- **Centralisation** offers control and standardisation; **decentralisation** utilises talent and local knowledge

- Goold and Campbell identified three major approaches to running divisionalised conglomerates: **strategic planning**, **strategic control** and **financial control**.

- Extended relationships are increasingly co-operative rather than adversarial. Various forms of partnership, alliance, consortium may lead to the development of a network organisation.

- The shamrock organisation, or flexible firm, has a core of permanent mangers and specialist staff supplied by a contingent workforce of contractors and part-time and temporary workers. This form is popular during recessions.

- A virtual organisation is a geographically distributed network with little formal structure, probably held together by IT applications, partnerships and collaboration.

- *Henry Mintzberg's* theory of organisational configuration is a way of expressing the main features by which both formal structure and power relationships are expressed in organisations. He suggests that there are five ideal types of organisation, each of which configures five standard components in a significantly different way. Each component of the organisation has its own **dynamic**, which **leads to a distinct type of organisation**. The sixth type is the missionary organisation.

- *Chandler* concluded that structure is determined by strategy. JS&W suggest that practical combinations of structures, processes and relationships are few and those that succeed tend to be robust and difficult to change because their dynamic interactions tend to produce **reinforcing cycles of behaviour**. Strategy and structure thus tend to support and preserve one another.

Quick Quiz

1   What are the three components of an organisation's configuration?

2   What specific features does a transnational have?

3   What are the perspectives of the standard balanced scorecard and how do they fit together?

4   What are the three strategic management styles identified by Goold and Campbell?

5   What are the five organisational components described by Mintzberg?

Answers to Quick Quiz

1   Structures, processes and relationships

2   Independent national operating companies that also provide expertise used globally; as a result global, or at least regional, scale economies; a global parent that establishes the basic roles of the national units and supports the systems, relationships and culture that enable them to work together.

3   The innovation perspective's measures of skills and processes should support the internal business perspective's measures of quality, efficiency and timeliness, which support the customer perspective's measures of relationships and loyalty, which support the overall financial perspective measure, ROCE.

4   Strategic planning, strategic control, financial control.

5   Strategic apex, middle line, operating core, technostructure, support services.

Now try the questions below from the Exam Question Bank

Number	Level	Marks	Time
Q7	Preparation	n/a	36 mins

Part D
Business processes

Business processes

Topic list	Syllabus reference
1 The background to process change	D1(b), D2(a)
2 The process-strategy matrix	D1(c)
3 A process redesign methodology	D1(a), (f)
4 Process commoditisation and outsourcing	D1(d), (e)

Introduction

Strategies are, to some extent at least, delivered by means of processes. We have already seen how processes fit with structures and relationships in configurations and we have examined control processes in some detail. In this chapter and the next we go on to examine processes in the wider sense, the contribution they make to organisations and strategy and, overall, how they may be improved and made more effective.

Study guide

		Intellectual level
D1	**The role of process and process change initiatives**	
(a)	Advise on how an organisation can reconsider the design of its processes to deliver a selected strategy	3
(b)	Appraise business process change initiatives previously adopted by organisations	3
(c)	Establish an appropriate scope and focus for business process change using Harmon's process-strategy mix	3
(d)	Explore the commoditisation of business processes	3
(e)	Advise on the implications of business process outsourcing	3
(f)	Recommend a business process redesign methodology for an organisation	2

Exam guide

The syllabus places considerable emphasis on processes. This is a very practical topic and it is easy to see that the Examiners will have plenty of scope for practical questions based on it. An obvious route would be to ask you to use the process-strategy matrix to select processes for improvement and the process redesign methodology discussed in section 3 to show how to proceed.

1 The background to process change

Business processes of all kinds have been subject to efforts towards their improvement for many years. The industrial revolution brought new techniques for manufacturing and also for administration. *Josiah Wedgewood* is best known for innovation in pottery and ceramic goods but he also made rapid strides in the development of cost accountancy, including the establishment of standard costs, for example. Other important figures in the history of management innovation include the experts known to us as the Scientific Management school and figures such as *Henry Ford, Alfred Sloan* and *Peter Drucker*. The search for better ways of doing things has been going on for a long time. In this section (which is largely based on Chapter 1 of *Business Process Change* by *Paul Harmon*) we will revise some of the important steps along the way.

1.1 Organisations as systems

> **FAST FORWARD**
>
> General system theory would see the organisation as an **open system**, interacting with its environment.

1.2 Systems theory

Key term

> *Curtis* defines a **system** as a collection of interrelated parts which taken together forms a whole such that:
>
> (a)   The collection has some purpose
> (b)   A change in any of the parts leads to or results from a change in some other part or parts.

An organisation is a type of system.

1.3 Open and closed systems

General systems theory makes a distinction between open, closed and semi-closed systems.

(a) **A closed system is isolated from its environment and independent of it**, so that no environmental influences affect the behaviour of the system, nor does the system exert any influence on its environment.

(b) **An open system is connected to and interacts with its environment**. It takes in influences from its environment and also influences this environment by its behaviour. An open system is a stable system which is nevertheless continually changing or evolving.

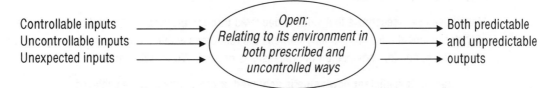

(c) **Few systems are entirely closed**. Many are **semi-closed**, in that their relationship with the environment is in some degree restricted. An example of a semi-closed system might be a pocket calculator. Its inputs are restricted to energy from its batteries and numerical information entered to it in a particular way (by the operator depressing a sequence of keys). The calculator is restricted in what it will do.

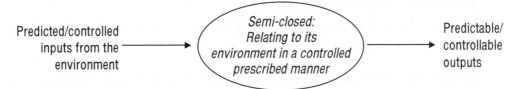

Social organisations, such as businesses and government departments, are by definition open systems.

Organisations have a variety of interchanges with the environment, obtaining inputs from it, and generating outputs to it.

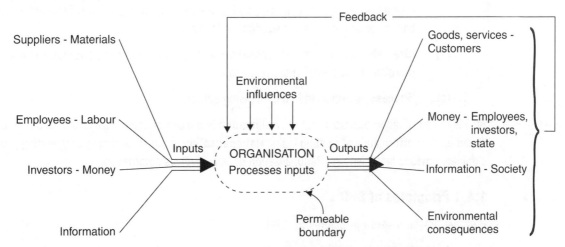

This general background is clearly linked to *Porter's* **value chain** model, which shows how the functioning of the **internal sub-systems** of the organisation contribute to its overall capability to add value. The ways in which the system and its sub-systems function constitute the organisation's **processes and relationships**. The value chain was discussed in detail earlier in this Study Text.

1.4 Business process re-engineering

Business process re-engineering is a useful approach based on challenging basic assumptions about business methods and even the objectives they are designed to achieve. IT can be very useful here, but simply to automate a process is not the same as re-engineering it.

Business process re-engineering involves fundamental changes in the way an organisation functions. For example, processes which were developed in a paper-intensive processing environment may not be suitable for an environment which is underpinned by IT.

Why focus on processes?

Many businesses recognise that value is delivered **through processes,** but still define themselves in terms of their functional roles. To properly harness the resources within a business a clear agreement of the management and implementation of processes is needed. **Without this focus** on processes:

(a)   It is **unclear how value is achieved** or can continue to be achieved.

(b)   The **effects of change** on the operation of the business are **hard to predict**.

(c)   There is no basis to achieve **consistent** business improvement.

(d)   **Knowledge is lost** as people move around or out of the business.

(e)   Cross-functional interaction is not encouraged.

It is **difficult to align the strategy** of an organisation with the people, systems resources through which that strategy will be accomplished.

The main writing on the subject is *Hammer and Champy's Reengineering the Corporation* (1993), from which the following is taken.

Key term

> **Business Process Re-engineering** is the fundamental rethinking and radical redesign of business processes to achieve dramatic improvements in critical contemporary measures of performance, such as cost, quality, service and speed.

The key words here are **'fundamental'**, **'radical'**, **'dramatic'** and **'process'**.

(a)   **Fundamental** and **radical** indicate that BPR assumes nothing: it starts by asking basic questions such as 'why do we do what we do', without making any assumptions or looking back to what has always been done in the past.

(b)   **'Dramatic'** means that BPR should achieve 'quantum leaps in performance', not just marginal, incremental improvements.

(c)   **'Process'** is explained in the following paragraphs.

BPR is not automation or rationalisation. **Automation** is the use of computerised working methods to speed up the performance of existing tasks. **Rationalisation** is the streamlining of operating procedures to eliminate obvious inefficiencies. Rationalisation usually involves automation.

1.4.1 Principles of BPR

Hammer presents **seven principles** for BPR.

(a)   Processes should be designed to achieve a desired **customer-focused outcome** rather than focusing on existing **tasks**. The whole process should be **market driven**.

(b)   Personnel who use the **output** from a process should **perform** the process. For example, a company could set up a database of approved suppliers; this would allow personnel who actually require supplies to order them themselves, perhaps using on-line technology, thereby eliminating the need for a separate purchasing function.

(c)   Information processing should be **included** in the work that **produces** the information. This eliminates the differentiation between information gathering and information processing.

(d)   **Geographically-dispersed** resources should be treated as if they are **centralised.** This allows the benefits of centralisation to be obtained, for example, economies of scale through central negotiation of supply contracts, without losing the benefits of decentralisation, such as flexibility and responsiveness.

(e)   Parallel activities should be **linked** rather than **integrated.** This would involve, for example, co-ordination between teams working on different aspects of a single process.

(f)   Workpeople should be **self-managing**, exercising greater autonomy over their work. The traditional distinction between workers and managers can be abolished: decision aids such as expert systems can be provided where they are required.

(g)   Information should be captured **once** at **source.** Electronic distribution of information makes this possible.

1.4.2 Is there a BPR methodology?

Davenport and *Short* prescribe a **five-step approach** to BPR.

Step 1   Develop the **business vision and process objectives**. BPR is driven by a business vision which implies specific business objectives such as cost reduction, time reduction, output quality improvement, Total Quality Management and empowerment.

Step 2   **Identify the processes** to be redesigned. Most firms use the 'high impact' approach, which focuses on the most important processes or those that conflict most with the business vision. Lesser number of firms use the exhaustive approach that attempts to identify all the processes within an organisation and then prioritise them in order of redesign urgency.

Step 3   Understand and **measure the existing processes** – to ensure previous mistakes are not repeated and to provide a baseline for future improvements.

Step 4   **Identify change levers**. Awareness of IT capabilities could approve useful when designing processes.

Step 5   Design and **build a prototype** of the new process. The actual design should not be viewed as the end of the BPR process – it should be viewed as a prototype, with successive alterations. The use of a prototype enables the involvement of customers.

1.5 IT and BPR

IT is not the solution in itself, it is an **enabler**. BPR uses IT to allow an organisation to do things that it is not doing already. For example, teleconferencing reduces the cost of travelling to meetings – a re-engineering approach takes the view that teleconferencing allows more frequent meetings.

As *Hammer* and *Champy* put it, 'It is this disruptive power of technology, its ability to break the rules that limit how we conduct our work, that makes it critical to companies looking for competitive advantage.'

1.5.1 Problems with BPR

There are concerns that BPR has become misunderstood. According to an independent study of 100 European companies, BPR has become allied in managers' minds with narrow targets such as **reductions in staff numbers** and other **cost-cutting** measures.

In addition to this perception about headcount, several other criticism have been levelled at the way the idea has been implemented.

(a)   Any successful BPR programme is likely to result in significant **changes** that will affect staff widely.

(b)   BPR as practised is a kind of **scientific management**: a rational approach to improving efficiency. It neglects the direct link to **effectiveness** originally envisaged and may, by reducing the number of managers in an organisation, reduce innovation and creativity at the same time. *Hamel and Prahalad* call this process **hollowing out**.

(c)   While BPR practice generally seeks to empower workers, it assumes they will work within structures and systems imposed by others. This places strict limits on the scope for releasing their potential with such modern ideas as **teamworking** and **coaching**.

(d)   Established systems often have valuable but unrecognised features, particularly in the area of **control**. When a process is re-engineered from scratch, particularly when done with a view to cutting costs, such desirable features as segregation of duties and management supervision may be lost.

1.6 Workflow systems

FAST FORWARD

Workflow systems and enterprise resource planning automate existing manual processes. The software engineering approach improves on this and can substitute software for some human interventions.

The first software-based **workflow systems** appeared in the early 1990s. They were essentially systems for the automation of document flows and were based on electronic copies of scanned original documents. The early systems had no potential for improvements to major organisation processes.

Subsequently, **enterprise resource planning** (ERP) systems were developed to provide a menu of communication and control links between **software application packages**. ERP worked best in well-understood applications such as accounting and stock management. We discuss the adoption of software packages later in this Study Text.

Like the original workflow systems, ERP systems are essentially a form of **automation of existing processes** and therefore **qualitatively different from BPR**, as discussed above.

1.7 Software engineering

The application of software to business processes has continued, with efforts being made to extend its potential scope to include aspects that would normally require human intervention, such as decision-making. The **software engineering** approach emphasises system, efficiency and consistency; there is also a focus on refining business analysts' inputs into software development.

1.8 The Rummler-Brache methodology

FAST FORWARD

The Rummler-Brache methodology sees processes as cross-functional wholes and considers them from three structural levels and three design perspectives.

In 1990, *Rummler and Brache* published *Improving Performance: how to Manage the White Space on the Organisation Chart*. As its title suggests, this book was about designing and managing business processes as **cross-functional wholes**. The authors suggested that organisational process change must be considered at three different structural levels and *at the same time* from three separate perspectives: there are thus **nine areas of concern**, all of which must be addressed satisfactorily if a programme of process change is to be successful.

Structural levels

    (a)   The organisation as a whole

    (b)   The process

    (c)   The job or performance level

Perspectives

    (a)   Goals and measures of achievement

    (b)   Design and implementation of processes

    (c)   Management

Effective organisations will have strong links both up and down the structural levels and across the perspectives. For example, process goals and measures must not only relate accurately to both overall organisational and detailed job goals and measures; they must also form part of a well-designed and implemented process that is managed to operate efficiently.

1.9 Quality improvement methods

FAST FORWARD

> There has been a series of quality improvement initiatives including Total Quality, Six Sigma and ISO 9000 certification.

There were a number of attempts to introduce a systematic approach to improving quality of output in the 1990s. **Statistical process control**, **total quality management** and all the implications of the **Toyota system of manufacturing** fall under this general heading, as do **Six Sigma**, which used a statistical approach to measurement, and **ISO 9000**. The implementation of ISO 9000 has developed from the simple documentation and management of procedures to a more change-oriented system. At the same time, there has been significant cross-fertilisation between these various initiatives. Quality management methods, including ISO 9000 and Six Sigma, are discussed later in this Study Text.

1.10 The Internet

FAST FORWARD

> The influence of the Internet has moved beyond unwieldy and expensive EDI, enabling extensive and cheap communication.

Electronic data interchange was the main networking technique for integrating large-scale corporate IT systems in the early 1990s. It was rather unwieldy and expensive to operate and so was only used by larger companies and their more important suppliers. The growth of the Internet and of its **World Wide Web** aspect in particular means that similar capabilities are now available at much reduced cost. Despite the setback caused by the bursting of the **dotcom bubble**, the Internet has had a major effect on business processes. Larger organisations use it to manage and circulate information, as well as making extensive use of it for retailing, while many small businesses trade exclusively over the Web.

1.11 The effect of business consolidations

FAST FORWARD

> Business considerations and the dispersal of manufacturing bring new demands for software integration and operations control and co-ordination.

Extensive redesign of processes often takes place as a result of **mergers and acquisitions**. There has been significant growth in this kind of process development as a result of accelerating globalisation. The acquisition of **foreign subsidiaries**, in particular, usually leads to extensive work to integrate systems or to redesign and replace them where they are incompatible.

At the same time, large scale manufacturing operations have become much more dispersed as work is transferred to low-wage economies in order to control costs. Controlling and co-ordinating such dispersed and complex operations have required the development of new, standardised systems.

1.12 The current position

Improvement projects should be tied to specific performance goals. Change management must be to a high standard. IT specialists must take a strategic view if they are to make appropriate input.

Harmon makes several comments about the current state of the art of business process change.

First, he emphasises the need to tie improvement projects to **specific corporate goals**: if this is not done, the project will lose focus, develop a life of its own and solve unimportant problems as a result.

Second, he remarks on the difficulty of installing new processes when the operational staffs and managers do not support the changes involved. Considerable effort must be expended on **change management**, including obtaining 'buy-in' and **aligning incentives** with the new processes.

The **role of IT specialists** is a third concern. Harmon feels that they have a special contribution to make because of the ubiquity of IT systems within the organisation: IT specialists are increasingly required to take a strategic view of the corporation as a whole so that they can support the line managers who have responsibility for operating and improving business processes. At the same time it is necessary for those line managers to understand the difficulties and concerns of the IT specialists.

1.12.1 Terminology

Harmon suggests three terms:

*   **Process improvement** is a tactical, incremental technique.

*   **Process re-engineering** is a strategic level rethinking of core processes.

*   **Process redesign** is for intermediate scale processes that need significant change.

Harmon suggests a specific terminology for process change efforts that emphasises the scale of what is contemplated.

(a) **Process improvement** is a **tactical level**, **incremental** technique that is appropriate for developing smaller, stable existing processes.

(b) **Process reengineering** is used at the **strategic level** when major environmental threats or opportunities mandate fundamental re-thinking of large scale, core processes that are critical to the operation of the value chain.

(c) **Process redesign** is an intermediate scale of operation appropriate for **middle sized processes** that require **extensive improvement or change**.

2 The process-strategy matrix

The process strategy matrix analyses processes in terms of their **complexity** on one axis and their **strategic importance** (the value they add) on the other.

It is clear from the overall account given above, that there are a number of options available when the need for process change is established. Harmon describes a tool intended to aid consideration of these options by categorising the organisation's identified processes into four groups. This is the **process-strategy matrix**, which is yet another two axis matrix.

The degree of **process complexity and dynamics** is plotted on the vertical axis; the horizontal axis shows the degree of **strategic importance of the process**. Process 'dynamics' means the extent to which the process is subject to adjustment in response to external stimuli. The effect of this analysis is to create four classes of processes, each of which is amenable to a particular improvement strategy.

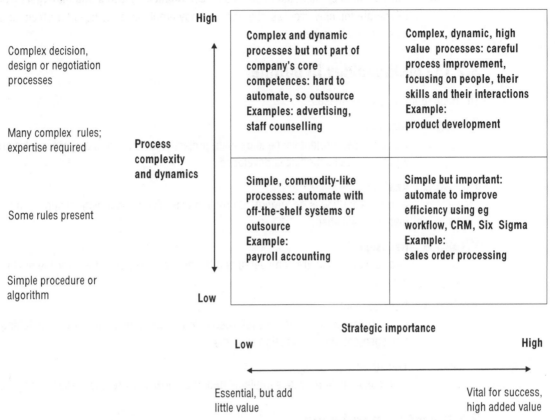

The process-strategy matrix

3 A process redesign methodology

FAST FORWARD

Harmon proposes a methodology for process redesign. This methodology has much in common with the **project management techniques** dealt with later in this Study Text. It has five phases: planning, analysis, redesign, development and transition.

Exam focus point

It is very easy to envisage that the Examiner might set a question that requires you to describe how a specific process redesign project might proceed. If you cannot recall exactly how Harmon's methodology proceeds, you could base a good answer on general principles of project management.

Harmon proposes a **business process redesign** methodology. It is clear from its nature that it is best fitted to the category of work described in Section 1.12.1 (c) above. That is to say, it seems appropriate for 'middle sized processes that require extensive improvement or change'.

The methodology is over-complex for **process improvement** (an 'incremental technique ... for developing smaller, stable existing processes'): indeed, Harmon covers process improvement in an earlier part of his book. Nevertheless, passing reference to major strategic change suggests that he does envisage its use at the other end of the scale, for **process reengineering** ('fundamental re-thinking of large scale, core processes').

3.1 Advantages of having a methodology

(a)   A plan provides **discipline** for the overall process and helps to prevent it from losing focus.

(b)   Successful implementation depends on **acceptance by staffs and managers** who will have to operate the new process: the methodology emphasise the need for obtaining support at all appropriate stages.

3.2 The methodology in outline

The methodology has five phases.

Phase 1   **Planning**
Goals are set, project scope is defined, project team members and other roles are identified and the overall schedule is developed.

Phase 2   **Analysis**
Current workflow is documented, problems identified and a general approach to a redesign plan is established.

Phase 3   **Redesign**
Possible solutions are considered and the best chosen; objectives for the next phase are defined.

Phase 4   **Development**
All functional implications are followed through, aspects are improved, including management and information systems.

Phase 5   **Transition**
The redesigned process is implemented; modifications are undertaken as required.

3.3 Initiating a redesign

Major process redesign can be very expensive in terms of managers' and specialists' time and it is, therefore, likely that redesign projects will only be undertaken when called for by managers at the **strategic apex**. Harmon calls these managers the **executive committee**. He also suggests that there may be a **process architecture committee** responsible for the organisation's responses to perceived threats and opportunities; this committee takes specific responsibility for the effectiveness of business processes overall. Under this structure, the executive committee would set overall goals and strategies, delegating decisions about process development to the process architecture committee.

Harmon recommends that the organisation be **structured around its systems and processes** rather than functionally. Where this is done, a process that is selected for redesign will have a process manager in charge of it; this manager becomes the **project sponsor** for the redesign project. More traditionally structured organisations will have to appoint a project sponsor. The project sponsor does not undertake detailed redesign work: this role is concerned with overall decision-making and championing the redesign at the highest levels.

A **process redesign steering committee** is required. This body has high level representation of all the departments involved in the process. It has two main functions. The first is to be responsible for approving the work of the redesign team. The second is to ensure that managers and staff affected by the redesign support the changes to be made and will implement them.

A **project facilitator** must be appointed to act as project manager. This important role may be allocated to a consultant since skill at facilitating project redesign is required, rather than familiarity with the specific business processes under consideration. In any case, it is important that the facilitator remains neutral and is not committed to any functional or departmental group.

3.4 Planning

The facilitator and the redesign team need a **project charter** or overall plan to define the scope of their work; this should include an account of how the process they design supports the organisation's overall strategy and goals and how it relates to other processes and stakeholders.

Ideally, this plan will have been defined at a higher echelon of management, such as the executive committee or the process architecture committee. If this has not been done, it will be for the project sponsor, facilitator and the steering committee, once appointed to develop this plan themselves. The facilitator will then take charge of the outline plan and refine it after appropriate consultation.

The planning phase ends with the agreement of a **detailed project plan**, including **time and cost budgets**, at the executive committee level. To reach this stage, the project sponsor, facilitator and steering group must produce extensive documentation. This will state the project's assumptions, goals, constraints, scope and success measures. It will outline the changes that are required and how they fit in with the rest of the organisation. It is particularly important that resource and systems constraints are considered in detail.

At the same time, the members of the **process redesign team** must be identified.

3.5 Analysing the existing process

This phase may not be present in all projects.

    (a)   Some organisations may already have full analysis documentation.
    (b)   There may not be an existing process.
    (c)   It may be decided to omit this phase if radical change is envisaged.

Where this phase is undertaken, it results in the **full documentation** of the processes and sub-processes concerned. This involves the use of process flow diagrams and organisation charts. Goals, activities, inputs and outputs are identified, named and described in detail. Known problems with the system are noted, as are descriptions of past attempts to improve them. It is also necessary to consider **how the process is managed**, what personal managerial responsibilities are involved and whether improvements to the management system are required. In particular, **performance measures and incentives** should be examined.

When the analysis is complete, the **project goals and assumptions** should be re-examined and revised as necessary. A coherent and robust redesign plan may then be created and presented to higher management. Approval by those who must later implement and manage the new design is essential and support from these senior managers is an indispensable output from this stage.

3.6 Designing the new process

Design of the new process itself is only part of this phase: there are other important aspects.

    (a)   Design of **supporting management roles and responsibilities** is required, as are the supporting performance measures.

    (b)   Rationalisation of **reporting responsibilities** may be possible and desirable. A new organisation structure may result.

    (c)   Where very complex processes are concerned, it may be appropriate to **run simulations and prepare cost estimates** on two or more possible new designs. This is likely to require the use of software tools.

    (d)   The new design must be **fully documented**.

The final essential output from this phase is, once again, approval from senior management. To achieve this it will be necessary to explain the new process in detail.

3.7 Development

This phase of the process follows the design through into all of its **functional and resource implications**. New IS resources of hardware and software are specified and designed; job descriptions are created and staff training provided; other necessary resources are acquired. The **project sponsor** has the role of co-ordinating the provision of the resources needed.

At this stage, the implications of organising by processes rather than by functions become apparent. The new process is more likely to be effective if it and the staff and resources committed to it are managed by a process manager rather than by a group of separate functional managers. This is, therefore the time at which a change to a **process structure** is best made; this would be a major project in its own right.

The development phase ends when all the new arrangements have been tested and found satisfactory and the new process is ready for installation.

3.8 Transition

The success of the transition phase depends on successful **change management**: it can be harmed or even prevented by opposition or passive resistance. There must be support from the top and close liaison with the managers who have to make the new process work. This may lead to revisions to the process. Eventually this phase merges into routine monitoring of the process for efficiency and potential further improvements.

FAST FORWARD ≫

4 Process commoditisation and outsourcing

Outsourcing enables organisations to benefit from their suppliers' scale economies

The establishment of standards for processes will make the easier to outsource. Some processes may thus be commoditised.

Outsourcing should have the major advantage of reducing the workload or the organisation's managers thus freeing more time to concentrate on core competences.

Generally speaking, outsourcing is appropriate for peripheral activities: to attempt to outsource core competences would be to invite the collapse of the organisation. However, it can be difficult to identify with clarity just what an organisation's core competences are and it is not too difficult to imagine an organisation whose core competence was, in fact, outsourcing. Certainly the motor manufacturing industry seems to be moving in this direction.

A further advantage of outsourcing is that external suppliers may capture **economies of scale** and experience effects that mean that costs may be reduced by using their services rather than in-house provision.

Outsourcing can be used for peripheral activities, such as catering, and, less commonly, for mission-critical ones such as IT services. Getting the best out of outsourcing depends on **successful relationship management** rather than through the use of formal control systems.

Successful outsourcing depends on three things.

(a) The ability to **specify with precision** what is to be supplied: this involves both educating suppliers about the strategic significance of their role and motivating them to high standards of performance.

(b) The ability to **measure** what is actually supplied and thus establish the degree of conformance with specification

(c) The ability to **make adjustments elsewhere** if specification is not achieved.

There are also **practical considerations** relating to outsourcing.
- It can save on costs by making use of a suppliers' economies of scale.
- It can increase effectiveness where the supplier deploys higher levels of expertise.
- It can lead to loss of control, particularly over quality.
- It means giving up an area of threshold competence that may be difficult to reacquire.

Outsourcing of non-core activities is widely acknowledged as having the potential to achieve important cost savings. However, process outsourcing is still uncommon because of the difficulty of assessing the cost-effectiveness of what is purchased: cost should be fairly clear, but the quality of what is purchased is extremely difficult to assess in advance. *Davenport* suggests that the adoption of **process standards** will overcome this problem. We can see this idea at work in the current use of quality standards (discussed in detail later in this Study Text). Such standards enable businesses to outsource with confidence to suppliers having the proper quality certification.

The establish of standards for a wide range of processes will have important consequences, since processes themselves will become commodities.

- Prices of outsourced processes will fall.
- The flow of jobs offshore will accelerate.
- The basis of competition will change.
- The quality of process performance will improve.

Chapter Roundup

- General system theory would see the organisation as an **open system**, interacting with its environment.

- Business process re-engineering is a useful approach based on challenging basic assumptions about business methods and even the objectives they are designed to achieve. IT can be very useful here, but simply to automate a process is not the same as re-engineering it.

- Workflow systems and enterprise resource planning automate existing manual processes. The software engineering approach improves on this and can substitute software for some human interventions.

- The Rummler-Brache methodology sees processes as cross-functional wholes and considers them from three structural levels and three design perspectives.

- There has been a series of quality improvement initiatives including Total Quality, Six Sigma and ISO 9000 certification.

- The influence of the internet has moved beyond unwieldy and expensive EDI, enabling extensive and cheap communication.

- Business considerations and the dispersal of manufacturing bring new demands for the software integration and operations control and co-ordination.

- Improvement projects should be tied to specific performance goals. Change management must be to a high standard. IT specialists must take a strategic view if they are to make appropriate input.

- Harmon suggests three terms:

    - **Process improvement** is a tactical, incremental technique.
    - **Process re-engineering** is a strategic level rethinking of core processes.
    - **Process redesign** is for intermediate scale processes that need significant change.

- The process strategy matrix analyses processes in terms of their **complexity** on one axis and their **strategic importance** (or the value they add) on the other.

- Harmon proposes a methodology for process redesign. This methodology has much in common with the **project management techniques** dealt with later in this Study Text. It has five phases: planning, analysis, redesign, development and transition.

- **Outsourcing** enables organisations to benefit from their suppliers' scale economies

    The establishment of standards for processes will make the easier to outsource. Some processes may thus be commoditised.

- There are also **practical considerations** relating to outsourcing.

    - It can save on costs by making use of a suppliers' economies of scale.
    - It can increase effectiveness where the supplier deploys higher levels of expertise.
    - It can lead to loss of control, particularly over quality.
    - It means giving up an area of threshold competence that may be difficult to reacquire.

    The establishment of standards for processes will make the easier to outsource. Some processes may thus be commoditised.

Quick Quiz

1 Define BPR in one sentence.

2 What are the structural levels specified in the Rummler-Brache methodology?

3 What are the perspectives specified in the Rummler-Brache methodology?

4 Arrange Harmon's three specified approaches to process change in ascending order of scale.

5 What are the axes of the process-strategy matrix?

6 What is the process-strategy matrix's prescription for dealing with processes that are complex and dynamic but add little value

7 What are the phases of Harmon's process redesign methodology?

Answers to Quick Quiz

1 BPR is the fundamental rethinking and radical redesign of business processes to achieve dramatic improvements in performance.

2 The organisation as a whole, the process, the job or performance level

3 Goals and measures; design and implementation; management

4 Process improvement, process redesign, process reengineering

5 Process complexity and dynamics; and strategic significance

6 Such processes are difficult to automate: they should be outsourced.

7 Planning, analysis, redesign, development, transition

Now try the questions below from the Exam Question Bank

Number	Level	Marks	Time
Q8	Preparation	n/a	15 mins

Improving processes

Topic list	Syllabus reference
1 Managing and measuring processes	D2(a)
2 Process redesign patterns	D2(b)-(e)
3 Standard software packages	D3(b), (d)
4 Establishing software requirements	D3(a)
5 Choosing research techniques	D3(a)
6 Assessing software packages	D3(c)
7 Selecting software packages	D3(c)

Introduction

Having established a framework for the consideration of process change, we may now proceed further into the practical detail of how to go about it. We start with some further, simple ideas and then proceed to the main subject of this chapter, the selection of software packages.

Study guide

		Intellectual level
D2	**Improving the processes of the organisation**	
(a)	Evaluate the effectiveness of current organisational processes	3
(b)	Describe a range of process redesign patterns	2
(c)	Establish possible redesign options for improving current processes of an organisation	2
(d)	Assess the feasibility of possible redesign options	3
(e)	Assess the relationship between process redesign and strategy	3
D3	**Software solutions**	
(a)	Establish information system requirements required by business users	2
(b)	Assess the advantages and disadvantages of using a generic software solution to fulfil those requirements	2
(c)	Establish a process for evaluating, selecting and implementing a generic software solution	2
(d)	Explore the relationship between generic software solutions and business process redesign	2

Exam guide

Your examiner is known to be interested in software approaches to process change, so we confidently await regular demonstrations of this interest in the form of questions that address the material in this chapter.

1 Managing and measuring processes

FAST FORWARD

> Organisations should be structured around processes rather than functions. This means that the hierarchy of management objectives and performance measures will be similarly structured. Process improvement becomes part of every manager's task.

As we noted earlier, *Harmon* recommends a management structure based on processes rather than functions, since it is the efficiency of the organisation's processes that determine its success. In practical terms, this can lead to a **matrix structure**.

This approach implies that the **hierarchy of objectives** should also be structured on process lines, as should the organisation's **measures of performance** (we mentioned this approach early in Chapter 1). Objectives and performance measures flow down in a co-ordinated way from mission to major processes, to sub-processes, to activities and to individual tasks. The roles of managers at all levels are thus built around process performance: they plan, set targets, provide training, measure performance and take control action in terms of the **processes for which they are responsible**. This approach fits well with the balanced scorecard approach.

Harmon says:

> If an organisation establishes process measures that extend from the process to the activity, and if managers continuously check these measures and take actions when there are deviations, then process improvement becomes part of every manager's job. In effect, **measures determine how the activity should be performed** (emphasis added).

This has a vital implication for process improvement: any changes made at a lower level **must be followed through** into the detail of management responsibility at **higher levels**. The immediate supervisor has to deal with a different way of doing things and achieve different outcomes. The supervisor's manager needs to know about these changes in the supervisor's role and so on up the hierarchy.

2 Process redesign patterns

In the previous chapter we considered a proposed general approach to the project management of the activities involved with the redesign of a process. In this section, we will look more closely at the techniques that are available for use in the redesign activity itself. *Harmon* calls these techniques **redesign patterns**.

Key term

A **process redesign pattern** is a general approach to redesigning processes for their improvement.

FAST FORWARD

Harmon describes four **basic redesign patterns**.

(a)   **Re-engineering** starts with a clean sheet of paper.
(b)   **Simplification** eliminates redundant process elements.
(c)   **Value-added analysis** eliminates activities that do not add value.
(d)   **Gaps and disconnects** targets problems at departmental boundaries.

The feasibility of any proposed redesign must be considered.

2.1 Re-engineering

We introduced BPR in the previous chapter, using these words: **'business process re-engineering** is the fundamental rethinking and radical redesign of business processes to achieve dramatic improvements in critical contemporary measures of performance, such as cost, quality, service and speed.'

The BPR approach is used when large-scale change is to be introduced. The aim is to achieve major efficiency improvements. This pattern is hardly **redesign** at all, since its philosophy is to question all assumptions and start from scratch. Re-engineering can achieve **very large-scale improvements**, but it is inevitably **highly disruptive** and has a **high risk of dramatic failure**.

2.2 Simplification

Simplification is a far less radical pattern of redesign. It proceeds on the assumption that most established business processes are likely to have developed **elements of duplication or redundancy**. This assumption is probably most valid in relation to large-scale processes that cut across departmental or functional boundaries and it is, therefore, in such instances that simplification is most likely to be fruitful approach. The effort involved is usually moderate.

The simplification approach commences with **identification and modelling** of all the systems, activities and sub-processes involved in the business process under investigation. Each element is then subject to challenge: it may not actually be necessary; it may provide information that is available elsewhere; it may be a bottleneck; it may repeat something done in another place; Whenever possible, activities are removed from the process so that duplication and unnecessary complexity are gradually eliminated. This pattern is likely to produce **improvements**, though their **scale can vary widely**, from the relatively minor to the impressive.

Judgement and flexibility are needed to use this approach, since apparently similar activities may incorporate subtle differences that are important in one departmental context but not in another. An element of redesign may be required in addition to simple cuts: for example, it may be possible to achieve a net saving by designing a single process to replace two existing ones.

2.3 Value-added analysis

The aim of value-added analysis is to eliminate processes that do not add value. Value-added analysis approaches processes from the point of view of the customer. Here, 'customer' means whoever receives the output of the process, so internal customers are included.

Value adding activities satisfy three conditions.

- The customer is willing to pay for the output.
- The process changes the output in some way.
- The process is performed correctly at the first attempt.

Four categories of activity are defined as **non-value-adding**.

- Preparation and set-up activities
- Control and inspection activities
- Movement of a product
- Activities that result from delay or failure of any kind

There is a third category: **value-enabling activities**. These are essential preliminaries to value-adding activities. If you think about this for a moment, you will see that, just as with the simplification approach, judgement is required here: an obvious instance lies in the area of preparation and set-up. We have defined such activities as non-value-adding, but, surely, they are essential preliminaries? An example might help here.

 Case Study

When *Toyota* restarted car production cars in the late 1940s, the prevailing western technology for producing body panels was based on extremely careful set-up of presses and very long production runs. Set-up had to be painstaking in order to avoid sub-standard output, some of which might not be discovered until it had been incorporated into a part-finished car. The problem was the alignment of the press dies. These weighed many tons and so took a team of specialists up to a day to reposition. In these circumstances, very long production runs were required to make the whole process economic. This implied the use of a large number of presses in order to provide the hundreds of different panels required and often led to excessive stock holdings.

Toyota was not able to use this system: it had only a few presses and could only sell a few thousand cars each year. *Taiichi Ohno*, the chief production engineer, therefore developed a system using simple adjustment mechanisms and roller mountings for the dies. This made it possible for ordinary production workers to change dies in a tiny fraction of the time previously thought necessary. An unexpected bonus of this approach was that, since the output panels were needed for immediate assembly, any misalignmant or other fault was discovered immediately and wastage was thus reduced.

How does this example help us? It is clear that Ohno's system of changing dies is an essential, minimal, value-enabling preliminary to the value activity of pressing body panels; the traditional way is extremely expensive and, with its natural consequences of over-stocking and high wastage, adds little if any value.

Bearing in mind that the overall intention is to eliminate non-value-adding activities, we may thus suggest that where preparation and set up are concerned, we should aim to ensure that they qualify as value-enabling activities by making them as simple and cost effective as possible.

The Toyota example Illustrates another aspect of the importance of processes and process redesign. This is the link between processes and strategy. The standard process was created in the context of the strategy of the US motor industry of the time: this involved vast volumes and was to some extent a seller's market, so healthy margins would easily absorb the waste inherent in the method. Toyota could not pursue this strategy: it was forced to minimise costs and maximise its utilisation of its resources. The redesign of the pressing process helped it to do so.

Like the simplification approach, value-added analysis commences with **identification and modelling** of all the systems, activities and sub-processes involved in the business process under investigation. Each element is then **categorised** according to the criteria discussed above. Harmon suggests that, typically, only 20% of the activities making up a process are identifiable as value-adding, with most of the remainder falling into the value-enabling category. When all of the clearly value-adding and value-enabling activities have been identified, the reminder may be examined in detail. The Toyota body press example above indicates how careful consideration can lead to the development of new methods that eliminate much non-value-adding work in preliminary activities.

(a) It may be possible to minimise control and inspection activities by processes of **empowerment**.

(b) Physical movement of products can be minimised by careful **workplace layout**, which is an aspect of production engineering. **Workflow systems** eliminate transit time for documents by scanning all documents to produce electronic copies which are transferred at the click of a mouse.

(c) Activities that result from delay or failure require careful investigation to establish **patterns or modes of failure** that may be subject to correction. Again, empowerment may offer some potential for making improvements. This is especially true in the whole area of customer complaints, where a rapid satisfactory resolution is a powerful tool for improving customer loyalty.

This improvement pattern is capable of producing results on a scale similar to similar to that achieved by the simplification approach; that is to say, varying between extensive and fairly small.

2.4 Gaps and disconnects

In the previous chapter we discussed *Rummler and Brache* and their book *Improving Performance: how to Manage the White Space on the Organisation Chart*. In this book, the authors suggest that a major problem with many processes is likely to be failures of communication between business departments and functions. These failures can produce continuing **gaps and disconnects** both in the processes themselves and in the management of those processes.

This approach commences in the usual way, with **identification and modelling** of the selected process, but its focus of is occasions when information or materials pass from one department or function to another, since this is where gaps and disconnects are to be found.

Rummler identifies over thirty potential areas in which gaps and disconnects are likely to occur. These are fairly evenly divided between the three levels we mentioned when discussing the book in the previous chapter.

(a) The organisation as a whole
(b) The process
(c) The job or performance level

It is only at the second and third of these levels that problems relating to actual **workflow** and **activities** appear. At the organisational level, they are entirely concerned with the **design of processes** and the **monitoring** and **control** of **process outcomes**. These are clearly **management activities**.

2.5 Feasibility

The purpose of considering feasibility is not so much to find out if a proposed project can achieve its objective as to establish whether or not it can do so in a **cost-effective** manner. Given sufficient resources, most proposals that lie outside the realms of fantasy can be implemented but **not all are worth undertaking**. The feasibility study is the mechanism by which the organisation filters out proposals that would cost too much, cause too much disruption, make excessive demands on human and other resources or have side effects whose undesirability outweighs their advantages. The assessment of feasibility can be broken down into a number of areas.

2.5.1 Technical feasibility

The assessment of technical feasibility will depend on the nature of the technology involved.

    (a)   Does all the necessary technology exist or is significant **innovation** required?

    (b)   Is the technology mature enough to use or is further **development** likely to be required?

    (c)   How **specialised** is the required technology and is **the expertise** to make use of it available?

Technical feasibility also includes **technical matters that do not relate to technology**; that is to say, matters of technical expertise, such as marketing, financial strategy and human resource management. We might wish to know, for example, whether it were feasible to communicate effectively with a particular identified market segment.

2.5.2 Social feasibility

Any change is likely to have effects upon people, both those in the organisation concerned and those outside it. The social feasibility of a project depends on the nature and extent of those effects. There are obvious human resource management implications to most projects, in the area of forming, leading and motivating the project team. The progress and outcome of a process improvement project may also have important consequences for employees outside the team, such as increased demand for certain categories of staff, redundancies, training requirements and changed work patterns.

2.5.3 Environmental concerns

Consideration of a project in environmental terms is usually not so much about feasibility as about **acceptability**. Several different stakeholder groups are likely to have environmental concerns and their opinions and reactions may affect both the progress of a project itself and the desired characteristics of its deliverables.

2.5.4 Financial feasibility

It is appropriate to submit proposed changes to **cost-benefit analysis**, though this can be very difficult when the benefits are largely in intangible form. Part of the difficulty lies in identifying the benefits and part in assigning monetary values to them. Dealing with intangible or qualitative benefits is likely to be particularly important in the public and voluntary sectors, where objectives such as improved road safety or education are common.

3 Standard software packages

FAST FORWARD

> ERP systems are based on limited, standardised modules. This means that the organisation must adapt to the standard system rather than designing its own most appropriate and efficient process. However, the alternative, adapting a standard package to local requirements, destroys the advantages of purchasing the standard package and introduces further complications. Nevertheless, packages have their own disadvantages.

The use of computers to automate business processes began over half a century ago in the UK. *J Lyons & Co* had made many improvements in its administrative techniques and set about developing its own computer in association with Cambridge University. The result was the **LEO 1 computer**: LEO stands for *Lyons Electronic Office*. LEO 1 ran its first payroll in December 1953. The LEO system was the archetypal **tailored**, or **bespoke**, IS; not only was the software created specifically for the company's purposes, the hardware was too.

In the forty years that followed, computers were widely utilised for a wide range of business procedures, including the well-known manufacturing and resource control systems, **MRP** and **MRPII**. The result of this process was the widespread acquisition of standardised software packages by large companies from the 1990s onward. These packages were originally standalone applications for such business functions as accounting and HRM but their vendors developed their products into packages that could deal with major parts of a business's system infrastructure in an integrated way. By extension from the MRP acronym, these integrated systems became known as **enterprise resource planning** (ERP) systems.

3.1 ERP – general characteristics

In general, standard ERP packages are robust systems that incorporate wide experience of business procedures and their automation. They are, however, based on **standardised modules** and are not necessarily optimised for any given commercial application. Claims by vendors that their products can give a competitive edge are questionable: competitors can easily buy the same product. The best that can be said is that an ERP system should provide an effective way of doing things.

The standardised, one size fits all nature of ERP software also means that attempting to improve business processes by installing it **reverses the normal method**. As *Harmon* says, with ERP 'you begin with a solution'. Rather than analysing what happens currently and then developing an improved system, ERP forces the organisation to adjust itself to the requirements of the software.

Exam focus point

> Be prepared to contrast Harmon's reservations about standard packages with Davenport's view that process standards will have a positive effect on how business is conducted. There is merit in both views but specific problems and context may lead to one conclusion or the other.

Because of this generic nature, many clients insist on having their ERP software tailored to fit their own existing systems. This is generally a **mistake**.

- The cost advantage of buying off the shelf is destroyed.
- Introduction is delayed.
- Reliability is reduced.
- New versions of the same software will be useless until they too have been modified.

A **middle course** between utilising a standard package and developing a bespoke application is to **purchase the source code** for a package and **modify it in-house** as required. This destroys the advantages of purchasing a standard package and adds its own disadvantages.

- Internal developers are initially unfamiliar with the programs and data structures.
- Pre-existing errors in the source code will not be fixed by the vendor.
- Upgrades issued by the vendor cannot be relied on to work properly.
- The underlying design may not in fact have the necessary development potential.

Generally it is cheaper and more effective to redesign the organisation's processes to fit a standard package than to do the opposite.

3.2 Advantages of software packages over in-house development

(a) **Cost savings** should be available because the vendor can spread the cost of systems development over a large number of installations.

(b)   **Time savings** should be very significant, since developing a new application can be extremely time consuming.

(c)   **Quality** should be guaranteed both by the vendor and, except for launch customers, by earlier installation by other customers.

(d)   **Documentation and training** should be immediately available and of high quality since these are important selling points.

(e)   **Maintenance support** should be good and would normally include help desk service and routine software amendments to correct faults as they become apparent.

(f)   Comprehensive **package evaluation** should be possible. This might include use for a trial period and visits to existing installations.

3.3 Disadvantages of software packages

(a)   **Property rights** over the software usually reside with the supplier. This has three important potential consequences for the user.

  (i)   The supplier controls future development of the software.

  (ii)   The supplier controls the support available and may discontinue it, forcing the customer to purchase an upgrade.

  (iii) The supplier may sell the product rights to another supplier, perhaps to the prejudice of the customer.

(b)   The **financial stability** and survival of the supplier is not guaranteed.

(c)   **Competitive advantage** cannot be obtained from standard software packages available to all.

(d)   **Inadequate performance** is quite likely: the customer may have to accept restricted functionality or pay for tailored amendments, with the accompanying disadvantages already discussed. Further problems may be caused by unwanted standard features: these may cause difficulties in training and implementation.

(e)   **Legal redress** for lack of functionality will almost certainly not be available.

(f)   **Changing requirements** can erode a package's functionality. Potential purchasers evaluate a package against their current requirements. These may change as time passes or may not have been properly specified in the first place. In either case, the package fails to provide full satisfaction.

4 Establishing software requirements

FAST FORWARD

The first phase of any IS project is likely to be the collection of information. There are seven techniques.

- Interviews
- Questionnaires
- Written questions
- Observation
- Protocol analysis
- Workshops
- Prototyping

Each technique has its advantages and disadvantages, so it will be normal to use a combination of them.

When an organisation contemplates the acquisition or development of a new IS, whether a component or a complete system, the first stage of the project is the **collection of information** so that system requirements may be firmly established. This must be done carefully and with an insistence on the verification of data: personal impressions and opinions are of little value. Also, it may be necessary to revisit work that has already been done in order to extend or confirm the data.

It is important that analysts have adequate face-to-face communication skills, since much of their work will involve close contact with the staff whose work they investigate. Staff may be suspicious, taciturn or otherwise unco-operative and analysts may have to work hard to gain their confidence. An important aspect of this process is initial research undertaken in order to become familiar with the basics of the business systems in use.

Skidmore and Eva describe seven techniques for fact gathering.

4.1 Interviews

Interviews allow analysts and stakeholders to meet and are thus particularly appropriate during the early stages of investigation. Interviews are used to collect information and promote understanding of a range of topics.

- The business background and technical context and constraints
- Current procedures and data flows
- Known problems with the existing system
- Requirements for the new system

Interviews must be **carefully planned and conducted** if they are to produce satisfactory results.

(a) It is important not to **rush to conclusions** at this early stage. Solutions based on incomplete information are unlikely to be appropriate.

(b) Projects to introduce new systems can be **unsettling for staff** since they often lead to job losses and other unwelcome changes. Interviewers must be careful to avoid any element of interrogation or criticism and should be appreciative of interviewees' assistance.

(c) Interviewers should make **comprehensive notes** during interviews and write them up promptly.

(d) It is usual to start at the top with the project sponsor and work down the hierarchy through managers to the staff that actually operate the existing system. This allows for the establishment of **an overview that is gradually supplemented with more detailed information**.

(e) Interviews should take place in the interviewee's workplace. This enhances **interviewee confidence**, ensures that current **documents** are available and allows for the initial observation of **working conditions and practices**.

(f) Interview preparation should include the establishment of clear **objectives** and the preparation of an agenda and questions. The agenda should be sent to the interviewee in sufficient time to allow for suitable preparation.

(g) Interviews must be controlled if they are to be effective. A rambling conversation is unlikely to produce the required information. A possible sequence is **context-detail-problems-requirements**.

    (i) During the **context** phase, interviewees describe their current roles and tasks.
    (ii) Further **detail** of procedures, documents and records is then elicited.
    (iii) **Problems** and how they arise may then be discussed.
    (iv) Finally, a wish list of **requirements** for the new system can be considered.

(h)   **Question technique** is an important aspect of control and there is a range of question types that may be used.

    (i)   **Closed questions** use words such as 'when', 'who' and 'how many' and require short, simple, positive answers. They are used to obtain basic facts and as a means of controlling the interviewee who likes to answer at length.

    (ii)   **Open questions** invite discursive answers and use words such as 'tell me about'. These questions allow the interviewer to obtain detailed information about procedures and problems. They are also useful for encouraging interviewees who are reluctant to speak.

    (iii)   **Anecdotal questions** are a kind of open question: the interviewer invites the respondent to provide illustrations or examples of the way in which events have occurred in the past.

    (iv)   **Probing questions** are used to obtain more details about an earlier answer. These questions promote a fuller consideration of a topic.

    (v)   **Verification questions** are a kind of probing question: they ask for specific confirmation of the interviewer's impression on a topic and use such phrases as 'would it be correct to say that ...'.

    (vi)   **Sequencing questions** are used to establish the correct order of events in a procedure.

4.2 Questionnaires

Questionnaires do not permit the use of question types other than closed, nor do they permit the interpretation of body language. However, they can be useful for gathering data from a large number of geographically scattered respondents and, with careful design, may be used to assess attitudes and aspirations. Also, they are not affected by distortions and errors introduced by the interviewer. **Question design** is obviously of great importance.

(a)   The questionnaire should be as short as possible and the questions should be both **concise and precise**.

(b)   Each question should ask for a single, separate response and not combine two queries.

(c)   **Leading questions**, which are those that suggest a particular response, must not be used.

(d)   Questions must use words and expressions that the respondents will **understand immediately**, including local jargon and technical terms where applicable.

(e)   The **method of response**, such as box ticking or number circling, must be made clear.

Once drafted, questionnaires should be **tried out** on sample of respondents to ensure that it works. This trial should include an analysis of responses.

4.3 Written questions

Written questions may be used when a person is not available for interview, or as a supplement to an earlier interview. They differ from questionnaires in that they can be **tailored to specific purposes** and allow for **open questions**.

4.4 Observation

Observation of working processes is an important tool for collecting information and works well as a complement to interviewing. It can be carried out **informally**, such as when visiting the workplace for other purposes, or **formally**, in which case the prior agreement of managers and staff is required.

Observation may be used to establish the detail of document flows, by following an example through all the processes it is subject to, and for understanding how processes and people interact by observing a workplace as a whole.

4.5 Protocol analysis

Protocol analysis starts with a person **performing a task and describing what is happening**. It combines the interaction of the interview techniques with the generation of data that cannot be explained in words alone. It also ensures that nothing is taken for granted by the person providing the information, since the demonstration includes all aspects of what has to be done.

4.6 Document analysis

Document analysis is very important since all formal transactions are likely to be recorded on a document of some kind. The analyst should obtain copies of all types of documents in use. The documents themselves must be assessed for **usability and relevance** to current procedure and analysed to establish the size and format of the **data fields** they contain. The **use** of the documents must also be established. This will include such matters as volumes and frequencies of use, the purpose of each, where the data comes from, who is responsible for completing it, where, how and for how long it is filed and so on.

4.7 Workshops

Workshops are particularly useful when there are **too many stakeholders** to interview individually; when **project scope is unclear**, as may be the case with new systems; and when there is disagreement about **system requirements**. A workshop run by a skilled facilitator can resolve this kind of problem and lead to acceptable consensus. Workshops also allow for creative interaction and can achieve more than other methods.

A series of workshops may be required, probably starting with senior stakeholders in order to decide high-level objectives and requirements. This stage may be followed by workshops for users to deal with more detailed matters.

Ideally, workshops will take place off-site in order to avoid disruption.

4.8 Prototyping

Prototyping is carried out using software to present a mock-up of how the eventual system will look and work. Users can then comment. This is very useful when the proposed system specification is very complex or when it lacks detail or precision. Another approach is to demonstrate an existing package that offers some of the required functionality, though it must be made clear that this is not being proposed as a solution.

4.9 Investigations when computers are already in use

The techniques discussed above may need some modification or change of emphasis when computers are already in use.

(a) Interviews and questionnaires will largely concern the functionality of the existing system.

(b) Observation is likely to be screen and keyboard based and will require attention to seating for observer and operator.

(c) Document analysis will relate to screen layouts in use. Storage will probably be in database form and investigation will require interviews with technical staff.

5 Choosing research techniques

The research techniques discussed above have distinct characteristics that make each of them more or less suitable as circumstances vary. Skidmore and Eva provide an assessment based on six specific problems that may occur.

(a) Staff may be **averse to change** and find it difficult to contribute ideas about future requirements and possible developments. Skidmore and Eva call this **present orientation**.

(b) Staff may be **vague** in their responses.

(c) The may be an element of '**taken for granted**' in staff's approach to existing systems: this results in failure to specify all aspects of the current situation.

(d) Much knowledge is **tacit** and is difficult to elicit in words.

(e) When a largely or completely **new system** is proposed, staff may have little concept of what it might achieve, except in the broadest terms.

(f) The analyst may be **inexperienced** in the work context under investigation and misunderstand or misinterpret raw information.

Using these criteria we may analyse the techniques discussed as good (G), very good (VG), or not good (NG) as shown in the table below.

	Change aversion	Vagueness	Taken for granted	Tacit knowledge	New system	Inexperience
Interview	G	G	G	NG	G	G
Observation	NG	G	VG	G	NG	VG
Protocol analysis	NG	NG	VG	VG	G	VG
Document analysis	G	NG	G	G	NG	VG
Workshop	VG	NG	VG	NG	VG	G
Prototype	VG	NG	VG	G	VG	G

6 Assessing software packages

FAST FORWARD

Software packages maybe assessed against ten high-level requirement categories, each of which is made up of more detailed specific requirements. Not all high-level categories will receive the same weighting.

Imperatives are non-negotiable, absolute requirements and must be established very early on in the project.

Skidmore and Eva suggest that software packages may be assessed against ten high-level categories of requirement.

- Functional requirements
- Non-functional requirements
- Technical requirements
- Design requirements
- Supplier stability requirements
- Supplier citizenship requirements
- Initial implementation requirements
- Operability requirements
- Cost constraints
- Time constraints

These high-level categories will not all be equally significant and it is an important early task to allocate **relative weights** to them, according to their individual importance to the customer. These weightings will be used later in a quantitative assessment of candidate packages. A convenient way to represent this is with a score out of a total of 100. A general indication of likely weighting for each high level requirement is given in the discussion below.

Each high-level requirement is essentially a **category of more detailed requirements**, each of which must be specified very carefully and given its own weighting: these weightings will also be used in the detailed evaluation of packages.

A further early consideration is the establishment of **imperatives**. Imperatives are **non-negotiable**, **absolute requirements** that candidate packages **must** satisfy. The role of imperatives is to reject unsuitable packages from further consideration, so they must be carefully considered and not established unless definitely applicable. Imperatives are likely to arise in **technical**, **supplier** and **cost** requirements.

6.1 Functional requirements

Functional requirements are the things the new software must do to **support business or operational functions**. These requirements are established using the investigative techniques already discussed. They will normally be given a very high relative weight. Both **current** and **anticipated future** requirements must be considered. Typical weighting overall: 30

6.2 Non-functional requirements

Non-functional requirements are so called simply to distinguish them from functional requirements; they are **not** non-essential and **must** be supported by the package. Their point of distinction is that they do not relate directly to business functionality. Examples are legal compliance, archiving and audit requirements. Non-functional requirements are also established using the investigative techniques already discussed. Typical weighting overall: 10

6.3 Technical requirements

Technical requirements relate to the details of IT and might include preferences such as the hardware platform to be used, the operating system to be supported and the software development language to be used. Some technical requirements might well be **imperatives**. Typical weighting overall: 10

6.4 Design requirements

Flexibility is an important feature for a package, since current requirements may develop into rather different ones in the future. There are three main factors that determine flexibility.

(a) **Architecture** is the internal structure of the system and how its parts interact. Problems of compatibility can limit future development, but the Open Applications Group of suppliers work to open architecture standards that allow their products to be linked to one another without difficulty.

(b) The **internal design** of such elements of package software as files and databases has a significant affect on flexibility: modular design is desirable, as is simplicity of code.

(c) A high degree of **configurability** will allow a package to be tailored to user requirements without expensive code modifications. Ideally, a package should be configurable without programmer intervention.

Typical weighting for design requirements overall: 5

6.5 Supplier stability requirements

Purchasers will require that that support should be available into the future, so they will be concerned that their chosen supplier is financially stable and unlikely to go out of business. They will also wish to purchase from a well-established supplier with a good reputation in the industry. A wide range of factors and considerations will influence a decision here.

(a) **Size and location** may be important: a small local supplier, or at least one with a local office, may provide a more personal service; a much larger one may have more experience and be more stable.

(b) Aspects of **financial stability**, such as profitability, turnover and length of successful trading history, may be **imperatives**. Similar considerations may apply to the supplier's **legal status**, **ownership** and **structure**.

(c) A good **reputation in the industry** for expertise, service and fair dealing will be desirable.

(d) **Accreditation** as a provider of certain hardware and software products may be required, as may wider industry accreditations.

(e) **Quality assurance** will be an important consideration and possibly an **imperative**: it may be appropriate to inspect the provider's procedures and certification.

(f) The use of **automated software tools** may be an indicator of the supplier's technical maturity.

(g) Vendors must have proper **insurance cover**.

(h) **Dispute resolution** should be the subject of a robust and equitable procedure.

(i) Here may be **outstanding issues** such as pre-existing litigation, takeover possibilities and directors' involvement in insolvency proceedings to take into account.

Typical weighting for supplier stability requirements overall: 15

6.6 Supplier citizenship requirements

The topics dealt with under the heading of citizenship might also be called matters of **social responsibility**. Purchasers might wish to take account of policy and practice on a range of issues.

- Diversity
- Health and safety
- Trade unions
- Charities and donations
- Sustainability and the environment

Typical weighting for supplier citizenship requirements overall: 2

6.7 Initial implementation requirements

It is vital that the installation stage of a new package is carried out successfully. This requires skill and involves several important processes.

(a) The **creation of new files** and possibly the **conversion of old ones** will be required. Many commercial applications are based on extensive files of, for example, customer data. Before a new application can start processing, the basic file structures must therefore be created. Where it is intended that pre-existing data should be available for processing, the existing files must be loaded, possibly after being converted to a new, compatible format. File conversion is a complex and time consuming process and assistance from the contractor may be an **imperative**.

(b) **Installation** might be required of the supplier; this might include initial loading, testing and troubleshooting. Both the software package and any hardware required should be installed by the package supplier in order to avoid disputes over responsibility for problems.

(c) **Implementation** is the introduction of the new system into service. It may be achieved by simply changing from the old to the new at a given point in time, such as the start of work on a particular day, or there may be a period of parallel running. The first method is likely to require technical support, possibly from vendor staff on site. Parallel running requires extra staff, which the vendor may be able to supply.

(d) **Training** in the new system will be required: its nature, content, cost and location must all be considered.

Typical weighting for initial implementation requirements overall: 10

6.8 Operability requirements

Implementation requirements continue beyond the initial phase and into the productive life of the system.

(a) **Documentation** should be clear, complete, easy to use, helpful and kept up to date.

(b) Continuing **support** will be required and considerations will include such matters as helpline availability, response times and policy on support for superseded versions of software.

(c) **Upgrade policy** includes such matters as cost, frequency, documentation and method of distribution.

(d) **Legal protection** is required to cover the possibility of the supplier's business being wound up. The source code should be lodged **in escrow**.

Typical weighting for operability requirements overall: 2

6.9 Time and cost constraints

Overall requirements relating to time and, particularly, cost will almost certainly be **imperatives**. However, it may also be appropriate to consider time and cost **trade-offs** against other issues in the overall requirement.

Typical weighting for cost constraints: 20; for time constraints: 2

7 Selecting software packages

The process of selecting a package may be thought of as falling into five phases.

- Obtaining tenders
- First pass selection
- Second pass selection
- Implementation
- The long-term relationship

Skidmore and Eva suggest that once the evaluation requirements have been set, the process of selecting a package may be thought of as falling into five phases.

- Obtaining tenders
- First pass selection
- Second pass selection
- Implementation
- The long-term relationship

7.1 Identifying potential suppliers

The selection procedure is built around a detailed **invitation to tender** (ITT), but before this can be issued, potential suppliers must be identified. One way to do this is to **advertise the general system requirement** in the trade press and ask for responses from suppliers. This very open approach may be legally required, particularly in the public sector, but it may attract an unmanageably large number of responses, many of which may be of little value. Some less appropriate suppliers may be weeded out by making a small charge for the issue of the ITT.

A more structured approach is to **research the market** using trade directories, Internet searches and personal business awareness.

In either case, the aim should be to identify a reasonable number of potential suppliers for further consideration. Some allowance must be made for wastage in the early stages, so, if, say, eight to twelve formal tenders are required, it may be necessary to identify fifteen to twenty candidates.

7.2 The invitation to tender

When a suitable number of potential suppliers has been identified, ITTs may be issued to them. The ITT is a fairly complex document and will include a number of sections. These are described below.

- (a) **Administrative information**
  - Where, how, to whom and by when the tender should be submitted
  - Procedure for dealing with queries
  - Rules about tendering
  - Confidentiality arrangements
- (b) Information about the **client organisation**
- (c) **The project**
  - **Objectives**
  - **Scope**
  - Project **imperatives** as described earlier
  - **Project owner**
  - Access to **client resources**, such as staff and existing systems

(d)   The **response format** may be specified, especially if it is intended to make comparisons using standardised numerical scores.

(e)   **Package requirements** will be stated in terms of the ten requirement categories discussed in Section 5 above

(f)   Client **project management** procedures

(g)   An exposition of the **evaluation procedures** that will be used to assess the tenders

The ITT is likely to be accompanied by a request for detailed information about the tendering organisation, including such items as legal, financial, employment and trading status and policies.

7.3 First pass selection

The object of the first pass selection is to produce a short list of, say, three candidate tenders that can be subjected to further evaluation. The first pass is based largely on information provided in the tenders that is relevant to the ten requirement categories. This must be assessed against each component of those ten categories. The quantitative analysis is extensive and a spreadsheet is commonly used to carry out the weighting arithmetic and to record the various scores.

7.3.1 Functional and non-functional requirements

Functional and non-functional requirements are considered separately but using the same quantitative method. The ITT asks suppliers to rate their products against the various functional and non-functional requirements. The rating is carried out by estimating the effort required to modify the package to fit the various components of each high-level requirement. Skidmore and Eva suggest a five point scale.

Score	
4	No modification required
3	Up to one day's work required
2	Two to five days' work required
1	Six to ten days' work required
0	More than ten days' work required

The suppliers' scores are multiplied by the requirement ratings and the results summed to provide a total assessment for each of the two high-level requirements.

7.3.2 Technical and design requirements

It will be possible to assess conformity with many **technical** and **design** requirements as a **simple positive or negative**, scoring 4 or 0 respectively; other aspects may require a degree of judgement. Assessment will be based on the tenders or on supplementary information obtained from suppliers. Scores are evaluated as above.

7.3.3 Supplier and implementation requirements

There are four high-level requirements in this group: supplier **stability** and **citizenship**; and **initial implementation** and **operability**. It will be possible to assess many items from the tenders; others will require subjective assessment in a facilitated workshop attended by suitable members of staff. Scores are evaluated in the usual way.

7.3.4 Cost

If all the tenders satisfy the **cost imperative**, they may be graded relative to the cheapest. Cost (and time) trade-offs may also be assessed.

7.4 Second pass selection

There are **two elements** to the second pass selection.

First, the quantitative assessment outlined above is used to create a **shortlist** of candidate packages that may be then examined further.

This further examination is based on an objective reassessment of those elements of the first pass that were based on the suppliers' claims. It is carried out by running each package through a series of **specific test scenarios**; a **user panel** then awards scores for each function. The demonstration can be provided by the suppliers performing against a script or by client staff using demonstration packages. The second method tends to be more convenient.

The **second element** of the second pass selection concerns **reference sites** and **financial investigation**.

(a)   Reference sites are places where the packages are already installed and in operation. Suppliers should provide information about these sites in their tenders. Reference sites should be visited and assessed in detail.

(b)   Financial investigation should be undertaken in order to check the information provided by the suppliers.

Either of these aspects of assessment may lead to significant adjustment to earlier scores and even reveal that one or more imperatives have not been satisfied.

7.5 Implementation

Because packages, by their very nature, may be expected to be fully functional and because of the work done during the assessment, it should not be necessary to include much **testing** in the initial implementation. Testing is likely to be restricted to volume running, checking interfaces with other systems and final usability checking.

Similarly, **standard package documentation** is unlikely to require much adjustment, though there may be some work required to integrate it with existing process documentation.

Training in the use of the package should be provided by the vendor, though the user will be responsible for training in the organisation's wider processes that relate to the package.

File creation and **conversion** are likely to be more involved, as already discussed. These are specialised jobs and vendor assistance is likely to be necessary. Vendors may quote a low price for this service as an inducement to buy.

7.6 Managing the long-term relationship

Buying a package tends to make the user organisation dependent on the supplier, bringing an inevitable element of risk. Nevertheless, the user can do several things to redress the balance.

(a)   Maintain a good relationship, avoiding conflict
(b)   Make supplier evaluation a continuing process to obtain early warning of potential problems
(c)   Maintain an escrow agreement
(d)   Have a contingency plan to migrate to another supplier

Chapter Roundup

- Organisations should be structured around processes rather than functions. This means that the hierarchy of management objectives and performance measures will be similarly structured. Process improvement becomes part of every manager's task.

- Harmon describes four **basic redesign patterns**.

  (a) **Re-engineering** starts with a clean sheet of paper.
  (b) **Simplification** eliminates redundant process elements.
  (c) **Value-added analysis** eliminates activities that do not add value.
  (d) **Gaps and disconnects** targets problems at departmental boundaries.

  The feasibility of any proposed redesign must be considered.

- ERP systems are based on limited, standardised modules. This means that the organisation must adapt to the standard system rather than designing its own most appropriate and efficient process. However, the alternative, adapting a standard package to local requirements, destroys the advantages of the purchasing the standard package and introduces further complications. Nevertheless, packages have their own disadvantages.

- The first phase of any IS project is likely to be the collection of information. There are seven techniques.

  - Interviews
  - Questionnaires
  - Written questions
  - Observation
  - Protocol analysis
  - Workshops
  - Prototyping

  Each technique has its advantages and disadvantages, so it will be normal to use a combination of them.

- Software packages maybe assessed against ten high-level requirement categories, each of which is made up of more detailed specific requirements. Not all high-level categories will receive the same weighting.

  Imperatives are non-negotiable, absolute requirements and must be established very early on in the project.

- The process of selecting a package may be thought of as falling into five phases.

  - Obtaining tenders
  - First pass selection
  - Second pass selection
  - Implementation
  - The long-term relationship

Quick Quiz

1   What are the three conditions that value adding activities satisfy?

2   What is protocol analysis?

3   How do non-functional requirements differ from functional requirements?

4   What is an imperative?

5   What is a reference site?

Answers to Quick Quiz

1   The customer is willing to pay for the output; the process changes the output in some way; the process is performed correctly at the first attempt.

2   A task is performed and, at the same time, the process is explained by the performer.

3   Both are essential and must be supported. However, non-functional requirements do not relate directly to business functionality. An example is legal compliance.

4   An essential, non-negotiable requirement.

5   A place where a software package is already installed and in operation that may be visited to carry out an assessment.

Part E
E-business

E-Business

Topic list	Syllabus reference
1 Principles of e-business	E1(1), (b)
2 Organisations and their customers	E1(c), (d)
3 Hardware and software infrastructure	E1(e)
4 IT and strategy	E1(f)
5 Supply chain management	E2(a)–(d)
6 E-procurement	E2(e), (f)

Introduction

Your syllabus includes an extensive section on e-business. This is a relatively new, rapidly expanding and fundamentally important aspect of strategic implementation. Indeed, in many organisations, it may be regarded as a fundamental aspect of strategy and certainly of the business model. In this chapter and the next we will consider this vital new area of business.

Study guide

		Intellectual level
E1	**Principles of e-business**	
(a)	Discuss the meaning and scope of e-business.	
(b)	Advise on the reasons for the adoption of e-business and recognise barriers to its adoption.	
(c)	Evaluate how e-business changes the relationships between organisations and their customers.	
(d)	Discuss and evaluate the main business and marketplace models for delivering e-business.	
(e)	Advise on the hardware and software infrastructure required to support e-business.	
(f)	Advise on how the organisation can utilise information technology to help it deliver a selected strategy.	
E2	**E-business application: upstream supply chain management**	
(a)	Analyse the main elements of both the push and pull models of the supply chain.	
(b)	Discuss the relationship of the supply chain to the value chain and the value network.	
(c)	Assess the potential application of information technology to support and restructure the supply chain.	
(d)	Advise on how external relationships with suppliers and distributors can be structured to deliver a restructured supply chain.	
(e)	Discuss the methods, benefits and risks of e-procurement.	
(f)	Assess different options and models for implementing e-procurement.	

Exam guide

We would expect aspects of e-business to be relevant to many questions both in Section A of your exam and in Section B. We would also expect that from time to time there might be complete questions on this topic, especially in Section B.

1 Principles of e-business

1.1 E-business – meaning and scope

FAST FORWARD

> Electronic business, or e-business, is the automation of business processes of all types through electronic means. This may be rrestricted to email or may extend to a fully-featured website or an e-marketplace. E-business that includes a financial transaction is known as e-commerce. E-business is radically different from ordinary business and brings six categories of benefit.
>
> Costs are reduced.
> Capability is increased.
> Communications are improved.
> Control is enhanced.

Customer service is improved.
Competitive advantage may be achieved, depending on competitors' reactions.

Adoption of e-business methods may be hindered by a range of obstacles including lack of skills; lack of Internet use and awareness among businesses and the wider population; and feats about privacy, effectiveness, cost, security and so on.

Key term

E-business has been defined by IBM as 'the transformation of key business processes through the use of Internet technologies'.

E-business processes include not only on-line marketing and sales, but supply-chain and channel management; manufacturing and inventory control; financial operations; and employee workflow procedures across an entire organisation. Essentially, e-business technologies empower customers, employees, suppliers, distributors, vendors and partners by giving them powerful tools for information management and communications.

There are **different levels of e-business**; some businesses do not need a website but deal all day with other businesses and customers online *via* email and an e-marketplace. Other businesses have a website that helps them sell their products all around the world. It is up to each business to determine what level of e-business is right for it.

E-business is often confused with **e-commerce**.

(a)   Any transaction with an electronic process using Internet technologies is **e-business**.

(b)   If there is a **financial transaction** involved with the electronic process using Internet technologies it is **e-commerce**. For example, buying a book on *Amazon.com* is both e-commerce and e-business. Creating a map with directions from your office to the post office on *Yahoo.com* is e-business (no e-commerce is involved).

E-commerce has many aspects.

(a)   Electronic ordering of goods and services that are delivered using traditional channels such as post or couriers (indirect electronic commerce)

(b)   On-line ordering, payment and delivery of intangible goods and services such as software, electronic magazines, entertainment services and information services (direct electronic commerce)

(c)   Electronic fund transfers (EFT)

(d)   Electronic share trading

(e)   Commercial auctions

(f)   Direct consumer marketing and after-sales service

There are several features of e-business and the Internet that make it radically different from what has gone before.

(a)   It **challenges traditional business models** because, for example, it enables suppliers to interact directly with their customers, instead of using intermediaries such as retail shops, travel agents, insurance brokers, and conventional banks.

(b)   Although the Internet is global in its operation, its benefits are not confined to large (or global) organisations. **Small companies** can move instantly into a global market place, either on their own initiative or as part of a **consumer portal**.

(c)   It offers a **new economics of information** because, with the Internet, much information is free of charge to the user. Those with Internet access can view many of the world's major newspapers and periodicals without charge.

(d) It supplies an almost incredible **level of speed** of communication, giving virtually instant access to organisations, plus the capacity to complete purchasing transactions within seconds.

(e) It has created **new and cheaper networks of communication** – between organisations and their customers (either individually or collectively), between customers themselves (through mutual support groups), and between organisations and their suppliers.

(f) It stimulates the appearance of **new intermediaries** and the disappearance of some existing ones. Businesses are finding that they can cut out the middle man, with electronic banking, insurance, publishing and printing as primary examples.

(g) It has led to **new business partnerships** through which small enterprises can gain access to customers on a scale which would have been viewed as impossible a few years ago.

(h) Work is becoming **independent of location**. Clerical, administrative and knowledge work can be done at any location. This can reduce establishment and travelling costs, especially if people work at home, but the loss of personal interaction can affect **motivation** and **job satisfaction**.

(i) The **nature of work** is changing since increased quantities of available data and more powerful methods of accessing and analysing it mean that greater attention can be paid to **customising product offerings to more precisely defined target segments**.

1.2 Adopting e-business

Driven by competitive pressures, companies are employing e-business for a variety of purposes.

(a) **Increase revenues** through optimal customer and partner management

(b) **Reduce costs** through automated sales, administration and service activities

(c) Enable greater **channel efficiency** and effectiveness: efficiency benefits arise from improved communication using email and other Internet technologies and effectiveness benefits obtain from the ability to gather information.

(d) Gain **visibility**

(e) **Control and automate** customer and partner facing operations

The e-business **adoption pyramid** illustrates the order in which e-business facilities tend to be adopted.

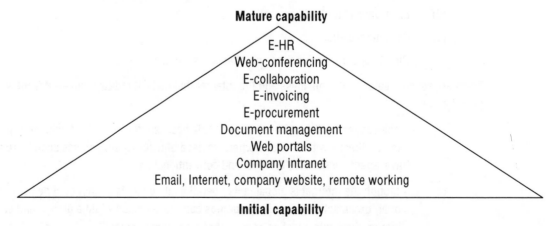

Mature capability

E-HR
Web-conferencing
E-collaboration
E-invoicing
E-procurement
Document management
Web portals
Company intranet
Email, Internet, company website, remote working

Initial capability

Most businesses start with the key e-business facilities of email, Internet and company websites and in addition, many also have remote working facilities. These facilities seem to constitute the key communication tools essential for businesses in the present technological environment.

Benefits of e-business

(a) **Cost reduction** – in procurement and reduced headcount needed to handle consumer and business enquiries. Cost of sales and promotion may be reduced and lower prices passed on to customers.

(b) **Capability** – may be able to increase penetration in new countries and may help reduce the amount of goods stored.

(c) **Communication** – to customers can be improved with updates of product or service information.

(d) **Control** – the web site can be used to monitor interest in product or service from customers.

(e) **Customer service** – many basic enquiries about products can be dealt with on the web site. Opening times (for stores or offices) and special offers can be promoted. This may reduce the number of phone enquiries. Business customers can use the e-commerce system to track delivery and manage inventory better through reducing time for ordering.

(f) **Competitive advantage** – will be dependent on the use of e-commerce by competitors.

1.3 Barriers to e-business and e-commerce adoption

Barriers (also referred to as obstacles, impediments or hindrances) to e-business adoption work differently according to perception, country, economic issues, technology, culture, law and ethics and organisational type.

The barriers to e-business appear greater to organisations with just a few employees. They use **three arguments**:

- E-business is not relevant to them.
- Staff do not have the required skills and knowledge.
- Their customers do not use e-business.

1.3.1 Other barriers

(a) **Country** – successful e-business depends on a critical mass of Internet users, which has not been reached in many countries. Also, the combination of connection and usage charges tends to inhibit the uptake of the Internet in many countries and, by extension, reduces e-commerce activity. Obviously, as more people go online and charges become competitive, the value of the whole network and the opportunities for e-business will increase tremendously and this initial barrier will be overcome.

(b) **Economic issues** – much of the consumer world still pays cash, rather than taking credit. The lack of ability or interest in credit transactions is an enormous barrier to e-commerce. Also, the issue of transaction security over the Internet is of concern to many consumers.

(c) **Culture** – different languages and cultural platforms compound the complexity of doing e-business overseas. Cultural features such as risk aversion, attitudes to privacy and lifestyle differences may impact Internet usage. The use of *Hofstede's* cultural dimensions can help e-businesses to understand their customers better. For example, cultures rating high on **uncertainty avoidance** and low on **individualism** are likely to be difficult markets for introducing consumer e-business.

(d) **Organisational type** – surveys of sectors such as retail, tourism and manufacturing have identified a number of major concerns including: privacy, trust, uncertainty of financial returns and lack of reliable measurement, fraud, lack of support and system maintenance. For small and medium-sized enterprises there is a wide range of barriers.

(i) Cost of implementation

(ii) Need for immediate return on investment

(iii) Complexity of technologies like electronic data interchange (EDI) which could require new skills

(iv) Lack of organisational readiness with many small and medium-sized enterprises having limited existing IT resources

(v) Lack of perceived benefits

(vi) Lack of assertiveness by the owner/manager

(vii) Security, including confidentiality and fraud

2 Organisations and their customers

FAST FORWARD

Both businesses and customers can originate e-commerce activity; thus there are four main categories: B2B, B2C, C2B and C2C. **Channel structures** are the means by which products and services are delivered to customers. **Disintermediation** removes intermediaries from supply channels while **reintermediation** establishes new ones. **Countermediation** is the creation of a new intermediary by an established company to compete *via* a business with established intermediaties.

2.1 Varieties of e-commerce

Ecommerce can be divided into four main categories.

B2B (Business-to-Business) – involves companies doing business with each other, as when manufacturers sell to distributors and wholesalers sell to retailers. Pricing is based on quantity of order and is often negotiable.

B2C (Business-to-Consumer) – involves businesses selling to the general public, typically through catalogues with **shopping cart software**.

C2B (Consumer-to-Business) – a consumer posts his project with a set budget online and within hours companies review the consumer's requirements and bid on the project. The consumer reviews the bids and selects the company that will complete the project.

C2C (Consumer-to-Consumer) – an excellent example of this is found at *eBay*, where consumers sell their goods and services to other consumers. Another technology that has emerged to support C2C activities is that of the payment intermediary *PayPal*. Instead of purchasing items directly from an unknown, un-trusted seller, the buyer can instead send the money to Pay Pal, who forward it to the vendor's account.

The transaction alternatives between businesses and consumers are shown in the matrix below:

Delivery by

		Business	Consumer
Exchange initiated by	Business	BSB Business models eg *VerticalNet.com*	B2C Business models eg *Amazon.com*
	Consumer	C2B Business models eg *Priceline.com*	C2C Business Models eg *eBay.com*

Companies using internal networks to offer their employees products and services online (but not necessarily via the Internet) are engaging in **B2E** (Business-to-Employee) e-commerce.

Other forms of e-commerce that involve transactions with the government include:

- **G2G** (Government-to-Government)
- **G2E** (Government-to-Employee)
- **G2B** (Government-to-Business)
- **B2G** (Business-to-Government)
- **G2C** (Government-to-Citizen)
- **C2G** (Citizen-to-Government)

B2M (Business to Machine) is a fast emerging area within e-commerce. The general idea is that companies can link to **remote machines** via the Internet. For example, with this technology, owners of vending machines know exactly how much stock is in each machine and their accounting system produces a restocking report advising the delivery driver accordingly. In this manner, companies can monitor their machines remotely to determine if they need repairing or restocking. This information is then used to schedule efficient delivery before the stock runs out.

2.2 Market place channel structures

Channel structures are the means by which a manufacturer or selling organisation delivers products and services to its customers. The simplest channel structure is **direct**: the business deals directly with the customer without the assistance of any **intermediaries**. The more complex the channel structure, the more intermediaries (wholesalers and/or retailers) are used in the supply chain. Intermediaries offer a wide range of services and facilities: they include agents, traders, brokers, dealers, wholesalers/distributors and providers of specialised information.

The main changes to channel structures facilitated through the Internet include **disintermediation** (direct selling), **reintermediation** (new intermediaries) and **countermediation** (the creation of a new intermediary by an established company)

2.2.1 Disintermediation

Disintermediation is the removal of intermediaries in a supply chain that formerly linked a company to its customers. Instead of going through traditional distribution channels, with intermediaries such as a distributor, wholesaler, broker or agent, companies may now deal with every customer directly via the Internet.

2.2.2 Examples

You can already bypass publishers to get a book printed at tiny cost through self-publishing sites such as *Lulu.com*. Gambling is being changed by online sites arranging bets directly between individuals, not through bookmakers. In the UK voice communication is being revolutionised by enabling people to use free Internet telephony systems such as *Skype* rather than *BT*. Even benevolent intermediaries such as libraries may be under threat if all reference books are scanned by Google and made available to everyone.

Disintermediation may be initiated by **consumers** because they are aware of **supply prices** direct from the manufacturer or wholesaler. Alternatively, it may be instigated by the author or creator of a work, such as *Steven King* selling his books directly to the public. There are also third party aggregators or buyer's clubs that link consumers with producers to obtain lower prices.

Reverse auction sites that allow consumers to specify an item they wish to purchase, allowing producers and others to bid on the item.

Traditional value chain in publishing

E-market value chain – Amazon

E-market value chain - the print on-demand paradigm

2.2.3 Reintermediation

Reintermediation is the establishment of new intermediary roles for traditional intermediaries that were disintermediated. In some cases, a new element of a supply chain simply replaces a single displaced element, such as Amazon.com replacing retailers. In other cases, a reintermediating entity replaces multiple supply chain elements. These new intermediaries do one of two things.

(a)   Provide customers with **new, important value-added services** not provided in the new direct customer-supplier relationship. An example is *Kelkoo* which is a shopping/price comparison search engine.

(b)   Provide customers with **more efficient means** of transacting business.

The ever-increasing number of 'hubs', 'portals', 'aggregators', 'clearinghouses' and 'exchanges' shows that entirely new ways of doing business are being created. Those organisations (or individuals) clever enough to recognise the opportunities provided by the Web and are reinventing themselves as 'cybermediaries' or 'infomediaries' – intermediaries offering value-added services to consumers and vendors over the Internet.

2.2.4 New types of intermediary

Search engines and directories – search engines, such as Google and *Alta Vista* provide search facilities based on data generated by software engines, that search the web. Directories such as Yahoo provide a general index of a large variety of different sites.

Search agents (Search bots) gather material from other sites. For example *Shopbot* searches across online shops.

Portals provide a gateway to the Web and may also offer **signposting**, selected **links** and other services to attract users. Internet Service Provider's (ISP) home pages such as www.AOL.com are an example of portals, and the large ISPs offer a wide range of added value services. Variations on the portal as gateway are: a horizontal portal or user customised gateway (eg *my Yahoo*); a vertical portal or special interest portal eg, *CNET* – a portal for users interested in developments in IT; and an enterprise information portal, which is an organisation's home page for employees, including corporate info and selected links.

'E-tailers' or consumer shopping sites such as Amazon. While starting as simply a bookshop on the web it has added a variety of products and types of services. By contrast, *Tesco* is an offline retailer which is offering web-based order and delivery services.

Malls are sites that group together different online stores as tenants. An example is the *Scottish Shopping Mall* (www.scottish-retailer.com). Malls provide cyber-infrastructure, but do not own inventory or sell products directly.

Auction sites such as eBay support online auctions.

Publisher web sites are traffic generators that offer content of interest to consumers.

Virtual resellers are intermediaries that exist to sell to consumers. They are able to obtain products directly from manufacturers, who may hesitate to go directly to consumers for fear of **alienating retailers** upon which they still largely depend.

Web site evaluators are may direct consumers to a producer's site *via* a new type of site that offers some form of evaluation, which may help to reduce some of the risk.

Forums, **fan clubs**, and **user groups** can play a large role in facilitating customer-producer feedback and supporting market research.

Financial intermediaries. Any form of e-commerce will require some means of making or authorising payments from buyer to seller.

2.2.5 Countermediation

Countermediation is the creation of a new intermediary by an established company in order to compete *via* e-business with established intermediaries. Examples include *B&Q* setting up *diy.com* to help people who want to do their own DIY, *Boots* setting up *handbag.com*, and *Opodo.com* which has been set up by a collaboration of nine European airlines. *Tescodiets.com* which was bought from *eDiets* is another example of a countermediation strategy. Countermediation also refers to possible partnerships with another independent intermediary eg, mortgage broker *Charcol* and *Orange*, which was Freeserve.

2.2.6 Example

Airlines. The impact of the Internet is seen clearly in the transportation industry. Airlines now have a more effective way of bypassing intermediaries (ie travel agents) because they can give their customers immediate access to flight reservation systems. *EasyJet*, was the first airline to have over half of its bookings made online.

Travel agents. The Internet has also produced a new set of online travel agents who have lower costs because of their ability to operate without a High Street branch network. Their low-cost structure makes them a particularly good choice for selling low margin, cheap tickets for flights, package holidays, cruises and so forth.

In 2004 *BA* stopped paying commission to travel agents for flight bookings, intending to move to an entirely Internet-based system for bookings. In 2005 the European industry saw significant consolidation when *Sabre Holdings*, the US owner of *Travelocity*, bought *Lastminute.com*.

Tesco is already the UK's largest Internet grocery business, but other companies are rapidly developing new initiatives. *Waitrose@work* allows people to order their groceries in the morning (typically through their employer's intranet communication system) and then have them delivered to the workplace in the afternoon: this approach achieves significant distribution economies of scale for Waitrose.

Financial services. The impact of the Internet is especially profound in the field of financial services. New intermediaries enable prospective customers to compare the interest rates and prices charged by different organisations for pensions, mortgages and other financial products. This means that the delivering companies are **losing control of the marketing** of their services, and there is a **downward pressure on prices**, especially for services which can legitimately be seen as mere commodities (eg house and contents insurance).

2.3 Business models for e-commerce

FAST FORWARD

> Rappa describes nine business models. E-commerce business models may also be categorised by characteristics such as value proposition, revenue model and market opportunity.

Knowledge brought forward from earlier studies

Business model was defined earlier in this Study Text.

Rappa classified nine generic business models:

1	Brokerage model	Those that bring buyers and sellers together and facilitate transactions (often fee based)
2	Advertising model	Supported by advertising revenue, a Web site will provide content and services together with advertising (eg banner ads)
3	Infomediary model	Collecting data about consumers and their purchasing habits and selling this information to other businesses
4	Merchant model	Selling of goods and services on the traditional retail model
5	Manufacturer model	Direct selling by the creator of a product or service to consumers, cutting out intermediaries
6	Affiliate model	Offering financial incentives to affiliated partner sites
7	Community model	Where users themselves invest in a site, eg by the contribution of content, money or time. This can be combined with other models, eg advertising or subscription
8	Subscription model	Where consumers (users) pay for access to the site, usually for high added-value content, eg financial information, newspapers, journals
9	Utility model	A model based on metered usage or pay-as-you-go

Other ways of categorising an e-commerce business model

(a) **Value proposition** defines how a company's product or service fulfils the need of customers

(b) **Revenue model** describes how the firm will earn revenue, produce profits, and produce a superior return on invested capital. The five primary revenue models are advertising, subscription, transaction fee, sales and the affiliate revenue model.

(c) **Market opportunity** refers to the company's intended **market space** and the overall potential financial opportunities available to the firm in that market space.

(d)   **Competitive environment** refers to the other companies operating in the same market space selling similar products.

(e)   **Competitive advantage** is achieved by the firm when it can produce a superior product and/or bring the product to market at a lower price than most, or all, of its competitors.

(f)   **Market strategy** the plan that details exactly how the organisation intends to enter a new market and attract new customers.

(g)   **Organisational development** describes how the company will organise the work to be accomplished.

(h)   **Management team**: employees of the company responsible for making the business model work.

3 Hardware and software infrastructure

System architecture is the arrangement of software, machinery and tasks in an information system needed to achieve a specific functionality.

The **Internet** enables computers across the world to communicate via telecommunications links.

The **World Wide Web** is a navigation system within the Internet. It is based on a technology called **hypertext** which allows documents stored on host computers on the Internet to be linked to one another.

An **intranet** is used to disseminate and exchange information 'in-house' within an organisation.

An **extranet** is used to communicate with selected people outside the organisation.

In general, all of the machines on the Internet can be categorised into two types: servers and clients. The machines that provide services to other machines are servers. And the machines that are used to connect to those services are clients.

Each machine on the Internet is assigned a unique address called an IP address.

There are several levels to the interaction between a client and a server, from the physical pieces of wire making the connection, through the transfer and checking of data, security problems of access and logging on, to the final presentation to and interaction with the user. The International Standards Organisation (ISO) has defined seven levels in a standard called Open Systems Interconnection.

A **protocol stack** is a group of protocols that all work together to allow software or hardware to perform a function. The TCP/IP protocol stack is a good example. It uses four layers that map to the OSI model.

Alternatives to PC-based Internet access include interactive digital television and wireless or mobile access.

3.1 E-commerce infrastructure

Many technologies must be integrated for supporting e-business:

• PC	• E-mail	• Database management software
• Modem	• Internet and Web protocols	• Shopping cart software
• Routers	• Web connectivity software	• Shipment tracking software
• Servers		

System architecture is the arrangement of software, machinery and tasks in an information system needed to achieve a specific **functionality**.

The table below shows how the different components of the e-business infrastructure relate to each other. They can be shown as different layers with defined interfaces between each layer.

E-business architecture	Infrastructure	Players
E-business services – Application layer	E-commerce software systems Customer Relationship Management system Performance enhancement Supply chain management, data mining and content management systems	*Microsoft, IBM, Ariba, BroadVision* *Peoplesoft, Siebel* *Cash Flow, Akamai*
Systems software layer	Web browser, operating systems, server software and standards, networking software and database management systems Encryption software	*Microsoft, Sun, Linux* *Oracle, Sybase, IBM, Microsoft.* *Verisign, Checkpoint*
Transport or network layer	Web servers. Physical network – routers and transport standards (TCP/IP)	*IBM, Dell, Sun.* *Cisco, Lucent*
Storage/physical layer	Permanent magnetic storage on web servers. Optical backup. Temporary storage in RAM	
Content and data layer	Web content for Internet, intranet and extranet sites. Customers' data. Transactions data. Payment systems. Streaming media solutions. Hosting services	*PayPal, CyberCash* *Microsoft, Real Networks, Apple* *IBM, Interland, WebIntellects*

The **application layer** uses business rules to determine pricing based on various discount strategies for different types of customers

The **data layer** retrieves basic price and product description information from a company-wide database

3.2 The Internet

The **Internet** enables computers across the world to communicate via telecommunications links. Information can be exchanged through e-mail or through accessing and entering data via a **website**: a collection of screens providing information in text and graphic form, any of which can be viewed by clicking the appropriate link (shown as a button, word or icon) on the screen.

The **World Wide Web** is a navigation system within the Internet. It is based on a technology called **hypertext** which allows documents stored on host computers on the Internet to be linked to one another. When you view a document that contains **hypertext links**, you can view any of the connected documents or pages simply by clicking on a link. The web is the most powerful, flexible and fastest growing information and navigation service on the Internet. In order to 'surf' or navigate the web, users need a **web browser** that interprets and displays hypertext documents and locates documents pointed to by links. *Internet Explorer* is the browser from *Microsoft*: alternatives include *Mozilla Firefox* and *Enigma*.

Access to the Internet will become easier and easier. Most new PCs now come pre-loaded with the necessary software, and cheaper Internet devices are beginning to reach the market: Microsoft and *America Online* (AOL), among others, have been exploring inexpensive 'set-top' TV/Internet connections. Developments in telecom networks are already rendering modems unnecessary. Personal digital assistants (PDAs) such as the *Palm Pilot*, wireless Internet-compatible cellular phones and wireless laptop connections (such as *Apple's* 'air port') allow users to surf the Web and send and receive e-mail from almost any location, without cords or cables.

While we tend to use the terms Internet and World Wide Web interchangeably, the Internet describes the entire system of networked computers and the World Wide Web describes the method used to access information contained on computers connected to the Internet. The availability of a common Internet infrastructure – of computers, networks and protocols – and the development of an easy to use **graphical user interface** (GUI) have been the catalysts for the growth of e-commerce. It has created an open community that is easy to join and easy to use.

Most large communications companies have their own dedicated **communication backbones** connecting various regions. In each region, the company has a Point of Presence (POP). The POP is a place for local users to access the company's network, often through a local phone number or dedicated line. There is no overall controlling network. Instead, there are several high-level networks connecting to each other through Network Access Points or NAPs.

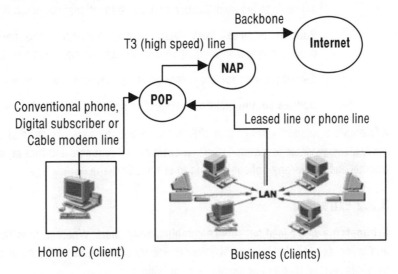

Physical and network infrastructure components of the Internet.

3.3 Intranets and extranets

'Inter' means 'between': 'intra' means 'within'; ''extra' means 'outside'. This may be a useful reminder of some of the inter-related terminology in this area.

(a) The **Internet** is used to disseminate and exchange information among the public at large.

(b) An **intranet** is used to disseminate and exchange information 'in-house' within an organisation. Only employees are able to access this information.

(c) An **extranet** is used to communicate with selected people outside the organisation.

3.3.1 Intranets

An **intranet** is an internal network used to share information. Intranets utilise Internet technology and protocols. The **firewall** surrounding an intranet fends off unauthorised access.

The idea behind an intranet is that companies set up their own mini version of the Internet. Each employee has a browser, used to access a server computer that holds corporate information on a wide variety of topics, and in some cases also offers access to the Internet.

Potential applications include company newspapers, induction material, online procedure and policy manuals, employee web pages where individuals post details of their activities and progress, and internal databases of the corporate information store.

Intranets are used for many purposes.

(a) **Performance data:** linked to sales, inventory, job progress and other database and reporting systems, enabling employees to process and analyse data to fulfil their work objectives

(b)   **Employment information:** online policy and procedures manuals (health and safety, disciplinary and grievance), training and induction material, internal contacts for help and information

(c)   **Employee support/information:** advice on first aid, healthy working at computer terminals, training courses offered and resources held in the corporate library and so on.

(d)   **Notice boards** for the posting of messages to and from employees: notice of meetings, events, trade union activities

(e)   **Departmental home pages:** information and news about each department's personnel and activities to aid identification and cross-functional understanding

(f)   **Bulletins or newsletters:** details of product launches and marketing campaigns, staff moves, changes in company policy links to relevant databases or departmental home pages

(g)   **E-mail** facilities for the exchange of messages between employees in different locations

(h)   **Upward communication:** suggestion schemes, feedback, questionnaires

A **firewall** is a security device that effectively isolates the sensitive parts of an organisation's system from those areas available to external users. It examines all requests and messages entering and exiting the Intranet and blocks any not conforming to specified criteria.

3.3.2 Extranets

Extranets are web based but serve a combination of users. Whereas an intranet resides behind a **firewall** and is accessible only to people who are members of the same company or organisation, an **extranet** provides various levels of accessibility to **outsiders**.

Only those outsiders with a valid **username** and **password** can access an extranet: varying levels of access rights enable control over what people can view. Extranets are becoming a very popular means for business partners to exchange information. They can share data or systems to provide smoother transaction processing and more efficient services for customers. An extranet may be used for a variety of purposes.

(a)   To provide a pooled service which a number of business partners can access and exchange **news** which is of use to partner companies and clients

(b)   To share **training** or **development resources**

(c)   To publicise loyalty schemes, sponsorships, exhibition attendance information and other **promotional tools**

(d)   To exchange potentially large volumes of **transaction data** efficiently

(e)   To provide **online presentations** to business partners and prospects

The basic components of an Extranet are an always on Internet connection via a **router**, an HTTP server, a firewall and the essential data and files. All the infrastructure and applications can sit inside the firewall or outside in a secure area called a demilitarised zone (DMZ). An organisation could connect its browser based purchase order system to the product catalogue database on a supplier's Intranet (see diagram below).

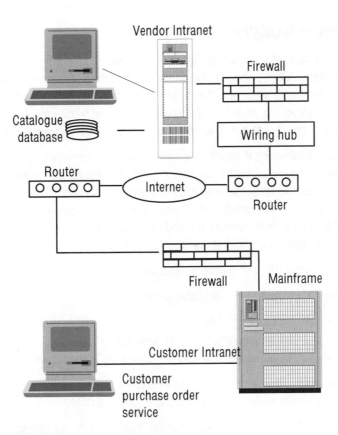

3.4 Electronic mail

The term **electronic mail** is used to describe various systems for sending data or messages electronically *via* a telephone or data network and a central server computer. E-mail has replaced letters, memos, faxes, documents and even telephone calls, combining many of the possibilities of each medium with new advantages of speed, cost and convenience. Messages are written and read in a special program such as *Microsoft Outlook Express* (for an individual) or part of a groupware package such as *Microsoft Exchange* or *Novell* if used in a large company. This software has convenient features such as: message copying (to multiple recipients); integration with an address book (database of contacts); automatic alert messages sent when the target recipient is unable to access his or her e-mail immediately, with alternative contact details; stationery and template features, allowing corporate identity to be applied; facilities for mail organisation and filing.

Some web sites eg, *Hotmail* and Yahoo provide free e-mail facilities and only require a Web browser.

3.5 Client/server architecture

In general, all of the machines on the Internet can be categorised into two types: servers and clients. The machines that provide services to other machines are servers. And the machines that are used to connect to those services are clients. It is possible and common for a machine to be both a server and a client, but for our purposes here you can think of most machines as one or the other.

A server machine may provide one or more services on the Internet. For example, a server machine might have software running on it that allows it to act as a Web server, an e-mail server and a file transfer protocol (FTP) server. Clients that come to a server machine do so with a specific intent, so clients direct their requests to a specific software application running on the overall server machine. For example, if you are running a Web browser on your machine, it will most likely want to talk to the Web server application on the server machine; your Telnet application will want to talk to the Telnet server and your e-mail application will talk to the e-mail server.

Internet protocol (IP)

To keep all of these machines straight, each machine on the Internet is assigned a unique address called an IP address. A server has a static IP address that does not change very often. A home machine that is dialling up through a modem often has an IP address that is assigned by the ISP when the machine dials in. That IP address is unique for that session — it may be different the next time the machine dials in. This way, an ISP only needs one IP address for each modem it supports, rather than one for each customer.

As far as the Internet's machines are concerned, an IP address is all you need to talk to a server but because most people have trouble remembering the strings of numbers that make up IP addresses, and because IP addresses sometimes need to change, all servers on the Internet also have human-readable names, called domain names. For example, www.amazon.com is a permanent, human-readable name. It is easier for most of us to remember than it is to remember 72.21.203.1; you can type the URL http://72.21.203.1 and arrive at the machine that contains the Web server for Amazon's home page.

When you type a URL into a browser, the following steps occur.

The browser breaks the URL into three parts:

- The protocol ('http')
- The server name ('www.amazon.com')
- The file name (where applicable eg, gp/homepage.html)

The browser communicates with a name server to translate the server name, 'www.amazon.com', into an IP address, which it uses to connect to that server machine.

The browser then forms a connection to the Web server at that IP address on port 80.

Following the HTTP protocol, the browser sends a GET request to the server, asking for the file http://www.amazon.com/gp/homepage.html'.

The server sends the HTML text for the Web page to the browser.

The browser reads the HTML tags and formats the page onto your screen.

3.5.1 Open Systems Interconnection (OSI) standard

There are several levels to the interaction between a client and a server, from the physical pieces of wire making the connection, through the transfer and checking of data, security problems of access and logging on, to the final presentation to and interaction with the user. Each level has its own standards, and many standards encompass several levels. In an attempt to bring some order to this, the International Standards Organisation (ISO) has defined seven levels in a standard called Open Systems Interconnection (OSI). At each layer, certain things happen to the data that prepare it for the next layer. The seven layers are:

Application	Layer 7 actually interacts with the operating system or application whenever the user chooses to transfer files, read messages or perform other network-related activities
Presentation	Layer 6 takes the data provided by the Application layer and converts it into a standard format that the other layers can understand
Session	Layer 5 establishes, maintains and ends communication with the receiving device
Transport	This layer maintains flow control of data and provides for error checking and recovery of data between the devices. Flow control means that the Transport layer looks to see if data is coming from more than one application and integrates each application's data into a single stream for the physical network.
Network	Layer 3 deals with the routing from one point in a network to another. It determines the way that the data will be sent to the recipient device. Logical protocols, routing and addressing are handled here

BPP))))
LEARNING MEDIA

Data-link	Layer 2 defines the rules for sending and receiving information between two specific nodes on a network
Physical	This is the level of the actual hardware. It defines the physical characteristics of the network such as connections, voltage levels and timing.

3.5.2 Protocol stacks

A **protocol stack** is a group of protocols that all work together to allow software or hardware to perform a function. The TCP/IP protocol stack is a good example. It uses four layers that map to the OSI model as follows:

Network Interface	Combines the Physical and Data layers and routes the data between devices on the same network. It also manages the exchange of data between the network and other devices.
Internet	Corresponds to the Network layer. The Internet Protocol (IP) uses the IP address, consisting of a Network Identifier and a Host Identifier, to determine the address of the device it is communicating with.
Transport	Corresponding to the OSI Transport layer, this is the part of the protocol stack where the Transport Control Protocol (TCP) can be found. TCP ensures that connection is maintained and that data is transferred correctly
Application	Combines the Session, Presentation and Application layers of the OSI model. Protocols for specific functions such as e-mail (Simple Mail Transfer Protocol, SMTP) and file transfer (File Transfer Protocol, FTP) reside at this level.

As you can see, it is not necessary to develop a separate layer for each and every function outlined in the OSI Reference Model. But developers are able to ensure that a certain level of compatibility is maintained by following the general guidelines provided by the model.

3.6 Alternative Internet access technologies

Alternatives to PC-based Internet access include interactive digital television and wireless or mobile access.

3.6.1 Interactive digital television (iDTV)

iDTV is displayed using a digital signal delivered by a range of media including cable, satellite and terrestrial (by aerial). Consumer interactions are provided by a remote control which enables users to select different viewing options through signals sent to a set top box. From a marketing perspective, a key aspect is how the return path to the provider operates. This is required to provide interactions which involve exchange of information such as a consumer completing an online offer form in response to an interactive TV ad or a purchase transaction. For satellite or terrestrial viewers, the return path is provided by the phone line and requires a dial-up and local-call charge in the same manner as the Internet. This currently acts as a barrier in comparison with cable which is an always-on, two-way connection.

3.6.2 Mobile or wireless commerce (m-commerce)

When wireless devices are used for e-commerce applications, this is referred to as mobile commerce or m-commerce.

As well as offering voice calls, mobile phones are used for e-mail and short message service (SMS) (commonly known as 'texting') that lets users receive and send short text messages to other cell phones.

Mobile phone characteristics

- They can be accessed from anywhere.
- Their users can be reached when they are not in their normal location.
- It is not necessary to have access to a power supply or a fixed line connection.
- They provide security, since each user can be identified by their unique identification code.

In 1999, the first of a new generation of mobile phones, known as **Wireless Application Protocol** (WAP) phones was introduced that offered the opportunity to access information on web sites specially tailored for display on the small screens of mobile phones. WAP pages are accessed using wireless techniques from a **WAP gateway** that is connected to a traditional web server where the WAP pages are hosted.

In 2001, new services became available on **General Packet Radio Service** (GPRS). This is approximately five times faster than GSM and is an always-on service charged according to usage. Display is still largely text-based and based on the WAP protocol.

In 2003, the third generation (3G) of mobile phone technology became available based on **Universal Mobile Telephone System** (UMTS). UMTS is a realisation of a new generation of broadband multi-media mobile telecommunications technology with high speed data transfer enabling video calling. 3G technologies enable network operators to offer users a wider range of more advanced services while achieving greater network capacity through improved spectral efficiency. Many facilities available from a desktop PC are offered on a handheld unit.

3.6.3 WiFi Internet access

Wireless Fidelity (WiFi) is a technology that facilitates the mobile use of laptop computers and personal handheld devices away from the home or office. WiFi networks are created through an array of local **hotspots** throughout metropolitan areas.

Hotspots can now be found in most major airports, hotels, bookstores, coffee houses, shopping centres, and even car dealerships.

Municipal WiFi is a newer application that is gaining popularity quickly. Numerous cities across the country are partnering with ISPs such as *EarthLink* to build wireless networks that blanket every inch of their city.

This new technology removes the need to be near a localised hotspot and provides wireless access to all residents and businesses within the city limits including open spaces such as parks and highways.

4 IT and strategy

FAST FORWARD

The Internet has the capacity to transform many businesses *via* the introduction of new technology and skills and, eventually, the re-positioning of the offering to fit the new market conditions.

A **strategy for e-commerce** should be considered at the highest level of management and it is particularly necessary that it should conform to the standard criteria for strategic choice: suitability, acceptability and feasibility.

Suitability for most companies, e-commerce will be a supplement to more traditional operations, with the website forming a supplementary medium for communication and sales.

Acceptability. The e-commerce strategy must be acceptable to important stakeholders. Distributors are particularly important here.

Feasibility. Feasibility is a matter of **resources**. The fundamental resource is cash, but the availability of the skilled labour needed to establish and administer a website will be crucial to the e-commerce strategy.

4.1 Strategy for e-commerce

The Internet has the capacity to transform many businesses *via* the introduction of new technology and skills and, eventually, the re-positioning of the offering to fit the new market conditions. Commentators highlight so-called **megatrends** which, coupled with the Internet, are changing the face of organisations.

(a)   New **distribution channels**, revolutionising sales and brand management

(b)   The continued **shift of power** towards the consumer

(c)   **Growing competition** locally, nationally, internationally and globally

(d)   An acceleration in the **pace of business**

(e)   The **transformation of companies** into 'extended enterprises' involving 'virtual teams of business, customer and supplier' working in collaborative partnerships

(f)   A re-evaluation of how companies, their partners and competitors **add value** not only to themselves but in the wider environmental and social setting

(g)   Recognition of **knowledge** as a strategic asset

Most experts agree that a successful strategy for e-commerce cannot simply be bolted on to existing processes, systems, delivery routes and business models. Instead, management groups have, in effect, to start again, by asking themselves **fundamental questions**.

- What do customers want to buy from us?
- What business should we be in?
- What kind of partners might we need?
- What categories of customer do we want to attract and retain?

In turn, organisations can visualise the necessary changes at **three interconnected levels**.

Level 1 – The simple **introduction of new technology** to connect electronically with employees, customers and suppliers (eg through an intranet, extranet or website)

Level 2 – **Re-organisation** of the workforce, processes, systems and strategy in order to make best use of the new technology

Level 3 – **Re-positioning** of the organisation to fit it into the emerging e-economy.

So far, very few companies have gone beyond levels 1 and 2. Instead, pure Internet businesses such as Amazon and AOL have emerged from these new rules: unburdened by physical assets, their competitive advantage lies in **knowledge management** and **customer relationships**.

4.2 Building an e-commerce strategy

A **strategy for e-commerce**, while not necessarily constituting the organisation's overall strategy, is likely to have wide implications and to involve and affect more than one function or department within the organisation. It should, therefore, be considered at the highest level of management and it is particularly necessary that it should conform to the **standard criteria for strategic choice**: suitability, acceptability and feasibility. It should work well with any existing operations; be acceptable (to distributors in particular) and not make impractical demands for cash and skilled labour.

4.2.1 Suitability

There are a few large organisations, such as Amazon, whose overall strategy is based on e-commerce. However, for most companies, e-commerce will be a **supplement to more traditional operations**, with the website forming a supplementary medium for communication and sales. It is important that the e-commerce strategy supports the overall strategy generally. One way of approaching this would be to consider the **extended marketing mix** and the need for **balance**, **consistency** and **mutual support** between the elements. A very simple example would consider the question of whether to confine the website to an essentially communications role, or to incorporate a fully featured on-line shopping facility. A specialist chain store dealing in, say, camping and outdoor equipment would expect to expand its market if it developed on-line shopping. On the other hand, a manufacturer of specialist luxury goods, such as the most expensive fountain pens, would probably have a policy of distributing through carefully selected retailers. It is unlikely that on-line shopping would appeal to the target market segment: they would probably enjoy the shopping experience and would want to try the products before they bought them.

4.2.2 Acceptability

The e-commerce strategy must be **acceptable to important stakeholders**. Distributors are particularly important here. Pursuing our luxury goods example, we would expect that retailers chosen for their attractive premises, skilled and attentive staff and air of luxury would be unhappy to find their position usurped by a website.

4.2.3 Feasibility

Feasibility is a matter of **resources**. The fundamental resource is cash, but the availability of the **skilled labour** needed to establish and administer a website will be crucial to the e-commerce strategy. It may be appropriate to employ **specialist consultants** for these purposes.

Under this heading, we might identify the following points for consideration.

(a)   The first thing to do is to try to establish precise **objectives** for the new strategy element. It may not be possible to do this conclusively and consideration of objectives may have to proceed alongside the processes outline below, all passing through several iterations.

(b)   An estimate and analysis of **costs** and **benefits** should be undertaken. This should cover all the possible options, such as what services are to be offered, whether a full catalogue is to be put online, whether Internet selling is envisaged, whether a search function is required and so on.

(c)   A detailed **budget** should be prepared, probably using estimates from the cost and benefit analysis. Where Internet selling is to be offered, **pricing policy** must be established: there is a theory that customers expect goods and services to be discounted when sold online, since they are aware that administrative costs are likely to be lower than in more traditional forms of distribution.

4.3 Strategy process models for e-business

FAST FORWARD

IT has the capacity to transform businesses. Corporate and e.business strategies thus become complementary, each supporting and influencing the other.

The traditional landscape of the business environment has changed from being a market**place** to one that is more of a market**space** – an information and communication-based electronic exchange environment. The impact of this is evident in the following changes.

(a)   The **content of transaction is different:** information about a product often replaces the product itself

(b)   The **context of transaction is different:** an electronic screen replaces the face-to-face transaction

(c)   The **enabling infrastructure of transactions is different:** computers and communications infrastructure may replace typical physical resources especially if the offering lends itself to a digital format.

The significant issue faced by managers today is one of **transformation**: 'How do I transform the brick and mortar company of yesterday to the click and mortar company of today in order to be competitive in the inevitable digital economy of tomorrow?'

Until the emergence of e-business, IS have largely played a **facilitative** (and relatively peripheral) role in business, focusing on improving operational efficiencies, cost structures, and effectiveness. Now, however, it would be fair to claim that e-business would not be possible if it were not for the information systems that facilitate it. The role of IS has become central to e-business.

E-business strategy is defined as the approach by which the application of internal and external electronic communications can support and influence corporate strategy. There is a **two-way relationship** between corporate and e-business strategies, with e-business strategy not only supporting corporate strategy but influencing or impacting it.

Differences between traditional business strategy and e-business strategy

	Traditional business strategy	E-business strategy
Planning horizons	Predictability and long-term execution plans	Adaptability and responsiveness within a short time period
Process models	Prescriptive strategy: the three elements (analysis, development and implementation) are linked together sequentially	Emergent strategy: the distinction between the three elements may be less clear and they are interrelated
Planning cycles	One time development effort	Iterative strategic development because the pace of change is rapid
Power base	Positional power and strength in the market place	Success based on manipulation of critical information
Core focus	Production and factory goods orientation	Customer orientation

According to *Kalakota and Robinson* **continuous planning with feedback** has evolved as the strategy of choice for the fluid and volatile e-environment. This method of continuous planning with feedback is structured around four steps.

Step 1   **Knowledge building and capability evaluation:** identify and acquire a comprehensive understanding/vision of customer needs. Develop a clear understanding of what capabilities are needed in order to address the identified customer needs. Communicate this understanding of customer needs to all employees of the organisation.

Step 2   **Develop a comprehensive e-business design:** this entails developing the competence to address customer needs. If the customer wants self-service, then the business design must provide and facilitate it.

Step 3   **E-business blueprint:** the vital link between the e-business design, the business goals, and the technology foundation. If a self-service business model is to be implemented, then the e-business blueprint helps determine the required application framework. It maps the projects and performance milestones that must be achieved.

Step 4   **Application development and deployment:** translate the key milestones and projects into integrated applications. There should be two feedback loops:

      (a)   At the micro level, employees know how their individual job performance impacts corporate objectives.

      (b)   At the macro level, feedback on the overall corporate objectives is provided. This facilitates an understanding about what is working and what is not so that refinements/remedial actions may be undertaken.

4.4 Stage models

Skidmore and Eva argue that the selection and prioritisation of IS developments is strongly influenced by the level of *IT maturity* that an organisation has reached, so this should be one of the first issues to be determined for understanding effective project selection.

Several stage models have been proposed for in assessing maturity of capability. Such models can also be used as guides to future development.

Richard Nolan is considered to be the first researcher to provide a structured outline to explain the computing evolution within organisations. The original model consisted of 4 stages:

1   **Initiation stage.** The technology is placed in the organisation to automate clerical operations.

2   **Contagion stage.** There is rapid and uncontrolled growth in the number and variety of applications of the particular technology, as users become more familiar with applications and demand more; the wider benefits of technology are perceived by more staff.

3   **Control stage**. Management now gains control over the technology's resources by implementing formal control processes and standards that stifle almost all new projects.

4   **Integration stage.** The use of the new technology increases rapidly, providing new benefits and supporting the overall business strategy.

Later, due to the emergence of new applications such as database systems, the initial model was altered to include two new phases:

5   **Data administration stage.** Emphasis is placed on information requirements rather than just processing requirements; data handled by the new technology is recognised as an important resource and so efforts are made to *manage* it.

6   **Maturity stage.** The IS/IT planning is brought into line with business planning and development. Data resources are flexible and information flows mirror the real-world requirements of the firm. The firm will be using a variety of applications to support its information needs.

In general, these stages of computer development show how information technologies and organisational and managerial strategies evolve with time.

Nolan's model was frequently adjusted and presented under different forms and versions.

New maturity models, better adapted to the realities of electronic commerce, have been developed by other researchers and practitioners. Recent research on growth phases and electronic commerce has shown the usefulness of these models in describing the company position in terms of electronic commerce development and of its possible development in the future. Besides its descriptive aspect, studies of **maturity models** help companies choose adequate strategies for moving into new, more advanced phases.

Exam focus point

These models do not conform to the five stage **capability maturity model** scheme presented elsewhere in this Study Text.

Rayport and Jaworski suggest a four-stage model of the evolution of Internet-based B2B e-commerce, believing that, in general, an organisation goes through these stages in utilising the Internet for its business-to-business activities:

1	**Emission – Broadcast**	The company begins by creating an **informational website** for its clients
2	**Interaction**	Using the Internet for **interaction with customers** such as emails, customer survey and feedbacks
3	**Transaction**	The use of the Internet to take, manage and support **transactions with customers** such as online ordering systems
4	**Collaboration**	The use of the Internet to provide **inter-organisational activities**, that can be accessed and utilised by the company and its trading partners

The model of *Rao et al* suggests the following stages of e-commerce development and their characteristics:

Stage 1	Stage 2	Stage 3	Stage 4
Presence	**Portals**	**Transaction integration**	**Company integration**
Content	Profiles	B2B/B2C	B2B
Window to the Web	2-way communications	Communities	Full integration
No integration	E-mail	E-marketplaces	E-business
E-mail	Order placing	Auctions	Uses e-commerce systems to manage CRM and supply chain
	Cookies	3rd party emarketplaces	
	No on-line financial transactions	Low-level collaboration	Value chain integration
		On-line financial transactions	High-level collaboration

Stages of growth models give a better understanding of the factors influencing the strategy an organisation is considering and so management are able to do a more successful job of planning. The management principles will differ from one stage to another and different technologies and perhaps different areas of the organisation are in differing stages at any one time. Therefore these models also make explicit the need for a portfolio of strategies to cater for these differences.

The stages approach is useful for several purposes.

(a) A small or medium sized enterprise may use it for comparison with its major competitors; it may indicate gaps and lead to strategic actions.

(b) It can provide a roadmap to assist companies to determine whether or not it is sensible to progress to a subsequent stage.

(c) It can explain past, current and future involvement in e-business.

(d) It can be used for guidance and direction as to where to proceed further, as well as where an organisation might focus its goals and resources.

(e) It can help an organisation reduce the complexity of its e-business initiatives by breaking them into smaller, more flexible and manageable portions. By doing so, an organisation is able to focus more on the task at hand, constantly evaluating and assessing the progression of its e-business initiatives.

(f) It can assist in identifying phases of development required and provide milestones that can be understood by management.

(g) It may help control costs and allow for alteration during the development process.

5 Supply chain management

A **supply chain** encompasses all activities and information flows necessary for the transformation of goods from the origin of the raw material to when the product is finally consumed or discarded.

A supply chain always includes push and pull elements. The pull based element is particularly relevant on IS for feedback and control, since it aims to eliminate buffer stocks by increasing responsiveness.

5.1 Supply chain basics

Key supply chain activities include production planning, purchasing, materials management, distribution, customer service, and sales forecasting. These processes are critical to the success of any operation whether they are manufacturers, wholesalers, or service providers.

Electronic commerce and the Internet are fundamentally changing the nature of supply chains, and redefining how consumers learn about, select, purchase, and use products and services. The result has been the emergence of new business-to-business supply chains that are consumer-focused rather than product-focused. They also provide customised products and services.

5.2 Push and pull models of the supply chain

5.2.1 Traditional supply chain – push model

In a supply chain based on the **push model**, an organisation produces goods according to schedules based on historical sales patterns.

A push-based supply chain is slow to respond to changes in demand, which can result in overstocking, bottlenecks and delays, unacceptable service levels and product obsolescence. Where there are several links in the distribution chain, the system's inability to respond to variations in consumption leads to the establishment of buffer stocks at each stage of distribution. Poor co-ordination can lead to large fluctuations in the levels of these buffer stocks, even where actual consumption patterns vary only marginally. This kind of unco-ordinated amplification of minor feedback signals is called the 'bull whip effect'.

Features of a push system

- Forecasts of sales drive production and replenishment
- Long term forecasts
- Inventory pushed to next channel level, often with the aid of trade promotions
- Inability to meet changing demand patterns
- Potential product obsolescence
- Excessive inventory and low service levels
- Bull whip effect

5.2.2 The pull model

Driven by e-commerce's capabilities to empower clients, many companies are moving to a customer-driven **pull model**, where production and distribution are **demand driven**. The consumer requests the product and 'pulls' it through the delivery channel. There is an emphasis on the supply chain's **delivering value to customers** who are actively involved in product and service specifications.

This new business model is less product-centric and more directly focused on the individual consumer. To succeed in the business environment, companies have recognised that there is an ongoing **shift in the balance of power** in the commerce model, from suppliers to customers.

Features of a pull system

- Demand drives production and replenishment
- Centralisation of demand information and of replenishment decision-making
- Reduced product obsolescence
- Expanded ability to meet changing demand patterns
- Lower inventories and higher service levels
- Reduced bull whip effect

In the pull model, customers use electronic connections to pull whatever they need out of the system. The push model involves a linear flow that keeps many members of the supply chain relatively isolated from end users. With the new customer-driven pull model, it is no longer a linear process. The new supply chain has each participant scrambling to establish direct electronic connections to the end customer. The result is that electronic supply-chain connectivity gives end customers the opportunity to become better informed through the ability to research and give direction to suppliers. Ultimately, customers have a direct voice in the functioning of the supply chain.

E-commerce creates a much more efficient supply chain that benefits both customers and manufacturers. Companies can better serve customer needs, carry less stock and send products to market more quickly.

5.2.3 IS implications

Push-based systems rely less on sophisticated IS support, since high stock levels are used to cope with variations in customer demand. Pull-based systems, like Just-in-Time (JIT), need accurate and quick information on actual demand to move inventory and schedule production in the chain: therefore, they require integrated internal systems and linkages throughout the supply chain.

A supply chain is almost always a **combination of both push and pull**, where the interface between the push-based stages and the pull-based stages is known as the push-pull boundary. An example of this would be *Dell's* **build-to-order** supply chain. Inventory levels of individual components are determined by forecasting general demand, but final assembly is in response to a specific customer request. The push-pull boundary would then be at the beginning of the assembly line. At this point on the supply chain timeline, it is typically coordinated through a **buffer inventory**.

5.3 Relationship with the value chain and the value network

FAST FORWARD

IS may be used to improve the working of the links between activities in the value chain and between value chains in the value network. One important consequence of this is that improved communication with customers results, making it easier for them to purchase.

Knowledge brought forward from earlier studies

The **value chain** concept has already been described in detail in this Study Text. Here is the diagram to refresh your memory.

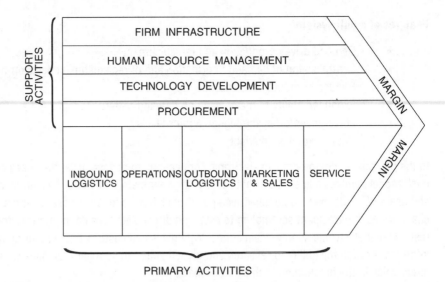

5.3.1 Using the value chain with IS

Management can use this model to assess the degree of **effectiveness** and **efficiency of resource use**.

(a) **Efficiency** is the measure of how well the resources are being used and measures could include profitability, capacity use and yield gained from that capacity

(b) **Effectiveness** is the assessment of how well the resources are allocated to the most competitively significant activities within the value chain.

An analysis of resource utilisation

(a) **Identify the value activities.** This stage should include an assignment of costs and added value and an identification of the **critical activities**. These are the various value activities, which underpin the production and delivery of products or services, including the supply and distribution chains.

(b) **Identify the cost or value drivers.** The factors that sustain the competitive position are called **cost drivers** or **value drivers**. For example, e-commerce allows transportation companies of all sizes to exchange cargo documents electronically over the Internet. It enables shippers, freight forwarders and trucking firms to streamline document handling without the monetary and time investment required by the traditional document delivery systems. By using e-commerce, companies can reduce costs, improve data accuracy, streamline business processes, accelerate business cycles, and enhance customer service.

(c) **Identify the linkages.** An organisation's value activities and the linkages between them are sources of **competitive advantage**. There may be important links between the primary activities. For example, good communications between sales, operations and purchasing can help cut stocks; the purchase of more expensive or more reliable machinery and equipment may lead to cost savings and quality improvements in the manufacturing process. Competitors can often imitate the separate activities of an organisation but it is more difficult to copy the linkages within and between value chains.

5.3.2 Value network

> A **value network** can be defined as the links between an organisation and its strategic and non-strategic partners that form its external value chain. Activities that add value do not stop at the organisation's boundaries.

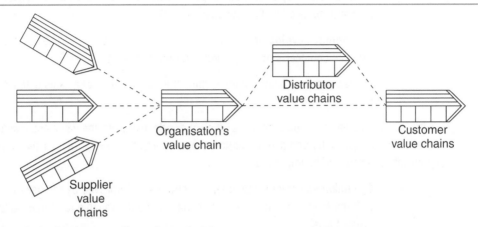

The impact of e-business on the value network

E-business is a vital element in the value network. It will help companies deliver better services to their customers, accelerate the growth of the e-commerce initiatives that are critical to their business, and lower their operating costs.

Using the Internet for e-business will allow customers to access price information, place delivery orders and track shipments. The Internet makes it easier for customers to do business with companies. For example, anything that simplifies the process of arranging transportation services will help build companies' business and enhance shareholder value. The only tools needed to take advantage of this solution are a personal computer and an Internet browser. By making more information available about the commercial side of companies, businesses will make their web site a place where customers will not only get detailed information about the services the company offers, but also where they can actually conduct business with the company. Ultimately, web sites can provide a universal, self-service system for customers. E-commerce functions are taking companies a substantial step forward by providing customers with a faster and easier way to do business with them.

5.4 Impact of IT on the value chain

Value chain analysis can be used to assess the impact of IS/IT and identify processes within the value chain where it can be used to add value

(a) **Inbound logistics** covers receiving, storing and handling raw material inputs. The use of IT includes stock control and systems such as Material Requirements Planning (MRP), Enterprise Resource Planning (ERP) and JIT.

(b) **Operations** are concerned with the transformation of the raw material inputs into finished goods or services. IT can be used to automate and improve tasks; examples include robots, process control, and machine tool control, Computer Aided Manufacturing (CAM), Computer Integrated Manufacturing (CIM) and Enterprise Resource Planning (ERP)

(c) **Outbound logistics** is concerned with the storing, distributing and delivering the finished goods to the customers. IT makes it possible to follow the progress of goods from pickup to delivery.

(d) **Marketing and sales** are responsible for communication with the customers. Supermarkets use EPOS systems information on stocks to aid speedy ordering and replenishment.

(e) **Service** covers all of the activities that occur after the point of sale eg, installation, repair and maintenance. Customer databases allow organisations to sell after-sales services.

Alongside all of these primary activities are the secondary, or support, activities of procurement, technology, human resource management and corporate infrastructure.

(a) At the inbound logistics stage of **procurement**, IT can automate purchasing decisions and can be used as a link to a supplier with EDI.

(b) **Technology development** includes Computer Aided Design (CAD) aiding operations to produce engineer's drawings and component design.

(c) **Human resource** applications include the maintenance of a skills database and staff planning.

Having identified areas that could be more efficient or effective from the value chain analysis, the IS/IT strategy can be used to try and determine how those activities, and in particular the competitively significant activities, can be improved.

(a) Can **linkages** between the different activities be improved by the use of IT? For example, information from support activities may be made available to primary activities on a more timely basis.

(b) Can IS/IT improve the **information flow** through the primary activities? For example, linking sales and marketing with operations or outbound logistics using a central database to provide sales and marketing with on-line details of products being produced.

(c) Can more effective **links** be formed with external entities? For example, can inbound logistics be improved by using EDI?

(d) Can IS/IT be used to **decrease the cost** of any activity? For example, is there room for more automation or transformation of activities, or even re-engineering using currently available IT tools and techniques?

5.5 Taking advantage of IT

Porter and Millar advocate five steps that senior executives may follow to take advantage of opportunities that the information revolution has created.

Porter and Millar advocate five steps that senior executives may follow to take advantage of opportunities that the information revolution has created.

Step 1 **Assess information intensity**. A high level of information content in either products or processes indicates that IT can play a strategic role.

Step 2 **Determine the role of IT in industry structure**. IT may have the potential to radically change the way in which the industry operates, including changing the basis of competition and moving its boundaries.

Step 3 **Identify and rank the ways in which IT might create competitive advantage**. Possible value chain-based applications include opportunities for reducing cost or enhancing differentiation and establishing new links between activities. There may also be opportunities to enter new market segments and to introduce new products.

Step 4 **Investigate how IT might spawn new businesses**. These might be based on the exploitation of new categories of information and the sale of information-processing capacity.

Step 5   **Develop a plan to exploit IT**. Effectively, this is the creation of a comprehensive strategy and has implications for most parts of the organisation.

For any organisation it is possible to assess the **information content** (the information intensity), of the value chain activities and linkages. *Porter and Millar's* **information intensity matrix** considers the role of IT and suggests how it can be exploited for competitive advantage. The matrix evaluates the information intensity of the value chain (how product value is transformed through activities and linkages in the value chain) against that of the product (what the buyer needs to know to obtain the product and to use it to obtain the desired result). When assessing the degree of information in the product, oil, for example, has a low information content while banking has a high information content.

The degree of information in the value chain also varies. It is low in the case of a cement manufacturer who makes a simple product in bulk, but high in the case of a complex, sophisticated process such as oil refining.

Information content of the product

	Low	High
High	Oil refining	Banking, Airlines
Low	Cement	Fashion

Information intensity of the value chain

If the information content of the **product** is high, IT can be used to **enhance product delivery** as, for example, with Internet sites for newspapers. When the information in the **value chain** is high, it implies that sophisticated information systems are required to **manage the linkages** optimally.

The segment where the information content of both the product and the value chain are **high** includes banking and financial services. For example, ATMs, credit cards, debit cards and customer databases have all been integrated to give a much more personalised service as well as lowering service costs. There are banks in the UK such as *First Direct* that have no branches and retail on line, through ATMs and 24 hour telephone phone links.

The segment where the information content of both the product and the value chain are **low** contains traditional process-manufactured, widely available commodity products with several potential producers, such as bricks and cement. The fact that information content is low does not mean that there is no scope for exploiting IT to achieve a business advantage. Firms in this segment might be low-cost producers who are looking for linkages in the value chain to contribute to overall cost leadership. For example, there could be a niche market for specialist bricks for example in garden design, where expertise is in short supply. Information about their use could provide added value. The production process offers little scope for IT but, since the process is presumably well known and closely controlled, information could be used to provide a more efficient operation. For example, airline pilots are encouraged to use autopilot to fly planes because consumption of fuel increases by as much as 30% during a manually controlled flight.

5.6 Restructuring the supply chain

Supply chain management options can be portrayed as a continuum from **vertical integration** to **virtual integration**.

Vertical integration has been extensively discussed elsewhere in this Study Text.

Vertical disintegration means that various diseconomies of scale or scope have broken a production process into separate companies, each performing a limited subset of activities required to create a finished product.

A **virtually integrated company** is one in which **core** business functions, as well as non-core functions, take place in external organisations. Virtually integrated companies are so tightly organised that it is often difficult to determine where one legal entity ends and another starts.

Supply chain management options can be portrayed as a continuum from **vertical integration** to **virtual integration**.

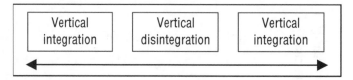

5.6.1 Vertical integration

Vertical integration a style of ownership and control with companies united through a hierarchy and sharing a common owner. It has been extensively discussed elsewhere in this Study Text.

5.6.2 Vertical disintegration

Vertical disintegration is a specific organisational form of production. As opposed to integration, in which production occurs within a single organisation, vertical disintegration means that various diseconomies of scale or scope have broken a production process into separate companies, each performing a limited subset of activities required to create a finished product.

One major reason for vertical disintegration is to **share risk**. Also, in some cases, smaller firms can be more responsive to changes in market conditions. Vertical disintegration is thus more likely when operating in volatile markets. Stability and standardised products more typically engender integration, as it provides the benefits of scale economies.

5.6.3 Example

Filmed entertainment was once highly vertically integrated into a handful of large studios that handled everything from production to theatrical presentation. After the Second World War, the industry was broken into small fragments, becoming highly vertically disintegrated, with specialised firms that only performed certain tasks such as editing, special effects, trailers and so on.

5.6.4 Virtual integration

A **virtually integrated company** is one in which **core** business functions, as well as non-core functions, take place in external organisations. Virtually integrated companies are so tightly organised that it is often difficult to determine where one legal entity ends and another starts. As a result, they operate as a single organisation with shared goals, processes and (sometimes) corporate cultures.

5.6.5 Example

An example of this restructuring is what has happened in the car industry. *Henry Ford's* original vision included controlling as many aspects of the end vehicle production as possible; from the production of raw materials in steel mills and rubber plantations, through all of the design, manufacturing, assembly and distribution activities. He managed a truly vertically integrated supply chain. Today the vision for most automotive vehicle manufacturers is to become virtual companies, owning only the brand and the customer. The design, system development, product sourcing, logistics, and even final assembly can all be outsourced to supply chain partners. Increasingly the goal is to replace physical assets with information in such a way that every member of this extended supply chain benefits. This forces the move from an environment of 'hard wired integration', where relationships are arms-length and adversarial, even across functional boundaries within the organisation, to an environment based on 'negotiated sourcing', where non-core activities are outsourced and collaborative partnerships are the norm.

5.6.6 Two kinds of integration

In most industries today it is not enough simply to optimise internal structures and infrastructures based on business strategy. The most successful manufacturers seem to be those that have carefully linked their internal processes to external suppliers and customers in **unique supply chains**. Upstream and downstream integration with suppliers and customers has emerged as an important element of manufacturing strategy. Typically, the goal is to create and coordinate manufacturing processes seamlessly across the supply chain in a manner that most competitors cannot very easily match

At the tactical level, the literature suggests that there are **two interrelated forms of integration** that manufacturers regularly employ.

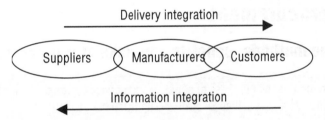

1   Co-ordinating and integrating the **forward physical flow** of deliveries between suppliers, manufacturers and customers, using just-in-time, mass customisation in the supply chain or by exploiting third party logistics

2   Backward co-ordination of information technologies and the flow of data for customers to suppliers

Information technologies allow multiple organisations to co-ordinate their activities in an effort to truly manage a supply chain. Integration using IT includes electronic data interchange (EDI) as well as sharing data for traditional planning and control systems.

According to *Hayes and Wheelwright* if this need to develop shared operational activities is accepted, then the strategic issues become **direction**, **degree** and **balance**.

(a)   In which **direction** should integration progress, towards customers and/or towards suppliers?

(b)   To what **degree** of integration should such activity be developed? How far should the company take downstream or upstream integration?

(c)   To what extent does each stage of the supply chain focus on supporting the total supply chain?

The fundamental concerns of direction and degree are the boundaries of the firm and whether the organisation should broaden or narrow the span of its operations, whereas balance deals with the resulting vertically linked activities, in terms of how dependent the suppliers and customers are on the firm, relative to how dependent the firm is on its suppliers and customers.

The challenges for manufacturing firms are shifting from **internal efficiency** to **supply chain efficiency**. The outward-shifting focus to the supply chain calls for information technology support systems that can handle information exchange between supply chain partners. The information can be integrated through ordinary means of communications such as telephone, fax and e-mail; it can also be integrated through dedicated supply chain planning software.

E-business is revolutionising the way supply chains are configured and managed and, in response, many supply chains are becoming more virtual. They are developing into looser affiliations of companies, organised as a supply network, where direct ownership is changing dramatically.

In all sectors, e-business is increasing the pressure for supply chain responsiveness in three ways.

(a) **Increased competition**. Easier market entry enables new entrants to steal significant market share at the expense of unresponsive existing suppliers.

(b) **Increased volumes and speed of data**. There is a requirement to gather, process and act on massively increasing volumes of data in a rapid and intelligent manner.

(c) **More demanding customer requirements**. These include reduced cost, shorter lead times and reliability of supply.

Additionally, what is not well recognised is the increased capability of customers to bypass their traditional supplier and **cut out the middle man**. This threat is equally applicable right along the supply chain, with the consumer bypassing the retailer, and businesses bypassing tiers of their suppliers. To remain in the chain, companies do not just have to demonstrate the value they add, but also demonstrate their ability to manage their own suppliers.

6 E-procurement

6.1 The methods, benefits and risks of e-procurement

FAST FORWARD

E-procurement is the purchase of supplies and services through the Internet and other information and networking systems, such as Electronic Data Interchange (EDI).

It is typically operated through a secure website, possibly using a paperless system based on a purchasing card. It brings time and efficiency improvements but it also brings threats to control and security. Implementation may proceed according to a variety of models, but initially it is easiest to introduce IS to only part of the improvement cycle.

An important part of many B2B sites, e-procurement is also referred to by other terms, such as **supplier exchange**.

Traditionally, e-procurement has been seen as a simple process from creation of need to placing an electronic purchase order with a supplier and the possible payment by BACS. Today the transactional process is considered to be only part of the e-procurement function. It includes purchasing, transportation, goods receipt and warehousing before the goods are used. A properly implemented system can connect companies and their business processes directly with suppliers while managing all interactions between them. This includes management of correspondence, bids, questions and answers, previous pricing, and multiple emails sent to multiple participants.

It focuses on the complete purchasing mix, or the 'five rights of purchasing', which are that goods and services must be delivered:

- At the right **time**
- In the right **quantity**
- In the right **quality**
- At the right **price**
- From the right **vendor**

6.1.1 Methods

Typically, e-procurement websites allow authorised and registered users to log in using a password. The supplying organisation will set up its website so that it recognises the purchaser once logged in and presents a list of items that the purchaser regularly buys. This saves searching for the items required and also avoids the need to key in name, address and delivery details. Depending on the approach, buyers or sellers may specify prices or invite bids. Transactions can be initiated and completed. Once the purchases are made the organisation will periodically be billed by the supplier. Ongoing purchases may qualify customers for volume discounts or special offers.

A very limited form of electronic procurement is the **purchasing card**, which is a paperless purchase and payment system aimed at the end-user who can now order and pay for goods directly with a small number of suppliers. Buyers identify themselves with their card number when placing an order; the supplier checks the purchase card number and, if correct, authorises it with the bank. The bank pays the supplier in 2 to 5 days, and the supplier ships the goods.

6.1.2 Benefits of e-procurement

Cost reduction	Might include process efficiencies, reduction in the actual cost of goods and services and reduced purchasing agent overheads
Reduced stock levels	Knowing product numbers, bid prices and contact points can help businesses close a deal while other suppliers are struggling to gather their relevant data
Control	The ability to control parts inventories more effectively
Wider choice of supplier	In theory, resources can be sourced from suppliers anywhere in the world, perhaps at much lower prices than could be obtained if the organisation only considered local suppliers.
Improved manufacturing cycles	Moving to e-sourcing speeds up the sourcing process dramatically but the increased efficiency and speed can also put the rest of a supply chain in chaos if it is not prepared to step up its performance to meet the increased speed in the purchasing link of the chain.
Intangible benefits	Staff are able to concentrate on their prime function and there is financial transparency and accountability.
Benefits to suppliers	Reduction in ordering and processing costs, reduced paperwork, improved cash flow and reduced cost of credit control

6.1.3 Risks of e-procurement

(a) **Control.** If anyone can order goods from anywhere there is a major risk that unauthorised purchases will be made. There is also an increased likelihood that purchases will be made from suppliers who cannot deliver the required quality (or cannot deliver at all!)

(b) **Organisational risk.** In moving to an e-procurement tool, an adopting company will make a substantial investment in the software, but for any number of reasons the implementation may never take flight. Users may not adapt to it well. Suppliers may reject the technology or new process. Technical issues may stall the implementation. Also, managing the internal processes around the changeover is challenging

(c) **Data security.** Putting a company's spending online means dealing with the security issues that come with any Internet-related deployment. This brings up questions like: Who has access to our data? Where is it stored? How is it protected? What happens if we change providers? Do we get our data back? Do they sell spending data to our competitors?

(d)   **Management loses spending control.** There is a perceived risk that moving to e-procurement will put spending decisions in the wrong hands internally and management will lose decision-making control over who spends how much on what.

(e)   **Supply chain problems.** Moving to e-sourcing speeds up the sourcing process dramatically but the increased efficiency and speed can also destabilise rest of a supply chain if it is not able to step up its performance to meet the increased speed in the purchasing link of the chain.

6.2 Options and models for implementing e-procurement

Model	How it works	Examples
Public Web	Individual buyers find individual suppliers on the web and make a purchase. There is no structural relation between buyer and supplier	Webshops like *www.amazon.com*
Exchange	Suppliers and buyers trade through a third party open marketplace. They have no structural relationship even though they may regularly deal with each other.	*www.autobuytel.com*
Supplier centric	An individual supplier gives access to buying organisations for a pre-negotiated product range. Buyer and supplier have a contractual relationship	*www.dell.com* *www.cisco.com*
Buyer centric	Individual companies have contracts with a number of different suppliers. The catalogue and ordering system are maintained within the buying organisation. The system is fully integrated into corporate financial control and reporting systems.	Many software suppliers
B2B Marketplace	An independent third party has agreements with a number of buying and supplying organisations. Buyers and supplier deal with each other through a marketplace. Both are bound by agreements with the marketplace	*www.productview.com*

In terms of the options available to organisations, historically, it has been easier to implement systems that only cover part of the procurement cycle.

For example, buyers may choose a minimal involvement such as a stock control system or a Web based catalogue or they may integrate the entry of the order through a database workflow system. Some networked accounting systems allow staff in the buying department to enter an order, which can then be used by accounting staff to make payment when the invoice arrives.

Enterprise Resource Planning (ERP) systems integrate all the facilities. Such integrated business software systems power a corporate information structure, thus helping companies to control their inventory, purchasing, manufacturing, finance and personnel operations. They allow an organisation to automate and integrate most of its business processes, share common data and practices across the whole enterprise and produce and access information in a real-time environment. ERP may also incorporate transactions with an organisation's suppliers. They help large national and multinational companies in particular to manage geographically dispersed and complex operations. For example, an organisation's UK sales office may be responsible for marketing, selling and servicing a product assembled in the US using parts manufactured in France and Hong Kong. ERP enables the organisation to understand and manage the demand placed on the plant in France.

Chapter Roundup

- Electronic business, or e-business, is the automation of business processes of all types through electronic means. This may be rrestricted to email or may extend to a fully-featured website or an e-marketplace. E-business that includes a financial transaction is known as e-commerce. E-business is radically different from ordinary business and brings six categories of benefit.

  Costs are reduced.
  Capability is increased.
  Communications are improved.
  Control is enhanced.
  Customer service is improved.
  Competitive advantage may be achieved, depending on competitors' reactions.

  Adoption of e-business methods may be hindered by a range of obstacles including lack of skills; lack of Internet use and awareness among businesses and the wider population; and feats about privacy, effectiveness, cost, security and so on.

- Both businesses and customers can originate e-commerce activity; thus there are four main categories: B2B, B2C, C2B and C2C. **Channel structures** are the means by which products and services are delivered to customers. **Disintermediation** removes intermediaries from supply channels while **reintermediation** establishes new ones. **Countermediation** is the creation of a new intermediary by an established company to compete *via* a business with established intermediaties.

- Rappa describes nine business models. E-commerce business models may also be categorised by characteristics such as value proposition, revenue model and market opportunity.

- **System architecture** is the arrangement of software, machinery and tasks in an information system needed to achieve a specific functionality.

  The **Internet** enables computers across the world to communicate via telecommunications links.

  The **World Wide Web** is a navigation system within the Internet. It is based on a technology called **hypertext** which allows documents stored on host computers on the Internet to be linked to one another.

  An **intranet** is used to disseminate and exchange information 'in-house' within an organisation.

  An **extranet** is used to communicate with selected people outside the organisation.

  In general, all of the machines on the Internet can be categorised into two types: servers and clients. The machines that provide services to other machines are servers. And the machines that are used to connect to those services are clients.

  Each machine on the Internet is assigned a unique address called an IP address.

  There are several levels to the interaction between a client and a server, from the physical pieces of wire making the connection, through the transfer and checking of data, security problems of access and logging on, to the final presentation to and interaction with the user. The International Standards Organisation (ISO) has defined seven levels in a standard called Open Systems Interconnection.

  A **protocol stack** is a group of protocols that all work together to allow software or hardware to perform a function. The TCP/IP protocol stack is a good example. It uses four layers that map to the OSI model.

  Alternatives to PC-based Internet access include interactive digital television and wireless or mobile access.

- The Internet has the capacity to transform many businesses *via* the introduction of new technology and skills and, eventually, the re-positioning of the offering to fit the new market conditions.

A **strategy for e-commerce** should be considered at the highest level of management and it is particularly necessary that it should conform to the standard criteria for strategic choice: suitability, acceptability and feasibility.

Suitability for most companies, e-commerce will be a supplement to more traditional operations, with the website forming a supplementary medium for communication and sales.

Acceptability. The e-commerce strategy must be acceptable to important stakeholders. Distributors are particularly important here.

Feasibility. Feasibility is a matter of **resources**. The fundamental resource is cash, but the availability of the skilled labour needed to establish and administer a website will be crucial to the e-commerce strategy.

- IT has the capacity to transform businesses. Corporate and e-business strategies thus become complementary, each supporting and influencing the other.

- *Skidmore and Eva* argue that the selection and prioritisation of IS developments is strongly influenced by the level of *IT maturity* that an organisation has reached, so this should be one of the first issues to be determined for understanding effective project selection.

  Several stage models have been proposed for in assessing maturity of capability. Such models can also be used as guides to future development.

- A **supply chain** encompasses all activities and information flows necessary for the transformation of goods from the origin of the raw material to when the product is finally consumed or discarded.

  A supply chain always includes push and pull elements. The pull based element is particularly relevant on IS for feedback and control, since it aims to eliminate buffer stocks by increasing responsiveness.

- IS may be used to improve the working of the links between activities in the value chain and between value chains in the value network. One important consequence of this is that improved communication with customers results, making it easier for them to purchase.

- *Porter and Millar* advocate five steps that senior executives may follow to take advantage of opportunities that the information revolution has created.

- Supply chain management options can be portrayed as a continuum from **vertical integration** to **virtual integration**.

  Vertical integration has been extensively discussed elsewhere in this Study Text.

  Vertical disintegration means that various diseconomies of scale or scope have broken a production process into separate companies, each performing a limited subset of activities required to create a finished product.

  A **virtually integrated company** is one in which **core** business functions, as well as non-core functions, take place in external organisations. Virtually integrated companies are so tightly organised that it is often difficult to determine where one legal entity ends and another starts.

- **E-procurement** is the purchase of supplies and services through the Internet and other information and networking systems, such as Electronic Data Interchange (EDI).

  It is typically operated through a secure website, possibly using a paperless system based on a purchasing card. It brings time and efficiency improvements but it also brings threats to control and security. Implementation may proceed according to a variety of models, but initially it is easiest to introduce IS to only part of the improvement cycle.

Quick Quiz

1   What distinguishes e-commerce from e-business?

2   What is disintermediation?

3   How does the infomediary model of e-business work?

4   What is system architecture?

5   What are the six stages of the IS evolution model associated with Nolan?

6   Is the bull whip effect associated with the push model or the pull model of the supply chain?

7   What are the axes of Porter and Millar's information intensity matrix?

8   What are the models available for implementing e-procurement?

Answers to Quick Quiz

1   E-business involves transactions over the Internet. If an e-business transaction is of a financial nature, it is e-commerce.

2   The removal of intermediaries from a supply chain

3   The infomediary collects data about consumers and their purchasing habits and sells it to other businesses.

4   The arrangement of software, machinery and tasks in an information system needed to achieve a specific functionality

5   Initiation, contagion, control, integration; and subsequently, data administration and maturity

6   The push model

7   Information content of the product and information intensity of the value chain

8   Public web, exchange, supplier centric, buyer centric, B2B market place

Now try the questions below from the Exam Question Bank

Number	Level	Marks	Time
Q9	Examination	10	18 mins

11

E-marketing

Topic list	Syllabus reference
1 E-marketing	E2(a), (b)
2 Customer relationship management	E2(b), (c), (d), (e)
3 Software and CRM	E2(f)

Introduction

This second chapter on e-business is largely concerned with marketing aspects and the way that various aspects of Internet technology can be used to build and maintain marketing relationships.

Study guide

		Intellectual level
E3	**E-business application: downstream supply chain management**	
(a)	Define the scope and media of e-marketing	
(b)	Highlight how the media of e-marketing can be used when developing an effective e-marketing plan	
(c)	Explore the characteristics of the media of e-marketing using the '6I's of Interactivity, Intelligence, Individualisation, Integration, Industry structure and Independence of location	
(d)	Evaluate the effect of the media of e-marketing on the traditional marketing mix of product, promotion, price, place, people, processes and physical evidence	
(e)	Assess the importance of on-line branding in e-marketing and compare it with traditional branding	
E4	**E-business application: customer relationship management**	
(a)	Define the meaning and scope of customer relationship management	
(b)	Explore different methods of acquiring customers through exploiting electronic media	
(c)	Evaluate different buyer behaviour amongst online customers	
(d)	Recommend techniques for retaining customers using electronic media	
(e)	Recommend how electronic media may be used to increase the activity and value of established, retained customers	
(f)	Discuss the scope of a representative software package solution designed to support customer relationship management	

Exam guide

This is very practical material relating to strategic implementations or, as JS&W put it, **strategy into action**. As such, it could well be examined in a dedicated question requiring in-depth knowledge, probably in Section B. It also lends itself to a less demanding coverage as part of a large question, perhaps in Section A.

1 E-marketing

FAST FORWARD

E-marketing is the application of IS and Internet techniques to the achievement of marketing objectives. Most marketing activities can be enhanced by the use of such techniques, including branding, customer service and sales.

1.1 E-marketing – scope and media

Key term

E-marketing is described by *Chaffey* in *E-business and E-commerce Management* as 'the application of the Internet and related digital technologies to achieve marketing objectives'.

Marketing objectives include identifying, anticipating and satisfying customer requirements profitably.

- **Identifying** – using the Internet to find out customers' needs and wants

- **Anticipating** – the demand for digital services

- **Satisfying** – achieving customer satisfaction raises issues over whether the site is easy to use, whether it performs adequately and how are the physical products dispatched.

Essentially, e-marketing means using digital technologies to help sell goods or services. The basics of marketing remain the same – creating a strategy to deliver the right messages to the right people. What has changed is the number of options available. These include pay per click advertising, banner ads, e-mail marketing and affiliate marketing, interactive advertising, search engine marketing (including search engine optimisation) and blog marketing.

Though businesses will continue to make use of traditional marketing methods, such as advertising, direct mail and PR, e-marketing adds a whole new element to the marketing mix and is a valuable complement. It gives businesses of any size access to the mass market at an affordable price and, unlike TV or print advertising, it allows truly personalised marketing.

1.1.1 Key marketing functions the Internet can perform

(a) **Creating company and product awareness** – communicating essential information about the company and its brands. Such information may have a financial orientation to help attract potential investors, or it may focus on the unique features and benefits of its product lines.

(b) **Branding** – is a marketing communications activity. The intent is to have the public perceive a brand in a positive manner. With the amount of advertising being devoted to the Internet increasing each year, the frequency of visits to a site will also increase. Consequently, a web site will play a more prominent role in building brand image. Online communications should therefore be similar in appearance and style to communications in the traditional media so as to present a consistent brand image.

(c) **Offering incentives** – many sites offer discounts for purchasing online. Electronic coupons, bonus offers, and contests are now quite common. Such offers are intended to stimulate immediate purchase before a visitor leaves a web site and encourage repeat visits.

(d) **Lead generation** – the Internet is an interactive medium. Visitors to a site leave useful information behind when they fill in boxes requesting more information (eg, name, address, telephone number, and e-mail address). A site may also ask for demographic information that can be added to the company's database. This information is retained for future mailings about similar offers, or they can be turned over to a sales force for follow-up if it is a business-to-business marketing situation.

(e) **Customer service** – in any form of marketing, customer service is important. Satisfied customers hold positive attitudes about a company and are apt to return to buy more goods. Right now, customer service is perceived as a weak link in Internet marketing. Customers are concerned about who they should call for technical assistance or what process to follow should goods need to be returned. Some customer service tactics commonly used include frequently asked questions (FAQs) and return e-mail systems. It is apparent that organisations will have to spend more time and money developing effective customer service systems.

(f) **E-mail databases** – organisations retain visitor information in a database. E-mailing useful and relevant information to prospects and customers helps build stronger relationships. An organisation must be careful that it does not distribute spam on the Internet. Spam refers to the delivery of unsolicited or unwanted e-mail.

(g)   **Online transaction** – organisations are capable of selling online if the web site is user friendly. Sites that are difficult to navigate create frustration in visitors. Presently, the business-to-business market is booming with business transactions. Organisations in the supply chain are linking together to achieve efficiencies in the buying-selling process.

1.1.2 Specific benefits of e-marketing

(a)   **Global reach** – a website can reach anyone in the world who has Internet access. This allows you to find new markets and compete globally for only a small investment.

(b)   **Lower cost** – a properly planned and effectively targeted e-marketing campaign can reach the right customers at a much lower cost than traditional marketing methods.

(c)   **The ability to track and measure results** – marketing by email or banner advertising makes it easier to establish how effective your campaign has been. You can obtain detailed information about customers' responses to your advertising.

(d)   **24-hour marketing** – with a website your customers can find out about your products even if your office is closed.

(e)   **Personalisation** – if your customer database is linked to your website, then whenever someone visits the site, you can greet them with targeted offers. The more they buy from you, the more you can refine your customer profile and market effectively to them.

(f)   **One-to-one marketing** – e-marketing lets you reach people who want to know about your products and services instantly. For example, many people take their mobile phone and Personal Digital Assistant (PDA) wherever they go. Combine this with the personalised aspect of e-marketing, and you can create very powerful, targeted campaigns.

(g)   **More interesting campaigns** – e-marketing lets you create interactive campaigns using music, graphics and videos. You could send your customers a game or a quiz – whatever you think will interest them.

(h)   **Better conversion rate** – if you have a website, then your customers are only ever a few clicks away from completing a purchase. Unlike other media which require people to get up and make a phone call, post a letter or go to a shop, e-marketing is seamless.

Together, all of these aspects of e-marketing have the potential to add up to more sales.

As a component of e-commerce it can include information management; public relations; customer service and sales

1.2 Developing an effective e-marketing plan

It is important to recognise that planning for e-marketing does not mean starting from scratch. Any online e-communication must be **consistent with the overall marketing goals** and **current marketing efforts** of the organisation.

The key strategic decisions for e-marketing are common with strategic decisions for traditional marketing. They involve selecting target customer groups and specifying how to deliver value to these groups. Segmentation, targeting, differentiation and positioning all contribute to effective digital marketing.

The **SOSTAC ® planning framework** developed by Paul Smith provides a structured and effective approach to marketing strategy. It can be used by managers in the private, public and non-profit sectors.

S = Situation Analysis	Where are we now? What is the external environment in which we are operating? What are our own strengths and weaknesses?
O = Objectives	Where do we want to get to? What is our goal?
S = Strategies	How do we get there? What do we need to do to be successful?
T = Tactics	What are the individual steps we need to take to achieve our objective?
A = Actions	What are the things we need to do? What is our 'to-do' list? Who will do what?
C = Control	What will we measure to know we are succeeding? How will we know when we have arrived?

The planning framework is expanded in the diagram below to show the techniques/actions that make up each stage:

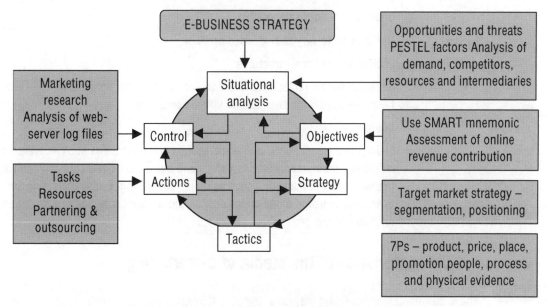

Framework for e-marketing planning

In developing an effective e-marketing plan, the media of e-marketing used at certain stages will include the following.

Competitor analysis	Scanning competitor Internet sites.
	Competitor benchmarking to compare e-commerce services within a market.
	Competitive intelligence systems give a structured approach to monitoring and disseminating information on competitor activities
Intermediary analysis	Identify and compare intermediaries for a marketplace
	Search portals and look for new approaches for traffic building
	Research whether competitors are using disintermediation or reintermediation

Internal marketing audit	Focus on e-market measurement:
	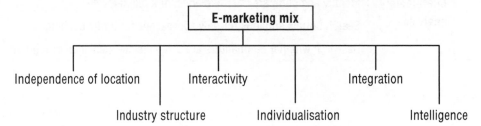
	Channel promotion — Acquisition costs, Referrers
	Channel behaviour — Who? How?
	Channel satisfaction — Opinions? Attitudes? Brand impact?
	Channel outcomes — Leads? Sales?
	Channel profitability — ROI? Profitability?
	Applying web analytics tools to measure the contribution of leads, sales and brand involvement currently delivered by online communications such as search engine marketing, online advertising and E-mail marketing in conjunction with the web site
	Create online CRM capabilities to understand customers' characteristics, needs and behaviours and to deliver targeted, personalised value
Objective setting	Online revenue contribution
Strategy	Identify target market by assessing size, segments, needs and competitive action
	Online value proposition (OVP)
Tactics	Use Internet to vary the extended product
	Look at new channel structures
	Research people replacements: autoresponders, e-mail notification, call-back facility, FAQs, on-site search engines and virtual assistants
	Branding
	Managing the continuous online marketing communications such as search engine marketing, partnerships, sponsorships and affiliate arrangements and campaign-based E-marketing communications such as Online advertising, E-mail marketing and microsites to encourage usage of the online service and to support customer acquisition and retention campaigns

1.3 Characteristics of the media of e-marketing

FAST FORWARD

The employment of e-marketing may be analysed and planned using the six Is.

- Independence of location
- Industry structure
- Integration
- Interactivity
- Individualisation
- Intelligence

The six Is of marketing developed at Cranfield by *McDonald and Wilson* in 1999, summarise the ways in which the Internet can add customer value and hence improve the organisation's marketing effectiveness.

```
                        E-marketing mix

Independence of location        Interactivity              Integration

        Industry structure           Individualisation          Intelligence
```

By considering and questioning each of these aspects of the new media marketing managers can develop plans to accommodate the characteristics of the new media.

Independence of location	Do you exploit any opportunities to deliver information-based products and services electronically? Electronic media gives the possibility of communicating globally –giving opportunities of selling into markets that may not have been previously accessible.
Industry structure	Industry restructuring includes the following: Redesigning business processes redrawing the market map in form of new market segments or increasing the marketing boundaries adopting IT enabled services (ITeS).
Integration	Do you have detailed knowledge of individual customers, influencers or consumers? Do you share this knowledge across all customer-facing parts of the business? Advertising products/services on the Web is easy. It is more difficult, but absolutely crucial to gather vital customer information, obtain customer feedback, use existing knowledge about the customer and exploit the Web's interactive nature to add value through product configuration, online pricing and so on.
Interactivity	Do you use interactive media to allow your customers to communicate with you? Do you listen to what they say and respond appropriately in a continuing dialogue? Traditional media are mainly 'push' media –the marketing message is broadcast from company to customer – with limited interaction. On the Internet it is usually a customer who seeks information on a web – it is a 'pull' mechanism. The growing use of carefully targeted direct mail as a means of communicating with individual customers has led some to call this 'the age of addressability'
Individualisation	Do you use your customer knowledge to tailor products and services to the needs of particular individuals or segments? Do you tailor all your communications to the characteristics of the recipients? Communications can be tailored to the individual unlike traditional media where the same message is broadcast to everyone
Intelligence	Do you inform your marketing strategy with intelligence gleaned from your operational systems at the customer interface eg, through analysis of customer needs, segmentation, prioritising segments according to customer lifetime value etc? The Internet can be used as a low cost method of collecting marketing information about customer perceptions of products and services. The web site also records information every time a user clicks on a link. Log file analysers will identify the type of promotions or products customers are responding to and how patterns vary over time

Example

The best-known example of electronic commerce – book-selling, exemplifies how the Internet can be used for an interactive dialogue with a known customer.

Web sites such as *Amazon.com* exploit the web's interactive nature to allow the customer to search for books on particular topics, track the status of an order placed earlier, and ask for recommendations of books similar to their favourites, read reviews placed by other customers, and so on. The web site builds knowledge of the customer which allows it, for example, to notify them by e-mail if a new book appears on a topic of particular interest.

1.4 E-marketing and the 7Ps

More specific concepts for the development of e-marketing may be based on the seven Ps.

- The augmented **product** can be extended through web information and interactivity.
- **Pricing** can be made transparent; dynamic pricing may be used.
- The global reach of the Internet has great implications for **place**, with the creation of new marketplaces and channel structures.
- **Promotion** can be previously targeted *via* customer databases.
- **People** can be replaced by software to a varying extent.
- **Processes** may be automated.
- **Physical evidence** consists of the customer's experience of using the organisation's e-marketing tools in general and of its website in particular

Marketing on the Internet brings many new opportunities not readily available or affordable using conventional marketing methods.

The marketing mix is the combination of marketing activities that an organisation engages in so as to best meet the needs of its targeted market. Because of changes in the market and the behaviour of the customers, future marketing should focus more on delivering value to the customer and become better at placing the customer – and not the product – in the centre. In some texts, the 4 Ps have been renamed the 4 Cs.

- Product becomes **customer value**
- Place becomes **customer convenience**
- Promotion becomes **customer communication**
- Price becomes **customer cost**

Another change because marketing has expanded into service delivery, means the original 4Ps of the marketing mix have been joined by three more Ps (Dibb and Simkin, 1994) (see diagram below):

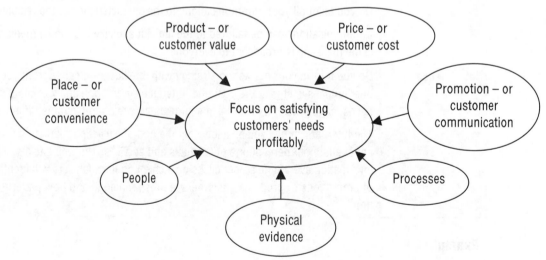

In this section we can show how e-commerce provides the opportunities for the marketer to vary the seven elements of the marketing mix.

1.4.1 Product (or customer value)

This is the element of the marketing mix that involves researching customers' needs and developing appropriate products. *Philip Kotler,* in *Principles of Marketing,* devised a very interesting concept of benefit building with a product. He suggested that a product should be viewed in three levels.

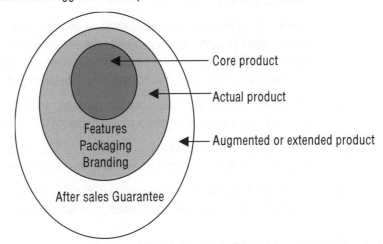

Core product – what is the core benefit the product offers? Customers who purchase a camera are buying more then just a camera they are purchasing memories.

Actual product – all cameras capture memories. The strategy at this level involves organisations **branding**, **adding features** and benefits to ensure that their product offers a differential advantage from their competitors.

Augmented or **extended product**: What additional non-tangible benefits can you offer? Competition at this level is based around after sales service, warranties, delivery and so on.

What does buying products online offer over one to one sales?

(a)   The ability to deliver interactivity and more detailed information through the Internet is the key to enhancing the augmented or extended product offering online.

(b)   The buyer knows immediately about product features, the facts, not a sales person's interpretations.

(c)   The buying process is customised for returning visitors, making repeat purchases easier. Organisations can also offer immediately ancillary products along with the main purchase. *EasyJet* for example can readily bundle its flights, hotels and car hire through suitable design of its web site

(d)   The product can also be customised to consumers needs eg *www.nike.com* offer customised trainers to users online. Users can design and see their trainers online before they order

1.4.2 Price (or customer cost)

The Internet has made pricing very competitive. Many costs such as store cost and staff cost have disappeared for completely online stores, placing price pressures on traditional retailers.

(a)   The Internet increases customer knowledge through **increased price transparency** since it becomes much quicker to shop around and compare quoted prices by visiting supplier web sites. Even more significant is the use of price comparison sites by consumers. Sites such as *Kelkoo.com* give a single location that empowers the consumer to quickly find out the best price from a range of suppliers for a range of products from books and CDs to white goods. Such easy access to information helps to maintain prices within the online world.

(b)   **Dynamic pricing** gives the ability to test prices or to offer differential pricing for different segments or in response to variations in demand. For some product areas such as ticketing it may be possible to dynamically alter prices in line with demand. *Tickets.com* adjusts concert ticket prices according to demand and have been able to achieve 45% more revenue per event as a result.

(c)   Different types of pricing may be possible on the Internet, particularly for digital, downloadable products. Software and music has traditionally been sold for a continuous right to use. The Internet offers new options such as payment per use; rental at a fixed cost per month or a lease arrangement. Bundling options may also be more possible.

(d)   The growth of online auctions also helps consumers to dictate price. The online auction company *eBay* has grown in popularity with thousands of buyers and seller bidding daily.

(e)   E-pricing can also easily reward loyal customers. Technology allows repeat visitors to be tracked, easily allowing loyalty incentives to be targeted towards them.

(f)   Payment is also easy; *PayPal* or online credit cards allow for easy payments. However the downside to this is Internet fraud, which is growing rapidly around the world.

1.4.3 Place (or customer convenience)

Allen and Fjermestad argue that that the Internet has the greatest implications for **place** in the marketing mix since it has a global reach.

E-Business Models

Types of marketplaces	Set up by	Main aim
Controlled by sellers	Single vendor seeking many buyers	To retain value and power in any transaction
Controlled by buyers	One or more buyers	To shift value and power in marketplace onto the buyer's side Buyer intermediaries can also be there to act as agents
Neutral marketplaces	Third party intermediaries to match many buyers to many sellers	To match buyers to sellers at an auction Commission based

Choosing a marketplace depends on four factors:

- Are there transactions or benefits to be realised?
- Is electronic market for product developing quickly?
- Does company have substantial market share or buying power?
- Would a neutral intermediary be beneficial?

Types of e-commerce marketplace

- B2C and B2B (can be combined or separate eg, *Dell*)
- C2C
- auctions, (*eBay, QXL*)
- consumer reviews (*Bizrate*),
- Games etc (*There.com*)
- C2B
- Customer bids (*priceline*)

New channel structures – strategies need to be developed for the following forms.

(a)   **Distintermediation** – is there an option for selling direct? When assessing this option there will be a number of barriers and facilitators to this change. A significant threat arising from the introduction of an Internet channel is that while disintermediation gives a company the opportunity to sell direct and increase profitability on products, it can also threaten distribution arrangements with existing partners.

(b)   **Reintermediation** – new intermediaries created through re-intermediation, for example Lastminute.com or JamJar.com, should be evaluated for suitability for partnering with for affiliate arrangements. These intermediaries receive a commission on each sale resulting from a referral from their site.

(c)   **Countermediation** – should the organisation partner with another independent intermediary, or set up its own independent intermediary? For example, a group of European airlines have joined forces to form *Opodo* which is intended to counter independent companies such as *Lastminute.com* or eBookers offering discount fares.

Navigation – there are three aspects of navigation that are key to achieving competitive advantage online.

(a)   **Reach** – this is the potential audience of the e-commerce site. Reach can be increased by moving from a single site to representation with a large number of different intermediaries.

(b)   **Richness** – this is the depth or detail of information which is both collected about the customer and provided to the customer. This is related to the product element of the mix.

(c)   **Affiliation** – this refers to whose interest the selling organisation represents – consumers or suppliers. This particularly applies to retailers. It suggests that customers will favour retailers who provide them with the richest information on comparing competitive products.

Localisation – providing a local site, usually a language specific version, is referred to as localisation. A site may need to support customers from a range of countries; they may have different product needs, language differences and cultural differences.

1.4.4 Promotion (or customer communication)

Marketing communications are used to inform customers and other stakeholders about an organisation and its products.

(a)   There are new ways of applying each of the elements of the **communications mix** (advertising, sales promotions, PR and direct marketing), using new media such as the web and e-mail. Most organisations today have some form of webpage used in most if not all advertisements. Placing banner advertisements on other web pages is a common form of e-promotion. Web public relations (WPR) is another approach to promoting online. Newsworthy stories based on product or service launches can be placed on the company's webpage, or WPR articles sent to review sites for consumers to read.

(b)   The Internet can be used at different stages of the **buying process**. For instance, the main role of the web is often in providing further information rather completing the sale. Think of car purchase. Many consumers will now review models online, but most still buy in the real world.

(c)   Promotional tools may be used to assist in different stages of **customer relationship management** from customer acquisition to retention. In a web context this includes gaining initial visitors to the site and gaining repeat visits using eg, direct e-mail reminders of site proposition and new offers.

(d)   The Internet can be integrated into **campaigns**. For example, we are currently seeing many direct response print and TV ad campaigns where the web is used to manage entry into a prize draw and to profile the entrant for future communications.

These general technological trends impact across the promotional mix.

Promotion activity	Impact/opportunity	Examples of supporting technology
Advertising	Reach more customers worldwide Target audiences more specifically Increase response via interactivity	Websites and ads Specialist TV channels Direct Response TV, SMS text messaging
Sales promotion	Target segment/individual interests and preferences Facilitate/motivate response Online discounts (lower admin costs)	Customer databases, EPOS data Online entry/coupons Online transaction
Direct marketing	Personalised, one-to-one messages Permission-based database/contacts to enhance response rate Speed and interactivity of response Direct response/transaction	Database E-mail, website, SMS requests for info E-mail + website links E-commerce sites
PR and publicity	Speed of information dissemination and response to crisis/issues	E-mail media releases and online information
Marketing/sales support	Publicising sponsorships Publicising exhibition attendance Up-to-date information for sales force & call centre staff	Website Website/e-mail clients Access to product/stock and customer database
Internal marketing	Staff access to information relevant to their jobs Co-ordination/identification of dispersed offices and off-site staff	Intranet newsletters, bulletins, policy info E-mail, tele– and video-conferencing
Network marketing	Supplier/client access to information relevant to business relationship	Extranet: access to selected information

1.4.5 People

The **people** element of the marketing mix is the way an organisations' staff interact with customers and other stakeholders during sales and pre and post sales. *Smith and Chaffey* (2001) suggest that online, part of the consideration for the people element of the mix is the consideration of the tactics by which people can be replaced or automated.

(a)   **Autoresponders** automatically generate a response when a company e-mails an organisation, or submits an online form.

(b)   **E-mail notification** may be automatically generated by a company's systems to update customers on the progress of their orders. Such notifications might show, for example, three stages: order received; item now in stock; order dispatched.

(c) **Call-back facility** requires that customers fill in their phone number on a form and specify a convenient time to be contacted. Dialling from a representative in the call centre occurs automatically at the appointed time and the company pays

(d) **Frequently Asked Questions (FAQ)** can pre-empt enquires. The art lies in compiling and categorising the questions so customers can easily find both the question and a helpful answer

(e) **On site search engines** help customers find what they are looking for quickly. Site maps are a related feature

(f) **Virtual assistants** come in varying degrees of sophistication and usually help to guide the customer through a maze of choices.

1.4.6 Process

The **process** element of the marketing mix is the internal methods and procedures companies use to achieve all marketing functions such as new product development, promotion, sales and customer service. The restructuring of the organisation and channel structures described for product, price, place and promotion all require new **processes**.

Exam focus point

> Note the link here to process redesign.

1.4.7 Physical evidence

The physical evidence element of the marketing mix is the tangible expression of a product and how it is purchased and used. In an online context, physical evidence is customers' experience of the company through the web site and associated support. It includes issues such as ease of use, navigation, availability and performance. Responsiveness to e-mail enquiries is a key aspect of performance. The process must be right to enable an acceptable response within the notified service standards such as 24 hours.

1.4.8 Example

A university can put its reading list on a website and students wishing to purchase any given book can click directly through to an online bookseller such as Amazon.com. The university gets a commission; the online bookseller gets increased business; the student gets a discount. Everyone benefits except the traditional bookshop.

Benefits of e-marketing
It promotes **transparent pricing** – because potential customers can readily compare prices not only from suppliers within any given country, but also from suppliers across the world.
It facilitates **personalised attention** – even if such attention is actually administered through impersonal, yet highly sophisticated IT systems and customer database manipulation.
It provides sophisticated **market segmentation** opportunities. Approaching such segments may be one of the few ways in which e-commerce entrepreneurs can create **competitive advantage**.
The web can either be a **separate** or a **complementary** channel.
A new phenomenon is emerging called **dynamic pricing**. Companies can rapidly change their prices to reflect the current state of demand and supply.

These new trends are creating **pressure** for companies. The main threat facing companies is that **prices will be driven down by consumers' ability to shop around**.

1.5 Comparison of traditional and on-line branding

FAST FORWARD

IT and the Internet have particular implications for branding.

- The domain name is a vital element of the brand
- Brand values are communicated within seconds *via* the experience of using the brand website
- Online brands may be created in four ways
  - Migrate the traditional brand
  - Extend the traditional brand
  - Partner with an existing digital brand
  - Create a new digital brand

Key term

A **brand** is a name, symbol, term, mark or design that enables customers to identify and distinguish the products of one supplier from those offered by competitors.

A brand is a tool which is used by an organisation to differentiate itself from competitors. For example, what is the value of a pair of *Nike* trainers without the brand or the logo?

The value of brands in today's environment is phenomenal. Brands have the power of instant sales; they convey a message of confidence, quality and reliability to their target market, which is particularly important in e-commerce where there are often concerns over privacy and security.

Aspects of a well-formed brand in traditional delivery channels
Brand name awareness – achieved through marketing communications to promote the brand identity and the other qualities of the brand
Perceived quality – awareness counts for nothing if the consumer has had a bad experience of a product or associated customer service
Positive brand associations – include imagery, the situation in which a product is used, its personality and symbols
Brand loyalty – the commitment of a segment to a brand

These customer touch-points combine to build a good brand presence. However, screen-based delivery adds a new level of complexity to the problem. For the first time customers are interacting in machine-mediated experiences as opposed to human-mediated. How can a machine be made to express a company's positive brand attributes, like respect and reliability, the same way a person does?

There are essential elements common to both traditional media and new screen-based systems. A successful brand, online or off, represents an entire customer experience. In a brick-and-mortar environment this includes such matters as: how the customer is welcomed into the store; how products are packaged and presented and how staff and customers interact.

These elements can be translated to the online shopping experience to include the e-tailer's home or welcome page web site design and page navigation and online support.

1.5.1 Visual identity

An effective visual identity is important online, as is a memorable **domain name**. The one big difference in branding on the internet from branding in conventional marketing is introduced by domain names. For example, the domain name *www.coca-cola.com* is fast becoming the brand first seen by the consumer rather than the distinctive red and white label on the can. Unfortunately, there are a limited number of names available, and each name has been given to the first applicant. The World Intellectual Property Organisation has now taken up this issue, at least in terms of the worst exploitative excesses. Even so there may be many legitimate claimants for a .com name who operate in very different sectors, and the

BPP LEARNING MEDIA

new extensions (such as *.biz* and *.TV*) do not totally resolve the problem. Every supplier still wants *.com* since this is where the customers look first.

Despite these similarities, online branding differs in important ways from traditional branding and must be approached differently. A company's entire character, identity, products, and services, can be communicated in seconds on the web and customers make judgments just as fast.

1.5.2 Online brand options

Migrate traditional brand online – this can make sense if the brand is well known and has a strong reputation eg, *Marks & Spencer*, *Orange* and *Disney*. However, there is a risk of jeopardising the brand's good name if the new venture is not successful.

Extend traditional brand – a variant. For example, *Aspirin's* land based brand positioning statement is 'Aspirin – provides instant pain relief''. Management felt it did not hold true for a meaningful web presence, because you can't get instant pain relief on the web. So it was changed to 'Aspirin – your self help brand' which offered visitors to their web site what they described as 'meaningful health oriented intelligence and self help'.

Partner with existing digital brand – co-branding occurs when two businesses put their brand name on the same product as a joint initiative. This practice is quite common on the Internet and has proved to be a good way to build brand recognition and make the product or service more resistant to copying by private label manufacturers. A successful example of co-branding is the *Senseo* coffeemaker, which carries both the *Philips* and the *Douwe Egberts* brands. Another is the *Braun* and *Oral B* plaque remover

Create a new digital brand – because a good name is extremely important, some factors to consider when selecting a new brand name are that it should suggest something about the product, be short and memorable, be easy to spell, translate well into other languages and have an available domain name

2 Customer relationship management

FAST FORWARD

Customer Relationship Management (CRM) is the establishment, development, maintenance and optimisation of long-term mutually valuable relationships between consumers and organisations.

It has three phases: acquisition, retention and extension. An accurate and detailed on-line database if fundamental to customer relationship management.

2.1 Meaning and scope of customer relationship management

Key term

Customer Relationship Management (CRM) is the establishment, development, maintenance and optimisation of long-term mutually valuable relationships between consumers and organisations.

What CRM involves	Company benefits realised as a result
• Organisations must become 'customer centric' • Organisations must be prepared to adapt so that they take customer needs into account and then deliver them • Market research must be used to assess customer needs and satisfaction	• Improved customer retention • Improved cross selling • Improved profitability (per customer and in general)

Dave Chaffey outlines three phases of CRM in E-Business and E-Commerce Management

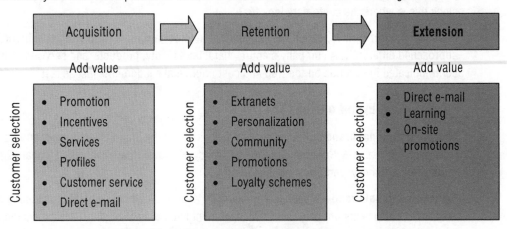

Chaffey's three phases of customer relationship management

Customer acquisition is the process of attracting customers for their first purchases.

Customer retention ensures that customers return and buy for a second time. The organisation keeps them as customers. This is most likely to be the purchase of a similar product or service, or the next level of product or service.

Customer extension introduces products and services to loyal customers that may not wholly relate to their original purchases. These are additional, supplementary purchases.

In recent times emphasis has increased on building and maintaining good long-term relationships with customers. This is because such relationships are more profitable than constantly searching for new customers, owing to repeat purchasing and ease of service.

2.1.1 The nature of the customer

Not all customers are the same. Some appear for a single cash transaction and are never seen again. Others make frequent, regular purchases in large volumes, using credit facilities and building up a major relationship. Yet another type of customer purchases infrequently but in transactions of high value, as, for instance, in property markets. This variation will exist to a greater or lesser extent in all industries, though each will have a smaller typical range of behaviour. However, even within a single business, customers will vary significantly in the frequency and volume of their purchases, their reasons for buying, their sensitivity to price changes, their reaction to promotion and their overall attitude to the supplier and the product.

Segmentation of the customer base can have a major impact on profitability, perhaps by simply tailoring promotion to suit the most attractive group of customers.

The **stakeholder concept** suggests a wider concern than the traditional marketing approach of supplying goods and services which satisfy immediate needs. The supplier-customer relationship extends beyond the basic transaction. Today's highly competitive business environment means that customers are only retained if they are very satisfied with their purchasing experience. Any lesser degree of satisfaction is likely to result in the loss of the customer. Companies must be active in monitoring customer satisfaction because very few will actually complain. They will simply depart. Businesses which use intermediaries must be particularly active, since research shows that even when complaints are made, the principals hear about only a very small proportion of them.

Research indicates that **the single largest reason why customers abandon a supplier is poor performance by front-line staff**. Any scheme for customer retention must address the need for careful selection and training of these staff. It is also a vital factor in **relationship marketing**.

2.1.2 Intermediaries

Many businesses sell to intermediaries rather than to the end consumer. Some deal with both categories; they have to recognise that **the intermediary is just as much a customer as the eventual consumer**. We have discussed the impact of the **strategic customer** elsewhere in this Study Text. Intermediaries who do not take title to goods are equally worthy of consideration. Examples are manufacturers who maintain their own sales organisation but appoint agents in geographically remote areas and companies who combine autonomous operations with franchising. While it is reasonable to give the highest priority to the needs of the **ultimate consumer** and insist on some control over the activities of the intermediary, it must be recognised that he will only perform well **if his own needs are addressed**. For instance, a selling agent who has invested heavily in stock after being given exclusive rights in an area should be consulted before further demands are made on his cash flow by the launch of a new product.

2.2 Relationship marketing

Relationship marketing is defined very simply by *Grönroos* as the management of a firm's market relationships

Kotler says 'marketing can **make promises** but only the whole organisation can **deliver satisfaction**'. *Adcock* expands on this by remarking that relationship marketing can only exist when the marketing function fosters a customer-oriented **service culture** which supports the network of activities that deliver value to the customer.

Relationship marketing is thus as much about **attitudes** and **assumptions** as it is about techniques. The marketing function's task is to inculcate habits of behaviour at all levels and in all departments that will enhance and strengthen the alliance. It must be remembered, however, that the effort involved in long-term relationship building is **more appropriate in some markets than in others**. Where customers are purchasing intermittently and switching costs are low, there is always a chance of business. This tends to be the pattern in commodity markets. Here, it is reasonable to take a **transactions approach** to marketing and treat each sale as unique. A **relationship marketing approach** is more appropriate where switching costs are high and a lost customer is thus probably lost for a long time. Switching costs are raised by such factors as the need for training on systems; the need for a large common installed base and high capital cost and the incorporation of purchased items into the customer's own designs.

2.2.1 Differences between transactional and relationship marketing

Transactional	Relationship
Importance of single sale	Importance of customer relation
Importance of product features	Importance of customer benefits
Short time scale	Longer time scale
Less emphasis on service	High customer service
Quality is concern of production	Quality is concern of all
Competitive commitment	High customer commitment
Persuasive communication	Regular communication

2.2.2 Implementing relationship marketing

The conceptual or philosophic nature of relationship marketing leads to a simple principle, that of **enhancing satisfaction by precision in meeting the needs of individual customers**. This depends on extensive two-way communication to establish and record the customer's characteristics and preferences and build a long-term relationship. *Adcock* mentions three important practical methods which contribute to this end.

- Building a customer database
- Developing customer-oriented service systems
- Extra direct contacts with customers

Modern **computer database systems** enable the rapid acquisition and retrieval of the individual customer's details, needs and preferences. Using this technology, relationship marketing enables the sales person to greet the customer by name, know what he purchased last time, avoid taking his full delivery address, know what his credit status is and what he is likely to want. It enables new products to be developed that are precisely tailored to the customer's needs and new procedures to be established that enhance his satisfaction. It is the successor to **mass marketing**, which attempted to be customer-led but which could only supply a one-size-fits-all product. The end result of a relationship marketing approach is a mutually satisfactory relationship that continues indefinitely.

2.2.3 Lifetime value

In determining which customers are worth the cost of long-term relationships, it is useful to consider their lifetime value. This depends on three things.

- Current profitability computed at the customer level

- The propensity of those customers to stay loyal

- Expected revenues and costs of servicing such customers over the lifetime of the relationship

Building relationships makes most sense for customers whose **lifetime value** to the company is the highest. Thus, building relationships should focus on customers who are currently the most profitable, likely to be the most profitable in the future, or likely to remain with the company for the foreseeable future and have acceptable levels of profitability.

Relationship marketing is grounded in the idea of establishing a **learning relationship** with customers. At the lower end, building a relationship can create cross-selling opportunities that may make the overall relationship profitable. For example, some retail banks have tried selling credit cards to less profitable customers. With valuable customers, customer relationship management may make them more loyal and willing to invest additional funds. In banking, these high-end relationships are often managed through private bankers, whose goals are not only to increase customer satisfaction and retention, but also to cross-sell and bring in investment.

2.2.4 Software

The goal of relationship management is to increase customer satisfaction and to minimise any problems. By engaging in 'smarter' relationships, a company can learn customers' preferences and develop trust. Every contact point with the customer can be seen as a chance to record information and learn preferences. Complaints and errors must be recorded, not just fixed and forgotten. Contact with customers in every medium, whether over the Internet, through a call centre, or through personal contact, is recorded and centralised.

Many companies are beginning to achieve this goal by using customer relationship management (CRM) software. Data, once collected and centralised, can be used to customise service. In addition, the database can be analysed to detect patterns that can suggest better ways to serve customers in general. A key aspect of this dialogue is to learn and record preferences.

2.2.5 Example

The *Ritz Carlton Hotel* makes a point of observing the choices that guests make and recording them. If a guest requests extra pillows, then extra pillows will be provided every time that person visits. At upmarket retailers, personal shoppers will record customers' preferences in sizes, styles, brands, colours and price ranges and notify them when new merchandise appears or help them choose accessories.

2.3 Different methods of acquiring customers through exploiting electronic media

Electronic media may be used to acquire customers by using a wide range of techniques. These vary from analogues of traditional mass-communications methods such as advertising and newsletters, through specialised on-line forms such as search engine registration, to previously targeted means such as personalised emails and website messages to logged in return customers.

Techniques to achieve acquisition include traditional on-line mass media techniques and specialised on-line techniques.

(a) **Search engine registration and directories** provide an index of content on registered sites that can be searched by keyword. Skilled website design can put a supplier high up among search results.

(b) **Newsgroups and forums** providing expert opinion and useful help are a way for businesses to communicate with their peers and customers in an informal environment.

(c) **Newsletters** allow an organisation to send news about the company, new products or services and any new information that has been posted on the web site.

(d) **Link building and partnership campaigns** can greatly benefit a business, significantly boosting its online presence. Reciprocal links are an exchange of links between two site owners. Types of link building include article and press release syndication, e-mail campaigns and directory submission. Affiliate networks are based on paying commission on sales referred from other sites.

(e) **Viral marketing** is about creating a buzz about products or services. Viral marketing relies on word of mouth or, in the online sense, getting people to share the online application with others. This can be achieved by providing web pages that can easily be sent to other people, for example. For businesses, viral marketing can emphasise the value of their goods or services, promote special offers and generate interest in the business or their products and services through word of mouth.

(f) **Banner advertising** is similar to advertisements seen in newspapers and magazines. They are the graphical strips commonly seen across the top of website pages. Many companies use banner advertising in affiliate programs, e-mails and related web sites. Depending on what medium is chosen to place the banner, the organisation could pay by impression, mile, click or action.

(g) **E-mail** marketing represents the single largest shift in the way humans communicate since the invention of the telephone.

2.4 Differences in buyer behaviour

The processes involved in making a purchase may be complex or relatively simple depending on the nature of the need.

The greatest contrast lies between business and consumer purchases. On-line purchaser behaviour is complicated by the special conditions of the on-line environment.

Segmentation of on-line consumer purchasers may be based on general on-line activity and the degree of confidence and competence displayed.

An important part of the marketing process is to understand why a customer or buyer makes a purchase. Without such an understanding, businesses find it hard to respond to the customer's needs and wants.

Research suggests that customers go through a five-stage decision-making process in any purchase. This is shown in the diagram below:

The model implies that customers pass through all stages in every purchase. However, in more routine purchases, customers often skip or reverse some of the stages.

Step 1 The buying process starts with **need recognition**: for example, I am hungry, we need a new sofa, I have a headache, or responds to a **marketing stimulus**, as, for example, when passing a restaurant and being attracted by the smell.

Step 2 The customer then needs to decide how much information (if any) is required. If the need is strong and there is a product or service that meets the need close to hand, then a purchase decision is likely to be made there and then. If not, then the process of **information search** begins. A customer can obtain information from personal, commercial, public and experiential sources.

Step 3 In the **evaluation** stage, the customer must choose between the alternative brands, products and services. Where a purchase is 'highly involving' the customer is likely to carry out extensive evaluation.

Step 4 The purchase decision is made

Step 5 The final stage is the post-purchase **evaluation of the decision**. It is common for customers to experience concerns after making a purchase decision. This arises from the phenomenon known as **cognitive dissonance**. This occurs when the customer receives different information from two trusted sources and experiences confusion and a lack of certainty. The customer, having bought a product, may feel that an alternative would have been preferable. In these circumstances that customer will not repurchase immediately, but is likely to switch brands next time.

2.4.1 Types of buying behaviour

Types of buying behaviour – there are four typical types of buying behaviour based on the type of products that is to be purchased.

(a) **Complex buying behaviour** occurs when the individual purchases a high value brand and seeks a lot of information before the purchase is made.

(b) **Habitual buying behaviour** occurs when the individual buys a product out of habit, such as newspaper.

(c) **Variety seeking buying behaviour** occurs when the individual likes to shop around and experiment with different products.

(d) **Dissonance reducing buying behaviour** occurs when buyer are highly involved with the purchase of the product, because the purchase is expensive or infrequent. There is little difference between existing brands. An example would be buying a diamond ring since there is perceived to be little difference between existing diamond brand manufacturers.

2.4.2 Business and consumer markets

The major differences in buyer behaviour are between the B2B and B2C markets

Differences	B2B	B2C
Market structure	Fewer buyers but larger purchases Demand largely derived from consumer demand eg, car industry buys steel because consumers buy cars	Many buyers with smaller purchases
Nature of the buying unit	Buying unit differs – more rational approach, more people involved	Individuals or families
Type of purchase	Purchase products to meet specific business needs – want a customised product package Emphasise economic benefits	Purchase products to meet individual or family needs Purchase from intermediaries
Type of buying decision	Business purchases involve a more complex decision-making process with formal, lengthy purchasing policies.	Buy on impulse or with minimal processes
Communication differences	Existing customers can be contacted directly. Information is placed on the web to support customers and encourage loyalty Web site content should be tailored to the needs of users, influencers and deciders	Promoting the web site uses methods such as banner ads and search engines

2.4.3 Internet consumers

Segmentation using buyer behaviour – there have been many studies to identify the behaviour of different groups of Internet user.

One study identified six different groups of active Internet users and their motivations

- **Simplifiers** – easier than the real world
- **Surfers** – new experiences
- **Bargainers** – good deals
- **Connectors** – chatroom users
- **Routiners** – news, stock prices, finance
- **Sportsters** – sports news

Netpoll has established a different user typology:

(a) **Gameboy** – Still at school and living at home. Accesses the Internet mainly at home. Into playing online games. Thinks he is pretty Net-savvy.

(b) **CyberLad** – Basically 'loaded man' online. Accesses at work and at home. Bit of a Jack the lad and thinks he knows it all as far as the Net is concerned.

(c) **Net Sophisticate** – Straddles the border between cool and nerd. Could be a gee-whiz creative at agency or unemployed and living at home with mum.

(d) **CyberSec** – Works as a PA to the boss of a small organisation. Super-competent, well turned out and also very much 'one of the girls' Accesses the Internet only at the office

(e) **Hit 'n' Runner** – Can be either be male or female. Successful professional or high-flying marketing exec. Accesses the Internet at work and only for information. Very impatient if finding information is difficult or if the site is slow to download.

(f) **InfoJunky** – Either male or female. Possibly a middle-rank civil servant or a partner at a small firm of solicitors. Is under the impression that the time spent online is a big benefit to the job. Given that he/she gets side-tracked, this is very debatable.

(g) **CyberMum** – Married with kids and works in a 'caring' profession. Her husband thought it would be a good idea if they got online when he started spending one week in four at company HQ in Holland, so that they could exchange email messages. She would like to be able to shop online, if only she knew how it worked.

2.5 Retaining customers using electronic media

FAST FORWARD

Retention of on-line customers may be based on careful use of customer databases and by offering wider benefits. Databases allow for personalised communications, promotions and offers. Wider benefits may be offered by access to extranets and on-line communities.

Much has been written about how to attract customers using search engines, indexes, portals and other advertising media etc but far less has been written about how to persuade them to remember any site and return to it when they need another item or, more especially, to return to that site when they do not need anything but may be susceptible to impulse purchases. This factor has been called **stickiness**.

Customer retention marketing is a tactically-driven approach based on customer behaviour. It is the core activity going on behind the scenes in:

- **relationship marketing**

- **loyalty marketing**

- **database marketing**

- **permission marketing** – consumers giving their consent to receive marketing information improves the targeting and relevance of promotional messages, thus improving response and conversion rates.

The basic philosophy is that active customers are happy (retained) customers; and they like to win. They like to feel they are in control and smart about choices they make, and they like to feel good about their behaviour.

Marketers take advantage of this by offering **promotions** of various kinds. These promotions range from discounts and sweepstakes to loyalty programs and higher concept approaches such as thank-you notes and birthday cards. Retaining customers means keeping them active otherwise they will slip away and eventually no longer be customers.

Other techniques for retaining customers include personalisation, the use of extranets, on-line communities, on-line sales promotions and opt-in e-mail marketing.

2.5.1 Personalisation

Database, document generation and web technologies have improved the ease and sophistication of targeting and personalisation of contact between organisations and customers. Here are some examples.

(a)   Allowing users to customise web pages for their personal interests and tastes

(b)   Making individually-targeted product offers and recommendations based on browsing/buying behaviour

(c)   Sending personally addressed and targeted-content messages to customers

(d)   Encouraging users/customers to form **virtual communities** (for example, using chat rooms, discussion boards and newsgroups)

2.5.2 Extranets

For many companies, extranets are still only web-based systems that provide password-protected areas allowing users (customers, resellers) to fill out forms or perform simple online transactions. HTTP-based extranets allow companies to deliver information through a browser interface but offer very limited ability to interact with core business systems and applications.

On the customer side, extranets offer secure tunnels to remote databases, which let users access inventory data, examine special discounts, view delivery status, research products, place and fulfills orders, and collaborate via a secure internet connection. By opening customer access in this way, extranets offer businesses a significant customer retention opportunity — the customer is almost literally attached to the business.

2.5.3 On-line communities

A community is a multi-way online environment where members encourage each other to contribute content and interact.

According to a top e-business technology consultant, the most important objective for a small business when establishing a business presence online is to create a community where people interested in the product or service can feel at home 'hanging out'.

Interactivity benefits

(a)   Within commercial sites, community members account for one-third of all users, but two thirds of all transactions

(b)   Active posters make nine times as many visits to a website as passive users

(c)   Active members are twice as loyal to a site as all other users.

Types of community are shown below

Communities of purpose where members share a vocation or profession	**Communities of circumstance** where members share a personal situation

Communities of purpose
where members share
a common objective

Communities of interest where members share a hobby or interest	**Communities of geography** where members live in the same area

Some sites are inherently sticky because they serve a particular natural community, for example, a fan club or football team. These will generate their own news regularly and will be visited frequently by both dedicated and lukewarm adherents without special stimulus. Other sites are also going to attract regular visitors because of their nature, such as *Amazon*, *ebay* and *Loot*, whose primary purpose is well known and is of frequent use for certain people. Revenue there comes from direct sales or commission on transactions or even from advertisers based on the number of visitors.

2.5.4 Opt-in email

Opt-in-email promotional emails that have been requested by the individual receiving them. Unlike promotional e-mails that get sent out to large lists of recipients without regard to whether or not they want the information, opt-in emails are only sent to people who specifically request them.

Opt-in emails are targeted and often personalised and carry information about specific topics or promotions that users are interested in learning about. Typical opt-in emails contain newsletters, product information or special promotional offers. For example, if a user frequented a Web site that sold books and music online, that user could opt in to receive announcements when his or her favourite author or musician released new material. The promotional email may even present the recipient with a special promotional offer to purchase the product at a discount available only to those on the opt-in list.

2.6 Increasing the activity and value of established, retained customers

Customer activity may be enhanced by the use of datamining and cookies.

CRM is concerned with the creation, development and enhancement of individualised customer relationships with carefully targeted customers and customer groups

Paul Postma, in *The New Marketing Era* highlights two major shifts in the way customer information is used in the new marketing era.

(a) 'In a traditional market approach, people have all sorts of ideas about the target group, or they think up some obvious target group for a certain product. Without a marketing database, people are able to approach this target group only as a generic whole, by choosing the correct advertising medium and tailoring the creative ideas to the prescribed target group. In the new approach…we no longer calculate the market from within the company, but instead communicate, listen and record. The **database** will teach us what the market has to say…'

(b) 'In the new marketing era, we are shifting from derivative and self-reported information to **behavioural analysis**... Information technology makes it possible to determine behaviour, even at an individual level, and even in mass markets. This information is by far the most trustworthy when forecasting future behaviour.'

2.6.1 Database marketing

Database marketing has been defined by *Shaw and Stone* as 'an interactive approach to marketing, which uses individually addressable marketing media and channels to extend help to a company's target audience, stimulate their demand and stay close to them by recording and keeping an electronic database memory of customer, prospect and all communication and commercial contacts, to help them improve all future contacts and ensure more realistic planning of all marketing'.

A database, in marketing terms, is a collection of data that can be organised to give marketing information. The customer database is one example.

Allen et al suggest the following projects which can be conducted using database marketing techniques.

Project	Method
Identify the best customers	Use RFM analysis (Recency of the latest purchase, Frequency of purchases and Monetary value of all purchases) to determine which customers are most profitable to market to.
Develop new customers	Collect lists of potential customers to incorporate into the database.
Tailor messages based on customer usage	Target mail and e-mail based on the types and frequency of purchases indicated by the customer's purchase profile.
Recognise customers after purchase	Reinforce the purchase decision by appropriate follow-up.
Cross-sell related and complementary products	Use the customer purchase database to identify opportunities to suggest additional products during the buying session.
Personalise customer service	Online purchase data can prompt customer service representatives to show that the customer is recognised, his needs known and his time (for example, in giving details) valued.
Eliminating conflicting or confusing communications	Present a coherent image over time to individual customers – however different the message to different customer groups. (For example, don't keep sending 'dear first-time customer' messages to long-standing customers!) Remember the Integrated Marketing Communications approach.

New data management techniques have been developed to provide marketers with better and quicker access to data analysis.

2.6.2 Datamining

Datamining is a set of statistical techniques that are used to identify trends, patterns and relationships in data.

Datamining techniques have been available for many years, but they have only recently grown popular, as more data is being created, data processing power (in the form of computers) is becoming more accessible and data mining software tools are becoming available. Most data mining models are of one of two types:

(a) **Predictive:** using known observations to predict future events (for example, predicting the probability that a recipient will opt out of an e-mail list)

(b)   **Descriptive:** interrogating the database to identify patterns and relationships (for example, profiling the audience of a particular advertising campaign).

The logical extension of database marketing is referred to by Kotler as **customer specific marketing** and by *Peppers and Rogers* as **one-to-one marketing**. The company collects data on individual customers, their past web-browsing and purchase habits, demographic and even psychographic characteristics. It is then possible to customise or personalise the organisation-customer interface to suit individual customer profiles: whether on the telephone (using Computer Telephony Integration), by mail (using data merged from database files into word-processing programmes), by email (ditto) or by website (personalising and customising pages for known surfers).

2.6.3 Cookies

Cookies are a technology that allows a website to remember individual visitors' surfing and/or purchase history and preferences. This information is placed on the visitor's hard disk and when he revisits the site, it references the cookie and is able to show the visitor product selections and recommendations, and offer personalised welcomes and streamlined ordering (through remembering names, addresses, and credit card details).

3 Software and CRM

FAST FORWARD

There are four main areas of CRM automation.

- **Sales** – lead management, order tracking, sales support
- **Service** – help desk, FAQs problem resolution
- **Marketing** – prospect database, campaign management
- **Reporting** – presentation of performance data

E-commerce systems must be integrated with back office systems such as inventory management and sales ledger.

Systems choice is subject to considerations previously dealt with, concerning design, integration, modality and customisation.

There are three aspects of CRM that can each be implemented in isolation from one another:

(a)   **Operational CRM** provides support to 'front office' business processes, including sales, marketing and service. Each interaction with a customer is generally added to a customer's contact history, and staff can retrieve information on customers from the database as necessary. Many call centres use some kind of CRM software to support their call centre agents.

(b)   **Collaborative CRM** covers the direct interaction with customers. This can include a variety of channels, such as Internet, email, automated phone/ Interactive Voice Response (IVR).

(c)   **Analytical CRM** analyses customer data for a variety of purposes eg, risk assessment and fraud detection, in particular for credit card transactions

Many businesses invest in a CRM system to improve their customer services. The CRM system brings information like customer data, sales patterns, marketing data and future trends together with the aim of identifying new sales opportunities, delivering improved customer service, or offering personalised services and deals.

In addition to improving sales and profitability, the CRM system is very effective in handling customer complaints and can have a tremendous effect on a company's reputation.

Whilst IT and software are not the entire story for CRM, they are vital to its success. CRM software collects data on consumers and their transactions. Huge databases store data on individuals and groups of individuals. Organisations will track individuals, and try to market products and services to them based upon similar buyer behaviour seen in other individuals.

The customer interacts with the company via e-mail, telephone, web or face-to-face, through the company's back office, sales team, marketing division and so on. As the interaction progresses to a sale, service query or quote the information from that interaction is stored and fed through middleware into a **database**. This data can then be drawn upon by sales, service, marketing or business to add a greater functionality to those departments.

Major areas of CRM focus on service automated processes, personal information gathering and processing, and self-service. It attempts to integrate and automate the various customer serving processes within a company. It typically involves four general areas.

(a) **Sales automation** including lead management, order tracking and sales support, plus integration with desktop applications to share contacts, send email and manage calendars

(b) **Service management** including basic helpdesk functionality, case management, escalation with basic workflow, problem ticket tracking and FAQs

(c) **Marketing automation** to manage a database of prospects. Further down the line more sophisticated campaign management can be brought into play to track the origin and status of prospects and monitor marketing effectiveness

(d) **Management reporting**, including easy to understand graphical views of different slices of the data such as by territories or order status

These areas should all be focused around building a single view of the customer. Integration should initially be sought between key modules.

Typical CRM objectives include reducing customer complaints, increasing communication with customers, increasing customer loyalty, and of course, increasing the variety or volume of products sold. Good sales people will know what their customers' requirements are, and when they are needed, but in a channel sales environment it is necessary to apply this level of knowledge company-wide to maximise opportunities for sale. Managers selecting CRM systems will be concerned with the following key technical issues:

- CRM applications
- Integration with back-office systems
- The choice of single-vendor solutions or a more fragmented choice

3.1 CRM applications

(a) **Electronic marketing**: a high volume of all communication takes place via email. A basic application for any CRM system would be to send an email to any customer who had previously purchased certain items which would lead the organisation to believe that they may be interested in related items. CRM systems allow this list to be created in minutes and campaigns put into action instantly. A logical extension of this strategy is to send them a way of ordering as well as a promotional message, as research has shown that this can treble the effectiveness of the campaign.

(b) **Target mailing** will reduce costs and increase response rate. A simple example of this is to send this season's catalogue to customers who purchased from the last catalogue. To achieve this, the mailing lists need to be linked to sales history.

(c)   **Sales analysis** is widely used by large sophisticated channel marketing businesses, but this strategy is basically simple and easy to implement using an integrated CRM system. For example, it should be easy to generate a list of customers who have not purchased for over a year. These could then be targeted by email, direct mail or telephone by asking them if they want to receive the next catalogue, and offering them some sort of discount to become a customer again. It is also possible to understand simple relationships; for example anybody purchasing a computer printer must need to buy toner cartridges. A simple gap analysis allows a list to be formed of the details of anyone who has purchased a printer without toner cartridges, and thus provides a targeted list for a sales campaign. Again a fully integrated CRM system will enable this.

(d)   **Order building**: another role for the CRM system should be to provide the organisation's order taker or website with key data about each customer. Customers placing orders can then be reminded of their usual order requirements, any related products on offer and further product information. As well as increasing sales, this also helps to build the customer relationship.

Integrated CRM software is also known as **front office solutions**. This is because they deal directly with the customer eg, applications for sales, marketing and customer service

Many call centres use CRM software to store all of their customers' details. When a customer calls, the system can be used to retrieve and display information relevant to the customer. By serving the customer quickly and efficiently, and also keeping all information on a customer in one place, a company aims to make cost savings, and also encourage new customers.

CRM solutions can also be used to allow customers to perform their own service *via* a variety of communication channels. For example, you might be able to check your bank balance via your WAP phone without ever having to talk to a person, saving money for the company, and saving you time.

A CRM solution is characterised by its functionality.

(a)   **Scalability** is the ability to be used on a large scale and to be reliably expanded to whatever scale is necessary.

(b)   **Multiple communication channels** provide the ability to interface with users *via* different devices such as phone, WAP, Internet and so on.

(c)   **Workflow** is enhanced by the ability to route work automatically through the system to different people based on a set of rules.

(d)   **Databases** provide centralised storage (in a data warehouse) of all information relevant to customer interaction.

(e)   **Customer privacy** is enhanced by, for example, data encryption and the destruction of records to ensure that they are not stolen or abused.

Integration with back-office systems

For CRM to be truly effective, the e-commerce platform must be seamlessly incorporated into the back office system (finance, payroll and HR applications). A simple example is that when product information in the back office system is altered (such as stock levels), this should also update the website. When customers place orders on the web, they should be able review their order history whether placed on the website or over the telephone.

When contemplating a CRM system, management will have previously invested in systems for other business functions. These legacy systems will be at the application and database levels within the organisation and it will not be financially viable to abandon these applications so their integration is a vital part of the decision to implement a CRM system.

3.2 The choice of single-vendor solutions or a more fragmented choice

CRM software is available either as a complete purchase from a software vendor or outsourced from an application service provider, or ASP. ASPs host the CRM applications and sell subscription-based services. ASPs are more affordable than standalone software and require little maintenance on the organisation's part. However, ASPs are often static in what they offer and will not provide the level of customisation offered by purchased software.

CRM software is often sold in modules, so checking on modular availability can help trim costs. Before shopping, think about the organisation's goals. Is retaining existing customers important? Reducing time in the sales cycle? Or is it more valuable to expand into an online market? The data that is collected, analysed, and reported on should directly support these objectives. CRM systems typically offer so many tracking options that it is easy to get caught up in data overload, collecting every possible piece of information about each and every customer, potential customer, and transaction. But it is far wiser to save time, effort, and money by deciding in advance what information is most worthwhile to collect, how it will be measured and what will be done with it.

In an ideal world, the organisation would choose to have a single integrated database such that any employee would have total visibility about a customer and could access all visit, sales and support histories; the system would be bought from a single vendor for ease of implementation and support.

In reality, most organisations will have different applications for different communications channels, separate databases in different functional areas and multiple vendors. E-commerce systems are often separate from traditional systems. Such fragmentation makes implementation and maintenance of such systems a headache for managers and will often result in poor levels of customer service for the customer. The solution that many companies are looking to move to is close to the situation above.

However, the best option might be to adopt a CRM system phase by phase. The company needs to identify the areas where the return on investment would be highest and adopt CRM technology there.

Another good approach is to automate one of the key departments with an inexpensive CRM solution and if the project becomes successful adopt a cross-company CRM solution.

For either of these options the present customer related information that is going to be integrated with the CRM system should be carefully analysed, consolidated, structured and cleaned up prior to adoption.

Chapter roundup

- E-marketing is the application of IS and Internet techniques to the achievement of marketing objectives. Most marketing activities can be enhanced by the use of such techniques, including branding, customer service and sales.

- The employment of e-marketing may be analysed and planned using the six Is.

  - Independence of location
  - Industry structure
  - Integration
  - Interactivity
  - Individualisation
  - Intelligence

- More specific concepts for the development of e-marketing may be based on the seven Ps.

  - The augmented **product** can be extended through web information and interactivity.

  - **Pricing** can be made transparent; dynamic pricing may be used.

  - The global reach of the Internet has great implications for **place**, with the creation of new marketplaces and channel structures.

  - **Promotion** can be previously targeted *via* customer databases.

  - **People** can be replaced by software to a varying extent.

  - Processes may be automated.

  - **Physical evidence** consists of the customer's experience of using the organisation's e-marketing tools in general and of its website in particular

- IT and the Internet have particular implications for branding.

  - The domain name is a vital element of the brand

  - Brand values are communicated within seconds *via* the experience of using the brand website

  - Online brands may be created in four ways

    - Migrate the traditional brand
    - Extend the traditional brand
    - Partner with an existing digital brand
    - Create a new digital brand

- **Customer Relationship Management** (CRM) is the establishment, development, maintenance and optimisation of long-term mutually valuable relationships between consumers and organisations.

  It has three phases: acquisition, retention and extension. An accurate and detailed on-line database if fundamental to customer relationship management.

- Electronic media may be used to acquire customers by using a wide range of techniques. These vary from analogues of traditional mass-communications methods such as advertising and newsletters, through specialised on-line forms such as search engine registration, to previously targeted means such as personalised emails and website messages to logged in return customers.

- The processes involved in making a purchase may be complex or relatively simple depending on the nature of the need.

  The greatest contrast lies between business and consumer purchases. On-line purchaser behaviour is complicated by the special conditions of the on-line environment.

  Segmentation of on-line consumer purchasers may be based on general on-line activity and the degree of confidence and competence displayed.

- Retention of on-line customers may be based on careful use of customer databases and by offering wider benefits. Databases allow for personalised communications, promotions and offers. Wider benefits may be offered by access to extranets and on-line communities.

- Customer activity may be enhanced by the use of datamining and cookies.

- There are four main areas of CRM automation.

  - **Sales** – lead management, order tracking, sales support
  - **Service** – help desk, FAQs problem resolution

  - **Marketing** – prospect database, campaign management
  - **Reporting** – presentation of performance data

  E-commerce systems must be integrated with back office systems such as inventory management and sales ledger.

  Systems choice is subject to considerations previously dealt with, concerning design, integration, modality and customisation.

Quick Quiz

1   What are the six I's?

2   What might be added to a core product to create an actual product?

3   What are the three phases of CRM identified by Chaffey?

4   What are the five phases of making a purchase?

5   What is permission marketing?

6   What is scalability?

Answers to Quick Quiz

1   Independence of location, industry structure interactivity, individualisation, integration and intelligence

2   Extra features, packaging, branding

3   Acquisition, retention, extension

4   Need recognition , information search, evaluation of alternatives, purchase decision, post purchase evaluation

5   Customers give their consent to receiving marketing communications in the future

6   A software attribute that enables use on a range of scales

Now try the questions below from the Exam Question Bank

Number	Level	Marks	Time
Q10	Examination	25	45 mins

Part F
Quality Issues

Quality

12

Topic list	Syllabus reference
1 Quality and strategy	F1
2 The terminology of quality management	F1(a)
3 The ISO 9000:2000 series of standards	F1(d)
4 The quality management system	F1(d)
5 Quality in information systems development	F2(a), (b), (c)
6 Capability Maturity Model Integration	F2(d)
7 Six Sigma	F3(a), (b), (c), (d), (e)

Introduction

The achievement of a consistent, desired level of quality is a vital feature of putting strategy into action. It is important to understand that consistency of *satisfactory* quality is, for most organisations, more important and appropriate than striving for the *highest* quality and sometimes failing to achieve it. In this chapter we will examine some modern approaches to quality management. These approaches to quality tend to have common features, so make sure you understand the areas in which they differ.

Study guide

		Intellectual level
F1	**Quality control, quality assurance and quality management systems**	
(a)	Discriminate between quality, quality assurance, quality control and a quality management system	2
(b)	Assess the relationship of quality to the strategy of an organisation	3
(c)	Appraise quality initiatives previously adopted by organisations	2
(d)	Advise on the structure and benefits of a quality management system and quality certification	3
F2	**Quality in the information systems development lifecycle**	
(a)	Justify the need and assess the characteristics of quality in computer software and the implications of these characteristics for testing, liability and ownership	3
(b)	Discuss the stages of systems development through the medium of the V lifecycle model	2
(c)	Advise on how the V lifecycle model defines and partitions testing and contributes to improved computer software quality	3
(d)	Discuss how the process of computer software development process might be improved through the application of the Capability Maturity Model Integration (CMMI) process	2
F3	**Quality Initiatives: Six Sigma**	
(a)	Define the scope, principles and objectives of Six Sigma	2
(b)	Discuss the team roles typically required by Six Sigma	2
(c)	Outline the Six Sigma problem-solving process (DMAIC)	2
(d)	Discuss the significance and implications of measurement in the Six Sigma problem-solving process	2
(e)	Explain the application of Six Sigma within e-business, the value chain and process redesign	2

Exam guide

The topics in this chapter provide plenty of scope for question requirements based on the explaining the various methodologies, but it is unlikely that a complete question would be so simple. Expect to be asked for recommendations as to which scheme would be best suited to the conditions in a question scenario and to explain your choice.

The examiner has indicated that questions on quality will be set in Section B of the examination. Such questions may deal exclusively with quality or they may cover other topics such as IT or business process change as well. it is also inevitable that some aspects of quality will be present in the Section A scenario.

1 Quality and strategy

> Quality management has developed from an inspection-based process to a philosophy of business that emphasises customer satisfaction, the elimination of waste and the acceptance of responsibility for conformance with quality specifications at all stages of all business processes.

1.1 Traditional approaches to quality

There has been a rise in awareness of quality and the systems that support it, to the extent that it has become of **strategic significance**. Quality is now considered to be of fundamental importance to many organisations. Indeed, many firms pursue a **strategy of differentiation based on high quality**.

There was a time when quality was not measured as an output target, and when managers considered it something to be added on to a product rather than something that was integral to it. Quality control applied largely to manufacturing and meant **inspection**, or identifying when defective items are being produced at an unacceptable level.

There are many problems with this approach.

(a) The inspection process itself **does not add value**: if it could be guaranteed that no defective items were produced, there would be no need for a separate inspection function.

(b) The **production of substandard products is a waste** of raw materials, machine time, human effort and overhead cost.

(c) The inspection department takes up possibly expensive **land and warehousing space**.

(d) The production of defects is **not compatible with newer production techniques** such as just-in-time: there is no time for inspection.

(e) **Working capital is tied up** in stocks that cannot be sold.

In other words, the inspection approach builds **waste** into the process, which is not acceptable: the resources it consumes can be put to better use.

1.2 The development of quality management

Quality management is not new. Below, we give a brief guide to some of the major ideas behind the development of quality management. An important theme running through this process is the gradual expansion of the quality idea from a **technique** forming part of the management of manufacturing output to its current status as a **philosophy of business** and vital component of strategy. Partly as a result of this development, the threshold level of quality capability has gradually risen, so that high quality standards are now taken for granted.

1.3 Deming

W Edwards Deming is one of the founding fathers of the quality movement. Deming's first job in this field was to use **statistical process control** to raise productivity in US factories during World War II. His ideas were adopted in Japan, once he was able to convince Japanese business leaders of their merits. Deming has asserted that over 90% of a company's problems can be corrected only by management, as management has the sole authority to change the system.

Deming's book *Out of the Crisis* listed fourteen points for managers to adopt to improve quality and competitiveness. These are summarised as follows.

(a)   Improving products and services must be a constant purpose of the organisation

(b)   Eliminate all waste. (This was especially important in Japan, which has few sources of raw materials).

(c)   Cease depending on mass inspection to achieve quality. This ties up resources and working capital in stocks.

(d)   Price should not be the only consideration in choosing a supplier. Quality and reliability are also important.

(e)   Improve the systems for production and service delivery. This reduces waste and enhances quality by ensuring the production system works optimally.

(f)   Train people so they are better at working, and understand how to optimise production.

(g)   Lead people.

(h)   'Drive out fear'.

(i)   Break down barriers between staff areas.

(j)   Get rid of slogans, exhortations, targets. These can be alienating.

(k)   Get rid of numerical quotas. These encourage the wrong attitude to production.

(l)   Enable people to take pride in work.

(m)   Encourage 'education and self improvement for everyone'.

(n)   Action should be taken to accomplish quality objectives.

The abandonment of mass inspection to assess quality implies that quality must be built in from the beginning, not added on at the end.

1.4 Crosby

Philip B Crosby is chiefly known for two concepts.

(a)   **Zero defects**: there should never be any defects in a product. Some consider this to be an impossible ideal, and invoke the concept of diminishing returns. Alternatively it can be seen as a slogan to employees.

(b)   **Right first time** is another idea which holds that a product should not have to be corrected once it is built. It is thus a corollary of the zero defects concept.

Crosby proposes four standards that flesh out these concepts.

(a)   Quality is **conformance to requirements**.
(b)   The system for advancing quality is **prevention**, not appraisal.
(c)   The **goal** should be zero defects.
(d)   The importance of quality is measured by the cost of *not* having quality.

Crosby's ideas demonstrate a fundamental shift from a 'supervisory' culture of quality assurance to one where each individual takes full responsibility for his work: **quality is everyone's responsibility**.

1.5 Juran

Joseph Juran's book *Quality Control Handbook* was published in 1951. He also worked with Japanese industrialists in the years immediately after World War II, and, with Deming, is credited with increasing Japan's industrial competitiveness.

While Deming's ideas are wide ranging and expand into considerations of leadership and management style, Juran was concerned with identifying **specific improvements for enhancing quality**. Juran's ideas are different in the following ways.

(a) The best approach to enhancing quality is to 'identify specific opportunities, evaluate their viability by using conventional methods such as return on investment, plan the selected project carefully, monitor their results'.

(b) Juran believes in the law of **diminishing returns**: there is an economic level of quality beyond which it is pointless to strive, because the costs outweigh the benefits.

(c) Juran believes that most quality problems derive from management systems and processes rather than poor workmanship.

Juran defines quality as 'fitness for use', which includes two elements.

(a) **Quality of design,** which can include the customer satisfactions built into the product.
(b) **Quality of conformance,** in other words a lack of defects in the finished goods.

1.6 Feigenbaum

Armand Feigenbaum appended the word 'total' to quality, thus emphasising the relevance of quality issues to **all areas of the operations of a business**. He is also noted for assessing the economic value of quality, as the value of many quality improvement measures are not exactly self-evident. In other words he stressed the importance of identifying the **costs** of quality, and the lack of quality, to prove that, in economic and accounting terms, 'prevention is better than cure'.

This involves changing the role of the quality control function (which inspected and rejected output) to one in which quality provided an effective system for quality maintenance.

(a) An **inspection role** is carried out after the event, after the wasteful and substandard production.

(b) A **planning role** would involve the design of systems and procedures to reduce the likelihood of sub-optimal production.

1.7 Ishikawa

The quality philosophy has been implemented most famously in Japan. According to some commentators **design quality** rather than **conformance quality**, has been responsible for much of the success of Japanese firms in some industries.

Ishikawa is noted for proposing **quality circles**, which are groups of selected workers delegated with the task of analysing the production process, and coming up with ideas to improve it. Success requires a commitment from the circle's membership, and a management willingness to take a back seat.

Quality circles are mainly management stimulated. Whatever the stated reasons are for instituting quality circles, the real reason for having quality circles is to motivate employees to improve quality.

2 The terminology of quality management

FAST FORWARD

'Quality' does not mean 'high quality'. It is the degree to which a set of inherent characteristics fulfils requirements. **Quality control** satisfies quality requirements, while **quality assurance** gives confidence that quality requirements will be satisfied. That is, quality control is about activities such as supervision and measurement, while quality assurance is about things that make those activities effective, such as training and quality records.

The word **quality** is used in several ways in everyday speech: it is used most precisely to mean simply the **nature** of a thing or to refer to one of its specific **characteristics**. However, the word is also used, rather imprecisely, to indicate that a thing possesses a high degree of excellence or is of **good** quality, the word **good** being understood. Thus, if people speak of 'a quality product', we understand them to mean that the product is made to high standards and will give good service.

We must discard this everyday imprecision when we begin to consider quality in its more technical sense. This is because the real world of business has room for a **wide range of different products**, each providing a **different combination of price and relative quality**. People flying first class expect a greater degree of comfort and service than is provided to passengers in tourist class, and rightly so: they have paid a much higher fare. But this does not mean that tourist class passengers are not equally entitled to the proper level of service that they, in turn, have paid for. **Quality** does not mean 'the best': it means what is right and proper under the circumstances.

This concept of quality is adopted in the International Organisation for Standardisation (ISO) definition.

Key term

Quality is 'the degree to which a set of inherent characteristics fulfils requirements'.   *ISO*

Exam focus point

The various ISO definitions given in this chapter are worth committing to memory. This is because questions on this part of the syllabus are likely to be quite practical and knowledge-based. A good definition is often an excellent way to start an answer to such a question (so long as it is relevant).

The ISO definition is a little open-ended, in that its full meaning depends on what the **requirements** are, but we can deal with that.

(a)   In a **retail context**, we might suggest that those requirements are the same thing as **reasonable customer expectations**, bearing in mind that these will inevitably reflect the price paid, to some extent at least.

(b)   Within the organisation or within a value system or network, the concept of the **internal customer** is relevant, and we may say that proper requirements reflect **fitness for purpose**, which must, in its turn, reflect the same reasonable expectations of the **strategic customer** (defined earlier in this study text). Here we might usefully introduce the concept of **design specification**, which should provide a clear specification of what is required.

(c)   In a **not-for-profit** scenario, a similar concept applies, though we might speak of the reasonable expectations of the relevant **stakeholders**.

2.1 Managing quality

If an organisation is to deliver products and services of the necessary level of quality, it must actively manage all the factors that have an impact on quality. In fact, there are very few aspects of any organisation that can be regarded as having no influence on quality, so an effective **quality management system** (QMS) is likely to have complex ramifications. The ISO definition of QMS is, perhaps, over-simplistic: 'a management system to direct and control an organisation with regard to quality'. A fuller definition is provided by *Tricker and Sherring-Lucas*.

> A **quality management system** is the organisational structure of responsibilities, activities, resources and events that together provide procedures and methods of implementation to ensure the capability of an organisation to meet quality requirements.
> *Tricker and Sherring-Lucas*

This definition gives a good indication of what is involved in a QMS. Much of it is present in organisations that do not claim to have a QMS as such: the difference is that the organisation that uses a QMS manages these common elements in a way that contribute to quality management. For example, any manufacturing organisation, no matter how rudimentary, will perform the activity of **procurement**. Procurement as part of a QMS will, for example, take positive steps to ensure that purchased materials conform consistently to the appropriate quality standards; non-QMS procurement may or may not do the same, but even if it does, it is unlikely that the procedures concerned will be documented and applied consistently.

The quality management system pervades the whole organisation since it is unlikely that there will be any of its aspects that do not have the potential to affect the quality of its outputs. Two very obvious features are the **quality manual** and the job of **quality manager**, but many other elements have their part to play. These include staff and management generally, customer requirements, supplier inputs, product design and development and customer service activities.

Quality management systems are discussed in more detail later in this chapter.

2.2 Quality assurance and quality control

Quality assurance (QA) and quality control (QC) are important aspects of the QMS.

> **Quality control** is the 'part of quality management focussed on fulfilling quality requirements'.
>
> **Quality assurance** is the 'part of quality management focussed on providing confidence that quality requirements will be fulfilled'.
> *ISO 9000:2000*

These two definitions are worth thinking about, especially if you have fallen into the common habit of thinking that **quality assurance** is just a more up to date version of **quality control**.

Quality control is about the things the organisation has to do to be sure that the quality of its output is as it should be. It is about activities such supervision, inspection, checks and measurements and applies to all parts of the organisation's value chain.

If QC is about fulfilling quality requirements, it is clear from the definition of **quality assurance** that it is about providing confidence that all the necessary QC activities are operating as they should and that a proper level of quality is therefore being achieved. QA is therefore concerned with the things that make quality control systems and activities effective. These things include quality policies; relevant management and training; and documentation such as quality records.

Tricker and Sherring-Lucas say that the **purpose** of QA is twofold:

(a) To provide assurance to a customer that the standard of workmanship within a contractor's premises is of the desired level and that all products leaving that particular firm are at, or above, a certain fixed minimum level of specification

(b) To ensure that manufacturing and service standards are uniform between an organisation's departments or offices and that they remain constant despite changes in personnel.

2.3 Quality certification

If an organisation's QMS is to provide a proper level of assurance to existing and potential customers, it is necessary for the organisation to achieve **quality certification**. This is an externally provided acknowledgement that the QMS is adequate in its provisions and its operation. Certification can only be provided by **accredited certification bodies**.

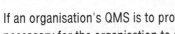

3 The ISO 9000:2000 series of standards

FAST FORWARD

The ISO 9000:2000 series has three parts

- ISO 9000:2000 is fundamentals and terminology.
- ISO 9001:2000 specifies essential features of quality management systems.
- ISO 9004:2000 provides guidelines for performance improvement.

We have already made reference to the ISO 9000:2000 series of quality standards: it is important that you understand what these standards are.

The ISO 9000:2000 series is the latest development in a line of quality standards that is directly descended from the British Standards Institution's (BSI) BS 5750 series of standards, which was published in 1979. The first ISO 9000 series of standards was very closely based on BS 5750 and was published in 1987. These standards were adopted without change, but under different names, by both the BSI and the European standards body. Improved versions were published in 1994 and widely adopted.

The layout of the standards was changed in 2000 and their content was improved yet again. The ISO 9000:2000 series now comprises three main standards.

(a)   **ISO 9000:2000 Quality Management Systems – Fundamentals and vocabulary** describes the fundamentals of QMS and defines related technical terms.

(b)   **ISO 9001:2000 Quality Management Systems – Requirements** is a specification of the essential features of a QMS intended to demonstrate an organisation's capability to provide products that meet the requirements of both customers and any applicable regulations.

(c)   **ISO 9004:2000 Quality Management Systems – Guidelines for performance improvement** provides guidance on QMS, including processes for continual improvement.

(The apparent gap between 9001 and 9004 is deliberate and arises from the combination of the 1994 standards 9001, 9002 and 9003 into a single standard, ISO 9001:2000.)

4 The quality management system

We have already provided a definition of QMS. Its rather general nature is inevitable, since there is no single approved model for a QMS. However, all QMS should be designed around the eight quality management principles given in ISO 9001:2000.

- Customer focus
- Leadership
- Involvement of people [1]
- Process approach [2]
- Systems approach to management [3]
- Continual improvement
- Factual approach to decision making
- Mutually beneficial supplier relationships

Notes

(1)   When we go on to discuss job design in a later chapter, you will see how the influence of Japanese management practice has led to the now commonly adopted principle that **quality is everybody's concern**. An important result of this approach is increased employee involvement in quality management through such mechanisms as **quality circles**.

(2)   This means managing related activities and resources as integrated processes.

(3)   This means managing groups of related processes as integrated systems

4.1 The costs of quality

Part of the purpose of quality management is to manage both the **cost of failure** and the cost of **inspection** and **presentation** so as to minimise quality related cost overall. An effective QMS will also improve the organisation's ability to deliver satisfactory outputs; it should lead to enhanced staff commitment; and it should improve relationships with customers.

Operating a QMS inevitably incurs cost. *Juran* analyses the costs associated with quality management into four types.

(a) **Inspection** or **appraisal costs** are incurred in establishing the **extent of conformance** to quality standards and include the costs of such activities as testing, inspection and the calibration of measuring equipment.

(b) **Prevention costs** are incurred in activities intended to ensure that quality is maintained: such activities include quality training, supplier surveys, quality planning and the work of quality improvement teams.

Taken together, these two categories make up the **cost of operating a QMS**. Against them must be set the **costs of quality failure**.

(a) **Internal failure costs** are incurred when a quality failure is discovered before the product or service is delivered to the customer. Examples are the costs of scrap, rework and re-inspection.

(b) **External failure costs** are incurred when a quality failure is incurred after the product or service has been delivered to the customer. Examples are the costs of complaint processing, warranty claims and product recalls.

Part of the skill of quality management is the minimising of these costs **in total**. The more rigorous the QMS, the lower the eventual costs of failure are likely to be, but the higher the costs of prevention and appraisal. The aim must to achieve a sensible balance between the two categories.

4.2 The advantages of having a QMS

An effective QMS, as well as minimising quality-related costs will have other important advantages.

(a) An improvement in the organisation's ability to deliver outputs of consistently satisfactory quality

(b) An improved level of staff commitment based on pride in work

(c) Improved customer relationships, with fewer complaints and increased turnover

4.3 The quality manual

An organisation's quality manual specifies its quality management system.

ey term

A **quality manual** is 'a document specifying the quality management system of an organisation'.

ISO 9000:2000

The ISO definition given above implies that there are two important aspects to the nature of the quality manual. The first is that it contains **practical details and instructions** for the operation of quality procedures and systems, so it is an everyday working document within the organisation. The second is that it is an important aspect of the design of the QMS and, as such, provides much of the **quality assurance** sought by external agencies such as customers and certification bodies. The quality manual is fundamental to quality management.

The quality manual is likely to contain a wide range of material: this can be grouped into a number of categories.

(a)   **Policies** relating to quality

(b)   The **organisation structure** that relates to quality management: this is likely to be identical with the overall structure of the organisation, or nearly so.

(c)   Details of **quality procedures**: this category includes a wide range of documentation.

Keeping the quality manual up to date is one of the responsibilities of the **quality manager**.

4.4 Policies relating to quality

> Quality policies may include a mission statement, a corporate policy statement and process specific polices.
>
> A **quality process** is a statement of the specified way to carry out an activity or a process
>
> There are two types of quality process: **core business processes** and **supporting processes**.

Key term

> **Quality policies** define 'the overall intentions and direction of an organisation related to quality as formally expressed by top management'.
>
> *ISO 9000:2000*

Statements of **quality policy** may be divided into three types.

(a)   The **mission statement** is a brief statement of overall quality policy and commitment set down at the most senior level of management. It will probably refer to customer satisfaction, ISO 9000 and the importance of good quality practice.

(b)   The **corporate policy statement** expands upon the mission statement. Tricker and Sherring-Lucas suggest that the eight quality principles already mentioned provide a good basis for drafting this policy. They also state that it should conform to five requirements.

(i)   It should be appropriate to the needs of the organisation and its customers
(ii)   It should involve all members of the organisation
(iii)   It should provide an outline of the organisation's goals and objectives
(iv)   It should be communicated and implemented throughout the organisation
(v)   It should be understood by everyone involved

(c)   **Process-specific policies** will relate directly to the organisation's processes and quality requirements. They should be adequate to manage quality in all key processes.

4.4.1 Processes and procedures

The words **process** and **procedure** are used in very specific ways in quality management practice based on the ISO 9000:2000 series; it is important that you understand these usages and how they differ from the everyday meanings of these words.

In ordinary use, **process** and **procedure**, while, perhaps, not quite interchangeable, can be used with very similar meanings: we might, for example, speak of a company's accounting processes or its accounting procedures and mean much the same thing. This is not the case in quality management. The difference is summarised in the definitions given below.

Key terms

> A **quality process** is 'a set of inter-related or interfacing activities which transform inputs into outputs'.
>
> A **quality procedure** is the 'specified way to carry out an activity or a process'.

4.4.2 Quality processes

The definition of **quality process** will remind you of our discussion in an earlier chapter of the model of an organisation as an **open system** interacting with its environment. Here, we may consider a quality procedure to be a **subsystem** of the overall organisational system. We must consider **ten elements** in this subsystem.

(a) The first three of these elements are the **process** itself, the **inputs** into it and the **outputs** from it.

(b) The next two elements are **suppliers**, from whom inputs are obtained, and **customers,** to whom outputs are delivered. Both customers and suppliers may be internal to the organisation, since many processes are operated in co-ordinated chains.

(c) **Inputs** is used in a very narrow sense and must not be confused with the next element, the **resources** that are required to make the process work. For example, in a simple manufacturing operation, **inputs** would be parts and raw materials, while the labour and machinery required to process them would be **resources**.

(d) Similarly, **controls** constitute a separate element: they are applied to the process but are separate from both **inputs** and **resources**.

(e) There are three further elements. The **purpose** of the process is a statement of what it is intended to achieve. The **process owner** is accountable for the operation of the process as a whole. **Performance targets and measures** are established and enforced by the **controls**.

Quality processes are divided into two types: **core business processes** and **supporting processes**. The concept is similar to that of primary and support activities in the **value chain model**, but the definitions are rather different.

(a) **Core business processes** combine in a logical sequence that proceeds from a market opportunity through to the delivery of a satisfactory product or service. The process owner for the overall sequence of core business processes would normally be the CEO or equivalent.

(b) **Supporting processes** supplement the core business processes by providing the necessary infrastructure. These processes will be owned by functional directors or managers.

Both core business processes and supporting processes must be fully documented, possibly using diagrams in a hierarchy of detail.

4.4.3 Quality procedures

FAST FORWARD

ISO 9001:2000 mandates a minimum of six specific written quality procedures. These cover two QMS processes and four MAI processes.

- Control documents
- Control records
- Internal audit
- Product failures
- Corrective action
- Preventive action

Quality procedures are the **detailed instructions** that lay down precisely **how** and **to what standards** quality processes are to be operated. They are only prepared where they are necessary and only in the detail that is needed in practice. A quality procedure may be very simple, or quite complex, possibly containing such items as lists of abbreviations, amendment records, distribution lists, statements of responsibility and examples of relevant forms as well as the detailed process instructions themselves. The detailed technical requirements and specialist procedures are normally contained in subsidiary **work instructions**.

ISO 9001:2000 requires that, as a minimum, **written procedures** must exist to control **two QMS processes** and **four processes relating to measurement, analysis and improvement** (MAI).

4.4.4 Compulsory QMS processes

Control of documents

It is important to ensure that only the latest issue of quality related documents such as drawings and instructions is used. Such documents must also be approved before use and subject to periodic review.

Control of records

Records are important both for purposes of quality assurance and for the future development of improved procedures. Procedures must be laid down to ensure that proper records are kept and to specify details of storage, retrieval, retention period and eventual disposal.

4.4.5 Compulsory MAI processes

Internal audit

Internal quality audit is required by ISO 9001:2000. The internal audit procedure must specify audit responsibilities, the frequency and extent of audit and the means of dealing with procedural failures.

Product failures

Defective or damaged products must not be delivered or used. Such products must be dealt with in one of three ways.

(a) **Rectification** followed by checking to ensure quality conformance
(b) '**Use under concession**' allows for a formal authorisation to make use of the product.
(c) **Prevention of use**, usually by quarantine and controlled disposal

Corrective action

A procedure is required to identify occasions of quality failure, investigate them, deal with the causes so as to prevent recurrence and verify that the new arrangements operate satisfactorily. All this must be properly recorded.

Preventive action

Appropriate efforts should be made to prevent the occurrence of quality failure. Potential instances should be identified, preventive action taken and reviewed and the whole process recorded.

4.4.6 Other necessary processes

While not specifically mandated as such, the standard implies that two other areas should be documented. These are **communication with customers** and the **evaluation and selection of suppliers**.

4.4.7 Quality objectives

The corporate policy statement and process-specific policies are likely to include **quality objectives**. These objectives should relate to the variables that determine whether or not proper quality is achieved. They should be written using *Drucker's* **SMART** model, which was discussed earlier in this Study Text.

5 Quality in information systems development

Four aspects of quality are particularly important in software.

- Functionality
- Reliability
- Usability
- Build quality (flexibility, expandability, portability, ease of maintenance)

Low quality in IS development produces systems that are difficult to use, maintain and enhance.

Your syllabus requires you to have some knowledge of quality management in information systems (IS) development. The complexity and internal integration of many IS makes them particularly susceptible to undesirable effects caused by defects of design and coding in particular. If you have used a PC at all you are likely to have had experience of the frustration and delay caused by defects in even such well-established systems as *Microsoft Windows*.

The material in this section is based on *Introducing Systems Development* by *Skidmore* and *Eva*.

5.1 Consequences of low quality in IS

Poor design and coding produce IS that are difficult to use, maintain and enhance. This has undesirable consequences.

(a) **Excessive costs** are incurred in correcting defects and adding or improving features to make the systems usable.

(b) **User confidence** is undermined.

(c) **Business efficiency** is harmed, with harmful effects on customer satisfaction and thence on profitability and even on the continuing existence of the organisation.

5.2 Features of good software

Four aspects of quality are particularly important in software.

(a) **Functionality** is the ability of the system to perform the tasks expected of it. It should do what the user wants it to do.

(b) **Reliability** means that the system keeps working and is not out of service frequently or for extended periods. Also, it does not produce unexpected or bizarre outputs.

(c) **Usability** means that the system is easy to use effectively.

(d) **Build quality** is evidenced by such features as ease of **maintenance**, **flexibility** in use, **expandability** and **portability** between platforms.

Failures of **functionality** and **reliability** give rise to the undesirable consequences already mentioned. Lack of **usability** will make operation of the system complex and costly in staff time; it will also require the provision of **extensive training** to users. Poor **build quality** will damage prospects for further overall system development in the future, as well as complicating maintenance and upgrades.

5.3 Systems development and the V model

FAST FORWARD

The **V model** of system development and testing requires the design of the system testing regime and the design of the system itself to be run as two linked and converging streams.

The term **'systems development lifecycle'** describes the stages a system moves through from inception until it is discarded or replaced. Traditional lifecycle models such as *Royce's* **waterfall model** break the systems development process into **sequential stages** – with the output from a stage forming the input to the following stage. The **spiral approach** involves carrying out the same activities over a number of cycles in order to clarify requirements and solutions.

In the early days of computing, systems development was **piecemeal**, involving automation of existing procedures rather than forming part of a planned strategy. The consequences were often poorly designed systems, which cost too much to make and which were not suited to users' needs.

This led to the development of generic models of the systems development such as that developed by the National Computing Centre in the 1960s. This saw the development process as commencing with the identification of a problem or opportunity and moving through a **logical sequence of stages** including a feasibility study, systems analysis, design and implementation, to conclude with review and maintenance. *Royce* described a similar sequence known as the **waterfall model**.

The term 'waterfall model' is now used to describe any system development model that is made up of a number of sequential stages – regardless of the name given to the stages.

The waterfall approach is an efficient means of computerising existing procedures within easily defined processing requirements. It works reasonably well where the system requirements are well understood by users and developers. However, it has serious disadvantages.

(a)   Sequential models restrict user input throughout much of the process. This often resulted in substantial and costly modifications late in the development process. It becomes increasingly difficult and expensive to change system requirements the further a system is developed.

(b)   Time overruns are common. The sequential nature of the process means a hold-up on one stage stops development completely.

(c)   Time pressure and lack of user involvement often resulted in a poor quality system and blame for the developers.

(d)   Operations and maintenance are treated as if they are an identifiable and finite stage with a distinct start and end. Maintenance is in fact continuous and open-ended.

These problems have led to the development of models that acknowledge the **cyclic nature of systems development**, such as *Birrel and Ould's* **'b' model** and various **spiral models**. These represent an evolutionary approach to systems development. They acknowledge that it is necessary to carry out the same activities over a number of cycles in order to clarify requirements and solutions.

In the spiral model, the development process starts at the centre, where system requirements are not well defined. They are refined with each rotation around the spiral. The longer the spiral, the more complex the system and the greater the cost.

Within each cycle of development there will be standard phases. Most of these are well illustrated by the **Structured Systems Analysis and Design Method** (SSADM). This was originally designed for use by the UK Government, but is now widely used in many areas of business.

5.3.1 SSADM

SSADM covers five stages from the early and middle stages of the systems development process. SSADM refers to stages as modules.

Module	Comment
Feasibility study	SSADM may be adopted without conducting a feasibility study, or after a study has been conducted. If the study is conducted under SSADM, it focuses on investigating system requirements and conducting a cost-benefit analysis
Requirements analysis	Involves an analysis of current operations followed by the development and presentation of options for the new system.
Requirements specification	This stage involves defining the data and processes that will be used in the new system. The systems specification document will be produced.
Logical system specification	This focuses initially on technical options for hardware and communications technology. Then the user interface and associated dialogue is designed. Logical rules for processing are established.
Physical design	The logical data structure is converted to actual physical data specifications, for example database specifications.

To these stages we only need to add the process of coding to have a fairly full picture of systems development up to the point at which testing commences.

5.3.2 Testing

Testing is a major aspect of quality control in the development of IS because of the complexity inherent in them. That complexity also means that testing cannot be regarded as something that is done when all the other aspects of a IS development project are complete: it must be incorporated at each stage of development. This approach is the essence of the **V model** of IS development.

5.4 The V model

The **V model** is the German federal standard for IS development projects. Its strength is that it requires the design of both **the testing regime** and of **the system itself** to be run as **two linked and converging streams**.

Thus, the first major process in developing a new system is likely to be the investigation and agreement of **user requirements**, while the very last major process before ongoing maintenance and development is likely to be some kind of **user acceptance test**. Clearly, the essence of success in the acceptance test is that the system meets the user requirements as originally specified. Therefore, the two elements of initial specification and final acceptance are very closely linked: the V model acknowledges this by requiring that they are developed in parallel. This principle is then applied as the design of the system moves through its various stages until the fundamental process of writing, configuring or customising code is reached.

Staff involved in testing may make a further contribution by the process of **verification**, which is applied at each stage of system specification.

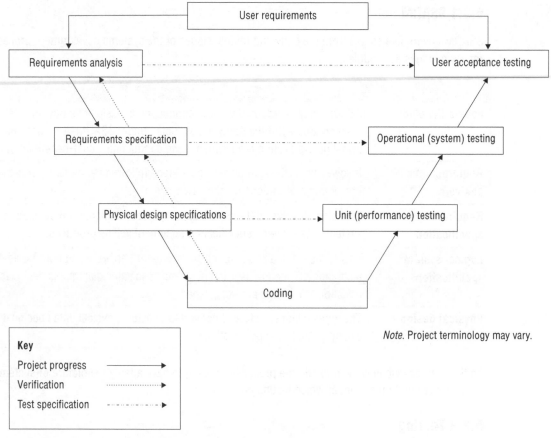

Note. Project terminology may vary.

There are three main benefits to using the V model approach.

(a)   It provides a formal basis for planning testing.
(b)   It enforces the design of test requirements before testing starts.
(c)   It requires that each stage of testing should be specified separately.

5.5 Static and dynamic testing

Static testing (or non-execution testing) consists of reviewing documents and logical models. Generally, it is the form of testing (or verification) employed on the downward, left-hand leg of the V model. **Dynamic testing** is used on the software code itself and involves running the programs and applications with live data inputs to ensure that outputs are as expected. This is the form of testing employed on the right-hand, upward leg of the V model. However, the code will first of all be subjected to a comprehensive static test in the form of a detailed inspection.

5.5.1 Unit testing

Unit testing (performance testing) is carried out by programmers to ensure that the **code functions as intended** and includes tests of such things as interfaces, error routines and integrity of data storage.

5.5.2 Operational testing

Operational testing (system testing) aims to ensure that the product meets the **requirements specified** for it. Specific tests will be made of business functionality; stability and reliability; usability and integration with other systems.

5.5.3 User acceptance testing

User acceptance testing is similar in nature to operational testing, using realistic input values and should be carried out with the same rigour. It tends to detect three types of error.

(a) **Failure to meet business requirements** may arise from poor or incorrect definition in the first place or from failure of any of the preceding test phases.

(b) **Usability problems** may emerge and lead to retraining of staff, changes to business processes or changes to the system.

(c) **Compatibility and performance problems** may arise when users run the new system on a variety of hardware configurations and in tandem with a range of linked software such as screensavers and other applications.

5.5.4 Load testing

Load testing (stress, volume, performance testing) is used to ensure that the system can handle the required volume of data inputs and outputs and can run the required number of peripherals such as terminals and printers. Load testing requires the use of computer-based tools such as simulations of operator inputs.

5.6 The limitations of testing

FAST FORWARD

It is not possible to guarantee that no faults will be found in a system, no matter how much testing is carried out.

Even when software testing is well-organised and properly conducted, it is not possible to offer a guarantee that no faults exist as a result. This is partly because of the extreme internal complexity of modern systems, with their multitudinous, inputs, responses and interfaces, and partly because application software depends on other elements, such as the compiler used, the network software and the operating system.

This practical limitation on software quality has several implications.

(a) Since testing can never be regarded as finished, the time allocated to it must be subject to some degree of negotiation.

(b) A maintenance contract will be essential for any application package.

(c) The supplier must attempt to manage the user's expectations, so that the usual disclaimer of liability for loss does not come as too much of a shock.

5.7 Quality, liability and ownership

As mentioned above, customer expectations about quality must be managed. This is one important aspect of the supplier-user relationship: other areas in which the relationship must be very carefully specified include **ownership** and **liability**. The supply contract will specify in detail what is supplied and may emphasise what is not included. Ownership of the **source code** is likely to reside with the supplier, the user merely purchasing the right to make use of a specified number of copies or use permissions. **Liability** of the supplier is likely to be strictly defined, largely because of the limitations on quality outlined above.

6 Capability Maturity Model Integration

A **capability maturity model** is a conceptual framework of organisational competence that can be used to assess an organisation's ability to deliver its product.

Five levels of maturity are commonly used in such models, ranging from an initial capability to optimisation of processes by continuous improvement.

The latest generic iteration is CMMI, which can be used for evaluation and organisational development. It is not a quality certification system like ISO 9000:2000, though external appraisal may be undertaken.

Earlier in this chapter, we discussed the ISO 9000:2000 approach to quality management. In that discussion, we showed that the essence of the system is the specification, standardisation and documentation of the **processes**, or working practices, used in the organisation.

This section is concerned with an approach to quality management that is rather different, but which is also based on **the importance of standardised processes**.

Key term

A **capability maturity model** is a conceptual framework of organisational competence that can be used to assess an organisation's ability to deliver its product.

Several capability maturity models (CMM) have been developed; all descend from an original version developed for the US Air Force at the *Carnegie-Mellon Software Engineering Institute* (SEI). This original model was intended to assist in the **evaluation of software contractors** and was described in *Managing the Software Process* by *WS Humphrey*.

The concept of the CMM has had its widest application in the fields of software and systems engineering, but it has also been applied in other fields: we will encounter the **project management maturity model** later in this study text, for example.

6.1 Levels of maturity

It is a common feature of CMM that they define **five levels of capability maturity** that an organisation may attain in the efficiency and completeness of its working practices. Here is an example of what may be expected at each of five levels.

(a)   **Level 1** represents an **initial capability**, where processes are not standardised and success depends on the professional competence of the people involved. Projects tend to come in late and over budget and there is little organisational learning.

(b)   At **Level 2** by contrast, success becomes to some extent **repeatable** and the organisation has some established procedures for project management, such as the use of time and cost plans and development milestones and review points. However, cost and time overruns are still likely.

(c)   At **Level 3**, standard processes are **defined**, **consistent** across the organisation and subject to **continuing improvement**. The critical distinction from level 2 is that, while standards and procedures may be tailored to suit a project, they are all based on a comprehensive established library rather being largely designed afresh for each project.

(d)   **Level 4** requires the consistent and effective **management** of activity. Management set **quantified quality goals** and use **quantitative techniques** to control work. The critical distinction from level 3 is that performance is quantitatively rather than merely qualitatively predictable.

(e) Organisations at **Level 5** seek to **optimise** their processes through continuous improvement that is fed back into their system. They establish and revise quantitative process improvement objectives and measure their actual improvements against them. The critical distinction from level 4 is that process improvement aims to shift the mean of performance outcomes upwards rather than merely overcoming specific problems.

6.2 CMMI

The spread of CMM has produced a fragmented and somewhat confusing body of models and in 2006, SEI released a new version intended to draw the threads together. This new version is known as **Capability Maturity Model Integration** (CMMI).

The original CMM was designed in response to a need for **evaluation**; inevitably, the idea has been taken up and used as a basis for **organisational development**. As a result, the content of the CMMI framework can be likened to the syllabus for an examination. It provides organisations with detail of what they should do in order to improve and it forms the basis for appraisal of their success. However, **CMMI appraisal is not analogous to ISO 9000:2000 certification**, though organisations that are appraised in the most formal and demanding way can use the result for marketing purposes.

The aim of CMMI is **process improvement**. Twenty two specific **process areas** are defined, each with one to four **goals**; each goal is supported by a number of specific **practices**. There are also five **generic goals** supported by seventeen **generic practices**: generic goals and practices are part of every process area.

It is possible to approach the process areas in two ways. They can be used to define five levels of maturity, in the traditional way, or to define **four functional areas**.

- Process management
- Project management
- Engineering
- Support

Exam focus point

A Pilot Paper Section B question offered fifteen marks for an explanation of the five CMMI levels and their implications for the scenario organisation.

7 Six Sigma

FAST FORWARD

Six Sigma is a quality management system that grew out of statistical quality techniques. The overall aim is a very high and consistent standard of quality output. It tends to take the form of specific improvement projects that follow a standard five phase pattern.

- **Define** requirements
- **Measure** performance
- **Analyse** the process
- **Improve** the process
- **Control** the new process

It depends to some extent on charismatic leadership

- **Master Black Belts** are in-house consultants in Six Sigma and spend all of their time on it. They are especially skilled in the statistical techniques involved and will contribute to several projects simultaneously.

- **Black Belts** also spend all of their time on Six Sigma and lead specific projects.

- **Green Belts** also lead projects. They are managers who retain other job responsibilities alongside Six Sigma.

Six Sigma is a quality management methodology developed at *Motorola* in the late 1980s. Originally, it was set of statistics-based techniques used by managers to assess manufacturing process performance. It has mutated into a widely applicable process improvement system with links to process re-engineering. Both *Harmon* and *Pande and Holpp* describe Six Sigma as the latest development in an evolutionary process that began with Scientific Management and continued through lean manufacturing and TQM.

Knowledge brought forward from earlier studies

In Chapter 8 we mentioned *Harmon's* classification of process change work.

(a)   **Process improvement** is a tactical level incremental technique that is appropriate for developing smaller, stable existing processes.

(b)   **Process reengineering** is used at the strategic level when major environmental threats or opportunities mandate fundamental re-thinking of large scale, core processes that are critical to the operation of the value chain.

(c)   **Process redesign** is an intermediate scale of operation appropriate for middle-sized processes that require extensive improvement or change.

Pande and Holpp think that Six Sigma is applicable to all three approaches and declare that 'achieving the goal of Six Sigma requires more than small, incremental improvements; it requires breakthroughs in every area of an operation'. They emphasise Six Sigma's track record of producing major return on investment and its effects on management methods.

On the other hand, Harmon describes Six Sigma as typically employed in **process improvement projects**. He goes on to say that it is very good at 'describing how to think about measuring process and activity outcomes' and 'how to use statistical techniques to analyse (*sic*) the outcomes and decide on corrective action'.

Pande and Holpp identify six themes in Six Sigma.

- Genuine focus on the customer
- Data– and fact-driven management
- Processes as the key to success
- Proactive management
- Boundaryless collaboration
- Perfectionism combined with tolerance of failure

7.1 The Six Sigma concept

The essence of Six Sigma is to improve a process to the extent that there is only the tiniest probability that it will produce unsatisfactory outputs. Note that we speak of probability: there are no certainties in this sort of work and we need to look a little further at **probability** to understand what is going on.

7.1.1 The normal distribution

The kind of probability we are concerned with is based on variation of a characteristic within a population. The population might be, say, men in the UK and the characteristic might be, say, height. Equally well, the population might be all the widgets a factory produces in a year and the characteristic might be their weight in grams. The important point about these two characteristics is that they **vary** from individual to individual and their variation is **normally distributed**.

Normal distribution of a population variable implies that its magnitude tends to clump around the mean, but there are also likely to be individual cases that are quite a long way from the mean. If we draw a graph

BPP
LEARNING MEDIA

to show the **frequency** with which actual measurements occur in a normally distributed variable, it will be a **bell shaped curve** such as the one below.

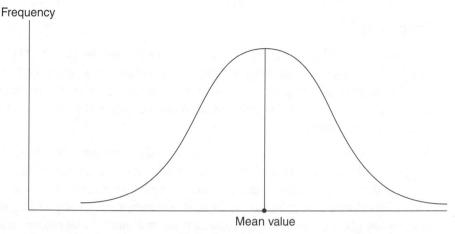

A good way to visualise the way the normal distribution works is to imagine **looking down vertically on a football pitch** with a large number of people standing on it. We have measured all these people's height and worked out the mean.

We persuade all the people whose height is **equal to the mean** to line up one behind the other **along the half way line**, starting from one of the touch lines; then the people who are one centimetre taller than the mean line up immediately to their right and those who are one centimetre shorter line up on their left, both starting from the same touch line. Then we repeat the process with those who are two centimetres taller and two centimetres shorter and so on, until everyone is in place.

If we then look down on the **shape of our crowd**, we will find that it is very close indeed to the curve shown above. We have drawn a graph using the touch line as the x axis and the centre line as the y axis. The people of mean height will be the most numerous and they will be at the centre of the curve. Taller and shorter people will be fewer in number and the greater the difference from the mean, the fewer people there will be. Eventually, as we move out towards the goal lines at either end, there might only be one or two people who are sufficiently tall or short to qualify.

It would probably take several thousand people to make this demonstration work. Even so, they would represent only a **sample** of the entire population of the country, so it is unlikely that we would encounter anyone who was outstandingly tall or short. But such people do exist and we cannot say for certain where the final limits of human height lie. The same is true of all normally distributed variables and so the tails of the normal curve never actually meet the x axis of our graph.

Standard deviation

However, we can say some other very precise things about our normally distributed variable. We can work out a measure of the variable called the **standard deviation**. How this is done need not concern us here, so long as we understand what it tells us. The standard deviation gives us an indication of the **dispersion** of the variable; that is to say, whether the curve is very tall and narrow, with most of the population values very close to the mean, or very low and flat, covering a wide range of measurements. The smaller the standard deviation, the taller and narrower the curve.

The standard deviation is interesting when we come to consider **probability**. The area under a part of the curve defined by a given number of standard deviations from the mean is easily obtained from mathematical tables. So, for example, if we take the part of the curve that lies within **two standard deviations** on either side of the mean, we find that approximately **95%** of the population will lie under it.

Going back to our height example, if the mean is 170 cm and the standard deviation is 10 cm, we can say that approximately 95% of people are between 150 cm and 190 cm tall. If we include everybody within **three standard deviations**, using the tables, we can say that over 99% of the population will be between 140 cm and 200 cm tall.

This is all very comforting and precise, but what does it have to do with **probability**, which, you may recall, was why we started on the normal distribution in the first place?

Probability

To deal with probability, we have to turn the concept on its head. We started off by describing the normal curve in terms of a **very large number of people** and we have discussed how it defines one of their variable characteristics: height in our example. We now think about what it can tell us about a **single individual**. While it cannot tell us anything absolutely precisely, it can tell us something useful with a certain degree of probability.

If we know, for example, that a person is a member of the population whose height we measured earlier, we can say **with 95% probability** that his or her height must lie in the range 170 cm to 190 cm. That is, we know that 95% of the population lie within that range, so a randomly chosen individual must therefore have a **95% chance** of being in that section of the population and, equally, of lying in that height range. Another way of using the same facts would be to say that our randomly chosen person has **only a 5% chance of lying outside** that height range.

7.1.2 Probability and process quality

The probability aspect of the normal distribution becomes very important for **process quality** when we start to think about product characteristics. We said that the essence of Six Sigma is to improve a process to the extent that there is only the **tiniest probability** that it will produce **unsatisfactory outputs**. In other words, we want to **control** things like widget weight so that it has only a tiny percentage chance of lying outside the acceptable limits.

We have spoken of 95% and 99% probability, both of which are regarded as pretty close to certainty. However, for Six Sigma we want to do better. The area under the normal curve out to three standard deviations includes well over 99% of all individual occurrences. If we extended the curve out to six standard deviations, the occurrences that were not covered would be **very, very few** indeed. This is the principle of Six Sigma: reduce the probability of defects to the minute level defined by the area **more than six standard deviations from the mean** (The Greek letter sigma in its lower case form (σ) is the usual mathematical symbol for standard deviation, hence six sigma)

In fact, the distribution used in the statistical theory that underpins Six Sigma differs slightly from the normal curve because of a phenomenon called long run process drift. Using this approach, only **3.4 items in a million** will lie outside the limit of six standard deviations either side of the mean. The goal of Six Sigma, therefore is to **reduce failures to a rate of less than 3.4 in a million**.

An important implication of this approach is that success is represented by a **band of quality** rather than a single specification. That band is defined as six standard deviations either side of the mean. Fairly obviously, if the measurements that correspond to those limits are close together, the standard deviation of the permitted measurements will be **very small** and the graph of the overall distribution will be very tall and thin.

Tolerances

It may be easiest to think about this in terms of a simple manufactured component, such as the piston in a single cylinder petrol engine. If the piston is too big, it will bind in the cylinder, or, possibly not even fit into it at all. If it is too small, it will both fail to capture the power generated from burning the fuel and it will move in an irregular fashion and cause excessive wear in the cylinder.

However, this does not mean that all pistons must be absolutely identical to the limit of measurement. Between the unacceptable extremes outlined above, there will be **a range of dimensions that are acceptable**. This range will be very narrow indeed, but it will exist. In fact, the specification for the piston diameter will probably be given with a *tolerance* such as 'plus or minus four thousandths of an inch'.

Whatever the physical dimensions of the permitted tolerance, Six Sigma requires that they must equate to plus or minus six standard deviations from the mean of the entire output of pistons if the manufacturing process is to qualify as operating at the Six Sigma level of quality.

This principle can be extended to processes other than manufacturing so long as some form of quantitative measurement is possible.

7.2 Process improvement with Six Sigma

As indicated above, Harmon suggests that Six Sigma is best applied to the **incremental improvement of fairly narrowly defined processes and sub-processes**; it is not an appropriate approach to process re-engineering or radical redesign. However, it must always be clear how the target process relates to the wider functional and strategic background.

An important feature of the system is its emphasis on the importance of basing management on **well-substantiated data** rather than opinion and intuition.

7.2.1 Organising Six Sigma

When an organisation decides to commit to Six Sigma, it will normally appoint an overall **implementation leader** and form a **steering committee** at a senior level to provide a vision for the process and to oversee it. One of the principal responsibilities of this committee will be to nominate process areas for improvement. Each area will constitute a separate project and will have its own Six Sigma **project team** and **sponsor** or **champion**. The sponsor will be a member of the steering committee or may be the process sponsor (the process owner in ISO 9000:2000 terms). The project team will be made up of **staff experienced in the process** under review; for smaller scale projects, they will be the staff actually operating the process.

Staff involved in the **leadership of projects** may possess varying grades of qualification in Six Sigma.

(a) **Master Black Belts** are in-house consultants in Six Sigma and spend all of their time on it. They are especially skilled in the statistical techniques involved and will contribute to several projects simultaneously.

(b) **Black Belts** also spend all of their time on Six Sigma and lead specific projects.

(c) **Green Belts** also lead projects. They are managers who retain other job responsibilities alongside Six Sigma.

A Six Sigma project is likely to entail a large amount of training, both for the various leader grades and for the process operating staff who make up the project teams. **Empowerment** is a feature of the system in that improvements are expected to flow from the bottom upwards. Team members are expected to commit to and take responsibility for the improvement work they are involved in.

Basic **project management techniques** are used in Six Sigma. Project management will be discussed in detail later in this Study Text: here we may simply mention that each improvement project will have a **charter** that defines its purpose, scope, assumptions and constraints in broad terms. This document will be subject to revision during the life of the project as its assumptions are challenged.

7.2.2 Six Sigma project phases

Six Sigma process improvement projects follow a **five phase** pattern known by the acronym DMAIC.

- **Define** customer requirements.
- **Measure** existing performance.
- **Analyse** the existing process.
- **Improve** the process.
- **Control** the new process.

7.2.3 Define

The definition phase is a planning phase and includes project definition and the documentation of the existing process. Typically this will take one to two weeks, with the team meeting two or three times each week. A project charter may be provided by the project sponsor, but it may be necessary for the team to negotiate project scope and goals. The establishment of precise **customer requirements** from the process in question is an essential part of this phase. *Kano* divides customer requirements into three levels.

- **Basic** requirements are the minimum the customer will accept.
- **Satisfiers** improve the quality of the customer's experience.
- **Delighters** are totally unexpected by the customer.

Both external and internal customers may be vague in stating their requirements so careful research and logical definition are required.

A further important output from this phase is careful documentation of the process as it exists, probably using some form of **flow diagram**.

7.2.4 Measure

In the measure phase, statistical tools to assess current performance are selected using black belt expertise. Harmon, quoting *Eckes*, suggests three measurement principles.

- Only measure what the customer thinks is important.
- Do not measure things that the customer is satisfied with.
- Only measure things that can be improved.

There are three main areas for measurement.

- **Inputs** such as raw materials and product specifications
- **Process elements** such as cost, time, skills and training
- **Outputs and customer satisfaction**

Fairly clearly, outputs and customer satisfaction derive from and are determined by inputs and processes. According to Pande and Holpp, it is common to represent this relationship as an equation $Y=f(X)$, where Y represents outputs and X represents inputs and processes. Y is then used in the jargon to mean goal or objective.

7.2.5 Analyse

Each element of the process may be assessed into one of three categories.

- **Value adding**
- **Necessary support** to value adding activities
- **Non-value adding**

Establishing the status of the various aspects of the process will require the use of a range of techniques including statistical analysis, *Pareto* analysis and the **fishbone analysis** discussed later in this Study Text.

Analysis should produce a list of problem causes and potential areas for improvement.

7.2.6 Improve

It may be particularly appropriate to **revisit the project charter** at the beginning of this phase, so as to incorporate any implications of the information obtained.

Improving the process demands a degree of **creative thought**. This can, to some extent, be guided by the wider experience of the team and its expert consultants. The problems identified in the analysis phase will indicate fruitful areas for consideration.

It is common for the people closely involved with the operation of a process to develop ideas for its improvement almost as soon as the possibility is raised. There is often value in these ideas, not least because of the great intimacy their authors have with the details of the process and its organisational setting.

Nevertheless, it is important that all proposals for improvement are subjected to a **rational review** so that their implications may be considered in as much detail as possible. **Cost** and **resource** consequences are of particular importance.

Implementation of the agreed improvements will require careful planning, probably small scale piloting and selling to stakeholders who were not involved in the project.

7.2.7 Control

Controlling processes is a **routine and continuing part of the management role**. When a process has been improved, it will probably be necessary to maintain some of the measurement processes used during the improvement effort in order to exercise control. However, the **cost of monitoring** must be considered, so it is likely that the extent of measurement will be minimised. Some processes can be monitored automatically, with control systems that generate exception reports automatically.

7.3 Applying Six Sigma

Your syllabus guide requires you to be able to apply Six Sigma ideas in three specific contexts.

7.3.1 E-business

Much e-business effort will relate to systems development, which has its own quality disciplines, as we have seen. Nevertheless, whether dealing with physical products or intangible services, there will be many aspects of an e-business operation that will be capable of improvement using Six Sigma. Physical products have to be procured, stored, picked, packed and delivered, for example, while services have to be designed and possibly tailored. In all cases there has to be provision for dealing with customer problems and complaints. All of these are mainstream e-business activities to which Six Sigma could be applied.

7.3.2 The value chain

As you know, the value chain is made up of value activities. In turn, those activities may be broken down into processes and sub-processes. Six Sigma is applicable at every level of this model.

7.3.3 Process improvement

We have already discussed process improvement in detail.

Chapter Roundup

- Quality management has developed from an inspection-based process to a philosophy of business that emphasises customer satisfaction, the elimination of waste and the acceptance of responsibility for conformance with quality specifications at all stages of all business processes.

- 'Quality' does not mean 'high quality'. It is the degree to which a set of inherent characteristics fulfils requirements. **Quality control** satisfies quality requirements, while **quality assurance** gives confidence that quality requirements will be satisfied. That is, quality control is about activities such as supervision and measurement, while quality assurance is about things that make those activities effective, such as training and quality records.

- The ISO 9000:2000 series has three parts

    - ISO 9000:2000 is fundamentals and terminology.
    - ISO 9001:2000 specifies essential features of quality management systems.
    - ISO 9004:2000 provides guidelines for performance improvement.

- Part of the purpose of quality management is to manage both the **cost of failure** and the cost of **inspection** and **presentation** so as to minimise quality related cost overall. An effective QMS will also improve the organisation's ability to deliver satisfactory outputs; it should lead to enhanced staff commitment; and it should improve relationships with customers.

- An organisation's quality manual specifies its quality management system.

- Quality policies may include a mission statement, a corporate policy statement and process specific polices.

    A **quality process** is a statement of the specified way to carry out an activity or a process

    There are two types of quality process: **core business processes** and **supporting processes**.

- ISO 9001:2000 mandates a minimum of six specific written quality procedures. These cover two QMS processes and four MAI processes.

    - Control documents
    - Control records
    - Internal audit
    - Product failures
    - Corrective action
    - Preventive action

- Four aspects of quality are particularly important in software.

    - Functionality
    - Reliability
    - Usability
    - Build quality (flexibility, expandability, portability, ease of maintenance)

    Low quality in IS development produces systems that are difficult to use, maintain and enhance.

- The **V model** of system development requires the design of the system testing regime and the design of the system itself to be run as two linked and converging streams.

- The term **'systems development lifecycle'** describes the stages a system moves through from inception until it is discarded or replaced. Traditional lifecycle models such as *Royce's* **waterfall model** break the systems development process into **sequential stages** – with the output from a stage forming the input to the following stage. The **spiral approach** involves carrying out the same activities over a number of cycles in order to clarify requirements and solutions.

- It is not possible to guarantee that no faults will be found in a system, no matter how much testing is carried out.

- A **capability maturity model** is a conceptual framework of organisational competence that can be used to assess an organisation's ability to deliver its product.

  Five levels of maturity are commonly used in such models, ranging from an initial capability to optimisation of processes by continuous improvement.

  The latest generic iteration is CMMI, which can be used for evaluation and organisational development. It is not a quality certification system like ISO 9000:2000, though external appraisal may be undertaken.

- Six Sigma is a quality management system that grew out of statistical quality techniques. The overall aim is a very high and consistent standard of quality output. It tends to take the form of specific improvement projects that follow a standard five phase pattern.

  - **Define** requirements
  - **Measure** performance
  - **Analyse** the process
  - **Improve** the process
  - **Control** the new process

  It depends to some extent on charismatic leadership

  - **Master Black Belts** are in-house consultants in Six Sigma and spend all of their time on it. They are especially skilled in the statistical techniques involved and will contribute to several projects simultaneously.

  - **Black Belts** also spend all of their time on Six Sigma and lead specific projects.

  - **Green Belts** also lead projects. They are managers who retain other job responsibilities alongside Six Sigma.

Quick Quiz

1 What is the difference between quality control and quality assurance?

2 Which document specifies an organisation's quality system?

3 What is the difference between a quality process and a quality procedure?

4 What is the V model of IS development?

5 As well as defining five levels of maturity, CMMI process areas can be used to define four functional areas. What are they?

6 What is the standard five phase pattern for process improvement under Six Sigma?

7 What failure rate does Six Sigma aim to achieve?

Answers to Quick Quiz

1   Quality control is about fulfilling quality requirements while quality assurance is about providing confidence that quality requirements will be fulfilled.

2   The quality manual

3   A process transforms inputs into outputs while the related procedure specifies how it should be performed.

4   The V model requires that the system and the regime for testing it be designed in parallel.

5   Process management, project management, engineering and support

6   Define requirements, measure performance, analyse the process, improve the process, control the new process

7   Less than 3.4 in a million.

Now try the question below from the Exam Question Bank

Number	Level	Marks	Time
Q11	Exam	25	45 mins

BPP
LEARNING MEDIA

Part G
Project management

13

Project management

Topic list	Syllabus reference
1 The nature of project management	G1(a), (b)
2 The project lifecycle	G1(d), (e), (f)
3 Strategic aspects of the project plan	G1(e), G2(c)
4 Practical aspects of project planning	G1(e)
5 Project management	G2(a), (b)
6 Controlling projects	G1(c), G2(c), (d) G3(a)–(e)

Introduction

Project management is an important aspect of strategy into action. In the first place, many organisations' business consists largely of projects: civil engineering contractors and film studios are two obvious examples. Secondly, even where operations are more or less continuous, the need for continuing strategic innovation and improvement in the way things are done brings project management to the forefront of attention. Finally, even relatively low-level, one-off projects must be managed with a view to their potential strategic implications.

Study guide

		Intellectual level
G1	**Identifying and initiating projects**	
(a)	Determine the distinguishing features of projects and the constraints they operate in	2
(b)	Discuss the relationship between organisational strategy and project management	2
(c)	Identify and plan to manage risks	2
(d)	Advise on the structures and information that have to be in place to successfully initiate a project	3
(e)	Assess the importance of developing a project plan and discuss the work required to produce this plan	3
(f)	Explain the relevance of projects to process re-design, e-business systems development and quality initiatives	2
G2	**Managing and leading projects**	
(a)	Discuss the organisation and implications of project-based team structures	2
(b)	Establish the role and responsibilities of the project manager and the project sponsor	2
(c)	Identify and describe typical problems encountered by a project manager when leading a project	2
(d)	Advise on how these typical problems might be addressed and overcome	3
G3	**Monitoring, controlling and concluding projects**	
(a)	Monitor the status of a project and identify project risks, issues, slippage and changes and the likely achievement of business benefits	2
(b)	Formulate response for dealing with project risks, issues, slippage and changes	2
(c)	Establish mechanisms for successfully concluding a project	2
(d)	Discuss the meaning and benefits of an end-project review, including benefits realisation	2
(e)	Evaluate how project management software may support the planning and monitoring of a project	3

Exam guide

The examiner has indicated that the importance of project management will be recognised both by Section B questions and issues in the Section A scenario. It is possible that topics that have been examined in the old syllabus Paper 2.1 *Information systems*, such as project initiation, project slippage, project completion and risk management, will re-emerge in your exam in a more complex and substantial form.

You should also remember that project management is also linked very closely to the business process change, IT and quality issues dealt with your syllabus. Its treatment here builds on the syllabus for Paper F1 *Accountant in Business*, Section E of which deals with leading and managing individuals and teams.

1 The nature of project management

A **project** is an undertaking that has a beginning and an end and is carried out to meet established goals within cost, schedule and quality objectives. It often has the following characteristics:

- A defined beginning and end
- Resources allocated specifically to it
- Intended to be done only once (although similar separate projects could be undertaken)
- Follows a plan towards a clear intended end-result
- Often cuts across organisational and functional lines

1.1 What is a project?

To understand project management it is necessary to first define what a project is.

A **project** is 'an undertaking that has a beginning and an end and is carried out to meet established goals within cost, schedule and quality objectives'. (Haynes, *Project Management*)

Resources are the money, facilities, supplies, services and people allocated to the project.

In general, the work which organisations undertake involves either **operations** or **projects**. Operations and projects are planned, controlled and executed. So how are projects distinguished from 'ordinary work'?

Projects	Operations
Have a defined beginning and end	On-going
Have resources allocated specifically to them, although often on a shared basis	Resources used 'full-time'
Are intended to be done only once	A mixture of many recurring tasks
Follow a plan towards a clear intended end-result	Goals and deadlines are more general
Often cut across organisational and functional lines	Usually follows the organisation or functional structure

An activity that meets the first four criteria above can be classified as a project, and therefore falls within the **scope of project management**. Whether an activity is classified as a project is important, as projects should be managed using **project management techniques**.

Common examples of projects include:

- Producing a new product, service or object
- Changing the structure of an organisation
- Developing or modifying a new information system
- Implementing a new business procedure or process

Maylor has described a project in **systems** terms as a process of conversion. This provides a useful overview of the concept.

1.2 What is project management?

Project management is the combination of systems, techniques, and people used to control and monitor activities undertaken within the project. It will be deemed successful if it is completed at the specified level of **quality**, **on time** and within **budget**. Achieving this can be very difficult: most projects present a range of significant challenges.

Key term

> **Project management**: Integration of all aspects of a project, ensuring that the proper knowledge and resources are available when and where needed, and above all to ensure that the expected outcome is produced in a timely, cost-effective manner. The primary function of a project manager is to manage the trade-offs between performance, timeliness and cost.
>
> *(CIMA Official Terminology)*

The objective of project management is a successful project. A project will be deemed successful if it is completed at the **specified level of quality**, **on time** and **within budget**.

Constraint	Comment
Quality	The end result should conform to the project specification. In other words, the result should achieve what the project was supposed to do.
Budget	The project should be completed without exceeding authorised expenditure.
Timescale	The progress of the project must follow the planned process, so that the 'result' is ready for use at the agreed date. As time is money, proper time management can help contain costs.

Quality, **cost** and **time** are regarded as the yardsticks against which project success is measured. It is common to add a fourth constraint, **scope**, and even to use it to **replace quality** as a fundamental constraint and target. The **scope** of a project is, in simple terms, all the work that is to be done and all the deliverables that constitute project success. Under this analysis, the quality constraint is restricted to a narrower meaning and the difference between scope and quality becomes the difference between doing a job and doing it well – or badly.

1.2.1 Projects present some management challenges

Challenge	Comment
Teambuilding	The work is carried out by a team of people often from varied work and social backgrounds. The team must 'gel' quickly and be able to communicate effectively with each other.
Expected problems	Expected problems should be avoided by careful design and planning prior to commencement of work.
Unexpected problems	There should be mechanisms within the project to enable these problems to be resolved quickly and efficiently.
Delayed benefit	There is normally no benefit until the work is finished. The 'lead in' time to this can cause a strain on the eventual recipient who is also faced with increasing expenditure for no immediate benefit.
Specialists	Contributions made by specialists are of differing importance at each stage.
Potential for conflict	Projects often involve several parties with different interests. This may lead to conflict.

1.2.2 A note on terminology

Unfortunately, the terminology used in project management is not standardised, as we have already seen in the case of **scope** and **quality**. This is partly because large organisations develop their own methodologies and partly because there are at least two major, widely used methodologies that are taught as professional disciplines. These are **PRINCE2**, developed in the UK and used globally, and the **project management body of knowledge** (PMBOK) approach and terminology developed by the US Project

Management Institute (PMI). Your syllabus does not mandate the use of any specific scheme of terminology, so we will use a selection of technical terms as they become appropriate in the discussion that follows. Where there are equivalents or near-equivalents, we will give them in brackets, together with their provenance, where appropriate, thus: '... project charter (PRINCE2: project initiation document)...'.

1.3 Projects and strategy

FAST FORWARD

Adaptation to environmental change makes project management an important feature of strategic implementation. Also, strategic management thinking can be a useful input into project management. Strategic project management envisages strategy as a stream of projects intended to achieve organisational breakthroughs.

1.3.1 Linking projects with strategy

Grundy and Brown see three links between **strategic thinking** and **project management**.

(a) Many projects are undertaken as **consequences of the overall strategic planning process**. These projects may change the relationship between the organisation and its environment or they may be aimed at major organisational change.

(b) Some important projects arise on a bottom-up basis. The need for action may become apparent for operational rather than strategic reasons: such projects must be given careful consideration to ensure that their overall effect is **congruent with the current strategy**.

(c) Strategic thinking is also required at the level of the **individual project**, in order to avoid the limitations that may be imposed by a narrow view of what is to be done.

1.3.2 Project managing strategy

Project management in its widest sense is fundamental to much strategy. This is because very few organisations are able to do the same things in the same ways year after year. Continuing **environmental change** forces many organisations to include extensive processes of **adaptation** into their strategies. Business circumstances change and new conditions must be met with new responses or initiatives. Each possible new development effectively constitutes a project in the terms we have already discussed.

Grundy and Brown suggest three reasons for taking a project management view of strategic management.

(a) Much strategy appears to develop in an incremental or fragmented way; detailed strategic thinking may be best pursued through the medium of a **strategic project** or group of projects. Project management is a way of making *ad hoc* strategy more deliberate and therefore better-considered.

(b) **Strategic implementation** is more complex than strategic analysis and choice; a project management approach, as outlined above, has an important role to play here, but must become capable of handling more complex, ambiguous and political issues if it is to play it effectively. When an apparent need for a project emerges, it should be screened to ensure that it supports the overall strategy.

(c) Even at the smaller, more traditional scale of project management, **wider strategic awareness is vital** if project managers are to deliver what the organisation actually needs

Of course, not all new developments are recognised as worthy of project management. For example, the installation of a new, shared printer in an office would probably be regarded as a matter of routine, though it would no doubt have been authorised by a responsible budget holder and installed and networked by a suitable technician. There would probably have been a small amount of training associated with its use and maintenance and it might have been the subject of a health and safety risk assessment. All these processes taken together look like a project, if a very small one.

In contrast to the multitude such small events, modern organisations are likely to undergo significant change far less often, but sufficiently frequently and with developments that have sufficiently long lives for project management to be an **important aspect of strategic implementation**. Project management and **change management** are thus intimately linked.

An atmosphere of change and continuing development will be particularly evident in relation to information systems and technology, organisation structure and organisation culture.

1.3.3 Project management as a core competence

FAST FORWARD

> Kerzner suggests that where project management is a core competence, a continuous improvement approach should be taken to developing and consolidating the methodology.

Project management can be a **core strategic competence** for companies working in such industries as consulting and construction. Such companies must ensure that they maintain and improve their project management abilities if they are to continue to be commercially successful.

Kerzner describes a five level **project management maturity model** of continuous organisational improvement in the methodology of project management. Organisations should aspire to progress to the highest level, which is a state of **continuous improvement**. The five levels need not necessarily follow one another in a linear fashion: they may overlap, but the degree of overlap allowed is reflected in the risk associated with the overall process.

Level 1   **Common knowledge**

The importance of project management to the organisation is understood and training in the basic techniques and terminology is provided.

Level 2   **Common processes**

The processes employed successfully are standardised and developed so that they can be used more widely, both for future projects and in concert with other methodologies such as total quality management.

Level 3   **Singular methodology**

Project management is placed at the centre of a single corporate methodology, achieving wide synergy and improving process control in particular. A separate methodology may be retained for IS matters.

Level 4   **Benchmarking**

Competitive advantage is recognised as being based on process improvement and a continuing programme of benchmarking is undertaken.

Level 5   **Continuous improvement**

Benchmarking information is critically appraised for its potential contribution to the improvement of the singular methodology.

Models such as Kerzner's are a guide to progress; in particular they indicate corporate training needs and career development routes for project managers.

1.3.4 Strategic project management

Grundy and Brown suggest that it is often appropriate for organisations to combine project management and strategic management into a process that they call **strategic project management**. This envisages strategy as a **stream of projects**.

> **Strategic project management** is the process of managing complex projects by combining business strategy and project management techniques in order to implement the business strategy and deliver organisational breakthroughs.
> *Grundy and Brown*

The link between strategy and project is most clearly seen in the concept of the **breakthrough project**.

> A **breakthrough project** is a project that will have a material impact on either the business's external competitive edge, its internal capabilities or its financial performance.
> *Grundy and Brown*

Breakthrough projects are a feature of the Japanese technique of *hoshin* or 'breakthrough management'. *Hoshin* requires that there should be not more than three concurrent breakthrough projects. This has distinct advantages.

- Resources are concentrated where they will do the most good.
- Projects of marginal value are avoided.
- Managerial attention remains focussed.

The link from strategy to project management is a process influenced by both **internal** and **external change**. Vision gives rise to ideas for **strategic breakthroughs**. These lead to the establishment of **strategic programmes** and these, in turn generate **strategic projects**.

2 The project lifecycle

> The project life cycle concept describes the progression of many projects through four stages: definition, design, delivery and development.

Projects may be thought of as having a **lifecycle**. This concept is useful for understanding the processes involved in project management and control, since the resources required and the focus of management attention vary as projects move from one stage to the next.

2.1 A typical four stage project lifecycle

Maylor describes a typical four stage project lifecycle.

2.1.1 Project definition

Project definition is the first stage. Its essential element is the definition of the purpose and objectives of the project. This stage may include abstract processes of conceptualisation, more rigorous analysis of requirements and methods, feasibility studies and, perhaps most important, a definition of scope. The scope of a project in this sense is what is included and what is not, both in terms of what it is intended to achieve and the extent of its impact on other parts of the organisation, both during its execution and subsequently.

The project definition stage may also include the procedures required for **project selection**. We will discuss this further below, but for now we may simply point out that an organisation may be aware of a larger number of worthwhile projects than it has resources to undertake. Some rational process for deciding just which projects will proceed is therefore required.

2.1.2 Project design

The project design phase will include detailed planning for **activity**, **cost**, **quality** and **risk**. Final project authorisation may be delayed until this stage to ensure that the decision is taken in the light of more detailed information about planned costs and benefits.

2.1.3 Project delivery

The project delivery phase includes all the work required to deliver the planned project outcomes. Planning will continue, but the emphasis is on getting the work done. Sub-phases can be identified.

(a)   The people and other resources needed initially are assembled at **start up**.

(b)   Planned project activities are carried out during **execution**.

(c)   **Completion** consists of success or, sometimes, abandonment.

(d)   The delivery phase comes to an end with **handover**. This is likely to include **project closure** procedures that ensure that all documentation, quality and accounting activities are complete and that the customer has accepted the delivery as satisfactory.

2.1.4 Project development

Handover brings the delivery phase to an end but the project continues through a further stage of management largely aimed at **improving the organisation's overall ability to manage projects**.

(a)   There should be an **immediate review** to provide rapid staff feedback and to identify short-term needs such as staff training or remedial action for procedure failures.

(b)   **Longer-term review** will examine the project outcomes after the passage of time to establish its overall degree of success. **Lifetime costs** are an important measure of success. There should also be longer-term review of all aspects of the project and its management, perhaps on a functional basis.

It is tempting to ignore the need for project review, especially since, done properly, it imposes significant costs in terms of management time and effort. It is, however, essential if the organisation is to improve the effectiveness of its project management in the future.

2.2 Project definition

Grundy and Brown summarise the process of project definition as the preparation of answers to a series of questions.

- What opportunities and threats does the project present?
- What are its objectives?
- What are its potential benefits, costs and risks?
- What is its overall implementation difficulty?
- Who are the key stakeholders?

A number of techniques that aid analytical thinking may be used when addressing these questions.

2.2.1 Defining the key issues – fishbone analysis

Fishbone analysis (root-cause, cause and effect or *Ishikawa* diagram analysis) is useful for establishing and analysing key issues. It can be used both on existing problems, opportunities and behavioural issues, and on those that may be anticipated, perhaps as a result of the construction of a scenario.

The essence of fishbone analysis is to break a perceived issue down into its smallest underlying causes and components, so that each may be tackled in a proper fashion. It is called fishbone analysis because the overall issue and its components are traditionally analysed and presented on a diagram such as the one below.

Fishbone analysis

The major issue or problem is shown at the right hand side of the page and the perceived causes and influences are shown, in no particular order, on the 'bones' radiating from the central spine. Each 'bone' can be further analysed if appropriate. It is common to use familiar models such as the Ms list of resources (men, money, machines and so on) to give structure to the investigation, though not necessarily to the diagram. The fish bone diagram itself is not, of course, essential to the process of analysis, but it forms a good medium for brainstorming a problem and for presenting the eventual results.

2.2.2 Determining performance drivers

Many strategic projects are aimed at or include improving some aspect of the performance of a department, activity or function: **performance driver analysis** is useful in such cases; essentially it is another brainstorming and presentation technique. It has a lot in common with the **force field analysis** we will encounter later in this Study Text, during our consideration of the management of change. The essential difference between the two is that force field analysis is concerned with factors affecting future change activity, while performance driver analysis is used to identify the factors that account for past (and current) performance.

The essence of the technique is to identify two groups of performance related influences: those that **enable good performance** and those that **hinder or prevent it**. The factors in these two groups are drawn as arrows against a baseline, the length of each arrow representing the perceived strength of the influence it represents.

Performance driver analysis

2.2.3 Gap analysis

Gap analysis is widely used in business strategy to focus attention on the **anticipated gap** between **desired** future strategic performance and **likely** future performance if there is no intervention. It can be used in a similar way in project selection and definition as a route to establishing both what projects should be undertaken and what their scope should be.

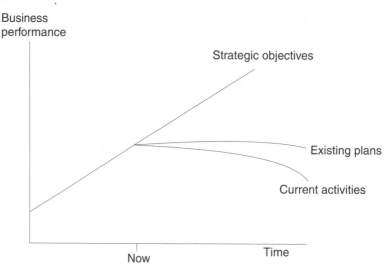

Gap analysis

2.2.4 From – to analysis

From – to analysis is appropriate for establishing the scope of strategic projects concerned with **organisational change** or **operational improvement**. The essence of the technique is to both define the **current state** ('from this') and the **desired state** ('to this') of relevant issues such as management style, control methods, power structures, communications practices, working methods, cost base and customer service. Deciding which issues are relevant is as important as deciding what should be done about them, so **fishbone analysis** might lead in to this technique. From-to analysis would supplement **gap analysis** by looking at the gap from a different perspective.

2.2.5 Stakeholder analysis

We will cover stakeholder analysis later in this chapter.

2.3 Initiating a project

FAST FORWARD

Limits to resource availability mean that not all potential projects will be undertaken; rational methods are used to select projects.

Project initiation tasks include the appointment of project manager and sponsor; stakeholder analysis and the definition of project scope. The business case explains why the project is needed, while the project charter gives authorisation for it to be undertaken.

2.3.1 Project selection

As already mentioned, it is likely that an organisation will be aware of a greater number of potentially advantageous projects than it has resources to undertake. It is therefore necessary to **select projects carefully** in order to make the best use of those limited resources. Project assessment and selection is analogous to strategic choice, not least because many projects are of strategic significance. The techniques used for making strategic choices are, therefore also applicable. The criteria of **suitability**,

acceptability and **feasibility** are applicable to many project choice problems, perhaps reinforced by the use of more detailed assessment techniques such as those below.

(a) **Risk/return analysis** using DCF, expected values and estimates of attractiveness and difficulty of implementation

(b) **Weighted scoring** of project characteristics

(c) Assessment of **organisational priority**

(d) **Feasibility studies** addressing technical, environmental, social and financial feasibility; such studies are costly and time-consuming and are likely to be restricted to front-running project proposals.

(e) **SWOT analysis**, assessing the strengths and weaknesses of individual projects against the opportunities and threats facing the organisation.

2.3.2 Project initiation tasks

When a project has been approved in general terms, it should be the subject of a number of management processes and tasks in order to start it up and move it into the execution phase. The exact nature of these processes may well vary from project to project and according to the particular project management methodology adopted. *Schwalbe* lists **pre-initiating tasks** and **initiating tasks**. The pre-initiating tasks follow on directly from the formal project selection process.

2.3.3 Pre-initiating tasks

Pre-initiating tasks are the responsibility of the senior managers who decide that the project should be undertaken.

(a) Determination of project scope, quality, time and cost **goals**

(b) Identification of the **project sponsor**

(c) Selection of the **project manager**

Note: The roles and responsibilities of the project manager and project sponsor are discussed later in this chapter.

(d) **Senior management meeting** with project manager to review the process and expectations for managing the project

(e) Decision whether the project actually needs to be divided into two or more smaller projects

2.3.4 Initiating tasks

Initiating tasks are carried out by the **project manager**.

(a) Identification of **project stakeholders** and their characteristics
(b) Preparation of a **business case** for the project
(c) Drafting of a **project charter** (PRINCE2: project initiation document)
(d) Drafting an initial statement of **project scope**
(e) Holding a **project initiation meeting** (PMBOK: 'kick-off' meeting)

2.4 Stakeholder analysis

Project stakeholders are the individuals and organisations that are involved in or may be affected by project activities and outcomes.

We discussed the strategic importance of stakeholders earlier in this Study Text. Fairly obviously, where a project is of strategic significance, stakeholders will be considered at several points during the development of the strategy. The stakeholder concept can also be applied to the management of projects of less overall significance. This would form part of that strategic approach to project management advocated by Grundy and Brown. It is important to understand who has an interest in a project, because part of the responsibility of the project manager is **communication** and the **management of expectations**. An initial assessment of stakeholders should be made early in the project's life, taking care not to ignore those who might not approve of the project, either as a whole, or because of some aspect such as its cost, its use of scarce talent or its side-effects. Each stakeholder's degree of interest in and support for (or opposition to) the project should be estimated

2.5 Preparation of a business case

When the project selection process is complete and a project selected for action, there is likely to be a great deal of information available to justify the decision to proceed. However, it is unlikely that a full account of the project has been prepared. A **business case** is a reasoned account of **why** the project is needed, **what** it will achieve and **how** it will proceed. The business case is a fundamental component of the PRINCE2 methodology, which is built on the assumption that a project is, in fact, **driven by its business case**. An important use of the business case in any project is to maintain **focus** and prevent **mission creep** by regular reference back to it. It is possible that final approval for a large project will depend upon the preparation of a satisfactory business case.

A business case is not, of course, something that is confined to commercial organisations: the principles are equally applicable to any organisation undertaking a project.

2.5.1 Typical content of a business case

- Background to the project and reasoning behind it
- Overall objectives and success criteria
- Important assumptions and constraints
- Project scope
- Summary budget
- Time estimate
- Summary risk analysis

2.6 The project charter

The **project charter** (or project initiation document) complements the business case: while the business case explains the **need** for work on the project to start, the charter gives **authorisation** for work to be done and resources used. The charter also has an important role in internal communication within the organisation, since it can be given wide distribution in order to keep staff informed of what is happening. The exact content of a charter will vary from organisation to organisation and from project to project, but some elements are likely to be present in all charters.

- Project title
- Project purpose and objectives
- Project start date and expected finish date
- Details of the project sponsor and project
- Authorisation by the main stakeholders

Other elements of information may be included.

- Outline schedule of work
- Budget information
- Outline of project scope and work sequence
- Further details of roles and responsibilities

2.7 Statement of project scope

As we have already indicated, the word 'scope' is used in project management to mean both the outcomes that are required and the work that is to be done to achieve them. It is obviously of great importance that everyone involved in a project should have a common understanding of these matters. If this common understanding is not reached, sooner or later there will be acrimonious disputes. A careful specification of project scope is therefore of great importance and the project management methodology in use may require that this be a separate document. Equally, it may be that the business case and the project charter between them provide a clear statement of agreed scope. Under the **PRINCE2** methodology, the **business case** performs the role of a statement of project scope.

It is likely that in larger projects it will become necessary to **adjust the project scope**. This might occur, for example, if resources are unavoidably reduced or it becomes clear that a feasibility study was too optimistic or too pessimistic. When a change to project scope becomes apparent, it is important that it is **clearly stated** and that the revision is **approved by the interested stakeholders**.

2.8 Terminology again

If you have been paying attention you will have noticed that there has been a certain amount of overlap in our account so far of the processes involved in getting a project off the ground. For example, there have been a couple of mentions of stakeholders and the whole problem of scope has been approached from several different directions. We make no apology for this – it is the result of the variety of project methodologies in use in the real world.

xam focus oint

> Prepare your own summary of the activities and processes involved in project selection, definition, and initiation, mentioning each one just once. This will provide you with essential information for dealing with any question that involves the early stages of a project.

3 Strategic aspects of the project plan

FAST FORWARD

> Many large-scale projects, particularly those involving major change, are strategically significant and project management can merge into strategic management. Force field analysis identifies enablers, constraints and showstoppers.

The unique nature of each project means that careful planning is an essential component of project management. Many project cost and time overruns and outright failures can be traced to failures of planning.

Project management as a discipline is commonly associated with fairly clearly defined issues such as preparing for a conference, organising an office move or installing a new IT system. Projects such as these can be of strategic importance, but even when they are, there is often an unspoken assumption that once the go-ahead is given, the job of project management is essentially one of detailed planning, organisation and control, with, perhaps, a little trouble-shooting thrown in. It is important to understand that this is unlikely to be the case with truly strategic projects: with projects such as the turn-round of an underperforming division or an initial move into a foreign market, **project management and strategic management are likely to merge into one another**. As a corollary, we can say that at the level of the strategic project, project planning is likely to make use of a strategic planning approach. A failure to think strategically is likely to lead to project failure.

3.1 Why do projects go wrong?

Project planning is fundamental to project success. **Realistic timescales** must be established, use of **shared resources** must be planned and, most fundamental of all, jobs must be done in a sensible **sequence**. However, even if all these aspects are satisfactory there are other potential pitfalls that the project planner must avoid or work around. Here are some examples.

(a) **Unproven technology**

Then use of **new technological developments** may be a feature of any project. The range of such developments extends from fairly routine and non-critical improvements, through major innovations capable of transforming working practices, costs and time scales, to revolutionary techniques that make feasible projects that were previously quite impracticable. As the practical potential of a technical change moves from minor to major, so too moves its potential to cause disruption if something goes wrong with it. A classic example is *Rolls Royce's* attempt to use carbon fibre in the design of the *RB211* engine in the early 1970s. Not only did the project fail to meet its objectives, its failure led to the company's financial failure and subsequent takeover by government.

(b) **Changing client specifications**

It is not unusual for clients' notions of what they want to evolve during the lifetime of the project. However, if the work is to come in on time and on budget, they must be **aware** of what is **technically feasible**, **reasonable** in their **aspirations**, **prompt** with their **decisions** and, ultimately, **prepared to freeze the specification** so that it can be delivered. The failure of the *TSR2* aircraft project forty years ago was in large part caused by major, unrealistic changes to specification.

Note that the term 'client' includes *internal* specifiers.

(c) **Politics**

This problem area includes politics of all kinds, from those internal to an organisation managing its own projects, to the effect of national (and even international) politics on major undertakings. Identification of a senior figure with a project; public interest and press hysteria; hidden agendas; national prestige; and political dogma can all have deleterious effects on project management. **Lack of senior management support** is an important political problem.

3.2 Force field analysis

Grundy and Brown suggest that force field analysis can be useful in project planning. This is an important example of the **close relationship between project management and strategic management** that appears in their analysis.

The emphasis of force field analysis is an assessment of the **degree of difficulty** that implementing a project is likely to encounter: the problems discussed above, and any of a wide range of other attitudes and conditions will affect the degree of difficulty encountered and this will be particularly the case with projects of a strategic nature. It is important that such matters are carefully considered as part of the planning process and force field analysis is one way of doing this.

The essence of force field analysis is the identification and assessment of the underlying forces tending to promote successful implementation or to hold it back. These forces may be referred to as **enablers** and **constraints**. The overall potential of each force must be estimated. As in the performance driver analysis already discussed, it is usual to show enablers and constraints as arrows against a baseline in a visual presentation.

A degree of objectivity can be brought into this analysis by seeking to **expose implicit assumptions** about these factors and the overall situation. This process can be moved forward by asking three questions.

- What is it about each force that allows it to be identified as an enabler or a constraint?
- How great is its potential influence on the change process?
- What other, less obvious factors does it depend on?

A further important part of the overall analysis is the identification of potential **showstoppers**. These are constraints that can make implementation so difficult as to cause overall project failure. These factors must be continuously monitored.

Management of constraints includes two important possibilities.

(a) It may be possible to turn one of the constraints around and turn it into a driver. Changing the mind of an unsympathetic stakeholder would be a good example.

(b) Careful examination of the context of the project may reveal **latent enablers** that could be called into play. For example, there may be sympathetic stakeholder groups whose driver potential has been ignored.

3.3 More on stakeholders

We suggested that a preliminary stakeholder analysis should form part of the project definition phase. It is appropriate to take this further at the planning stage. The project manager should be prepare to deal with varying degrees of support for the project. A **stakeholder grid** of the type discussed earlier in this study text should be prepared and an assessment made of overall stakeholder attitudes. This process should be repeated as required to reflect the changes that are likely to occur as the project progresses and stakeholders' attitudes develop.

4 Practical aspects of project planning

FAST FORWARD

> Work breakdown structure is an analysis of the work involved in a project into a structure of phases, activities and tasks. **Dependencies** determine the order in which tasks must be carried out, while **interactions** between tasks affect them without imposing order.

4.1 Work breakdown structure

Work breakdown structure (WBS) is fundamental to traditional project planning and control. Its essence is the **analysis** of the work required to complete the project into **manageable components**.

A good way to approach WBS is to consider the **outputs** (or 'deliverables') the project is required to produce. This can then be analysed into physical and intangible components, which can in turn be further analysed down to whatever level of simplicity is required. Working backwards in this way helps to **avoid preconceived ideas** of the work the project will involve and the processes that must be undertaken. This approach, called product breakdown, is the basis of project planning under the PRINCE2 system.

The WBS can allow for several levels of analysis, starting with major project phases and gradually breaking them down into major activities, more detailed sub-activities and individual tasks that will last only a very short time. There is no standardised terminology for the various levels of disaggregation, though an **activity** is sometimes regarded as being composed of **tasks**.

The delivery phase of many projects will break down into significant stages or sub-phases. These are very useful for control purposes, as the completion of each stage is an obvious point for reviewing the whole plan before starting the next one.

4.1.1 Dependencies and interactions

A very important aspect of project planning is the determination of **dependencies** and **interactions**. At any level of WBS analysis, some tasks will be dependent on others; that is to say, **a dependent task cannot commence** until the task upon which it depends is completed. Careful analysis of dependencies is a major step towards a workable project plan, since it provides an **order in which things must be tackled**. Sometimes, of course, the dependencies are limited and it is possible to proceed with tasks in almost any order, but this is unusual. The more complex a project, the greater the need for analysis of dependencies.

Interactions are slightly different; they occur when tasks are linked but not dependent. This can arise for a variety of reasons: a good example is a requirement to share the use of a scarce resource.

The output from the WBS process is a list of tasks, probably arranged hierarchically to reflect the disaggregation of activities. This then becomes the input into the planning and control processes described below.

4.2 The project budget

FAST FORWARD

> The **project budget** plans the allocation of resources to the project and forms a basis for their control. Budgeting may be top-down or bottom-up.

Key term

> **Project budget.** The amount and distribution of resources allocated to a project.

Building a project budget should be an orderly process that attempts to establish a realistic estimate of the cost of the project. There are two main methods for establishing the project budget; **top-down** and **bottom-up**.

Top-down budgeting describes the situation where the budget is imposed 'from above'. Project managers are allocated a budget for the project based on an estimate made by senior management. The figure may prove realistic, especially if similar projects have been undertaken recently. However the technique is often used simply because it is quick, or because only a certain level of funding is available.

In **bottom-up budgeting** the project manager consults the project team, and others, to calculate a budget based on the tasks that make up the project. WBS is a useful tool in this process.

4.3 Gantt charts

FAST FORWARD

> A Gantt **chart** shows the deployment of resources over time.

A **Gantt chart**, named after the engineer *Henry Gantt* who pioneered the procedure in the early 1900s, is a horizontal bar chart used to plan the **time scale** for a project and to estimate the **resources** required.

The Gantt chart displays the time relationships between tasks in a project. Two lines are usually used to show the time allocated for each task, and the actual time taken.

A simple Gantt chart, illustrating some of the activities involved in a network server installation project, follows.

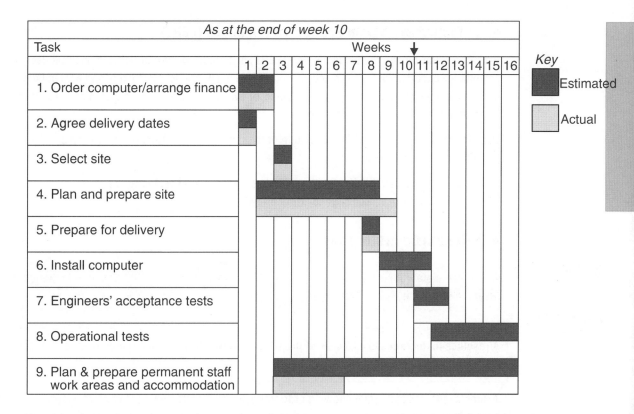

The chart shows that at the end of the tenth week Activity 9 is running behind schedule. More resources may have to be allocated to this activity if the staff accommodation is to be ready in time for the changeover to the new system.

Activity 4 had not been completed on time, and this has resulted in some disruption to the computer installation (Activity 6), which may mean further delays in the commencement of Activities 7 and 8.

A Gantt chart does not show the interrelationship between the various activities in the project as clearly as a **network diagram** (covered later in this chapter). A combination of Gantt charts and network analysis will often be used for project planning and resource allocation.

4.4 Network analysis

FAST FORWARD

Network analysis illustrates interactions and dependencies. It is used to plan the sequence of tasks making up project scope and to determine the critical path. PERT uses probabilities to make estimates of likely completion and milestone dates.

Network analysis, also known as **Critical Path Analysis** (CPA), is a useful technique to help with planning and controlling large projects, such as construction projects, research and development projects and the computerisation of systems.

CPA aims to ensure the progress of a project, so the project is completed in the **minimum amount of time**. It pinpoints the tasks **on the critical path**, which is the longest duration sequence of tasks in the project; a delay to any of these tasks would **delay the completion** of the project as a whole. The technique can also be used to assist in **allocating resources** such as labour and equipment.

xam focus
oint

Critical path analysis is employed in most complex projects but it is a specialised process and you will not be required to use it in the exam.

4.4.1 Project evaluation and review technique (PERT)

Project evaluation and review technique (PERT) is a modified form of network analysis designed to account for **uncertainty**. For each activity in the project, **optimistic**, **most likely** and **pessimistic** estimates of times are made, on the basis of past experience, or even guess-work. These estimates are converted into a mean time and also a standard deviation.

Once the mean time and standard deviation of the time have been calculated for each activity, it should be possible to do the following.

(a)   Establish the duration of the critical path using **expected times**.
(b)   Calculate a **contingency time allowance**.

4.5 Resource histogram

FAST FORWARD

A resource **histogram** is a useful planning tool that shows the amount and timing of the requirement for a resource (or a range of resources).

Key term

A resource **histogram** shows a view of project data in which resource requirements, usage, and availability are shown against a time scale.

A simple resource histogram showing programmer time required on a software development program is shown below.

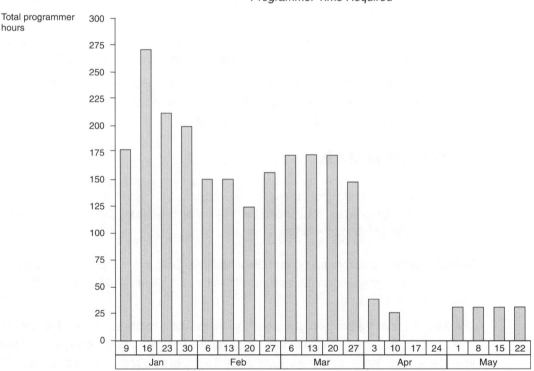

Programmer Time Required

Some organisations add another bar (or a separate line) to the chart showing resource availability. The chart then shows any instances when the required resource hours exceed the available hours. Plans should then be made to either obtain further resource for these peak times, or to re-schedule the work plan. Alternately the chart may show times when the available resource is excessive, and should be re-deployed elsewhere. An example follows.

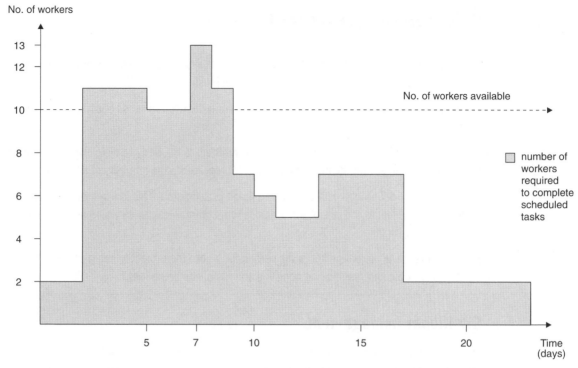

No. of workers

No. of workers available

number of workers required to complete scheduled tasks

Time (days)

The number of workers required on the seventh day is 13. Can we re-schedule the non-critical activities to reduce the requirement to the available level of 10? We might be able to re-arrange activities so that we can make use of the workers available from day 9 onwards.

4.6 Project management software

Project management software can be used to produce detailed project planning documentation, to update plans and to produce reports.

Project management techniques are ideal candidates for computerisation. Schwalbe discusses three categories of software after noting that many project managers simply use basic applications such as *MS Word* and *Excel* to prepare documentation and support decisions.

4.6.1 Low-end software

Low-end software assist with basic functions such as publishing and creation of Gantt charts. It may provide enhancements to *Word* and *Excel*.

4.6.2 Mid-range software

Mid-range software can handle larger projects and multiple users. It will produce Gantt charts and network diagrams and will assist with critical path analysis, resource allocation and project status tracking. *MS Project* is typical of this class of software.

4.6.3 High end software

High-end software can handle very large projects and dispersed user groups. These packages can also summarise the information held about a portfolio of projects on an enterprise wide basis and may be integrated with wider ERP systems.

5 Project management

Key terms

> The **project sponsor** provides and is accountable for the resources invested into the project and is responsible for the achievement of the project's business objectives.
>
> The **project manager** takes responsibility for ensuring the desired result is achieved on time and within budget.
>
> The **Project Board** (PMBOK: project steering committee) is the body to which the project manager is accountable for achieving the project objectives. It represents the interests of the project sponsor.
>
> **Project champion.** Sometimes a project champion is appointed. This is a senior manager whose role is to represent the project to the rest of the organisation, communicating its vision and objectives and securing commitment to them.
>
> **Project owner.** The project owner is the person for whom the project is being carried out and as such he is interested in the end result being achieved and his needs being met.

5.1 Higher management

In all but the smallest organisations, it is likely that the project manager will be appointed by and be responsible to a higher level of management. Resources must be allocated to the project by a person or group with the power to do so and the project manager must be subject to supervision.

It is common to refer to the person or group providing the resources as the **project sponsor**, though the term **investment decision-maker** has also been used. The project sponsor may, in fact, be the strategic apex body of the organisation, or may be a person or committee at a lower level; the essential feature is that the project sponsor has the budgetary capability to authorise the project.

The project sponsor will not be involved in the management of the project and may not have the capacity to provide effective supervision for the project manager. Under these circumstances, the project sponsor may appoint a **project owner**, whose role will be to review project plans and progress at regular intervals and to arbitrate on any conflicts that may arise between project and line management. Of course, in smaller organisations, the roles of project sponsor and project owner may be combined.

Exam focus point

> Some organisations use the terms project owner and project sponsor in a way exactly opposite to the usage we have outlined here! An example is the Scottish Executive construction works procurement guidance, which makes the project owner subordinate to the investment decision-maker and superior to the project sponsor. Be careful in your use of these terms and explain what you mean when you use them.

5.1.1 The project manager

FAST FORWARD

> The person who takes ultimate responsibility for ensuring the desired result is achieved on time and within budget is the **project manager**. **Duties** of the project manager include: Planning, teambuilding, communication, co-ordinating project activities, monitoring and control, problem-resolution and quality control.

Some project managers have only one major responsibility: a specific project. However, anyone responsible for a project, large or small, is a project manager. As result, many project managers, will have routine work responsibilities outside their project goals, which may lead to conflicting demands on their time.

The role a project manager performs is in many ways similar to those performed by other managers. There are however some important differences, as shown in the table below.

Project managers	Operations managers
Are often **generalists** with wide-ranging backgrounds and experience levels	Usually specialists in the areas managed
Oversee work in **many functional areas**	Relate closely to technical tasks in their area
Facilitate, rather than supervise team members	Have direct technical supervision responsibilities

5.2 The responsibilities of a project manager

A project manager has responsibilities to both management and to the project team.

5.2.1 Responsibilities to management

- Ensure resources are used efficiently – strike a balance between cost, time and results
- Keep management informed with timely and accurate communications
- Manage the project to the best of his or her ability
- Behave ethically, and adhere to the organisation's policies
- Maintain a customer orientation (whether the project is geared towards an internal or external customer) – customer satisfaction is a key indicator of project success

5.2.2 Responsibilities to the project and the project team

- Take action to keep the project on target for successful completion
- Ensure the project team has the resources required to perform tasks assigned
- Help new team members integrate into the team
- Provide any support required when members leave the team either during the project or on completion

5.3 Duties of a project manager

The project manager's responsibilities give rise to a number of fairly standard duties and managerial activities

Duty	Comment
Outline planning	See above for project definition and initiation
Detailed planning	Work breakdown structure, budgeting, resource requirements, network analysis for scheduling.
Obtain necessary resources	Resources may already exist within the organisation or may have to be bought in. Resource requirements unforeseen at the planning stage will have to be authorised separately by the project board or project sponsor.
Teambuilding	Build cohesion and team spirit in the project team.
Communication	Keep all stakeholders suitably informed and ensure that members of the project team are properly briefed. Manage expectations.
Co-ordinating project activities	Co-ordination will be required between the project team, external suppliers, the project owner and end-users.
Monitoring and control	Monitor progress against the plan, and take corrective measures where needed.

Duty	Comment
Problem-resolution	Even with the best planning, unforeseen problems may arise.
Quality control	Understand and manage quality procedures; agree and manage any appropriate trade-off of functionality against achieving deadlines.

It is also possible to view the **process of project management** as having **five stages**.

- Initiation
- Planning
- Leadership
- Controlling
- Completing

The first, second, fourth and fifth of these phases correspond closely to the phases of the **project life cycle**, which was discussed earlier in this chapter. The third phase, leadership, forms a major part of the subject matter of this section.

5.4 The skills required of a project manager

Project managers require the following **skills**: Leadership and team building, organisational ability, communication skills (written, spoken, presentations, meetings), some technical knowledge of the project area and inter-personal skills.

To perform these duties and meet these responsibilities, a project manager requires a wide range of skills.

Skill	Application to project management
Leadership and team building	A participative style of leadership is appropriate for much of most projects, but a more autocratic, decisive style may be required on occasion.
	Be **positive** (but realistic) about all aspects of the project
	Understand where the project fits into the **big picture**
	Delegate tasks appropriately – and not take on too much personally
	Build team spirit through **co-operation** and recognition of achievement
	Do not be restrained by organisational structures – a high tolerance for ambiguity (lack of clear-cut authority) will help the project manager
Organisational	Ensure all project **documentation** is clear and distributed to all who require it
	Use project management **tools** to analyse and monitor project progress
Communication and negotiation	**Listen** to project team members
	Use **persuasion** to coerce reluctant team members or stakeholders to support the project
	Negotiate on funding, timescales, staffing and other resources, quality and disputes
	Ensure management is kept **informed** and is never surprised
Technical	By providing (or at least providing access to) the **technical expertise** and experience needed to manage the project

Skill	Application to project management
Personal qualities	Be **flexible**. Circumstances may develop that require a change in plan
	Show **persistence**. Even successful projects will encounter difficulties that require repeated efforts to overcome
	Be **creative**. If one method of completing a task proves impractical a new approach may be required
	Patience is required even in the face of tight deadlines. The 'quick-fix' may eventually cost more time than a more thorough but initially more time-consuming solution
Problem solving	Only the very simplest projects will be without problems. The project manager must bring a sensible approach to their solution and **delegate** as much responsibility as possible to team members so that they become used to **solving their own problems.** By the nature of a project there is always uncertainty and risk in a project. The project manager needs to be able to react to these situations fast, and adopt an efficient problem solving attitude so as not to hold up the project at key moments.
Change control and management	Major projects may be accompanied by the kind of far-reaching **change** that has wide-ranging effects on the organisation and its people. Here, however, we are concerned with **changes to the project itself**. Changes can arise from a variety of sources (not least the intended end-users) and have the potential to disrupt the progress of the project. They must be properly authorised, planned and resourced and records kept of their source, impact and authorisation if the project is not to become unmanageable. **Change control** is one of the components of the **PRINCE2** project management system

5.5 Leadership style

As in other forms of management, different project managers have different styles of leadership. There is no single best leadership style, as individuals react differently to different styles on different occasions. The key is adopting a style that suits both the leader and the team and that is appropriate to the current situation.

The leadership style adopted will affect the way decisions relating to the project are made. Although an autocratic style may prove successful in some situations, such as very simple or repetitive projects, a more consultative style has the advantage of making team members feel more a part of the project. This should result in greater **commitment**.

Not all decisions will be made in the same way. For example, decisions that do not have direct consequences for other project personnel may be made with no (or limited) consultation. A **balance** needs to be found between ensuring decisions can be made efficiently, and ensuring adequate consultation.

The type of people that comprise the project team will influence the style adopted. For example, professionals generally dislike being closely supervised and dictated to. Some people however, prefer to follow clear, specific instructions and not have to think for themselves.

Project management techniques encourage **management by exception** by identifying, from the outset, those activities which might threaten successful completion of a project.

5.6 Organising for projects – the matrix structure

Many projects are organised as stand-alone enterprises, with their own dedicated staff. However, much project management is undertaken within a framework of routine operations, with staff being seconded to the project from their own departments or functions. This gives rise to a **matrix structure**. In general terms, a matrix structure provides for the formalisation of management control between different functions, whilst at the same time maintaining functional departmentation. This approach is widely used as a general approach to management in complex organisations. It is particularly suitable for structuring the management of projects. Many projects are **interdisciplinary**, and might require, for instance the contributions of an engineer, a scientist, a statistician and a production expert, who would be appointed to the team while retaining membership and status within their own functional department. A matrix approach enables such specialists to receive management and leadership inputs from both the project manager and their own functional manager.

5.7 The project team

FAST FORWARD

Project managers should have some understanding of the way that groups of people interact at work.

Teams enable people's talents and efforts to be combined and teamwork can have a motivating effect, Tuckman identified four stages in team development.

- Forming
- Storming
- Norming
- Performing

However, teams bring their own problems, including disharmony, risky shift, groupthink and political conflict. Handy suggests a contingency approach to team leadership. Belbin identified nine roles played by team members.

• Co-ordinator	• Shaper
• Plant	• Monitor-evaluator
• Resource investigator	• Implementer
• Team worker	• Finisher
• Specialist	

Key term

> A **group** is 'any collection of people who perceive themselves to be a group'.

Unlike a random collection of individuals, a group shares a common sense of identity and belonging. They have certain attributes that a random crowd does not possess.

(a)   A **sense of identity**. There is awareness of membership and acknowledged boundaries to the group which define it.

(b)   **Loyalty to the group**, and acceptance within the group. This generally expresses itself as conformity or the acceptance of the norms of behaviour and attitudes that bind the group together and exclude others from it.

(c)   **Purpose and leadership**. Most groups have an express purpose, whatever field they are in: most will, spontaneously or formally, choose individuals or sub-groups to lead them towards the fulfilment of those goals.

A **primary working group** is the immediate social environment of the individual worker. A **formal group** used for particular objectives in the work place is called a **team**. Project teams fall into this category by definition. Although many people enjoy working in teams, their popularity in the work place arises because of their effectiveness in fulfilling the organisation's work.

5.7.1 Aspects of teams

Key term

> A **team** is a 'small number of people with complementary skills who are committed to a common purpose, performance goals and approach for which they hold themselves mutually accountable'. (*Katzenbach and Smith*, 1994)

(a) **Work organisation.** Teams combine the skills of different individuals and avoid complex communication between different business functions.

(b) **Control.** Fear of letting down the team can be a powerful motivator, hence teams can be used to control the performance and behaviour of individuals. Teams can also be used to resolve **conflict**.

(c) **Knowledge generation**. Teams can generate ideas.

(d) **Decision-making.** Teams can be set up to investigate new developments and decisions can be evaluated from more than one viewpoint.

(e) **Communication.** Team work can enhance the flow of information.

(f) **Social needs.** People generally have a need for company and social interaction.

5.7.2 Multi-disciplinary teams

Many project teams will be deliberately structured as multi-disciplinary teams. Multi-disciplinary teams bring together individuals with different skills and specialisms, so that their skills, experience and knowledge can be pooled or exchanged. Team working of this kind encourages freer and faster communication between disciplines in the organisation.

(a) Team working increases workers' **awareness of their overall objectives** and targets.

(b) Team working **aids co-ordination**.

(c) Team working **helps to generate solutions to problems**, and suggestions for improvements, since a multi-disciplinary team has access to more 'pieces of the jigsaw'.

5.7.3 Development of the team

The **performance** and **effectiveness** of teams is influenced by a range of factors.

(a) **Size** is important: larger groups can do more work, but individual productivity tends to fall. This is called the **Ringelmann effect**. This effect is held to be the product of **social loafing**, which arises when group members believe they will not receive a fair share of reward if they make a great effort, nor appropriate blame if they make an inadequate one.

(b) **Cohesion** enhances output. Cohesion is reduced by membership turnover and if members have divided loyalties. Similarity of status enhances cohesion.

(c) **Group roles**. Groups often develop roles that are played by individuals spontaneously. More formal roles are acknowledged by mechanisms such as election. Personal predisposition and talent are important in the emergence of such figures as leaders and nurturers in groups. We return to this concept later when we discuss the work of *Belbin* on team roles.

Four stages in team development were identified by *Tuckman*. Project managers should be aware of these stages and be prepared to manage and exploit them

Step 1 **Forming**

The team is just coming together, and may still be seen as a collection of individuals. Each member wishes to impress his or her personality on the group. The individuals will be trying to find out about each other, and about the aims and norms of the team. There will at this stage probably be a wariness about introducing new ideas. The objectives being pursued may as yet be unclear and a leader may not yet have emerged. This period is essential, but may be time wasting: the team as a unit will not be used to being autonomous, and will probably not be an efficient agent in the planning of its activities or the activities of others.

Step 2   Storming

This frequently involves more or less open conflict between team members. There may be changes agreed in the original objectives, procedures and norms established for the group. If the team is developing successfully this may be a fruitful phase as **more realistic targets** are set and **trust** between the group members **increases**.

Step 3   Norming

A period of settling down: there will be agreements about work sharing, individual requirements and expectations of output. **Norms and procedures** may evolve which enable methodical working to be introduced and maintained.

Step 4   Performing

The team sets to work to execute its task. The difficulties of growth and development no longer hinder the group's objectives.

5.7.4 Characteristics of the ideal functioning team

(a)   Each individual gets the support of the team and a sense of identity and belonging that encourages loyalty and hard work on the group's behalf.

(b)   Skills, information and ideas are shared, so that the team's capabilities are greater than those of the individuals. **Synergy** is achieved through the pooling of skills.

(c)   New ideas can be tested, reactions taken into account and persuasive skills brought into play in group discussion for **decision making** and **problem solving**. The team provides a focus for **creativity** and **innovation**, especially in multi-disciplinary teams.

(d)   Each individual is encouraged to participate and contribute and thus becomes personally involved in and committed to the team's activities. Equally, control and discipline are enhanced by commitment to the team's expectations.

(e)   Goodwill, trust and respect can be built up between individuals, so that communication is encouraged and potential problems more easily overcome. This can contribute to **empowerment** when responsibility and authority are delegated to self-managing teams.

5.7.5 Problems with teams

Unfortunately, team working is rarely such an undiluted success. There are certain constraints involved in working with others.

(a)   Awareness of **group norms** and the desire to be acceptable to the group may **restrict individual effort**.

(b)   **Too much discord**. Where an individual is a member of more than one group, conflicting roles and relationships can cause difficulties in communicating effectively.

(c)   **Personality problems** will arise if one member dislikes or distrusts another; is too dominant or so timid that the value of his ideas is lost; or is so negative in attitude that constructive communication is rendered impossible.

(d)   **Rigid leadership** and procedures may stifle initiative and creativity in individuals. Team working requires that managers share power with the team. Some managers find this difficult to do. Also, a coaching style of management is most appropriate for teams and this must be learned.

(e)   **Differences of opinion** and political conflicts of interest are always likely.

(f) **Too much harmony**. Teams work best when there is room for disagreement. They can become dangerously blinkered to what is going on around them, and may confidently forge ahead in a completely **wrong** direction. *I L Janis* describes this as **groupthink**. The cosy consensus of the group prevents consideration of alternatives, constructive criticism or conflict. Alternatively, efforts to paper over differences may lead to bland recommendations without meaning

(g) **Corporate culture and reward systems**. Teams will fail if the company promotes and rewards the individual at the expense of the group. Similarly, when team rather than individual output is measured, it is easier for un-motivated individuals to get by with minimal effort.

(h) **Too many meetings**. Teams should not try to do everything together. Not only does this waste time in meetings, but team members are exposed to less diversity of thought. Decision-making by teams can be excessively time-consuming and may not offer any advantage over the normal process of decision-making by individual managers after consultation.

(i) **Powerlessness.** People will not bother to work in a team or on a task force if its recommendations are ignored.

(j) **Risky shift**. Group processes are such that individual characteristics can be reinforced and become exaggerated. A good example is the way that a group of risk-averse individuals may adopt a far less risk-averse approach to collective decision-making.

5.7.6 Creating an effective work team

The management problem is how to create effective, efficient work teams. *Handy* takes a contingency approach to the problem of team effectiveness.

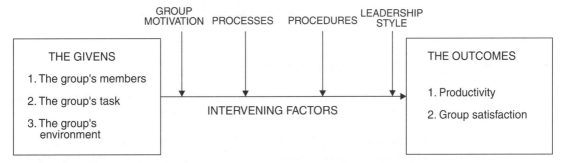

Management can operate on both 'givens' and 'intervening factors' to affect the 'outcomes'.

5.8 The givens

5.8.1 The team

Belbin, in a study of business-game teams at Carnegie Institute of Technology in 1981, drew up a list of the most effective character-mix in a team. This involves eight necessary roles that should played by team members.

Member	Role
Co-ordinator	Presides and co-ordinates: balanced, disciplined, good at working through others
Shaper	Highly strung, dominant, extrovert, passionate about the task itself, a spur to action
Plant	Introverted, but intellectually dominant and imaginative; source of ideas and proposals but with disadvantage of introversion

Member	Role
Monitor-evaluator	Analytically (rather than creatively) intelligent; dissects ideas, spots flaws; possibly aloof, tactless – but necessary
Resource-investigator	Popular, sociable, extrovert, relaxed; source of new contacts, but not an originator; needs to be made use of
Implementer	Practical organiser, turning ideas into tasks; scheduling, planning and so on; trustworthy and efficient, but not excited; not a leader, but an administrator
Team worker	Most concerned with team maintenance – supportive, understanding, diplomatic; popular but uncompetitive – contribution noticed only in absence
Finisher	Pushes the team to meet deadlines, attend to details; promotes urgency and follow-through; not always popular

The **specialist** joins the group to offer expert advice when needed. Notice that one team member may play two or more roles.

5.8.2 The task

The nature of the task must have some bearing on how a group should be managed.

(a)   If a job must be done urgently, it is often necessary to dictate how things should be done, rather than to encourage a participatory style of working.

(b)   Jobs which are routine, unimportant and undemanding will be insufficient to motivate either individuals or the group as a whole.

5.8.3 The environment

The team's environment relates to factors such as the physical surroundings at work and to inter-group relations.

5.8.4 Intervening factors and outcomes

Processes and procedures. Research indicates that a team that tackles its work systematically will be more effective than one that lives from hand to mouth, and muddles through.

Motivation and leadership style. High productivity outcomes may be achieved if work is so arranged that satisfaction of individuals' needs coincides with high output. Where teams are, for example, allowed to set their own improvement goals and methods and to measure their own progress towards those goals, it has been observed (by *Peters and Waterman* among others) that they regularly exceed their targets. The **style of leadership** adopted by the team leader can also affect its outcome. This depends on the circumstances.

Individuals may bring their own **hidden agendas** to groups for satisfaction. These are personal goals that may have nothing to do with the declared aims of the team, such as protection of a sub-group, impressing superiors and pursuit of inter-personal rivalry.

6 Controlling projects

Progress reports should report progress towards key **milestones**. Slippage may be managed with a number of options, including incentives, working smarter, extra resources and rescheduling. Project changes must be carefully considered, communicated, documented and controlled. Risk management involves risk assessment and recording, and action to reduce, avoid, transfer or absorb risks.

6.1 Progress reports

Key term

> A **progress report** shows the current status of the project, usually in relation to the planned status.

The frequency and contents of **progress reports** will vary depending on the length of, and the progress being made on, a project. The report is a control tool intended to show the discrepancies between where the project is, and where the plan says it should be. A common form of progress reports uses two columns – one for planned time and expenditure and one for actual. Any additional content will depend on the format adopted. Some organisations include only the 'raw facts' in the report, and use these as a basis for discussion regarding reasons for variances and action to be taken, at a project review meeting. Other organisations (particularly those involved in long, complex projects) produce more comprehensive progress reports, with more explanation and comment.

The report should monitor progress towards key milestones.

Key term

> A **milestone** is a significant event in the life of the project, usually completion of a major deliverable.

A progress report may include a **milestone slip chart** which compares planned and actual progress towards project milestones. Planned progress is shown on the X-axis and actual progress on the Y-axis. Where actual progress is slower than planned progress slippage has occurred.

Milestone slip chart

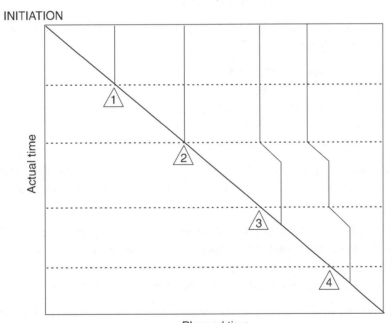

On the chart above milestones are indicated by a triangle on the diagonal planned progress line. The vertical lines that meet milestones 1 and 2 are straight – showing that these milestones were achieved on time. At milestone 3 some slippage has occurred. The chart shows that no further slippage is expected as the progress line for milestone 4 is the same distance to the right as occurred at milestone 3. The progress report should also include an updated budget status – such a report could adopt the format shown in the following example.

6.2 Dealing with slippage

When a project has slipped behind schedule there are a range of options open to the project manager. Some of these options are summarised in the following table.

Action	Comment
Do nothing	After considering all options it may be decided that things should be allowed to continue as they are.
Add resources	If capable staff are available and it is practicable to add more people to certain tasks it may be possible to recover some lost ground. Could some work be subcontracted?
Work smarter	Consider whether the methods currently being used are the most suitable – for example could prototyping be used.
Replan	If the assumptions the original plan was based on have been proved invalid a more realistic plan should be devised.
Reschedule	A complete replan may not be necessary – it may be possible to recover some time by changing the phasing of certain deliverables.
Introduce incentives	If the main problem is team performance, incentives such as bonus payments could be linked to work deadlines and quality.
Change the specification	If the original objectives of the project are unrealistic given the time and money available it may be necessary to negotiate a change in the specification.

6.3 Project change procedure

Some of the reactions to slippage discussed above would involve changes that would significantly affect the overall project. Other possible causes of changes to the original project plan include:

- The availability of new technology
- Changes in personnel
- A realisation that user requirements were misunderstood
- Changes in the business environment
- New legislation eg Data protection

The earlier a change is made the less expensive it should prove. However, changes will cost time and money and should not be undertaken lightly. When considering a change an investigation should be conducted to discover:

(a) The **consequences of not implementing** the proposed change.
(b) The **impact of the change** on time, cost and quality.
(c) The expected **costs and benefits** of the change.
(d) The **risks** associated with the change, and with the status-quo.

The process of ensuring that proper consideration is given to the impact of proposed changes is known as change control. Changes will need to be implemented into the project plan and communicated to all stakeholders.

6.4 Risk management

Projects and other undertakings carry an element of **risk**, for example the risk of an inappropriate system being developed and implemented. Risk management is concerned with identifying such risks and putting in place policies to eliminate or reduce these risks. The identification of risks involves an overview of the project to establish what could go wrong, and the consequences. Risk management may be viewed as a six-stage process:

Stage 1   Plan the risk management approach.

It is appropriate to determine the degree of **risk aversion** that will apply. The general rule is that as risk increases so do potential returns. Minimising risk is expensive, so the degree of risk acceptable to the project sponsor and project board should be considered at an early stage.

Stage 2   Identify and record risks.

Existing plans for time, costs and quality should be examined for risk potential. The critical path, cost estimates and quality assumptions should be examined with particular care. It will be useful for project staff to brainstorm and external advice may be sought: this could come from non-project staff within the organisation or from external sources.

Identified risks are recorded in a **risk register**. Schwalbe suggests the detail shown below should be recorded for each risk event in the risk register.

(a)   An identification number

(b)   A probability

(c)   A name

(d)   A description

(e)   The root cause

(f)   Possible indicators and symptoms: these are factors that tend to increase the chance that the risk event will occur.

(g)   Potential impact

(h)   Potential responses

(i)   An owner: this person monitors the risk event

(j)   Current status: this will change as the project progresses; eventually the risk may become irrelevant.

Stage 3   Assess the risks.

There are two aspects to the assessment of risk.

(a)   The **probability** that the risk event will actually take place
(b)   The **consequences** of the risk event if it does occur

Several quantitative techniques may be useful in assessing risk, including expected values, sensitivity analysis, Monte Carlo simulation and programme evaluation and review technique (PERT). PERT requires the application of probabilities to the time planned for the activities identified in the critical path analysis.

The likelihood and consequences of risks may be plotted on a matrix. This approach allows unquantifiable risks to be considered alongside those to which a numerical value can be given.

Risk Assessment Matrix

Potential impact			
High	M	H	VH
Med	L	M	H
Low	VL	L	M
	Low	*Med*	*High*

Threat likelihood

Stage 4   Plan and record risk responses.

Developing a risk **contingency plan** that contains strategies for risks that fall into the VH segment should have priority, followed by risks falling into the two H segments. Following the principle of **management by exception**, the most efficient way of dealing with risks outside these quadrants may be to do nothing unless the risk presents itself. Extra time and finance should be held in reserve for dealing with likely contingencies.

Dealing with **risk** involves four strategies.

(a)   **Avoidance**: the factors that give rise to the risk are removed.

(b)   **Reduction** or **mitigation**: the potential for the risk cannot be removed but analysis has enabled the identification of ways to reduce the incidence and/or the consequences.

(c)   **Transference**: the risk is passed on to someone else, perhaps by means of insurance, or possibly by building it into a supplier contract.

(d)   **Absorption**: the potential risk is accepted in the hope or expectation that the incidence and consequences can be coped with if necessary.

Stage 5   Implement risk management strategies.

Stage 6   Review the risk management approach and actions for adequacy.

Risk management is a continuous process. Procedures are necessary to regularly review and reassess the risks documented in the risk register.

6.5 Project completion

> The project completion report shows the project outcomes, and any continuing issues. There should be a post-completion audit process to examine the degree of success achieved, review methods and organisation and note lessons for future reference.

> The **completion report** summarises the results of the project, and includes client sign-off.

On project completion the project manager will produce a completion report. The main purpose of the completion report is to document (and gain client sign-off for) the end of the project.

The report should include a summary of the project outcome.

(a)   Project objectives and the outcomes achieved

(b)   The final project budget report showing expected and actual expenditure (If an external client is involved this information may be sensitive – the report may exclude or amend the budget report)

(c)   A brief outline of time taken compared with the original schedule

The completion report will also include provision for any continuing issues that will need to be addressed after completion. Such issues would be related to the project, but not part of the project. (If they are part of the project the project is not yet complete!) An example such of an issue would be a procedure for dealing with any 'bugs' that become apparent after a new software program has been tested and approved.

Responsibilities and procedures relating to any such issues should be laid down in the report.

The manager may find it useful to distribute a **provisional report** and request feedback. This should ensure the version presented for client sign-off at the completion meeting is acceptable to all parties.

A more detailed review of the project follows a few months after completion, the post-completion audit.

6.5.1 The post-completion audit

> The **post-completion audit** is a formal review of the project that examines the lessons that may be learned and used for the benefit of future projects.

The audit looks at all aspects of the project with regard to two questions.

(a)   Did the end result of the project meet the client's expectations?

(i)   The actual design and construction of the end product
(ii)   Was the project achieved on time?
(iii)   Was the project completed within budget?

(b)   Was the management of the project as successful as it might have been, or were there bottlenecks or problems? This review covers:

(i)   Problems that might occur on future projects with similar characteristics.
(ii)   The performance of the team individually and as a group.

In other words, any project is an **opportunity to learn how to manage future projects more effectively**.

The post-completion audit should involve input from the project team. A simple questionnaire could be developed for all team members to complete, and a reasonably informal meeting held to obtain feedback, on what went well (and why), and what didn't (and why).

This information should be formalised in a report. The post-completion audit report should contain the following.

(a)   A **summary** should be provided, emphasising any areas where the structures and tools used to manage the project have been found to be unsatisfactory.

(b)   A **review of the end result** of the project should be provided, and compared against the **results expected**. Reasons for any **significant discrepancies** between the two should be provided, preferably with suggestions of how any future projects could prevent these problems recurring.

(c)   A **cost-benefit review** should be included, comparing the forecast costs and benefits identified at the time of the feasibility study with actual costs and benefits.

(d)   **Recommendations** should be made as to any steps which should be taken to improve the project management procedures used.

Lessons learnt that relate to the way the project was managed should contribute to the smooth running of future projects.

A starting point for any new project should be a review of the documentation of any similar projects undertaken in the past.

6.5.2 Benefits realisation

It is obviously important that the benefits expected from the completion of a project are actually enjoyed. Benefits realisation is concerned with the planning and management required to realise expected benefits. It also covers any required organisational transition processes.

The UK Office of Government Commerce has identified a **six stage procedure for benefits realisation**. This is most relevant to projects aimed at process improvement and changing the organisation's way of doing things

Stage 1   **Establishing benefits measurement**

Measure the start state and record it in the **benefits profile**. The benefits profile defines each anticipated benefit and is used to track progress towards its realisation. Determine how benefit realisation will be measured. Benefits may be complex and spread across departments: designing usable and realistic measures may be difficult.

Stage 2   **Refining the benefits profile**

The benefits profile should be refined and controlled throughout the life of the project. Project managers should conduct regular benefits profile reviews in collaboration with key stakeholders.

Stage 3   **Monitoring benefits**

There should be regular monitoring of benefits realisation. It must be accepted that some projects will only be beneficial in enabling other projects to be successful.

Stage 4   **Transition management**

Projects are likely to bring change and this must be managed in a proper way. Effective communications and will be required as will the deployment of good people skills

Stage 5   **Support for benefit realisation**

Benefits realisation will mainly accrue after the end of the project. Where a project brings changes in methods and processes, there is likely to be a period for settling-down before benefits are fully realised. During this period, costs may rise and problems may occur. Careful management is required to overcome these short-term effects. A philosophy of continuous improvement is required if further benefits are to be achieved.

Stage 6   **Measuring the benefits**

Benefits achieved should be established by comparison with the pre-improvement state recorded in the benefits profile.

Chapter Roundup

- A **project** is an undertaking that has a beginning and an end and is carried out to meet established goals within cost, schedule and quality objectives. It often has the following characteristics:

    - A defined beginning and end
    - Resources allocated specifically to it
    - Intended to be done only once (although similar separate projects could be undertaken)
    - Follows a plan towards a clear intended end-result
    - Often cuts across organisational and functional lines

- **Project management** is the combination of systems, techniques, and people used to control and monitor activities undertaken within the project. It will be deemed successful if it is completed at the specified level of **quality**, **on time** and within **budget**. Achieving this can be very difficult: most projects present a range of significant challenges.

- Adaptation to environmental change makes project management an important feature of strategic implementation. Also, strategic management thinking can be a useful input into project management. Strategic project management envisages strategy as a stream of projects intended to achieve organisational breakthroughs.

- Kerzner suggests that where project management is a core competence, a continuous improvement approach should be taken to developing and consolidating the methodology.

- The project life cycle concept describes the progression of many projects through four stages: definition, design, delivery and development.

- Limits to resource availability mean that not all potential projects will be undertaken; rational methods are used to select projects.

    Project initiation tasks include the appointment of project manager and sponsor; stakeholder analysis and the definition of project scope. The business case explains why the project is needed, while the project charter gives authorisation for it to be undertaken.

- Many large-scale projects, particularly those involving major change, are strategically significant and project management can merge into strategic management. Force field analysis identifies enablers, constraints and showstoppers.

- Work breakdown structure is an analysis of the work involved in a project into a structure of phases, activities and tasks. **Dependencies** determine the order in which tasks must be carried out, while **interactions** between tasks affect them without imposing order.

- The **project budget** plans the allocation of resources to the project and forms a basis for their control. Budgeting may be top-down or bottom-up.

- A Gantt **chart** shows the deployment of resources over time.

- **Network analysis** illustrates interactions and dependencies. It is used to plan the sequence of tasks making up project scope and to determine the critical path. PERT uses probabilities to make estimates of likely completion and milestone dates.

- A resource **histogram** is a useful planning tool that shows the amount and timing of the requirement for a resource (or a range of resources).

- **Project management software** can be used to produce detailed project planning documentation, to update plans and to produce reports.

- The person who takes ultimate responsibility for ensuring the desired result is achieved on time and within budget is the **project manager**. **Duties** of the project manager include: Planning, teambuilding, communication, co-ordinating project activities, monitoring and control, problem-resolution and quality control.

- Project managers require the following **skills**: Leadership and team building, organisational ability, communication skills (written, spoken, presentations, meetings), some technical knowledge of the project area and inter-personal skills.

- Project managers should have some understanding of the way that groups of people interact at work.

  Teams enable people's talents and efforts to be combined and teamwork can have a motivating effect, Tuckman identified four stages in team development.

  - Forming
  - Storming
  - Norming
  - Reperforming

  However, teams bring their own problems, including disharmony, riskshift, groupthink and political conflict. Handy suggests a contingency approach to team leadership. Belbin identified nine roles played by team members.

  - Co-ordinator
  - Plant
  - Resource investigator
  - Team worker
  - Specialist

  - Shaper
  - Monitor-evaluator
  - Implementer
  - Finisher

- Progress reports should report progress towards key **milestones**. Slippage may be managed with a number of options, including incentives, working smarter, extra resources and rescheduling. Project changes must be carefully considered, communicated, documented and controlled. Risk management involves risk assessment and recording; and action to reduce, avoid, transfer or absorb risks.

- The project completion report shows the project outcomes, and any continuing issues. There should be a post-completion audit process to examine the degree of success achieved, review methods and organisation and note lessons for future reference.

Quick Quiz

1   What are the three main measures of project success?

2   What are the two main project management methodologies in the UK and the US?

3   What is a breakthrough project?

4   What are four phases of a typical project lifecycle?

5   What does a Gantt chart do?

6   Who provides the resources needed for a project?

7   What are the four stages of team development identified by Tuckman?

8   What is a milestone?

9   What are the four risk management strategies?

10   What is the main benefit of carrying out a post-completion audit?

Answers to Quick Quiz

1   Quality, cost and time

2   PRINCE2 and PMBOK

3   One that will have a material effect on either the business's external competitive edge, its internal capabilities or its financial performance

4   Definition, design, delivery, development

5   It shows the deployment of resources over time

6   The project sponsor

7   Forming, storming, norming and performing

8   A significant event in the life of the project, usually completion of a major deliverable

9   Avoidance, mitigation, transference, absorption

10   The opportunity make the management of future projects more effective

Now try the questions below from the Exam Question Bank

Number	Level	Marks	Time
Q12	Examination	20	36 mins

Part H
Finance

14

Finance

Introduction

Finance may be regarded as the fundamental business resource, since it provides access to all other more specific resources, to the extent that they are available. The organisation's financial position will be a major part of the strategic position and will also constitute a strong influence on the process of strategic choice. Finance is thus of inherent strategic significance and several aspects of financial management are properly the concern of the managers at the strategic apex.

All of the material in this section of this Study Text should be familiar to you from your previous studies so dealing with it should be a matter of revision and consolidation on knowledge.

Study guide

		Intellectual level
H1	**The link between strategy and finance**	
(a)	Explain the relationship between strategy and finance.	3
	(i) Managing the value	
	(ii) Financial expectations of stakeholders	
	(iii) Funding strategies	
H2	**Finance decisions to formulate and support business strategy**	
(a)	Determine the overall investment requirements of the business.	2
(b)	Evaluate alternative sources of finance for these investments and their associated risks.	3
(c)	Efficiently and effectively manage the current and non-current assets of the business from a finance and risk perspective.	2
H3	**Financial implications of making strategic choices and of implementing strategic actions**	
(a)	Apply efficiency ratios to assess how efficiently an organisation uses its current resources.	2
(b)	Apply appropriate gearing ratios to asses the risks associated with financing and investment in the organisation.	2
(c)	Apply appropriate liquidity ratios to assess the organisation's short-term commitments to creditors and employees.	2
(d)	Apply appropriate profitability ratios to assess the viability of chosen strategies.	2
(e)	Apply appropriate investment ratios to assist investors and shareholders in evaluating organisational performance and strategy.	2

Exam guide

P3 is not a strategic financial management paper and we do not expect the examiner to present technically difficult questions on finance. Judging from the pilot paper, we would suggest that you are likely to encounter numerical analysis of some kind in Question 1, as was the pattern in old syllabus exams. However, there is no certainty that this analysis will be of a financial kind. There is also a strong likelihood that financial matters will appear in other questions, but here the topic is more likely to be the mutual impact of finance and strategy on one another, rather than on computations.

1 Finance and strategy

FAST FORWARD

In commercial organisations, managing for value is about creating shareholder value, while in the public sector, it is about obtaining value for money. Managers must understand the key cost and value drivers affecting their operations. Financial risk is determined exclusively by gearing, but there are several sources of business risk. Financial risk may be balanced against business risk, so that overall risk is managed.

JS&W suggest that organisations of all types must deal with three broad issues of finance.

- **Managing for value**
- **Funding**
- **Financial expectations of stakeholders**

1.1 Managing for value

For commercial organisations, managing for value is about **creating value** for shareholders, while in the public sector, it is about **obtaining best value** for the money spent.

1.1.1 Shareholder value

Shareholder value depends on long-term capacity to generate cash. This will enable the payment of dividends, which, in turn, will drive up the market value of the business, offering capital gain as an alternative form of value. Ability to generate cash is influenced by three main factors.

(a) **Funds from operations**, which are determined by sales revenues and costs

(b) The net cost of financing the **capital base of fixed and current assets** required to support operations: an important aspect of this factor is the efficiency with which these assets are used.

(c) **Capital structure** (gearing), which will determine the company's **cost of capital** (and its financial risk)

1.1.2 Best value in the public sector

Most public sector managers are concerned only with managing their budgeted cash spending. However, they should understand the significance of the factors outlined above as they apply to their responsibilities. A good example is the need for efficient exploitation of fixed assets.

1.1.3 Drivers of cost and value

Value creation does not occur and costs do not arise evenly across the organisation, so managers should have a firm grasp of the **key cost and value drivers** affecting their operations. Some of these may be outside the organisation, elsewhere in the value network, so the ability to influence suppliers and distributors may be crucial to success. This will depend on **relative bargaining power**, as discussed elsewhere in this Study Text.

Choice of **generic strategy** interacts with cost and value: strict control of cost is obviously fundamental to cost leadership, while differentiation will inevitably have cost implications associated with such matters as brand communications, product quality and customer service.

The structure of costs and value creation is likely to **change over time**, as, for example, illustrated by the cost and profit aspects of the **product life cycle**. The cash flow aspect of the **Boston matrix** analysis also illustrates this.

1.2 Funding strategies

There are likely to be several considerations relevant to funding decisions for commercial organisations. Among these are: the ownership structure; whether a company is quoted or privately held; and, perhaps most significantly, the attitude of the owners and senior managers to **risk**. One of the most important commercial funding decisions is **capital structure**, or **gearing**. Gearing up, with a high proportion of loan capital, enables holders of equity to benefit significantly when overall returns are in excess of the cost of debt, since the surplus accrues to them. The natural corollary to this is, however, that when times are hard and returns are depressed below the rate payable to lenders, it is the holders of equity that have to find the shortfall. This is **financial risk**.

The level of gearing and thus the degree of financial risk accepted will be influenced by management's beliefs about the prospects for the company and the future movement of interest rates; these, in turn, depend to some extent on the future state of the economy generally.

Financial risk cannot be considered in isolation. There are several other important sources of risk, including political change and the dangers inherent in the physical environment. However, it is likely to be **business risk** that will require the most careful consideration. Business risk is the total of all the uncertainties that exist in any business venture and thus includes such aspects of uncertainty as sales success, public image, changes in the bargaining power of suppliers and so on.

1.2.1 Managing risk

JS&W point out that financial risk can, to some extent, be balanced against business risk in order to produce an acceptable level of risk overall. If business risk is perceived as being low, a higher level of financial risk may be acceptable and gearing increased Similarly, if business risk increases, a proportionate response might be to aim to pay off an element of debt. The ability to **adjust the level of dividend paid** may be a useful adjunct to this concept.

JS&W illustrate the relationships involved here using the four cases of the Boston matrix, which parallel the life cycle model to some extent. We summarise their illustration in the table below.

	Launch (Question mark)	Growth (Star)	Maturity (Cash Cow)	Decline (Dog)
Business risk	Very high	High	Medium to low	Low
Financial risk, therefore	Keep very low	Keep low	May be increased	Can be high
Funding	Venture capital	Equity	Debt and equity	Secured Debt
Dividends	Nil	Nominal, if any	High	Total

1.2.2 Conglomerates

A large company is likely to seek a balanced portfolio of businesses at different stages of their lives. It is important that such conglomerates consider the **overall risk profile** of their operations. They should then adjust their funding strategy using the ideas illustrated above.

1.2.3 Funding and strategy

Funding arrangements can be a major influence on strategy.

   (a)   A **highly geared company** is likely to avoid high levels of business risk.

   (b)   The **form of ownership** may be changed in order to gain access to new sources of funds.

   (c)   A strategy based on **acquisitions** may be driven by the need to reinvest surplus funds or to demonstrate a high level of growth to the market; wider strategic considerations may be neglected as a result.

1.3 Stakeholders' financial expectations

We discussed the general expectations of stakeholders earlier in this Study text. These will inevitably make demands on available funds, some directly, as in employees' expectations for proper wages and salaries, and some more indirectly, as in various expectations of socially responsible action.

There will also be expectations of **solvency** and **liquidity** on the part of trading partners and providers of loan finance. Customers will expect **good value** in their purchases. This also applies to public sector organisations.

2 Financial management decisions

FAST FORWARD

In seeking to attain the financial objectives of the organisation or enterprise, a financial manager has to make decisions on three topics.

- Investment
- Financing
- Dividends

These three policy areas interact and decision makers must also manage the interactions.

2.1 Investment, financing and dividend decisions

Maximising the wealth of shareholders generally implies maximising profits consistent with long-term stability. Often short-term gains must be sacrificed in the interests of the company's long-term prospects. In the context of this overall objective of financial management, there are three main types of decisions facing financial managers: **investment** decisions, **financing** decisions and **dividend** decisions.

2.2 Investment decisions

The financial manager will need to **identify** investment opportunities, **evaluate** them and decide on the **optimum allocation of scarce funds** available between investments.

Investment decisions may be on the undertaking of new **projects** within the existing business, the **takeover** of, or **merger** with, another company or the **selling off** of a part of the business. Managers have to take decisions in the light of strategic considerations such as whether the business intends to **expand internally** (through investment in existing operations) or **externally** (through expansion).

2.3 Financing decisions

Financing decisions include those for both the long term (**capital structure**) and the short term (**working capital management**).

The financial manager will need to determine the **source, cost** and effect on **risk** of the possible sources of long-term finance. A balance between **profitability** and **liquidity** (ready availability of funds if required) must be taken into account when deciding on the optimal level of short-term finance.

2.4 Interaction of financing with investment and dividend decisions

When taking financial decisions, managers will have to fulfil the **requirements of the providers of finance**, otherwise finance may not be made available. This may be particularly difficult in the case of equity shareholders, since dividends are paid at the company's discretion; however if equity shareholders do not receive the dividends they want, they will sell their shares, the share price will fall and the company will have more difficulty raising funds from share issues in future.

Although there may be risks in obtaining extra finance, the long-term risks to the business of **failing to invest** may be even greater and managers will have to balance these risks. Investment may have direct consequences for decisions involving the **management of finance**; extra working capital may be required if investments are made and sales expand as a consequence. Managers must be sensitive to this and ensure that a balance is maintained between receivables and inventory, and cash.

A further issue managers will need to consider is the **matching** of the **characteristics** of investment and finance. **Time** is a critical aspect; an investment which earns returns in the long-term should be matched with finance which requires repayment in the long-term.

Another aspect is the **financing of international investments**. A company which expects to receive a substantial amount of income in a foreign currency will be concerned that this currency may weaken. It can hedge against this possibility by borrowing in the foreign currency and using the foreign receipts to repay the loan. It may though be better to obtain finance on the international markets.

2.5 Dividend decisions

Dividend decisions may affect the view that shareholders have of the long-term prospects of the company, and thus the **market value of the shares**.

2.6 Interaction of dividend with investment and financing decisions

The amount of surplus cash paid out as **dividends** will have a direct impact on **finance** available for **investment**. Managers have a difficult decision here; how much do they pay out to shareholders each year to keep them happy, and what level of funds do they retain in the business to invest in projects that will yield long-term income. In addition funds available from retained profits may be needed if debt finance is likely to be unavailable, or if taking on more debt would expose the company to undesirable risks.

3 Cash forecasts

FAST FORWARD

Cash forecasting should ensure that sufficient funds will be available when needed, to sustain the activities of an enterprise at an acceptable cost.

3.1 Cash budgets

Key term

A **cash budget** (or **forecast**) is a detailed budget of estimated cash inflows and outflows incorporating both revenue and capital items. *(CIMA Official Terminology)*

Cash forecasts (or budgets) are used to plan the structure of an organisation's finances.

- How much cash is required
- When it is required
- How long it is required for
- Whether it will be available from anticipated sources

A company must know **when** it might need to borrow and **for how long**, not just **what amount** of funding could be required.

3.2 Cash forecasts based on the balance sheet

The balance sheet based forecast is produced for **management accounting purposes** and so not for external publication or statutory financial reporting. **It is not an estimate of cash inflows and outflows**. A number of sequential forecasts can be produced, for example, a forecast of the balance sheet at the end of each year for the next five years.

As an estimate of the company's balance sheet at a future date, a balance sheet based forecast is used to identify either the **cash surplus** or the **funding shortfall** in the company's balance sheet **at the forecast date**.

As part of a business's risk analysis, different forecasts should be prepared with **changing financial** or **business variables**. The links between these variables and the figures in the forecasts may not be straightforward.

3.3 Sensitivity analysis

In a well-designed forecast a great number of **'what-if'** questions can be asked and answered quickly by carrying out **sensitivity analysis** and changing the relevant data or variables. In a cash flow forecast model, managers may wish to know the cash flow impact if sales growth per month is nil, $1/2$%, 1%, $1\frac{1}{2}$%, $2\frac{1}{2}$% or minus 1% and so on.

However, businesses will also want to estimate the magnitude of changes in sales and ultimately profits if economic or business variables change. This will be more problematic.

3.4 Changes in economic variables

Businesses need to be aware of likely changes in inflation, interest rates and so on. Governments and central banks issue regular updates and forecasts, and the financial press is also helpful.

However businesses will also need to forecast:

(a)   How the **predicted changes** will **affect demand**. The links may not be easy to forecast. Businesses should consider separately the effect of major increases on each type of product.

(b)   How the **business** will **respond to changes in variables**. For example will the business automatically adjust prices upwards by the rate of inflation, or will it try to hold prices? What will its competitors do? If raw material prices increase, will the business try to change suppliers? What effect will this have on payment patterns?

3.5 Changes in business variables

Economic variables will clearly impact upon business variables such as **sales volumes** or **profit margins**. Businesses need to be aware of the other factors, such as changes in the competitive environment that could affect these variables and how this effect might work. The original forecast should itself have been based on **demand forecasts,** determined by market surveys and statistical models based on past changes in demand. However if factors such as taste change, businesses need to recognise this might not just require marginal changes in forecasts, but a re-visiting of the base data, since the changes will ultimately render the previous surveys or models redundant.

4 Financing requirements

Cash deficits will be funded in different ways, depending on whether they are short or long-term. Businesses should have procedures for investing **surpluses** with appropriate levels of risk and return.

4.1 Deficiencies

Any forecast **deficiency** of cash will have to be funded.

(a)   **Borrowing**. If borrowing arrangements are not already secured, a source of funds will have to be found. If a company cannot fund its cash deficits it could be wound up.

(b)   The firm can make arrangements to **sell any short-term marketable financial investments** to raise cash.

(c) The firm can delay payments to suppliers, or pull in payments from customers. This is sometimes known as **leading and lagging**.

Because cash forecasts cannot be entirely accurate, companies should have **contingency funding**, available from a surplus cash balance and liquid investments, or from a bank facility. The approximate size of contingency margin will vary from company to company, according to the cyclical nature of the business and the approach of its cash planners.

Forecasting gives management time to arrange its funding. If planned in advance, instead of a panic measure to avert a cash crisis, a company can more easily choose when to borrow, and will probably obtain a lower interest rate.

4.2 Cash surpluses

Many cash-generative businesses are less reliant on high quality cash forecasts. If a **cash surplus** is forecast, having an idea of both its size and how long it will exist could help decide how best to invest it.

In some cases, the amount of **interest** earned from surplus cash could be significant for the company's earnings. The company might then need a forecast of its interest earnings in order to indicate its prospective **earnings per share** to stock market analysts and institutional investors.

5 Obtaining equity funds

FAST FORWARD

Companies seeking extra equity finance can obtain it by **retaining cash** in the business for investment or by **issuing shares**.

5.1 Retained profits

For many businesses, the cash needed to finance investments will be available because the earnings the business has made have been retained within the business rather than paid out as dividends. We emphasised earlier that this interaction of investment, financing and dividend policy is the most important issue facing many businesses.

5.1.1 Advantages of using retentions

(a) Retentions are a **flexible source** of finance; companies are not tied to specific amounts or specific repayment patterns.

(b) Using retentions does **not involve** a **change in the pattern** of **shareholdings**.

5.1.2 Disadvantages of using retentions

(a) As mentioned above, shareholders may be **sensitive** to the **loss of dividends** that will result from retention for re-investment, rather than paying dividends.

(b) Not so much a disadvantage as a misconception, that retaining profits is a cost-free method of obtaining funds. There is an **opportunity cost** in that if dividends were paid, the cash received could be invested by shareholders to earn a return.

5.2 Ordinary (equity) shares

Key terms

> **Equity** is the issued ordinary share capital plus reserves, statutory and otherwise, which represent the investment in a company by the ordinary shareholders.

> **Equity share capital** is a company's issued share capital less capital which carries preferential rights. Ordinary share capital normally comprises ordinary shares. *(CIMA Official Terminology)*

Ordinary (equity) shares are those of the owners of a company.

The ordinary shares of UK companies have a nominal or 'face' value, typically £1 or 50p. Outside the UK it is not uncommon for a company's shares to have no nominal value.

The market value of a quoted company's shares bears **no relationship** to their **nominal value**, except that when ordinary shares are issued for cash, the issue price must be equal to or (more usually) *more than* the nominal value of the shares.

5.3 Reasons for share issues

A new issue of shares might be made in a variety of different circumstances.

(a) The company might want to **raise more cash**, for example for expansion of its operations.

(b) The company might want to issue new shares partly to raise cash but more importantly to obtain a **stock market listing**. When a UK company is floated, for example on the main stock market, it is a requirement of the Stock Exchange that at least a minimum proportion of its shares should be made available to the general investing public if the shares are not already widely held.

(c) The company might issue new shares to the shareholders of another company, in order to **take it over**.

6 Bank loans

FAST FORWARD

> Bank loans tend to be a **source** of **medium-term finance**, linked with the purchase of specific assets. Interest and repayments will be set in advance.

6.1 Loans and overdrafts

Banks often provide term loans as medium or long-term financing for customers. The customer borrows a fixed amount and pays it back with interest over a period or at the end of it. This contrasts with an overdraft facility, when a customer, through its current account, can borrow money on a short-term basis up to a certain amount. Overdrafts are repayable on demand.

6.2 Loan or overdraft

A customer might ask the bank for an overdraft facility when the bank would wish to suggest a loan instead; alternatively, a customer might ask for a loan when an overdraft would be more appropriate.

(a) In most cases, when a customer wants finance to help with day to day trading and cash flow needs, an **overdraft** would be the **appropriate method** of financing. The customer should not be short of cash all the time, and should expect to be in credit in some days, but in need of an overdraft on others.

(b) When a customer wants to borrow from a bank for only a **short period of time**, even for the purchase of a major asset such as an item of plant or machinery, an overdraft facility might be more suitable than a loan, because the customer will stop paying interest as soon as his account goes into credit.

(c)   When a customer wants to borrow from a bank, but cannot see its way to repaying the bank except over the course of a few years, the **medium– or long-term nature** of the financing is best catered for by the provision of a loan rather than an overdraft facility.

6.2.1 Advantages of an overdraft over a loan

(a)   The customer **only pays interest when it is overdrawn**.

(b)   The bank has the flexibility to **review** the customer's overdraft facility periodically, and perhaps agree to additional facilities, or insist on a reduction in the facility.

(c)   An overdraft can do the same job as a loan: a facility can simply be **renewed** every time it comes up **for review**.

(d)   Being short-term debt, an overdraft will not **affect** the calculation of a company's **gearing**.

6.2.2 Advantages of a loan over overdraft

(a)   Both the customer and the bank **know exactly** what the repayments of the loan will be and how much interest is payable, and when. This makes planning (budgeting) simpler.

(b)   The customer does not have to worry about the bank deciding to reduce or **withdraw** an overdraft facility before he is in a position to repay what is owed. Overdrafts are normally **repayable on demand**. There is an element of 'security' or 'peace of mind' in being able to arrange a loan for an agreed term.

(c)   Loans normally carry a **facility letter** setting out the precise terms of the agreement.

6.3 Bank loan or other loan capital

A choice businesses often have is whether to seek funding through a bank loan or through other types of loan capital.

6.3.1 Advantages of bank loan over other forms of loan capital

(a)   **Flexibility**. It may be possible to alter the terms of the bank loan as the finance requirements of the company change.

(b)   **Confidentiality**. Although the bank will require information, the customer will not have to fulfil the publicity requirements that an issue of loan stock on the financial markets would need.

(c)   **Speed**. It will be rather quicker to arrange a bank loan than fulfilling all the requirements of a public issue.

(d)   **Costs**. A bank loan will mean that the issue costs of loan stock are avoided.

6.3.2 Disadvantages of bank loan over other forms of loan capital

(a)   **Restrictions**. Restrictions such as collateral and possible restrictive covenants are required, as opposed to none for certain types of loan capital.

(b)   **Financial information**. Detailed financial information such as budgets and management accounts may have to be submitted periodically to the bank, whereas other lenders will not require information in this detail.

6.4 Time scale of loan

For purchases of a non-current asset the **term of the bank loan should not exceed** the **economic or useful life** of the asset purchased with the money from the loan. A business manager will often expect to use the revenues earned by the asset to repay the loan, and obviously, an asset can only do this as long as it is in operational use.

7 Loan capital

7.1 Loan stock

The term **bonds** is used to mean the various forms of long-term debt a company may issue, such as loan stock, which may be **redeemable** or **irredeemable**.

ey term

Loan capital (or loan stock) is debentures and other long-term loans to a business.

(CIMA Official Terminology)

Loan capital or stock has a **nominal value**, which is the debt owed by the company, and interest is paid at a stated **'coupon'** on this amount. For example, if a company issues 10% loan stock, the coupon will be 10% of the nominal value of the stock, so that £100 of stock will receive £10 interest each year. The rate quoted is the gross rate, before tax.

ey term

Stock is an amount of fully paid up capital, any part of which can be transferred.

(CIMA Official Terminology)

Unlike shares, debt is often issued **at par**, ie with £100 payable per £100 nominal value. Where the coupon rate is fixed at the time of issue, it will be set according to prevailing market conditions given the credit rating of the company issuing the debt. Subsequent changes in market (and company) conditions will cause the market value of the bond to fluctuate, although the coupon will stay at the fixed percentage of the nominal value.

8 Ratio analysis

Ratios provide a means of systematically analysing financial statements. They can be grouped under the headings **profitability**, **liquidity**, **gearing** and **shareholders' investment**. It is important to calculate **relevant ratios** and to take into account the **limitations** of **ratio analysis.**

8.1 Uses of ratio analysis

Businesses carry out ratio analysis in order to **measure the progress of the enterprise** and of individual subsidiaries, so that managers know how well the company concerned is doing. The financial situation of a company will also obviously affect its share price. Is the company profitable? Is it growing? Does it have satisfactory liquidity? Is its gearing level acceptable? What is its dividend policy?

The key to obtaining meaningful information from ratio analysis is **comparison**: comparing ratios over time within the same business to establish whether the business is improving or declining, and comparing ratios between similar businesses to see whether the company you are analysing is better or worse than average within its own business sector.

A vital element in effective ratio analysis is understanding the **needs of the person** for whom the ratio analysis is being undertaken. **Investors** for example will be interested in the **risk and return** relating to their investment, so will be concerned with dividends, market prices, level of debt vs. equity and so on. **Suppliers** and **loan creditors** are interested in receiving the payments due to them, so will want to know how liquid the business is. **Managers** are interested in ratios that indicate how well the business is being run, and also how the business is doing in relation to its **competitors**.

<table>
<tr><td>**Exam focus point**</td><td>Try not to be too mechanical when working out ratios, and think constantly about what you are trying to achieve. You will only obtain credit in the exam for calculating ratios that are relevant.</td></tr>
</table>

8.2 Limitations of ratio analysis

Although ratio analysis can be a very useful technique, it is important to realise its limitations.

(a) **Availability of comparable information**

When making comparisons with other companies in the industry, industry averages may hide **wide variations** in figures. Figures for 'similar' companies may provide a better guide, but then there are problems identifying which companies are similar, and obtaining enough detailed information about them.

(b) **Use of historical/out-of-date information**

Comparisons with the previous history of a business may be of limited use, if the business has recently undergone, or is about to undergo, **substantial changes**. In addition, ratios based on published accounts suffer from the disadvantage that these accounts are filed some months after the end of the accounting period. Comparisons over time may also be distorted by **inflation**, leading to assets being stated at values that do not reflect replacement costs, and revenue increasing for reasons other than more sales being made.

(c) **Ratios are not definitive**

'Ideal levels' vary industry by industry, and even they are not definitive. Companies may be able to exist without any difficulty with ratios that are rather worse than the industry average.

(d) **Need for careful interpretation**

For example, if comparing two businesses' liquidity ratios, one business may have higher levels. This might appear to be 'good', but further investigation might reveal that the higher ratios are a result of higher inventory and receivable levels which are a result of poor working capital management by the business with the 'better' ratios.

(e) **Manipulation**

Any ratio including profit may be distorted by **choice of accounting policies**. For smaller companies, working capital ratios may be distorted depending on whether a big customer pays, or a large supplier is paid, before or after the year-end.

(f) **Ratios lack standard form**

For example, when calculating **gearing** some companies will include bank overdrafts, others exclude them.

<table>
<tr><td>**Exam focus point**</td><td>Bear these limitations in mind when calculating and interpreting ratios, as examiners' reports give many examples of misapplication of ratio analysis, and over-simplistic and misleading interpretations.

Financial data will frequently be provided in the exam, particularly in Question 1 and you should aim to make the best possible use of it. Examiner's reports for Paper 3.5 suggest that candidates often ignore valuable information contained in the numerical data given.</td></tr>
</table>

8.3 Broad categories of ratios

Ratios can be grouped into the following four categories:

- Profitability and return
- Debt and gearing
- Liquidity: control of cash and other working capital items
- Shareholders' investment ratios (or 'stock market ratios')

The *Du Pont* system of ratio analysis involves constructing a pyramid of interrelated ratios like that below.

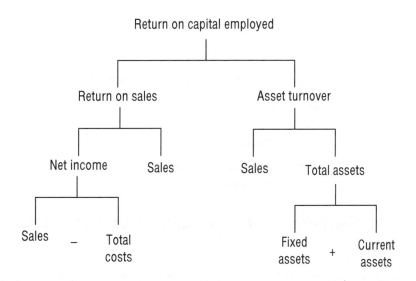

Such **ratio pyramids** help in providing for an overall management plan to achieve profitability, and allow the interrelationships between ratios to be checked.

Although you will have encountered most or all of the ratios that we are about to define before, make sure you know how to calculate them in the exam. One suggestion is to list all the ratios you need to know on a single sheet of paper and go through that sheet over and over again.

8.4 Profitability and return: the return on capital employed (ROCE)

A company ought of course to be profitable, and obvious checks on **profitability** are:

- Whether the company has made a profit or a loss on its ordinary activities
- By how much this year's profit or loss is bigger or smaller than last year's profit or loss

It is impossible to assess profits or profit growth properly without relating them to the amount of funds (the capital) employed in making the profits. An important profitability ratio is therefore **return on capital employed (ROCE)**, which states the profit as a percentage of the amount of capital employed. **Profit** is usually taken as profit on ordinary activities before interest and taxation (PBIT), and **capital employed** is shareholders' capital plus long-term liabilities and debt capital. This is the same as total assets less current liabilities.

The underlying principle is that we must compare like with like, and so if capital means share capital and reserves plus long-term liabilities and debt capital, profit must mean the profit earned by all this capital together. This is PBIT, since interest is the return for loan capital.

$$\text{Thus ROCE} = \frac{\text{(PBIT)}}{\text{Capital employed}}$$

Capital employed = Shareholders' funds plus current liabilities plus any long-term provisions for liabilities and charges.

8.4.1 Evaluating the ROCE

What does a company's ROCE tell us? What should we be looking for? There are three comparisons that can be made.

    (a)   The **change** in ROCE from one year to the next

    (b)   The **ROCE** being **earned** by other companies, if this information is available

    (c)   A comparison of the ROCE with **current market borrowing rates**

        (i)   What would be the cost of extra borrowing to the company if it needed more loans, and is it earning an ROCE that suggests it could make high enough profits to make such borrowing worthwhile?

        (ii)   Is the company making an ROCE which suggests that it is making profitable use of its current borrowing?

8.5 Analysing profitability and return in more detail: the secondary ratios

We may analyse the ROCE, to find out why it is high or low, or better or worse than last year. There are two factors that contribute towards a return on capital employed, both related to turnover.

8.5.1 Profit margin

A company might make a high or a low profit margin on its sales. For example, a company that makes a profit of 25p per £1 of sales is making a bigger return on its turnover than another company making a profit of only 10p per £1 of sales.

8.5.2 Asset turnover

Asset turnover is a measure of how well the assets of a business are being used to generate sales. For example, if two companies each have capital employed of £100,000, and company A makes sales of £400,000 a year whereas company B makes sales of only £200,000 a year, company A is making a higher turnover from the same amount of assets. This will help company A to make a higher return on capital employed than company B.

Profit margin and asset turnover together explain the ROCE, and if the ROCE is the primary profitability ratio, these other two are the secondary ratios. The relationship between the three ratios is as follows.

Profit margin × Asset turnover = ROCE

$$\frac{\text{PBIT}}{\text{Sales}} \times \frac{\text{Sales}}{\text{Capital employed}} = \frac{\text{PBIT}}{\text{Capital employed}}$$

It is also worth commenting on the **change in turnover** from one year to the next. Strong sales growth will usually indicate volume growth as well as turnover increases due to price rises, and **volume growth** is one sign of a prosperous company.

8.6 Debt and gearing ratios

Debt ratios are concerned with how much the company **owes in relation to its size** and whether it is getting into heavier debt or improving its situation.

(a) When a company is heavily in debt, and seems to be getting even more heavily into debt, banks and other would-be lenders are very soon likely to refuse further borrowing and the company might well find itself in trouble.

(b) When a company is earning only a **modest profit** before interest and tax, and has a **heavy debt burden**, there will be very little profit left over for shareholders after the interest charges have been paid.

8.6.1 The debt ratio

The **debt ratio** is the **ratio** of a **company's total debts** to its **total assets**.

(a) **Assets** consist of non-current assets at their balance sheet value, plus current assets.
(b) **Debts** consist of all payables, whether current or non-current.

You can ignore long-term provisions and liabilities, such as deferred taxation.

There is no absolute rule on the **maximum safe debt ratio**, but as a very general guide, you might regard 50% as a safe limit to debt. In addition, if the debt ratio is over 50% and getting worse, the company's debt position will be worth looking at more carefully.

8.6.2 Capital gearing

Capital gearing is concerned with the amount of debt in a company's **long-term** capital structure. **Gearing ratios** provide a long-term measure of liquidity.

$$\text{Gearing ratio} = \frac{\text{Prior charge capital (long-term debt)}}{\text{Prior charge capital} + \text{equity (shareholders' funds)}}$$

Prior charge capital is long-term loans and preferred shares (if any). It does not include loans repayable within one year and bank overdraft, unless overdraft finance is a permanent part of the business's capital.

8.6.3 Operating gearing

Operating gearing measures the proportion of fixed costs to total costs. High operating gearing means that a high proportion of cost is fixed. This has implications for business risk in that if turnover falls, there is little automatic relief in the reduction of variable costs. Operating gearing can be calculated as $\frac{\text{Contribution}}{\text{PBIT}}$.

8.6.4 Interest cover

The **interest cover** ratio shows whether a company is earning enough profits before interest and tax to pay its interest costs comfortably, or whether its interest costs are high in relation to the size of its profits, so that a fall in profit before interest and tax (PBIT) would then have a significant effect on profits available for ordinary shareholders.

$$\text{Interest cover} = \frac{\text{PBIT}}{\text{Interest charges}}$$

An interest cover of 2 times or less would be low, and it should really exceed 3 times before the company's interest costs can be considered to be within acceptable limits. Note it is usual to exclude preference dividends from 'interest' charges.

8.6.5 Cash flow ratio

The **cash flow ratio** is the ratio of a company's net annual cash inflow to its total debts:

Net annual cash inflow
Total debts

(a)   **Net annual cash inflow** is the amount of cash which the company has coming into the business each year from its operations. This will be shown in a company's cash flow statement for the year.

(b)   **Total debts** are short-term and long-term payables, together with provisions for liabilities and charges.

Obviously, a company needs to earn enough cash from operations to be able to meet its foreseeable debts and future commitments, and the cash flow ratio, and changes in the cash flow ratio from one year to the next, provides a useful indicator of a company's cash position.

8.7 Liquidity ratios: cash and working capital

Profitability is of course an important aspect of a company's performance, and debt or gearing is another. Neither, however, addresses directly the key issue of liquidity. **A company needs liquid assets so that it can meet its debts when they fall due.**

Liquidity is the amount of cash a company can obtain quickly to settle its debts (and possibly to meet other unforeseen demands for cash payments too). **Liquid funds** consist of:

(a)   **Cash**

(b)   **Short-term investments for which there is a ready market,** such as investments in shares of other companies. (Short-term investments are distinct from investments in shares in subsidiaries or associated companies.)

(c)   **Fixed term deposits** with a bank or building society, for example six month deposits with a bank

(d)   **Trade receivables.** (These are not cash, but ought to be expected to pay what they owe within a reasonably short time.)

(e)   **Bills of exchange receivable.** (Like ordinary trade debtors, these represent amounts of cash due to be received soon.)

If an analysis of a company's published accounts is to give us some idea of the company's liquidity, profitability ratios are not going to be appropriate for doing this. Instead, we look at **liquidity ratios** and **working capital turnover ratios.**

Liquidity ratios

The **current ratio** is defined as:

Current assets
Current liabilities

In practice, a current ratio comfortably in excess of 1 should be expected, but what is 'comfortable' varies between different types of businesses.

The **quick ratio**, or **acid test ratio**, is:

Current assets less inventory
Current liabilities

This ratio should ideally be at least 1 for companies with a slow stock turnover. For companies with a fast stock turnover, a quick ratio can be less than 1 without suggesting that the company is in cash flow difficulties.

An excessively large current/quick ratio may indicate a company that is **over-investing in working capital**, suggesting poor management of debtors or stocks by the company.

We can calculate **turnover periods** for stock, debtors and creditors (debtor and creditor days). If we add together the stock days and the debtor days, this should give us an indication of how soon stock is convertible into cash. Both debtor days and stock days therefore give us a further indication of the company's liquidity.

Question	Ratios

Calculate liquidity and working capital ratios from the accounts of a manufacturer of products for the construction industry, and comment on the ratios.

	20X8	20X7
	£m	£m
Revenue	2,065.0	1,788.7
Cost of sales	1,478.6	1,304.0
Gross profit	586.4	484.7
Current assets		
Inventory	119.0	109.0
Receivables (note 1)	400.9	347.4
Short-term investments	4.2	18.8
Cash at bank and in hand	48.2	48.0
	572.3	523.2
Current liabilities		
Loans and overdrafts	49.1	35.3
Corporation taxes	62.0	46.7
Dividend	19.2	14.3
Payables (note 2)	370.7	324.0
	501.0	420.3
Net current assets	71.3	102.9

Notes

	20X8	20X7
	£m	£m
1 Trade debtors	329.8	285.4
2 Trade creditors	236.2	210.8

Answer		

	20X8	*20X7*
Current ratio	$\dfrac{572.3}{501.0} = 1.14$	$\dfrac{523.2}{420.3} = 1.24$
Quick ratio	$\dfrac{453.3}{501.0} = 0.90$	$\dfrac{414.2}{420.3} = 0.99$
Debtors' payment period	$\dfrac{329.8}{2,065.0} \times 365 = 58$ days	$\dfrac{285.4}{1,788.7} \times 365 = 58$ days
Stock turnover period	$\dfrac{119.0}{1,478.6} \times 365 = 29$ days	$\dfrac{109.0}{1,304.0} \times 365 = 31$ days
Creditors' turnover period	$\dfrac{236.2}{1,478.6} \times 365 = 58$ days	$\dfrac{210.8}{1,304.0} \times 365 = 59$ days

As a manufacturing group serving the construction industry, the company would be expected to have a comparatively lengthy debtors' turnover period, because of the relatively poor cash flow in the construction industry. It is clear that the company compensates for this by ensuring that they do not pay for raw materials and other costs before they have sold their stocks of finished goods (hence the similarity of debtors' and creditors' turnover periods).

The company's current ratio is a little lower than average but its quick ratio is better than average and very little less than the current ratio. This suggests that stock levels are strictly controlled, which is reinforced by the low stock turnover period. It would seem that working capital is tightly managed, to avoid the poor liquidity which could be caused by a high debtors' turnover period and comparatively high creditors.

Creditors' turnover is ideally calculated by the formula:

$$\frac{\text{Average creditors}}{\text{Purchases}} \times 365$$

However, it is rare to find purchases disclosed in published accounts and so cost of sales serves as an approximation. The creditors' turnover ratio often helps to assess a company's liquidity; an increase in creditor days is often a sign of lack of long-term finance or poor management of current assets, resulting in the use of extended credit from suppliers, increased bank overdraft and so on.

8.8 Stock market ratios

The final set of ratios to consider are the ratios which help equity shareholders and other investors to assess the value and quality of an investment in the ordinary shares of a company.

We shall then consider their significance in the analysis of performance.

Dividend yield $= \dfrac{\text{Dividend per share}}{\text{Market price per share}}$

Interest yield $= \dfrac{\text{Interest payable}}{\text{Market value of loan stock}}$

Earnings per shares $= \dfrac{\text{Profit after tax, extraordinary items and preference dividends}}{\text{Number of equity shares in issue and ranking for dividend}}$

Price/Earnings ratio $= \dfrac{\text{Market value per share}}{\text{Earnings per share}}$

$$\text{Dividend cover} = \frac{\text{Earnings available for distribution to ordinary shareholders}}{\text{Actual dividend for ordinary shareholders}}$$

Investors are interested in:

- The value (market price) of the securities that they hold
- The return that the security has obtained in the past
- Expected future returns
- Whether their investment is reasonably secure

8.8.1 Dividend and interest yields

In practice, we usually find with quoted companies that the **dividend yield** on shares is less than the interest yield on debentures and loan stock (and also less than the yield paid on gilt-edged securities). The share price generally rises in most years, giving shareholders **capital gains**. In the long run, **shareholders will want the return on their shares**, in terms of **dividends received** plus **capital gains**, to exceed the return that investors get from fixed interest securities.

8.8.2 Earnings per share (EPS)

EPS is widely used as a measure of a company's performance and is of particular importance in comparing results over a period of several years. A company must be able to sustain its earnings in order to pay dividends and re-invest in the business so as to achieve future growth. Investors also look for **growth** in the EPS from one year to the next.

Question	Earnings per share

Walter Wall Carpets plc made profits before tax in 20X8 of £9,320,000. Tax amounted to £2,800,000.

The company's share capital is as follows.

	£
Ordinary share (10,000,000 shares of £1)	10,000,000
8% preference shares	2,000,000
	12,000,000

Required

Calculate the EPS for 20X8.

Answer

	£
Profits before tax	9,320,000
Less tax	2,880,000
Profits after tax	6,520,000
Less preference dividend (8% of £2,000,000)	160,000
Earnings	6,360,000
Number of ordinary shares	10,000,000
EPS 63.6p	

EPS must be seen in the context of several other matters.

(a) EPS is used for **comparing the results** of a company over time. Is its EPS growing? What is the rate of growth? Is the rate of growth increasing or decreasing?

(b)   Is there likely to be a significant **dilution** of EPS in the future, perhaps due to the exercise of share options or warrants, or the conversion of convertible loan stock into equity?

(c)   EPS should not be **used blindly** to compare the earnings of one company with another. For example, if A plc has an EPS of 12p for its 10,000,000 10p shares and B plc has an EPS of 24p for its 50,000,000 25p shares, we must take account of the numbers of shares. When earnings are used to compare one company's shares with another, this is done using the P/E ratio or perhaps the earnings yield.

(d)   If EPS is to be a reliable basis for comparing results, it must be **calculated consistently**. The EPS of one company must be directly comparable with the EPS of others, and the EPS of a company in one year must be directly comparable with its published EPS figures for previous years. Changes in the share capital of a company during the course of a year cause problems of comparability.

Note that EPS is a figure based on **past data**, and it is easily manipulated by changes in accounting policies and by mergers or acquisitions.

8.8.3 Price/earnings ratio

The P/E ratio is, simply, a measure of the relationship between the **market value** of a company's shares and the **earnings** from those shares.

The value of the P/E ratio reflects the market's appraisal of the shares' future prospects. In other words, if one company has a higher P/E ratio than another it is because investors either expect its earnings to **increase faster** than the other's or consider that it is a **less risky** company or in a more 'secure' industry.

One approach to assessing what share prices ought to be, which is often used in practice, is a P/E ratio approach:

(a)   The relationship between the EPS and the share price is **measured** by the **P/E ratio**.

(b)   There is no reason to suppose, in normal circumstances, that the P/E ratio will vary much over time.

(c)   So if the EPS goes up or down, the share price should be expected to move up or down too, and the new share price will be the new EPS multiplied by the constant P/E ratio.

For example, if a company had an EPS last year of 30p and a share price of £3.60, its P/E ratio would have been 12. If the current year's EPS is 33p, we might expect that the P/E ratio would remain the same, 12, and so the share price ought to go up to 12 × 33p = £3.96.

Changes in the P/E ratios of companies over time will depend on several factors.

(a)   If **interest rates go up**, investors will be attracted away from shares and into debt capital. Share prices will fall, and so P/E ratios will fall.

(b)   If **prospects** for **company profits improve**, share prices will go up, and P/E ratios will rise. Share prices depend on expectations of future earnings, not historical earnings, and so a change in prospects, perhaps caused by a substantial rise in international trade, or an economic recession, will affect prices and P/E ratios.

(c)   **Investors' confidence** might be changed by a variety of circumstances, such as:

(i)   The prospect of a change in government

(ii)   The prospects for greater exchange rate stability between currencies

8.8.4 The dividend cover

The dividend cover is the number of times the actual dividend could be paid out of current profits and indicates:

(a) The **proportion** of distributable profits for the year that is being **retained** by the company

(b) The level of **risk** that the company will **not be able to maintain the same dividend** payments in future years, should earnings fall

A high dividend cover means that a high proportion of profits are being retained, which might indicate that the company is investing to achieve earnings growth in the future.

9 Comparison of accounting figures

FAST FORWARD

Ratio analysis often forms the basis of comparisons with performance over time or with other companies.

9.1 Results of the same company over successive accounting periods

Useful comparisons over **time** include:

- **Percentage growth** in **profit** (before and after tax) and percentage growth in turnover
- **Increases or decreases** in the **debt ratio** and the gearing ratio
- **Changes** in the **current ratio**, the stock turnover period and the debtors' payment period
- **Increases** in the **EPS**, the dividend per share, and the market price

The principal advantage of making comparisons over time is that they give some indication of progress: are things getting better or worse? However, there are some weaknesses in such comparisons.

(a) The effect of **inflation** should not be forgotten.

(b) The progress a company has made needs to be set in the context of **what other companies have done**, and whether there have been any **special environmental or economic influences** on the company's performance.

9.1.1 Allowing for inflation

Ratio analysis is not usually affected by **price inflation**, except as follows.

(a) **Return on capital employed** (ROCE) can be misleading if fixed assets, especially property, are valued at **historical cost net of depreciation** rather than at current value. As time goes by and if property prices go up, the fixed assets would be seriously undervalued if they were still recorded at their historical cost.

(b) Some growth trends can be misleading, in particular the **growth in sales turnover**, and the **growth in profits or earnings**.

9.2 Comparisons between different companies in the same industry

Making comparisons between the results of different companies in the same industry is a way of assessing which companies are outperforming others.

(a) Even if two companies are in the **same broad industry** (for example, retailing) they might not be direct competitors. Even so, they might still be expected to show **broadly similar performance**, in terms of growth.

(b) If two companies are **direct competitors**, a comparison between them would be particularly interesting.

Comparisons between companies in the same industry can help investors to rank them in order of desirability as investments, and to judge relative share prices or future prospects. It is important, however, to make comparisons with caution: **a large company and a small company in the same industry might be expected to show different results**, not just in terms of size, but in terms of:

(a) **Percentage rates of growth** in sales and profits

(b) **Percentages of profits re-invested** (Dividend cover will be higher in a company that needs to retain profits to finance investment and growth.)

(c) **Fixed assets** (Large companies are more likely to have freehold property in their balance sheet than small companies.)

9.3 Comparisons between companies in different industries

Useful information can also be obtained by comparing the financial and accounting ratios of companies in different industries. An investor ought to be aware of how companies in one industrial sector are performing in comparisons with companies in other sectors. For example, it is important to know:

(a) Whether sales growth and profit growth is higher in **some industries** than in others (For example, how does growth in the financial services industry compare with growth in heavy engineering, electronics or leisure?)

(b) How the **return on capital employed** and **return on shareholder capital compare** between different industries

(c) How the **P/E ratios and dividend** yields vary between industries

Chapter Roundup

- In commercial organisations, managing for value is about creating shareholder value, while in the public sector, it is about obtaining value for money. Managers must understand the key cost and value drivers affecting their operations. Financial risk is determined exclusively by gearing, but there are several sources of business risk. Financial risk may be balanced against business risk, so that overall risk is managed.

- In seeking to attain the financial objectives of the organisation or enterprise, a financial manager has to make decisions on the following subjects.

    - Investment
    - Financing
    - Dividends

    These three policy areas interact and decision makers must also manage the interactions.

- **Cash forecasting** should ensure that sufficient funds will be available when needed, to sustain the activities of an enterprise at an acceptable cost.

- As part of a business's risk analysis, different forecasts should be prepared with **changing financial** or **business variables**. The links between these variables and the figures in the forecasts may not be straightforward.

- **Cash deficits** will be funded in different ways, depending on whether they are short or long-term. Businesses should have procedures for investing **surpluses** with appropriate levels of risk and return.

- Companies seeking extra equity finance can obtain it by **retaining cash** in the business for investment or **issuing shares**.

- Bank loans tend to be a **source** of **medium-term finance**, linked with the purchase of specific assets. Interest and repayments will be set in advance.

- The term **bonds** describes various forms of long-term debt a company may issue, such as loan stock, which may be **redeemable** or **irredeemable**.

- **Ratios** provide a means of systematically analysing financial statements. They can be grouped under the headings **profitability**, **liquidity**, **gearing** and **shareholders' investment**. It is important to calculate **relevant ratios** and to take into account the **limitations** of **ratio analysis.**

- **Ratio analysis** often forms the basis of comparisons with performance over time or with other companies.

Quick Quiz

1   What do JS&W consider to be the three main issues in strategic finance?

2   What is the name of the type of risk associated with gearing?

3   How might a company fund a forecast cash deficiency?

4   What are the advantages of using retained profits as a source of equity funds?

5   What is loan capital?

6   What is the formula for capital employed used in the ROCE calculation?

7   What is operating gearing?

8   Is inflation relevant to the calculation of ROCE?

Answers to Quick Quiz

1   Managing for value; funding; financial expectations of stakeholders

2   Financial risk

3   By borrowing; by selling marketable investments; and by managing cash flows to creditors and from debtors

4   Retained profits are flexible in that there is no specific schedule of repayments. Also, there is no change in the pattern of shareholdings.

5   Debentures and other long-term loans to a business

6   Shareholders' funds plus current liabilities plus any long-term provisions for liabilities and charges

7   The proportion of total costs that is made up of fixed costs

8   Yes: the use of historic cost net of depreciation would be misleading.

Now try the questions below from the Exam Question Bank

Number	Level	Marks	Time
Q13	Examination	25	45 mins

Part I
People

15

Leadership, performance and reward

Topic list	Syllabus reference
1 Strategic leadership	I1(a), (b)
2 Human resource planning	I2(a)
3 Appraisal and performance management	I2(b)–(d)
4 Reward management	I3(a)–(d)

Introduction

This is the first of two chapters concerned with human resource management topics. In this chapter we consider the various aspects of leadership and motivation. Appraisal and reward are the practical activities that derive from these wider topics and they have a direct influence on performance. In Chapter 15 we will look in more detail at human resource development, a third major influence on performance.

Study guide

		Intellectual level
I1	**Strategy and people: leadership**	
(a)	Explain the role of visionary leadership and identify the key leadership traits effective in the successful formulation and implementation of strategy and change management.	3
(b)	Apply and compare alternative classical and modern theories of leadership in the effective implementation of strategic objectives.	3
I2	**Strategy and people: performance management**	
(a)	Explain how the effective recruitment, management and motivation of people is necessary for enabling strategic and operational success.	3
(b)	Discuss the judgemental and developmental roles of assessment and appraisal.	3
(c)	Evaluate the concept of performance management and explore its relationship with strategic management.	3
(d)	Advise on the relationship of performance management to performance measurement (performance rating) and determine the implications of performance measurement to quality initiatives and process re-design.	3
I3	**Strategy and people: reward management**	
(a)	Explore the meaning and scope of reward management and reward practices.	2
(b)	Discuss and evaluate different techniques of reward and their relationship to job.	
(c)	Discuss and evaluate different techniques of reward and their relationship to job design, appraisal and deployment of staff.	2
(d)	Explore the principles and difficulty of aligning reward practices with strategy.	2
(e)	Advise on the relationship of reward management to quality initiatives, process re-design and the harnessing of e-business opportunities.	3
I4	**Strategy and people: job design**	
(a)	Assess the contribution of four different approaches to job design (scientific management, job enrichment, Japanese management and re-engineering).	3
(b)	Explain the human resource implications of knowledge work and post-industrial job design.	2
(c)	Discuss the tensions and potential ethical issues related to job design.	2
(d)	Advise on the relationship of job design to quality initiatives, process re-design, project management and the harnessing of e-business opportunities.	3
I5	**Strategy and people: staff development**	
(a)	Discuss the emergence and scope of human resource development, succession planning and their relationship to the strategy of the organisation.	2
(b)	Advise and suggest different methods of establishing human resource development.	3

		Intellectual level
(c)	Advise on the contribution of competency frameworks to human resource development.	3
(d)	Discuss the meaning and contribution of workplace learning, the learning organisation, organisation learning and knowledge management.	3

Exam guide

The examiner views the human resource as being of great strategic significance and clearly linked to strategic capability, the resource-based view of strategy and the idea of strategic development as a learning process. We anticipate that these will be common themes in questions. In particular, as outlined in the introduction to this chapter, the Examiner presents appraisal, reward and human resource development as three major inputs to performance. A fourth input, selection, is not included in your syllabus.

1 Strategic leadership

Knowledge brought forward from earlier studies

Paper F1, *Accountant in Business*, includes a section called 'Leading and managing individuals and teams'. This forms an important background to the material below.

FAST FORWARD

The study of leadership has produced a wide range of theories; these may be analysed into four main groups.

- Trait theories
- Behavioural theories
- Contingency theories
- Transformational theories

1.1 Trait theories

Trait theories are based on the idea that some people are inherently suited to positions of leadership because they possess **appropriate personal qualities**. This approach can be seen as rooted in a class-based social structure, but extensive attempts were made to define specific leadership qualities. However, there was little agreement as to what those qualities actually were. This approach was overtaken in the mid-twentieth century by the belief that leaders were to be identified by what they did rather than by who they were. Leadership came to be seen as a matter of **behaviour** and could therefore be taught.

Nevertheless, personal qualities and their development form a continuing strand in the progress of thought on leadership and research has identified a number of traits that have been linked to leadership effectiveness with reasonable consistency, including emotional maturity and tolerance of stress. There is also evidence of a genetic basis for leadership ability differences.

1.2 Behavioural theories

Behavioural theories are linked to the two contrasting approaches to dealing with subordinates described by *McGregor's* **Theory X** and **Theory Y**: at one extreme is an emphasis on power and control, at the other a commitment to co-operation and participation . This may be extended into the familiar spectrum of leadership styles first explicitly described by *Tannenbaum and Schmidt*, but clearly identifiable in earlier work by *Lewin* and *Likert*. The most widely used of these behavioural approaches is the **management grid** devised by *Blake and Mouton*; This rejects the idea of a single spectrum and classifies behaviour on two scales representing **concern for tasks** and **concern for relationships**.

1.3 Contingency theories

Contingency theory as applied to leadership suggests that no one style is likely to be entirely appropriate for all circumstances. For example, in an emergency, an autocratic approach is likely to be far more effective than an approach based on consultation and participative decision-making. The setting for the exercise of leadership will vary from case to case. In particular, the nature of the group and its needs and desires are critical.

1.3.1 Adair

Adair's action-centred, or situational model sees the leadership process in a context made up of three main variables, all of which are interrelated and must be examined in the light of the whole situation. These are **task needs**, the **individual needs** of group members, and the **needs of the group** as a whole. The total situation dictates the relative priority that must be given to each of the three sets of needs. Effective leadership is identifying and acting on that priority to create a balance between the needs. Adair's model is unusual in that it integrates both the **needs of the individual** and the **dynamics of the group**.

1.3.2 Fiedler

Fiedler found that people become leaders partly because of their own attributes and partly because of the nature of the **situation** they find themselves in. Leadership style depends on the personality of the leader, which is fixed. The extent to which the situation favours the leader depends on three things.

(a) **Position power**. This is the same thing as organisational authority.

(b) **Task structure**. Work is easier to organise and accountability easier to determine when the task is clear, well defined and unambiguous. The quality of performance is difficult to control when the task is vague and unstructured.

(c) **Leader-subordinate relations**. The leader's task is eased when subordinates have trust and confidence in him or her.

Fiedler found that a **task-oriented** approach was most productive when the situation was either **very favourable** to the leader or **very unfavourable**. In less extreme cases, a more **people-centred** approach was more effective.

1.3.3 Hersey and Blanchard

Hersey and Blanchard developed a model of leadership which appears to **map style theories on to the grid** suggested by Blake and Mouton. The leader should determine the **maturity** of followers. Maturity has three components.

(a) **Achievement motivation** (can the followers set high but realistic goals?).

(b) **Responsibility** (willingness and ability to assume it).

(c) **Education/experience**. Maturity in practice is divided into psychological maturity (eg attitude to work) and job maturity (eg problem solving ability).

Where maturity is high, the manager need exert little effort in support of either task or relationships and may **delegate** to a great extent.

Where maturity is low, on the other hand, an **autocratic** approach may be required, with great attention to the task but little need for attention to relationships.

Followers of moderate maturity will probably respond well to a high degree of concern for relationships combined with a moderate degree of attention to the task. **Participative** approaches are useful here.

1.4 Transformational theories

All of the models so far considered may be referred to collectively as **transactional theories** of leadership. This term is used to distinguish them from more recent approaches that have come to be known as **transformational theories** of leadership. Transformational theories generally accept that the world is a much less stable place than it was and that changes of all kinds are frequent and far-reaching. It is necessary for leaders of all kinds to accept this and to provide leadership that will help their organisations to respond in creative and effective ways.

John van Maurik lists five main expectations of modern leaders.

- To **change** organisations and systems from within
- To **empower** others
- To work through **teams** in delayered environments
- To provide **clarity of purpose** and direction
- To drive forward adventurous, **visionary strategies**

There are thus three main themes within this school of thought.

- **Teams**
- **Change**
- **Vision**

There has been a wide range of writing and thinking on these themes: we might give special mention to *Belbin's* description of **ideal team membership** and Senge's work on the **learning organisation**.

2 Human resource planning

FAST FORWARD

People are fundamental to any organisation. The **manpower planning** approach suffers from disadvantages that are similar to those of the national planning approach to strategy. A more diagnostic approach lays more emphasis on the complexity of **human behaviour**.

Psychological contracts may be **coercive**, **calculative** or **co-operative**. The contract is perceived as coercive when the individual perceives if as unequal and exploitative. The co-operative contract exists when the individual identifies with the organisation and its goals.

People are essential, indeed, fundamental, to any organisation. The strategic significance of having the right people working effectively increases as technology becomes more complex, knowledge work increases in importance and strategy relies more and more on the talents and creativity of human beings. An important aspect of human resource management (HRM), therefore, consists of the various activities that attempt to ensure that the organisation has the people it needs when it needs them. These activities include **recruitment**, **retention** and, when necessary, **reduction** of headcount.

2.1 Rational planning and diagnostic planning

Early attempts to systematise staff planning in the 1960s and 1970s relied on a top-down, 'manpower planning' approach that fitted well with the then-popular rational planning approach to strategy. This attempted to forecast future requirements for all grades and types of staff, to analyse existing staff into the various categories required and to forecast the resulting surpluses or shortfalls. Recruitment, retention and reduction were then planned as required to meet the overall requirement. Extensive work was done on statistical tools and measures to support this method, leading to **PC-based personnel information systems** that could provide extensive detail on such matters as staff turnover, absenteeism and retention.

This approach suffered from the same disadvantages that we have seen in connection with the rational approach to strategy itself. In particular, it failed to pay sufficient attention to the **complexity of human behaviour**, emphasising systems rather than actually managing people in an effective way. As a result, a more **diagnostic** approach was developed. This attempts to look behind the raw data and to discern the factors that lead to variation in such matters as turnover, retention and absenteeism. As a result, 'planning becomes integrated into the whole process of management of the employment relationship . . . Importantly, manpower planning has a part to play in bridging the gap between the needs of the organisation (as defined by senior management) and the needs of individual employees' (*Gold*).

2.2 Human resource planning

Both the rational and diagnostic approaches are used to support an existing strategy. The use of the term 'human resource planning' to replace 'manpower planning' reflects a move to a co-ordinated bundle of HRM practices that make the links between strategy, structure and people more explicit. One important result of this change is an acknowledgement that HR practices based on high involvement, commitment and reward tend to be more effective than the alternative approach based on low pay, low job security and work intensification. However, basing HRM methods on the former approach requires that senior management accept that individual and collective knowledge and skill constitute an important element of strategic capability. Many organisations do not accept this and see their people mainly as a cost driver that must be controlled.

2.3 Psychological contracts

A **psychological contract** exists between individuals in an organisation and the organisation itself.

(a) The individual expects to derive certain benefits from membership of the organisation and is prepared to expend a certain amount of effort in return.

(b) The organisation expects the individual to fulfil certain requirements and is prepared to offer certain rewards in return.

Three types of psychological contract can be identified.

(a) **Coercive contract**. This is a contract in which the individual considers that he or she is being forced to contribute his efforts and energies involuntarily, and that the rewards he receives in return are inadequate compensation.

(b) **Calculative contract**. This is a contract, accepted **voluntarily** by the individual, in which he expects to do his job in exchange for a readily identifiable set of rewards. With such psychological contracts, motivation can only be increased if the rewards to the individual are improved. If the organisation attempts to demand greater efforts without increasing the rewards, the psychological contract will revert to a coercive one, and motivation may become negative.

(c) **Co-operative contract**. This is a contract in which the individual identifies himself with the organisation and its goals, so that he/she actively seeks to contribute further to the achievement of those goals. Motivation comes out of success at work, a sense of achievement, and self-fulfilment. The individual will probably want to share in the planning and control decisions which affect his work, and **co-operative contracts are therefore likely to occur where employees participate in decision making**.

Motivation happens when the psychological contract is viewed in the same way by the organisation and by the individual and when both parties are able to fulfil their side of the bargain: the individual agrees to work, or work well, in return for whatever rewards or satisfactions are understood as the terms of the 'contract'.

An important aspect of how employees perceive the equity of their relationship with their employers lies in the way they perceive their material rewards. *Adams* and *Salomon* suggest that this perception will always be coloured by comparisons with other people. There are many classes of person with whom comparison could be made, such as employees doing the same work, those doing different work and those working for other organisations. Comparisons will also be made between the employee's pay and the company's profits; between the employee's pay and his perception of his needs; and so on.

2.4 Recruitment and selection

The psychological contract comes into existence during the processes of recruitment and selection. The co-operative contract may be considered to be the most appropriate for highly-skilled knowledge workers, such as professionally qualified accountants, but the calculative contract is probably at least as important. The potential for the calculative contract to degenerate into a coercive contract emphasises the importance of a clear understanding of the **mutual obligations** that exist within employment. This understanding should be based on equitable recruitment and selection procedures and developed within the employment relationship.

3 Appraisal and performance management

FAST FORWARD

Appraisal has several purposes, including the improvement of individual performance; motivation; communication; selection for promotion; and the determination of individual reward.

It is also fundamental to **performance management**, forming a link between the individual and overall strategy. Within this wider setting, appraisal may be seen as having two immediate purposes:

- Judgement
- Development

While the need for some kind of performance assessment is widely accepted, appraisal systems are frequently disparaged as bureaucratic, ineffective and largely irrelevant to the work of the organisation. Partly as a response to this view, modern approaches attempt to enhance the relevance of appraisal by linking it to organisational strategy and objectives. This emphasises the use of appraisal as an **instrument of control over the workforce**. However, running in parallel with this trend is an awareness, among HR professionals at least, that appraisal systems are fundamental to the aspirational model of HRM outlined above and to the co-operative psychological contract.

3.1 The purpose of appraisal

The purpose of appraisal is usually seen as the **improvement of individual performance**, but it may also be regarded as having close links to a wide range of other HR issues, including discipline, career management, motivation, communication, selection for promotion and determining rewards. It is also fundamental to the notion of **performance management**, which may be regarded as being based on a direct link from each employee to the requirements of business strategy.

Within this wider paradigm, regular appraisal interviews can be seen as serving two distinct purposes.

- (a) **Judgement**: appraisal supports the making of largely administrative decisions about pay, promotion and work responsibilities. These decisions have to be made on the basis of judgements about the appraisee's behaviour, talent, industry and value to the organisation. Such judgements can be uncomfortable for both appraiser and appraisee and lead to hostility and aggression.

- (b) **Development**: appraisal can contribute to **performance improvement** by establishing development needs, progress and opportunities. This is the more supportive aspect of appraisal, but still requires the appraiser to make decisions about the appraisee.

'The tension between appraisal as a judgemental process and as a supportive development process has never been resolved and lies at the heart of most debates about the effectiveness of appraisal at work.' (Gold)

Feedback on performance has been widely regarded as an important aspect of the participative style of management, which, in turn, has been promoted as having potential to motivate higher performance. However, the link between feedback and motivation is not simple and an important aspect of the judgemental part of appraisal is its potential to **demotivate**.

Meyer et al studied appraisal at GEC in 1965. Gold suggests that their findings are still relevant and provides a summary.

   (a)   Criticism often has a negative effect on motivation and performance.

   (b)   Praise has little effect, one way or the other.

   (c)   Performance improves with specific goals.

   (d)   Participation by the employee in goal-setting helps to produce favourable results.

Exam focus point

> Points (c) and (d) above are regarded as of great importance by the Examiner in connection with much of the material covered in earlier chapters. Their impact on business process redesign is particularly significant.

   (e)   Interviews designed primarily to improve performance should not at the same time weigh salary or promotion in the balance.

   (f)   Coaching by managers should be day to day rather than just once a year.

More recently, *Campbell and Lee* have pointed out the ways in which discrepancies may arise between people's own opinions of their performance and those of their supervisors.

   (a)   **Information**. There may be disagreement over what work roles involve, standards of performance and methods to be used.

   (b)   **Cognition**. The complexity of behaviour and performance leads to different perceptions.

   (c)   **Affect**. The judgemental nature of appraisal is threatening to the appraisee and, possibly, to the appraiser.

One approach to mitigating the undesirable effects of judgemental appraisal has been the use of **multisource feedback**, including 360 degree appraisal, in order to provide a demonstrably more **objective** review. Such approaches have tended to be used principally for appraisal of managers. Multisource feedback can be seen as empowering for staff; reinforcing for good management behaviour (since it shows managers how they are seen by others); and likely to improve the overall reliability of appraisal. However, research has shown that the effects can vary significantly.

3.2 Performance management

FAST FORWARD

> Performance management attempts to integrate HRM processes with the strategic direction and control of the organisation by incorporating agreed goals and control measures. There are several approaches to performance rating.
>
> * Inputs and personal qualities
> * Results and outcomes
> * Behaviour in performance

Performance management systems represent the rational, efficiency-driven aspect of HRM. They attempt to integrate HRM processes with the strategic direction and control of the organisation. This means that the same kind of **cybernetic control model** is used for performance management as is used for overall strategic and operational control of the organisation.

Step 1   Goals are set.

Step 2   Performance is measured and compared with target.

Step 3   Control measures are undertaken in order to correct any shortfall.

Step 4   Goals are adjusted in the light of experience.

You will be familiar with this kind of management control in business organisations, where the balanced scorecard, for example, is often used as the basis for such an approach. Gold highlights the **Best Value** framework introduced into the UK public sector in 1997.

Performance management requires that the strategic objectives of the organisation are broken down into layers of more and more detailed sub-objectives, so that individual performance can be judged against personal goals that support and link directly back to corporate strategy. This kind of cascade of goals and objectives was discussed earlier in this Study Text.

The performance management system, though it emphasises the control aspects of appraisal must also allow for the **development** aspect of appraisal, providing for coaching and training where needed.

3.3 Performance rating

Intimately linked with the definition of goals is the creation of suitable **performance indicators**. Several different approaches have been used at various times.

3.3.1 Inputs or personal qualities

The diagnosis of **personality traits** such as loyalty, leadership and commitment really requires the use of valid psychometric methods by qualified specialists. When managers attempt to perform this task, bias, subjectivity, and other effects will tend to **undermine the reliability of the output**.

3.3.2 Results and outcomes

Where the cybernetic model is implemented, objective assessment of performance against work targets can be a **reliable method of rating**. Performance against quantified work objectives, such as number of sales calls made, can be used alongside measures of progress within competence frameworks and the overall picture can be enriched with qualitative measures and comments. A **fundamental problem** with this approach is the importance of the way in which objectives are set. Ideally, they should be agreed at the outset, but this requires a degree of understanding of the complexity and difficulty of the work situation that neither party to the appraisal may possess.

Exam focus point

> This approach can be used effectively in the context of both quality management and business process re-design.

3.3.3 Behaviour in performance

Appraisal may be based more on how appraisees carry out their roles than on quantified measures of achievement. This is particularly relevant to managerial and professional activities such as communication, planning, leadership and problem resolution.

Behaviour-anchored rating scales (BARS) enable numerical scoring of performance at such activities. A numerical scale from, say, one to seven, is 'anchored' against careful descriptions of the kind of behaviour that would lead to a maximum or minimum score. This is the kind of scale satirised by the well known parody that has 'leaps tall buildings at a single bound' at the top and 'walks into walls' at the bottom. Appraisers then judge just where the appraisee falls against each scale.

Behavioural observation scales (BOS) are slightly different in two respects.

(a)   They break aspects of behaviour down into sub categories: skill at developing people, for example might be assessed against such activities as giving praise where due, providing constructive feedback and sharing best practice.

(b)   Appraisers assess the actual frequency with which such activities are performed against the frequency of opportunities to undertake them. The scores are recorded on numerical scales anchored by 'never' and 'always'.

Both BARS and BOS can enhance objectivity in appraisal and in self-appraisal.

4 Reward management

FAST FORWARD

Employment is an economic relationship: labour is exchanged for reward. **Extrinsic rewards** derive from job context and include pay and benefits. **Intrinsic rewards** derive from job content and satisfy higher level needs. reward interacts with many other aspects of the organisation. Reward policy must recognise these interactions, the economic relationship and the psychological contract.

There are five elements to Bratton's model of reward management.

- The strategic perspective
- Reward objectives
- Reward options
- Reward techniques
- Reward competitiveness

Employment is fundamentally an economic relationship: the employee works as directed by the employer and, in exchange, the employer provides reward. The relationship inevitably generates a degree of tension between the parties, since it requires **co-operation** if it is to function, but it is also likely to give rise to **conflict** since the employee's reward equates exactly to a cost for the employer.

Key term

Reward is 'all of the monetary, non-monetary and psychological payments that an organisation provides for its employees in exchange for the work they perform'.   *Bratton*

Rewards may be seen as **extrinsic** or **intrinsic**.

(a)   **Extrinsic rewards** derive from the **job context**: such extrinsic rewards include pay and other material benefits as well as matters such as working conditions and management style.

(b)   **Intrinsic rewards** derive from **job content** and satisfy higher-level needs such as those for self esteem and personal development.

The organisation's reward system is based on these two types of reward and also includes the policies and processes involved in providing them.

Reward is a fundamental aspect of HRM and of the way the organisation functions. It interacts with many other systems, objectives and activities.

- It should support the overall strategy.
- It is a vital part of the psychological contract.
- It influences the success of recruitment and retention policies.
- It must conform with law.
- It consumes resources and must be affordable
- It affects motivation and performance management.
- It must be administered efficiently and correctly.

The dual nature of reward mentioned earlier – a benefit for the employee, a cost for the employer – means that the parties in the relationship have divergent views of its purposes and extent. Employees see reward as fundamental to their standard of living: inflation, comparisons with others and rising expectations put upward pressure on their notion of what its proper level should be. Employers, on the other hand, seek both to control their employment costs and to use the reward system to influence such matters as productivity, recruitment, retention and change.

4.1 A reward management model

Bratton proposes a model of reward management based on five elements.

(a) The **strategic perspective**
(b) Reward **objectives**
(c) Reward **options**
(d) Reward **techniques**
(e) Reward **competitiveness**

4.2 The strategic perspective

> Knowledge brought forward from earlier studies

You will recall from your studies for paper F1 that contingency theory as applied to management suggests that techniques used should be appropriate to the circumstances they are intended to deal with: there is unlikely to be a single best option that is appropriate to any context.

A **contingency approach to reward** accepts that the organisation's strategy is a fundamental influence on its reward system and that the reward system should support the chosen strategy. Thus, for example, cost leadership and differentiation based on service will have very different implications for reward strategy (and, indeed, for other aspects of HRM). A firm aiming for cost leadership would have to keep its payroll costs under very tight control. However, it would not wish to sacrifice its chosen level of quality by employing the cheapest labour and neglecting to provide training. Therefore, it would aim to minimise training costs by recruiting experienced staff, bargain hard over benefits and pay rates and achieve economies of scale where possible.

A firm aiming to differentiate on quality, on the other hand, would aim to recruit and train staff to provide a high level of satisfactory customer interaction; to deploy as much talent as possible to product development and to reward high performance with a range of attractive benefits

Also, reward must be linked to and support achievement of the cascade of goals and objectives discussed earlier. Reward is therefore an important element of overall strategic control.

4.3 Reward objectives

The reward system should pursue three behavioural objectives.

(a) It should support **recruitment and retention**.
(b) It should **motivate** employees to high levels of performance.
(c) It should promote **compliance** with workplace rules and expectations.

4.3.1 Recruitment and retention

The reward system should support **recruitment and retention**. Several influences are important here. Employees will certainly assess their pay and material benefits against what they believe to be the prevailing market rate. They will also take account of disadvantageous factors, such as unpleasant working conditions in their assessment of the degree of equity their reward achieves for them. Finally, they will be very sensitive to comparisons with the rewards achieved by other employees of the same organisation. Failure to provide a significant degree of satisfaction of these concerns will lead to enhanced recruitment costs.

4.3.2 Motivation

The reward system should **motivate employees** to high levels of performance.

Knowledge brought forward from earlier studies

You will recall from your studies for Paper F1 that motivation has been the subject of much research and many theories. It is a very complex topic and impossible to sum up in a few words. However, we can say with reasonable confidence that the relationship between reward and motivation is far from simple and that there is no more than a very limited degree of correlation between pay levels and work performance.

Despite the apparently tenuous link between performance and level of pay, traditional pay systems have featured incentives intended to improve performance; also there has been a tendency for British and North American companies to adopt systems of individual performance related pay intended to support overall organisational objectives rather than simply to incentivise individual productivity.

4.3.3 Compliance

The reward system should **promote compliance** with workplace rules and expectations. The psychological contract is complex and has many features, including material rewards. The incentives included in the reward system play an important role in **signalling to employees the behaviour that the organisation values**. It is also an important contributor to the way employees perceive the organisation and their relationship with it.

4.4 Reward options

Material reward may be divided into three categories.

(a)   **Base pay** is a simply established reward for the time spent working.

(b)   **Performance pay** is normally added to base pay and is intended to reward performance learning or experience.

(c)   **Indirect pay** is made up of benefits such as health insurance, child care and so on.

4.4.1 Base pay

Base pay is usually related to the value of the job, as established by a simple estimate, a scheme of **job evaluation** or reference to prevailing employment market conditions. It is **easy to administer** and shows a **commitment by the employer** to the employee that goes beyond simple compensation for work done. A distinction may be made between hourly or weekly paid **wages** and monthly paid **salary**. The latter is normally expressed as an annual rate

4.4.2 Performance pay

Performance pay takes many forms, including **commission**, **merit pay** and **piecework pay**.

Performance pay differs from base pay in that it can be designed to support **team working** and **commitment to organisational goals**. Team working is supported by a system of bonuses based on team rather than individual performance; the size of the team may vary from a small work group to a complete office or factory. Overall organisational performance is supported by various schemes of **profit sharing**, including those that make payments into pension funds or purchase shares in the employing company.

4.4.3 Indirect pay

Benefits can form a valuable component of the total reward package. They can be designed so as to resemble either base pay or, to some extent, performance pay. A benefit resembling base pay, for example, would be use of a subsidised staff canteen, whereas the common practice of rewarding high-performing sales staff with holiday packages or superior cars looks more like performance pay.

There is a trend towards a **cafeteria** approach to benefits. Employees select the benefits they require from a costed menu up to the total value they are awarded. This means that employees' benefits are likely to match their needs and be more highly valued as a result.

4.5 Reward techniques

The reward system must attempt to achieve **internal equity**; that is to say, when employees make comparisons between their own rewards and those of others, they conclude that the overall structure is fair. If internal equity is not achieved, employees will conclude that the psychological contract has been breached and their behaviour will be affected. They may become less co-operative or they may leave.

Three techniques contribute to the establishment of internal equity.

4.5.1 Job analysis

Job analysis is the 'systematic process of collecting and evaluating information about the tasks, responsibilities and the context of a specific job' (Bratton). The data collected during job analysis are used to prepare job descriptions, job specifications and job performance standards. (Note that in practice the terms job description and job specification may be used loosely: a *job specification* is often referred to as a *person specification*, while the *Hays* recruitment website, for example uses the term *job specification* to mean exactly what Bratton means by *job description*). This information is useful in itself for a range of HRM purposes, including recruitment and training needs analysis, and it also forms the basis for **job evaluation**.

Note also that job analysis is a important aspect of quality and process re-design initiatives and is almost certainly required when e-business methods are adopted.

4.5.2 Job evaluation

Job evaluation is 'a systematic process designed to determine the relative worth of jobs within a single work organisation' (Bratton). The process depends on a series of subjective judgements and may be influenced by organisational politics and personal preconceptions. In particular, it can be difficult to separate the nature of the job from the qualities of the current incumbent.

Evaluation may be carried out in four ways.

(a) **Ranking** simply requires the arrangement of existing jobs into a hierarchy of relative value to the organisation.

(b) **Job-grading** starts with the definition of a suitable structure of grades in a hierarchy; definitions are based on requirements for skill, knowledge and experience. Each job in the organisation is then allocated to an appropriate grade.

(c) **Factor comparison** requires the allocation of monetary value to the various factors making up the content of a suitable range of benchmark jobs. This method is complex and cumbersome.

(d)   **Points rating** is similar to factor comparison, but uses points rather than monetary units to assess the elements of job content.

4.5.3 Performance appraisal

Performance appraisal has already been discussed in detail.

4.6 Reward competitiveness

The level of rewards an organisation offers will inevitably be subject to factors external to the organisation.

(a)   The **labour market** as it exists locally, nationally and perhaps globally, as relevant to the organisation's circumstances

(b)   The pressure for **cost efficiency** in the relevant industry or sector

(c)   **Legislation** such as the level of any applicable minimum wage

4.7 Setting reward levels in practice

Many companies use commercially available **survey data** to guide the overall level of the rewards they offer. This approach can be combined with the reward techniques outlined above.

An element of **flexibility** must be incorporated to reflect both the different levels of skill, knowledge and experience deployed by people doing the same work and their effectiveness in doing it.

Governments influence pay levels by means other than outright legislative prescription.

(a)   They affect the demand for labour by being major employers in their own right.

(b)   They can affect the supply of labour by, for example, setting down minimum age or qualification requirements for certain jobs.

(b)   Their fiscal and monetary policies can lead them to exert downward pressure on public sector wage rates.

4.7.1 Problems with reward systems

Reward systems are subject to a range of pressures that influence their working and affect the psychological contract.

(a)   Where **trade unions** are weak, as in the UK, employers have more freedom to introduce performance related pay.

(b)   **Economic conditions** may prevent employers from funding the rewards they might wish to provide in order to improve commitment. The result would be disappointment and dissatisfaction.

(c)   Performance pay systems are prone to **subjective and inconsistent** judgement about merit; this will discredit them in the eyes of the employees.

Chapter Roundup

- The study of leadership has produced a wide range of theories; these may be analysed into four main groups.

    - Trait theories
    - Behavioural theories
    - Contingency theories
    - Transformational theories

- People are fundamental to any organisation. The **manpower planning** approach suffers from disadvantages that are similar to those of the national planning approach to strategy. A more diagnostic approach lays more emphasis on the complexity of **human behaviour**.

    Psychological contracts may be **coercive**, **calculative** or **co-operative**. The contract is perceived as coercive when the individual perceives if as unequal and exploitative. The co-operative contract exists when the individual identifies with the organisation and its goals.

- Appraisal has several purposes, including the improvement of individual performance; motivation; communication; selection for promotion; and the determination of individual reward.

    It is also fundamental to **performance management**, forming a link between the individual and overall strategy. Within this wider setting, appraisal may be seen as having two immediate purposes:

    - Judgement
    - Development

- Performance management attempts to integrate HRM processes with the strategic direction and control of the organisation by incorporating agreed goals and control measures. There are several approaches to performance rating.

    - Inputs and personal qualities
    - Results and outcomes
    - Behaviour in performance

- Employment is an economic relationship: labour is exchanged for reward. **Extrinsic rewards** derive from job context and include pay and benefits. **Intrinsic rewards** derive from job content and satisfy higher level needs. reward interacts with many other aspects of the organisation. Reward policy must recognise these interactions, the economic relationship and the psychological contract.

    There are five elements to Bratton's model of reward management.

    - The strategic perspective
    - Reward objectives
    - Reward options
    - Reward techniques
    - Reward competitiveness

Quick Quiz

1   What are the three types of psychological contract?

2   What is the probable effect of praise on performance?

3   State two methods used to quantify behaviour in role.

4   What are the elements of Bratton's model of reward management?

5   What are the three categories of material reward?

Answers to Quick Quiz

1   Coercive, calculative and co-operative

2   Nil

3   Behaviour-anchored rating scales and behavioural observation scales

4   Strategic perspective, reward objectives, reward options, reward techniques and reward competitiveness

5   Base pay, performance pay and indirect pay

Now try the questions below from the Exam Question Bank

Number	Level	Marks	Time
Q14	Examination	10	18 mins

16

Job design and staff development

Introduction

In this second chapter on human resource management we look at a series of topics related to the way an organisation's people contribute to its success. We discussed the organisation's side of the bargain – leadership and reward – in the previous chapter. Here, we explore the wide range of approaches used to manage the workforce's efforts.

Study guide

		Intellectual level
I4	**Strategy and people: job design**	
(a)	Assess the contribution of four different approaches to job design (scientific management, job enrichment, Japanese management and re-engineering)	3
(b)	Explain the human resource implications of knowledge work and post-industrial job design	2
(c)	Discuss the tensions and potential ethical issues related to job design	2
(d)	Advise on the relationship of job design to quality initiative, process re-design, project management and the harnessing of e-business opportunities	3
I5	**Strategy and people: staff development**	
(a)	Discuss the emergence and scope of human resource development, succession planning and their relationship to the strategy of the organisation	2
(b)	Advise and suggest different methods of establishing human resource development	3
(c)	Advise on the contribution of competency frameworks to human resource development	3
(d)	Discuss the meaning and contribution of workplace learning, the learning organisation, organisation learning and knowledge management	3

Exam guide

There is much very practical detail in this chapter and it is easy to envisage a complete question covering both principles and how to embody them in a work situation.

1 Job design

FAST FORWARD

Job design is essentially about organising work and that has always been a major role of management. Four approaches are identified.

- **Scientific Management** is an engineering approach that seeks to apply a single, ideal solution to any given piece of work. It leads to work study, deskilling, efficiency and alienation.

- **Job enrichment** attempts to overcome the undesirable effects of the Scientific Management approach by making work more meaningful for the worker.

- The **Japanese model** emphasises enhanced worker responsibility in pursuit of higher quality and reduced waste.

- **Re-engineering** pursues major improvements in organisational systems while, at the same time, empowering workers to make the best use of their skills and abilities.

- Managers should be as humane as possible when undertaking job design.

Key term

Job design is the process of combining tasks and responsibilities to form complete jobs and the relationship of jobs in the organisation.

Bratton

The importance of job design as a managerial responsibility has been apparent ever since there have been organised societies. *Adam Smith* described the economic advantages of job specialisation in *The Wealth of Nations*; in the later nineteenth century **organising** a structure of tasks and jobs was identified by *Fayol* as one of the functions of management. A little later, *Frederick Taylor* founded his business and the approach still known as **Scientific Management** on the careful consideration and control of individual job content and technique.

Your syllabus requires us to consider four different approaches to job design.

- Scientific Management
- Job enrichment
- The Japanese model
- Re-engineering

1.1 Scientific Management

Frederick W Taylor argued that management should be based on 'well-recognised, clearly defined and fixed principles, instead of depending on more or less hazy ideas.' He was an engineer by training and mostly concerned with an **engineering efficiency** approach to production in order to increase productivity. His methods were later applied to many other types of work.

Taylor's early experience convinced him that workers had a natural tendency to do the minimum they could get away with: he described workers as 'marking time' or 'soldiering', rather than working productively. Since managers had very poor knowledge of how much output could reasonably be expected from a worker, the result was large scale under-achievement. It was always his principle that there was 'one best way' of doing a given job and the main thrust of much of his early work was therefore careful experimentation and measurement to find the **most effective methods**. This approach was the basis of what later became the widely used discipline of **work study**.

1.1.1 Principles of Scientific Management

Taylor described four ideas as the principles of his method.

(a) **The development of a true science of work**. 'All knowledge which had hitherto been kept in the heads of workmen should be gathered and recorded by **management**. Every single subject, large and small, becomes the question for scientific investigation, for reduction to law.'

(b) **The scientific selection and progressive development of workers:** workers should be carefully trained and given jobs to which they are best suited.

(c) **The bringing together of the science and the scientifically selected and trained men**. The application of techniques to decide what should be done and how, using workers who are both properly trained and willing to maximise output, should result in maximum productivity.

(d) **The constant and intimate co-operation between management and workers:** 'the relations between employers and men form without question the most important part of this art.'

1.1.2 Scientific Management in practice

Trade unionists, politicians of the left and those sympathetic to their ideas see Scientific Management as an extremely undesirable development, since it **minimised worker autonomy** and **maximised management control**. (This point of view can often be identified by the use of the term 'Taylorism' rather than Scientific Management.)

(a)   **Work study techniques** established the 'one best way' to do any job. No discretion was allowed to the worker. Preparation and servicing tasks were allocated to unskilled workers. Subsequently, *Henry Ford's* approach to mass production broke each job down into its smallest and simplest component parts: these single elements became the newly-designed job. This process of **deskilling** makes such work unfulfilling and boring but very productive.

(b)   **Planning the work and doing the work were separated.** First line management of work groups might involve several 'functional foremen,' each responsible for a different aspect of planning and controlling the work. Workers lost any control over what they did.

(c)   **Workers received large pay increases** as the new methods greatly increased productivity and profits.

(d)   All aspects of the **work environment** were tightly controlled in order to attain maximum productivity.

Despite the views of the detractors of Scientific Management, there is much that is relevant today in this approach and the pursuit of productivity through efficiency of method is still a major preoccupation for management at all levels. The whole field of process redesign, for example is essentially an application of the basic idea of improving performance in a designed way, as is much of the detail of modern quality management. However, we may identify two important and linked differences.

(a)   The Scientific Management approach was for an external expert to prescribe the improvement: the modern approach is to involve the people concerned with the process.

(b)   Taylor promoted the idea of 'one best way': modern approaches accept that more than one solution may be valid.

Also, there are genuine problems with Scientific Management in a modern setting.

(a)   The **alienation** and **boredom** associated with the production-line approach lead to high levels of **labour turnover** and **absenteeism**.

(b)   While basic labour costs may fall, there is a penalty to pay in **increased costs of planning and supervision**.

(c)   Lack of **job satisfaction** can lead to lack of **commitment** and thence to **quality problems**.

1.2 Job enrichment

1.2.1 The human relations background

The development of the **human relations** school of thought can be traced back to experiments carried out in the early 1920s at *Western Electric's* Hawthorne plant in Chicago. The original experiments seemed to show that there was no clear relationship between improvements made to working conditions and productivity. Subsequent research extending over many years indicated the complex interplay of social, material and personal factors in determining much workplace behaviour and its influence on productivity. Awareness of **social and individual psychology** became a fundamental aspect of management technique, with an emphasis on measures such as employee **counselling** and the satisfaction of **social needs**. There was also an understanding that **financial reward alone** would be unlikely to motivate workers to high levels of output. However, the theory did not produce reliable results when applied in practical terms.

1.2.2 Motivation and job design

'Neo-human relations' was used by *Rose* as a label for the later work of psychologists such as *Maslow*, *McGregor* and *Herzberg*. These authors are best known in the wider field of management studies for their ideas about **motivation** and the potential of work and the work situation to provide higher psychological satisfactions. One important aspect of this consideration of work and motivation has been an emphasis on the **importance of job content** and a move towards **job enrichment**.

1.2.3 Job enrichment

Job rotation and **job enlargement** are simple approaches to the redesign of jobs.

(a) **Job rotation**, or periodic movement around a group of different de-skilled tasks, can go some way towards reducing monotony and boredom, but offers little extra satisfaction.

(b) **Job enlargement** reverses the process of de-skilling by combining a number of linked processes together in one job. This is in direct opposition to Ford's production line approach.

A more sophisticated approach is known as **job enrichment**: this may be distinguished from job enlargement in that the latter brings tasks together on a horizontal axis, while job enrichment involves an element of vertical amalgamation: an enriched job includes some elements of **responsibility for planning and control**.

Hackman and Oldham suggest that five core characteristics are required in enriched jobs if they are to produce positive outcomes.

(a) The job requires the use of a **range of skills and talents**

(b) **Task identity** (sometimes called **closure**): the job includes all the tasks needed to complete an identifiable product or process.

(c) **Task significance**: the job has an impact on other people's lives or work.

(d) **Autonomy**: workers have a degree of discretion in scheduling and organising their work.

(e) **Feedback**: workers are provided with information on the results of their performance.

These elements should lead to **three desirable psychological states**.

- Experience of **meaningful work**
- Experience of **responsibility for outcomes**
- Knowledge of **actual results**

These, in turn, should produce **desirable outcomes**.

- High productivity and quality
- High job satisfaction and low absenteeism and labour turnover

However, this desirable progression, from job enrichment to desirable outcomes is subject to the effect of **moderators**.

- The level of knowledge and skill possessed by the employee
- The strength of the employee's need for growth in the job
- The influence of the work context over satisfaction

Thus, an ignorant, clumsy and unambitious person working in unsatisfactory conditions is unlikely to demonstrate the desired outcomes when his job is enriched.

Exam focus point

> If you consider the processes involved in job enrichment, you should discern potential links to quality methods, process redesign and the changes inherent in adopting and e-business method. Each of these aspects of strategic implementation can provide extensive opportunities for job enrichment.

1.3 The Japanese model

Japanese industry has had enormous influence on western manufacturing practice. **Lean production** or 'the Toyota system' have been widely adopted and developed in an attempt to achieve Japanese levels of productivity and quality. *Bratton* suggests that three notable elements of the Japanese production model contribute to its influence on job design.

- Flexible manufacturing
- Quality methods
- Minimisation of waste

1.3.1 Flexible manufacturing

Flexibility of manufacturing means the ability to produce relatively small batches of a range of products without incurring excessive **set-up** costs. The principal features of the Japanese method of achieving this are multi-skilled workers and careful shop floor layout that makes a range of machinery and equipment available to each of them. **Machine cells** are a common feature of this approach. This approach stands in strong contrast to both the principles of Scientific Management and the assembly line layout; it inevitably brings a high degree of **job enrichment** through the **variety of work** and the **skills needed** to perform it.

1.3.2 Quality methods

As already discussed in our earlier general coverage of quality methods, Japanese manufacturers paid close attention to statistical quality control and *Deming's* other principles and methods very early in that country's post-1945 recovery. One of the results of this focus was the development of the **total quality** approach. This puts quality at the heart of the manufacturing process by abolishing inspection as an independent function and separate process within the organisation and making production workers responsible for the quality of their own output. This feature, together with participation in activities aimed at achieving **continuous improvement**, also produces job enrichment.

1.3.3 Minimisation of waste

Incorporating quality responsibility into production work is also an example of the Japanese approach to waste: separate inspection processes (and the rework they lead to) add no value: therefore they are abolished. The **just in time** philosophy is a further example. Stocks of materials, components and work-in-progress must be financed with capital that could be better employed earning a return elsewhere: stocks are therefore cut to an absolute minimum and capital released. To achieve this, the *kanban* system is used. A kanban is a signal calling for productive effort: a series of kanbans flows back from the final customer through all the various manufacturing and logistic stages of production: as a result, production is **pulled through** the factory by demand, **not pushed** by production schedule. This again places **enhanced responsibility** on individuals and work groups to respond appropriately. It is also a good illustration of one application of e-business methods: the use of electronic data interchange to link stages in the value network.

1.3.4 The problem of control

Bratton points out that the job enriching effects described above combine to make the company heavily **dependent on its workers**. In order to counterbalance this, Japanese companies have made use of a set of **social mechanisms that enhance the commitment** of their workers. The basic aim is the promotion of a **sense of community** that provides a socialisation into the norms of loyalty and motivation. Work groups tend to develop their means of disciplining members felt not to be conforming.

1.4 Re-engineering

Knowledge brought forward from earlier studies

We looked at business process change in more detail earlier in this Study Text, including a discussion of business process re-engineering (BPR) as it affects job design. You should refer to our earlier discussion and consider how BPR may be said to fit into the job design spectrum.

1.5 Ethics and job design

Knowledge brought forward from earlier studies

When we discussed ethics, we dealt with two important matters that are directly related to job design.

(a)   One formulation of the **categorical imperative** is that people should not be treated simply as means to an end but as an end in themselves.

(b)   Natural law theory imposes a duty to respect the rights of others.

The managerial priorities of **control** and **cost reduction** can drive the process of job design towards infringement of these ethical principles.

(a)   Jobs may be **deskilled** and organised in ways that prevent workers from deriving any satisfaction or fulfilment from them.

(b)   Jobs may be automated or outsourced out of existence, thus bringing significant disruption and stress to workers' lives.

(c)   Work groups may be broken up, limiting the potential of work to fulfil this is a difficult and complex problem: managers should seek to balance their organisational responsibilities and the effect of their actions on their workers, seeking a humane course of action where possible.

1.6 An overview of job design

FAST FORWARD

Productivity through **work specialisation** leads to mechanisms of close managerial control: together, these forces produce **job dissatisfaction** and **poor motivation**. All job design must attempt to reconcile these forces.

All job design must attempt to **reconcile two forces** that tend to work in opposition to one another.

(a)   The need to **break work up** in order to exploit specialisation and the division of labour so as to maximise productivity

(b)   The need to **integrate** and **control** the highly differentiated activities that result from (a)

From the point of view of the worker, specialisation can produce fragmented, unsatisfying work and poor social interaction, which, combined with its resultant control-based style of management, leads to low levels of **motivation and commitment**.

Scientific Management was based on extremes of specialisation and management control and ignored the potential psychological effects on the work force. Later developments have produced a different balance.

1.7 Summarising four approaches to job design

	Features	Assumptions about motivation	Job design
Scientific Management	Prescribed standard methods	Pay – piecework	Extreme specialisation Split of planning and doing
Human relations/ job enrichment	Work groups Combination of tasks Some control over planning	Social needs Achievement, growth, responsibility	Less extreme, with some control tasks shifted downwards
Japanese style	JIT, TQM, consensus, lifetime employment, loyalty	Social processes of clan control	Multi-skilling to achieve flexibility
BPR	Strong leadership from the top	Emphasis on market discipline and serving the needs of the customer	Process teams

Exam focus point

Your syllabus specifically mentions the relationship of job design to quality, process design, project management and e-business. Your examiner ahs said that the project management reference is not required, but you should be aware that the other three elements of strategic implementation mentioned are likely to involve a need for some degree of job redesign. You should bear this in mind when answering questions that deal with those three elements.

2 HRM and knowledge work

FAST FORWARD

Knowledge work has become a major part of the economies of developed countries. This has had important effects on the way organisations work and are managed, with a shift away from procedure and control towards a looser, more flexible system based on problem solving and empowerment.

Knowledge brought forward from earlier studies

We discussed organisational learning and knowledge management earlier in this Study Text, when we were considering strategic capability. You should refer back in order to refresh your memory.

Recent years have seen a shift of manufacturing to low-cost sites in developing countries and a consequent decline in the West. As a result, service industries have become far more important to the economies of developed countries. This trend has been accompanied by the recognition of the **knowledge worker** as a vital feature of modern business. This has two important implications.

(a)   Knowledge is recognised as a **vital asset** and crucial to business success. Organisations must therefore acquire, organise, manage and exploit knowledge if they are to survive.

(b)   This vital asset, knowledge, fundamentally exists in the brains of knowledge workers and is controlled by them. If the organisation is benefit, its workers must be organised and managed in a way that will **stimulate both learning and creativity**.

These factors have led to a shift away from the classic bureaucratic structure of management and organisation, which was built around the careful planning and control of procedures and operations, to a looser, 'post-modern', 'post-bureaucratic' or 'post-industrial' approach that emphasises information sharing, flexibility and empowerment.

2.1 The move to knowledge work

	From	To
Type of work	Individual	Project teams
Focus	Task performance	Customers, problems, opportunities
Skills and knowledge	Narrow	Specialist but with wide interest
Feedback and results	Rapid	Slow
Employee loyalty	Organisation and career within it	Peers, profession
Contribution to success	Individual support to the wider strategy	A few major successes

2.2 Impact on the organisation

Bratton, quoting *Hecksher*, suggests that as organisations evolve to take account of these changes they will display five features.

(a)   **Organisational dialogue and trust** reduces the scope for managerial control and direction and enables a wide range of bottom up and lateral inputs. This feature depends on:

(b)   **Sharing of information** about the organisation's operations, problems and opportunities.

(c)   **Principle-based management** replaces management based on formal rules and procedure and leads to greater flexibility and adaptation.

(d)   **Communication flows and decision-making** are built around projects and problem-solving rather than hierarchical routine.

(e)   **Peer evaluation** of performance replaces formal credentials and supervisor opinion.

3 Staff development

FAST FORWARD

Human resource development should be seen as an investment in strategic capability since it improves both skills and commitment. It may be approached top-down, in the form of **human capital theory**, or bottom-up through **empowerment**. In the UK, governments encourage rather than enforce HRD efforts, despite concerns about low levels of skills. This voluntarist approach has led to an emphasis on useful, workplace competence-based qualifications.

The traditional personnel management function of training is now supplemented and may be replaced by the wider concept of **human resource development** (HRD).

(a)   The view of training as a **cost** is being replaced with a view of HRD as an **investment in strategic capability**.

(b)   Investment in **employee learning** and recognition of the **competitive advantage conferred by upgraded skills** triggers the creation of an internal market in such qualities with consequent implications for other HR activities such as recruitment, retention and reward.

(c)   Organisations seeking to benefit from employee loyalty and commitment find that HRD can enable employees to contribute to the **development and success of strategy and operations**.

This **wider vision of HRD** can link to the organisation's strategy in two ways: these correspond to the traditional 'top-down' model of strategy as a controlled response to environmental change and the emergent or 'bottom-up' model.

(a)   Under the **top-down** model, the organisation's senior managers are responsible for recognising new, more general and wide-ranging environmental factors that mandate HRD effort. For example, technological developments may lead to the recognition of a skills gap and the need for staff training.

(b)   Under the **bottom-up** model, empowered employees recognise individual gaps in skills, knowledge or capability and take steps to resolve them through discussion, co-operation and the development of new methods. An example would be the improvement of a product as a result of customer contact and internal consultation and action.

It is appropriate for organisations to utilise both approaches, though this requires senior management effort to reconcile them and enable them to work in a synergistic fashion rather than interfering with each other.

A traditional view of the place of HRD in strategic management is that it **responds to imperatives** generated by the strategic management process, whatever form that takes. Some HRD professionals would argue that HRD should be a major component of that process in order to create a learning culture as a basis for more effective strategy. This is not yet a popular approach in the UK.

3.1 Establishing HRD

The prevailing view of HRD in UK commercial organisations is **human capital** theory. This sees investment in HRD as analogous to investment in other assets and judges its value in terms of return on investment. This approach requires clear evidence of probable benefit before investment is made in HRD and restricts developmental activities that have uncertain though possibly important benefits. The extreme case of this view is the drive to reduce training costs and ensure control of work practices through **deskilling** and careful **job design**.

The alternative view is a **developmental humanistic** approach, as discerned by *Gold and Smith*. This approach features empowerment; lifelong learning and the learning organisation; productivity through a sense of meaningful work; and learning as a way of both coping with change and fulfilling ambitions. Advocates of this approach accept that it is necessary to present its advantages in terms that relate to human capital theory if it is to be adopted.

The benefit of an active commitment to HRD may be considered at three levels.

(a)   **The individual's** job prospects and potential income are enhanced by vocational and academic qualifications.

(b)   **The organisation** may find that recruitment, adaptation to change, staff turnover and productivity are enhanced by good HRD, but *Machin and Vignoles* have suggested that any causal relationship that exists may in fact work in the reverse sense; that is, it may just be that profitable and productive firms do more HRD.

(c)   At the **national economic and social level**, there is a link between general education and economic growth, but it is difficult to establish one between training and growth.

In general, the UK displays a **voluntarist approach** to HRD, in that the role of government is to encourage rather than to enforce HRD. This contrasts with the **interventionist approach** current in France, under which the government imposes a training levy based on payroll value and uses the funds to reimburse employers that undertake training. This system was tried in the UK by the Labour government of the late 1960s and later abolished because the system inevitably imposed a **deadweight cost of administration** in addition to the cost of any HRD actually undertaken. A company undertaking all of the HRD deemed appropriate would only be reimbursed with 97.5% of the levy it had paid, the balance being consumed by government in administering the scheme.

3.2 Competence frameworks

The dominance of the voluntarist view in the UK has led government to promote HRD within a market-led framework. Research commissioned by the National Skills Task Force indicates that there is a major shortage of technical skills but that employers either fail to recognise this or work around it by concentrating on low skill-content products. Government has responded to this problem with a range of supply-side measures and exhortation. Measures have included infrastructure improvements, including a network of institutions to co-ordinate national initiatives, and the development of a comprehensive national scheme of **competence based qualifications**.

ey term

> **Competences**, in the sense used here, are 'the required outcomes expected from the performance of a task in a work role, expressed as performance standards with criteria'.   *Gold*

The emphasis on workplace performance reflects the human capital approach to HRD.

The qualifications themselves are called national vocational qualifications (NVQs) in England and Wales and Scottish vocational qualifications (SVQs) in Scotland. There has been criticism of the N/SVQ approach because of their emphasis on outcomes measured against standards rather than on knowledge and understanding. It has also been suggested that they have simply added to the number of qualifications available rather than rationalising them overall.

Institutions

The UK national structure of institutions concerned with HRD includes the Qualifications and Curriculum Authority, which oversees all standards in both education and training, and a number of Regional Development Agencies and Learning and Skills Councils, which promote and oversee all education and training after the age of 16 years.

3.3 Workplace learning

Advocates of HRD suggest that learning is fundamental if the organisation is to cope with environmental change, uncertainty and complexity. HRD practitioners place the following concepts under the umbrella of workplace learning.

- Organisational learning
- Knowledge management
- The learning organisation
- E-Learning

Organisational learning, the learning organisation and knowledge management are dealt with elsewhere in this Study Text. E-learning is an effective way to acquire knowledge and non-manipulation skills using interactive software.

3.4 Succession planning

FAST FORWARD

> Succession planning not only provides for continuity of leadership, if also facilitates management development at all levels.

Key term

> **Succession planning** is undertaken in order to ensure continuity in the organisation's leadership. It involves the systematic identification, assessment and development of managerial talent at all levels.

Succession planning should be an integral part of the HR plan and should support the organisation's chosen strategy. The developed plan should also be compatible with any changes that that are foreseen in the way the organisation operates. It is likely that strategic objectives will only be obtained if management development proceeds in step with the evolution of the organisation.

3.4.1 Benefits of succession planning

(a)   The development of managers at all levels is likely to be improved if it takes place within the context of a succession plan. Such a plan gives focus to management development by suggesting objectives that are directly relevant to the organisation's needs.

(b)   Continuity of leadership is more likely, with fewer dislocating changes of approach and policy.

(c)   Assessment of managerial talent is improved by the establishment of relevant criteria.

3.4.2 Features of successful succession planning

(a)   The plan should focus on future requirements, particularly in terms of strategy and culture.

(b)   The plan should be driven by top management. Line management also have important contributions to make. It is important that it is not seen as a HR responsibility.

(c)   Management development is as important as assessment and selection.

(d)   Assessment should be objective and preferably involve more than one assessor for each manager assessed.

(e)   Succession planning will work best if it aims to identify and develop a leadership *cadre* rather than merely to establish a queue for top positions. A pool of talent and ability is a flexible asset for the organisation.

Case Study

Succession planning

Few large companies approach their succession planning with care.

When Sir Richard Greenbury stepped down as chairman of Marks and Spencer last year, it took the retailer months to find a successor. Other companies that have struggled to find new leaders include Barclays and Reed Elsevier, the publisher.

When Bob Ayling was sacked as chief executive of British Airways earlier this year, one of the many criticisms directed at him was that he had sidelined any rivals and failed to groom a successor.

Michael Skapinker, Financial Times, 13 July 2000

Chapter Roundup

- Job design is essentially about organising work and that has always been a major role of management. Four approaches are identified.

  - **Scientific Management** is an engineering approach that seeks to apply a single, ideal solution to any given piece of work. It leads to work study, deskilling, efficiency and alienation.

  - **Job enrichment** attempts to overcome the undesirable effects of the Scientific Management approach by making work more meaningful for the worker.

  - The **Japanese model** emphasises enhanced worker responsibility in pursuit of higher quality and reduced waste.

  - **Re-engineering** pursues major improvements in organisational systems while, at the same time, empowering workers to make the best use of their skills and abilities.

  - Managers should be as humane as possible when undertaking job design.

- Productivity through **work specialisation** leads to mechanisms of close managerial control pull: together, these forces produce **job dissatisfaction** and **poor motivation**. All job design must attempt to reconcile these forces.

- **Knowledge work** has become a major part of the economies of developed countries. This has had important effects on the way organisations work and are managed, with a shift away from procedure and control towards a looser, more flexible system based on problem solving and empowerment.

- Human resource development should be seen as an investment in strategic capability since it improves both skills and commitment. it may be approached top-down, in the form of **human capital theory**, or bottom-up through **empowerment**. In the UK, governments encourage rather than enforce HRD efforts, despite concerns about low levels of skills. This voluntarist approach has led to an emphasis on useful, workplace competence-based qualifications.

- Succession planning not only provides for continuity of leadership, if also facilitates management development at all levels.

Quick Quiz

1   What are the meaningful psychological states that job enrichment is intended to produce?

2   What elements of the Japanese production model does Bratton identify as influencing the Japanese approach to job design?

3   What effects will the move to knowledge work have on the organisation?

4   How does human capital theory view the cost of HRD?

5   What are competences?

Answers to Quick Quiz

1   Experience of meaningful work; experience of responsibility for outcomes; knowledge of actual results

2   Flexible manufacturing; quality methods; minimisation of waste

3   Organisational dialogue and trust, which depends on sharing of information; principle-based management rather than procedure-based management; problem-solving and project-based communication-flows; peer evaluation of performance

4   As investment in assets

5   Competences, in the sense used here, are 'the required outcomes expected from the performance of a task in a work role, expressed as performance standards with criteria'.

Part J
Change and development

Managing strategic change

Introduction

It will be unusual for an organisation's strategy to remain unchanged for any appreciable period of time and the same is true of the methods and processes used for implementing it. The influence of environmental developments is such that strategies will inevitably change and evolve; the only question is how rapid the change will be.

The management of change is thus an integral and important part of strategic management and is the subject of this chapter. Following JS&W, we will start by considering the **diagnosis of change requirements**. The work to be done here consists of establishing the type of change required; exploring the organisational context and the cultural influences involved; and analysing the forces that support or hinder the change required.

We will then examine the impact of **management style** and the **roles played by** managers and other **agents of change**. There are a number of **levers of change** that managers can use and we consider these next. Finally, we consider the **common pitfalls** that have hampered change programmes in the past.

Study guide

		Intellectual level
C2	**Managing strategic change**	
(a)	Explore different types of strategic change and their implications	2
(b)	Determine the organisational context of change and use the cultural web to diagnose this organisational context	3
(c)	Establish potential blockages and levers of change	2
(d)	Advise on the style of leadership appropriate to manage strategic change	2
(e)	Specify organisational roles required to manage strategic change	2
(f)	Discuss levers than can be employed to manage strategic change	2

Exam guide

Change is a theme that appears frequently in old syllabus exams and there is every reason to believe that this will continue. It is very important to be aware that strategic change may be implicit in a scenario rather than being the explicit subject of a question requirement. You must be able to recognise the factors that drive change and constrain the ways in which it may be effected.

1 Diagnosis: situation analysis for change

FAST FORWARD

There are three main change management considerations.

- The type of change required, whether adaptation, evolution, reconstruction or revolution

- The wider context of change, including the time available; capability to implement change; capacity and readiness; and power

- Forces facilitating and blocking change

A wide range of stimuli may lead an organisation's managers to recognise the need for strategic change. Consideration of the broader contexts of the **environment** and the organisation's **strategic capability** may show that large scale developments are necessary; the need to put strategy into action may call for more detailed but no less far-reaching adjustment of processes, relationships, technologies and so on. In any event, the management of change starts with an understanding of **three main considerations**.

(a)   The **type** of change required
(b)   The **wider context** of the change
(c)   **Forces facilitating** and **blocking** change

1.1 Types of change

JS&W, quoting *Balogun and Hope Hailey* analyse change on two axes: these are its **scope** and its **nature**.

The **scope** of change is its extent: the measure of scope is whether or not the methods and assumptions of the existing **paradigm** must be replaced.

The **nature** of change may be incremental and built on existing methods and approaches, or it may require a 'big bang' approach if rapid response is required, as in times of crisis.

Scope of change

Nature of change		Realignment	Transformation
	Incremental	Adaptation	Evolution
	'Big bang'	Reconstruction	Revolution

(a) **Adaptation** is the most common type of change. It does not require the development of a new paradigm and proceeds step by step.

(b) **Reconstruction** can also be undertaken within an existing paradigm but requires rapid and extensive action. It is a common response to a long-term decline in performance.

(c) **Evolution** is an incremental process that leads to a new paradigm. It may arise from careful analysis and planning or may be the result of **learning processes**. Its transformational nature may not be obvious while it is taking place

(d) **Revolution** is rapid and wide ranging response to extreme pressures for change. A long period of **strategic drift** may lead to a crisis that can only be dealt with in this way. Revolution will be very obvious and is likely to affect most aspects of both what the organisation does and how it does them.

1.2 The context of change

The context of change is provided by the organisational setting; this has many aspects and can therefore be very complex. However, this complexity can be approached in a manageable way by considering it under eight general headings proposed by Balogun and Hope Hailey. One of the eight headings is **scope**: this has already been discussed. The rest are discussed below.

The headings represent a wide range of influences and the specific considerations affecting the impact of each may vary from organisation to organisation. For example, the first on the list, **time available**, may be largely determined by stakeholder sentiment in one organisation and by anticipated political change in a another, with different aspects of the market situation influencing both.

1.2.1 Aspects of context

(a) The **time available** may vary dramatically.

(b) The **preservation** of some organisational characteristics and resources may be required.

(c) **Diversity** of general experience, opinion and practice is likely to ease the change process: homogeneity in these factors is unlikely to do so.

(d) The **capability** to manage and implement change is obviously important. To a great extent, this depends on past experience of change projects, both among managers and among lower-level staff.

(e) **Capacity** to undertake change depends on the availability of resources, particularly finance and management time and skill.

(f) The degree of workforce **readiness** for change will affect its success. Readiness may be contrasted with **resistance** to change, which can exist at varying levels of intensity and may be widespread or confined to pockets.

(g) The **power** to effect change may not be sufficient to overcome determined resistance among important stakeholder groups. This can apply even at the strategic apex, where, for example, major shareholders, trustees or government ministers may constrain managers' freedom of action.

1.2.2 Questions

An examination of context leads to four questions.

(a)   Is the organisation able to **achieve** the change required?
(b)   Does the context affect the **means** by which change should be achieved?
(c)   Should the context itself be **restructured** as a preliminary to strategic change?
(d)   Will constraints present in the context make it necessary to proceed in **stages**?

1.3 Culture and change

If you think about the elements of context outlined above, you will quickly realise that they are all affected to some extent by **cultural considerations**. For example, even the adequacy or otherwise of the time available may be affected by culturally-influenced attitudes to speed of action, caution and risk.

The **cultural web** may be used as a tool to establish specific implications of the desired overall strategic change by facilitating comparison between the current position and the desired future outcome. For example, consideration of **power structures** may make it clear that there should be a move away from some aspects of uncontrolled **devolution of power** and towards a **clearer definition of responsibility**. Similarly, it might be decided that dress is a powerful **symbol** and that a corporate livery should be provided for customer-facing staff.

1.4 Forcefield analysis

Forcefield analysis consists of the identification of the factors that promote and hinder change. Promoting forces should be exploited and the effect of hindering forces reduced.

It is traditional to represent these forces by **arrows** whose individual dimensions correspond to their perceived strengths. Promoting and hindering forces are then shown pointing from opposite sides to a vertical linear datum line. This representation is useful for purposes such as brainstorming and staff briefings, but two lists in order of magnitude are just as useful for purposes of analysis. The example below concerns a public sector organisation that is introducing performance review.

Exam focus point	We have already encountered this kind of diagrammatic presentation when we were considering project management. Be aware that change management and project management are intimately linked: any project is quite likely to result in change, while change is often implemented through projects.

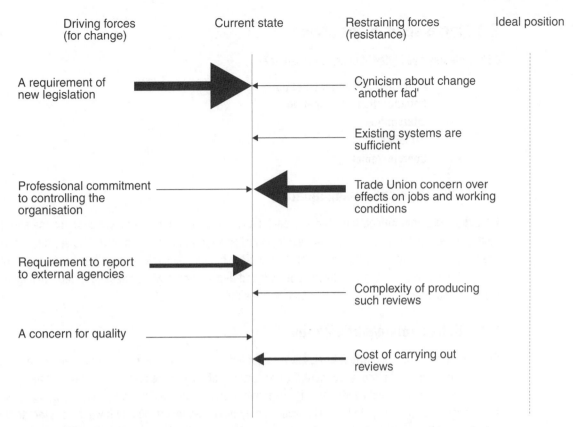

| Driving forces (for change) | Current state | Restraining forces (resistance) | Ideal position |

A requirement of new legislation — Cynicism about change `another fad'

Existing systems are sufficient

Professional commitment to controlling the organisation — Trade Union concern over effects on jobs and working conditions

Requirement to report to external agencies

Complexity of producing such reviews

A concern for quality

Cost of carrying out reviews

Senior (drawing on the advice of *Carnall* and *Huczyuski and Buchanan*) suggests a practical route to applying the force field analysis idea.

(a) Define the problem in terms of the current situation and the desired future state.

(b) List the forces supporting and opposing the desired change and assess both the strength and the importance of each one.

(c) Draw the force field diagram.

(d) Decide how to strengthen or weaken the more important forces as appropriate and agree with those concerned. Weakening might be achieved by persuasion, participation, coercion or bargaining, while strengthening might be achieved by a marketing or education campaign, including the use of personal advocacy.

(e) Identify the resources needed.

(f) Make an action plan including event timing, milestones and responsibilities.

JS&W state that, typically, elements of the **cultural web** emerge as important forces promoting or hindering change. The web can thus be used alongside forcefield analysis as a diagnostic tool.

2 Styles of change management

FAST FORWARD

There are five change management styles.

- Education and communication
- Collaboration/participation
- Intervention
- Direction
- Coercion/edict

Progression down the list of styles corresponds to progression through the four types of change noted above.

2.1 Five management styles

JS&W identify five styles of change management.

- **Education and communication**
- **Collaboration/participation**
- **Intervention**
- **Direction**
- **Coercion/edict**

2.1.1 Education and communication

Education and communication is an approach based on persuasion: the reasons for change and the means by which it will be achieved are explained in detail to those affected by it. It is appropriate when change is **incremental**. This style is time-consuming, but can be useful if there has been misinformation in the past. However, it is a top-down approach and depends on a **willingness** to accept management's plans as appropriate. This may not, in fact, be present.

2.1.2 Collaboration/participation

Collaboration, or **participation**, brings those affected by strategic change into the change management process, drawing them into issue identification, prioritisation and the creation of new routines to implement newly established strategy, for example. It may improve decision quality by bringing wider experience and knowledge to bear. However, it may be time-consuming and it will be **subject to the influence of the existing culture and paradigm**, which may limit its potential effectiveness. This approach is both ethical, in basic deontological terms, and advantageous in practice, since it can nurture a positive attitude, thus building both **readiness** and **capability** for change. It is suited to incremental change.

2.1.3 Intervention

Intervention is undertaken by a **change agent** (see below) who delegates some aspects of the change process to teams or individuals, while providing guidance and retaining overall control. Delegated aspects can include both design and implementation activities. Final responsibility for achieving the necessary change remains with the change agent, but this kind of participation can build **commitment** and a **sense of ownership**. This style is appropriate for incremental change.

2.1.4 Direction

Direction is a top-down style in which **managerial authority** is used to establish and implement a change programme based on a clear future strategy. It is thus suited to **transformational change**. It has the potential advantages of speed and clarity, but may lead to **resistance**. Its success depends in part on the adequacy of the proposed strategy: if this is inappropriate, the best managed of change programmes will not result in wider strategic success.

2.1.5 Coercion

Coercion is an **extreme form of direction**, being based on the use of power to impose change. It is likely to provoke opposition but may be the best approach in times of confusion or crisis.

2.2 Using styles

There may be advantage to making use of more than one of the change management styles outlined above

2.2.1 Context

Specific aspects of the organisational context already discussed will influence the use that can be made of the five styles. Clear and appropriate **direction** can be a strong motivating force and may enhance **readiness** to change, while **collaboration/participation** and **intervention** may help to build **capability** to change.

2.2.2 Scope and nature

Using Balogun and Hope Hailey's matrix (shown in Section 1.1), we might suggest that progression down the list of styles may correspond reasonably well with progression from top left to bottom right of the matrix. In **adaptation**, where time is not critical and the extent of the change required is small, styles from the collaborative-communicative end of the spectrum may be appropriate. **Revolution**, on the other hand will require a great element of **direction** and even of **coercion**. The intermediate cases are likely to require a combination of **participation** and **direction**, with the emphasis on the former in **evolution** and on the latter in **reconstruction**.

2.2.3 Power structures

In many cases it will be appropriate to **echo an organisation's normal power structure** when managing change. Direction or intervention are likely to be more suitable in a firmly hierarchical organisation than they would be in a network or learning organisation, except in time of crisis, for example.

2.2.4 Personality type

Management style is a tool. Good managers will be capable of using a **style appropriate to the conditions** they have to work in. However, many managers' personality types will incline them to the style with which they are most comfortable. This effect is likely to interact with the effect of power structure mentioned above.

2.2.5 Combining styles

It will often be appropriate to use a combination of styles in a change programme, taking different approaches with different stakeholders. Providers of capital are likely to respond better to **education and communication** than to **direction**, for example, while something approaching **coercion** may be necessary in some internal areas simply because of the pressure of time.

3 Change management roles

FAST FORWARD

A **change agent** is an individual or group that helps to bring about strategic change in an organisation.

Strategic leaders act as change agents in one of five styles

- Strategy
- Human assets
- Expertise
- Control
- Change

Middle managers implement and control top down change; translate overall change strategy for local contexts; and advise strategic managers.

Outsiders may be brought in at the strategic apex in order to re-make the paradigm. New middle managers can enhance change capability; consultants can fill planning and facilitating roles.

> A **change agent** is an individual or group that helps to bring about strategic change in an organisation.
>
> *JS&W (amended)*

Change agency is an activity that might be concentrated in one person, but which is just as likely to be spread among the members of a group, such as a project team or management staff generally. Outsiders, such as consultants, may share in change agency.

JS&W examine change agency by considering the roles played by three distinct groups.

- **Strategic leaders**
- **Middle management**
- **Outsiders**

3.1 Strategic leadership

> **Leadership** is the process of influencing an organisation (or group within an organisation) in its efforts towards achieving an aim or goal.
>
> *JS&W*

JS&W, quoting *Farkas and Wetlaufer*, identify **five approaches to strategic leadership**.

- **Strategy**
- **Human assets**
- **Expertise**
- **Control**
- **Change**

3.1.1 The strategy approach

The leader taking the strategy approach focuses on **strategic analysis** and the **formulation of strategy**. Other managers take responsibility for routine operations and for the management of change.

3.1.2 The human assets approach

The **development of the organisation's people** is the main activity of leaders who takes the human assets approach: other managers take responsibility for strategic management. Such leaders are concerned to recruit the right people and to develop an appropriate **culture**. Their approach to change management is to recruit people to whom the responsibility can be devolved.

3.1.3 The expertise approach

The expertise approach focuses on some form of **technical expertise as a source of competitive advantage** and concentrates on building expertise through systems and procedures. This focus also forms the basis of change management. Other managers also concentrate on their areas of expertise.

3.1.4 The control approach

The control approach is also known as the 'box' approach. The strategic leader following this approach concentrates on setting **procedures and control measures** and **monitoring performance** so as to achieve uniform, predictable performance. Other managers are expected to use this approach and change management is based on **careful control**.

3.1.5 The change approach

The leader using the change approach focuses on **continual change** and expends much effort on communication and motivation. Other managers are expected to act largely as **change agents**.

3.1.6 Charismatic and transactional leadership

We discussed leadership in general terms earlier in this Study Text. The five approaches outlined above may be fitted into a general model of leadership that recognises two general types: **charismatic** and **transactional**.

(a) **Transactional leaders** focus on systems and controls and generally seek improvement rather than change. This approach is also called **instrumental** leadership.

(b) **Charismatic leaders** energise people and build a vision of the future. Change management is a natural part of what they do. This approach is also known as **transformational** leadership and we referred to it in this way in our earlier discussion.

Using this analysis, we may say that the **control** approach is a form of **transactional leadership**, while the other four approaches fall into the **charismatic** category.

3.2 Middle management

Strategic leaders pursuing change may see their middle managers as implementers at best and possibly as potential blockers. Their commitment to change is important and they have significant roles to play in change management.

(a) **Implementation** and **control** where change is introduced in a top-down way

(b) **Translation** of the overall change strategy into forms suited to specific local contexts: this may require **reinterpretation** and **adjustment** of strategic factors such as relationships with suppliers and customers.

(c) Provision of **advice** to higher management on requirements for change and potential obstacles

3.3 Outsiders

Outsiders may contribute to the change process in a range of roles.

(a) A new **chief executive** may be appointed to bring a fresh point of view and break down the constraints of the existing paradigm. A **hybrid** chief executive is one who has appropriate experience of the industry, or even of the organisation, but is not part of the existing culture.

(b) New **managers** in other positions can enhance the capability to change and increase **diversity** of opinion and practice. However, their success is likely to depend on the visible backing of the chief executive.

(c) **Consultants** may be employed to fill a number of planning and facilitating roles. Like newly appointed managers, they bring a fresh approach and are not constrained by the existing paradigm. This enables them to challenge things that are taken for granted. Also, their appointment signals the importance of the change process.

(d) Other external **stakeholders** are capable of influencing change and may have a part to play.

4 Change management levers

A turnaround strategy is required when a business is in terminal decline. Such a strategy uses its own change management techniques. More widely applicable change management levers are often related to aspects of the cultural web.

- Challenging the paradigm
- Changing routines
- Use of symbolic processes
- Political activity and use of power structures
- Communication and monitoring
- Tactics, including careful timing, care over job losses and exploration of quick successes

Many of the levers that can be used to implement change are related to aspects of the **cultural web**. We will consider these in this section, but first we will consider the special case of **turnaround**.

4.1 Turnaround

When a business is in terminal decline and faces closure or takeover, there is a need for rapid and extensive change in order to achieve cost reduction and revenue generation. This is a **turnaround strategy**. JS&W identify **seven elements of such a strategy**.

4.1.1 Crisis stabilisation

The emphasis is on reducing costs and increasing revenues. An emphasis on reducing direct costs and improving productivity is more likely to be effective than efforts to reduce overheads.

    (a)   **Measures to increase revenue**

- Tailor marketing mix to key market segments
- Review pricing policies to maximise revenue
- Focus activities on target market segments
- Exploit revenue opportunities if related to target segments
- Invest in growth areas

    (b)   **Measures to reduce costs**

- Cut costs of labour and senior management
- Improve productivity
- Ensure clear marketing focus on target market segments
- Financial controls
- Strict cash management controls
- Reduce inventory
- Cut unprofitable products and services

Severe cost cutting is a common response to crisis but it is unlikely to be enough by itself. The **wider causes of decline** must be addressed.

4.1.2 Management changes

It is likely that new managers will be required, especially at the strategic apex. There are four reasons for this.

    (a)   The old management allowed the situation to deteriorate and **may be held responsible by key stakeholders**.

    (b)   **Experience of turnaround management** may be required.

    (c)   Managers brought in from outside will not be **prisoners of the old paradigm**.

    (d)   A **directive approach** to change management will probably be required.

4.1.3 Communication with stakeholders

The support of key stakeholder groups, such as the workforce and providers of finance, is likely to be very important in a turnaround; it is equally likely that stakeholders did not receive full information during the period of deterioration. A **stakeholder analysis** (discussed earlier in this Study Text) should be carried out so that the various stakeholder groups can be informed and managed appropriately.

4.1.4 Attention to target markets

A **clear focus on appropriate target market segments** is essential; indeed a lack of such focus is a common cause of decline. The organisation must become customer-oriented and ensure that it has good flows of marketing information.

4.1.5 Concentration of effort

Resources should be concentrated on the best opportunities to create value. It will almost certainly be appropriate to **review products and the market segments** currently served and eliminate any distractions and poor performers. A similar review of internal activities would also be likely to show up several candidates for **outsourcing**.

4.1.6 Financial restructuring

Some form of **financial restructuring** is likely to be required. In the worst case, this may involve trading out of insolvency. Even where the business is more or less solvent, capital restructuring may be required, both to provide cash for investment and to reduce cash outflows in the shorter term.

4.1.7 Prioritisation

The eventual success of a turnaround strategy depends in part on management's ability to **prioritise necessary activities**, such as those noted above.

4.2 Challenging the paradigm

The entrenched assumptions and habits of mind that JS&W refer to as **the paradigm** constitute an important obstacle to strategic change. The paradigm must, therefore, be **challenged** if change is to be achieved. There are several approaches to this process of challenge; JS&W give four examples.

(a) Newcomers to the organisation are likely to trust **objective evidence** that new conditions require new approaches. Unfortunately, evidence is rarely overwhelming, or even complete, and there is a natural tendency to reinterpret, discount or even deny it. Persistence is required when objective evidence is relied on.

(b) A **careful analysis** of just what is taken for granted, possibly through **workshop sessions**, may enhance an objective assessment of new ideas. The aim is to lead those involved to challenge their own assumptions.

(c) **Scenario construction** can be used to bring managers to a better understanding of changing conditions by presenting a range of possible futures and their implications for the organisation.

(d) It may be appropriate to take firm action to **bring senior managers close to the daily reality** of what the organisation does, perhaps by extended visits to places and processes with direct customer contact.

4.3 Changing routines

Routines are the **habitual behaviours** that members of the organisation display both internally and externally. They are *not* procedures or processes but the **wider ways of doing things** that are typical of the organisation. They are closely linked to the paradigm. The problem of routines is that they can subvert change efforts. For example, it is unlikely that simply explaining required new processes and procedures will lead to their effective adoption: existing routines will mould the way they are put into operation.

When a **top-down change programme** requires the introduction of new methods, the detail of implementation can be driven by the careful identification of **critical success factors** and the **competences** they demand.

When change is to be introduced in a **less directed** way, change agents may focus on routines, **extending** existing ways of doing things toward what is required and then 'bending the rules of the game' when sufficient stakeholder support has been created.

4.4 Symbolic processes

Symbols were mentioned earlier in this Study Text during our discussion of culture. Their importance in the context of change is that they can often be used as levers of change. However, it is important to understand that the significance of a given symbol may vary from person to person; this makes their use as a tool of management difficult.

(a)   New **rituals** can be introduced and old ones abolished in order to communicate and implement change. For example, the replacement of a strictly hierarchical approach to management with a culture of coaching and empowerment can be signalled and reinforced by the introduction of social occasions such as office parties that will allow staff to meet relatively informally.

(b)   Formal **systems and processes** can have symbolic aspects, typically when they signal status and power relationships, but also when they direct attention to new concerns, such as customer service.

(c)   Changes to **physical aspects** of the workplace can have strong symbolic effect, as, for instance, when open-plan offices or hot desking are introduced.

(d)   The **behaviour** of leaders and change agents has very powerful symbolic effect and must reflect intended change if the intention is not to be undermined: staff will respond far better to example than to edict.

(e)   **Language** can have symbolic significance beyond the bald meaning of the words used. Well chosen words can inspire and motivate change; similarly, the use of badly chosen words can undermine their inherent meaning.

(f)   **Stories** have an important symbolic role, but are not easy to exploit since much corporate communication is automatically dismissed as mere marketing puff.

4.5 Power and politics

Politics is about the exercise of **power** and the use of **influence**. Managers and other important individual stakeholders establish and exploit **power structures** and **networks of influence** that are intertwined with both formal hierarchies and the informal aspects of the organisation's life. The implementation of strategy is inevitably influenced by the operation of these structures and networks. Change management is also, therefore, subject to political influence and change managers should take due account of political processes.

JS&W suggest three objectives of **political activity** that may be sought by change managers.

- Building the **power base**
- Overcoming **resistance**
- Achieving **compliance**

Four **political mechanisms** may be used to exert influence in these areas.

- Manipulation of **resources**
- Relationships with **powerful groups and individuals** (elites)
- Exploitation of **subsystems**
- **Symbolic activity**

4.5.1 Resources

The ability to control the allocation of resources (or even merely to influence their allocation) is recognised as a distinct and important **form of power** within the organisation. It can be used both to **enable specific developments** in the change programme and, more subtly, to **build support and influence** that will assist with the processes of overcoming resistance and ensuring compliance.

4.5.2 Elites

Association with **respected and influential stakeholders** can enhance the personal status and thus the power base of the change agent. Similarly, association with a **high status change agent** can assist more junior managers to overcome resistance to change.

Sometimes it is necessary to **eliminate centres of resistance** by removing people from the organisation in order to ensure compliance with change requirements.

4.5.3 Subsystems

A power base can be established by building up **networks and alliances** among those sympathetic to change. It may then be possible to outmanoeuvre and marginalise the resistance. Equally, however, it may not; also, such manoeuvring by change agents may provoke stronger resistance. It will be useful to analyse power and influence using the stakeholder mapping model explained earlier in this Study Text.

4.5.4 Symbols

Change managers may utilise existing symbols and symbolic activities or challenge them as seems appropriate.

4.6 Communication and monitoring

It is obvious that change management must include effective communication and explanation of the **need for change**, what the plan is intended to **achieve** and what it involves. Good communication is a very important factor in overcoming resistance to change, particularly in the matter of building trust. Strategic complexity may make this difficult, but a clear vision must be provided.

A wide range of **communication media** is available and it is important that **appropriate selections** are made. Media that provide richness, immediacy and interactivity are appropriate when complex and important material is to be communicated, while more routine matters can be dealt with in less complex ways. It is important for change agents to be aware that what seems simple and routine to them may have significantly greater importance for ordinary members of the organisation.

The **intervention style** of change management inherently provides extensive means of communication in the form of the individuals and teams involved. These people form an important route through which information can flow into the organisation.

Communication efforts should include clear and plentiful opportunities and routes for **feedback**, so that omissions, poorly constructed messages, misunderstandings and anxiety can be dealt with.

Care must be taken with **emotional aspects** of communication so that appropriate media, language and symbols are used.

Monitoring of behaviour to ensure that required changes are not subverted is essential.

4.7 Tactics

The change process can be forwarded by the use of specific tactics of change management.

4.7.1 Timing

The time at which actions are taken can be selected for tactical effectiveness.

(a) A **crisis** can be used to justify extensive change, so monitoring a mounting crisis and delaying action until it is ripe may enhance acceptance.

(b) **Windows of opportunity** may occur, as, for example, when a takeover occurs.

(c) **Messages** about timing must be coherent so that, for example, rapid action is not undermined by the retention of procedures that enforce long time frames.

(d) Fear and anxiety about change as such may be reduced if unpleasant consequences can be **decoupled in time** from the main change programme: an example would be a programme of redundancy that does not commence until other change objectives such as the outcomes of product and market reviews have been implemented.

4.7.2 Job losses

The threat of job losses associated with change is likely to be bad for morale and to provoke resistance. Redundancy programmes must be managed with care.

(a) A single, rapid and extensive round of cuts is preferable to a long drawn out programme of smaller reductions: the former can be stressful but the latter creates **long-term uncertainty and anxiety**.

(b) Where **delayering** is required, it may be possible to concentrate the job losses among managers identified as being opposed to change: these are likely to be more senior figures.

(c) Those who lose their jobs should be dealt with as sympathetically and **compassionately** as possible; the provision of services such as outplacement, counselling and retraining may help.

4.7.3 Quick success

Momentum for change can be created by putting simple but highly visible improvements into successful operation. Even where the overall position is difficult and requires a complex solution, such **quick wins** are often available: it is common for them to emerge in the form of suggestions from the lower echelons of the organisation.

Even where there are no obvious easy options, it may be possible to create some by **concentrating the available resources** on specific problems rather than spreading them thinly.

5 Pitfalls of change management

Change programmes may be subverted and lead to unintended consequences. This has four implications for change management.

- Monitoring and control are vital.
- The existing culture must be understood.
- The organisation's people should be involved in the change process.
- The extent of the challenge must be recognised.

JS&W quote *Harris and Ogbonna*, who identify **eight unintended outcomes** of change programmes.

(a)   When change programmes extend into the longer-term, there is a danger that organisation members will come to view the initiatives as mere **ritual** with little real significance.

(b)   Change initiatives can be **hijacked** for unintended purposes: for example, improved technology provided to improve performance may be used simply to cut staffing levels, defeating the overall objective.

(c)   The successful introduction of new initiatives may suffer **erosion** from the effects of other events and processes, as, for example, when high staff turnover hampers staff development.

(d)   Recalcitrant staff may **reinvent** the nature and implications of the change programme in a way that accommodates previous undesirable practices. This is a failure of monitoring and control.

(e)   When change is imposed from the top down, its proponents may be seen as inhabiting an **ivory tower**, out of touch with operational reality and lacking in credibility as a result.

(f)   Change managers who pay insufficient attention to **symbols** can both fail to make the change relevant to day to day reality and succeed in sending the wrong messages.

(g)   If practical adjustments, to systems, for example, **do not fit well** with the overall intent of the change programme, staff are likely to become confused and demotivated.

(h)   Apparent **behavioural compliance** may disguise lack of commitment.

These problems underline the complexity of the change management task. JS&W identify four specific implications for change management.

(a)   **Monitoring** and **control** are vital aspects of change management, as is the flexibility to adjust programmes as they unfold.

(b)   It is essential to understand the **existing culture** and its effects, since they are highly likely to hinder planned change.

(c)   It will generally be advantageous to **involve the organisation's people** in the change process.

(d)   Change represents a **major challenge** and may be more difficult to implement than it seems at first.

Chapter Roundup

- There are three main change management considerations.

    - The type of change required, whether adaptation, evolution, reconstruction or revolution.

    - The wider context of change, including the time available; capability to implement change; capacity and readiness; and power

    - Forces facilitating and blocking change

- There are five change management styles.

    - Education and communication
    - Collaboration/participation
    - Intervention
    - Direction
    - Coercion/edict

    Progression down the list of styles corresponds to progression through the four types of change noted above.

- A **change agent** is an individual or group that helps to bring about strategic change in an organisation.

    Strategic leaders act as change agents in one of five styles

    - Strategy
    - Human assets
    - Expertise
    - Control
    - Change

    Middle managers implement and control top down change; translate overall change strategy for local contexts; and advise strategic managers.

    Outsiders may be brought in at the strategic apex in order to re-make the paradigm. New middle managers can enhance change capability; consultants can fill planning and facilitating roles.

- A turnaround strategy is required when a business is in terminal decline. Such a strategy uses its own change management techniques. More widely applicable change management levers are often related to aspects of the cultural web.

    - Challenging the paradigm
    - Changing routines
    - Use of symbolic processes
    - Political activity and use of power structures
    - Communication and monitoring
    - Tactics, including careful timing, care over job losses and exploration of quick successes

- Change programmes may be subverted and lead to unintended consequences. This has four implications for change management.

    - Monitoring and control are vital.
    - The existing culture must be understood.
    - The organisation's people should be involved in the change process.
    - The extent of the challenge must be recognised.

Quick Quiz

1   What is meant by the scope and nature of change?

2   Which styles of management are required to effect revolution?

3   What is a change agent?

4   What is the difference between charismatic leadership and transactional leadership?

5   What are the objectives of political activity that may be sought by change managers?

6   How can change managers create opportunities for early success?

Answers to Quick quiz

1   The scope of change is its extent; a crucial measure of scope is whether the existing paradigm must be charged. The nature of change may be instrumental or may require a 'big bang' approach.

2   Direction and, probably, coercion

3   A change agent is an individual or group that helps to bring about strategic change in an organisation

4   Transactional leaders focus on systems and controls, while charismatic leaders seek to energise people and build a vision of the future.

5   Building a powerbase; overcoming resistance; achieving compliance

6   By concentrating resources on potentially solvable problems rather than spreading them thinly.

Now try the questions below from the Exam Question Bank

Number	Level	Marks	Time
Q15	Examination	12	22 mins

18

Strategic development

Topic list	Syllabus reference
1 Intention, emergence and realisation	C3 (a)
2 Developing intended strategies	C3 (b)
3 Developing emergent strategies	C3 (c), (d)
4 Diversity of strategic processes	C3 (e)
5 Challenges and implications	C3 (e)

Introduction

We have covered a great deal of ground in this Study Text, but nearly all of our discussion has related to specific ideas that may be used when developing strategy; that is to say, we have concentrated on tools, models and techniques that may be used to create answers to specific strategic problems. We have said very little about the wider processes by which an overall strategy is designed. This final chapter attempts to round off our consideration of business strategy by looking at the ways in which strategies come into existence.

There are two principal classes of strategies: the intended and the emergent. We will start by contrasting these classes and discussing their relationship. Then we will look at each in more detail. The final sections of this chapter will examine some challenges and more general concepts relating to strategy development.

Study guide

		Intellectual level
C3	**Understanding strategy development**	
(a)	Discriminate between the concepts of intended and emergent strategies.	3
(b)	Explain how organisations attempt to put an intended strategy into place.	2
(c)	Highlight how emergent strategies appear from within an organisation.	3
(d)	Discuss how process redesign, quality initiatives and e-business can contribute to emergent strategies.	2
(e)	Assess the implications of strategic drift and the demand for multiple processes of strategy development.[3]	3

Exam guide

This is a rather theoretical chapter and the material it covers may seem rather obscure. However the Examiner has indicated that it is likely to appear in many examination case studies. Also, Section 5 has some useful detail on specific strategic challenges that could be useful in dealing with the kind of complex scenario typical of Section A questions.

1 Intention, emergence and realisation

Realised strategy may emerge from everyday actions and routine decisions, or it may be the result of considered intention. **Intended strategies** may also fail to be realised.

You will recall that in Chapter 1 of this Study Text, we explained the way that JS&W analyse strategy into three main elements: **strategic position**, **strategic choices** and **strategy into action**.

    (a)   The strategic managers must attempt to **understand** the organisation's strategic position.

    (b)   Strategic choices are about **scope**, the **direction** and **method** of development and how to achieve **competitive advantage**.

    (c)   Strategies must be made to **work in practice**. Major issues here include **structuring**, **enabling** and **change**.

This analysis is written in terms of **management**: that is to say, as though strategy is a project that managers work on and bring to completion in a deliberate and logical fashion. Understanding of strategic position informs strategic choice: together they give create an **intention**. The next stage, strategy into action is about how we **realise** that intention.

Strategy by intention

In our discussion of the **strategy lenses** we explained that this represents just one view of strategy and that there are other, equally valuable, views of its nature. These views describe what we may call **emergent strategy**. The essence of this kind of strategy is that it is not the result of any kind of top-down, intended managerial process. This kind of strategy comes about as a largely unintended result of the everyday activities, decisions and processes that take place at all levels of the organisation. Thus, realised strategy can **emerge** as well as arise from intention.

We also have to be aware that what managers intend **may not actually be realised**: plans may be unworkable for a variety of reasons, resources may be inadequate, important stakeholders may be obstructive and so on.

Our diagrammatic overview thus has to be amended to include these extra possibilities.

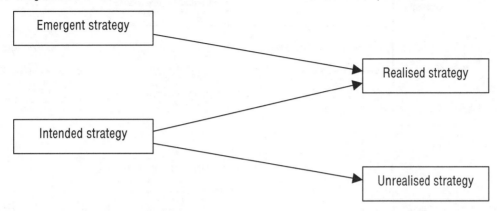

Strategy: a fuller picture

2 Developing intended strategies

FAST FORWARD

Intended strategies are developed in a systematic way, making use of rational procedures and, probably, specialist staff. This approach has advantages associated with system and method and disadvantages associated with ponderousness and inflexibility. More recently, workshops and project teams have been used to develop intended strategies and strategy consultants have been employed.

The development of intended strategies is associated with **strategic planning systems**. JS&W use the phrase 'systematised, step-by-step, chronological procedures' in their discussion of this idea. Typically, such a system will proceed in a linear fashion, starting from mission and objectives and working through to implementation and the feedback of performance review. Such a system is illustrated below.

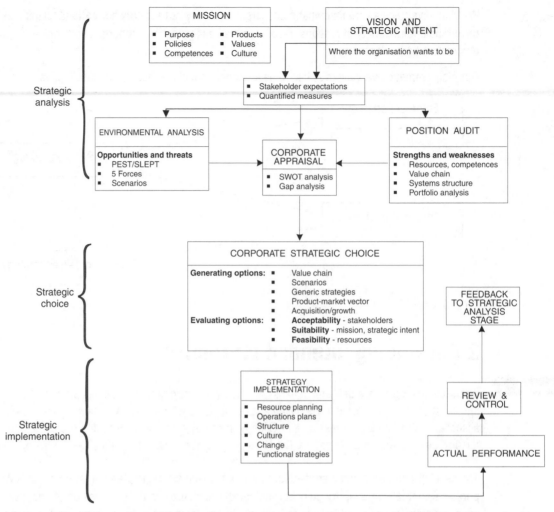

When you look at the detail of this model, you will recognise much that we have discussed in this Study Text. However, for the purposes of our current discussion, the important thing about this diagram is not the way it draws together a number of related ideas, but that **it represents the traditional view of how strategy is actually made**: it is a representation of a **corporate subsystem** that would have staff, managers, offices and interactions with other corporate systems.

The idea that strategy should be made in this way is no longer popular for reasons that will be reviewed later in this Section, but it does have its advantages, both for **determining** what the strategy should be and in **implementing** it.

2.1 Advantages of a formal system of strategic planning

Advantages	Comment
Provides a structure	Developing strategy is a complex task, with many variables to take into account. A formal system provides a structure for analysis and planning.
Risk management	A full scheme of strategic planning should both identify and help in managing these risks.
Stimulation of thought, challenge and questioning	The system of strategic planning provides a structure for discussion and can encourage creativity and challenges to the paradigm.
Decision-making	Companies cannot remain static – they have to cope with changes in the environment. The planning process draws attention to the need to change and adapt, not just to 'stand still' and survive.

Advantages	Comment
Control	Management control can be better exercised if targets are explicit.
Consistency	Plans for a range of business unit activities can be integrated and long-term and short-term objectives can be made consistent with one another. Otherwise, strategies can be rendered ineffective by budgeting systems and performance measures that have no strategic content.
Communication	Discussion at the various stages helps to make the reasoning behind strategy clear, while the creation of specific plans prompts appropriate dissemination.
Time horizon	Longer-term views can be built in to the system by setting a suitable time horizon for the planning period.
Co-ordination	Business unit plans, the use of resources and the activities of different business functions can be co-ordinated and directed towards a common goal.
Objectives	Managers are forced to define what they want to achieve.
Responsibility and involvement	A plan shows people where they fit in and what they have to do.

2.2 Criticisms of formal strategic planning

(a) Making strategic plans is not the same thing as managing strategy, which is the long-term scope and direction of the organisation. The complexity of the model shown above is capable of **distracting managers' attention** from controlling actual progress.

(b) It is also easy to confuse strategic planning and control with **budgetary processes**. There is an obvious relationship between the two, but they re not the same. The latter is a complex but routine activity; the former requires careful consideration of the kind of material dealt with in this Study Text.

(c) The best is the enemy of the good: there is no guarantee that a complex planning system will produce the perfect strategy and too much time and effort can be spent searching for it.

(d) A further problem with a complex and formal system of planning is that the various aspects of analysis that it involves can lead to a simple **acceptance of the current *realised* strategy**.

(e) A **split may develop** between the people responsible for **planning** and those responsible for **implementation**. Line managers may be too busy to take part in the planning process, while planners are unlikely to have the authority required to implement the plans they produce. The result is that planning becomes divorced from operational reality. This division can be reinforced if commercial confidentiality receives too much emphasis and planning is carried on in an atmosphere of secrecy.

(f) Particularly in very large organisations, the planning system may be **too extensive and complex** for even quite senior managers to understand the way it works. This hinders proper input and application.

(g) Very detailed analysis can lead to information overload; this, in turn, can prevent the planners from recognising major strategic issues when they arise.

(h) Over-formal planning systems and over-rigid control can hamper innovative thinking.

Possibly as a result of these problems, the use of formal strategic planning systems has declined markedly and it has been common for more responsibility for strategic decision-making to be devolved to line managers. Planning has become more informal and has tended to concentrate on discussion of key strategic issues and establishing overall strategic scope and direction.

2.3 Workshops and project teams

As formal planning systems have declined in importance, there has been a growth in the use of project teams and workshops to develop aspects of overall strategy. Such groups can be set up at almost any level in the organisation and can be particularly useful for keeping managers at the strategic apex in touch with current routine operational experience and problems. A wide range of specific purposes may be served using these methods.

(a)   A top management group might **set overall strategy** after considering reports from specialists, functions and business units.

(b)   **Strategic analysis** could be undertaken by more junior managers who then report upwards.

(c)   A cross-hierarchical group might be set up to **challenge current assumptions**.

(d)   Similar groups might be formed to **generate new ideas and approaches** to problems.

(e)   The planning of **strategic implementation** cannot be done by top management alone. Similarly, **monitoring progress** could be done in workshops.

(f)   Consideration of **factors blocking strategic change** could be carried out by a project team.

2.4 Strategy consultants

Strategy consultants have a range of roles to play in strategic management. Some of these are political, such as lending their authority to a new CEO who wishes to bring about change, or symbolic, as when their presence and activity emphasise the importance of a new approach. They can also assist with key aspects of the strategic management process.

(a)   **Strategic analysis and options generation** may be an appropriate task for consultants where the situation is confused or there is disagreement among top managers. Consultants may bring a fresh and impartial approach.

(b)   Consultants should bring **knowledge and experience** and can be transmitters of best practice between organisations.

(c)   Consultants may assist in the process of **strategic decision-making**. However, they should not exercise undue influence: responsibility for strategy should remain with the managers at the strategic apex of the client organisation.

(d)   **Strategic change** is a fruitful field for the employment of consultants, especially in such activities as coaching and training.

2.5 Imposed strategy

Powerful external stakeholders may be able to impose a strategy. This is most common in the public sector, where government may make generally applicable regulations that con strain strategic choice, or may take more specific action to force a particular strategy on to an organisation. Privatisation is an example of the way in which governments have imposed strategic change on organisations.

3 Developing emergent strategies

FAST FORWARD

Logical incrementalism develops strategy in small experimental steps. Resource allocation procedures may lead to the emergence of strategy, as may the cultural processes that make up the paradigm. However, an obsolete paradigm will lead to **strategic drift** and the emergence of inappropriate strategic moves. Strategies may emerge from the bargaining and negotiation associated with political activity.

The practices developed during detailed strategic implementation may also be a source of emergent strategies.

Realised strategy can emerge as well as arise from intention. However, this is not a random process: emergent strategies require extensive management if they are to be successful.

3.1 Logical incrementalism

ey term

> **Logical incrementalism** is the deliberate development of strategy by experimentation and learning from partial commitments.   *JS&W*

Quinn observed processes typical of logical incrementalism.

(a)   A **generalised view** of a desired future state and rather wide objectives

(b)   Constant **environmental scanning** rather than firm forecasts

(c)   A combination of building a **strong core business** on experience and **experimenting** with possible strategic options

(d)   'Subsystems' consisting of groups of people that experiment with products and markets

(e)   Employment of **formal and informal processes** to draw out patterns of development

Such an approach combines an element of intention with a significant amount of emergence. It allows for constant adjustment and testing of strategy, good quality of environmental information, readiness to change and continuing internal consultation.

3.2 Resource allocation routines

Bower and *Burgelman* concluded independently that strategy arises as a consequence of **competitive resource allocation** within organisations. Managers at lower and intermediate levels bid for resources for the projects they favour. The basic decision rules and the strategic context are set at the strategic apex, but strategy is determined by resource allocation decisions made at lower levels. JS&W quote the example of *Intel*, which in the 1980s switched from making memory chips to concentration on microprocessors in this fashion.

3.3 Cultural processes

The structures, assumptions, practices and processes that make up the paradigm and the wider cultural web may be sufficiently influential as to determine strategy, particularly in the shape of strategic responses to environmental changes. Experience of methods that have worked in the past can offer a comforting approach to dealing with new ambiguities and uncertainties. However, making strategy in this way can slow response to environmental change and lead to **strategic drift**.

Key term

> **Strategic drift** occurs when strategies progressively fail to address the strategic position of the organisation and performance deteriorates.   *JS&W*

JS&W suggest that **strategic drift** arises because of the tendency to prefer small adjustments to large ones. If performance deteriorates, the first reaction will be to impose tighter control over implementation. If this is ineffective, a new strategy may be developed. However, this will take place within the constraints of the cultural web. By the time the organisation's leaders understand and accept that cultural change is required, it may be too late.

3.4 The Icarus paradox

Miller describes the way in which a once successful paradigm becomes obsolete, referring to the effect as the **Icarus paradox**.

Miller suggests that when companies succeed, their success can lead to a kind of dislocated feedback of the qualities that made them succeed; this distortion then leads to failure.

Miller diagnoses four important aspects of this distortion.

(a)   **Leadership failures** occur when success reinforces top management's preconceptions, makes them over confident, less concerned for the customer's views, conceited and obstinate.

(b)   **Cultural domination** by star departments and their ideologies leads to intolerance of other ideas and reduces the capacity for innovative and flexible response.

(c)   **Power games and politics** are used by dominant managers and departments to resist change and amplify current strategic thinking.

(d)   **Corporate memory**, consisting of processes, habits and reflexes, is substituted for careful thought about new problems.

The interplay of these factors leads to decline, usually along one of four **trajectories**.

(a)   **Craftsman become tinkerers**. Quality driven engineering farms become obsessed with irrelevant technical detail.

(b)   **Builders become imperialists**. Acquisitive, growth driven companies over-expand into areas they cannot manage properly.

(c)   **Pioneers become escapists**. Companies whose core competence is technically superb innovation and state-of-the-art products lose focus and waste their resources on grandiose and impractical projects.

(d)   **Salesman become drifters**. Marketing oriented companies with stables of valuable brands become bureaucratic pursuers of sales figures whose market offerings become stale and uninspired.

3.5 Political processes

It is common to view organisations as arenas of political activity: we discussed the political aspects of change management earlier in this Study Text.

Key term

> The **political view** of strategy development is that strategies develop as the outcome of processes of bargaining and negotiation among powerful internal or external interest groups (or stakeholders).

The political view is reasonable, in that powerful executives are likely to defend and seek to extend their power and influence. It is probable that both information flows and strategic analysis will therefore be influenced by political manoeuvres. Existing strategies and potential challengers will become identified with particular factions and the outcome of strategic choice may amount to victory and defeat if compromise is not reached. It is reasonable to view the political processes of negotiation as a kind of emergent or incremental approach to making strategy.

Nevertheless, the political process is equally capable of leading to significant innovation, as powerful managers seek new ideas to enhance their own power.

We have said that emergent strategies are to be contrasted with intended strategies in that they come about as a result of the every day activities decisions and processes that take place at all levels of the organisation. In this context, it is important to remember the relational diagram of your syllabus: process change, quality initiatives and e-business are both the important elements of strategic implementation and sources from which unintended strategies are likely to emerge.

4 Diversity of strategic processes

FAST FORWARD

There is no single correct way to develop strategy and effective strategies may well result from the simultaneous working of more than one process.

We have examined a wide range of means of arriving at strategy and considered the advantages and disadvantages of each. The picture is complex and somewhat obscure, but we may offer some comments on the idea of strategic method, based, as usual, on JS&W.

(a)   There is **no single correct way** to develop a strategy.

(b)   Strategy development is likely to vary at different **times** and in different contexts.

(c)   Different managers will **perceive strategy development differently**. For example, top managers tend to see their strategic work as rational and intended; middle managers may be more aware of the impact of politics

(d)   It is unlikely that any organisation's strategy is the result of a single process; several are likely to be at work, and this may well produce a more successful outcome than a single approach.

5 Challenges and implications

FAST FORWARD

Organisational learning can form a strong base for the development of strategy, especially when environmental conditions are both complex and dynamic. Simple and static conditions permit a planning approach. Stable but complex environments promote decentralisation of strategic development.

Our discussion above raises some challenges and implications for the management of strategy development.

5.1 Strategic drift

We have discussed the nature of strategic drift already. The tendency to prefer small adjustments can lead to a growing mismatch between strategic posture and strategic reality. Cultural rigidity can also reduce the organisation's ability to innovate and confine it to simply **reacting** to its environment rather than **seeking to influence** it.

The challenge for strategic managers here is to promote the ability and inclination to challenge received wisdom in a creative and objective way. A strategy-making system that incorporates more than one of the approaches discussed in this chapter is more likely to be successful at this than concentrating on any one in particular.

5.2 The learning organisation

Continuing challenge to assumptions and search for improvement are typical of a **learning organisation**. We have already considered some aspects of organisational learning in our coverage of knowledge management earlier in this Study Text.

Key term

A **learning organisation** is capable of continual regeneration from the variety of knowledge, experience and skills of individuals within a culture that encourages mutual questioning and challenge around a shared purpose or vision.

JS&W

A learning organisation emphasises the **sharing of information and knowledge** both up and down the normal communication channels and horizontally through **social networks** and **interest groups**. It challenges notions of hierarchy and managers are facilitators rather than controllers. Such an organisation is inherently capable of change. The concept has much in common with that of **logical incrementalism**. The challenge is to combine the advantages of rational planning with the resilience and adaptability provided by the learning approach.

5.3 Uncertainty and complexity

Not only must strategy take account of environmental conditions, the system and methods used in its development must also be appropriate to those conditions. It is usual in this context to analyse an organisation's environment along axes of **complexity** and **change**.

Simple and static environments are amenable to analysis and forecasting based on history and leading indicators and the rational model of strategy is more or less appropriate. However, this approach becomes less useful as environmental conditions become more complex or more dynamic, or both simultaneously.

Organisational design becomes important in environments that are **reasonably stable** but display **significant complexity**. Decentralisation into specialised organisational parts will allow the various aspects of the environment to be dealt with separately as they evolve.

Relatively **simple environments** that are subject to **rapid change** will display **significant uncertainty**. Scenario planning may be a useful technique under these conditions. Extensive and continuous environmental scanning will be required and the creativity and cooperation typical of **logical incrementalism** and the **learning organisation** will be required.

Complex and dynamic environments present the greatest challenge. Decentralisation is also appropriate here, combined with an acceptance at the strategic centre that operation experience and learning present at the periphery represent the organisation's greatest strategic strength.

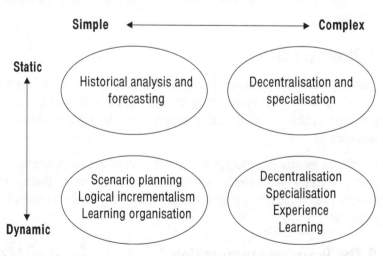

Environment and strategy development

5.4 Managing strategy development

As we have already indicated, the use of more than one approach is likely to be useful when an organisation develops its strategy. Also, the processes it uses are likely to vary with its circumstances. JS&W complete their consideration of the management of strategy development by considering some further, connected points.

(a) It will be necessary to select different development processes for different purposes in the same organisation. Co-ordination across SBUs will require a rational approach, but within each business unit a different approach, perhaps based on learning may be appropriate, for example.

(b) Managers responsible for strategy development must therefore take care to ensure that **appropriate processes are used in each separate context**.

(c) Managers at the **strategic apex** must consider their role, since there are several approaches they can use.

(d) In divisionalised organisations, it is likely that **different levels will use different strategic processes**, with an emphasis on rational planning at the centre and on experience and learning in the divisions.

(e) Therefore, managers at different levels must **understand the importance of the roles played at other levels**.

Chapter Roundup

- **Realised strategy** may emerge from everyday actions and routine decisions, or it may be the result of considered intention. **Intended strategies** may also fail to be realised.

- **Intended strategies** are developed in a systematic way, making use of rational procedures and, probably, specialist staff. This approach has advantages associated with system and method and disadvantages associated with ponderousness and inflexibility. More recently, workshops and project teams have been used to develop intended strategies and strategy consultants have been employed.

- **Logical incrementalism** develops strategy in small experimental steps. Resource allocation procedures may lead to the emergence of strategy, as may the cultural processes that make up the paradigm. However, an obsolete paradigm will lead to strategic drift and the emergence of inappropriate strategic moves. Strategies may emerge from the bargaining and negotiation associated with political activity.

    The practices developed during detailed strategic implementation may also be a source of emergent strategies.

- There is no single correct way to develop strategy and effective strategies may well be the result from the simultaneous working of more than one process.

- Organisational learning can form a strong base for the development of strategy, especially when environmental conditions are both complex and dynamic. Simple and static conditions permit a planning approach. Stable but complex environments promote decentralisation of strategic development.

Quick Quiz

1   The sources of realised strategy may be divided into two categories. What are they?

2   How might intended strategies be developed?

3   Theorists have described several sources of emergent strategies. What are they?

4   Under what environmental conditions is decentralisation an appropriate response?

5   Can you recommend a single mode of strategy development that will be satisfactory under most conditions?

Answers to Quick quiz

1   Intended strategies and emergent strategies

2   Typically, within planning departments, but more recently, through workshops and project teams and by employing consultants

3   Logical incrementalism, resource allocation routines, cultural processes and political processes

4   Complexity, whether static or dynamic

5   You might try, but would be ill-advised to do so.

Now try the questions below from the Exam Question Bank

Number	Level	Marks	Time
Q16	Examination	15	35 mins

This question is actually the first requirement of a much longer case study. The scenario is extensive, so we have allowed you extra reading time.

Exam question bank

1 Bartok Fuel

20 mins

Bartok Fuel is a private company run by two brothers, David and Sean Bartok. The company was founded in the 1960s by their father, Gerald, who started life with a petrol station and car repair workshop. After some years, Gerald expanded by buying a tanker and starting to distribute household fuel to customers. This part of the business has grown successfully and now has some 15 tankers and an annual turnover of £30 million.

In the 1960s, the car repair business included the manufacture of car windscreens. From this grew an element of the business, called Bartok Glass, which now makes sealed glass window units for the construction industry and has a turnover of about £8 million.

During the 1970s and 1980s Gerald had purchased a number of sites from which petrol was sold. These sites are still owned by the company but are now leased to other companies and used for a variety of purposes. The original garage no longer exists, but the company still operates a car dealership and repair workshop in the centre of Woking. This part of the business started in the 1990s and for some time was fairly profitable, particularly when it was a Jaguar dealership run by Gerald's younger son, Sean. However, due to changes in the market place, the Jaguar franchise had to be sold and the business now sells Fiat and Kia cars.

The fuel distribution and glass businesses continue to be fairly profitable under the management of the older brother David, but the car business is facing hard times. The car retail business is notoriously cut-throat, with margins as low as 2–3% and very high targets set by the manufacturers. The car dealership also deals in second hand cars and this area is slightly more profitable. This division now employs about 50 people.

David is the managing director of the company and at a recent board meeting he put forward a number of proposals for improving the profitability of the car dealership and garage. One suggestion is that the site should be sold for its development potential and the car dealership brought to an end.

A further option brought up by David is the potential for entering the emerging Far East market for fuel distribution. He has recently met a Malaysian entrepreneur who was visiting the UK, who is making considerable profits in this area and is looking for investment from a new partner. David is very keen on this option and is trying to push it through.

Required

(a)   Describe the approach to strategy that Bartok Fuel appears to have had in the past.

(b)   What factors should the Board to consider before making any decisions on the proposals to dispose of the Woking site for development and to enter the Far East fuel distribution market?

2 EMS

15 mins

The Environment Management Society (EMS) was established in 1999 by environment practitioners who felt that environmental management and audit should have its own qualification. EMS has its own Board who report to a Council of eight members. Policy is made by the Board and ratified by Council. EMS is registered as a private limited entity.

EMS employs staff to administer its qualification and to provide services to its members. The qualification began as one certificate, developed by the original founding members of the Society. It has since been developed, by members and officers of the EMS, into a four certificate scheme leading to a Diploma. EMS employs a full-time chief examiner who is responsible for setting the certificate examinations which take place monthly in training centres throughout the country. No examinations are currently held in other countries.

If candidates pass all four papers they can undertake an oral Diploma examination. If they pass this oral they are eligible to become members. All examinations are open-book one hour examinations, preceded by 15 minutes reading time. At a recent meeting, EMS Council rejected the concept of computer-based assessment. They felt that competence in this area was best assessed by written examination answers.

Candidate numbers for the qualification have fallen dramatically in the last two years. The Board of EMS has concluded that this drop reflects the maturing marketplace in the country. Many people who were practitioners in environmental management and audit when the qualification was introduced have now gained their Diploma. The stream of new candidates and hence members is relatively small.

Consequently, the EMS Board has suggested that they should now look to attract international candidates and it has targeted countries where environmental management and audit is becoming more important. It is now formulating a strategy to launch the qualification in India, China and Russia.

However, any strategy has to recognise that both the EMS Board and the Council are very cautious and notably risk averse. EMS is only confident about its technical capability within a restricted definition of environmental management and audit. Attempts to look at complementary qualification areas (such as soil and water conservation) have been swiftly rejected by Council as being non-core areas and therefore outside the scope of their expertise.

Required

Internal development, acquisitions and strategic alliances are three development methods by which an organisation's strategic direction can be pursued. Explain the principles of internal development and discuss how appropriate this development method is to EMS. **(8 marks)**

3 Competitor analysis

36 mins

From the 1980's onwards, organisations have been increasingly conscious of the need to develop appropriate competitive strategies. More recently, competition has increased in many areas due to factors such as a more global dimension to trade and an opening of new markets, It follows that, in order to gain and maintain competitive advantage, it may be worthwhile for organisations to identify and carefully consider the present and likely future activities of their competitors.

Required

(a) Evaluate the importance of competitor analysis, with reference to the benefits and potential dangers of undertaking such an exercise. **(10 marks)**

(b) Discuss the key issues to be addressed when conducting a competitor analysis, including potential data sources and tools that may be helpful. **(10 marks)**

(Total = 20 marks)

4 Firebridge Tyres Ltd

36 mins

Firebridge Tyres Ltd (FTL) is a wholly owned UK subsidiary of Gonzales Tyre Corporation (GTC) of the USA. FTL manufactures and sells tyres under a number of different brand names.

(a) Firespeed, offering high product quality, at a price which offers good value for money
(b) Freeway, a cheap brand, effectively a standard tyre
(c) Tufload, for lorries and commercial vehicles

FTL has good relationships with car firms and distributors.

GTC is rather less focused; not only does it make tyres and some other components, but it also owns a chain of car service centres specialising in minor maintenance matters such as tyre replacement, exhaust fitting, and wheel balancing.

FTL has experienced a fall in sales revenue, partly as a result of competition from overseas producers, in what is effectively a mature market. Moreover, sales of new cars have not been as high as had been hoped, and consumers are more reluctant than before to part with their money.

FTL's managers have had meetings with GTC's managers as to how to revive the fortunes of the company. FTL would like to export to the US and to Asia. GTC has vetoed this suggestion, as FTL's tyres would compete with GTC's. Instead, GTC suggests that FTL imitate GTC's strategy by running a chain of service stations similar to GTC's service stations in the US. GTC feels that vertical integration would offer profits in its own right and provide a distribution network which would reduce the impact of competition from other tyre manufacturers. GTC has no shortage of cash.

You are a strategic consultant to FTL.

Required

(a)   What are the principal factors in the external environment that would influence FTL's strategic choice?   **(6 marks)**

(b)   Describe the barriers to entry that FTL might face if it decided to enter the service centre business.
                                                                                                          (6 marks)

(c)   Does FTL's existing strategic capability give it a good chance of success in the service business?

                                                                                                          (8 marks)

                                                                                                  (Total = 20 marks)

5 Nadir Products: ethics   36 mins

John Staples is the Finance Director of Nadir Products plc, a UK-based company which manufactures and sells bathroom products – baths, sinks and toilets – to the UK market. These products are sold through a selection of specialist shops and through larger 'do-it-yourself' stores. Customers include professional plumbers and also ordinary householders who are renovating their houses themselves. The company operates at the lower end of the market and does not have a strong reputation for service. Sales have been slowly declining whereas those of competitors have been improving. In order to encourage increased sales the Board of Directors have decided to pay senior staff a bonus if certain targets are achieved. The two main targets are based on profit levels and annual sales. Two months before the end of the financial year the Finance Director asks one of his staff to check through the orders and accounts to assess the current situation. He is informed that without a sudden improvement in sales before the year end the important sales targets will not be met and so bonuses will be adversely affected.

The Finance Director has proposed to other senior staff that this shortfall in sales can be corrected by taking one of the following decisions.

1.   A significant discount can be offered to any retail outlet which takes delivery of additional products prior to the end of the financial year.

2.   Scheduled orders due to be delivered at the beginning of the next financial year can be brought forward and billed before the end of this year.

3.   Distributors can be told that there is a risk of price increases in the future and that it will be advisable to order early so as to circumvent this possibility.

The Board is not sure of the implications associated with such decisions.

Required

(a)   As a consultant, prepare a report for the Board of Nadir Products examining the commercial and ethical implications associated with each of the proposed options mentioned above.   **(8 marks)**

(b)   Assess the significance of the corporate social responsibility model for Nadir Products. **(12 marks)**

                                                                                                  (Total = 20 marks)

6 Acklington Antennas

Acklington Antennas Ltd is a UK company that designs and manufactures antennas for airborne navigation and communication systems. The industry is characterised by dedication to high technical standards because of the demands of aircraft safety. There are three main parts to the business: design and integration of antennas for new aircraft; aftermarket spares for existing systems; and sub-contract manufacture of other firms' designs.

Design of new installations is highly technical and very time consuming since it depends on extensive tests, including test flying. Globally, there are only three other manufacturers capable of this work.

The aftermarket operation includes spares for Acklington's own products and for antennas the company has designed to replace the other three manufacturers' own proprietary designs. Sales of the latter are somewhat price sensitive, but the aircraft spares market generally is characterised by the high prices charged to captive customers for approved spares.

Demand for subcontracting work tends to be intermittent but forms a profitable supplement to the manufacture of the company's own designs. Nobody in the industry thinks it odd that Acklington should both manufacture for and compete with other firms.

Acklington's market is now being threatened by Wizzomatic Inc, which is a subsidiary of a major US armaments group. Wizzomatic is offering a family of standardised antennas derived from its work for the US government. The antennas offer a substantial price advantage over most proprietary designs and are being promoted as suitable for most applications.

Required

(a)   Assess the strategic options available to Acklington Antennas.
(b)   Briefly describe how you would expect Acklington Antennas' marketing mix to be made up.

7 United Products

United Products (UP) was formed 46 years ago by the merger of two large commercial organisations: Bulk Foods and Rowbotham Enterprises. Over the years it has acquired and disposed of several businesses and now has operations in Europe and North America. It has wholly owned subsidiaries operating in flour milling; vineyards; grocery retailing; agricultural machinery manufacturing and distribution; chemicals (particularly fertilisers); publishing; film production; and forestry. It is also involved via joint ventures and partnerships in quarrying, electronics design and clothes retailing.

The company is regarded by investors as fairly safe but dull. Its growth has not kept pace with its competitors and some of its divisions' performance is distinctly poor.

UP is organised into divisions, some of which are product based and some geographically based. Control is devolved to the CEOs of each division, subject to the compilation and submission of detailed monthly performance reports to the corporate HQ in Fazackerley, near Liverpool in the UK. Corporate HQ requires that each division has identifiable managers responsible for production, sales and finance. These managers are frequently visited by senior members of the relevant head office staff. It is corporate policy to promote from within, and all divisional CEOs must have experience of working both at corporate HQ and in at least three divisions.

There has been a history of disputes between HQ and the divisions. Many have complained about the complexity of the monthly reports and the cost of compiling them. Some have said that they find HQ requirements and visits to be disruptive and counter-productive. However, the Corporate CEO, is very concerned about the tendency of the divisions to go their own way.

Required

(a)   Is the way UP is currently organised a sensible one?

(b)   What is a virtual organisation? Would such an approach be suitable for any of UP's operations?

8 BPR and supply chain   15 mins

ABC has a chain of twenty supermarkets. When stock items reach their re-order level in a supermarket the in-store computerised inventory system informs the stock clerk. The clerk then raises a request daily to the ABC central warehouse for replenishment of stocks via fax or e-mail. If the local warehouse has available stock, it is forwarded to the supermarket within twenty-four hours of receiving the request. If the local warehouse cannot replenish the stock from its inventory holding, it raises a purchase order to one of its suppliers. The supplier delivers the stock to the warehouse and the warehouse then delivers the required stock to the supermarkets within the area. The ABC area warehouse staff conduct all business communication with suppliers.

ABC recently contracted an IT consultant to analyse and make recommendations concerning their current supply chain briefly described above. Following the initial investigation the consultant reported.

'To enable an established traditional company like ABC to develop a Virtual Supply Chain system it may be necessary to employ a Business Process Re-engineering (BPR) approach.'

Required

With reference to the above scenario, describe what is meant by a Business Process Re-engineering approach.

9 Internet strategy

The SDW Company has been trading for one year. It provides an airline service between three major cities in the country in which it operates.

Mr M, the majority shareholder and Managing Director, is keen to expand its operations and, in particular, to use the Internet as the major selling medium. He has discovered, for example, that doubling sales on the Internet usually results in no additional costs. However, doubling sales using a call centre normally results in a doubling of staff and an increase in costs.

All tickets are currently sold via the company's call centre. The company has an Internet site although this is used for publicity only, not for sales or marketing. Competitors currently use a mixture of selling media, although detailed information on the success of each medium is not available to the SDW Company.

Mr M has asked you, as a qualified management accountant, to assist him in upgrading the company's Internet site and, in particular, showing how this will help to reduce operating costs.

Required

Advise Mr M on how to establish and implement an appropriate Internet strategy for the SDW Company.

10 DRB   45 mins

DRB Electronic Services operates in a high labour cost environment in Western Europe and imports electronic products from the Republic of Korea. It re-brands and re-packages them as DRB products and then sells them to business and domestic customers in the local geographical region. Its only current source of supply is ISAS electronics based in a factory on the outskirts of Seoul, the capital of the Republic of Korea. DRB regularly places orders for ISAS products through the ISAS web-site and pays for them by credit card. As soon as the payment is confirmed ISAS automatically e-mails DRB a confirmation of order, an order reference number and likely shipping date. When the order is actually despatched, ISAS send DRB a notice of despatch e-mail and a container reference number. ISAS currently organises all the shipping of the products. The products are sent in containers and then trans-shipped to EIF, the logistics company used by ISAS to distribute its products. EIF then delivers the products to the DRB factory. Once they arrive, they are quality inspected and products that pass the inspection are re-branded as DRB products (by adding appropriate logos) and packaged in specially fabricated DRB boxes. These products are then stored ready for sale. All customer sales are from stock. Products that fail the inspection are returned to ISAS.

Currently 60% of sales are made to domestic customers and 40% to business customers. Most domestic customers pick up their products from DRB and set them up themselves. In contrast, most business customers ask DRB to set up the electronic equipment at their offices, for which DRB makes a small charge. DRB currently advertises its products in local and regional newspapers. DRB also has a web site which provides product details. Potential customers can enquire about the specification and availability of products through an e-mail facility in the web site. DRB then e-mails an appropriate response directly to the person making the enquiry. Payment for products cannot currently be made through the web site.

Feedback from existing customers suggests that they particularly value the installation and support offered by the company. The company employs specialist technicians who (for a fee) will install equipment in both homes and offices. They will also come out and troubleshoot problems with equipment that is still under warranty. DRB also offer a helpline and a back to base facility for customers whose products are out of warranty. Feedback from current customers suggests that this support is highly valued. One commented that 'it contrasts favourably with your large customers who offer support through impersonal off-shore call centres and a time-consuming returns policy'. Customers can also pay for technicians to come on-site to sort out problems with out-of-warranty equipment.

DRB now plans to increase their product range and market share. It plans to grow from its current turnover of £5m per annum to £12m per annum in two years time. Dilip Masood, the owner of DRB, believes that DRB must change its business model if it is to achieve this growth. He believes that these changes will also have to tackle problems associated with

–   Missing, or potentially missing shipments. Shipments can only be tracked through contacting the shipment account holder, ISAS, and on occasions they have been reluctant or unable to help. The trans-shipment to EIF has also caused problems and this has usually been identified as the point where goods have been lost. ISAS does not appear to be able to reliably track the relationship between the container shipment and the Waybills used in the EIF system.

–   The likely delivery dates of orders, the progress of orders and the progress of shipments is poorly specified and monitored. Hence deliveries are relatively unpredictable and this can cause congestion problems in the delivery bay.

Dilip also recognises that growth will mean that the company has to sell more products outside its region and the technical installation and support so valued by local customers will be difficult to maintain. He is also adamant that DRB will continue to import only fully configured products. It is not interested in importing components and assembling them. DRB also does not wish to build or invest in assembly plants overseas or to commit to a long-term contract with one supplier.

Required

(a)   Draw the primary activities of DRB on a value chain. Comment on the significance of each of these activities and the value that they offer to customers.   **(9 marks)**

(b)   Explain how DRB might re-structure its upstream supply chain to achieve the growth required by DRB and to tackle the problems that Dilip Masood has identified.   **(10 marks)**

(c)   Explain how DRB might re-structure its downstream supply chain to achieve the growth required.   **(6 marks)**

(Total = 25 marks)

11 CMMI

45 mins

CCT Computer Systems plc specialises in the development and implementation of software for the logistics industry. After experiencing a number of years of growth and profitability the company is continuing to report growth in turnover but, for the last five quarters, it has also reported small losses. An investigation into this has revealed that costs have risen greatly in systems development and support and consequently margins have been eroded in recently completed projects. It appears that this trend is going to continue. Many people within the company attribute this worsening financial performance to a perceived reduction in software quality. Here are three testimonies received during the investigation

Amelia Platt: Software Development Manager CCT Computer Systems plc

'You have to remember that the original logistics system was developed by Ilya Borisova (the founder of CCT) and three of his friends from university days. They did not build the software with expansion or maintenance in mind. Also, it is difficult to know what some of the programs actually do, so making changes is a nightmare. Programmers make changes to program code without really knowing what the knock-on effect will be.'

Tony Osunda: General Manager QANDO logistics – a major customer

'We feel that the last project was most unsatisfactory. We specified our requirements very carefully but the delivered system did not work the way we wanted. We found it cumbersome to use and key areas of functionality were either wrong or missing altogether. After implementation, we asked for a number of changes so that the system would work as it should. We were originally asked to pay for these changes but we pointed out that they weren't really changes – they were things we had asked for all along. Eventually, CCT backed down and so we got the changes for free. The system works fine now, but it has been delivered late and we are still seeking compensation for this.

Carlos Theroux: One of the original programmers of the CCT logistics software solution: Now lead programmer CCT Computer Systems plc

'It is no fun here anymore. When we were smaller we could all dive in and solve the problems. When I joined we had three programmers, now we have one hundred and thirty. What do they all do? There is no work ethic. We all used to stay over until we got the problem solved. Now there is documentation, documentation and documentation. We have now adopted a formal project management method, more documentation! I am not sure this place suits me anymore.'

Required

(a) A perceived reduction in software quality is blamed by many people for the decline in profitability at CCT. Discuss the importance and characteristics of software quality and explain how each of these characteristics might be measured. **(10 marks)**

(b) Explain the levels within the Capability Maturity Model Integration (CMMI) process and discuss their implications for CCT. **(15 marks)**

(Total = 25 marks)

12 Project initiation

36 mins

Project management in the ABC company

Dave is the project manager in-charge of a project team installing new software in the ABC Company. The installation is currently three weeks behind schedule, with only seven weeks left before the installation should be complete. Due to the time constraints, Dave has cancelled all project meetings to try and focus his team on meeting the project deadlines. While this action has had some slight improvement in the amount of work being carried out, members of the team have been complaining that they cannot discuss problems easily. Most of the team are professional staff with appropriate project management qualifications.

Over the last week, both of the systems analysts have left to move onto other assignments due to double bookings by the project management company. This did not help the morale of the remaining team members. To try and compensate for the lack of staff, the project manager has asked two other team members with a small amount of systems analysis experience to continue their jobs. To try and impress upon them the seriousness of the situation, Dave also made these members responsible for any mistakes in the analysis documentation.

In the last few days, the working situation in the team has become significantly worse, with many minor quarrels and disagreements breaking out. Dave has chosen to ignore these problems, and simply asked the team to focus on completing the project.

Required

(a)   Identify and explain where the ABC Company project is being poorly managed.   **(10 marks)**

(b)   Explain how the project manager can help resolve these difficulties.   **(10 marks)**

(Total = 20 marks)

Guidance note

You may find it easier to structure your answer with headings for each problem you identify, and then in two separate paragraphs, answer the two parts of the question. This should ensure that actions to resolve the problem are included in your answer.

13 Educational institution   45 mins

You are a newly-appointed Finance Manager of an Educational Institution that is mainly government-funded, having moved from a similar post in a service company in the private sector. The objective, or mission statement, of this Institution is shown in its publicity material as:

'To achieve recognised standards of excellence in the provision of teaching and research.'

The only financial performance measure evaluated by the government is that the Institution has to remain within cash limits. The cash allocation each year is determined by a range of non-financial measures such as the number of research publications the Institution's staff have achieved and official ratings for teaching quality.

However, almost 20% of total cash generated by the Institution is now from the provision of courses and seminars to private sector companies, using either its own or its customers' facilities. These customers are largely unconcerned about research ratings and teaching quality as they relate more to academic awards such as degrees.

The Head of the Institution aims to increase the percentage of income coming from the private sector to 50% over the next five years. She has asked you to advise on how the management team can evaluate progress towards achieving this aim as well as meeting the objective set by government for the activities it funds.

Required

(a)   Discuss the main issues that an Institution such as this has to consider when setting objectives.

   Advise on

   - Whether a financial objective, or objectives, could or should be determined; and
   - Whether such objective(s) should be made public.   **(9 marks)**

The following is a list of financial and non-financial performance measures that were in use in your *previous company:*

FINANCIAL	NON-FINANCIAL
Value added	Competitive position
Profitability	Customer satisfaction
Return on investment	Market share

Required

(b)   Choose *two of each* type of measure, explain their purpose and advise on how they could be used by the Educational Institution over the next five years to assess how it is meeting the Head of the Institution's aims.

(16 marks)

Note: A report format is NOT required in answering this question.   **(Total = 25 marks)**

14 Coxford Doors   18 mins

Coxford Doors is a family owned wood products company, specialising in producing doors and windows to be sold directly to house builders. There are currently no sales directly to homeowners who may wish to purchase doors and windows to replace their existing ones. In recent years the industry has become much more competitive. Most of the customers are now large nationwide builders, the industry having gone through a period of consolidation. These customers generally require standardised products in large volume, and they buy on the basis of low prices and guarantees of regular delivery. This has put great pressure on companies such as Coxford Doors. This company is still operating as if it were dealing with the fragmented market of twenty years ago. The family, in seeking uninterrupted growth, has permitted the workforce to have a substantial degree of self-management. This has avoided industrial unrest but there have been disadvantages to this approach. This delegated decision-making has led to delays in manufacturing and problems with quality. There has appeared to be a lack of focus. Consequently the company has lost important contracts and is gradually seeing its sales volume and profits decline.

The family has employed Andrew Smith as the new Managing Director, giving him the responsibility for turning the company around. He has decided that power and control must now return to the centre. The passive style of management pursued in the earlier years is now giving way to a more centralised and autocratic approach. However it is obvious that such a change in management style could create even further problems for the company.

Required

Discuss the benefits and problems which this more direct style of management might bring to Coxford Doors.   **(10 marks)**

15 Auto Direct   22 mins

Mark Howe, Managing Director of Auto Direct, is a victim of his own success. Mark has created an innovative way of selling cars to the public which takes advantage of the greater freedom given to independent car distributors to market cars more aggressively within the European Union. This reduces the traditional control and interference of the automobile manufacturers, some of whom own their distributors. He has opened a number of showrooms in the London region and by 2004 Auto Direct had 20 outlets in and around London. The concept is deceptively simple; Mark buys cars from wherever he can source them most cheaply and has access to all of the leading volume car models. He then concentrates on selling the cars to the public, leaving servicing and repair work to other specialist garages. He offers a classic high volume/low margin business model.

Mark now wants to develop this business model onto a national and eventually an international basis. His immediate plans are to grow the number of outlets by 50% each year for the next three years. Such growth will place considerable strain on the existing organisation and staff. Each showroom has its own management team, sales personnel and administration. Currently the 20 showrooms are grouped into a Northern and Southern Sales Division with a small head office team for each division. Auto Direct now employs 250 people.

Required

Using appropriate strategies for managing change provide Mark with a brief report on how he should pursue his proposed growth plans.
(12 marks)

16 Lionel Cartwright

35 mins

Lionel Cartwright considers himself to be an entrepreneur. He has been involved in many business ventures, each with minimal planning. He claims that this allows him to respond quickly to changing circumstances. His father had left him a small road haulage firm – three lorries – but he soon sold this to a larger operator when he recognised that operating margins were low and competition was severe. With the money received he bought a fast-food franchise, realising that this was where there was likely to be substantial growth. However, the franchisor required Lionel to limit both his ambitions and ideas for expansion to the development of this single franchise site. Lionel did not like this constraint and sold out and moved on. He then invested his money in an internet firm, having identified the potential in this market. Unfortunately for Lionel his investment in the company was insufficiently large to permit him to have much say in the management of the company so he again sold out. He demonstrated his opportunism because he managed to sell his investment before the technology shares had fallen on the global stock exchanges. Lionel now has a cash sum of about £12 million seeking a suitable investment.

It is clear form Lionel's track record that he enjoys involvement in the management of businesses and he also prefers some element of control. He appears to have a skill in identifying potential growth markets and he also seems to have an intuitive knowledge of the market place. He is currently showing an interest again in the food/restaurant retailing market and he is looking at organic foods and juices (produce grown without the use of synthetic fertilisers or pesticides). He has noticed a growing trend in the USA for outlets selling fresh vegetable and fruit juices which are squeezed to the customer's demand, either to be consumed on premises or taken away for consumption, as is the case with many fast-food chains. This development is all part of the growing health-conscious climate. Lionel believes that the European market is ready for such a venture and this is his initial objective. He has already opened four outlets in central London. To acquire the leases, fit out the premises, train labour and buy stock plus some initial expenditure on marketing has already cost Lionel £3 million. He realises that to become profitable he must open several more outlets so as to gain from both the experience curve and from economies of scale. He estimates that about 30 outlets will provide him with the necessary critical mass. He believes that these outlets could be anywhere in Europe, given the right environment. He is confident that he has identified a transnational segment for a health focused nutritious juice – a segment of the market which is uniform, regardless of nationality. This is based upon the youth market which tends to have common tastes in both entertainment and leisure activities throughout Europe – France, Italy, Germany and the UK appear to be acceptable target areas. However this segment is believed to be relatively sophisticated and affluent so outlets, therefore, will need to be in expensive city-centre areas or in other similar type areas which this target market group might regularly visit.

One of the problems facing Lionel's new venture and one of the pressures pushing him towards expansion is the need for regular access to suitable organic raw materials. These are in short supply. With large UK supermarkets generating increasing competitive demand for organic produce Lionel is finding it difficult to find reliable, quality suppliers. His current demand is too low and he needs to guarantee his suppliers a larger volume of orders so as to maintain their interest. He can only do this if he can rapidly expand the number of outlets he has or if he increases the volume sold through each outlet. The latter option is not really feasible. The area which each outlet covers is limited and to expand demand might mean either lowering the image which the outlet has developed and/or lowering the price of the products. Given the relative elasticities of demand, although the volumes of sales may rise, the profitability of each outlet may actually fall.

Another problem which Lionel is facing is obtaining suitable sites for his outlets. It is essential that these are in the appropriate locations. His current ones are in central London where there is a young and affluent market and also where the tourist trade is high. Future sites need to be acquired if expansion is to be achieved. If he goes into the rest of Europe they will need to be in major city centres or in similar type sophisticated tourist areas. It is inevitable that the availability of these sites will be limited and the cost of acquisition will be expensive. In addition the juice enterprise needs to be marketed in a sympathetic way. The target clientele, being young, mobile and affluent will be easily deterred from buying the product if the marketing lacks subtlety. Consequently any rush towards expansion by using aggressive marketing techniques must be tempered with caution. It will be too easy to down-grade the enterprise's image, so damaging it in the eyes of its potential customers.

Lionel had made an effort to understand his core competences and he hoped that these would match the critical success factors needed for this industry. He believed that he had the necessary market knowledge, his operation was small enough to be flexible and responsive to sudden changes in market circumstances and he felt that he had the level of motivation required to be successful in such a fast-moving, consumer, non-durable industry.

After one year's operations the results from the four London outlets compared with a chain of similar outlets in the USA seem to demonstrate that Lionel's ambitions may be over-optimistic. Whilst recognising that the enterprise is still young (although there is the novelty attraction and also no near competition) the profits are nowhere near as attractive as those being obtained from a larger chain (20 outlets) in the USA. [See details in Table 1.]

If Lionel is to achieve his ambition of setting up a profitable chain of retail juice outlets he must seek expansion without alienating his customer-base. He can do this gradually and internally by funding any expansion through retained earnings. He could also attempt to acquire another retail/fast food chain and adapt it to this new format. Finally, he could seek some sort of alliance whereby he achieves expansion, using other people's efforts and resources, particularly financial ones. This could involve licensing or franchising agreements. Each of these modes of expansion has its own advantages, but there are also disadvantages associated with each.

Table 1

Details of performance of individual outlets in USA and in the United Kingdom

(£'000) (where appropriate)

All figures refer to the calendar year 2000

	UK outlet	USA outlet
Sales	600	750
Cost of materials	200	200
Labour costs	125	125
Rental/lease costs	125	85
Stocks held	30	20
Wasted materials as a % of sales	22	9
Varieties of products available for juicing (actual numbers)	14	25
Marketing costs allocated per unit	60	35
Administration costs allocated per outlet	20	10
Customers per week (actual numbers)	2,000	2,500
Size of store (square metres)	275	250
Numbers of staff	10	15
Number of hours open as a % of total hours available within any given week	40	65
Waiting time (from order to service) in minutes	15	8
Profit	70	295

Required

It appears that Lionel is a follower of the emergent school of strategy formulation as distinct from the rational model (planning) approach. Discuss the benefits that such an opportunistic approach may bring Lionel and comment on any problems he may experience with such an approach to setting strategy.

(15 marks)

Exam answer bank

1 Bartok Fuel

> **Top tips.** This is quite a simple question that offers a gentle introduction to the style of the examination. Part (c) is typical of the sort of question that usually forms one of the requirements of a 60 mark case study, being essentially a critical discussion of possible specific strategies. It is usually pretty clear what the overall worth of the proposals is, but not always. Discuss this sort of thing as rationally as you can, using simple models and pointing out any implications you can discern.

Part (a)

There would appear to be no real evidence of any formal strategic planning in the past. There is no mention of any mission statement or objectives for the company. The company seems to have moved from a garage and workshop into fuel distribution and glass manufacture almost by accident. These developments might have **emerged from patterns of behaviour** rather than any planning process and it could be argued that the company illustrates the emergent strategy model. However, there is also an element of **logical incrementalism** as the business has not strayed far from its origins but has taken small steps into new areas where it already has some knowledge and expertise.

It could also be argued that only a small number of strategic options were ever considered and the options that have been taken in the past have perhaps simply been accepted as satisfactory rather than embraced as ideal. This approach has been termed **bounded rationality** by *Herbert Simon*.

Part (b)

Each of the two strategies being considered requires very different considerations from the board.

If the Woking site is sold for its development potential, this will clearly be a boost to the company's cash flow. However, as we have no information about the company's current financial position, we cannot comment as to whether this is an element of the decision to sell. Nevertheless, the board must consider what use can be made of the funds received. It may be that the two options are related in David's mind and the funds from the sale of the Woking site are to be earmarked for investment in the Far East. In any case, the sale should only be considered further if it seems likely that the income can be invested in a way that will **generate a higher return** than the garage business currently achieves.

If the Woking site is to be shut down there are also considerable **human resource issues** to be addressed. The division employs 50 people who must either be made redundant or be re-employed in other areas of the business. In either case, the cost of redundancy payments or of retraining must be taken into account. The car dealership appears to be a fairly stand-alone element of the business but it must also be considered whether its closure will have any **knock-on effects** on the other parts of the company.

The proposed expansion into the Far East is fraught with potential problems. Bartok Fuel has always been a UK based business and therefore expansion abroad is a major issue. The results of a **PEST analysis** would be daunting. The company has no experience of doing business in any country in the Far East. It knows nothing of local business conditions or regulations. Language and culture are likely to present major difficulties.

All this is partially countered by the existence of a partner who knows the market and the culture of the Far East, but Bartok Fuel will still be making something of a leap in the dark. In fact, they would be **wholly dependent** on the probity, efficiency and goodwill of their partner. It would appear that the company's only real contribution will be to provide risk capital and the brothers must ask themselves if they really see that as their area of expertise – they are not running a bank, after all.

2 EMS

The decline in the number of people taking the qualification appears to be a reflection of the maturity of the marketplace. The large pool of unqualified environmental managers and auditors that existed when the qualification was launched has now been exploited. There are now fewer candidates taking the examinations and fewer members joining the EMS. The organisation's response to this has been to look for international markets where it can promote the qualifications it currently offers. It hopes to find large pools of unqualified environmental managers and auditors in these markets.

The scenario suggests that EMS currently has relatively limited strategic ambitions. There is no evidence that EMS plans to develop new qualifications outside its current portfolio. Indeed, attempts to look at complementary qualifications (such as soil and water conservation) have been rejected by Council. Hence, expansion into new strategic business markets does not appear to be an option.

Strategy Development

Internal development

Internal development takes place when strategies are developed by building on or developing the organisation's own capabilities. It is often termed organic growth. This is how EMS has operated up to now. The original certificates were developed by the founders of the Society. Since then, additional certificates have been added and the Diploma programme developed at the instigation of members and officers of the Society.

In many ways this type of organic growth is particularly suited to the configuration of the organisation, one where there is a risk-averse and cautious culture. The organic approach spreads cost and risk over time and growth is much easier to control and manage. However, growth can be slow and indeed, as in the case of EMS, may have ceased altogether. Growth is also restricted by the breadth of the organisation's capabilities. For example, EMS has not been able to develop (or indeed even consider developing) any products outside of its fairly restricted product range. Furthermore, although internal development may be a reasonable strategy for developing a home market it maybe an inappropriate strategy for breaking into new market places and territories. This is particularly true when, as it appears in the case of the EMS, internal resources have no previous experience of developing products in overseas markets.

In summary, internal growth has been the method of strategy development at EMS up to now, based on a strategic direction of consolidation and market penetration. There is no evidence that EMS is considering developing new products to arrest the fall in qualification numbers. However, the Board has suggested developing new markets for the current qualification range and India, China and Russia have been identified as potential targets. It seems unlikely that internal development will be an appropriate method of pursuing this strategic direction.

3 Competitor analysis

Part (a)

> **Top tips.** The requirement to deal with the *dangers* of competitor analysis is an odd one; it is difficult to see how a detailed knowledge of competitors could be harmful. Nevertheless, we are able to offer something as you will see.

Life in business is easiest for monopolists. The only constraint on the charges they make is the size of the market they wish to achieve; they need not bother themselves with their customers' detailed needs and preferences because there are no alternative products available to them. Competitors spoil this easy life. Competition is a constant threat to profit and even to survival. It is a sensible management that understands its competitors. Competitor analysis can offer strategic benefits.

Awareness of potential threats

Competitors are likely to have their own coherent plans for success. These plans represent specific threats; an understanding of their objectives, strategies and technical and economic capabilities enables us to prepare our responses in advance, thus limiting their ability to achieve success at our expense. At the same time, we can assess less immediate threats, separating the relatively innocuous from those that might become important in the future.

Awareness of potential targets

If we understand our competitors' strengths and weaknesses, we are able to design our strategy to exploit the one and avoid the other. Alternatively, we may be able to spoil their plans, exploit the markets they have created or adopt the methods they have used.

Awareness of potential responses

Even where competitors' own plans do not represent a particular threat, it is possible that they may respond to our plans in a way that will force them off track. We should consider potential competitor response when deciding our own strategy. This may enable us to avoid damaging head-on confrontation.

Strategic dangers

The chief danger to a company carrying out customer analysis is a loss of focus on its own strategy. Too great an emphasis on competitor capability and potential response may lead to the rejection of viable strategic options. Carried to extremes, this may produce a kind of paralysis, all possible courses seeming unviable.

There is also the possibility of diminishing returns if too many resources are devoted to the role.

Part (b)

Top tips. Even if you have never heard the phrase 'competitor analysis' you should be able to guess that competitors' current strengths and weaknesses and how they go about their business (their strategies, in other words) would be of interest.

Wilson and Gilligan suggest five main areas for competitor analysis.

Who are our competitors?

As well as the obvious competitors who serve the same markets with similar goods, we must be aware of the threat from companies whose products are quite different but satisfy the same needs; and those who compete for the same discretionary expenditure. An example of the first is skis and surf boards; and of the second, cinema tickets and shoes.

Competitors will be particularly deserving of our attention if they serve the same market as ourselves; use similar distribution methods; serve the same geographical area; use similar technology; have similar core competences; or are at a similar stage of the value system.

What are their objectives?

Stakeholders. Organisations' objectives are influenced by their stakeholders. A general profit-maximising objective may be undermined by top management priorities, such as status, dominance or devotion to technological advance.

Time frame. Strategies may concentrate on the long term or aim for short-term results: different actions will result.

Scale and focus. A large company that serves a market as part of a wider portfolio of activity or for some other purpose than maximising profit may not be as aggressive as a smaller operation that has no alternative but to succeed in that market.

What are their strategies and how successful are they?

Information from the trade and business press, trade associations and the sales force (who are in contact with mutual customers) may be supplemented by **competitor accounting**. This technique may be used to estimate the likely effect of a given strategy on a competitor's cost structure and revenue streams.

What are their strengths and weaknesses? As when considering competitor strategies, standard strategic analysis tools, such as the value chain and portfolio analysis, may be used. Information about capital structure and estimates of costs can be useful indicators.

What are they likely to do, particularly in response to our actions?

With established competitors it may be possible to forecast responses from past practice, but it is less easy to establish the reasons behind their action (or lack of it). Cost information is particularly useful.

(a)   High exit costs are likely to encourage a vigorous response, since market failure will cause the competitor will incur those high fixed costs.

(b)   High operational gearing encourages aggressive action to preserve high volumes to spread the high level of fixed costs over.

(c)   High costs generally make cost leadership impossible and make it difficult to respond to price cuts.

4 Firebridge Tyres Ltd

> **Top tips**. This is a fairly straightforward question on the environment and strategic capability. Part (a) may look very wide ranging and therefore rather daunting. This is a good example of the way in which the use of a model (such as PEST) can help you to organise your thoughts. You will see from our answer that a detailed knowledge of the motor industry is not required to answer this question.

Part (a)

Main factors in the external environment

The environment of an organisation is everything outside the boundaries of the organisation. Organisations are by definition open to the environment: it is the source of their inputs; it is the destination of their outputs; and it sets constraints over what the organisation can do. Some argue that the environment is increasingly a source of uncertainty for organisations, and that it is becoming harder to read. The degree of uncertainty it causes results from its complexity and the rate of change.

Hofer and Schendel argue that the very purpose of strategy is to secure some sort of environmental fit. This might be an extreme position, as it implies reaction to the environment rather than activity to shape environmental forces. However, any formal strategic planning process takes the environment into account.

As far as the general environment is concerned, we can analyse PEST and competitive factors.

Political and legal factors

Firebridge Tyres Ltd (FTL) operates in a stable political environment. Agreements between governments have opened up international markets, not only to FTL but to its competitors: however GTC does not want FTL to increase its exports outside Europe. There is no shortage of car service stations, a fragmented industry, so political interference is unlikely. Local government might determine the siting of certain activities. FTL is indirectly affected by government transport policy, if this affects the demand for and use of cars.

Economic factors

In the UK, tyres must be checked annually, as part of the MOT testing process. The overall level of economic activity determines transport use, which influences wear and tear of tyres. However, in times of hardship, people will be less likely to buy the premium brand range preferring to go for the lower cost Freeway range, cheaper overseas tyres, or even retreads. The general level of prosperity also influences the number of people in the population who use cars; rising incomes and wealth mean rising numbers of cars purchased, hence greater demand for tyres. People will also move to lower cost service options in hard times: FTL does not want a service business lumbered with heavy overheads. The UK market is much smaller than the US: GTC might be unrealistic in assuming that the same formula, which might depend on economies of scale, would work over in the UK.

Social factors

Social factors influence demand indirectly, *via* political pressure for legislation or changing patterns of demand. For examples, governments are more concerned with ecological issues. There are disposal problems with used tyres. This might affect what they are made of. Some can be burnt as fuel, but with landfill taxes increasing, recyclable tyres may be preferred. The proposed service business depends on patterns of car use. It may be that many drivers and will prefer a garage.

Technological factors

Tyres are a fairly mature technology, although there are improvements to be made to increase their grip, their longevity, and their recyclability. Any changes in the plastics and materials industry might be relevant. Also, if cars become lighter, lighter tyres will be needed.

The main factor in the environment is competition, which is impinging directly on FTL.

A number of service chains already exist in the UK, but otherwise the industry is fairly fragmented. Competition on price is important, but also on quality. However, FTL needs to assess how the competition will respond.

The competitive environment can be described using Porter's five forces model (barriers to entry– see below, substitute products, customer bargaining power, supplier bargaining power, competitive rivalry). There are few substitute products, but competitive rivalry is intense. Suppliers have low bargaining power probably.

Part (b)

Barriers to entry discourage new competitors to an industry. If they are low, it is easy to set up shop, but hard to discourage other people from doing so too. The main barriers to entry are described below.

Economies of scale

For some firms, a barrier to entry is the **size of the operation needed to be profitable**. Tyres are high volume, low margin products on the whole, and for most cases, the best way to make money is to manufacture in large quantities. A large plant implies high fixed costs and **a high breakeven point**. There is little evidence that significant economies of scale can be achieved in *servicing*. There are some service chains, but the industry seems fragmented.

Product differentiation

FTL already pursues this strategy by producing different tyres, directed at different segments. In service, differentiation might be achieved on the basis of FTL's **brand name**, and a promise of service quality. Advertising costs might be considerable, however, to build the brand.

Capital requirements

No new factories need to be built, of course, but FTL will have to acquire leases or freeholds of a number of properties in which to set up its service stations. Many of the prime spots might be taken over by petrol stations. Ideally FTL will be positioned near residential areas or near roads, to make them easy to find. The cost of this depends on the size of the operation that GTC is proposing.

Switching costs

Switching costs are minimal; new customers are easy to find, but hard to keep, unless service quality is better.

Distribution

The chain is basically a distribution outlet for FTL's tyres. The importance of choosing the right sites for distributing the service was identified above. Existing service providers know the market, but otherwise they have no special advantages.

Conclusion

Barriers to entry are fairly low. This will make it easy to set up business, but hard to make a profit perhaps, unless some unique lessons can be transferred from GTC, operating in a very different transport infrastructure.

Part (c)

Strategic capability and critical success factors

Strategic capabilities have four essential qualities.

- They produce effects that are valuable to buyers.
- They are **rare**.
- They are **robust** in that they are difficult for competitors to imitate
- They are **non-substitutable**.

Critical success factors, on the other hand, are product features that are particularly valued by a group of customers. Organisations must get these things right if they are to succeed. Some of these factors relate to physical products, but many depend on internal processes and the basic infrastructure of the business.

FTL is a manufacturing business, producing what is essentially a commodity product, tyres, and making a stab at product differentiation. This competence is not truly distinctive, as there are other tyre manufacturers in the world, but FTL has built up a market presence in Europe. The strategic capabilities that led to this position probably look something like those shown below.

(a)   Building a **brand** that consumers recognise, and preventing its erosion by competition
(b)   Good commercial relations with the distributors, who are the **strategic customers**
(c)   Making **incremental technical innovations** in order to encourage new sales

How do these relate to the proposed service centre business? A key problem is that services are a very different proposition to products. There are several possible resources and competences for the proposed servicing business.

(a)   A brand that customers recognise and choose, having realistic and satisfied expectations of what it offers

(b)   Well-chosen sites that are easily accessible, offer plenty of parking and are comfortable to wait in.

(c)   Well-trained staff who not only know how to change wheels and tyres, and do other repairs but who are able to demonstrate high standards of customer care

(d)   To be seen as preferable to the local garage in terms of the processes by which the service is provided

FTL's existing competences, at best, cover brand building. It has no experience in choosing and managing properties or customer service staff: US conditions are different, so a transfer of skills between the US and the UK firm may be hard to achieve. FTL runs a manufacturing business; a service business, based on a variety of intangibles such as staff courtesy, is a different proposition. The required cultures of the two businesses might conflict.

The firm might have to spend a lot of money on training, both technically and in terms of customer care. Also money would have to be spent on building the brand. However, GTC should be able to provide some expertise in building the service aspects.

In short, FTL's current strategic capability is not suited to this plan, given the fragmented nature of the industry. GTC may be able to provide some help, but GTC might end up investing more money and making short term losses, rather than the profits it is looking for.

FTL is in a difficult situation, because its managers are tied by the priorities of the US parent.

5 Nadir Products: ethics

Part (a)

> **Top tips**. While this question clearly has an important ethical slant, it is important to deal with the commercial impact of the proposed courses of action. If you feel your experience has not prepared you to do this, think in terms of stakeholder theory and ask yourself what connected stakeholders like customers are reasonably entitled to expect and how *you* would react to these ploys.
>
> Do not spend more than a minute on dealing with the report form requirement: a suitable heading and, perhaps, numbered paragraphs are all that are required. A short introductory paragraph giving the reason for the report is a good way to get started.

REPORT

To:	Board Members, Nadir Products plc
From:	A Consultant
Date:	December 2001
Subject:	Proposed adjustments to turnover reporting

You asked me to comment on the commercial and ethical implications of suggestions that had been made about the value of this year's turnover. There was concern that a current decline in sales will adversely affect the level of bonuses paid to senior staff.

My first comment is that the assumption behind the suggestions appears wrong. The aim of the bonus scheme was surely to provide an incentive for senior staff to take appropriate action to improve performance. If performance has not improved, it would be perverse to adjust the numbers so that they receive the bonuses anyway. There is an element of moral hazard here: if the bonuses are in effect guaranteed and not dependent on improved performance, the incentive effect disappears and the scheme might as well be abandoned.

I understand that there is concern that staff will be adversely affected by the downturn in sales value. However, I must point out the questionable nature of the suggestions from an ethical point of view. It is likely that the detailed proposals will create a conflict of interests since each has the potential to disadvantage shareholders. It would be ethically inappropriate to pursue any course of action that reduced shareholder value in order to enrich senior staff.

I will now examine the individual proposals.

Discount for additional sales. A discount is an unexceptional sales promotional device that may be used, for instance, to increase or defend market share or to shift excess stock. It has a cost, in the form of reduced margin, and it is a matter of commercial judgement to decide whether the benefit is greater than the cost. It may also have the effect of merely bringing sales forward in time, so that later trading periods suffer.

Of the three suggestions, this is the most defensible. However, it is quite *indefensible* if it is undertaken solely in order to boost bonuses, because of the conflict of interest discussed above.

Bringing forward scheduled orders is a form of window dressing. Your auditors will deploy checks on such activities as a matter of course, and may succeed in detecting this. The accounts would then have to be adjusted, since there is no commercial justification for the practice. It can be seen as detrimental to shareholders since the reported profit would be overstated and, while this may have a positive effect on share value in the short term, were it ever discovered, it would bring into question the company's corporate governance. Such a scheme is also likely to irritate customers who may respond by delaying payment and even seeking a new supplier. This would clearly disadvantage the company.

This suggestion is unacceptable on both ethical and practical grounds.

Warning of possible price rises. I take it as read that there are no actual plans to raise prices? If this is the case, to say that such plans exist is untruthful and therefore inappropriate for a company that wishes to maintain high ethical standards. Further, to hide behind a form of words such as 'there *may* be price rises' would be equally dishonest, since the intention would be to create a specific, incorrect impression in customers' minds. When the warning is eventually shown to be spurious, customers' estimation of the company will fall, with an eventual knock-on effect on turnover.

This ploy is comparable to the previous one in its potential effect on shareholders and customers but is even more unethical

Conclusion. None of the suggestions is acceptable ethically or commercially as a solution to the senior staff bonus problem.

Part (b)

The stakeholder view is that many groups have a stake in what the organisation does. This is particularly important in the business context, where shareholders own the business but employees, customers and government also have particularly strong claims to having their interests considered. It is suggested that modern corporations are so powerful, socially, economically and politically, that unrestrained use of their power will inevitably damage other people's rights. Under this approach, the exercise of corporate social responsibility constrains the corporation to act at all times as a good citizen. Particular emphasis is laid on the preservation of employment and protection of the environment.

We are not told the extent of Nadir Products operations. If as seems likely, they are largely confined to the UK, or at least to the EU, the company's activities will be subject to fairly demanding legal requirements concerning such basic aspects of good corporate citizenship. They must conform or court legal sanctions.

Another argument points out that corporations exist within society and are dependent upon it for the resources they use. Some of these resources are obtained by direct contracts with suppliers but others are not, being provided by government expenditure. Examples are such things as transport infrastructure, technical research and education for the workforce. Clearly, Nadir Products contributes to the taxes that pay for these things, but the relationship is rather tenuous and the tax burden can be minimised by careful management. The company can do as much or as little as it cares to in this connection.

Mintzberg suggests that simply viewing organisations as vehicles for shareholder investment is inadequate, since in practice, he says, organisations are rarely controlled effectively by shareholders. Most shareholders are passive investors. We do not know whether or not this is the case with Nadir Products.

Many organisations regard the exercise of corporate social responsibility as valuable in promoting a positive corporate image. The management of Nadir Products therefore may feel that it is appropriate to take an instrumental approach to such matters as sponsorship and charitable giving. Charitable donations and artistic sponsorship are useful media of public relations and can reflect well on the business. They can be regarded as another form of promotion, which like advertising, serves to enhance consumer awareness of the business. It would be necessary for the company to ensure that the recipients of its generosity were appropriate to its operations at the bottom end of the market: grand opera would probably be inappropriate.

The arguments for and against social responsibility are complex ones. However, ultimately they can be traced to different assumptions about society and the relationships between the individuals and organisations within it. It is unlikely to be something that need occupy a great deal of the time of Nadir Products' directors.

6 Acklington Antennas

Part (a)

> **Top tips**. We answer the first part of this question largely in terms of *Porter's* **generic strategies**. This is because of the nature of the scenario. There is mention of price sensitivity, to which cost is related; the market is clearly highly specialised, so the idea of a niche approach is relevant; and finally, the products tend to be highly differentiated.
>
> It would be possible to take a product-market growth vector approach, but that model would not be so appropriate. We are given no information relevant to market penetration; product development is clearly going on anyway; market development and diversification are high-risk strategies for such a specialised company working in such high technology. Generally, *Ansoff's* model is most useful for less specialised companies, particularly those working in consumer products and services.
>
> The possible solution of a reorganisation of the industry, however, could be applied just as easily to an analysis using the product-market model.

Acklington Antennas is under threat from a new entrant that appears likely to enjoy a substantial cost advantage because of high volumes and the prior amortisation of development costs. However, Wizzomatic's products, being standardised, are unlikely to be suitable for many specialised applications.

Wizzomatic appear to be seeking to establish themselves as the cost leaders within the industry, using their cost advantage to build up volume. Cost leaders tend to seek as much product standardisation as possible in order to obtain economies of scale and Wizzomatic seem to have a major advantage here.

It would therefore not be advisable for Acklington to meet the new entrant head on. The price cuts necessary to build the necessary volume would be likely to starve the company of cash, thus prejudicing its new design work. It would find itself in the classic 'stuck in the middle' trap, subject to continuing high costs but unable to raise its prices.

A much safer option for Acklington would be to pursue two specific target market segments.

- The new design market, where they have expertise and a reputation that Wizzomatic cannot challenge with its standardised products

- Those parts of the spares market that require more specialised products than Wizzomatic can supply.

The first of these options represents a strategy of differentiation, while the second is a niche strategy.

It is likely that if Wizzomatic succeeds in establishing itself in the market it has chosen, Acklington will see its volumes falling. This need not lead to a fall in turnover if it is able to penetrate its chosen segments more deeply. However, a fall in volume of standard antennas will mean an increase in fully absorbed cost per unit, with a knock-on effect on margin. It may be that Acklington will have to withdraw from the volume part of its business. This will lead to concomitant downsizing of its production capacity unless it succeeds in retaining much of its existing aftermarket business.

To expand its share of the new systems market, Acklington will have to increase its sales effort and its design and test capacity. We have no way of knowing how easy this will be, but we may speculate that the highly skilled staff required will be fairly difficult to find, while the design and test facilities are likely to be quite expensive. Depending on the company's access to investment funds, therefore, this strategy may require a long period of time to implement.

The niche spares market will probably be easier to expand initially, since Acklington is likely to have the manufacturing capacity available, as discussed above. An immediate problem here is likely to be that the other three established players may also be planning a similar strategy.

It is possible that the other three principal suppliers in the industry will also feel the heat of Wizzomatic's arrival. This is all the more likely if they too are unable to meet the challenge head on. It may be that this could be a cue for restructuring the industry, by merger or takeover. The aim would be to accumulate the resources necessary to compete with Wizzomatic rather than ceding dominance in the volume sales segments of the market.

A strategy of consolidation would not be easy to implement. It would probably involve painful rationalisation of several functions, with job losses and other staff upheaval. There would also be a probability of conflict between perceived winners and losers, which would be exacerbated if the rationalisation took the form of takeover rather than merger.

The aim of the consolidation would be for a larger, more efficient company to emerge, retaining the best of the products, people, markets and resources of its parents. A careful strategic analysis would be necessary to ensure that the new strategy built on strengths and avoided weaknesses. It may be, for example, that even a merged company would not dispute the volume market but would aim to dominate the new design market.

Part (b)

> **Top tips**. Acklington Antennas is a manufacturing company, so the basic 4 Ps mix is what is required here. With a question like this, which is only worth 8 marks, do not dwell too much on background explanations. Cut to the chase and make as many good valid points as you can. You don't need to know anything about aircraft communication systems. But you do need to be generally aware of the differences between consumer and industrial marketing.

Product

The product element of Acklington's marketing mix is relatively simple. A firm's product may be viewed as a solution to a customer's problem. Acklington's products are therefore of two basic types: the newly developed and very high-value added antennas designed for new aircraft; and the standard antennas produced either for use as spares or for supply to other businesses.

Quality is clearly a major issue affecting both types of product, because of the requirements of aircraft safety. The standard antennas must be produced to existing precise specifications, while the new designs must satisfy strict performance requirements before they are released to service.

Packaging is also likely to be important. Spares, in particular, must have a long shelf life and may be transported to any part of the world. The packaging will have to provide substantial protection against climatic variables such as heat and humidity, as well as against impact and abrasion.

Price

We are told that prices in the industry are generally high and that co-operation between suppliers is not unusual. While presumably not engaging in price-fixing, it seems that the small group of suppliers in the industry tend not to compete on price. It is likely that winning contracts for new systems design is likely to depend far more on long-term relationships with customers and proven technical quality. In the spares market, it would seem that Wizzomatic's arrival may shake up the existing rather cosy arrangements, both as far as supplies direct to users and subcontract manufacturing are concerned. So long as variable costs can be covered, Acklington may feel it can cut its prices in these markets in order to maintain its manufacturing capacity in being.

Acklington will have to establish exactly which of Wizzomatic's products are acceptable substitutes for its own and where there are gaps in Wizzomatic's standardised range. Those gaps can then be exploited with higher prices.

Promotion

Acklington's products are complex, expensive and sold to industrial buyers, so the company's main promotional effort is likely to go into personal selling by experienced sales engineers. There is also likely to be attendance at trade fairs and a small amount of reminder advertising in the specialist press. Public relations effort is likely to be minimal and also concentrated on the specialist press.

Distribution

Distribution to aircraft manufacturers is likely to be direct to the end user, without any use of intermediaries. The subcontract work will also go direct to the purchasers. Distribution of aftermarket spares may involve the use of intermediaries, since the products are highly standardised technically and may be sold globally without modification. Since the products are expensive, regional or national intermediaries may be able to provide a service by investment in spares inventories.

7 United Products

Part (a)

> **Top tips**. This is a wide ranging question and, perhaps, therefore, somewhat daunting. Remember that with this type of question there will be a lot of easy marks for explaining the basics. For example, a list of strengths and weaknesses would glean quite a few marks, though not 50%.
>
> In order to score well on this question you must do two slightly different things when you are applying your knowledge to the scenario: use the setting to illustrate your theory; and suggest ways in which the theory might be used to make improvements.
>
> Thus, for example, we say that the internal transfer and promotion from within policy is an example of the way that relatively junior managers can obtain good experience of real business problems. Similarly, we say that the detailed monthly reporting might be over-restrictive in its effects and, on examination, might prove to be unnecessarily expensive.
>
> Notice also that we begin with a comment about the very nature of UP's business, which you might think is a matter over and above the question of its organisation. Don't forget that there is scope in this exam for this sort of digression if you make it relevant to the scenario.

Divisionalisation is a common form of organisation structure in large organisations, especially those that encompass a wide variety of products, technologies and geographical locations. UP seems to qualify under all three of these categories. The form has been found to allow for overall control from the corporate headquarters without drowning it in the detail of micromanagement at long range.

The diversity of the company's operations is itself worthy of comment from a strategic point of view. There is obviously a tradition of having widely different operations and it is possible to discern some potential for synergy, in agriculture and retailing, for instance. However, the organisation is committed to managing a very wide range of technologies and markets and it may be that its lacklustre financial performance is linked to a lack of specialist knowledge among its senior managers. The policy of moving managers from division to division, while generally good for their personal development may actually hamper the progress of the more specialised operations.

It is generally considered that conglomerate diversification only adds value when the expertise of the corporate headquarters is such that its allocation of capital is more effective than would be achieved by a normally efficient capital market. Whether this is the case with United Products must be subject to some doubt. The less profitable divisions are protected from the disciplines of the market by the corporate HQ, while those with good prospects may find themselves starved of funds.

UP clearly displays one disadvantage of the divisional form. There is a tendency for the divisions to be more bureaucratic than they would be as independent organisations in order to service the demands of the corporate HQ's control procedures. UP takes this to an extreme, demanding monthly reports and carrying out frequent functional inspections rather than encouraging a responsive autonomy by the use of simple **key performance indicators**. The probable effect of this is to stifle the creativity and sense of ownership that flow from greater autonomy. This is most likely to be visible in the divisions that operate in complex, unstable environments, such as film-making, publishing and fashion retailing. A side effect is the absorption of an excessive degree of divisional revenue in management charges for HQ and in the divisional bureaucracies themselves.

Another problem of divisionalisation was referred to by *Mintzberg* as the pull to balkanise. This is the natural desire of the division heads for independence from central control. In an organisation like UP, with its rather bureaucratic approach, this might take the form conforming to the letter of the rules but manipulating activities and finances. So long as the reporting parameters fall within set limits, it may be possible to conceal unauthorised ventures for a long time, possibly with unfortunate consequences.

A final comment might be made about the mixture of divisional types: there are both product divisions and geographical divisions. This might be a sensible response to UP's geographical range and variety of products. On the other hand it might be a source of confusion and conflict between geographical and product based managers for control of particular operations. This will be particularly apparent when new markets are entered. The problem may be exacerbated by the management structures put in place for the various joint ventures. Overall, the potential for complexity and confusion is significant.

Part (b)

> **Top tips**. The idea of virtuality has become very fashionable and people tend to use the term rather loosely. The definition we give is academically correct. Be sure that you do not confuse the virtual organisation with *Handy's* concept of the **shamrock organisation**, which is merely an organisation that makes extensive use of self-employed and temporary staff in order to be able to control its labour costs in times of economic slowdown.

The idea of a virtual organisation or cybernetic corporation has attracted considerable attention as the usefulness of IT for communication and control has been exploited. The essence of the virtual organisation is the electronic linking of spatially dispersed components.

Such an organisation is a temporary or permanent collection of geographically dispersed individuals, groups, organisational units (which may or may not belong to the same organisation), or entire organisations that depend on electronic linking in order to complete the production process.

However, an organisation is not a virtual organisation merely because it uses IT extensively and has multiple locations. Many organisations fall into that category.

Also, organisations that make extensive use of temporary and self-employed labour are not necessarily virtual organisations because of that, though they may have some virtual characteristics.

UP almost certainly uses extensive IT systems for its internal communications. It would be surprising if it did not have an internal e mail system and it may well have a corporate intranet. However, it clearly has activities that are very real as opposed to virtual, such as its agricultural, extractive, manufacturing and retailing operations.

Of the activities we are told about, electronic design is perhaps the one most suited to the virtual approach. It may be possible for design engineers to work in isolation, using computer aided design equipment and communicating by e mail. However, where the design work requires a team effort, co-ordination may become a problem.

Publishing may also be a candidate, depending on the nature of what is published. Authors of books are likely to work alone, and editors may be able to do the same, as may their assistants and other specialists such as proof readers and indexers. The transmission of entire texts by electronic means is quite feasible and some specialist books are published by being printed on demand from computer memory.

8 BPR and supply chain

Top tips. Ensure you revise the features of supply chains in general, and virtual supply chains in particular. Remember at all times that the examiner is interested in your ability to apply your knowledge in a practical setting.

Business Process Re-engineering (BPR) is the fundamental rethinking and radical design of business processes to achieve dramatic improvements in critical contemporary measures of performance, such as cost, quality, service and speed.

In other words, BPR involves significant change in the business rather than minimal or incremental changes to processes. This is essentially different from procedures such as automation where existing processes are simply computerised. Although some improvements in speed may be obtained, the processes are essentially the same. For example, the local warehouse could use EDI to send an order to the supplier, which may be quicker than email. However, the process of sending the order and receiving the goods to the warehouse is the same.

Using BPR, the actual reasons for the business processes being used can be queried, and where necessary replaced with more efficient processes. For example, rather than stock being ordered from the store via the central warehouse, the supplier could monitor stocks in each store using an extranet. When goods reach re-order level, the supplier is aware of this and can send goods directly to the store. Not only does this provide stock replenishment much more quickly, it is also more cost effective for the supplier as the central warehouse effectively becomes redundant.

Key features of BPR involve the willingness of the organisation to accept change and the ability to use new technologies to achieve those changes. In the example, ABC may have to clearly explain the benefits to staff from the new systems, to ensure that they are accepted. ABC may also need to obtain additional skills in terms of IT and ability to implement and use those systems. New hardware and software will also certainly be required. The aim of BPR is to provide radical improvements in efficiency and cost savings of up to 90%. Amending the supply chain as noted above will help to these benefits.

9 Internet strategy

Top tips. Issues available for discussion are highlighted within the scenario, and range from the strategic to the operational. Your answer should identify a range of these issues and show why they are relevant to this particular situation.

The following issues should be considered when establishing and implementing an appropriate Internet strategy for the SDW company.

- **The Internet Strategy must support the overall business strategy**

    SDW has devised a business plan to expand operations beyond the three cities it currently flies between, and to introduce Internet sales. In the future Mr M wishes Internet sales to be the main selling media of SDW tickets.

    An Internet strategy should be established that supports these aims. Site capacity and response times must be able to cope with forecast site traffic.

- **The existing website**

  The current website is used for 'publicity'. As SDW has already established a web presence, it needs to consider whether this site address should be kept, and the site content modified/replaced, or whether a new address may also be required.

  As SDW does not have this type of expertise in-house, an external website development consultancy should be employed to explain the various options and recommend an appropriate course of action.

- **Integration and compatibility with other systems**

  To bring efficiency gains and lower the cost of processing a transaction, the on-line purchasing system must be integrated with other systems, such as ticketing, payment and accounting systems. Site security for on-line payments must be addressed by experts in the field.

  Supporting processes and procedures also need to be set up, for example a process that will enable paper tickets be delivered and possibly procedures for paperless 'e-ticketing'.

- **Impact upon other areas of the business**

  The move to e-commerce will impact upon other areas of SDW. The call centre is likely to be scaled down as increasing numbers of customers move to on-line purchase. This could potentially bring significant cost savings to SDW.

  The downsizing of the call centre should be anticipated and planned for. Staff should be kept fully informed, and realistic information provided about possible redundancies.

- **On-going site maintenance**

  Establishing the site is the first stage. SDW must also implement policies and procedures to ensure information (particularly fight schedules and prices) are kept up-to-date. This should be able to be performed in-house, following suitable training from the consultants who implemented the site.

- **Other implementation issues**

  Once built, tested and implemented, the site should be publicised. Thorough testing is essential as potential customers who encounter difficulties are unlikely to return to the site. A large-scale, highly advertised launch may best be avoided, as these often result in site overloading – giving a poor first impression to potential customers.

10 DRB

(a) A simple value chain of the primary activities of DRB is shown below.

Handling and storing inbound fully configured equipment Quality inspection	Re-branding of products Re-packaging of products	Customer collection Technician delivery and installation	Local advertising Web based enquiries support	On-site technical support Back to base
Inbound logistics	**Operations**	**Outbound Logistics**	**Marketing and sales**	**Service**

Comments about value might include:

Inbound logistics: Excellent quality assurance is required in inbound logistics. This is essential for pre-configured equipment where customers have high expectations of reliability. As well as contributing to customer satisfaction, high quality also reduces service costs.

Operations: This is a relatively small component in the DRB value chain and actually adds little value to the customer. It is also being undertaken in a relatively high cost country. DRB might wish to re-visit the current arrangement.

Outbound logistics: Customer feedback shows that this is greatly valued. Products can be picked up from stock and delivery and installation is provided if required. Most of the company's larger competitors cannot offer this service. However, it is unlikely that this value can be retained when DRB begins to increasingly supply outside the geographical region it is in.

Marketing and sales: This is very low-key at DRB and will have to be developed if the company is to deliver the proposed growth. The limited functionality of the web site offers little value to customers.

Service: Customer feedback shows that this is greatly valued. Most of the company's competitors cannot offer this level of service. They offer support from off-shore call centres and a returns policy that is both time consuming to undertake and slow in rectification. However, it is unlikely that this value can be retained when DRB begins to increasingly supply outside the geographical region it is in.

(b)   DRB has already gained efficiencies by procuring products through the supplier's web-site. However, the web site has restricted functionality. When DRB places the order it is not informed of the expected delivery date until it receives the confirmation email from ISAS. It is also unable to track the status of their order and so it is only when it receives a despatch email from ISAS that it knows that it is on its way. Because DRB is not the owner of the shipment, it is unable to track the delivery and so the physical arrival of the goods cannot be easily predicted. On occasions where shipments have appeared to have been lost, DRB has had to ask ISAS to track the shipment and report on its status. This has not been very satisfactory and the problem has been exacerbated by having two shippers involved. ISAS has not been able to reliably track the transhipment of goods from their shipper to EIF, the logistics company used to distribute their products in the country. Some shipments have been lost and it is time-consuming to track and follow-up shipments which are causing concern. Finally, because DRB has no long term contract with ISAS, it has to pay when it places the order through a credit card transaction on the ISAS website.

DRB has stated that it wishes to continue importing fully configured products. It is not interested in importing components and assembling them. It also does not wish to build or invest in assembly plants in other countries. However, it may wish to consider the following changes to its upstream supply chain:

- Seek to identify a wider range of suppliers and so trade through other sell-side web sites. Clearly there are costs associated with this. Suppliers have to be identified and evaluated and financial and trading arrangements have to be established. However, it removes the risk of single-sourcing and other suppliers may have better systems in place to support order and delivery tracking.

- Seek to identify suppliers who are willing and able to re-brand and package their products with DRB material at the production plant. This should reduce DRB costs as this is currently undertaken in a country where wage rates are high.

- Re-consider the decision not to negotiate long-term contracts with suppliers (including ISAS) and so explore the possibility of more favourable payment terms. DRB has avoided long-term contracts up to now. It may also not be possible to enter into such contracts if DRB begins to trade with a number of suppliers.

- Seek to identify suppliers (including ISAS) who are able to provide information about delivery dates prior to purchase and who are able to provide internet-based order tracking systems to their customers. This should allow much better planning.

- Consider replacing the two supplier shippers with a contracted logistics company which will collect the goods from the supplier and transport the goods directly to DRB. This should reduce physical transhipment problems and allow seamless monitoring of the progress of the order from despatch to arrival. It will also allow DRB to plan for the arrival of goods and to schedule its re-packaging.

DRB might also wish to consider two other procurement models; buy-side and the independent marketplace.

In the buy-side model DRB would use its web site to invite potential suppliers to bid for contract requirements posted on the site. This places the onus on suppliers to spend time completing details and making commitments. It should also attract a much wider range of suppliers than would have been possible through DRB searching sell-side sites for potential suppliers. Unfortunately, it is unlikely that DRB is large enough to host such a model. However, it may wish to prototype it to see if it is viable and whether it uncovers potential suppliers who have not been found in sell-side web sites searches.

In the independent marketplace model, DRB places its requirements on an intermediary web site. These are essentially B2B electronic marketplaces which allow, on the one hand, potential customers to search products being offered by suppliers and, on the other hand, customers to place their requirements and be contacted by potential suppliers. Such marketplaces promise greater supplier choice with reduced costs. They also provide an opportunity for aggregation where smaller organisations (such as DRB) can get together with companies that have the same requirement to place larger orders to gain cheaper prices and better purchasing terms. It is also likely that such marketplaces will increasingly offer algorithms that automatically match customers and suppliers, so reducing the search costs associated with the sell-side model. The independent marketplace model may be a useful approach for DRB. Many of the suppliers participating in these marketplaces are electronics companies.

(c) DRB's downstream supply chain is also very simple at the moment. It has a web-site that shows information about DRB products. Customers can make enquiries about the specification and availability of these products through an e-mail facility. Conventional marketing is undertaken through local advertising and buyers either collect their products or they are delivered and installed by a specialist group of technicians. DRB could tune its downstream supply chain by using many of the approaches mentioned in the previous section. For example:

- Developing the web site so that it not only shows products but also product availability. Customers would be able to place orders and pay for them securely over the web site. The site could be integrated with a logistics system so that orders and deliveries can be tracked by the customer. DRB must recognise that most of its competitors already have such systems. However, DRB will have to put a similar system in place to be able to support its growth plans.

- Participating in independent marketplace web sites as a supplier. DRB may also be able to exploit aggregation by combining with other suppliers in consortia to bid for large contracts.

- DRB may also consider participating in B2C marketplaces such as e-bay. Many organisations use this as their route to market for commodity products.

DRB may also wish to consider replacing its sales from stock approach with sales from order. In the current approach, DRB purchases products in advance and re-packages and stores these products before selling them to customers. This leads to very quick order fulfilment but high storage and financing costs. These costs will become greater if the planned growth occurs. DRB may wish to consider offering products on its website at a discount but with specified delivery terms. This would allow the company to supply to order rather than supply from stock.

11 CMMI

(a)   Software quality is notoriously difficult to define, but at least four issues deserve consideration.

Conformity to requirements

This is concerned with the software performing business functions correctly. It does what the user expects it to do and does not do what it is not expected to do. This issue is about meeting expectations. The conformity to requirements might be measured by the number of change requests submitted immediately after the system has gone live. If the system performs to requirements then there should be very few change requests until the system has been in operation for some time. Evidence at CCT suggests that this is a major issue. These problems are highlighted by Tony Osunda. He states that 'the delivered system did not work the way we wanted' and that 'key areas of functionality were either wrong or missing altogether'. The fact that changes were subsequently made for free indicates why margins are falling. Doing these would have significantly eroded into the projected profitability of the project.

Reliability

The software behaves consistently and reliably and so is available for the user. The reliability of software can be measured by availability and downtime. Indeed, reliability is often defined within service level agreements (SLAs). For example; the software must be available for 99% of the agreed service time, where service time is defined as 07.00 – 22.00, Monday to Friday. Reliability is relatively easy to measure because it concerns the availability of the software. There is no evidence at CCT that their software has reliability problems.

Usability

The ease of use of software is a major issue in software delivery and e-business development. The usability of software may be assessed in a number of ways. For example;

*   By logging the nature and number of calls to a HELP desk. This should be relatively low if the software is easy to use.

*   By observing users actually using the software and recording the problems and difficulties they encounter.

*   By using questionnaires to ask users how easy they have found the system to use.

There is some evidence that CCT software has usability problems. Crispin Peters-Ward stated that 'We found (the system) cumbersome to use.'

Degree of excellence

The software should exhibit elements of good build, such as maintainability, flexibility and expandability. This software quality is about long-term design potential. This is quite difficult to measure. However, there are technical measures which allow the modularity of the software to be assessed. If the modularity of the software is low then the software is likely to be easy to maintain and test. There is evidence that the CCT software has long-term design problems. Amelia Platt comments that the software was not built 'with expansion in mind. Also, it is difficult to know what some of the programs actually do, so making changes is a nightmare. Programmers make changes to program code without really knowing what the knock-on effect will be.' There are now one hundred and thirty programmers in the company. It is unlikely that they all understand how the software has been constructed. Hence, there is ample opportunity for introducing faults into the system.

Software quality is extremely important to end users. Users expect systems to perform functions correctly and reliably. They expect systems to be easy to use. Failure to fulfil these expectations may lead to frustration with the product, inefficient use of systems and the under-performance of organisations. In the extreme it may lead to organisational collapse and, where safetycritical software fails, to loss of life. The elements of product quality (degree of excellence) may not be immediately obvious to an end user. However, high maintenance costs become very clear to organisations over time, as they increasingly consume a company's operational budget.

(b) The Capability Maturity Model Integration (CMMI) is a process improvement approach that provides organisations with the essential elements of effective processes. It can be used to guide process improvement across a project, a division, or an entire organisation. It has five levels of capability. Organisations are encouraged to move up the levels and to eventually achieve capability level 5. A successful appraisal at this level would assist CCT in delivering quality software as well as publicly demonstrating their competence to do so. Many customers mandate that suppliers should be at a certain level in the CMMI assessment.

Capability level 0 is where there is an incomplete process which is either not performed at all or is partially performed. One or more of the specific goals of the process area are not satisfied. There is no evidence of such a process at CCT. Capability Level 1 is defined as performed. A performed process is a process that satisfies all of the specific goals of a process area such as software development. At this level the processes are performed informally, without following a documented process description or plan. The rigour with which these practices are performed depends on the individuals managing and performing the work and the quality of the outcomes may vary considerably. Successful outcomes for an organisation operating at level 1 depend upon the heroic efforts of individuals. Carlos Theroux alludes to these days at CCT; 'when we were smaller we could all dive in and solve the problems. We all used to stay over until we got the problem solved'.

A capability level 2 process is characterised as a managed process. A managed process is a performed (capability level 1) process that is also planned and executed in accordance with a defined procedure. A critical distinction between a performed process and a managed process is the extent to which the process is actually managed! A managed process is planned (the plan may be part of a more encompassing plan) and the performance of the process is managed against the plan. Corrective actions are taken when the actual results and performance deviate significantly from the plan. A managed process achieves the objectives of the plan and is documented as a standard for consistent performance. Carlos Theroux has alluded to the introduction of a project management methodology and its adoption will assist CCT to achieve capability level 2.

A capability level 3 process is characterised as a 'defined process.' A defined process is a managed (capability level 2) process that is tailored from the organisation's set of standard processes according to the organisation's tailoring guidelines.

It contributes work products, measures, and other process-improvement information to the organisational process. A critical distinction between a managed process and a defined process is the scope of the process descriptions, standards, and procedures. In software terms, capability level 3 is achieved when a defined engineering process is in place so that the process of software development (not just its management) is consistent and standard. At this level of capability, the organisation is interested in deploying standard processes that are proven and that therefore take less time and money than continually writing and deploying new processes. Another critical distinction is that a defined process is described in more detail and performed more rigorously than a managed process. CCT does not appear to be at this level at the moment. It could be argued that the problems in requirements functionality highlighted by Tony Osunda would not happen in a defined process.

A capability level 4 process is characterised as a 'quantitatively managed process.' A quantitatively managed process is a defined (capability level 3) process that is controlled using statistical and other quantitative techniques. Quantitative objectives for quality and process performance are established and used as criteria in managing the process. The quality and process performance are understood in statistical terms and are managed throughout the life of the process. A critical distinction between a defined process and a quantitatively managed process is the predictability of

BPP
LEARNING MEDIA

the process performance. A defined process only provides qualitative predictability. Clearly, CCT is not at this level yet. However, statistical analysis of faults, perhaps using Six Sigma principles, could deliver important quality improvements. The measurement of quality is fundamental to this level. Hence, the organisation must consider some of the issues raised in the answer to part a) of this question.

A capability level 5 process is characterised as an 'optimising process.' An optimising process is a quantitatively managed (capability level 4) process that is changed and adapted to meet relevant current and projected business objectives. An optimising process focuses on continually improving the process performance through both incremental and innovative technological improvements. A critical distinction between a quantitatively managed process and an optimising process is that the optimising process is continuously improved by addressing common causes of process variation. In a process that is optimised, common causes of process variation are addressed by changing that process. The process of continuous process improvement through quantitative feedback from the process itself is clearly not happening in CCT at present.

12 Project initiation

Leadership style

(a)   The leadership style of the manager is tending to be autocratic; that is team members are being told what to do without the opportunity to discuss the decisions being made. This leadership style tends to be appropriate for staff who need a lot of guidance through a project.

(b)   In this situation, most of the staff have professional qualifications, indicating that they are able to think though problems for themselves and monitor their own work effectively. A more appropriate management style would be participative. Dave could discuss the work to be done and then let staff carry out this work. This approach would benefit staff by providing them with more responsibility and benefit Dave by freeing up more time to monitor the overall progress of the project.

Lack of communication

(a)   The cancelling of project meetings can have an adverse effect on morale, as well as making communication between the team members more difficult. While it appears that more work will be carried out on the project, if staff feel that they are not being communicated to, or that they cannot discuss problems, then overall work efficiently is likely to suffer.

(b)   This problem is easy to resolve; Dave should re-introduce the team meetings and apologise for making the mistake of cancelling them in the first place. This will provide an appropriate channel of communication and help team members realise it was not their fault that the meetings were cancelled.

Lack of project updates

(a)   The other problem with cancelling team meetings is that project team members will not be aware of how the project is progressing overall. Team members may not feel motivated to work harder if they perceive that other members are not 'pulling their weight'. The possibility of conflicts within the team suggest that morale and trust may be low, and so motivation may be an issue.

(b)   Re-introducing the team meetings will assist communication and help all team members to see how the project is progressing. When all team members can see that everyone is working hard, then this will have a positive impact on morale and the overall amount of work being done.

Accountability for errors

(a)   Making team members accountable for errors is acceptable, where those members made mistakes in the first place. However, in this situation, the 'trainee' systems analysts were not responsible for a large percentage of the analysis work as this was carried out by the previous analysts.

(b)   Dave should really be grateful that these two team members are attempting to continue this important work, and not place hindrances in their way. An appropriate way of maintaining motivation would be to simply ask for explanation of any errors found; accountability for those errors can be decided later, if necessary.

Conflicts within the team

(a)   The number of small disputes within the team indicate that working relationships are not good. These problems will tend to affect overall communication and working efficiently within the team, as members will not feel that they can discuss problems with each other.

(b)   In this situation, Dave is wrong to ignore the problem; his team is already behind schedule and trying to hide the problem is more likely to make it worse. Dave must attempt to resolve the conflicts in some way, preferably by meeting and discussing with the team members why the conflicts are arising.

If the problems cannot be resolved, the project will continue to fall behind schedule. The conflicts and the lack of trained analysts may indicate that the project deadlines need to be moved, or the project cancelled until a full working team with good relationships can be used.

13 Educational Institution

> **Top tips.** The key to (a) was recognising the range of requirements that the Institution now has to fulfil – the needs of different stakeholders and the different objectives that should be met. You would have limited the marks you could earn if you had not discussed publicity of objectives. In (b) we have provided answers for all the measures, although you were only asked to discuss a selection. You need to think carefully about what could distort the measures used and how they might prompt action.

(a)   **Different stakeholders**

At present the government is the most important **external stakeholder**. However the government will become less important and private sector users more important as the proportion of income derived from private sector courses increases. In addition the Institution will also have to take into account the interests of staff (internal stakeholders) and public sector students.

Links between financing and objectives

The cash limits set by the government relate to the **effectiveness** of the Institution's operations. The limits that the Institution has to meet are determined by what its outputs are in terms of research publications and quality. The Institution will have to take into account the methods of **measuring** these non-financial objectives.

Use of finance

Fulfilling the government's requirements (and therefore obtaining finance) is the most important current objective. However the Institution should also consider how it makes the best use of the finance it obtains, and here financial objectives become important. It should be looking to **minimise costs** as far as possible. The Institution should have the objective of choosing the **most economical** option that does not compromise the achievement of the non-financial objectives. The Institution should also have the objective that the **expenditure** it undertakes produces the **maximum return** in terms of meeting the non-financial objectives.

Level of investment

The Institution also needs to consider how much to spend on **long-term investment** rather than spend its entire budget on short-term requirements. If the Institution does not invest in upgrading facilities, over time teaching and research quality will suffer as the best staff move to other institutions with better facilities, and the Institution fails to fulfil more demanding expectations of quality.

Advantages of publicising objectives

Publicising the above objectives seems unexceptionable, as the Institution will be demonstrating that it is trying to achieve **value for money** from its operations. Likewise publicising an **investment target** will indicate to prospective teachers and students the Institution's recognition that it needs to allocate resources to ensure that it keeps up with changing views on what constitutes **excellence.**

Disadvantages of publicising objectives

The main problem with publicising objectives is that the Institution may be judged on the basis of objectives which it does not have the freedom to set. As well as fulfilling government requirements on effectiveness, the Institution may also need to take into account **other government guidelines**, for example those relating to mix of students. In addition publicising objectives may **highlight conflicts** between serving the needs of the public sector and serving the needs of private sector clients.

(b) **Value added**

Value added can be defined in financial terms as **sales revenues** less **the cost of running courses** (lecturers' fees, costs of producing material, costs of facilities used). Sales revenues is not however the only measure of the success of an Educational Institution. Better measures may be percentages of students **passing their exams**. For non-exam private sector courses the measure should ideally relate to **enhanced job performance**.

Use of value added

The Institution will undoubtedly pay attention to revenues, but it will also need to measure the benefits students have gained from its courses. Benefits can be measured in a variety of ways; for non-exam courses they could take the form of students demonstrating improved skills or knowledge at the end of the course, for example by giving a presentation. Data about all the **costs directly related** to the courses will also be needed. Sophisticated measures such as **shareholder value added** can be used to measure the impact of **fixed and working capital investment**, and the Institution's **required rate of return**.

Profitability

Profitability can be used to **measure the returns** that the **resources input** are generating, **relative** to the **sales** made. Measured in these terms, profit measures by themselves do not take account of the **investment** used to generate the profits.

Use of profitability

Profits may be distorted by the **accounting policies**, the **method** used for **allocating the costs** of running the Institution or depreciation. Depreciation charges may be particularly problematic if many of the assets have not been purchased on the open market but provided by the government, and have **no resale value**. Provided though that profits are calculated on a **consistent basis** over the five year period, the **trend of profits** should indicate the Institution's progress towards its targets.

Profits should also be used in conjunction with measures of **quality**. If profits have been **increased** by **cutting costs** and running poorer quality courses, in time the increase may be negated by the **fall in turnover** resulting from customers looking elsewhere for higher quality training.

Profitability measures can also influence the **range** and **frequency** of courses run, with the **most profitable** courses being run more often. However past profits may not be the **best indication** of future prospects, and focusing on the performance of individual courses may **not highlight** the **links** between them.

Return on investment

Return on investment is calculated by **dividing profits** by the **value of assets used**.

Use of return on investment

Again the profit figures used may be subject to distortion, but return on investment does at least take into account the **resources needed** to generate profits. However the figures might be distorted by the methods used to **allocate assets**. Provided though the methods used are consistent, return on investment can be used as an indication of changing efficiency levels over time. Its use may however **restrict investment**, as managers seek to keep down levels of capital employed; this may not be in the Institution's best interests as it is trying to expand its courses programme.

Competitive position

There are various measures of competitive position that may be valuable to the Institution. These include the **number and variety of courses** offered by competitors, also the extent to which competitors are introducing **new courses,** the **standard of courses** offered and the **pricing structure** of courses.

Use of competitive position

The Institution can **benchmark** competitors by sending its **staff** on **competitors' courses**, and getting them to report on the standards of teaching, material and facilities. The feedback provided should indicate the Institution in what areas its **own courses** need to be **improved** to match those offered by competitors. Benchmarking may also highlight **strengths** of the Institution's courses compared with its competitors, and these **strengths** can be **emphasised** in **marketing literature.**

Customer satisfaction

Customer satisfaction is likely to be a key measure for the Institution. If customers are satisfied with the courses provided, they are likely to **book further courses** and also **recommend the courses** to others.

Use of customer satisfaction

The Institution can obtain feedback from customers **by review forms** at the end of every class. These should allow participants to **rank different aspects** of the courses (quality of teaching, quality of material, facilities provided). **Targets** could be set for the marks that should be achieved. These targets could be increased over time, and also improvements made to courses that failed to reach the targets. Alternative methods of assessing how customers' needs have been met include **internal peer reviews**, **quality audits**, and obtaining **feedback** from **private sector participants' employers**.

Another way of measuring satisfaction is to track the **level of bookings** from **previous participants** on Institution courses. In a competitive market, customers will only book again if they are happy with what they have received in the past.

Market share

Market share measures the **percentage share** that an organisation has in the **total market** for a good or service. It measures the **success** of the **sales performance**, **pricing strategy** and **product quality**.

Use of market share

The Institution will need to research who offers similar courses and **ascertain numbers** who go. The courses offered by others need to be tracked over time. In order to achieve its growth targets, it may be better for the Institution to concentrate on expanding courses in areas in which it currently has **low market share**, since there may be potential to attract customers away from competitors. **Market share targets** may be set as **subsidiary targets** to **growth targets**.

14 Coxford Doors

> **Top tips**. This rather unrealistic scenario turns the situation in the typical UK family run business on its head: one would normally find such a business falling behind because its autocratic management style and **power culture** were unsuited to a rapidly changing environment. Nevertheless, this question is a gift to the reasonably well prepared candidate. It is *almost* an invitation to write down all you know about participation and change management. Almost – but not quite: you must *always* relate your answer to the scenario!

This company seems to have operated more like a soviet than a business. No doubt there has been much job-satisfaction, but the company's ability to compete and add value has deteriorated.

A participatory style of management has been shown in many studies to enhance personal **motivation** and **commitment** to the organisation's mission. This occurs via the process of **internalisation**, whereby the members of the workforce adopt the corporate goal as their personal goal. This can lead to better industrial relations, higher quality and better service. However, there is no conclusive evidence that such an approach necessarily leads to improved overall performance. This is borne out by the situation at Coxford Doors.

Andrew Smith's style of management is likely to bring the focus that has been missing in the past. He will no doubt speed up the decision making process (probably by making most decisions himself) plan effectively and issue clear instructions. Confusion and delay should be reduced and control enhanced. This will improve the business's responsiveness and ability to satisfy customers.

However, Andrew Smith is likely to encounter resistance from a work force used to proceeding according to its own ideas of what is appropriate. Morale and loyalty are both likely to suffer from the loss of autonomy. There is likely to be a lack of co-operation and, possibly, active resistance to the new order. The commercial position might deteriorate further as a result.

Even if there is acceptance that the trading position demands change it is unlikely to be wholehearted. A strong undercurrent of resentment may be created, resurfacing at some time in the future, perhaps when the commercial situation has improved.

Routine changes are harder to sell than **transformational** ones if they are perceived to be unimportant and not survival-based.

Culture change is perhaps hardest of all, especially if it involves basic assumptions. This is certainly the case at Coxford Doors. However, the necessary precondition for change are in place. Andrew Smith is himself an **outsider**, prepared to challenge and expose, in a visible way, the existing behaviour pattern; his appointment will act as a **trigger**; and **alterations to the power structure** will be an inherent part of his actions.

The unfreeze stage is likely to include extensive **communication** and **consultation processes**, but the objective must be kept in sight; concern for proper treatment of employees must not be allowed to subvert the overall aim.

Change is the second stage of the process and is mainly concerned with introducing the new, desirable behaviours and approaches. This will involve retraining and practice to build up familiarity and experience. Individuals must be encouraged to take ownership of the new ways of doing things. For this to happen they must be shown to work.

Refreeze is the final stage, involving consolidation and reinforcement of the new behaviour. Positive or negative reinforcement may be used, with praise, reward and sanctions applied as necessary.

It will be important for Andrew Smith to retain **control of the process** at all times, since the company's history of participative management will tend to undermine his move towards a firmer style. He must make it clear from the outset that change must take place, while remaining flexible on the detail and the style of its introduction. It would be advisable to aim for an intermediate style of management, in which the workforce retain a voice. Operational control must be improved, but it should not be necessary to move to a completely autocratic way of doing things.

15 Auto Direct

Top tips. You must think hard about the wording of this question. Superficially, it asks you for a summary of change management strategies in a particular context, which would be a large job to do properly, but offers only twelve marks. The implication is that you must not descend into too much detail about any particular model or approach.

Managing Director, Auto Direct

Date

Report: Change management strategies and methods

The change that you are contemplating, while extensive, is incremental and does not involve the transformation of your organisation. It therefore falls into the category of **adaptation**, which implies that you may proceed step by step and leave your basic assumptions and approach unchanged.

It would be a very worthwhile exercise to consider some of the factors that might affect the success of your programme of change. Chief among these are likely to be the various human factors present in your staff.

Presumably you will include some element of promotion and cross-posting of your existing workforce in order to provide a basis of experience at your new sites, so you should consider the degree of **readiness** (or willingness) of your staff to undertake the development you plan.

You should also consider your company's managerial **capability** and **capacity** in terms of resources to undertake change. The former depends largely on past experience

While good **project management** of a programme of change is very important, it is the **human aspects of the change management process** that are crucial. This is because change will not happen unless people make it happen. A number of strategies are proposed for dealing with this aspect of change management.

Participation in decision-making is sometimes recommended as a way of improving motivation generally and may be useful in the context of change. It is probably advantageous to involve staff in decisions affecting them, their conditions and their work processes and at least hear what they have to say. However, participation is not a universal panacea and can be very **time consuming**. Also, the normal **management style and culture** of the organisation must be considered. It is probably inappropriate to promote participation exclusively in the context of change if staff are not used to it: their main reaction may be one of suspicious cynicism.

An **autocratic** approach, imposing change by means of **coercion** can work reasonably well in some circumstances, especially where the staff expect nothing else. It has the benefit of saving time and is probably the **best approach in times of crisis**. However, it does have the weakness of ignoring the experience and knowledge that staff may be able to offer.

In any event, **communication** with staff about the proposed change is commonly regarded as an essential process. Ideally, information will be provided as early as possible, explaining why change is necessary and the course that will be followed. Anxiety, particularly over job security, is common during change and a programme of communication and education can go a long way to allay it.

Sometimes neither participation nor coercion can resolve all problems and **negotiation** may be required. This is often the case when the labour force is strongly organised and when there is disagreement between management factions as to the best course to follow.

This has been a brief overview of some approaches to change management. You will no doubt be in a position to decide which are most appropriate to the circumstances of Auto Direct.

16 Lionel Cartwright

Top tips. It would be possible to take issue with the presumption that Lionel makes use of emergent strategies. Such strategies develop out of patterns of behaviour and *ad hoc* choices, perhaps made elsewhere in the organisation than at the strategic apex. Lionel's approach is more a kind of **freewheeling opportunism**. He spots an opportunity and then exploits it as best he can. No one else is involved and the process is as deliberate as he can make it within the limitations of his knowledge and experience.

In fact, in his own suggested solution, the Examiner who set this question talked about 'emergent or opportunistic strategy formulation' as though the two terms were interchangeable.

The rational approach to formulating strategy attempts to take into account all the factors that might bear on a business's strategic position by working through a series of linked processes. These commence with the definition of overall objectives and include consideration of the various aspects of the environment; assessment of the business's strengths, weaknesses and other characteristics; the generation and assessment of possible courses of action; and the establishment and operation of appropriate control mechanisms.

While exhaustive and logical, this approach is rather cumbersome and lacking in flexibility. As a result, it can become a recipe for rigidity, inhibiting the flow of strategic ideas. Typically, this occurs when too much faith is placed in the inevitability of the model's arriving at the only correct answer to the strategic problem. The assumption that there is a single acceptable route to a successful strategy tends to stifle invention and ignores the potential of hunch, expedient and opportunism.

A more flexible approach will exploit the potential of these factors, allowing strategy to develop or emerge in a less rigid fashion. Such an approach is clearly more in Lionel's style. He has made a series of successful strategic decisions, largely, it would seem, without entering into any extensive planning procedure.

It is fairly easy to discern why Lionel has adopted this approach to strategy. First, it is consistent with his self-image as an entrepreneur, quick to spot and seize profitable opportunities. His record of success in building up his capital must be a great satisfaction to him.

Connected with this is his apparent dislike of working in close co-operation with others. Lionel prefers to be sole master of his destiny, rather than one of a team; he has chosen to rely on his instincts.

He has not provided himself with the specialist advisers whose input would be necessary for a more considered approach. Indeed, he is probably the sort of person who would be rather bad at leading such a group.

So far Lionel has enjoyed success with his opportunistic approach but he should be aware that it has its disadvantages.

Any venture involving more than a few people in face-to-face contact with one another requires a degree of planning if it is to run smoothly. Lionel's plans for expansion beyond his current 4 outlets will require the acquisition and integration of significant resources. Quite apart from the potential need to raise further finance, which will be difficult without a clear business plan, Lionel may find his ad hoc approach hampering his ability to expand smoothly.

Another very important practical advantage of a planned, cohesive approach is that control becomes easier and more definite. If Lionel is unsure of just what he can realistically expect to achieve, he will have little ability to assess success or failure, since he will have no objective yardstick.

An allied problem over the longer term is that a clear vision of where he is going would allow Lionel to develop a depth and breadth of relevant knowledge and expertise. At the moment, he has no potential to develop his operations by learning from experience, except in the very widest sense. His experience in road haulage is unlikely to be very useful in sourcing high-quality fruits and vegetables, for example.

A final problem for Lionel to ponder is this: if he wishes to expand significantly, he will inevitably have to increase the number of his employees and eventually to hire at least a few with significant professional skills. His ability to attract, retain and work through these people is likely to depend in part on their having a clear idea of what they are supposed to be doing and where the organisation is going. So long as he is able to take all the decisions himself, the absence of a clear corporate plan will not matter so much; when significant delegation can no longer be avoided, it may seriously hamper his progress.

Pilot Paper

> **BPP Note.** The following pages contain the pilot paper questions and answers produced by the ACCA.

Pilot paper

Paper P3

Business Analysis

Time allowed

Reading and planning: 15 minutes
Writing: 3 hours

This paper is divided into two sections:

Section A – This ONE question is compulsory and MUST be attempted

Section B – TWO questions ONLY to be attempted

Do NOT open this paper until instructed by the supervisor.

During reading and planning time only the question paper may be annotated. You must NOT write in your answer booklet until instructed by the supervisor.

This question paper must not be removed from the examination hall.

Warning

The pilot paper cannot cover all of the syllabus nor can it include examples of every type of question that will be included in the actual exam. You may see questions in the exam that you think are more difficult than any you see in the pilot paper.

Section A – The ONE question in this section is compulsory and MUST be attempted.

The following information should be used when answering question 1.

The case study of this Business Analysis pilot paper is based on the one examined in Paper 3.5 – Strategic Business Planning and Development in June 2004. Slight amendments have been made to the scenario, questions and answers to reflect the Business Analysis syllabus and emphasis.

1   Introduction

Network Management Systems (NMS) is a privately owned hi-tech business set up in a location near London in 1993. NMS is the brainchild of a Canadian computer engineer, Ray Edwards. Ray is a classic hi-tech entrepreneur, constantly searching for ways to exploit technological opportunities and unafraid to take the risks associated with high technology start-ups. NMS's first product was a digital error detection box able to 'listen' to computer signals and detect faults. The original box, designed by Ray, was built on his kitchen table and manufactured in a garage. Ray is a flamboyant character and a committed entrepreneur. In his words an entrepreneur is "someone willing to work 18 hours a day for themselves … to avoid working eight hours a day for someone else!"

Structure of the business and key product areas

By 2006 NMS employed 75 full time employees in a new, purpose built factory and office unit. These employees were a mix of technically qualified engineers working in research and development (R&D), factory staff manufacturing and assembling the products and a small sales and service support team. In 2006, NMS had three distinct product/service areas.

One of the three products NMS produced was data communication components which it sold directly to original equipment manufacturers (OEMs) that used these components in their hardware. Both the OEMs and their customers were predominantly large international companies. NMS had established a good reputation for the quality and performance of its components, which were also competitively priced. However, NMS had less than 1% share of the UK market in this sector and faced competition from more than twenty suppliers, most of who also competed internationally. Furthermore, one of NMS's OEM customers accounted for 40% of its sales. The European market for data communications equipment had increased from $3.3 billion in 1999 to $8.0 billion in 2006. Forecasts for 2007 and beyond, predict growth from increased sales to currently installed networks rather than from the installation of new networks. The maturity of the technology means that product lifecycles are becoming shorter. Success comes from producing large volumes of relatively low priced reliable components. However, all new components have to be approved by the relevant government approval body in each country being supplied. Approval for new data communication equipment is both costly and time consuming.

NMS's second product area was network management systems – hence the name of the company. Fault detection systems were supplied directly to a small number of large end users such as banks, public utility providers and global manufacturers. NMS recognised the unique configuration of each customer and so it customised its product to meet specific needs and requirements. They have pioneered a "modular building block" design, which allows the customer to adapt standard system modules to fit their exact networking requirements. NMS products focused on solving network management problems and the success of its products was reflected in the award of the prestigious Government Award for Technology for "technological innovation in the prevention of computer data communication downtime". This was recognition of the excellence of the R&D engineers who developed the software and related hardware. It further enhanced NMS's reputation and enabled it to become a successful niche player in this low volume market with gross margins in excess of 40%. NMS only faces two or three competitors in a specialist market where there is no need to gain government approval for new products and systems.

Finally, the complexity of NMS products means that technical support is a third key business area. NMS has established a reputation for excellent technical support, reflecting Ray's continuing concern with customer care. However, it is increasingly difficult and costly to maintain this support because the company lacks a national network. All technical support is provided from its headquarters. This contrasts with the national and international distributed service structure operated by its large, international competitors.

Emerging problems

NMS's growth has made Ray increasingly concerned about the ability of NMS to identify market trends, scan its competitive environment and create marketing strategies and plans. NMS's market and sales planning only covers the year ahead. Larger competitors invest heavily in market research analysis and customer relationship marketing. Business-to-business marketing is becoming an increasingly complex and sophisticated activity in this sector.

Accurate sales forecasting is also a key input into production planning and scheduling. NMS manufactures 40% of the components used in its products. The rest of the components, including semiconductors and microprocessors, are bought in from global suppliers. Serious production problems result from periodic component shortages, creating significant delays in manufacturing, assembly, and customer deliveries. Furthermore, the growth of NMS has outstripped the largely manual control systems designed to support its production and sales operation.

Ray is acutely aware of his key role as founder and chairman of the firm. He is also finding the skills and attributes necessary for founding and growing the business are not appropriate in a mature business. He is heavily reliant on his extrovert personality and his ability to muddle through with informal, flexible systems. The limitation of this approach is now beginning to show. He is finding it increasingly difficult to cope with the day-to-day demands of running the business while at the same time planning its future. Functional departments in the shape of sales and marketing, technical (R&D), manufacturing and administration are in place but strategic planning, such as there is, is very much his responsibility.

Recruitment of high calibre staff is also a problem – NMS's small size and location means that it struggles to attract the key personnel necessary for future growth. Ray feels pressure on him to either develop the necessary skills himself, or to develop the right people with the right skills. In Ray's words, starting a business is like "building your own airplane and then teaching yourself how to fly".

One particular skill in short supply is the financial capability of dealing with growth. His negotiations with bankers and other financial intermediaries have become increasingly difficult and time consuming. The financial control information required to support growth and, more recently, to ensure survival is often inadequate. However, 2006 had started well, with NMS approached as a target for a possible acquisition by a major data communications company. The opportunity to realise some of the equity in the business had considerable appeal. Unfortunately, while protracted negotiations were taking place, a downturn in the global economy occured. Orders for NMS's products fell and the banks and venture capitalists supporting NMS through overdraft and long-term investment became much less sympathetic. The final insult occurred when Ray was approached by a venture capitalist with a management buyout proposal put together with NMS's financial director and sales manager. The value placed on the business was a derisory £50K. Ray was angry and hurt by the size of the offer and also at the disloyalty of his senior staff in seeking to buy the business. To make matters worse the uncertainty over the future of the business has led to a number of key members of staff deciding to leave the company. The financial director and sales manager are still both in post, but their future plans are uncertain. Financial data for NMS is presented in Table 1.

Ray's future at NMS

Ray is currently considering his future at NMS. He has identified three main exit options. The first is to personally lead the company out of its current problems, which he largely attributes to global economic slowdown, and to launch the business on the stock exchange as soon as its economic position improves. His second option is to sell the business for a figure which more accurately reflects its real value and to walk away and reflect on his future. His final option is to seek acquisition by one of his large customers (or competitors) and so become part of a much larger organisation. In such circumstances he would offer to stay on and develop NMS within the structures imposed by a parent organisation. By nature a fighter, the recent uncertainties over ownership and gloomy forecasts for the global economy have made him seriously reflect on his own priorities. His hands-on approach and involvement with all aspects of the business seems increasingly inappropriate for handling the problems of a hi-tech business such as NMS.

Table 1: Financial data for Network Management Systems

	2004	2005	2006	2007 (forecast)
Sales	£'000	£'000	£'000	£'000
UK sales	4,500	6,300	6,930	6,235
Export sales	300	500	650	520
Total sales	4,800	6,800	7,580	6,755
Cost of sales	2,640	3,770	4,550	4,320
Gross margin	2,160	3,030	3,030	2,435
Expenses				
Administration	500	630	700	665
Distribution	715	940	945	885
Marketing	50	60	70	70
R&D	495	590	870	690
Overheads	200	280	320	325
Operating profit	200	530	125	-200
Sales Interest paid	25	120	150	165
Net profit	175	410	-25	-365
Financing				
Long-term liabilities	160	750	1,000	1,100
Share capital and reserves	375	605	600	575
Other information				
Employees	50	60	75	60
% of orders late	5	7	10	6
Order book	4,725	4,150	3,150	2,500

Required:

(a) Assess the macro-environment of NMS by undertaking a **PESTEL** analysis. (10 marks)

(b) Using appropriate models and financial and quantitative data from the scenario, provide an environmental and financial analysis of NMS, highlighting problem areas. (25 marks)

(c) Ray is considering three main exit options from the business as it currently exists. Assess each of the three identified exit options in terms of their ability to solve the problems highlighted in your analysis and in terms of Ray's future role in the business. (15 marks)

(50 marks)

Section B – TWO questions ONLY to be attempted

2   The Environment Management Society (EMS) was established in 1999 by environment practitioners who felt that environmental management and audit should have its own qualification. EMS has its own Board who report to a Council of eight members. Policy is made by the Board and ratified by Council. EMS is registered as a private limited entity.

EMS employs staff to administer its qualification and to provide services to its members. The qualification began as one certificate, developed by the original founding members of the Society. It has since been developed, by members and officers of the EMS, into a four certificate scheme leading to a Diploma. EMS employs a full-time chief examiner who is responsible for setting the certificate examinations which take place monthly in training centres throughout the country. No examinations are currently held in other countries.

If candidates pass all four papers they can undertake an oral Diploma examination. If they pass this oral they are eligible to become members. All examinations are open-book one hour examinations, preceded by 15 minutes reading time. At a recent meeting, EMS Council rejected the concept of computer-based assessment. They felt that competence in this area was best assessed by written examination answers.

Candidate numbers for the qualification have fallen dramatically in the last two years. The Board of EMS has concluded that this drop reflects the maturing marketplace in the country. Many people who were practitioners in environmental management and audit when the qualification was introduced have now gained their Diploma. The stream of new candidates and hence members is relatively small.

Consequently, the EMS Board has suggested that they should now look to attract international candidates and it has targeted countries where environmental management and audit is becoming more important. It is now formulating a strategy to launch the qualification in India, China and Russia.

However, any strategy has to recognise that both the EMS Board and the Council are very cautious and notably risk-averse. EMS is only confident about its technical capability within a restricted definition of environmental management and audit. Attempts to look at complementary qualification areas (such as soil and water conservation) have been swiftly rejected by Council as being non-core areas and therefore outside the scope of their expertise.

Required:

Internal development, acquisitions and strategic alliances are three development methods by which an organisation's strategic direction can be pursued.

(a) Explain the principles of internal development and discuss how appropriate this development method is to EMS.   (8 marks)

(b) Explain the principles of acquisitions and discuss how appropriate this development method is to EMS.
                                                                                                                (8 marks)

(c) Explain the principles of strategic alliances and discuss how appropriate this development method is to EMS.   (9 marks)

(25 marks)

3   CCT Computer Systems plc specialises in the development and implementation of software for the logistics industry. After experiencing a number of years of growth and profitability the company is continuing to report growth in turnover but, for the last five quarters, it has also reported small losses. An investigation into this has revealed that costs have risen greatly in systems development and support and consequently margins have been eroded in recently completed projects. It appears that this trend is going to continue. Many people within the company attribute this worsening financial performance to a perceived reduction in software quality. Here are three testimonies received during the investigation

Amelia Platt: Software Development Manager CCT Computer Systems plc
"You have to remember that the original logistics system was developed by Ilya Borisova (the founder of CCT) and three of his friends from university days. They did not build the software with expansion or maintenance in mind. Also, it is difficult to know what some of the programs actually do, so making changes is a nightmare. Programmers make changes to program code without really knowing what the knock-on effect will be."

Tony Osunda: General Manager QANDO logistics – a major customer
"We feel that the last project was most unsatisfactory. We specified our requirements very carefully but the delivered system did not work the way we wanted. We found it cumbersome to use and key areas of functionality were either wrong or missing altogether. After implementation, we asked for a number of changes so that the system would work as it should. We were originally asked to pay for these changes but we pointed out that they weren't really changes – they were things we had asked for all along. Eventually, CCT backed down and so we got the changes for free. The system works fine now, but it has been delivered late and we are still seeking compensation for this."

Carlos Theroux: One of the original programmers of the CCT logistics software solution: Now lead programmer CCT Computer Systems plc
"It is no fun here anymore. When we were smaller we could all dive in and solve the problems. When I joined we had three programmers, now we have one hundred and thirty. What do they all do? There is no work ethic. We all used to stay over until we got the problem solved. Now there is documentation, documentation and documentation. We have now adopted a formal project management method, more documentation! I am not sure this place suits me anymore."

Required:

(a) A perceived reduction in software quality is blamed by many people for the decline in profitability at CCT. Discuss the importance and characteristics of software quality and explain how each of these characteristics might be measured.

(10 marks)

(b) Explain the levels within the Capability Maturity Model Integration (CMMI) process and discuss their implications for CCT.

(15 marks)

(25 marks)

4   DRB Electronic Services operates in a high labour cost environment in Western Europe and imports electronic products from the Republic of Korea. It re-brands and re-packages them as DRB products and then sells them to business and domestic customers in the local geographical region. Its only current source of supply is ISAS electronics based in a factory on the outskirts of Seoul, the capital of the Republic of Korea. DRB regularly places orders for ISAS products through the ISAS web-site and pays for them by credit card. As soon as the payment is confirmed ISAS automatically e-mails DRB a confirmation of order, an order reference number and likely shipping date. When the order is actually despatched, ISAS send DRB a notice of despatch e-mail and a container reference number. ISAS currently organises all the shipping of the products. The products are sent in containers and then trans-shipped to EIF, the logistics company used by ISAS to distribute its products. EIF then delivers the products to the DRB factory. Once they arrive, they are quality inspected and products that pass the inspection are re-branded as DRB products (by adding appropriate logos) and packaged in specially fabricated DRB boxes. These products are then stored ready for sale. All customer sales are from stock. Products that fail the inspection are returned to ISAS.

Currently 60% of sales are made to domestic customers and 40% to business customers. Most domestic customers pick up their products from DRB and set them up themselves. In contrast, most business customers ask DRB to set up the electronic equipment at their offices, for which DRB makes a small charge. DRB currently advertises its products in local and regional newspapers. DRB also has a web site which provides product details. Potential customers can enquire about the specification and availability of products through an e-mail facility in the web site. DRB then e-mails an appropriate response directly to the person making the enquiry. Payment for products cannot currently be made through the web site.

Feedback from existing customers suggests that they particularly value the installation and support offered by the company. The company employs specialist technicians who (for a fee) will install equipment in both homes and offices. They will also come out and troubleshoot problems with equipment that is still under warranty. DRB also offer a helpline and a back to base facility for customers whose products are out of warranty. Feedback from current customers suggests that this support is highly valued. One commented that "it contrasts favourably with your large customers who offer support through impersonal off-shore call centres and a time-consuming returns policy". Customers can also pay for technicians to come on-site to sort out problems with out-of-warranty equipment.

DRB now plans to increase their product range and market share. It plans to grow from its current turnover of £5m per annum to £12m per annum in two years time. Dilip Masood, the owner of DRB, believes that DRB must change its business model if it is to achieve this growth. He believes that these changes will also have to tackle problems associated with

–   Missing, or potentially missing shipments. Shipments can only be tracked through contacting the shipment account holder, ISAS, and on occasions they have been reluctant or unable to help. The trans-shipment to EIF has also caused problems and this has usually been identified as the point where goods have been lost. ISAS does not appear to be able to reliably track the relationship between the container shipment and the Waybills used in the EIF system.

–   The likely delivery dates of orders, the progress of orders and the progress of shipments is poorly specified and monitored. Hence deliveries are relatively unpredictable and this can cause congestion problems in the delivery bay.

Dilip also recognises that growth will mean that the company has to sell more products outside its region and the technical installation and support so valued by local customers will be difficult to maintain. He is also adamant that DRB will continue to import only fully configured products. It is not interested in importing components and assembling them. DRB also does not wish to build or invest in assembly plants overseas or to commit to a long-term contract with one supplier.

Required:

(a) **Draw the primary activities of DRB on a value chain. Comment on the significance of each of these activities and the value that they offer to customers.**   (9 marks)

(b) **Explain how DRB might re-structure its upstream supply chain to achieve the growth required by DRB and to tackle the problems that Dilip Masood has identified.**   (10 marks)

(c) **Explain how DRB might re-structure its downstream supply chain to achieve the growth required.**   (6 marks)

(25 marks)

Pilot Paper P3
Business Analysis

At the Professional level it is not always possible to publish a suggested answer which is fully comprehensive. Credit will be given to candidates for points not included in the suggested answers but which nevertheless, are relevant to the questions.

The suggested answers presented below give more detail than would be expected from a candidate under examination conditions. The answers are intended to provide guidance on the approach required from candidates, and on the range and depth of knowledge, which could be written by an excellent candidate.

1   (a)   The PESTEL framework may be used to explore the macro-environmental influences that might affect an organisation. There are six main influences in the framework: political, economic, social, technological, environmental and legal. However, these types are inter-linked and so, for example, political developments and environmental requirements are often implemented through enacting legislation. Candidates will be given credit for defining the main macro-environmental influences that affect NMS, rather than the classification of these influences into the PESTEL framework.

Political – NMS is situated in a country with a relatively stable political system. Like many industrialised countries, all political parties in this country appear to value and promote technology. Tax incentives and grants are often given to companies to invest in technology and research and development. These incentives are not only available to NMS, but also (in the United Kingdom) to their customers. This has helped fuel the growth in the data communications market and although evidence suggests that this growth is tailing off, investment is still significant. Government itself is a major investor in communications technology, often using such investments to facilitate economic growth in this sector. However, most governments are also anxious to set standards that any company supplying equipment that links into the national telecommunications network have to meet. There is evidence of government control in the shape of the approvals process. This may arise from fears about technical reliability and compatibility but it may also be designed to hinder competition from foreign suppliers. Finally, government may promote the recognition of technology through an awards scheme. NMS has received such recognition through a Government Award for Technology.

Economic – again a significant factor, in that the stage in the economic or business cycle can clearly affect buying decisions. The case study suggests that 2006 has seen a slight downturn in the UK and international economy and a consequent slowing down in large customers' commitment to long-term investment. The bad news is that customers can postpone such investment. The good news is that if innovation creates products and systems that bring cost and communication advantages to customers then eventually they will have to invest in them. Wage rates remain high in the United Kingdom and NMS may wish to re-consider their commitment to manufacturing 40% of their components in the United Kingdom. Labour costs (allied to compliance costs – see below) and legal obligations makes manufacturing in the UK extremely expensive. It is likely that many of their competitors source 100% of their components abroad and only assemble their products in the UK.

Social – communication and information exchange will continue to increase with consequent implications for companies supplying the products and systems to meet these growing needs. All evidence suggests that the social use of services on such networks will increase. Hence, although demand appears to be dropping off, new social uses for telecommunication networks might spark off a new wave of economic investment.

Technological – clearly a significant factor in shaping the life cycles of existing products and the introduction of new ones. The hi-tech sector is extremely innovative, with new and improved technologies constantly emerging. NMS must scan the marketplace for such technologies and identify how such they might affect the future of their products. NMS must also consider how such emergent technologies might be used in their own products.

Environmental issues – continue to have an impact on organisations. Organisations are encouraged by politicians and by legislation to reduce their emissions and improve their re-cycling. The cost of disposal of raw materials is also increasing. There is no direct evidence of such issues in the case study scenario. However, as a manufacturing company in the United Kingdom it is highly likely that NMS will be affected by such factors.

Legal – NMS operates in a country where there are many laws defining employer responsibilities and employee rights. It is likely that regulation will continue and the NMS will, like all organisations working in the European Union (EU), have to evaluate the benefits and cost of working within such legal structures. Some organisations seek to gain advantage by moving to countries where regulation is more lax and hence avoid the compliance costs incurred by their competitors. The case study scenario suggests that NMS has significant international competitors. It is likely that some of these will be based in countries where legislative requirements are less onerous.

(b)   Michael Porter provides, through his five forces model, a useful means of analysing the competitive environment. Analysis suggests the following key factors are shaping this environment.

Bargaining power of buyers

There is evidence that large industrial customers are becoming more cost conscious and this is likely to lead to increased price negotiation with their suppliers. At the same time customers are placing a premium on quality and service. Data communications products are becoming important in virtually every area of large organisations, causing greater sensitivity to price, quality and reliability. The end users of this equipment are becoming less technically proficient and more demanding, particularly in their unwillingness to adopt products that are difficult to use.

The supplying industry is relatively fragmented and so buyers have a wide choice and can compare competitors and exert buyer power on them. Information on NMS and their competitors' products and services is easily available to potential buyers. Buyer power is therefore likely to become more significant – particularly in view of the downturn in the global economy.

It is important to recognise that NMS is competing in two discrete markets. Firstly, data communications components, where with a 1% market share, they are at best a marginal supplier. The customers are OEMs who are large industrial buyers with the ability to demand a testing combination of low prices, high quality and reliability. This is expected both in terms of component performance and even more significantly, in view of recent manufacturing and assembly problems, guaranteed delivery. A combination of circumstances suggests that OEM's have significant bargaining power in this market. The OEM who accounts for 40% on the company's current sales is in a particularly strong position.

In the second market, where network management systems are supplied to large end users, buyers appear to have less bargaining power. NMS is a significant supplier in this market place with only two or three competitors. NMS is catering for each customer's specific network needs and so each solution is to some degree a bespoke solution. This makes it much harder for buyers to compare the prices of potential suppliers, particularly given the modular design of the NMS product. Furthermore, this product represents a relatively small part of the overall cost of the end user's investment in information and communication systems. This is also likely to make such products less price sensitive and hence provides an opportunity to generate good margins.

Bargaining Power of Suppliers

Evidence from the information provided gives no real insight into the bargaining power of suppliers but the purchase of components such as semiconductors and microprocessors is likely to be from major global companies such as Intel and, as a consequence, supplier power may be very significant. NMS, as a small company, will not have the power to exert buyer pressure on its suppliers, either in terms of price or delivery. Such components form 60% of current product production and problems over deliveries and scheduling are having significant impact on the company's ability to meet customer deadlines. Clearly an audit needs to be made of supplier performance and the opportunity, or otherwise, for NMS to concentrate on suppliers able to deliver on time. However, for a small company like NMS, the supplier is in an excellent bargaining position.

Threats from New Entrants

NMS is operating in an industry where the costs of entry are significant because it is capital and knowledge intensive. NMS has shown there is a place for smaller innovative companies able to identify specialist market niches. Economies of scale compel new entrants to enter at significant output levels or suffer a cost disadvantage. The products are complex and there is likely to be a significant learning curve with costs only falling as volume builds up over time. Large international customers (such as OEMs, banks, public utilities) are likely to be cautious in moving to new suppliers.

The need for government approval of new data communications equipment creates a process that is both lengthy and expensive and this creates a significant barrier to entry. New entrants may be discouraged by the considerable uncertainty surrounding the industry – both in terms of technology, user acceptance and the R&D investment necessary to create components and systems compatible with the OEM's equipment and end user systems. Furthermore, the need to offer comprehensive support, although something of a problem to a small company such as NMS, does also create a significant barrier to new entrants.

Evidence suggests that market knowledge as an input into product design and delivery is becoming more critical and NMS's ability to create a recognised brand with its end users is creating a competitive advantage. Finally, the barriers to exit from the industry in the shape of knowledge, skills and assets which are very industry specific also reduces the attractiveness of the market place to new entrants.

Rivalry among Competitors

Very different levels of competition are being experienced in the two market places NMS is operating in. Unfortunately the financial data given does not separate out the results from each market but it is clear that the high-volume, low-margin component business offers intense competition with buyers who are able to use their size to extract favourable prices. The ability of NMS to generate better market share and margins through product innovation in this market seems highly unlikely.

Intensity of rivalry in the network management systems market is significantly less because there are only two or three competitors in this specialist market. NMS is dealing with a small number of large end users and designing products specific to their needs. In Porter's terms, NMS are adopting a focused differentiation strategy. In these low-volume, high-margin markets the emphasis has to be on increasing the volume side of the business, but at the same time making sure they have the resources to handle new customers.

Threats from Substitutes

High-tech industries are, almost by their very nature, prone to new technologies emerging that threaten and then eventually replace the established technology. Hence it is important that companies in the industry have scanning systems in place to warn of such threats. NMS will need to ensure that it has innovative new products under development which incorporate any significant technological change. There is evidence that suggests that large successful, high-tech companies are particularly vulnerable to ignoring the challenge coming from disruptive new technologies. However, NMS being small may have a competitive advantage in its ability to respond quickly and flexibly to such change.

Financial Analysis

The significant slowdown in sales growth and its predicted decline in 2007 is a major cause for concern. The extent to which this is externally determined through the economic downturn, as opposed to internal management, product and sales force failings is difficult to determine. It would be useful to compare the performance of NMS with its competitors and the market place as a whole. Export sales continue to form less than 10% of total sales and this is worrying for a company operating in a global industry. It appears from the 2007 forecast, which predicts a more significant decline in export sales than home sales

f

that nothing is being done to address this. Equally concerning is the upward drift in the cost of sales over the 2004–2006 period. Evidence from the case suggests that supplier performance and consequent production scheduling problems needs to be investigated. The inevitable result of these revenue and cost trends is a falling gross margin.

Expenses do not seem to have been controlled, increasing at a faster rate than turnover. The impact of this on net profit is all too obvious. Failure to control expenses in a period of reduced growth suggests poor management control systems and inadequate management response. The forecast for 2007 suggests an increase in overhead expenses despite the decline in sales.

Commitment to research and development (R&D) in a hi-tech business is crucial to continued product innovation and NMS have maintained an R&D: Total sales ratio of 10% or more each year. However, R&D is notoriously difficult to predict in terms of its success and the timing of breakthroughs. The commitment of NMS should be applauded, but funding it from borrowing, as is increasingly occurring, could explain some of the problems the company is having with the banks and other financial intermediaries. Again, not untypical in a hi-tech business, there is little spending on marketing, perhaps because the company is under the impression that the products sell themselves. However, NMS could point out that the marketing spend was also relatively low at a time that they were relatively successful.

Perhaps one of the most worrying performance features is the slowing down in new business being generated. In 2004 unfulfilled orders virtually matched total sales but the forecast for 2007 sees that key ratio fall to barely one-third of total sales. This issue clearly has to be addressed.

Finally, in terms of measuring performance, the balanced scorecard could be used to good effect. Financially, the current position does not augur well – growth in turnover is slowing down, profitability is falling, the debt ratio is high and stock levels are worrying.

Customer measures are mixed – the company's products are well regarded but production scheduling problems are leading to increasing waiting time for customers. Market share in data communications is small and measuring the market share in network management systems is difficult because of the bespoke nature of the product. Technical support to customers is perceived as a key business area and NMS still has an excellent reputation for customer care.

There is a mixture of signals in terms of the progress being made with internal processes. Products are innovative and the ability to tailor the network management system means that end user needs are met. However, operational and management control processes appear weak – flexible but informal. Operations have a need for more sophisticated planning and scheduling systems and although post-sales performance in the shape of technical support looks good, this appears to be expensive to maintain.

Finally, from the perspective of learning/innovation, NMS has recognised the need to grow people in order to develop the business, but seems unable to recruit and retain the right calibre of people. Failure to do so will prevent Ray from being able to delegate to subordinates and focus his energies on the strategic threats to the survival of the company. Evidence suggests that a number of key personnel have left the company, hopefully not the innovative R&D engineers who gained the company its Government Award for Technology.

(c)   The decision of the founding owner-manager to leave the business is clearly a critical one, particularly in terms of a company such as NMS where the value of the business is very much linked to the founder's vision.

Any exit strategy must be carefully planned so as to not jeopardise the future of the business. In the strategy literature, considerable attention is paid to the entry barriers that do or do not discourage the entrance of new competitors. Exit barriers receive far less attention but are very relevant to an owner-manager such as Ray looking to leave the business as a going/ growing concern and realising a return on their personal investment – financial and emotional – in the business. As identified above there are barriers to entry into the industry but unfortunately for Ray there are significant barriers to exit as well – exit in this case referring to him rather than the business. The assets of the business are not easily put to alternative use. Alternative markets for the company's products are difficult to find. Above all in knowledge based, R&D intensive businesses such as NMS, these less tangible assets are very specific to the products, markets and customers that the firm currently has.

Johnson, Scholes and Whittington offer what is now regarded as the classic framework for choosing between strategic options or in their terms determining the 'success criteria' of suitability, acceptability and feasibility in choosing between options. Using their language – 'suitability is concerned with whether a strategy addresses the circumstances in which a company is operating (its environment, its resources/competences and the expectations of its stakeholders) – the strategic position or rationale of a strategy and whether it makes sense'. Alternative options can be ranked, decision trees drawn up or scenarios used to compare the relative suitability of each option in achieving a desired position. 'Acceptability is concerned with the expected performance outcomes of a strategy', where acceptability is measured against the rewards, risk and anticipated stakeholder reactions to the chosen option. 'Feasibility is concerned with whether the organisation has the resources and competencies to deliver a strategy' – and in particular the funding flows and resource deployment capabilities associated with each option.

The three identified exit strategies and an assessment of each option against the three success criteria is given below. Comparing the three options shows the inevitable uncertainties and trade-offs associated with having to make a choice. Ray will face an opportunity cost (the value of the best alternative option not chosen) whichever option he chooses. Such choices are particularly hard in the owner-managed business where there is a need to reconcile personal goals with the well-being of the business. Essentially Ray faces a difficult choice as to when he leaves the business and his degree of involvement in helping solve its current problems – is his presence a cost or benefit to the business?

Option 1: Turnaround and going public Suitability

This is clearly an ambitious long-term strategy, which will require significant time and effort to turn the company round. It is difficult to see who else could achieve this, other than Ray, and the retention of Ray's know-how may be crucial to success. Ray will need to address how he transfers that knowledge to key managers in the business.

Acceptability

This appears to be a relatively high risk and return option, which prolongs Ray's role in the business. The reactions of customers may be favourable, the reactions of the bank and venture capitalist less so, particularly as Ray has no track record in this area. He has no experience of floating a company on a stock exchange and of meeting shareholder expectations.

Feasibility

The willingness of the financial agencies to provide the necessary funding to support the recovery is open to question and may be a function of developing a coherent recovery plan including a phased withdrawal of Ray and the identification of able managers to succeed him.

Option 2: Outright sale

Suitability

This option depends on the ability to identify a suitable buyer able to put in the necessary resources to turn the company round. Selling out is not really a strategy for recovery, as it does not address the initial strategic problems identified in the analysis. It just transfers the problems to someone else.

Acceptability

This can be seen as a medium risk-low return option, but one which allows Ray to make a reasonably swift and clean exit from the business. The reaction of Ray's customers will be crucial to the success of this strategy. Given Ray's recognition of his management limitations in a mature company, banks and other financial stakeholders might find this approach very acceptable.

Feasibility

This depends on the ability to obtain a fair price for the business and for the new owners to have the necessary funds to carry out the necessary changes to NMS and the necessary resources to cope with Ray's departure from the firm. Failure to find a buyer may mean this is not the short-term solution that Ray is looking for. The (low) valuation of their companies is always an issue for entrepreneurs. Perhaps this is what was behind the protracted negotiations with a potential suitor in 2006?

Option 3: Friendly acquisition

Suitability

The support and resources of a large customer (or competitor) company may be just what NMS needs. Ray's expertise and technical knowledge could be useful to the new holding company and so he could therefore be retained in this business for an agreed length of time. This option should address the identified weaknesses regarding staff, systems and structure if the acquisition is properly implemented.

Acceptability

This is likely to be a medium risk and return strategy with any price premium for NMS dependent on the value placed on Ray's continued contribution. Its acceptability to Ray depends on his willingness to give up control. It is likely to find favour with the financial stakeholders. The problem may be Ray's ability to work in a corporate structure, particularly in the light of his declaration that an entrepreneur is "someone willing to work 18 hours a day for themselves.... to avoid working eight hours a day for someone else!"

Feasibility

Funding issues should not be a problem given the resources of the acquirer. The key problem will be in integrating Ray and the firm into a large company environment.

Clearly this is a complex set of options for Ray to consider, and it requires him to be clear about his personal goals and objectives and how far any strategy is either helped or hindered by his presence in the firm. Each option will have a different timescale for achieving Ray's goal of exiting from the business.

2   Context

The decline in the number of people taking the qualification appears to be a reflection of the maturity of the marketplace. The large pool of unqualified environmental managers and auditors that existed when the qualification was launched has now been exploited. There are now fewer candidates taking the examinations and fewer members joining the EMS. The organisation's response to this has been to look for international markets where it can promote the qualifications it currently offers. It hopes to find large pools of unqualified environmental managers and auditors in these markets.

The scenario suggests that EMS currently has relatively limited strategic ambitions. There is no evidence that EMS plans to develop new qualifications outside its current portfolio. Indeed, attempts to look at complementary qualifications (such as soil and water conservation) have been rejected by Council. Hence, expansion into new strategic business markets does not appear to be an option.

Strategy Development

(a)   Internal development

Internal development takes place when strategies are developed by building on or developing the organisation's own capabilities. It is often termed organic growth. This is how EMS has operated up to now. The original certificates were developed by the founders of the Society. Since then, additional certificates have been added and the Diploma programme developed at the instigation of members and officers of the Society.

In many ways this type of organic growth is particularly suited to the configuration of the organisation, one where there is a risk-averse and cautious culture. The organic approach spreads cost and risk over time and growth is much easier to control and manage. However, growth can be slow and indeed, as in the case of EMS, may have ceased altogether. Growth is also restricted by the breadth of the organisation's capabilities. For example, EMS has not been able to develop (or indeed even consider developing) any products outside of its fairly restricted product range. Furthermore, although internal development may be a reasonable strategy for developing a home market it maybe an inappropriate strategy for breaking into new market places and territories. This is particularly true when, as it appears in the case of the EMS, internal resources have no previous experience of developing products in overseas markets.

In summary, internal growth has been the method of strategy development at EMS up to now, based on a strategic direction of consolidation and market penetration. There is no evidence that EMS is considering developing new products to arrest the fall in qualification numbers. However, the Board has suggested developing new markets for the current qualification range and India, China and Russia have been identified as potential targets. It seems unlikely that internal development will be an appropriate method of pursuing this strategic direction.

(b) Mergers and Acquisitions
A strategy of acquisition is one where one organisation (such as EMS) takes ownership of other existing organisations in the target countries. One of the most compelling reasons for acquisition is the speed it allows an organisation to enter a new product or market area. EMS might look to acquire organisations already offering certification in its target markets. These organisations would then become the mechanism for launching EMS qualifications into these markets. In addition, it is likely that these organisations will have qualifications that the EMS does not currently offer. These qualifications could then be offered, if appropriate,in EMS's home market. This arrangement would provide EMS with the opportunity to quickly offer its core competences into its target markets, as well as gaining new competencies which it could exploit at home.

However, acquisitions usually require considerable expenditure at some point in time and evidence suggests that there is a high risk that they will not deliver the returns that they promised. It is unlikely that the EMS will have enough money to fund such acquisitions and its status as a private limited entity means that it cannot currently access the markets to fund such growth. Any acquisitions will have to be funded from its cash reserves or from private equity investment groups. Furthermore, acquisitions also bring political and cultural issues which evidence suggests the organisation would have difficulty with. Under achievement in mergers and acquisitions often results from problems of cultural fit. This can be particularly problematic with international acquisitions, which is exactly the type of acquisition under consideration here. So, although acquisitions are a popular way of fuelling growth it is unlikely that EMS will have either the cash or the cultural will to pursue this method of strategy development. There is no evidence that EMS has any expertise in acquiring organisations in it home market and so such acquisitions overseas would be extremely risky.

(c) Strategic Alliances
A strategic alliance takes place when two or more organisations share resources and activities to pursue a particular strategy. This approach has become increasingly popular for a number of reasons. In the context of EMS it would allow the organisation to enter into a marketplace without the large financial outlay of acquiring a local organisation. Furthermore, it would avoid the cultural dislocation of either acquiring or merging with another organisation. The motive for the alliance would be co-specialisation with each partner concentrating on the activities that best match their capabilities. Johnson, Scholes and Whittington suggest that co-specialisation alliances "are used to enter new geographic markets where an organisation needs local knowledge and expertise". This fits the EMS requirement exactly.

The exact nature of the alliance would require much thought and indeed different types of alliance might be forged in the three markets targeted by EMS. A joint venture is where a new organisation is set up jointly owned by the parents. This is a formal alliance and will obviously take some time to establish. EMS will have to contribute cost and resources to the newly established company, but such costs and resources should be much less than those incurred in an acquisition. However, joint ventures take time to establish and it may be not be an option if EMS wants to quickly move into a target marketplace to speedily arrest its falling numbers. A licence agreement could be an alternative where EMS licenses the use of its qualification in the target market. This could be organised in a number of ways. For example, a local organisation could market the EMS qualification as its own and pay EMS a fee for each issued certificate and diploma. Alternatively, the qualification may be marketed by the local organisation as an EMS qualification and EMS pays this organisation a licence fee for every certificate and diploma it issues in that country. This requires less commitment from EMS but it is likely to bring in less financial returns, with less control over how the qualification is marketed. Furthermore, if the qualification is successful, there is the risk that the local organisation will develop its own alternative so that it gains all the income from the transaction, not just a percentage of the transaction fee.

At first sight, the strategic alliance appears very appropriate to EMS's current situation. The licensing approach is particularly attractive because it seems to offer very quick access to new markets without any great financial commitment and without any cultural upheaval within EMS itself. However, the uptake of the qualification is unpredictable and the marketing and promotion of the qualification is outside the control of EMS. EMS may find this difficult to accept. Furthermore, the EMS will only be receiving a fraction of the income and so it must ensure that this fraction is sufficient to fuel growth expectations and service the newly qualified members in other countries. Finally, there is often a paradox in organisations where internal development has been the strategic method adopted so far. An organisation used to internal development and control often finds it difficult to trust partners in an alliance. Yet trust and cooperation is probably the most important ingredient of making such strategic alliances work.

3 **(a)** Software quality is notoriously difficult to define, but at least four issues deserve consideration.

Conformity to requirements

This is concerned with the software performing business functions correctly. It does what the user expects it to do and does not do what it is not expected to do. This issue is about meeting expectations. The conformity to requirements might be measured by the number of change requests submitted immediately after the system has gone live. If the system performs to requirements then there should be very few change requests until the system has been in operation for some time. Evidence at CCT suggests that this is a major issue. These problems are highlighted by Tony Osunda. He states that "the delivered system did not work the way we wanted" and that "key areas of functionality were either wrong or missing altogether". The fact that changes were subsequently made for free indicates why margins are falling. Doing these would have significantly eroded into the projected profitability of the project.

Reliability

The software behaves consistently and reliably and so is available for the user. The reliability of software can be measured by availability and downtime. Indeed, reliability is often defined within service level agreements (SLAs). For example; the software must be available for 99% of the agreed service time, where service time is defined as 07.00 – 22.00, Monday to Friday. Reliability is relatively easy to measure because it concerns the availability of the software. There is no evidence at CCT that their software has reliability problems.

Usability

The ease of use of software is a major issue in software delivery and e-business development. The usability of software may be assessed in a number of ways. For example;

- By logging the nature and number of calls to a HELP desk. This should be relatively low if the software is easy to use.
- By observing users actually using the software and recording the problems and difficulties they encounter.
- By using questionnaires to ask users how easy they have found the system to use.

There is some evidence that CCT software has usability problems. Crispin Peters-Ward stated that "We found (the system) cumbersome to use."

Degree of excellence

The software should exhibit elements of good build, such as maintainability, flexibility and expandability. This software quality is about long-term design potential. This is quite difficult to measure. However, there are technical measures which allow the modularity of the software to be assessed. If the modularity of the software is low then the software is likely to be easy to maintain and test. There is evidence that the CCT software has long-term design problems. Amelia Platt comments that the software was not built "with expansion in mind. Also, it is difficult to know what some of the programs actually do, so making changes is a nightmare. Programmers make changes to program code without really knowing what the knock-on effect will be." There are now one hundred and thirty programmers in the company. It is unlikely that they all understand how the software has been constructed. Hence, there is ample opportunity for introducing faults into the system.

Software quality is extremely important to end users. Users expect systems to perform functions correctly and reliably. They expect systems to be easy to use. Failure to fulfil these expectations may lead to frustration with the product, inefficient use of systems and the under-performance of organisations. In the extreme it may lead to organisational collapse and, where safety-critical software fails, to loss of life. The elements of product quality (degree of excellence) may not be immediately obvious to an end user. However, high maintenance costs become very clear to organisations over time, as they increasingly consume a company's operational budget.

(b) The Capability Maturity Model Integration (CMMI) is a process improvement approach that provides organisations with the essential elements of effective processes. It can be used to guide process improvement across a project, a division, or an entire organisation. It has five levels of capability. Organisations are encouraged to move up the levels and to eventually achieve capability level 5. A successful appraisal at this level would assist CCT in delivering quality software as well as publicly demonstrating their competence to do so. Many customers mandate that suppliers should be at a certain level in the CMMI assessment.

Capability level 0 is where there is an incomplete process which is either not performed at all or is partially performed. One or more of the specific goals of the process area are not satisfied. There is no evidence of such a process at CCT. Capability Level 1 is defined as performed. A performed process is a process that satisfies all of the specific goals of a process area such as software development. At this level the processes are performed informally, without following a documented process description or plan. The rigour with which these practices are performed depends on the individuals managing and performing the work and the quality of the outcomes may vary considerably. Successful outcomes for an organisation operating at level 1 depend upon the heroic efforts of individuals. Carlos Theroux alludes to these days at CCT; "when we were smaller we could all dive in and solve the problems. We all used to stay over until we got the problem solved".

A capability level 2 process is characterized as a managed process. A managed process is a performed (capability level 1) process that is also planned and executed in accordance with a defined procedure. A critical distinction between a performed process and a managed process is the extent to which the process is actually managed! A managed process is planned (the plan may be part of a more encompassing plan) and the performance of the process is managed against the plan. Corrective actions are taken when the actual results and performance deviate significantly from the plan. A managed process achieves the objectives of the plan and is documented as a standard for consistent performance. Carlos Theroux has alluded to the introduction of a project management methodology and its adoption will assist CCT to achieve capability level 2.

A capability level 3 process is characterized as a "defined process." A defined process is a managed (capability level 2) process that is tailored from the organisation's set of standard processes according to the organisation's tailoring guidelines.

It contributes work products, measures, and other process-improvement information to the organisational process. A critical distinction between a managed process and a defined process is the scope of the process descriptions, standards, and procedures. In software terms, capability level 3 is achieved when a defined engineering process is in place so that the process of software development (not just its management) is consistent and standard. At this level of capability, the organisation is interested in deploying standard processes that are proven and that therefore take less time and money than continually writing and deploying new processes. Another critical distinction is that a defined process is described in more detail and performed more rigorously than a managed process. CCT does not appear to be at this level at the moment. It could be argued that the problems in requirements functionality highlighted by Tony Osunda would not happen in a defined process.

A capability level 4 process is characterized as a "quantitatively managed process." A quantitatively managed process is a defined (capability level 3) process that is controlled using statistical and other quantitative techniques. Quantitative objectives for quality and process performance are established and used as criteria in managing the process. The quality and process performance are understood in statistical terms and are managed throughout the life of the process. A critical distinction between a defined process and a quantitatively managed process is the predictability of the process performance. A defined process only provides qualitative predictability. Clearly, CCT is not at this level yet. However, statistical analysis of faults, perhaps using Six Sigma principles, could deliver important quality improvements. The measurement of quality is fundamental to this level. Hence, the organisation must consider some of the issues raised in the answer to part a) of this question.

A capability level 5 process is characterized as an "optimizing process." An optimizing process is a quantitatively managed (capability level 4) process that is changed and adapted to meet relevant current and projected business objectives. An optimizing process focuses on continually improving the process performance through both incremental and innovative technological improvements. A critical distinction between a quantitatively managed process and an optimizing process is that the optimizing process is continuously improved by addressing common causes of process variation. In a process that is optimized, common causes of process variation are addressed by changing that process. The process of continuous process improvement through quantitative feedback from the process itself is clearly not happening in CCT at present.

4   (a)   A simple value chain of the primary activities of DRB is shown below.

Handling and storing inbound fully configured equipment Quality inspection	Re-branding of products Re-packaging of products	Customer collection Technician delivery and installation	Local advertising Web based enquiries	On-site technical support Back to base support
Inbound logistics	**Operations**	**Outbound Logistics**	**Marketing and sales**	**Service**

Comments about value might include:

Inbound logistics: Excellent quality assurance is required in inbound logistics. This is essential for pre-configured equipment where customers have high expectations of reliability. As well as contributing to customer satisfaction, high quality also reduces service costs.

Operations: This is a relatively small component in the DRB value chain and actually adds little value to the customer. It is also being undertaken in a relatively high cost country. DRB might wish to re-visit the current arrangement.

Outbound logistics: Customer feedback shows that this is greatly valued. Products can be picked up from stock and delivery and installation is provided if required. Most of the company's larger competitors cannot offer this service. However, it is unlikely that this value can be retained when DRB begins to increasingly supply outside the geographical region it is in.

Marketing and sales: This is very low-key at DRB and will have to be developed if the company is to deliver the proposed growth. The limited functionality of the web site offers little value to customers.

Service: Customer feedback shows that this is greatly valued. Most of the company's competitors cannot offer this level of service. They offer support from off-shore call centres and a returns policy that is both time consuming to undertake and slow in rectification. However, it is unlikely that this value can be retained when DRB begins to increasingly supply outside the geographical region it is in.

(b)   DRB has already gained efficiencies by procuring products through the supplier's web-site. However, the web site has restricted functionality. When DRB places the order it is not informed of the expected delivery date until it receives the confirmation e-mail from ISAS. It is also unable to track the status of their order and so it is only when it receives a despatch email from ISAS that it knows that it is on its way. Because DRB is not the owner of the shipment, it is unable to track the delivery and so the physical arrival of the goods cannot be easily predicted. On occasions where shipments have appeared to have been lost, DRB has had to ask ISAS to track the shipment and report on its status. This has not been very satisfactory and the problem has been exacerbated by having two shippers involved. ISAS has not been able to reliably track the transhipment of goods from their shipper to EIF, the logistics company used to distribute their products in the country. Some shipments have been lost and it is time-consuming to track and follow-up shipments which are causing concern. Finally, because DRB has no long term contract with ISAS, it has to pay when it places the order through a credit card transaction on the ISAS website.

DRB has stated that it wishes to continue importing fully configured products. It is not interested in importing components and assembling them. It also does not wish to build or invest in assembly plants in other countries. However, it may wish to consider the following changes to its upstream supply chain:

- Seek to identify a wider range of suppliers and so trade through other sell-side web sites. Clearly there are costs associated with this. Suppliers have to be identified and evaluated and financial and trading arrangements have to be established. However, it removes the risk of single-sourcing and other suppliers may have better systems in place to support order and delivery tracking.
- Seek to identify suppliers who are willing and able to re-brand and package their products with DRB material at the production plant. This should reduce DRB costs as this is currently undertaken in a country where wage rates are high.
- Re-consider the decision not to negotiate long-term contracts with suppliers (including ISAS) and so explore the possibility of more favourable payment terms. DRB has avoided long-term contracts up to now. It may also not be possible to enter into such contracts if DRB begins to trade with a number of suppliers.
- Seek to identify suppliers (including ISAS) who are able to provide information about delivery dates prior to purchase and who are able to provide internet-based order tracking systems to their customers. This should allow much better planning.
- Consider replacing the two supplier shippers with a contracted logistics company which will collect the goods from the supplier and transport the goods directly to DRB. This should reduce physical transhipment problems and allow seamless monitoring of the progress of the order from despatch to arrival. It will also allow DRB to plan for the arrival of goods and to schedule its re-packaging.

DRB might also wish to consider two other procurement models; buy-side and the independent marketplace.

In the buy-side model DRB would use its web site to invite potential suppliers to bid for contract requirements posted on the site. This places the onus on suppliers to spend time completing details and making commitments. It should also attract a much wider range of suppliers than would have been possible through DRB searching sell-side sites for potential suppliers. Unfortunately, it is unlikely that DRB is large enough to host such a model. However, it may wish to prototype it to see if it is viable and whether it uncovers potential suppliers who have not been found in sell-side web sites searches.

In the independent marketplace model, DRB places its requirements on an intermediary web site. These are essentially B2B electronic marketplaces which allow, on the one hand, potential customers to search products being offered by suppliers and, on the other hand, customers to place their requirements and be contacted by potential suppliers. Such marketplaces promise greater supplier choice with reduced costs. They also provide an opportunity for aggregation where smaller organisations (such as DRB) can get together with companies that have the same requirement to place larger orders to gain cheaper prices and better purchasing terms. It is also likely that such marketplaces will increasingly offer algorithms that automatically match customers and suppliers, so reducing the search costs associated with the sell-side model. The independent marketplace model may be a useful approach for DRB. Many of the suppliers participating in these marketplaces are electronics companies.

(c) DRB's downstream supply chain is also very simple at the moment. It has a web-site that shows information about DRB products. Customers can make enquiries about the specification and availability of these products through an e-mail facility. Conventional marketing is undertaken through local advertising and buyers either collect their products or they are delivered and installed by a specialist group of technicians. DRB could tune its downstream supply chain by using many of the approaches mentioned in the previous section. For example:

- Developing the web site so that it not only shows products but also product availability. Customers would be able to place orders and pay for them securely over the web site. The site could be integrated with a logistics system so that orders and deliveries can be tracked by the customer. DRB must recognise that most of its competitors already have such systems. However, DRB will have to put a similar system in place to be able to support its growth plans.
- Participating in independent marketplace web sites as a supplier. DRB may also be able to exploit aggregation by combining with other suppliers in consortia to bid for large contracts.
- DRB may also consider participating in B2C marketplaces such as e-bay. Many organisations use this as their route to market for commodity products.

DRB may also wish to consider replacing its sales from stock approach with sales from order. In the current approach, DRB purchases products in advance and re-packages and stores these products before selling them to customers. This leads to very quick order fulfilment but high storage and financing costs. These costs will become greater if the planned growth occurs. DRB may wish to consider offering products on its website at a discount but with specified delivery terms. This would allow the company to supply to order rather than supply from stock.

Pilot Paper P3
Business Analysis

1 **(a)** 1 mark for identifying an appropriate macro-environmental influence in each of the PESTEL areas – even if it is justifying the lack of influence. A further 4 marks are available for given credit to candidates who have extended their argument in selected areas of the framework. It must be accepted that each area of the PESTEL will have a differential effect. (10 marks).

 (b) 1 mark for each relevant point made in the competitive analysis of NMS (up to a maximum of 13 marks) and 1 mark for each relevant point made in the financial analysis of NMS (up to a maximum of 9 marks). A further 3 professional marks are available for such aspects as the structure, presentation and logical flow of the answer. (25 marks)

 (c) 1 mark for each relevant point up to a maximum of 5 marks for each of the three exit strategies. (15 marks)

(50 marks)

2 The question asks for principles and suitability.

 1 mark for each relevant point up to a maximum of 8 marks for internal development. There is a maximum of 4 marks for points relating to principles. (8 marks)

 1 mark for each relevant point up to a maximum of 8 marks for acquisitions. There is a maximum of 4 marks for points relating to principles. (8 marks)

 1 mark for each relevant point up to a maximum of 9 marks for strategic alliances. There is a maximum of 5 marks for points relating to principles. (9 marks)

(25 marks)

3 **(a)** 1 mark for each relevant point up to a maximum of 5 marks for identifying and discussing software quality. 1 mark for each relevant point up to a maximum of 5 marks for identifying appropriate measures. (10 marks)

 (b) 1 mark for each relevant point up to a maximum of 2 marks for introducing the CMMI concept. 1 mark for each relevant point up to a maximum of 2 marks for a description of each capability level (five levels)

 1 mark for each relevant point up to a maximum 3 marks for applying CMMI to the CCT scenario. (15 marks)

(25 marks)

4 **(a)** 1 mark for each relevant point up to a maximum of 3 marks for the value chain
 1 mark for each relevant point up to a maximum of 6 marks for the significance and value of the primary activities.
(9 marks)

 (b) 1 mark for each relevant point up to a maximum of 6 marks for identifying upstream changes.

 1 mark for each relevant point up to a maximum of 4 marks for identifying how these changes address problems experienced by DRB. (10 marks)

 (c) 1 mark for each relevant point up to a maximum of 6 marks for identifying upstream changes. (6 marks)

(25 marks)

Index

Note. **Key Terms** and their page references are given in **bold**.

Review Form & Free Prize Draw – Paper P3 Business Analysis (4/07)

All original review forms from the entire BPP range, completed with genuine comments, will be entered into one of two draws on 31 January 2008 and 31 July 2008. The names on the first four forms picked out on each occasion will be sent a cheque for £50.

Name: _____ Address: _____

_____

_____

How have you used this Text?
(Tick one box only)

☐ Home study (book only)

☐ On a course: college _____

☐ With 'correspondence' package

☐ Other _____

Why did you decide to purchase this Text? *(Tick one box only)*

☐ Have used BPP Texts in the past

☐ Recommendation by friend/colleague

☐ Recommendation by a lecturer at college

☐ Saw advertising

☐ Saw information on BPP website

☐ Other _____

During the past six months do you recall seeing/receiving any of the following?
(Tick as many boxes as are relevant)

☐ Our advertisement in *ACCA Student Accountant*

☐ Our advertisement in *Pass*

☐ Our advertisement in *PQ*

☐ Our brochure with a letter through the post

☐ Our website www.bpp.com

Which (if any) aspects of our advertising do you find useful?
(Tick as many boxes as are relevant)

☐ Prices and publication dates of new editions

☐ Information on Text content

☐ Facility to order books off-the-page

☐ None of the above

Which BPP products have you used?

Text	☑	Success CD	☐	Learn Online	☐
Kit	☐	i-Learn	☐	Home Study Package	☐
Passcard	☐	i-Pass	☐	Home Study PLUS	☐

Your ratings, comments and suggestions would be appreciated on the following areas.

	Very useful	Useful	Not useful
Introductory section (Key study steps, personal study)	☐	☐	☐
Chapter introductions	☐	☐	☐
Key terms	☐	☐	☐
Quality of explanations	☐	☐	☐
Case studies and other examples	☐	☐	☐
Exam focus points	☐	☐	☐
Questions and answers in each chapter	☐	☐	☐
Fast forwards and chapter roundups	☐	☐	☐
Quick quizzes	☐	☐	☐
Question Bank	☐	☐	☐
Answer Bank	☐	☐	☐
Index	☐	☐	☐

Overall opinion of this Study Text	Excellent ☐	Good ☐	Adequate ☐	Poor ☐

Do you intend to continue using BPP products?   Yes ☐   No ☐

On the reverse of this page are noted particular areas of the text about which we would welcome your feedback. The BPP author of this edition can be e-mailed at: glennhaldane@bpp.com

Please return this form to: Nick Weller, ACCA Publishing Manager, BPP Learning Media Ltd, FREEPOST, London, W12 8BR

Review Form & Free Prize Draw (continued)

TELL US WHAT YOU THINK

Please note any further comments and suggestions/errors below

Free Prize Draw Rules

1   Closing date for 31 January 2008 draw is 31 December 2007. Closing date for 31 July 2008 draw is 30 June 2008.

2   Restricted to entries with UK and Eire addresses only. BPP employees, their families and business associates are excluded.

3   No purchase necessary. Entry forms are available upon request from BPP Learning Media Ltd. No more than one entry per title, per person. Draw restricted to persons aged 16 and over.

4   Winners will be notified by post and receive their cheques not later than 6 weeks after the relevant draw date.

5   The decision of the promoter in all matters is final and binding. No correspondence will be entered into.

ACCA

PAPER P3

BUSINESS ANALYSIS

In this new syllabus first editi

- We discuss the best strategies fo
- We highlight the most important
- We signpost how each chapter li
- We provide lots of exam focus po
- We emphasise key points in regu
- We test your knowledge of what y
- We examine your understanding i
- We reference all the important top

BPP's **i-Learn** and **i-Pass** produ

FOR EXAMS IN DECEMB

LEARNING MEDIA

First edition April 2007

ISBN 9780 7517 3302 0

British Library Cataloguing-in-Publication Data
A catalogue record for this book
is available from the British Library

Published by

BPP Learning Media Ltd
BPP House, Aldine Place
London W12 8AA

www.bpp.com/learningmedia

Printed in Great Britain by
W M Print
45-47 Frederick Street
Walsall, West Midlands
WS2 9NE

Your learning materials, published by BPP Learning
Media Ltd, are printed on paper sourced from
sustainable, managed forests.

We are grateful to the Association of Chartered Certified
Accountants for permission to reproduce past
examination questions. The suggested solutions in the
exam answer bank have been prepared by BPP Learning
Media Ltd, unless where otherwise stated.